Baltic Cities

the Bradt Travel Guide

Neil Taylor

edition
1

www.bradtguides.com

Bradt Travel Guides Ltd, UK
The Globe Pequot Press Inc, USA

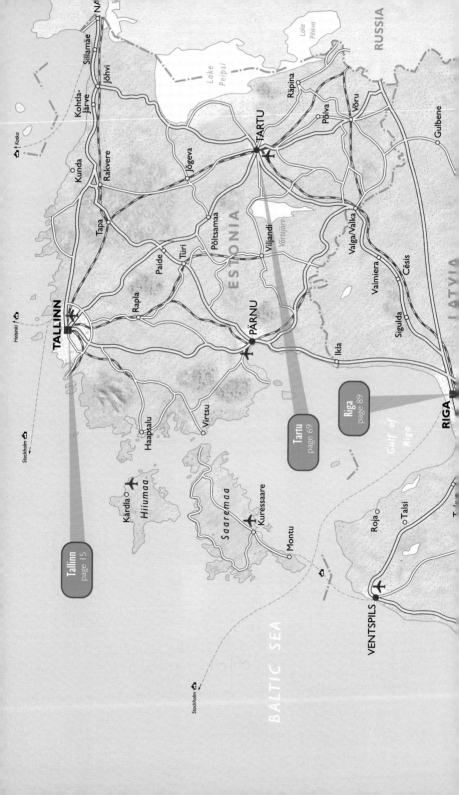

Baltic Citi
Don't
miss...

Café culture
Café in front of the former Orthodox cathedral, Kaunas (JS) page 225

Art Nouveau
Eisenstein building at 10b Elizabetes, Riga (CN) page 123

rks and gardens
Kadriorg Palace and
gardens, Tallinn
(AA/TCTO) page 60

Rivers and lakes
Pregel River and the old
German red-brick Gothic
cathedral, Kaliningrad
(JS) page 269

**Churches and
cathedrals**
Vilnius Cathedral
(CN) page 297

left **Old Town Hall, Kaunas**
(JS) page 223

above **Detail on Art Nouveau building, Tallinn**
(CN) page 46

below **Half-timbered houses, Klaipeda** (JS) page 242

top **Song Festival, Riga**
(CN) page 146

above **St Catherine's Passage, Tallinn**
(TV/TCTO)

right **St Casimir fair, Vilnius** (JS)

Authors and Contributors

Neil Taylor was from 1975 to 2005 director of Regent Holidays, a British tour company that has specialised in travel to the Baltic countries and Kaliningrad since 1991. He visits the area about four times a year and in 1999 his Bradt guide to Estonia was first published; it is now in its fourth edition. He is now a non-executive director of Martin Randall Travel, is on the Board of the Association of Independent Tour Operators (AITO), and writes and broadcasts on general travel trade topics. In 2000, Neil was awarded the Lifetime Achievement Award by the British Guild of Travel Writers.

Stephen Baister studied modern languages at Oxford and London universities and worked as a publisher before becoming a solicitor. While in practice, he represented a number of clients with interests in eastern and central Europe. He is the co-author of the Bradt guide to Latvia of which the fifth edition was published in 2007, and of the Bradt guide to Riga. He has a doctorate in east European law from University College London. He is now Chief Registrar in Bankruptcy in the High Court.

Howard Jarvis has been the chief editor of a number of publications in the Baltic countries, including *The Baltic Times*, the region's only weekly newspaper, and *VilniusNOW!*, a glossy monthly for business travellers. He has been a contributor at the Jane's Information Group since 2000 and has written numerous articles on developments in the Baltic region and Belarus. Based in Vilnius, he is now editor of *Baltic Stand By*, a travel industry magazine and website.

Brigita Pantelejeva, who helped to update the Kaunas chapter, has lived there all her life, except for one year when she was a high-school student in the United States at Green Bay, Wisconsin. This year abroad generated her interest in creative writing and in the English language. She is now taking a master's degree in linguistics at Kaunas University.

Chris Patrick has a degree in French and German from Oxford University. After graduation she lived and worked in Japan and travelled extensively in the Far East. She works now in international research and consultancy and has assisted a number of organisations from eastern Europe in doing business in the Far East. She first visited Latvia in 1989 and has returned many times since. She is co-author of the Bradt guide to Latvia, of which the fifth edition was published in 2007, and of the Bradt guide to Riga.

PUBLISHER'S FOREWORD

Hilary Bradt

The first Bradt travel guide was written in 1974 by George and Hilary Bradt on a river barge floating down a tributary of the Amazon. In the 1980s and '90s the focus shifted away from hiking to broader-based guides covering new destinations – usually the first to be published about these places. In the 21st century Bradt continues to publish such ground-breaking guides, as well as others to established holiday destinations, incorporating in-depth information on culture and natural history with the nuts and bolts of where to stay and what to see.

Bradt authors support responsible travel, and provide advice not only on minimum impact but also on how to give something back through local charities. In this way a true synergy is achieved between the traveller and local communities.

When we published our first guides to the Baltic countries in 1995 we never imagined that the region would become so popular. The last Soviet troops had only left the three republics during the previous year, and their psychological presence was still felt. My own visit to Tallinn a few years later showed me a vibrant city rejoicing in its independence. Now, of course, thousands of discerning travellers are drawn to explore the cities of the Baltic states, looking for something a little different. It's been quite a Cinderella story!

First edition October 2008

Bradt Travel Guides Ltd
23 High Street, Chalfont St Peter, Bucks SL9 9QE, England. www.bradtguides.com
Published in the USA by The Globe Pequot Press Inc, 246 Goose Lane,
PO Box 480, Guilford, Connecticut 06475-0480

British Library Cataloguing in Publication Data
A catalogue record for this book is available from the British Library •
ISBN-13: 978 1 84162 247 7

Photographs A Anušauskas/www.travel.lt (AA/TLT), Ain Avik/TCTO&CB (AA/TCTO), Stephen Baister and Chris Patrick (SC), Agnieszka i Wlodek Bilinscy/FotobankPoland (AWB), Tricia Hayne (TH), Estonian Tourist Board (ETB), *Hidden Europe* magazine (HE), Kaido Haagen (KH), Liepaja TB (LTB), Christian Nowak (CN), Jonathan Smith (JS), Gediminas Treciokas (GT), Joanna Vaughan (JV), Toomas Volmer/TCTO&CB (TV/TCTO), www.travel.lt (TLT)
Front cover Street lamp in Riga (Imants Urtans/Poligons Photo Index/Alamy)
Back cover Door of House of Blackheads, Tallinn (TH), Three Crosses Hill, Vilnius (JS)
Title page Art Nouveau, Riga (CN), Stained-glass window, Kaunas (JS), Viru Gate, Tallinn (TH)
Maps Terence Crump

Typeset from the author's disc by Wakewing
Printed and bound in India by Nutech Photolithographer, New Delhi

Acknowledgements

In preparing the text on Königsberg, I must give particular thanks to Lorenz Grimoni, Director of the Königsberg Museum in Duisburg. He gave me access to the museum archives which cover all aspects of pre-war life in the city and which house research done by Germans in Kaliningrad since 1990 when they were able to return there. Future generations in particular will be grateful for all the work done in the museum to preserve the memory of what had been an important German city. In Kaliningrad itself, my guide, Olga Danilova, has shared her enthusiasm, realism and knowledge on each of my visits. I owe Olga a great debt, as do most English-speaking visitors.

It is invaluable that Latvia and Lithuania now both have active tourist offices in London. Eva Staltmane and then her successor Brigita Stroda at the Latvia office have provided me with constant support, as have Indrė Trakimaitė and Vaida Andriuškevičiutė at the Lithuanian office. Particular thanks are due to Evita Valtere in Liepaja for helping me with a great deal of necessary background material.

Tricia Hayne, my former editor at Bradt, has kindly taken on yet again the unenviable task of compositing my stream of consciousness into a coherent narrative that actually makes sense. I just hope that my enthusiasm for this project makes up for my disorganisation in carrying it out. As this book crosses between five different languages, two members of the Bradt team take on particular importance in ensuring a high standard of accuracy. They are the typesetter Sally Brock and the cartographer Terence Crump, who can make or break a book like this. They have undoubtedly made it.

It was a brave decision of Hilary Bradt in the early 1990s to take the Baltic region seriously. I am grateful to her successors in the office, Donald Greig and Adrian Phillips, for continuing to show the company's commitment to the area.

LIST OF MAPS

Contents

AUTHOR'S STORY

I first visited the Baltic capitals in May 1992 and my addiction began at once. I would return that autumn with my first group. Travel was adventurous in those days, with long queues at proudly erected border posts, provisional currencies gradually giving way to permanent ones and local residents being as curious about us as we were about them. However, one impression that struck me then and which still remains is how different the countries are and how inappropriate the term 'Baltic' is. For several years a group tour in the area had to be largely restricted to the capitals as few hotels or restaurants elsewhere could adequately cater for groups. Individual travel hardly existed then. *Baltic Capitals* was written to cover tourism as it then stood.

I soon extended my travels throughout the region and began to realise that several other towns deserved almost the same attention that I had previously just given to the capitals and this book is the result. I would not now want to be in Vilnius without travelling as well to Kaunas and Klaipeda. Once in Klaipeda it would be absurd not to enjoy the coast road to Liepaja before returning to Riga. Future books will probably include Daugavpils and Narva as they continue their breakaway from a very Soviet past. I am sure that writing them will give me as great a pleasure as tackling this one has. I just hope that I have passed on my enthusiasm, without failing to be critical on the occasions when this has been necessary.

Introduction

'Baltic' is an adjective often used, but it is rarely liked by those on whom outsiders impose it. I therefore chose the term with some trepidation for the title of this book, particularly given the diversity of the cities covered in it. When he was foreign minister of his country, the President of Estonia Toomas Hendrik Ilves made the famous remark that the only thing that united the so-called Baltic countries was the Soviet occupation which had been inflicted on them from 1945 to 1991. Visitors to the area will immediately understand what he meant as they hear four seemingly unrelated languages, see all manner of architectural styles, and note the complete indifference that one country has for the others. This was in fact my immediate impression when I first came to the area in 1992 and why I went on to write *Estonia* for Bradt. Their *Latvia* and *Lithuania* guides appeared at the same time for this reason. However, many tourists now visit the area at the eastern end of the Baltic Sea and want one guidebook to the major cities that are featured by tour operators in either group or individual itineraries.

Tour operators and therefore travellers are no longer restricting visits to Tallinn, Riga and Vilnius, an itinerary that started life in Soviet times and just continued through the 1990s and the early years of this century. These three capitals must of course still be seen, and they all warrant repeat visits, but not at the expense of so much else that should now be included.

Developments in Tallinn, Riga and Vilnius have continued apace since independence in the early 1990s, but the other five cities covered in this book have gone through even more rapid transformation since 2000. In my early visits, I used to calculate my stays in hours. Now I plan them in days and return ever more often. Transport links make this easy and a pleasure. Who would have thought in 2000 that eight years later London would have a daily flight to Kaliningrad, and Liverpool a twice-weekly service to Kaunas? Equally I would not have anticipated a conference centre in Tartu, or a prison in Liepaja opening its doors to visitors happy to pay for overnight accommodation there. Future editions of this book will I am sure be as pleasantly demanding on me as this one has been. Studying politics along the Baltic Sea can be frustrating; travel never is.

Overview

WHEN TO GO

Most tourists to the Baltic countries visit in the summer months between late April and early October. July and early August are very busy in the cheaper hotels since this is the German and Scandinavian school holiday period. Temperatures in the summer can reach 25°C/80°F quite regularly, though they often hover around 20°C/70°F. Good weather can never be guaranteed in this area. Clouds can quickly congregate, turning a sunny morning into a dismal afternoon, but the reverse is equally true. Day trips should never be undertaken without a coat and strong shoes. Tallinn barely sees night-time around midsummer and the days are long in all four countries from May until September. The deluxe and business-class hotels often reduce their prices in July and August to attract tourists at a time when their normal clientele is absent.

More tourists are now seeing the attractions of winter visits to the cities in this region. Culture flourishes then, temperatures do not fall much below freezing, and queues are non-existent at the major sites. From western Europe, winter air fares have now dropped to a level which makes weekend breaks in these cities very popular. January and early February are best avoided because of the short hours of daylight then and the occasional bitter day, but other months should offer a pleasant stay. Christmas is now taken seriously in the Baltics and a well-planned short shopping trip around the Christmas markets should more than make up for the air fare.

PUBLIC HOLIDAYS

New Year's Day	1 January
Orthodox Christmas (Kaliningrad)	7 January
Independence Day (Lithuania)	16 February
International Women's Day	8 March
Restoration of Independence Day (Lithuania)	11 March
Easter	March/April
May Day (Estonia, Kaliningrad and Latvia)	1 May
Independence from USSR (Latvia)	4 May
Victory in Europe Day (Kaliningrad)	9 May
Independence Day (Kaliningrad)	12 June
Midsummer (Estonia and Latvia)	23–4 June
Mindaugas Day (Lithuania)	6 July
Assumption (Lithuania)	15 August
Restoration of Independence Day (Estonia)	20 August
All Saints' Day (Lithuania)	1 November
Day of Reconciliation (Kaliningrad)	7 November
Independence Day (Latvia)	18 November

Christmas Eve (Estonia, Lithuania and Kaliningrad)	24 December
Christmas Day	25 December
Boxing Day (Latvia)	26 December
New Year's Eve (Latvia)	31 December

Flags are displayed in the Baltic countries on 14 June, to commemorate those deported to Siberia on 14 June 1941 and in later deportations. They are also displayed on 23 August, to commemorate the signing between Germany and the USSR of the Molotov–Ribbentrop Pact on 23 August 1939, which enabled the USSR to incorporate the three Baltic countries in June 1940.

TIME ZONES

Before World War II, Estonia and Latvia were two hours ahead of GMT and Lithuania one hour ahead, as was East Prussia. During the Soviet occupation the three Baltic republics and the Kaliningrad region were forced to use Moscow time which is three hours ahead of GMT. Courageous local nationalists during this period would often keep their watches an hour behind Moscow time as an act of defiance to the USSR and of loyalty to the former regime. On regaining independence changing back the time was one of the first acts of the new governments and in the early '90s they all kept in step, to be joined later by Kaliningrad. In the mid '90s they tended to go their separate ways, causing havoc with bus and plane timetables, but fortunately since 2000 they have all agreed to work within the EU framework, so they are always two hours ahead of the time in Britain and one hour ahead of most of Europe.

RED TAPE

Estonia, Latvia and Lithuania abolished the Soviet visa system immediately after their independence in 1991. Since joining the EU they have implemented the same visa exemptions so citizens from all other EU countries, as well as from Australia, Canada, New Zealand and the USA do not need visas. Since December 2007, the three Baltic countries have been members of the Schengen Agreement, so nationals of those countries which do require visas need only one visa to cover Estonia, Latvia and Lithuania. Visa procedures for people who do need them are cumbersome, expensive and time-consuming.

Kaliningrad initially followed Russia by adopting the former Soviet visa system but a fall in the number of tourists forced them to break away from this in 1999. All tourists still need a visa, which is only granted on the basis of pre-booked accommodation, but it is now issued on arrival at the airport and at the land borders with Poland. Visas are *not* issued on the Lithuanian border so visitors entering Kaliningrad this way will need to apply several weeks in advance through a Russian embassy. Although the local authorities in Kaliningrad are eager to abolish visas for EU citizens, Moscow was still in 2008 refusing to let them do so.

CONSULAR HELP IN THE BALTICS Australia, Britain, most EU countries and the United States have consulates in each of the Baltic capitals except Kaliningrad. The British consulates can provide assistance to nationals of most Commonwealth countries in emergencies. Kaliningrad has seven consulates representing Belarus, Denmark, Germany, Latvia, Lithuania, Poland and Sweden. Nationals of other countries needing consular help have to turn to their embassy in Moscow. Given the complications of this, it is particularly important in Kaliningrad to ensure that all valuables and passports are safely stored in a hotel safe.

CURRENCY AND CHANGING MONEY Each country has its own currency and payment in any other one is not possible. All four currencies are convertible and can be exchanged throughout the Baltic countries. As banks and exchange bureaux do not usually charge commission, small amounts left over can be re-exchanged without difficulty. In Tallinn, Riga and Vilnius, banks and exchange bureaux change all major Western currencies. Those at airports are always open for incoming flights but at land borders and at railway and bus stations they tend to close between 20.00 and 08.00, even though many international buses and trains travel through the night. Exchange bureaux in the towns are usually open seven days a week from around 09.00 to 19.00. Most hotels change money, some at any time of day, but rates are always better in exchange bureaux. On day trips out of town, remember to change sufficient money before departure since exchange and credit card facilities may not be available *en route*.

In the Kaliningrad oblast, apart from at the land border with Lithuania, it is often possible to exchange only euros or US dollars into roubles although since 2006 more banks have started to change pounds, Polish zloties and Baltic currencies as well. It is forbidden to make any payments in foreign currency, although shops wanting custom from cruise passengers will often accept euros.

In the UK, Thomas Cook and HSBC sell all four currencies, but it is otherwise difficult to obtain them in advance in western Europe. Estonia, Latvia and Lithuania had originally planned to convert to the euro in 2008 as all three currencies had already by then been tied to the euro for several years. However because of high local inflation rates, this is now unlikely until around 2012. Tourists from Britain can obtain all three Baltic currencies at one of several exchange bureaux at Heathrow, Gatwick and Stansted airports before they leave, and from the post office. They are also available in Helsinki. It is always important to insist on receiving low-value notes when changing money as notes worth more than about £5/US$10 are often difficult to exchange in museums, cafés and kiosks where tourists are likely to spend most of their cash. For the latest exchange rates, check your daily newspaper or www.xe.com. The following gives an indication of the exchange rates at the time of publication.

EXCHANGE RATES

Estonia The Estonian kroon (EEK) has a fixed rate with the euro of 15.65EEK. In July 2008 exchange rates against the pound and US dollar were £1 = 19.70EEK, and US$1 = 9.90EEK. Notes are issued for 1, 2, 5, 10, 25, 50, 100 and 500EEK, although those for 1 and 2 kroon are now being replaced with coins. There are also coins for 10, 20 and 50 sents.

Latvia The lat (Ls) is the official currency of Latvia (in Latvian the singular is lats, the plural lati). There are 100 santimi to the lat (the singular is santims, the plural santimi). The lat is fixed to the euro with one euro being worth Ls0.70 and a dollar being worth Ls0.45 in July 2008. In contrast to Estonia, coins are issued up to Ls2 and notes from Ls5 upwards. As the lat is worth £0.90, the money there is convenient for British tourists to calculate as coins and notes come close to their British counterparts. Coins are issued for 1, 2, 5, 10, 20 and 50 santimi and for Ls1 and Ls2; notes for Ls5, Ls10, Ls20 and Ls50. (Gamblers and money-launderers may also find the Ls100 and Ls500 notes of use.) Outside Latvia, it is sometimes difficult to exchange coins so these should be re-exchanged before departure, and on the Latvian side of land borders.

Lithuania Having for nine years been tied to the US dollar, since February 2002 the lit (Lt) has been tied instead to the euro. The fixed rate is 3.45Lt = €1, so in July 2008 the pound was worth about 4.35Lt and the dollar about 2.20Lt. There are coins for 1, 2, 5,

10, 20 and 50 cents and also for 1Lt, 2Lt and 5Lt. There are notes for 10, 20, 50 and 100 lits. Those formerly in circulation for 1, 2 and 5 lits have been largely replaced by coins.

Kaliningrad Through much of the 1990s the Russian rouble fluctuated wildly against other currencies, but since 1998 it has been very stable against the US dollar at a rate of US$1 = R23–30. In July 2008, exchange rates were £1 = R46.50, and US$1 = R23.50 and €1 = R37. Coins are issued for 10, 20 and 50 kopeks and for 1, 2 and 5 roubles. Given the very low prices for most items of interest to tourists, the only notes likely to be of use are those for 10, 20 and 50 roubles, although higher denominations are issued.

CASH MACHINES
These are easily found all over the Baltic countries and their use is constantly spreading. In Kaliningrad, reliable ATMs are becoming more readily available. Cash machines generally take major credit cards such as MasterCard and Visa. Do, however, check before leaving home what charges your bank will make for such use.

CREDIT CARDS
Throughout the three Baltic countries the use of cards is as widespread as elsewhere with all major shops, restaurants and hotels taking them. They can be used in hotels in Kaliningrad, but not in many shops and only in a few restaurants. Major rail and bus stations accept cards, but smaller ones do not, nor can they be used to pay for fares on board.

TRAVELLERS' CHEQUES
These are useless throughout the Baltics. Only a few banks can exchange them; shops, hotels, restaurants and exchange bureaux will invariably refuse them. The easy availability of cash machines in Estonia, Latvia and Lithuania, and the very low cost of incidentals in Kaliningrad, makes their use superfluous. (Many local people do not write cheques any more as they only use electronic banking.)

BUDGETING
Whilst hotel costs are similar to those in western Europe, other expenses will be much lower, except at restaurants and clubs clearly geared to affluent foreigners. A bus or train ride of 200km may well cost only £8/US$16, a light lunch £3/US$6 and a taxi across town £5/US$10. With low sales taxes, petrol is about half the UK price and a carton of 200 cigarettes costs scarcely more than the price of a packet in Britain. In Kaliningrad, prices are even lower than in the other cities covered in this guide. Museums do charge admission fees, usually with reductions for children and for the elderly. The full charge is rarely more than £2/US$4 and often much less. Locally produced books and maps in English often offer good value. On day trips out, incidental costs will be much lower than in the larger towns and on these occasions it is worth looking out for souvenirs since their prices will be geared to local consumers. As more affluent tourists and business people tend to base themselves in the capitals, costs there tend to be much higher, but by following the guidelines given in this book, it should be possible to pay provincial prices in all of them.

Shoppers visiting more than one of the cities will save money by finishing their tour in Kaliningrad, where most souvenirs are much cheaper than further north. Amber is of course the obvious buy there, together with linen and vodka. Lithuania and Estonia produce tasteful items carved from juniper wood, whereas the best china and glass is sold in Riga. However, prices in Liepaja are geared to local people as the number of tourists there is still much lower than in the other towns described here.

Tipping Up to 10% is very welcome in restaurants, cafés and hairdressers if the service deserves it, but not otherwise. In Tallinn, many expats make a point of not tipping if the service it is not up to the mark, in the hope that it will improve on future occasions. In Riga and in some more expensive restaurants in Vilnius, menus will indicate whether service is included, so in such circumstances be sure not to tip twice!

WHAT TO TAKE

The shops are now so well stocked in all four countries, with prices usually much lower than those in western Europe, that there is no need to pack a range of supplies before departure. Long gone are the days when travellers took iron rations and a medicine chest to safeguard their survival. An umbrella is essential year-round as clouds can suddenly appear on even the nicest of days. Be prepared similarly for changes in temperature: a sweater may be needed in summer and a spring day can rapidly become a winter one. Tough footwear is always essential because of the uneven pavements and the number of sites away from main roads. Relatively formal wear is still the custom for concerts and plays. Westerners attending performances often stand out with their untidy, casual dress.

The foreign-language bookshops in the major cities of Estonia, Latvia and Lithuania are well supplied with English-language, light and serious reading matter but few English (or even German) books are sold in Kaliningrad. Local guides in Kaliningrad are always pleased to receive books in English and many find their way into school and college libraries.

GETTING THERE

✈ BY AIR Between 2006 and 2007, Air Baltic expanded massively and showed its determination not just to be a Latvian airline. Even though Vilnius will always play second fiddle to Riga in its operations, it became very keen to make Vilnius a second hub in the Baltics, starting flights from there eastwards and matching FlyLAL in the number of services provided to both London Gatwick and Dublin. Travellers to Ukraine, central Asia and the Caucasus will increasingly be changing planes in Riga and Vilnius and may well complete their holidays in these regions with a short Baltic city break. As SAS has a major shareholding in both Air Baltic and in Estonian Air, it will not allow these two to compete. British Airways abandoned Vilnius in 2006 and Riga in 2007.

Air Baltic was also busy at this time reinvigorating services within the Baltics so started flights from Riga to Kaliningrad, from Riga to Liepaja and between the three capitals. The year 2008 could well see them flying to Tartu and reopening the airport at Daugavpils. A special airpass was introduced in January 2008 for travellers flying into the region on Air Baltic. This allows eight local flights to be booked at a cost of €35 plus taxes for each sector, and all but the first sector can be open-dated.

Estonian Air continues its daily service to Tallinn from London Gatwick and flies three times a week to Dublin. The airline also flies twice daily between Tallinn and Vilnius.

Many airlines, but in particular, Finnair, SAS and Czech, offer a range of connections from UK regional airports such as Birmingham, Manchester and Glasgow via Copenhagen, Helsinki and Prague to the Baltic countries. These airlines also offer the best connections from North America to the Baltics. Travellers from Australia and New Zealand are best advised to travel to London and then to take separate tickets from there.

Fares of course vary enormously but early booking is always advisable to get the cheapest ones. It is easy for instance to reach anywhere in the Baltics from the UK in the summer for around £100 plus taxes if booked six months in advance, but these fares are likely to be £400 if booked at the last minute.

The large number of Latvians and Lithuanians working in Britain and Ireland since their EU accession in 2004 has led to a wide range of no-frills flights from Kaunas and

Riga to destinations all over the UK and to Dublin. Most of these are operated by Ryanair. To Estonia, easyJet operate a daily service from London Stansted.

BY TRAIN Editions of this book's predecessor, *Baltic Capitals*, could write off Baltic train services in a derisory couple of sentences. Now they will form an integral part of many travellers' itineraries. The year 2006 saw the start of a serious train service between Tallinn and Tartu, with first-class as well as economy-class carriages. A service abandoned several years ago between Riga and Liepaja was also reopened that year, at the same time as a faster train service began between Riga and Daugavpils. The abolition of border controls under the Schengen Agreement will surely lead to a direct train service between Riga, Valga and Tartu. Lithuania never neglected its train services in the way that Estonia and Latvia did, but it would be surprising if improvements are not made in the services between Vilnius and Kaunas and Vilnius and Klaipeda. There are no international services to Poland, but many trains from each of the Baltic countries operate to Russia and Belarus. The Tallinn–St Petersburg service, revived in 2007 with new rolling stock, also provides a comfortable way to travel between Tallinn and Narva. The abandonment of certain crucial sections of track will prevent the return of rail services between Tallinn, Riga and Vilnius.

BY BUS Eurolines has an extensive network of services to western Europe from the Baltics and some services to Russia. Eurolines and other local companies such as Ecolines also run express buses between the Baltic countries. These operate several times a day and are the most practical way of land travel between the major cities. They jump the queue at the Russian borders so timings are virtually guaranteed. The journey takes around five hours from Riga to either Vilnius or Tallinn. There is a through service from Vilnius to Tallinn and also routes from Riga to Kaunas and to Tartu. Reservations can be made abroad through travel agents (see opposite) and online bookings on some services became possible in 2007 through their websites (*www.eurolines.ee* & *www.ecolines.ee*). The fare from Riga to either Tallinn or Vilnius is around £10/US$20 one-way. English is spoken in all Eurolines offices.

In January 2008 Hansabuss started a two-class bus service between Tallinn and Riga, operating three times a day Monday–Friday and once a day at weekends, stopping *en route* in Pärnu. The one-way fare is about £17/$34 in tourist class, or £25/$50 in business class. Full details are on www.businessline.ee.

Local companies operate services from Kaliningrad to Nida, Vilnius and Riga which should be pre-booked in view of the visa stipulations. These, too, jump border queues so passengers who may have spent around £5/US$8 for their fare can have the pleasure of overtaking rich businessmen fuming in their Mercedes. There are some similar services to Poland but these are less regular nowadays as local travellers now require visas.

BY CAR The entry of the three Baltic countries into the EU has made driving from western Europe much easier. Basic UK insurance cover is now valid there (although still not in Kaliningrad). However with the massive reduction in air fares that took place in 2004–05, flying and then hiring a car locally makes much more sense. UK tour operators can easily arrange a fly-drive package, but for visitors staying largely in the capital cities cars are unlikely to be of use. Many of the sites are within walking distance of hotels and others are within easy reach by bus or taxi. For day trips off the beaten track hiring a car may be worthwhile but as prices for local guides and drivers are very reasonable it is often sensible to consider taking this route. Minor roads are not well signposted and local people in the countryside do not usually speak foreign languages.

BY FERRY In the summer, hovercraft and catamarans take between an hour and 90 minutes to link Tallinn and Helsinki. Larger boats, taking about three hours, operate year-round. Services start at around 08.00 in the morning and finish around 21.00 at night. Competition between the many companies operating these routes keeps prices down to about £12 one-way and £20 return. Some carriers offer a business class for about double this price, with a private lounge and free refreshments. A day and overnight ferry operates between Tallinn and Stockholm and a day one between Riga and Stockholm. Visitors from Britain and Ireland wanting to visit Sweden and the Baltic countries can obtain a three-sector ticket from SAS agents and then use one of these ferries. Several cruise liners visit Kaliningrad, Klaipeda, Liepaja, Riga and Tallinn as part of a tour around the Baltic Sea.

TOUR OPERATORS

UK

Baltic Adventures, 22 Westfield Dr, Harpenden, Herts AL5 4LP; ☎ 01582 462283; e info@balticadventures.co.uk; www.balticadventures.co.uk. Specialists for activity groups, team-building & incentive breaks.

Baltic Holidays 5 Wood Rd, Manchester M16 9RB; ☎ 0845 0705711; e info@balticholidays.com; www.balticholidays.com. Offers a very wide range of individual & group tours to all 3 Baltic countries & to Finland, Poland & Russia

Baltic Travel Company London Hse, 271–3 King St, London W6 9LZ; ☎ 08456 800642; e info@baltictravelcompany.com; www.baltictravelcompany.com

Baltics and Beyond 6 Airedale Terrace, Skipton, N Yorks BD23 2BA; ☎ 0845 094 2125; e info@balticsandbeyond.com; www.balticsandbeyond.com. Individual itineraries to the 3 Baltic countries plus Belarus & Kaliningrad.

Explore Worldwide Nelson Hse, 55 Victoria Rd, Farnborough, Hants GU4 7PA; ☎ 0870 333 4001; e info@explore.co.uk; www.exploreworldwide.com. Operates a 2-week group tour through the 3 Baltic countries, with departures throughout the summer.

Kirker Holidays 4 Waterloo Ct, 10 Theed St, London SE1 8ST; ☎ 020 7593 2288; e travel@kirkerholidays.com; www.kirkerholidays.com. Deluxe individual short breaks to the 3 Baltic capitals.

Martin Randall Travel Voysey Hse, Barley Mow Passage, London W4 4GF; ☎ 020 8742 3355; e info@martinrandall.co.uk; www.martinrandall.com. Australian office ☎ 7 33770141; e martinrandall@bigpond.com. Group tours to the Baltic countries for those interested in art, architecture & music.

Opera Tours The Tower, Mill La, Rainhill, Prescot, Merseyside L35 6NE; ☎ 0151 493 0382; e info@operasabroad.com; www.operasabroad.com. Individual packages including opera or concert tickets.

Regent Holidays Mezzanine Suite, Froomsgate Hse, Rupert St, Bristol BS1 2QJ; ☎ 0845 277 3387; e regent@regent-holidays.co.uk; www.regent-holidays.co.uk. Specialists for Kaliningrad as well as the Baltic countries. Group tours cover the 4 capitals; city breaks are available to each of them & tailor-made individual itineraries can cover any combination of the cities with the surrounding areas. Itineraries can also include Belarus, Finland, Poland & Russia.

Scantours 73 Mornington St, London NW1 7QE; ☎ 020 7554 3530; e info@scantoursuk.com; www.scantoursuk.com. Offers city breaks, group tours & individual arrangements to 3 of the Baltic capitals & also combinations with Denmark, Sweden & Finland.

Travel Editions 69–85 Tabernacle St, London EC2A 4BD; ☎ 020 7251 0045; e tours@traveleditions.co.uk; www.traveleditions.co.uk. Group tours, many arranged as newspaper readers' offers.

Vamos Travel 2 Styles Cl, Leamington Spa, Warks CV31 1LS; ☎ 0870 762 4017; e info@vamostravel.com; www.vamostravel.com. Specialises in stag weekends & sporting breaks.

IRELAND As direct flights started from Dublin to the Baltic capitals in 2004, tour operators soon followed with appropriate programmes for city breaks and longer stays. After an uncertain start, these flights are clearly here to stay, partly because of the large Baltic communities now established in Ireland. The two operators with the widest range of possibilities in 2008 were:

Arrow Tours 40 West St, Drogheda, Co Louth; ☎ 041 983 1177; www.arrowtours.ie

Citiescapes 6 Castle St, Bray, Co Wicklow; ☎ 01 276 1222; e book@citiescapes.ie; www.citiescapes.ie

With most flights from the UK to the Baltics leaving Gatwick in the early evening, and arrival of the return flight in the afternoon, it is not difficult to join UK tours from Ireland.

GETTING AROUND

✈ **BY AIR** Since 2006 there has been a considerable increase in the number of flights between Tallinn, Riga and Vilnius, partly because of the worsening road traffic and partly because of reduced fares now offered on these routes to travellers able to book well in advance. The Air Baltic Pass of up to eight coupons for these flights at a fixed price of €35 per journey (plus tax) will probably encourage more tourists to use them as an alternative to the bus. Domestic flights in Estonia operate between Tallinn and the islands of Hiiumaa and Saaremaa. Air Baltic fly five times a day from Riga to Liepaja, Monday to Friday, and twice daily at weekends. They may well in future fly to Riga from Tartu in Estonia. Air Baltic fly from Kaliningrad to Riga, but there are no flights to Vilnius or Tallinn from there.

BY TRAIN No trains link the capitals, expect for one between Vilnius and Kaliningrad, but the area has from around 2006 seen a great revival in rail services and hopefully the trend towards modern carriages and faster timings will continue. The morning and evening services between Tallinn and Tartu are now a great success, and much cheaper than the bus. At the time of writing in early 2008, Liepaja has just one fast train a day to Riga in the morning with a return in the evening, but it is likely that this service will soon be expanded. If bought in advance at the station, tickets cost a little less than when bought on the train itself. First-class between Tallinn and Tartu, for an extra €K50 or so, is certainly to be recommended, as is travel in the centre coach from Riga to Liepaja as it is video-free.

Several suburban services are of use to tourists, from Tallinn to Paldiski, from Riga to Jurmala, and from Kaliningrad to Svetlogorsk, in each case from the capital to a nearby town on the coast.

English is not often spoken in railway stations but timetables are clearly displayed, although in Kaliningrad this is of course in the Cyrillic alphabet. Russian is in fact the first language of most railway employees throughout the Baltics. Tickets for the suburban services mentioned above are sold on the train and at larger stations.

BY BUS The most convenient way to travel between all four cities is by bus. Most services are run by Eurolines and Ecolines. Baltic specialists abroad can pre-book these, and from 2007 it became possible to book some of these buses online (*www. eurolines.ee & www. ecolines.net*). In the winter, it is often possible to buy a ticket on the spot just before departure.

The journey time between Tallinn and Riga and also between Riga and Vilnius is around five hours. Buses operate about six times a day on both sectors and the one-way fare is around £10/US$20. There is a daily bus from Kaliningrad to Riga which takes around nine hours and one night bus between Kaliningrad and Vilnius which takes eight hours. The one-way fare on these routes is also around £10/US$20. For those in no rush between Kaliningrad and Vilnius, there are six buses a day between Kaliningrad and Klaipeda which run along the Curonian Spit. These then connect with hourly services between Klaipeda and Vilnius. Allow about ten hours for the whole journey. Scenically this a much more attractive option.

Extensive bus services operate in all eight cities and local maps will give details of current routings. In Tallinn, where several competing companies operate, service numbers change quite frequently so it is important to get an up-to-date map. In the other cities, a regular pattern has now been set so few changes are likely in the near future. In Kaunas, Liepaja, Riga and Vilnius, the airports are served by a good local bus service. This is less regular in Tallinn, but as several hotels have a minibus service and a taxi into town should not cost more than £5/US$10, this does not matter so much. In Kaliningrad there is a dedicated airport bus that runs from directly outside the terminal to the Kaliningrad Hotel in the town centre.

Tickets bought at kiosks in Kaunas, Liepaja, Tallinn, Tartu and Vilnius are cheaper than those bought on the bus. Further savings are available if tickets are bought in booklets of ten. There are also passes for periods as short as one hour and as long as 48 hours, which are certainly the best value for those needing to use public transport to reach their hotel. If most visits are within walking distance of a hotel, the booklets are good value for individual journeys. Tallinn and Riga have tourist cards (see pages 24 and 99) which include free public transport for the time of their validity.

Buses link the capitals with all other major cities in their respective countries on a very regular basis. For instance between Tallinn and Tartu, or Vilnius and Kaunas, services operate every half-hour. Timetables are displayed in the bus stations and in most cases the fare is paid directly to the driver, but tickets can also be bought beforehand in the bus station, which guarantees a seat.

BY TAXI Taxis used to be a nightmare throughout the Baltics but are now better regulated. Kaunas Airport and Tallinn harbour, however, remain places where taxis are best avoided. Taxis can be easily hailed in the streets and with the lively nightlife for which all Baltic cities are now renowned, they operate almost round the clock. Taxis ordered by phone are usually cheaper than those hailed on the street so visitors planning to make many such journeys should enquire on arrival about reliable companies. Within city limits, meter fares apply and this is also the case to and from the airports. It is important to ensure that the meter is put on when the journey starts, so that there can be no subsequent arguments about the fare.

Some of the deluxe hotels operate their own fleets of taxis. These, too, are metered; prices tend to be higher but then so is the comfort of the vehicles! Lengthy journeys which would be unthinkable by taxi in western Europe can be undertaken in the Baltics with costs being so much lower.

ACCOMMODATION

A massive programme of hotel renovation took place throughout the area following the demise of the Soviet Union. The cities approached this task in different ways. Tallinn and Riga started by renovating the large tower blocks bequeathed by the Soviet Union and several have now gone through two separate renovations since 1991. From the mid 1990s, smaller hotels opened in the old town centres and also in the more affluent suburbs. In Vilnius, the reverse process operated with new small hotels opening first and only in 2002 did renovation begin at the Lietuva Hotel. From around 2000, Tallinn started to invest again in new tower blocks and 2007 saw the opening of the Swissôtel, which became the tallest building in the town. In all three cities, visitors have for many years taken for granted proper plumbing, satellite television, English-speaking reception staff and varied menus in the restaurants. In Kaliningrad, the lack of investment incentives and the lower number of visitors has let modernisation proceed at a much slower pace so most hotels remain large and impersonal. However, 2006 saw the opening of several small ones, a trend that will hopefully continue. It is because hotel building started to take off in 2005 in the other cities now included in this book that they can finally be recommended as a base for a holiday, rather than just for a short stop.

It is always wise to pre-book hotels not only for the lower prices (see below) but also simply to secure a room. A relatively small conference or sporting event may lead

ACCOMMODATION PRICE CODES

Based on a double room in summer, including breakfast

$$$$$	£155+	$310+	€200+
$$$$	£116–155	$232–310	€150–200
$$$	£77–116	$154–232	€100–150
$$	£38–77	$77–154	€50–100
$	up to £38	up to $77	up to €50

to the whole town being full. Pre-booking in Kaliningrad is in any case essential to secure a Russian visa.

In their renovations many hotels are only putting in showers and not baths in the rooms. Tourists who prefer baths should ask their tour operator to stipulate this when making the booking.

ACCOMMODATION PRICES The bigger hotels rarely expect visitors to pay the prices given on their websites as most book through agents who have negotiated lower rates. Many smaller hotels now also prefer to use agents since the volume of regular business they provide compensates for the lower prices they pay. Four- and five-star hotels reduce their prices at weekends, over public holidays and in July–August when business traffic drops. Three-star hotels tend to raise their prices then since they cater largely for tourists. The prices given in this book are based on quoted prices for a double room in summer 2008. They will be lower in winter and, despite 10% inflation projected for the Baltic countries in 2008, could be lower in summer too, particularly in Riga and Tallinn which both saw about a thousand new rooms opening in 2007–08. Vilnius, though, may well be able to hold up its prices, bearing in mind that it has been designated European Capital of Culture in 2009, so is already in the midst of regular publicity.

EATING AND DRINKING

It is perhaps in restaurants and bars that the transformation from the old days became quickly apparent in Tallinn, Riga and Vilnius. *In Your Pocket* and the *City Paper* now list hundreds of choices in each city and what is gratifying is the number that still exist five or six years after opening. Every major cuisine is represented and, with the numbers of restaurants now available, advance booking is often not necessary. It is worth venturing outside the old city areas: the best food is often to be found in their immediate vicinity and there is little risk of seeing other tourists there, and certainly not large groups. Many are not immediately obvious, but they are highlighted in this book.

One has to be brutally honest about local food. Whilst there are many perfectly acceptable dishes, few are memorable. However, they should at least be made from fresh ingredients, now that these are available year-round. Thick soups can be recommended in winter as meals in themselves, and pancakes are served with a variety of savoury or sweet fillings. The ranges of coffee, cakes and ice cream available are one positive legacy of Soviet and German times.

Kaliningrad has made progress recently and there is sufficient choice to cover a stay of a week or so. Prices are so low that it would be invidious to complain about the quality; a wide menu can now be taken for granted but do not yet expect many non-Russian restaurants.

From about 2004 Tartu became gastronomically exciting and new restaurants open there every year, whereas none seems to close. Outside the other capitals, the best food remains in the hotels, although there are signs this may soon change.

Wine is quite expensive throughout the region and the quality unexciting. A wine list shows what is in stock from time to time, not what is regularly available. It is often better (and much cheaper) to drink local beer. Spirits are good everywhere with a wide local and international choice. Tourists who knew the old USSR will still find it hard to adjust to a small café in the Baltics offering a choice of malt whiskies, at prices half those charged in Scotland.

MEDIA AND COMMUNICATIONS

TELEPHONES Public telephones in all four countries are operated by cards which can be bought at local kiosks. Cards are not interchangeable so new ones have to be bought for each country. It is not possible to use credit cards, nor do any phones accept coins. Instructions are usually given in English in the phone booths. The procedure is the same in all four countries: the receiver is lifted, the card inserted and then the number dialled. As the call continues, the reducing value of the card is shown on the screen. Calls to western Europe cost around £0.60/US$1 a minute with reductions in the evenings and at weekends. With competition from mobile phone companies, prices are tending to fall. Prices from hotel rooms are of course higher than this but they are rarely exorbitant. Calls to local mobile phones can cost almost as much as international calls, particularly in Estonia. Calls can be made from all major post offices. As the use of mobile phones in all four countries is so prevalent now, public phone boxes are few and far between.

Dialling codes and information specific to the various countries are given in the individual city chapters later in the book. However, to make an international call from each of the four countries, dial 00 followed by the country code:

Australia	61	Ireland	353
Canada	1	Italy	39
Estonia	372	Latvia	371
Finland	358	Lithuania	370
France	33	UK	44
Germany	49	USA	1

POST AND COURIER Post from the three Baltic countries is transmitted quickly, reaching western Europe or America within four or five days. From Kaliningrad, post can travel via Warsaw or via Moscow so can take up to two weeks. Postage rates are fairly similar in all four countries, with higher charges applying for cards and letters sent beyond Europe. As post offices sell thick envelopes and parcel paper, it is easy to send home books and other bulky items bought during a tour. They also sell cards at very reasonable rates. The one at the top of Tallinn Old Town charges less than half the price demanded by sellers in the street outside! Stamps can naturally be used only in their country of origin so do not forget to use them before moving on.

All major courier companies such as DHL, Fedex and UPS have offices in each of the capitals.

NEWSPAPERS AND MAGAZINES The *In Your Pocket* series of mini-guides to each of the capitals provides invaluable information for each city, including listings of restaurants, museum opening hours, postage rates and details of public transport. Their irreverent style is a pleasant contrast to the minimal official tourist material that is produced locally. Where appropriate they can be highly critical. For Tallinn, Riga and Vilnius the guides are produced locally every couple of months, so are always up to date. Elsewhere they are published every six months or annually. Guides cost the equivalent of £1.50/US$3 each, and are available at many hotels and kiosks. They are also published in full on the website (*www.inyourpocket.com*) so this is worth consulting before departure.

The *Baltic Times* is published weekly in Riga (in English) and covers contemporary politics in the three main Baltic countries. The *Königsberg Express*, published monthly in German in Kaliningrad, fulfils a similar role there. European editions of the main American and British newspapers are available on the morning of publication in Tallinn, Riga and Vilnius, but not elsewhere. German papers occasionally reach Kaliningrad. In the winter they are sold in the Kaliningrad Hotel and in the summer also in Svetlogorsk.

The *City Paper*, published monthly in Tallinn, in a sense combines the *Baltic Times* and the *In Your Pocket* guides. Each issue costs about £1.50/US$3. It has useful background articles on contemporary politics, thoughtful restaurant reviews and practical information on the three main Baltic capitals. It is an excellent introduction to the area and earlier issues are covered on its website (*www.balticsworldwide.com*).

TELEVISION All hotels used regularly by foreign tourists now have satellite television, offering at least one English-language channel. Many offer both American and British channels, realising that most visitors have a clear preference for one or the other.

🏺 MUSEUMS

In all four countries, museums tend to have short opening hours and close at least one day a week. Monday is the most likely day for closure. Although opening times tend to change frequently, the *In Your Pocket* guides carry this information, as do the local tourist offices. Where museums have useful websites with details of their current opening hours, these are listed. It is rare for museums to open before 10.30 in the morning. Smaller ones are happy to open specially for groups and tour operators usually arrange this so that their party can have the building to themselves. This arrangement is particularly attractive at the Mentzendorf House and at the Rozentāls Museum in Riga, both of which can take around 25 people in comfort, but not more. Most have an admission charge, though this is rarely higher than the equivalent of £2/US$4. Pensioners are often admitted free of charge or at a reduced price.

HEALTH AND SAFETY

HEALTH No inoculations are required for visits to this area and hygiene standards in hotels and restaurants are high. Nevertheless, it would be wise here, as at home, to be up to date with immunisations against diphtheria, tetanus and polio. Tap water should not be drunk in Kaliningrad but is safe elsewhere in the Baltic countries. It is wise to carry a good insect repellent and to use it day and night if mosquitoes are around.

Local hospitals can be trusted to deal with any emergency; long gone are the days when foreigners flew to Helsinki or Stockholm for any minor ailment. EU passport holders are entitled to use health facilities in the Baltic countries on the same basis as residents, but this does not apply in Kaliningrad.

A full list of current travel clinic websites worldwide is available on www.istm.org. For other journey preparation information, consult www.tripprep.com. Information about various medications may be found on www.emedicine.com/wild/topiclist.htm.

DISABLED VISITORS The cobbled streets of the old towns are not the ideal place for those in a wheelchair or with limited mobility, but elsewhere the cities are as accessible as anywhere in the West. All newly built hotels and offices cater for wheelchairs.

CRIME This is much less of a problem than in most European capitals, although pickpockets are a threat in Tallinn and Riga old towns where the maze of small streets makes for an easy getaway. There have recently been attacks on rich foreigners in Tallinn leaving clubs late at night. Car theft is common throughout the area and cars should always be left overnight in a guarded hotel parking lot.

Passports and air tickets can fairly safely be left in hotel rooms, locked in cases. Otherwise the usual sensible precautions apply. Do not take out large sums of cash when walking around the main tourist areas. What might be a modest sum to a Western tourist can be a month's pay for a local youngster so it is not surprising that some will succumb to temptation when offered the chance.

MAJOR DATES IN BALTIC HISTORY

1201	Riga founded.
1221	First recorded demonstration in Riga against occupation.
1323	Vilnius documented for the first time in a letter by Grand Duke Gediminas, who made it Lithuania's capital.
1386	Royal union of Poland and Lithuania.
1410	Polish-Lithuanian army defeats the Teutonic Knights, ending German hegemony over the Baltic region.
1544	Founding of Königsberg University.
1569	Polish–Lithuanian Commonwealth formed.
1579	Founding of Vilnius University.
1581	Riga falls to the Polish–Lithuanian Commonwealth.
1600	Tallinn seized by the Swedes.
1621	Riga seized by the Swedes.
1710	Riga and Tallinn seized by the Russians.
1758–62	Russians occupy Königsberg for four years.
1794	Vilnius seized by the Russians.
1795	Polish–Lithuanian Commonwealth is wiped off the map; Vilnius becomes a provincial capital of the Tsarist Empire.
1808	Memel (Klaipeda) becomes the temporary capital of Prussia for a year after Napoleon occupies Berlin.
1812	Napoleon seizes Vilnius but his forces are driven back a few months later. Riga's wooden suburbs were burnt to prepare to defend the Old Town against Napoleon, who instead advanced towards Moscow.
1836	Richard Wagner moves to Königsberg from Magdeburg to marry and to escape his creditors. The following year he would move to Riga to take up an appointment as director of music (and also to be further from his creditors).
1873	First Song Festival held in Riga.
1918	Lithuanian independence is declared in Vilnius on 16 February, Estonian independence declared on 24 February in Tallinn, and Latvian independence in Riga on 18 November.
1920	In the Treaty of Tartu of 2 February 1920, the Treaty of Moscow of 12 July, and the Treaty of Riga of 1 August, the Soviet Union recognises the independence of each of the Baltic countries. Polish troops seize Vilnius on 9 October and it will remain under Polish occupation until autumn 1939. Kaunas is established as a temporary capital of Lithuania.
1923	On 19 January, Memel (Klaipeda) is incorporated into Lithuania.
1924	On 1 December an attempted coup d'état by the Communist Party of Estonia fails.
1933	In elections held on 5 March, the Nazis win 53% of the vote in Königsberg, one of the highest percentages anywhere in Germany.

1939	On 23 March, Nazi Germany occupies Memel (Klaipeda). Molotov–Ribbentrop Pact signed on 23 August. On 9 October, Hitler summons the Baltic-German communities of Tallinn and Riga 'back home' even though most had been settled in the Baltics for centuries.
1940	Between 14 and 16 June, the three Baltic countries are occupied by Soviet troops and by early August are formally incorporated into the USSR.
1941	The Baltic capitals each fall to the German army as it advances into Russia: Vilnius on 23 June, Riga on 1 July and Tallinn on 28 August.
1944	Reoccupation by Soviet troops of Vilnius on 7 July, of Tallinn on 22 September and of Riga on 13 October.
1945	On 10 April, General Lasch surrenders Königsberg to the Red Army.
1946	In July Königsberg is renamed Kaliningrad.
1947	In October the deportation begins of all remaining Germans in Kaliningrad.
1960	Tallinn, Riga and Vilnius are opened to foreign tourists for stays of no more than three nights. Kaliningrad will stay closed until 1988.
1965	A twice-weekly ferry service opens between Tallinn and Helsinki, which will remain the only link with the West until 1989.
1980	Olympic Games sailing and yachting events held in Tallinn.
1986	On 14 June, the first demonstration since the return of Soviet power in 1944 is held beside the Freedom Monument in Riga.
1987	German tourists allowed to return to Klaipeda.
1988	On 11 September Trivimi Velliste, a future foreign minister, publicly demands Estonian independence in front of an audience of 300,000 at the Song Festival Amphitheatre in Tallinn.
1989	A human chain of two million people links Vilnius, Riga and Tallinn on 23 August, the 50th anniversary of the signing of the Molotov–Ribbentrop Pact.
1990	11 March. The restoration of Lithuanian independence is declared in Vilnius by Vytautas Landsbergis from the same balcony used on 16 February 1918.
1991	Fourteen protestors defending the Vilnius television tower are killed by Soviet troops on 13 January. On 20 January five protestors would be similarly killed in Riga. 20–21 August. Following the unsuccessful coup in Moscow against President Gorbachev, Estonia and Latvia declare independence. Worldwide diplomatic recognition for all three Baltic countries follows within the next few days.
1993	On 31 August the last Soviet troops leave Lithuania; they would finally leave Latvia and Estonia in 1994.
2002	Eurovision Song Contest held in Tallinn. The 2003 one took place in Riga.
2004	The three Baltic countries join NATO in April and the EU in May.
2005	On 3 July, Gerhard Schröder and Jacques Chirac visit Kaliningrad, the first foreign heads of state to do so.
2006	On 14 March the former Estonian President, Lennart Meri, dies.
2007	On 21 December, border controls are abolished between the Baltic countries as they join the Schengen Agreement.
2009	Vilnius to be European Capital of Culture.
2011	Tallinn to be European Capital of Culture.
2012	Earliest possible introduction of the euro in the three Baltic countries.

2

Tallinn ESTONIA

Whether approached by air, land or sea, Tallinn is immediately identifiable as a capital that looks West rather than East. The departure board at the airport lists London, Copenhagen and Stockholm but rarely St Petersburg. The boats that fill the harbour, be they massive ferries or small yachts, head for Finland and Sweden, not Russia. The traffic jams that are beginning to block the main streets are caused by Volkswagens, Land Rovers and Saabs, not by Ladas. Links with the West are celebrated; those with Russia are commemorated. In May 1998, Tallinn celebrated its 750th anniversary since on 15 May 1248 it adopted Lübeck Town Law, which united most members of the Hanseatic League. A month later, as on every 14 June, flags were lowered in memory of those deported to the Soviet Union on 14 June 1941.

Immediately after independence Western goods started pouring into the shops, and Russian ones are now very hard to find. There is a similar reluctance to buy from any of the other former Soviet republics. Travel agents offer the same tempting prices for holidays in Turkey, Greece and Italy that are available in western Europe, but nobody is interested in St Petersburg or the Crimea. Architecturally, with the exception of the Alexander Nevsky Cathedral, it is the Germans, Swedes and Danes who have left their imposing mark on the churches and fortifications of the Old Town. Tallinn was always ready to defend itself but in the end never did so. The nearest it came to a major battle was at the conclusion of the Northern War in 1710, but plague had reduced the population from 10,000 to 2,000 so the Swedes offered little resistance to the army of Peter the Great. It has suffered many occupations but, apart from a Soviet bombing raid in 1944, the city has not been physically harmed as no battles were ever fought there.

The division in Tallinn between what is now the Old Town on the hill (Toompea) and the newer town around the port has survived political administrations of every hue. It has divided God from Mammon, Tsarist and Soviet governors from their reluctant Estonian subjects, and now the Estonian parliament from successful bankers, merchants and manufacturers who thrive on whatever coalition happens to be in power. Tallinn has no Capitol Hill or Whitehall. The parliament building is one of the most modest in the Old Town, dwarfed by the town walls and surrounding churches. When fully restored, the Old Town will be an outstanding permanent monument to Gothic and Baroque architecture, and a suitable backcloth to formal political and religious activity. Outside its formidable wall, contemporary Tallinn will change rapidly according to the demands of the new business ethos. For those arriving by sea, tower blocks now identify Tallinn just as much as the silhouette of the Old Town.

HISTORY

Written records on Tallinn date only from the 12th century although it is clear that a small port existed well before then. In 1219 the Danes occupied Tallinn and much of what is now northern Estonia, on the pretext of spreading Christianity. The name Tallinn dates from this time and in Estonian actually means 'Danish city'. Although this name was

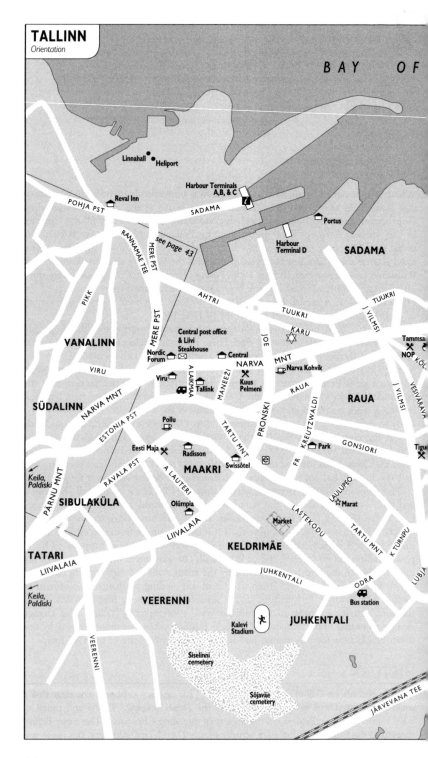

TALLINN
Orientation

BAY   OF

Linnahall   Heliport

Reval Inn

POHJA PST

RANNAMÄE TEE

PIKK

MERE PST

Harbour Terminals
A, B, & C

SADAMA

see page 43

Harbour
Terminal D

Portus

SADAMA

AHTRI

TUUKRI

J VILMSI

VANALINN

MERE PST

Central post office
& Liivi
Steakhouse

TUUKRI

KARU

JOE

NARVA

MNT

Tammsa

NOP
KÖL

Nordic
Forum

Central

VIRU

Viru

A LAIKMAA

Tallink

MANEEŽI

Narva Kohvik

Kuus
Pelmeni

RAUA

RAUA

J VILMSI

VESIVARAVA

SÜDALINN

NARVA MNT

ESTONIA PST

Pollu

PRONSKI

FR. KREUTZWALDI

Park

GONSIORI

Tigu

Eesti Maja

RÄVALA PST

Radisson

A LAUTERI

MAAKRI

Swissôtel

TARTU MNT

Keila,
Paldiski

PÄRNU MNT

SIBULAKÜLA

Olümpia

LIIVALAIA

Market

LAULUPEO

Marat

LASTEKODU

TARTU MNT

K TURNPU

KELDRIMÄE

TATARI

LIIVALAIA

JUHKENTALI

ODRA

LUBJA

Keila,
Paldiski

VEERENNI

VEERENNI

Kalevi
Stadium

JUHKENTALI

Bus station

Siselinni
cemetery

Sõjaväe
cemetery

JÄRVEVANA TEE

16

TALLINN

Viimsi

Maarjamae Palace

0 ——————— 400m
0 ——————— 400yds

N

Bradt

PIRITA TEE

Exhibition Centre

Narva

Song Festival
Amphitheatre

Russalka Memorial

NARVA MNT

NARVA MNT

KADRIORG

Kadriorg Park

KUREPOLLU

Narva

Spaghetteria

Cantina
Carramba

Lydia

Park

WEIZENBERG

Kadriorg
Palace

Peter the Great

VALGE

Poska
Villa

KOIDULA

Park

Mikkeli

KUMU

POSKA

UUSLINN

LAAGNA TEE

PAE

Kadriorg
Stadium

LAAGNA TEE

PAE

GONSIORI

TORUPILLI

PUNANE

PALLASTI

SIKUPILLI

LASNAMÄE

LASNAMÄE

MAJAKA

PAE

Narva

TARTU MNT

PETERBURI TEE

PETERBURI TEE

SUUR - SÕJAMÄE

Ülemiste

*Lake
Ülemiste*

TARTU MNT

Tartu, Airport

ÜLEMISTE

chosen to suggest only temporary occupation, it has been maintained. The first German merchants settled in 1228 and they were to maintain their economic domination until 1939, even during the long periods of Swedish and Tsarist rule. Their elaborate coats of arms, displayed in the Dome and Niguliste churches, were a formal expression of this power. When, for instance, the Swedes surrendered to the Russians in 1710, the capitulation documents confirmed that German would remain the official language of commerce. Reval, the German name for Tallinn, is sometimes seen in English publications; it probably comes from Revala, the old Estonian name for the surrounding area. A more colourful explanation is that it comes from the two German words *reh* and *fall*, meaning the falling of the deer as they attempt to escape the Danish occupation.

Peter the Great visited Tallinn on 11 different occasions, so crucial was the city as an ice-free port to his empire. In 1711 he joined Christmas celebrations in Town Hall Square. He instigated the permanent expansion of Tallinn beyond the city walls by building Kadriorg Palace near the coast about two miles from the Old Town. The previous history of constant warfare at least in the vicinity of the town had led to all buildings being makeshift wooden houses which could easily be burnt as a preliminary defence to the city. Tallinn was then to enjoy 200 years of peace and increasing prosperity. Architecturally, though, the Old Town has always remained the centre of Tallinn and its main attraction. Gert Walter, a Baltic German who settled in East Germany and could therefore return to Tallinn during the Soviet period, describes the Old Town as having 0.5% of the surface area of Tallinn but giving it its entire magic.

The completion of the railway link with St Petersburg in 1870 turned Tallinn into a major city. The port was enlarged to handle the increasing volume of goods that could now be brought there and factories were established to take advantage of the larger markets. In the 20th century, most events that would determine Estonia's future took place in Tallinn. Independence was declared there in 1918 and in 1991; German occupations were imposed there also in 1918 and again in 1941. The Soviets came in 1940 and then chased the Germans out in 1944. In the 20th century, the Russians and Germans between them occupied Tallinn seven times, and the country has been independent three times, although it has to be admitted that independence on the first occasion in 1918 lasted for only one day. Britain can claim considerable credit for ensuring that the next period of independence would last much longer – 20 years. Intervention by the Royal Navy during 1918–19 in the Gulf of Finland near Tallinn ensured that neither the Bolsheviks nor the Germans were able to conquer Estonia at that time.

The port always adapted to the political circumstances in which it found itself. During the first independence period from 1920 to 1940 it exported large quantities of timber and dairy products to Britain as the market to the new Soviet Union was lost. Passenger services linked it with all its Baltic neighbours. From 1945 until 1990 it would suffer a moribund 45 years with little international trade being allowed. Sections of the harbour area were closed to the public as a military area and regeneration of this area is still continuing in 2008. The twice-weekly ferry service that operated for Finnish visitors from the 1960s rapidly increased to a boat an hour during the 1990s as the notorious 'vodka tourists' poured in, together with some other visitors who had broader interests. Whilst 2.5 million passengers a year come to Tallinn on this route, the port has to battle hard with Russian, Latvian and Lithuanian ports for the transit traffic in goods from Russia and central Asia. Another battle, in which Tallinn has been tremendously successful, is first to encourage cruise ships to berth here, and then to extend their stay. After being rigidly controlled in St Petersburg, passengers enjoy the easy-going mixture of excursions and free time in the Old Town.

Between 1945 and 1990 the city's population doubled in size to 500,000, about 30% of the total population of Estonia. Since then, Tallinn's population, like that of the whole country, has dropped considerably as couples delay starting families and living on one's own becomes more popular. It is now approximately 380,000. The year 2002 was the first since 1990 when more births than deaths were registered and since then the populations of both the town and the country have remained static.

On 26 April 2007 a traffic island in central Tallinn suddenly became a major international news item. Until then, it had been the site of the Bronze Soldier, a monument erected in 1945 by the Soviet Union to commemorate their 'liberation' of Tallinn on 22 September 1944. Many formal ceremonies took place there in Soviet times, and after the restoration of independence in 1991 Soviet veterans tended to place wreaths there both on 9 May each year to commemorate the end of the war, and on 22 September. It was thought, too, that a number of bodies had been buried there in 1944 but they had never been identified. These were finally excavated at the time the monument was moved.

The Estonian government planned from early 2007 to move the monument to a military cemetery where, amongst others, some British sailors from the 1918–20 campaign were buried. There were two reasons for this decision. First, what had become a noisy traffic island was no place for a war memorial; and second, its prominence in the town centre was seen as an insult to Estonian sovereignty. Estonia could not forgive Soviet vandalism which led to the destruction of nearly all of the monuments to the fighting in 1918–20, but the government in no way wanted to emulate this behaviour. (Latvia and Lithuania did not have to face this issue since the equivalent monuments in Riga, Vilnius and Kaunas are a long way from the town centre.)

It has still not been established why on 26 April 2007 several hundred young Russian-speaking males went on the rampage in the streets near the monument, looting the shops and waving their stolen goods at press photographers and television crews. Their behaviour was an acute embarrassment to most Russian speakers in Estonia who either accepted the government view or, if not, would certainly not have wanted their views represented in this way. Many ethnic Russians, disgusted at the behaviour of this small minority, came to express their regrets the following morning to the shopkeepers who had been hit.

The Russian government banned the transmission of pictures from the demonstrations and cut a lot of railway transit traffic through Estonia, even though it was largely members of the Russian-speaking community who worked on the railways. Cyber attacks were launched on Estonia, which for two days seriously harmed communications between Estonia and the outside world and on the basis of misreporting in the Russian press, many Russian tourists cancelled their holidays in Estonia. President Putin asked them to visit Kaliningrad instead; perhaps some did so, but by Christmas the number of Russian visitors to Tallinn was not much lower than the 2006 figure. In the eyes of most ordinary Russians, the issue, like the soldiers formerly scattered across a traffic island, had been properly buried.

SUGGESTED ITINERARIES

DAY ONE Spend the whole day in the Old Town starting at the top of the Toompea Hill around 09.00 when the churches open but before the cruise passengers are brought there. An audio guide hired from the tourist office will provide a lively accompaniment of stories to this walk and this is included in the price of a Tallinn Card (see page 24). Start at the Alexander Nevsky Cathedral (page 55), continue to the Dome Church (page 56), walk down Lühike jalg ('Short Leg') and drop into the Adamson-Eric Museum (page 49) at the bottom of the hill to be amazed at how one man can produce art in so many shapes and forms. A visit to Niguliste Church (St Nicholas', page 57) should finish the morning.

Michael Bourdeaux

For 15 years after World War II, Tallinn was a closed city, nestling amongst the forest of defensive (offensive) weaponry trained on the NATO countries. Suddenly in 1960 it was opened to Western visitors. I was lucky enough to have been a student at Moscow University at the time, so in May 1960 I was perhaps the first British visitor. I not only went there by train from Leningrad but also stayed illegally in a private house for the first and only time during the 25 years that I knew the Soviet Union. Far from being worried that I would bring trouble on their heads, the occupants barred the exit and refused to let me out until I had agreed to stay for three nights, having found my own photograph displayed on their wall!

All of us, as if by common agreement, steered clear of the topic of the Soviet occupation but the family thoroughly organised my time for the next three days. After eight months in drab winter Moscow, the élan of ancient Tallinn in its bright spring colours took me into a new world. A visit on Sunday to Kaide's Lutheran church, Charles' Church, left mixed impressions. Strangely, the family did not want to accompany me. This huge church was about half full, with 40% of the congregation younger people, a far higher proportion than one saw in Russia. I tried to see the pastor after the service, but the corridor was blocked by dozens of young people waiting outside his door. None of these, to my surprise, would speak to me, although most must have known Russian. I surmised they were waiting for religious instruction, illegal under the Soviet system at the time, and were unwilling for a foreigner (or a Russian if they took me for one) to intrude.

On my final day, having purchased an air ticket to Riga, I was waiting on the tarmac beside a small aeroplane. An official came up to me, demanded my documents, took me inside and told me my intended flight was illegal for a foreigner. 'Our rules are less strict than yours in Britain for Soviet citizens,' he said. 'When I was there, I was prevented from visiting many places. You can go where you like, but not always by your chosen route. Visit Riga by all means, but you must do so by train via Leningrad.'

Spend midday around Town Hall Square and, if the weather permits, climb the Town Hall Tower for a view of contemporary Tallinn before going down to the basement (page 54) to see the exhibition on how the square has looked over the last 800 years. Do not forget to use the toilets here as they offer the best views of the foundations.

Continue the afternoon at the City Museum (page 49) and allow an hour to watch all the films which relive the bombing in 1944 and the independence demonstrations in 1988–91. Have a cup of tea in the café at the top and then finish up at the Maritime Museum (page 52) to see how and why so many nations fought for control of the harbour. Only the British (and the Estonians!) are presented in a favourable light. The latest exhibit covers the tragedy of the *Estonia* which sank in September 1994, claiming 850 lives. The two streets that link the museum to the Viru Gate, Uus and Müürivahe, are ideal for a final stroll, as they have a range of buildings to admire, but also small cafés and shops. Do take another walk around the Old Town after sunset to see the major buildings bathed in floodlight.

DAY TWO After a totally urban day, some greenery is called for, so start by taking the tram to Kadriorg Palace (page 64) and linger in the gardens before going in. Do not miss the porcelain at the Mikkeli Museum (page 65) before walking on to KUMU (page 50), the new art museum that opened in February 2006. A rest will be needed before setting off further out of town to the Song Festival Grounds (page 63). Try to imagine 5,000 people singing here, or come in July 2009 and see the real thing. Take the bus back to Vabaduse Väljak (Freedom Square), an area where there are many cafés for lunch. Look in at the Tallinn Art Hall to see which contemporary artists are in favour, and then face the Occupation Museum (page 53) which shows the horrors and banalities of life under the Soviet and German occupations between 1940 and 1991. Finish the afternoon at the National Library (page 52). Hopefully there will be a concert in the early evening either at Niguliste (page 57) or at the Dome Church (page 56). A Tallinn card (see page 24) will be invaluable for this two-day itinerary.

PRACTICALITIES

MONEY AND BANKING

Currency The Estonian kroon is tied to the euro at the rate of 15.65EEK. In July 2008 exchange rates against the pound and US dollar were £1 = 19.70EEK and US$1 = 9.90EEK.

Banks and credit cards The Hansapank at Vanu Turg 2 (*www.hansa.ee*) and the Äripank at Vana Viru 7, close to the Viru Gate, usually give the best exchange rate for pounds and dollars. The nearby Tavid exchange at Aia 5 (*www.tavid.ee*) is very useful for getting rid of unwanted notes from all over the world. During the day, their rates are as good as those at Äripank and they do not charge commission so even small amounts can sensibly be exchanged. Tavid is open around the clock, even at Christmas and New Year, but from 19.00 until 09.00 the following day during the week, and from 17.00 at the weekends, their rates worsen considerably, often by as much as 10%. Exchange rates can be checked on the relevant websites.

Elsewhere in the town, both at banks and exchange bureaux, the rate for pounds can vary enormously whereas that for the US dollar is less erratic and of course that for the euro will be most competitive as the exchange rate is fixed. There are many exchange bureaux and banks along Viru which leads from Viru Square to Town Hall Square. Check the rates before deciding which to use. The exchange bureaux are open daily from 10.00 until 19.00. Banks close at 17.00 or 18.00 and do not usually open at weekends, except for those branches based in large shopping centres which open on both Saturday and Sunday. ATMs (cashpoints) are available throughout the town.

Appalling rates for all currencies can always be guaranteed at the 'airside' bureau in Tallinn Airport and at the bus station, so these two outlets should be avoided. The bank 'landside' at the airport in the arrivals area usually has poor rates for buying EEK, but the one in the departure area is fine. Those at the railway station offer reasonable rates. Tourists are advised not to accept notes of 500EEK when changing money since they are often difficult to use as most transactions will involve much smaller sums or can be paid by credit card. At the time of publication, it was still uncertain when Estonia would join the euro. This had originally been planned for 2008 but high rates of inflation in 2006 and 2007, which were likely to continue in 2008, ruled this out. The year 2012 now seems the earliest practical date.

Local media The *Baltic Times*, published weekly on a Thursday, is the best English-language source of news for the three Baltic republics. It also lists exhibitions and concerts. *Tallinn In Your Pocket*, published every two months, is invaluable for its independent – and therefore irreverent – reviews on restaurants, museums and other sites. The *City Paper*, published monthly, covers Tallinn, Riga and Vilnius together in a similar way to *Tallinn In Your Pocket* but with the addition of political articles. The printed publication now concentrates more on background articles, but their website has a full and critical list of hotels and restaurants. Both the *City Paper* and *Tallinn In Your Pocket* are a welcome contrast to many worthy but dull local guidebooks. Travel agents abroad who specialise in the Baltics will be able to provide copies of both publications or they are available online (*www.inyourpocket.com* & *www.balticsworldwide.com*). Several free-of-charge listings magazines are circulated by hotels and local travel agents but as these are supported totally by advertising, they cannot really be trusted.

European editions of British and American newspapers are on sale in Tallinn at the larger hotels on the day of publication.

There are no local radio or television stations that transmit in English.

COMMUNICATIONS

Telephones Public phone boxes take phonecards, which can be bought at kiosks; they do not take cash or credit cards. Calls can also be made from post offices. Mark-ups on phone calls from hotel rooms vary enormously. Some hotels have wisely reduced prices to persuade visitors not to use their mobile phones; others have kept charges that were acceptable in the 1990s but are not any longer. As in Britain, there is now no distinction in Estonia between costs for local or national calls, although some hotels still maintain one.

From a phonebox, reckon to spend about 40p/80c a minute to phone a landline in Britain or North America.

Dialling To reach Tallinn by phone from abroad, first dial the international code 00, second the Estonia country code 372, and then the Tallinn seven-digit number. This will always begin with a '6'. A similar system operates in other areas of Estonia. For instance, all Tartu numbers begin with a '7'. To reach phones abroad from Tallinn dial 00 and then the relevant country code.

Mobile phones Most Estonians now have mobile phones, which are operated by a number of different companies. They each have a separate access code which is dialled after the 372 and which replaces the city code of 6. Despite the popularity of mobile phones, calls to and from them are still much more expensive than those to and from landlines.

Useful telephone numbers
Ambulance and Fire Brigade ☏ 112

Central Hospital ☏ 622 7070

City Tourist Office ☏ 645 7777

Police ☏ 110

Telephone Information ☏ 626 1111

POST The Central Post Office is at Narva mnt 1, opposite the Viru Hotel. It has relatively short opening hours (⊕ *08.00–20.00 Mon–Fri, 08.00–18.00 Sat*). It sells a wide range of postcards, changes money at acceptable rates and provides telephone services. Tourists often use the post office at the top of the Old Town at Lossi plats 4 beside the Alexander Nevsky Cathedral but this is only open 09.00–17.00 Monday–Friday. For collectors, it has a wide selection of stamps, and postcards are sold at much lower prices than those charged elsewhere in the Old Town. It does not provide exchange facilities. The postal service is extremely efficient, with cards reaching anywhere in Europe within a few days.

INTERNET All major hotels have a business centre offering a full range of services, including internet access, but the charges are high – usually around 100EEK per half-hour. Some hotels, such as the Meriton Grand and the Nordic Forum, have a computer for guests' use in the lobby which is free of charge. Terminals are also free of charge, but therefore often in use, at the National Library. Metro, the café beside the bus station under the Viru Centre (⏲ *07.00–23.00 Mon–Fri, 10.00–23.00 Sat/Sun*), can be recommended for those who prefer to make frequent short use of internet cafés. They have a 'season ticket' for ten hours costing only EEK100 which allows unlimited access for that time-frame. Otherwise they charge EEK35 an hour during the week and EEK20 an hour at weekends. Several computers are available free of charge in the departure lounge at Tallinn Airport.

EMBASSIES

🅔 **Canada** Toom-Kooli 13; ✆ 627 3311; f 627 3312; e tallinn@canada.ee

🅔 **Ireland** Vene 2; ✆ 681 1888; f 681 1899; e embassytallinn@eircom.net

🅔 **Latvia** Tõnismägi 10; ✆ 646 1313; f 631 1366

🅔 **Lithuania** Uus 15; ✆ 631 4030; f 641 2013; e amber@anet.ee; www.hot.ee/lietambasada

🅔 **Russia** Pikk 19; ✆ 646 4175; f 646 4178; e vensaat@online.ee; www.estonia.mid.ru

🅔 **UK** Wismari 6; ✆ 667 4700; f 667 4723; e information@britishembassy.ee; www.britishembassy.ee

🅔 **USA** Kentmanni 20; ✆ 668 8100; f 668 8134; e tallinn@usemb.ee; www.usemb.ee

HOSPITALS AND PHARMACIES The Central Hospital (✆ *620 7015*) on Ravi provides 24-hour emergency care and the 24-hour pharmacy (✆ *644 2282*) is at Tõnismägi 5. Long gone are the days when foreigners who fell ill demanded to be taken immediately to Helsinki.

RELIGIOUS SERVICES Tallinn now has an active religious life, with services held regularly at all the churches in the Old Town. An English-language service is held every Sunday at 15.00 at the Holy Ghost Church. Full details are available on www.eelk.ee/tallinna.puhavaimu. The synagogue opened in May 2007 at Karu 16, near the harbour, and details of services can be found on www.ejc.ee. There is currently no mosque in Tallinn.

TOURIST INFORMATION The Tallinn Tourist Board (⏲ *May–Sep 09.00–19.00 Mon–Fri, 10.00–19.00 Sat/Sun; closed national holidays: 23–24 Jun & 20 Aug*) has a shop front office on the corner of Kullassepa 4 and Niguliste 2 (St Nicholas') which sells a minimal range of books, maps and cards. They have up-to-date editions of *Tallinn In Your Pocket* and the *City Paper*, but for anything else, cross the road to the bookshop Raamatukoi. What is, however, useful is a large reference folder with timetables for ferries to Finland, buses out of Tallinn and local railways. There is a similar office in the ticket hall by the harbour. This office, like all other tourist offices around Estonia, has a website (*www.visitestonia.com*). Visiting these sites before departure will save a lot of time on arrival.

For tourists who arrive without having pre-booked any excursions, or who need to book further accommodation in the Baltic area, the tourist office can also advise on local operators with regular programmes. From 1 June to 15 September, Estonian Holidays operates a daily sightseeing walk in old Tallinn (€12 pp), departing from their office at 14.00. The tour lasts three hours and includes admission to the Dom Church.

TOUR OPERATORS Recommended ones include:

Baltic Tours Pikk 31; ✆ 630 0460; e incoming@baltictours.ee; www.bt.ee

Estonian Holidays Rüütli 28/30; ✆ 627 0500; e holidays@holidays.ee; www.holidays.ee

Estravel Suur-Karja 15; ✆ 626 6266; e sales@estravel.ee; www.estravel.ee

THE TALLINN CARD The card provides an ideal way for tourists spending two days or more in Tallinn to budget effectively for their sightseeing and entrance fees. A bus tour is included, as is an iPod walk around the Old Town, plus unrestricted use of public transport and entrance to all the major museums. Although charges for all of these have gone up considerably over the last few years, the card price has stayed the same since 2006. Full details of what is included can be seen on www.tallinn.ee/tallinncard. From January 2008 the cost is 130EEK for 6 hours, 350EEK for 24 hours, 400EEK for 48 hours and 450EEK for 72 hours.

TRANSPORT

TALLINN AIRPORT The airport is only 3–4km from the town centre. The current building dates originally from 1980 when Tallinn suddenly needed to show an international face for the Olympics (sailing events were held in the Baltic) and has been modernised on several occasions to meet the demands of Western travellers since independence. Major renovation is again under way, with plans to name the airport after Lennart Meri, Estonia's first president who died in March 2006. He will always be remembered there for holding a press conference outside the gents' toilets to show his dissatisfaction with their lack of cleanliness.

A local bus service operates to the town centre every quarter of an hour with the final stop behind the Viru Hotel. Several other hotels such as the Radisson and the Central are within walking distance of this stop. Tickets bought from the driver cost 20EEK and only local currency can be used. (Tickets bought from kiosks cost 13EEK individually or 90EEK if bought in a block of ten; these are available at the landside kiosk where arriving passengers leave the baggage hall.) During the day taxis are easily available. They are all metered and cost about 100EEK into town. Passengers arriving on late-evening flights, however, should pre-book a transfer through their travel agent as few taxis operate then and the bus service usually finishes around 23.30. The local bus from the airport passes the main bus station (Autobussijaam), which is useful for those wanting to continue journeys beyond Tallinn. Local buses, transfer coaches and taxis must be paid for in local currency.

There is an exchange bureau airside and also one landside in the arrivals area. The airside one offered outrageous rates throughout 2007, about 17.50EEK to the pound, when 23 EEK was easily available in the town centre. There are two banks landside and the one nearer to the departures area usually offers better rates. For travellers arriving from Britain on an Estonian Air flight from Gatwick, the Thomas Cook exchange bureau at Gatwick handles Estonian kroon. There is a cashpoint in the arrivals area. There is no tourist-information office or hotel-booking agency at the airport. American and British tourists plagued by high airport taxes at home will be relieved to hear that at Tallinn Airport they are minimal. Flight schedules are available on the website (*www.tallinn-airport.ee*).

TAXIS Taxis are all metered and have a minimum fare of 35EEK. Journeys within the town centre should not cost more than 50EEK. As taxis are reasonably priced and always metered, they can be considered for long journeys. For instance, one to Lahemaa National Park, about 100km from Tallinn, is unlikely to cost more than 1,000EEK.

Taxi companies called by phone are always cheaper than those that ply for hire on the street or park at ranks. Their cars are a little older but perfectly safe and all have meters. Taxi Raadio (✆ *601 5111*) are reliable and a journey to the airport with them rarely costs more than 60EEK.

LOCAL BUSES/TRAMS AND TROLLEYBUSES Many tourists to Tallinn never take either a bus or a taxi during their stay as the Old Town is very close to most of the hotels and the steep narrow roads conveniently restrict traffic to pedestrians anyway. Such visitors, however, miss everything that is cheaply and easily accessible by bus outside the Old Town. There are competing bus companies so exact routes and numbers change from time to time but services are frequent and the public transport map *Tallinn Ühistranspordi kaart*, published by Regio, is reprinted sufficiently often to be up to date. Some stops have maps but not all do and the names of the stops listed in the timetables are unlikely to mean much to visitors. The tram and trolleybus routes are of course fixed. In spring 2008 the flat fare was 13EEK for individual tickets bought from kiosks or 20EEK for tickets bought on the bus. A book of ten tickets bought at kiosks costs 90EEK, so buying one of these halves the cost of travel. Another useful ticket is the 24-hour one, costing 55EEK. (See also Tallinn Card, page 24.) Good bus services operate to Pirita and Rocca al Mare. Tram enthusiasts will be pleased at the number of places relevant to tourists which their routes pass.

CAR HIRE This is not advisable within Tallinn. Distances are so short and parking so difficult that public transport, taxis and bicycles are the sensible ways to get around. Visitors planning to travel to other towns can easily rely on buses but cars are very useful for seeing the coast and national parks. In the summer it is important to pre-book cars as demand invariably exceeds supply. Tour operators abroad can easily do this, as can the local agents listed above, or bookings can be made directly with the many international and local companies now involved in this business.

CYCLING This is a very sensible way of visiting the city, particularly as many places in the Old Town are difficult to reach by car and buses cannot travel on the narrow roads there. Much of the town is very flat and the rides out to Pirita or Rocca al Mare offer scenic and architectural perspectives not available in the centre. City Bike (*Uus 33;* ✆ *511 1819 or 683 6383;* e *mail@citybike.ee; www.citybike.ee*) have daily group tours around Tallinn and also arrange transport for cyclists to Lahemaa National Park or Paldiski. Their office is in the Old Town, where all their tours start and where their bicycles are kept. This is also a small hostel.

ACCOMMODATION

Tallinn now has about 60 hotels but they are often fully booked at weekends, during trade fairs and in the peak summer season. Pre-booking is therefore always advisable. Specialist travel agents abroad often have access to lower prices than those quoted by the hotels directly, and they may also have allocations at several hotels specifically reserved for them.

Among the newer establishments, the Merchant's House may well have many successors in future as hotels convert Old Town properties into quiet oases, shielded from the bustle outside. However, several hotels are taking advantage of the laxer planning environment recently introduced in Tallinn, with the council happy to see more skyscrapers and less control over renovation in the Old Town. In December 2007, the Swissôtel opened and is now the tallest building in the town, dominating the financial quarter near the harbour. About 1,000 new rooms became available during 2007, in all categories, so it is unlikely that more hotels will open in 2008, although several hotels currently open are planning extensions.

The recommendations that follow are obviously rather arbitrary and the omission of a hotel should in general be taken as resulting from lack of space rather than necessarily as a criticism. A number well away from the centre have been omitted even though their lower prices might well appeal. As prices in 2008–09 are likely to be so much lower than those charged until 2007, there will be less need to look around for good value. It can be assumed in all cases that the rooms in the hotels mentioned below have private facilities and free WiFi access, that the hotel accepts credit cards, and that it has a restaurant and bar. Many hotels have saunas which guests can use free of charge and the newer larger ones of course have spa centres too. Baths are rare in Estonian hotels, even in four–star establishments, so should be specifically requested.

LUXURY $$$$$

⌂ **Parkconsul Schlössle** (27 rooms) Pühavaimu 13/15; ☎ 699 7700; ℮ schlossle@ schlossle-hotels.com; www.schlossle-hotels.com. Until 2003, this hotel was in a class on its own but competition finally came with the opening of the Three Sisters, & more followed with the opening of the Telegraaf in April 2007. A townhouse owned by many successful Baltic Germans over the years, the Parkconsul Schlössle was converted into Tallinn's first truly luxurious hotel; any senior government minister from abroad always used to stay here. It is small enough to maintain the air of a gracious private residence. There is a small conference centre, but it seems incongruous. The hotel is a setting for constant but unostentatious indulgence, for champagne rather than wine &, until the 2007 smoking ban, for cigars rather than cigarettes. The restaurant, like all the best ones in Tallinn, is in a cellar & has an extensive menu. For those able briefly to abandon all this, the hotel is within walking distance of all the attractions in the Old Town. $$$$$

⌂ **Telegraaf** (80 rooms) Vene 9; ☎ 600 0600; ℮ info@telegraafhotel.com; www.telegraafhotel.com. When this hotel opened in April 2007, delayed partly to ensure that the 1917 façade remained intact, it brought several unique facilities to the Old Town, including an underground car park & a swimming pool. Room service is provided without a member of staff having to enter, by using a revolving cupboard.

FIRST CLASS $$$–$$$$

⌂ **Barons** (34 rooms) Suur-Karja 7; ☎ 699 9700; ℮ barons@baronshotel.ee; www.baronshotel.ee. For every bank that closes in Tallinn, a new hotel opens, but in this case it is on the same site. In fact, 13 different banks occupied the building during the 20th century, & some doors as a result do seem excessively secure. Visitors will find it hard to believe that Barons opened in 2003 rather than 1903, since the panelling, the minute lift, the sombre colour schemes & the illustrations of Tallinn are all from the earlier date. So is the name of the road: '*karja*' means 'to herd', as cattle used to be led to pasture along it. Whenever renovation is carried out, more & more papers from the early 20th century come to light. The view from many rooms & from the restaurant over the Old Town will again keep the 21st century away. For once it is sensible to go upstairs to eat in Tallinn, rather than downstairs. Do however avoid Fri & Sat nights,

The building was initially a post office but in Soviet times it monitored all the overseas phone calls made from Estonia. The restaurant fortunately provides a link with the Tsarist rather than the Soviet past, so that Russian food can be positively promoted. $$$$$

⌂ **Three Sisters** (23 rooms) Pikk 71; ☎ 630 6300; ℮ info@threesistershotel.com; www.threesistershotel.com. Perhaps because it is so luxurious, the hotel does not bother with an Estonian name as no Estonian could afford it; hosting Queen Elizabeth II in October 2006 was a great coup. It is clearly aiming to rival the Parkconsul & is to some extent modelled on it. Both buildings have a history of over 500 years & both can claim famous rather than notorious owners. Here a library is the dominating public room & a member of staff escorts guests into the lift for the 1-floor journey down to the restaurant. With only a small number of rooms, one even with a piano, the atmosphere of a 19th-century townhouse is still maintained. Computers & plenty of other 21st-century paraphernalia are available if needed, but it seems a pity to let modernity intrude. Estonians who wish to impress their friends on the cheap come for lunch here & linger over a £5/US$10 club sandwich. Foreigners come in the evening for pumpkin soup, pork with chanterelle mushrooms & a particular rarity in Estonia, homemade ice cream. $$$$$

when the hotel is an oasis of quiet against a backdrop of raucous behaviour in the surrounding bars. No rooms have baths but the suites have jacuzzis. $$$$

⌂ **Domina City** (68 rooms) Vana-Posti 11–13; ☎ 681 3900; ℮ city@domina.ee; www.dominahotels.com. The Italian management here is reflected in the ample use of marble in the reception area & in the range of wildly abstract art in the restaurant. When they first opened in 2002, it was a radical gesture to have 2 non-smoking floors, but others followed suit & now smoking is banned in all public areas. Like all good restaurants in Tallinn, the one here is built into a brick-lined cellar. Lovers of Soviet memorabilia should note the red star on the roof. The most important extra here is the soundproofing, sadly necessary at weekends as the hotel is situated directly opposite Tallinn's largest & noisiest nightclub. $$$$

🏠 **Domina Ilmarine** (150 rooms) Pohja 23; ☎ 614 0900; e ilmarine@domina.ee; www.dominahotels.com. What was Estonia's major machine-tool factory from the Tsarist period until World War II, which then turned to making hearing aids in Soviet times, is an unlikely background for a modern, hygienic & well-lit hotel, but that is the fact. So well regarded was the business during Estonia's first period of independence that both the president & the prime minister invested in it. Being just outside the Old Town, the hotel has space & uses it well. The rooms are big, as are the public areas, & there is ample parking for coaches & private cars. Double glazing prevents any traffic noise from causing a disturbance. Part of the hotel is allocated to flats for long-stay guests. $$$$

🏠 **Nordic Forum** (267 rooms) Viru Väljak 3; ☎ 622 2900; e forum@nordichotels.eu; www.nordichotels.eu. This hotel opened in December 2007, exactly when it said it would, which is a great rarity in Tallinn, where delays of more than a year are very common. It stares across at the Viru with which it will undoubtedly strongly compete. Being only just outside the Old Town, tourists will not object to the short walk there & for business people the walk to the new financial centre is equally convenient. Those who can afford it should book one of the corner suites with their wide views of the Old Town & their equally generous saunas. The business centre is free of charge to hotel guests, as is the top-floor swimming pool. Appropriate at a time when visitors are becoming increasingly conscious of the environment, nature is the dominating theme on the walls & in the carpets. Nordic Hotels also own the Bellevue in Riga (see page 103). $$$$

🏠 **Kalev Spa** (100 rooms) Aia 18; ☎ 649 3300; e kalevspa@kalevspa.ee; www.kalevspa.ee. Around 2000, Estonians suddenly discovered they needed to keep healthy, so spas & gyms sprung up around the country, particularly on the coast. This spa hotel, which opened in January 2006, is the first one in a town centre so its facilities, including a very welcome swimming pool, are geared as much to residents as to visitors from outside. Their use, however, is free of charge to hotel guests. The restaurant overlooks the swimming pool, which must make over-indulgent diners feel guilty. $$$

🏠 **Meriton Grand** (165 rooms) Toompuiestee 27; ☎ 667 7000; e hotel@meritonhotels.com www.meritonhotels.com. Travellers who came to Tallinn in the early 1990s will remember the grim Hotel Tallinn that used to besmirch this site. Luckily all traces of it were removed before this new hotel opened in 1999. Being immediately below the Old Town & having more than ample rooms, it appeals both to business travellers & to tourist groups. It is tempting to spend much of a stay in this hotel in the lift, since it offers one of the best views of Toompea Hill at the top of the Old Town. British tourists are drawn by the high proportion of rooms with baths. During 2008, a spa hotel was under construction behind the current building. $$$$

🏠 **Olümpia** (400 rooms) Liivalaia 33; ☎ 631 5333; e olympia@revalhotels.com; www.revalhotels.com. Built originally for the Olympic Games in 1980, this hotel is now the firm favourite of foreign business visitors to Tallinn. With the range of restaurants & conference facilities it offers, some never leave the hotel during their stay in Tallinn. They are often joined by the local expat community which has a particular affinity for the '60s music played in the Bonnie & Clyde nightclub. At w/ends & during the summer, rates drop to attract tourists paying their own way. All of the rooms are now at least 4-star standard & the reception staff work very quickly during the arrival & departure 'rush hours'. The restaurant on the top floor offers excellent views of the Old Town, as do many of the rooms. The newspaper shop always stocks up-to-date British newspapers, a rarity in Tallinn. Tourists who want to arrive or leave in greater style than a local taxi is able to provide can hire the hotel's 9m-long Lincoln which costs about £50/US$80 an hour. $$$$

🏠 **Radisson** (280 rooms) Rävala pst 3; ☎ 682 3000; e info.tallinn@radissonsas.com; www.tallinn.radissonsas.com. All the main central Tallinn hotels that opened during the 1990s were conversions of existing buildings. In 2000, the Radisson dramatically broke away from that tradition by not only starting from scratch but also by constructing what was until early 2006 the tallest building in Tallinn. (It was then overtaken by the Swissôtel.) This gave it the advantage of not having to make any compromises & a purpose-built formula was worked out to appeal to both the business & the leisure traveller. It has often pioneered what other hotels are then forced to copy, such as free WiFi for all guests. One original feature has been a special low check-in for small children, with toys around should there be any delay. Cultured guests will appreciate the paintings in the lobby area by Kaido Ole, one of Estonia's best-known contemporary artists. The rooftop café, Lounge 24, gives excellent photo opportunities towards both the Old Town & the new financial area growing up (literally) in the immediate vicinity of the hotel. For tourists wanting a more unusual photo, Tallinn Central Prison is easily visible from here, too. The restaurants & Lounge 24 have been priced to cater for local patrons, so are not as expensive as might be expected in a 4-star hotel. $$$$

⌂ **Reval Park** (121 rooms) Kreutzwaldi 23; ☏ 630 5305; e sales@revalhotels.com; www.revalhotels.com. Formerly the dreaded Kungla Hotel, which could barely claim 2-star status, the hotel was transformed within a few weeks during the summer of 1997 & has never looked back. It has pioneered rooms for non-smokers, for the disabled & for those with allergies as well as round-the-clock gambling, fortunately in a casino with a separate entrance. The casino presumably helps to keep the rooms so reasonably priced. Rooms are larger here than in most other hotels & the restaurant has very low prices for excellent food. Walking to the Old Town is just about possible & indeed essential as the surroundings are very bleak. The guarded car park is free of charge to hotel guests. $$$

⌂ **St Petersbourg** (27 rooms) Rataskaevu 7; ☏ 628 6500; e stpetersbourg@schlosse-hotels.com; www.schlosse-hotels.com. The St Petersbourg is under the same management as the deluxe Schlössle Hotel & suits those who want a comfortable Old Town address but do not miss luxury. The small number of rooms is certainly a draw. It may well be the oldest hotel in Tallinn, as it has had this leading position under every single regime of the 20th century, but within its class it is very expensive. Its location near to many famous clubs & restaurants appeals to visitors who can dispense with sleep for much of the night. It is one of the very few hotels in Tallinn to offer a babysitting service. $$$$

⌂ **Santa Barbara** (53 rooms) Roosikrantsi 2a; ☏ 640 7600; e reservations @stbarbara.ee; www.stbarbara.ee. The austere limestone façade from the turn of the century hides a very professional operation which used to be run by the Scandic group. Now independent, the hotel has stayed at the same level. The cellar restaurant is completely German, with no intrusion from Estonia or anywhere else. The staff get to know all the guests, many of whom are now regulars, which makes the hotel difficult to book for first-time visitors. $$$

⌂ **Savoy** (40 rooms) Suur-Karja 17–19; ☏ 680 6604; f 680 6601; e savoy @tallinnhotels.ee; www.savoyhotel.ee. This hotel, which opened in May 2006, is under the same management as the Portus in the harbour, but the style is so completely different that it is probably just as well that the 2 hotels are a good mile apart. (The Hotel Bern, halfway between them on Aija, is also under the same management.) Their respective clients would mix as well as beer on wine. The Old Town location, the 19th-century building & baths in nearly all of the rooms will appeal to older tourists wanting a leisurely stay, as will the thick wooden shutters in the summer, which keep out the

strong early-morning light. The charger for laptop computers & for mobile phones has cleverly been put into the safe, so that these items can be safely left on charge in the rooms. Its bar has original features, too, such as high armchairs rather than stools. Standing here would be out of the question. It is hard to think of a greater contrast to the stag bars 100m or so away. $$$$

⌂ **Scandic Palace** (87 rooms) Vabaduse Väljak; ☏ 640 7300; e palace@scandic-hotels.com; www.scandic-hotels.com. The hotel brochure claims it has offered 'excellent service since 1937' & this is probably true. Although many other hotels now match its facilities, Estonians are very loyal to it as the hotel was one of the few links from the first independence period that remained throughout the Soviet era. Embassies were briefly set up in the hotel in 1991 before foreign legations could reclaim their pre-war buildings. It is now equally conveniently situated for tourists interested in the Old Town & business visitors needing the government ministries. In 1997 President Meri opened the new presidential suite which for several years was the most expensive room in Tallinn, but the remaining 86 rooms have always been modestly priced. The hotel is run by the Scandic group that also operates the Santa Barbara in Tallinn & the Ranna in Pärnu. $$$$

⌂ **Swissôtel** (238 rooms) Tornimäe 3; ☏ 624 0000; e tallinn@swissotel.com; www.tallinn.swissotel.com. It is not surprising that the Radisson should in 2008 have a competitor arising almost next door; what is surprising is that it should have taken 8 years for another international chain to embark on this competition. Its aim is to be international in a new context for Estonia, looking east just as much as looking west. All the staff are as fluent in Russian as they are in English & all the printed materials are in 3 languages. Rooms start at the 12th floor & continue to the 29th, with executive ones being on floors 27–29. There are no sgl rooms as such, just dbls with separate baths & showers; only the few twins have just a shower. There are many novelties for Tallinn, setting a new 5-star level. Not only are tea- & coffee-making facilities in each room standard, but so is an espresso machine; every room has an iron & ironing board, & fresh flowers. Adaptors are not needed as all rooms are equipped with 3 sockets (to meet the needs of European, British & American plugs), both in the room & in the safe, which has a connection for recharging mobile phones & laptop computers.

The 11th floor is for keeping fit, but with a view. The sauna looks over the former Soviet officers' club & towards the airport; the gym towards the Old Town.

Only the swimming pool does not offer a view. There is a weighing-machine beside the lift, to check how effective exercising has been. Facilities on this floor are free of charge to hotel guests.

Tallinn's highest restaurant is on the top floor of the hotel, but surprisingly is open only in the evenings, & not on Sun or Mon. Perhaps this is taking exclusivity a little too far & it is to be hoped that a more broad-minded approach will follow. The 8th floor Café Swiss, however, is open from 06.30 to midnight with a buffet or à-la-carte option for each of the 3 meals. If power b/fasts are to take off in Estonia, it will probably be from here. $$$$ exc b/fast.

⌂ **Tallink** (300 rooms) Laikmaa 5; ☏ 630 0800; e hotel@tallink.ee; www.bwhoteltallink.com. If this hotel had been located anywhere else in Tallinn, it would have been considered enormous. However, as it overlooks the Viru, with its 500 rooms, it seems merely large. Being closely linked to the ferry company that operates to Helsinki, it is very much an outpost of Finland in Tallinn. Everything works & the light colours are appealing, particularly in winter, but perhaps more could have been done to broaden its appeal. The bus from the airport stops outside its door & some higher rooms have good views over the Old Town. $$$$

⌂ **Viru** (500 rooms) Viru Väljak 4; ☏ 630 1390; e viru.reservation@sok.fi; www.viru.ee. Being the centre of the tourism trade for much of the Soviet era, the enormous Viru initially found it hard to redefine its role in the face of competition & ever-rising standards. By 2000 it had finally undergone a complete renovation & can now serve both business clients & fastidious tourists. It has become very biased towards Finnish clients, particularly since its takeover by the Finnish chain Sokos. Some of these guests can provide unwanted liveliness late on Fri & Sat evenings. Its location is excellent for the Old Town & for local shops. Tourists determined to have a bath rather than a shower are more likely to succeed here. Since late 2005 the hotel has been fighting for permission to build a complete new extension to the hotel in the neighbouring Tammsaare Park. $$$$

⌂ **Viruinn** (15 rooms) Viru 8; ☏ 644 9167; e viruinn@viruinn.ee; www.viruinn.ee. It is perhaps surprising that this is the first hotel in Tallinn to convert an old townhouse as carefully as possible into a boutique hotel. It opened in 2006, with beams obstructing everywhere & access difficult for both the old & the very young, given the number of stairs & corridors. Needless to say, there is no lift. However the fit middle-aged will enjoy an escape from all-too-modern Viru St back into the 19th century. Good soundproofing ensures their isolation. The Al Sole café downstairs provides a halfway house between the old & the new with light meals & cakes worthy of its more famous competitors. $$$$

TOURIST CLASS $$–$$$

⌂ **Bern** (50 rooms) Ala 10; ☏ 680 66 30; e bern @tallinnhotels.ee; www.bern.ee. Halfway between the Portus & the Savoy, both in a geographical & in a hierarchical sense, this hotel opened in 2007 to join the other 2 in the Tallinn Hotel group. Although a completely new building, it is in the Old Town, but most of its rooms overlook a courtyard. As it is set back from the street, noise is not a problem. Welcome extras are free landline phone calls within Estonia, & laptop computers loaned free of charge. And to use the word yet again, children stay free of charge until their 17th birthday. Rooms vary a lot in size, but not in facilities or in comfort. The basement restaurant, at its best in winter when a real fire burns, has more style & space than one would expect in a 3-star hotel, & its extensive wine list is a very pleasant surprise. $$$

⌂ **Central** (247 rooms) Narva mnt 7; ☏ 633 9800; e sales@revalhotels.com; www.revalhotels.com. This hotel became an immediate favourite of tour operators from abroad when it opened in 1995 as it had no Soviet past to eliminate, & regular improvements have followed. Staff were immediately aware of the demands & eccentricities of Western tourists, who have been catered for in the café/restaurant ever since. The hotel offers disabled access & 1 room in the new wing is adapted for use by disabled guests. A computer is available free of charge to guests. The Central is within easy walking distance of the Old Town & the main post office. Although it opened in what was then a rundown part of town, the surrounding area is becoming increasingly attractive, with more shops & restaurants opening every year. $$

⌂ **L'Ermitage** (91 rooms) Toompuiestee 19; ☏ 699 6400; e reservations@lermitagehotel.ee; www.lermitagehotel.ee. Although on a main road, this hotel is in many respects quieter than others as it is so well soundproofed; late-night revellers do not get this far from the Old Town as they would actually have to walk for 10mins. It appeals to groups as coaches can stop directly in front & isn't too big to seem impersonal. Those lucky enough to get a high room at the front will be rewarded with excellent views of the town walls. $$$

⌂ **Imperial** (32 rooms) Nunne 14; ☏ 627 4800; e imperial@baltichotelgroup.com; www.baltichotelgroup.com. Like the Konventa Sēta in

Riga Old Town, this hotel is built into the town wall, which is therefore being preserved as part of it. Although on one of the few real roads in the Old Town, the location is quiet. During 2005 the hotel was considerably upgraded, leading to the demise of the stag parties which previously had been tolerated here. Rooms vary greatly in size & protruding beams sometimes add more of a medieval ambience than some guests would wish. Massive discounts are often available in winter here, together with late check-outs, useful for those booked on the afternoon flight to London. $$$

🏠 **Merchant's House** (37 rooms) Dunkri 4–6; 📞 697 7500; e info@merchantshousehotel.com; www.merchantshouse.com. In summer 2005 a formula that has worked so well in Riga at the Gutenbergs finally reached Tallinn – 14th–16th-century woodwork & frescoes have been integrated into a hotel that will satisfy even the most fastidious customer. Rooms vary in size & shape, as do the corridors, but short detours to reach them are a small price to pay for such a special environment. Given the round-the-clock activity on Dunkri it is good that only 3 of the rooms face it, & that the library, which also does so, is well soundproofed. The 'winter' restaurant is amongst the cellars of the basement; the 'summer' one in the courtyard onto which most rooms look. Tallinn's first ice bar is on the ground floor & on a similar theme it is worth mentioning that all rooms are air-conditioned, an important asset for several weeks during the summer. The temptations at the ice bar can be viewed on the obvious website address: www.icebar.ee. $$$$

🏠 **Meriton Old Town** (40 rooms) Lai 49; 📞 614 1300; e hotel@grandhotel.ee. This hotel opened in March 2004 & is under the same management as the Meriton Grand, but has deliberately been pitched at a very different clientele. Those who normally shun 2- or 3-star hotels may well accept such a standard here, given the view that most rooms have over the Old Town, of St Olav's Church, or towards the harbour. There is also the added appeal of the hotel being built into the city wall. Being on the edge of the Old Town, the place is quiet yet with a reasonably central location, within walking distance of many museums & shops. It is worth paying the slightly higher costs for the rooms on the 4th floor, with their larger size, their baths rather than showers & above all for the views. The basement rooms make up for the total lack of a view with the skilfully implanted use of the old city wall. For anyone willing to risk turning up after midnight without a reservation, rooms are then sold at half-price. $$

🏠 **Mihkli** (84 rooms) Endla 23; 📞 666 4800; e mihkli@uniquestay.com; www.uniquestay.com. The

bland location of the hotel on a busy road should not put off anyone from entering. Whilst it is only a few minutes walk from the Old Town, & on a number of bus routes elsewhere, the range & low prices charged for an array of spa treatments, & also for the Tricky Ants dinner show, probably entice many guests never to leave. The hotel is a social centre in its own right & also a venue for small conferences. Effective sound-proofing keeps the outside world at bay. By 2008, Unique Hotels had completed their total transformation from the drab Soviet leftover they bought in 2006, so 13 Zen rooms had appeared, & free computers were in each room, together with tea & coffee, also free of charge. In brief, darkness has turned into light here. In 2008, Unique opened the restored Vihula Manor in Lahemaa National Park, about an hour's drive from Tallinn, so offer 'town & country' packages linking the 2 hotels. $$$

🏠 **Old Town Maestro** (23 rooms) Suur-Karja 10; 📞 626 2000; e maestro@maestrohotel.ee; www.maestrohotel.ee. Having opened in 2001, this small hotel now has its regulars who want straightforward furnishings, peace & quiet, & yet an Old Town location. Rooms are much bigger than might be expected from a converted townhouse but the lift is much smaller – it can take only one person with a case at a time. The road is traffic-free but that does mean wheeling cases along the cobbles on arrival & departure. The reception area doubles up as a bar, which adds to the family atmosphere. The sauna & the business centre are, surprisingly, side by side on the top floor. Photographers should bring their cameras for the unusual views over the town from the staircase & the sauna. $$$.

🏠 **Pirita Convent Guesthouse** (21 rooms) Merivälija 18; 📞 605 5000; e pirita@osss.ee; www.osss.ee. For anyone determined to have quiet at night, this is undoubtedly the place to go for. The nuns stay up for latecomers so ideal guests are those who have dinner here & then go to their rooms. The yachting harbour of Pirita is 3km northeast of the town & the ruined convent with this new guesthouse is set well back from the main road. Prices, too, are provincial rather than Tallinn. Tourists with a car will be happy with the space here & others will be pleased that after 500 years a religious order is finally active on the site again. An extensive programme of concerts takes places in the chapel. $$

🏠 **Portus** (107 rooms) Uus Sadama 23; 📞 680 6600; e portus@tallinnhotels.ee; www.portus.ee. Regular visitors to Tallinn will remember this hotel as the Saku, named after the brewery & which provided a glass of beer at check-in. If the ambience is slightly more sober now, this is undoubtedly a hotel for the young & lively. Rooms have their numbers painted on them, so that guests with uncertain late-night vision can still hopefully find the right one. The beer store has been converted into a children's playroom but the corridors are still painted red, orange & yellow. It is in the port, beside Terminal D, so convenient for those also visiting Helsinki. Bus no 20 stops outside the door for those who would rather avoid the 15min walk to the Old Town & bus no 2 goes to the bus station & the airport from here. The Italian restaurant offers a surprisingly good meal for starting or finishing a visit to Tallinn. $$$

⌂ **Poska Villa** (8 rooms) Poska 15; ☎ 601 3601; e poskavilla@hot.ee; www.hot.ee/poskavilla. For those who prefer the quiet ambience of Kadriorg to the pace of central Tallinn, this villa with its garden is ideal. The tram into town is about 10mins' walk from the house, but probably more enticing is Kadriorg Park with its palace, museums & now KUMU. $$

⌂ **Salzburg** (53 rooms) Pärnu mnt 555; ☎ 650 3965; e info@salzburg.ee; www.salzburg.ee. This used to be the Peoleo Hotel until 2006 when it was drastically modernised & renamed. The dreary location of course remains, at the edge of Tallinn's shopping malls on the outskirts of the town, but everything possible has been done to compensate for it. Rooms are half the price they would be in town & a wide range of facilities is offered. For those hiring a car it is ideal, with ample safe parking space & no traffic delays when arriving or leaving. $$

⌂ **Shnelli** (124 rooms) Toompuiestee 37; ☎ 631 0100; e reservations@gohotels.ee; www.gohotels.ee. As part of the much-needed renovation of the railway station, this hotel opened beside it in 2005. It is a straightforward 3-star place with the 'green' rooms facing the park below the Old Town & the 'blue' hopefully facing a blue sea & sky, but also overlooking the platforms of the railway station. The former obviously cost rather more. The railway theme predominates in the photos on the walls & even in the design of the corridor carpets. A covered walkway links the hotel to the station & its restaurant; as with stations everywhere now, the trains are less important than the shops to which most of the space has been let. The restaurant is much cheaper than any in the Old Town & particularly at w/ends offers a pleasantly quiet environment for a meal. The few trains now running from here will certainly not provide any disturbance. Single visitors hoping to change their status whilst in Tallinn may want to take advantage of the rooms let only to 2 people after midnight for 500EEK. $$

⌂ **Skane** (38 rooms) Kopli 2c; ☎ 667 8300; e info@hotelskane.eu; www.hotelskane.eu. Being just over the railway & the tramlines from the Old Town, this hotel is literally on the wrong side of the tracks.

Hopefully gentrification of the surrounding area will not take too long & it can then look the Old Town in the face. In the meantime, guests can enjoy prices that are half of those charged by hotels just 500m away & the walk into the Old Town is very short. A tram & bus stop are on the doorstep. No rooms have baths, but all have BBC TV. $$

⌂ **Susi** (100 rooms) Peterburi 48; ☎ 630 3300; e susi@susi.ee; www.susi.ee. An estate agent would probably describe this location as 'unprepossessing' since it is surrounded by factories & a petrol station & is on the wide St Petersburg motorway. It is also literally the high point of Tallinn, at 55m above sea level. On 14 May 1343, the St George's Night rebellion took place here. It had started further north on 23 April & this was the nearest point to Tallinn that Estonian forces would reach. Over 10,000 were killed in a desperate attempt to overthrow the Teutonic Knights. A plaque in the hotel lobby commemorates the battle, as does the park on the other side of the road where there are several further monuments. The hotel is more comfortable & more modern than any of the other tourist-class hotels outside the centre & is easily accessible by tram. The pictures displayed on its staircase put many of Tallinn's museums to shame. There are oils, lithographs & watercolours showing contemporary & historical Tallinn; other pictures are of country scenes. They are well lit & sensibly framed & of course can be seen 24 hours a day. Should the lift break down, this gallery is more than adequate compensation. The hotel suits many groups as parking is easy, as is access to the airport & to the Tartu road. $$

⌂ **Taanilinna** (20 rooms) Uus 6; ☎ 640 6700; e info@taanilinna.ee; www.taanilinna.ee. Perhaps they were daring, perhaps they were foolish, but in June 2002 Tallinn saw its first hotel with Russian-speaking reception staff & with brochures in English & Russian. The spelling 'Hotell' was the only concession made to Estonia at the time, although the website now has an Estonian section. Visitors who do not care about this will like the prices, the small number of rooms, the location in one of the few quiet streets in the Old Town & the use of wood rather than of stone. The terrace sadly looks out onto the back of a supermarket & a dreary block of flats but in future years this view may well change. The wine cellar is an unexpected bonus in a hotel of this size & category & is most welcome given the lack of other watering holes in the immediate vicinity. $$$

⌂ **Ülemiste** (120 rooms) Lennijamaa tee 2; ☎ 603 2600; e sales@ylemistehotel.ee; www.ylemistehotel.ee. This hotel opened beside the airport in 2004 in what was then a very bleak location but the development since then of the Ülemiste shopping centre beside it has greatly enhanced the potential pleasure of a stay here. Prices in these shops are of course much lower than those charged in the town centre. Great advantage has been taken of all the space available so expect a larger lobby, rooms & even corridors than elsewhere in Tallinn. Those able to indulge in the more expensive rooms at the top of the hotel will be rewarded with views across Ülemiste Lake. The location is very convenient given the number of flights arriving late & leaving early. It is a 400m walk to the terminal or one stop on the local bus. In the winter the hotel offers a late check-out at 15.00 to passengers taking the London flight at 16.15. For those prepared to take quite a risk, rooms are offered at half-price to walk-in passengers who arrive after midnight. $$

🏠 **Unique** (67 rooms) Paldiski mnt 3; 🕿 660 0700; e info@uniquestay.com; www.uniquestay.com. Tallinn hotels have tended to copy each other once a successful formula has been found. The larger ones inevitably copy models from abroad & the smaller ones try to recreate a 1930s ambience even though modern technology is around if guests need it. When the Unique opened in spring 2003, it clearly wanted to break away from anything that had ever been tried before. Each room has its own flat-screen computer which can be used free of charge around the clock. It also has tea & coffee. The lighting in the corridors comes from the floor rather than the ceiling. Orange rather than green

or brown is the predominant colour. Originally restricted to 17 rooms at Paldiski 3, the hotel added another 50 in April 2004 in its new building on the corner of Paldiski & Toompuiestee & plans for a further extension were in hand in 2008. Several of these rooms, the Zen rooms, are as original as their predecessors, with whirlpool baths, adjustable lighting & gravity-free chairs. This is also the first hotel in Tallinn with an Estonian restaurant! The chain plans to expand both within Tallinn & to the neighbouring Baltic countries. $$$.

🏠 **Vana Wiru** (80 rooms) Viru 11; 🕿 669 1500; e hotel@vanawiru.ee; www.vanawiru.ee. Viru St is always full of tourists but most will not know of the existence of this hotel as its entrance is at the back. Potential guests should not be deterred by the fact that the building dates from the 1950s, normally the worst period of Soviet architecture. Its vast marble lobby suggests luxury but in fact most of the rooms are of a standard size & with showers rather than baths. Few have good views but with a location beside the city wall, one can forgive anything. It is certainly worth paying more for the junior suites on the 5th floor which do have extensive views over the Old Town. Shopaholics should enquire about the 10% discount the hotel arranges for its guests at the nearby Kaubamaja department store. Groups will like the convenient coach park right beside the entrance. $$$

✕ EATING AND DRINKING

There is now such a choice of restaurants in Tallinn that it is invidious to attempt a shortlist. Every major nation is represented and more unusual ones include Argentina, Georgia, Lithuania and Scotland. Hawaiian and Thai food appeared for the first time in 2000, Czech and Arabic food followed in 2002 and by 2003 Russian food had also staged a comeback, having been completely rejected in the years immediately following independence. By 2005, they were joined by an African, an Armenian and a Korean one. Tallinn's first Jewish restaurant opened in 2007 and the first Portuguese one in 2008. Given that by 2007 there were few new nationalities to represent, entrepreneurs started to take the risk of opening premises outside the town centre. This has on the whole proved successful as both residents and tourists are happy to take a bus or tram to save money, have space and above all to have quiet. As smoking was banned in all public places from summer 2007, this applies to restaurants unless they can offer a totally enclosed space away from the main area.

Detailed descriptions of restaurants appear in the *City Paper*, shorter ones in *Tallinn In Your Pocket*. A dark entrance, down poorly maintained stairs in a side street, is usually a clear indication that good food and value lies ahead. Bright lights at street level should be avoided. At the time of writing, nobody has opened a revivalist Soviet restaurant, though the success of such ventures in Riga and in former East Berlin must in due course tempt some embittered members of the Russian-speaking community in Tallinn.

Most of the following restaurants have been open for several years and are popular with tourists, expats and local residents. I have, however, deliberately tried to include

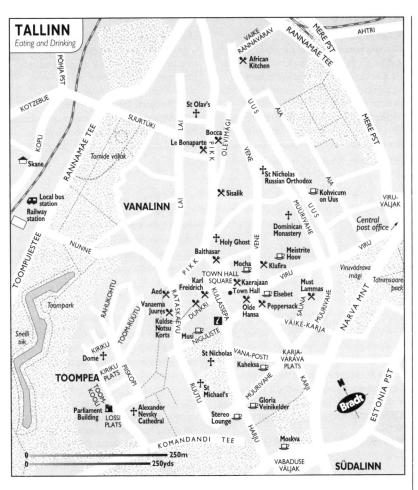

TALLINN
Eating and Drinking

POHJA PST

KOTZEBUE

KOPLI

Skane

RANNAMÄE TEE

SUURTÜKI

Tornide väljak

LAI

St Olav's

VÄIKE-RANNAVÄRAV

RANNAMÄE PST

MERE PST

AHTRI

African
Kitchen

UUS

AIA

Bocca
Le Bonaparte

OLEVIMÄGI

PIKK

VENE

MERE PST

St Nicholas
Russian Orthodox

Sisalik

AIA

Kohvicum
on Uus

VIRU-
VÄLJAK

Local bus
station
Railway
station

TOOMPUIESTEE

VANALINN

LAI

NUNNE

Toompark

Snelli
tiik

KIRIKU
Dome

TOOMPEA

KIRIKU
PLATS

PISKOPI

TOOM-
KOOLI

Parliament
Building

LOSSI
PLATS

RAHUKOHTU

TOOM-RÜÜTLI

Holy Ghost

Balthasar

PIKK

Karl
Freidrich

Aed

Vanaema
Juures

Kuldse
Notsu
Korts

RATASKAEVU

TOWN HALL
SQUARE

Mocha

DUNKRI

Kaerajaan

Town Hall

Olde
Hansa

Musi

NIGULISTE

KULLASSEPA

Dominican
Monastery

MÜÜRIVAHE

Meistrite
Hoov

Klafira

Elsebet

Peppersack

VIRU

Must
Lammas

SAUNA

VÄIKE-KARJA

Central
post office

VIRU

Viruvärava
mägi

NARVA MNT

MÜÜRIVAHE

Tammsaare
park

St Nicholas

Kaheksa

ALEXANDER
Nevsky
Cathedral

VANA-POSTI

St
Michael's

RÜÜTLI

Stereo
Lounge

MÜÜRIVAHE

HARJU

KARJA-
VÄRAVA
PLATS

KARJI

Gloria
Veinikelder

Moskva

KOMANDANDI   TEE

0   250m
0   250yds

VABADUSE
VÄLJAK

SÜDALINN

ESTONIA PST

Bradt

N

2

some that are not well known abroad and which cannot afford to advertise. I have also gambled on some recent openings in the expectation that they will outlive this edition of the book. Apologies in advance to the many other excellent restaurants that, with more space, would also have been included. Websites are listed so that menu planning can begin abroad and not just at the table. Restaurants are on the whole very good at keeping these up to date, and for those in a rush it is possible to pre-book not only a table but also the meal. Eating in hotels is popular in Tallinn and some of their restaurants are covered in the hotel descriptions in the previous chapter.

Prices quoted are for three courses without wine. From 2007, many Tallinn restaurants greatly increased the prices of their wines, although not of beer and soft drink, in several cases exceeding what is normal in central London. For those unhappy drinking beer with a meal, it therefore makes sense to check wine prices as well as food ones before settling down.

At lunchtime many cheaper restaurants have a dish of the day – *päevapraad* – and in late 2007 it was possible to pay 40EEK (about £2/€4) for a substantial portion of meat and vegetables. This word is often not translated, presumably in the hope that foreigners will instead happily pay three times as much for similar dishes on the main menu.

Almost all restaurants are open seven days a week from 12.00 until 23.00.

RESTAURANTS

✗ **Aed** Ratskaevu 8; ✎ 626 9088;
www.restoranaed.ee. This is not a vegetarian restaurant
at all, but it is the next best thing for those who want
one, given its extensive choice of appropriate dishes.
Although carnivores are equally welcome here, it is the
vegetables & the sauces that diners remember,
considering the lack of quality in these elsewhere in
Tallinn. Its opening during the bitter winter of early
2006 made this an even more effective selling point.
Now its sensible wine prices are an added bonus. If the
courtyard at the back were a little bigger, one could
imagine all the herbs used in the cooking having grown
there in pots. The large TV screens do not show
football matches, nor shrieking rock stars, but a
constantly changing selection of classical paintings.
350EEK.

✗ **African Kitchen** Uus 34; ✎ 644 2555;
www.africankitchen.ee. This restaurant became so
popular during 2005 that it was hard to believe that it
only opened around Christmas 2004. The crowds
continued to pour in during 2006 & 2007 so doubtless
2008 will be the same. It is cheap & cheerful, but so
much more as well. The menu is diverse, the website to
the point & equality across the continent is assured by
offering one cocktail, & only one, from each of 25
different African countries & all at the same price.
Come here with a group, or be willing to become part
of one; this is not the place for dining à deux. Live music
is played, with no extra cost, every Fri & Sat evening.
200EEK.

✗ **Balthasar** Raekoja Plats 11; ✎ 627 6400;
www.restaurant.ee. Garlic dominates every course
here, even the ice cream, but above all in the salads.
Whilst other dishes do appear on the menu, they tend
to be as appetising as a vegetarian option in a
steakhouse. Opening in early 2000, the restaurant took
over the top floor of the former pharmacy (see page
54) & has kept as much of the original wooden
furnishings as was practical. With the restaurant's views
over Town Hall Square, it is tempting to linger here but
it also offers a quiet respite over lunch between
morning & afternoon sightseeing tours. The range of
short drinks at the bar can be equally tempting at other
times of day. 350EEK.

✗ **Bocca** Olevimägi 9; ✎ 641 2610; www.bocca.ee. A
passer-by on the pavement here who happened to
notice the plain-glass windows with the 2 canvas panels
behind them would not believe that during 2003 Bocca
got more publicity abroad than all other Tallinn
restaurants put together. Only the cars parked outside
suggest considerable opulence inside. Critics liked the
modern minimalist layout against the medieval backdrop

of very solid limestone. They liked the changing lighting
schemes – & the fact that plenty of modest pasta dishes
were available if octopus & veal seemed unnecessarily
extravagant. The glitterati have moved on now, but
standards here have stayed the same. 600EEK.

✗ **Le Bonaparte** Pikk 45; ✎ 646 4444;
www.bonaparte.ee. The formal restaurant at the back &
the easy-going café at the front are both French
through & through. The décor is very domestic & totally
unpretentious. The care & flair all go into the food,
which is still too rare in Tallinn, whether it is a simple
cake in the café or an elaborate pâté at the start of a
serious meal. Other unusual touches are the individual
towels in the toilets & coat-warmers for visitors in
winter. Prices in both the restaurant & the café are
fortunately very Estonian. Those who want to take
France home with them can buy a range of cheeses &
bread at the counter. 450EEK.

✗ **Cantina Carramba** Weizenbergi 20a; ✎ 601 3431;
www.carramba.ee. Opening in Kadriorg outside the
town centre in 2004 was certainly a gamble, but it has
definitely paid off. The variety of Mexican food, not to
mention its low cost, is certainly worth the 10min tram
ride it may take to get here. Onion rings in beer dough
is one of many original dishes served. Helpful to
newcomers are the little pepper symbols beside many
dishes on the menu: 1 indicates a medium dose where 3
is really strong. As it's open through the day, an
afternoon at the Palace or KUMU could pleasantly end
with an early supper here. Do bear in mind that
although the cuisine is Mexican, the portions are
certainly American. 250EEK.

✗ **Controvento** Katariina käik; ✎ 644 0470;
www.controvento.ee. Uniquely in Tallinn, this restaurant
could maintain a review written when it first opened in
1992. It has retained the same menu, the same décor &
probably many of the same clients, who want no-
nonsense home cooking in an Italian bistro & no attempts
to emulate temporary culinary fads. Prices have increased
somewhat but they remain modest in comparison with
the competition in the Old Town. 300EEK.

✗ **Eesti Maja** Lauteri 1; ✎ 645 5252;
www.eestimaja.ee. Do not expect quick service here or
even staff with much English, but instead be ready for
enormous portions & rich food at each course. It would
be hard to spend more than £7/US$14 a head & many
eat their fill for much less. Side rooms seating around
8–10 people are useful for private functions. One
houses a collection of photographs from the 1920s. The
vegetable soup makes a good meal in itself at lunchtime.
In 2007 another restaurant opened under the same
ownership: Toompea Eesti Maja (see below). 200EEK.

✕ **Fahle** Tartu 84a; ☏ 603 0588; www.fahlerestoran.ee. For years, the abandoned Fahle building was an embarrassing eyesore for tourists as they drove into Tallinn from the airport. Few could have guessed it was one of Tallinn's most successful factories as a paper-mill from 1900 until 1940. Gentrification came suddenly in 2007 with the cleaning of its limestone façade & the addition of glass-fronted luxury flats above the former roof. A spacious restaurant, which has kept the limestone surroundings, is a welcome part of the complex, particularly for those eager to escape w/kend crowds in the Old Town. 300EEK

✕ **Golden Dragon** Pikk 37; ☏ 631 3506; www.goldendragon.ee. This is a straightforward Chinese restaurant in the best sense of the term. The cooking is fine, the menu enormous, the prices reasonable & the service adequate. The lanterns dangle against a background of Estonian limestone. Modern China & modern Estonia of course share an obsession for piped music so be ready for any meal to be spoilt on this score. The entrance is in a courtyard, through a heavy door & down a tortuous staircase. This complication fortunately keeps out the more raucous tourists. 200EEK.

✕ **Kaerajaan** Raekoja Plats 17; ☏ 615 5400; www.kaerajaan.ee. The opening of this large formal restaurant on Town Hall Square in March 2008 perhaps signifies the end of the stag era in Tallinn. Taking as its name an Estonian folk dance & playing music which only older local people can recognise is a sure indication that anyone under 25 should stay away, particular if they just want a beer. 450EEK

✕ **Karl Friedrich** Raekoja Plats 5; ☏ 627 2413; www.restaurant.ee. The grand location on Town Hall Square might suggest ostentation & prices to match but fortunately this has not happened. Each floor caters for a different age group but it is the top floor that is recommended; the long walk up & down is well worthwhile. Oldies should book well in advance for a table overlooking the square & enjoy a lingering lunch or dinner. It became a pepper restaurant in 2005 so expect this ingredient even in a crème brulée or a chocolate mousse. At the same time, the kitchen moved upstairs so diners on that floor see all their food being prepared. Perhaps they went for pepper to compete with the garlic restaurant over the square? 450EEK.

✕ **Klafira** Vene 4; ☏ 667 5144; www.klafira.ee. If Soviet Russia has been banished for good from Estonia, the Tsarist aristocracy is making an effective comeback here instead. Perhaps they were wise to wait until 2000, nine years after the re-establishment of Estonian independence, before doing so. Their food is strictly Russian, their wine is sensibly French. That rich Estonians

are first willing to come & then even to speak Russian to the staff shows the high standards the restaurant has set. Allow a full evening here & do not consider the cost beforehand. The menu is expensive by Estonian standards, but not by London or New York ones. If there is music, it is live & lively, so those unhappy with this should check first on timings. 500EEK.

✕ **Kuldse Notsu Korts** (The Golden Pig) Dunkri 8; ☏ 628 6567; www.notsu.ee. Although this restaurant belongs to the luxury St Petersbourg Hotel next door, the two establishments have nothing in common. This country restaurant, with low ceilings & long wooden tables, seems pleasantly incongruous in the middle of the Old Town. However, this is precisely its appeal. It offers varied Estonian fare – thick mushroom soups, pork in innumerable guises & apples in almost as many. Drink apple juice or beer rather than wine. Estonians have in general fled from the Old Town as far as eating is concerned but they still come here in large numbers, which must be a recommendation. 300EEK.

✕ **Liivi Steakhouse** Narva mnt 1; ☏ 625 7377; www.steakhouse.ee. Everything is wonderfully predictable here, so this is the place to be unadventurous. All styles of steak are on the menu & they can be accompanied by a wide range of red wines. The starters are pâtés & soups & the sweets apple pie or ice cream. Situated opposite the Viru Hotel in a complex that also houses the main post office, it has very varied but always conventional clientele. 350EEK.

✕ **Lydia** Koidula 13a; ☏ 629 8990; www.lydia.ee. Lydia pioneered the idea of genteel suburban dining in Tallinn & the proportion of locals to foreigners shows how successful they have been. Kadriorg, where Lydia is based, is perhaps only just a suburb as it is so close to the town centre. A meal here makes sense after enjoying the luxury of Kadriorg Palace, KUMU & the porcelain collection at the Mikkel Museum. The décor of paintings & flowers lends itself to a leisurely rather than a rushed lunch or dinner. Many of the ingredients are local, but the sauces are French so are ample in their portions & contain appropriate quantities of alcohol. 350EEK

✕ **Must Lammas** (The Black Sheep) Sauna 2; ☏ 644 2031; www.mustlammas.ee. For years this Georgian restaurant was called Exit but it changed its name in early 2001. Luckily little else has changed in the intervening years. All guests are greeted with portions of firewater & strips of salted beef as the menus are handed out. Eat meat, meat & more meat all evening, topped, if you did not have lunch, with some ice cream drenched in brandy. Start with stuffed vine leaves & move on to beef & pork stews. Vegetarians keep out. 300EEK.

✕ NOP Köleri I; ☎ 603 2270; www.nop.ee. Although in a modest wooden building in Kadriorg, outside the city centre, & despite closing every day at 20.00, this combined shop & restaurant specialising in organic foods became an instant success when it opened early in 2008. To foreigners, NOP is translated as 'natural organic produce'. For Estonians they think of the word *noppima* which means to 'pick' fruit & berries. The menu changes daily but carnivores will always be as happy as vegetarians here. 200EEK

✕ Olde Hansa Vanaturg I; ☎ 627 9020; www.oldehansa.com. Ignore the silly name & the silly costumes worn by the staff but enjoy the candles (there is no electric light) & the genuinely Estonian live music. Some tables are for 2 but don't venture in for a quiet, intimate evening. This is really a party venue so come as a group & with a very empty stomach. Portions are enormous, even for soup & ice cream. 350EEK.

✕ Peppersack Viru tänav 2; ☎ 646 6900; www.peppersack.ee. Johan Peppersack was one of Tallinn's best mayors when Estonia was ruled by the Swedes in the 16th & 17th centuries. He fought the occupiers for money & autonomy with a tenacity that no other mayor could equal in the subsequent 400 years. He would not have tolerated the mess Polish restorers, local Estonians & the Soviet occupiers got into when they tried & failed to restore the building in time for the 1980 Olympics. The compromise between Polish Baroque & the former Gothic is still there. Perhaps it is better to look at the live entertainment, which can feature fencers, troubadours or martial artists (check the website if it matters which). The menu is extensive but many find it easiest just to order one of the feasts at a fixed price which includes 3 courses & drink. Several of these are fish-based & 1 is vegetarian. 350EEK.

✕ Sisalik (Lizard) Pikk 30; ☎ 646 6542; www.sisaliku.ee. This is probably the only restaurant in Tallinn that has the linguistic & gastronomic daring to have a website in French. It is quite right that they should, since this is provincial France transposed to medieval Tallinn. The frogs' legs on the menu prove the point. The tortuous stone steps leading down to the basement location are distinctly Estonian (or Scots) but then France takes over. Those who know 'Les Amis' in Vilnius (page 189) will appreciate the need for a similar restaurant here. The menu is large enough to meet all

tastes but small enough to ensure that mistakes are not made & that nothing synthetic is ever offered. The really greedy do not immediately walk out onto Pikk after eating here. They 'go to Belgium' upstairs at the café Anneli Viik for coffee & chocolate. 300EEK.

✕ Spaghetteria Weizenbergi 18; ☎ 601 3636; www.restorankadriorg.ee. People-watching from restaurants in the town centre tends to involve horror at the misbehaving foreigners or concern for the rushing Estonians. The location of this restaurant, on a first floor above the tram stop for Kadriorg Park, gives views of a totally different kind. People who come here have time, & are relaxed; raucous stag parties would never find their way. Looking inwards is the kitchen, which forms the centre of this floor. The food is of course Italian, but it is perhaps significant that the wine list is much longer than the menu. Priorities here are clearly Italian, too. 250EEK.

✕ Tigu Vilmsi 45; ☎ 5666 8493; www.tigukohvik.ee; ⏰ 17.00–22.00 Tue–Sat, closed Sun & Mon. A restaurant with only 5 tables is usually worth a journey, & this one is no exception. The outside façade is so drearily Soviet, it can easily be missed. The menu is only in Estonian, but the food is entirely French, as is the internal décor. Opening hours were in early 2008 simply eccentric, but the food is such that everybody fits in. It is linked with Sisalik in town, which would otherwise be its only competitor. 300EEK.

✕ Toompea Eesti Maja Toompea 8; ☎ 644 4423. Under the same ownership as Eesti Maja, & close to the Occupation Museum, this new restaurant opened in 2007. Service is quicker than at the older restaurant, but diners are welcome to linger. 200EEK.

✕ Vanaema Juures (Grandma's Place) Rataskaevu 10/12; ☎ 626 9080. This is probably Tallinn's most famous restaurant but not even a visit from Hillary Clinton has gone to its head. The valid & repeated descriptions of it – good home cooking, a traditional décor & a cosy atmosphere – degenerate into cliché but few would dispute them. The furnishings & photographs from the previous independence period (1918–40), together with discreet music from that time, deter the young & raucous, but others will immediately appreciate the originality of total Estonian surroundings. Unfortunately, Grandma had not got around to having a website by 2008 so presumably never will. 350EEK.

CAFÉS AND BARS There is little distinction between cafés and bars in Tallinn as no licence is needed to serve alcohol. Self-service at a counter remains common although practice varies as to whether clients then wait for the drinks or whether they are brought to the table. Establishments that open only in the evening are listed in the entertainment section. Those below are open all day and usually in the evening as well.

Piped music is largely unavoidable but perhaps readers can help find a café where all music is banned so peace and quiet is assured. The success of those listed here should ensure that they are all around during the currency of this book, although be prepared for name changes if a new owner takes over.

✗ **Elsebet** Viru 2. Lunch on the run is not yet a Tallinn phenomenon, despite the serious business environment. However, those who want to bring London practice with them can race into the ground floor here & will be out in 5mins at most with a range of sandwiches, quiches & cakes. The more sensible visitor will forget b/fast in the hotel for once to arrive here with a camera at 08.00 so that a window table on the first floor will be theirs. Stay for a couple of hours to see the last of yesterday's drunks being picked up, the Tallinn elite coming out of their expensive flats & the first of the cruise parties meandering towards Town Hall Square. Don't forget a zoom lens to catch unsuspecting faces & Tallinn's windows & roofs.

♀ **Gloria** Veinikelder Müürivahe 2; www.gloria.ee. It seems a shame to ignore Estonia while in Tallinn but that is what anyone who comes here has to do. Forget vodka or the local Vana Tallinn & concentrate on the 2,000 different bottles not only of wine but also of cognac & whisky. Many foreigners justify their presence in this wine bar by pointing out that they can enjoy their 'own' drinks here at prices much lower than those charged at home. That the bar is called 'Napoleon' shows where most of these 2,000 bottles come from.

🍴 **Jõujaam** (Power Station) Väike Karja 8. Perhaps where Stereo Lounge (see page 38) started many others will follow, but for the moment it is only here that a white background has again emerged in the heart of the Old Town. The pictures & the décor all centre on the theme of generation & high & low voltage reveal the size of the dishes. The smaller ones are in fact the most original; a hot salad of beans, pears & ham or a cheese-based vegetarian wrap will be remembered for longer than the Adenauer pork chop or the Kekkonen steak. Hopefully these references to politicians famous in the 1950s will keep the clientele quieter & older than those usually seen in Old Town bars.

🍴 **Kaheksa** Vana-Posti 8. Kaheksa means 'eight' but nobody seems to know the reason for this name. The austere granite Sõprus Cinema to which this is an adjunct is a surprising backcloth but indoors a totally tropical environment is created. The décor is light, as are the drinks, most of which are rum & coconut based. Teetotallers can hide their abstinence behind fruit-smoothies which really are light desserts. From about 2002, a Caribbean theme hit Tallinn & here it is at its best. Perhaps a visit in midwinter is inadvisable as leaving will be a blow; wait until the summer when the outside will from time to time rival the interior. Given its proximity to Hollywood, one of Tallinn's largest nightclubs, the clientele here is inevitably young, particularly in the early evening.

🍴 **Kohvicum** Uus 16; www.kohvik.ee. This is in the basement of the Music Academy (Muusikamajas) but is open to the public although few tourists track it down. Its warmth is welcome in winter & so is the opposite in summer. It is run by the Kehrwieder group who own a number of dependable cafés around Tallinn. The location is most useful, given the few other cafés in this part of the Old Town. The website gives a full list of the Kehrwieder outlets & a map showing their locations.

🍴 **Kuus Pelmeni** (Six Dumplings) Narva 8. Six is in fact a modest portion here, & given the self-service & low prices, it is worth going for a dozen, which means roughly 1 of each filling offered. With almost a similar number of sauces, it would be possible to make up over a hundred separate dishes, even before the vegetables are taken into account. Simply because it is about 400m from the Viru Gate, only locals know it but foreigners will get a surprised welcome & as 2 meals here cost the same as a beer in the Old Town, more must in due course follow.

🍴 **Maiasmokk** (Sweet Tooth) Pikk 16. It is nice to find a café that is unashamedly old-fashioned. The panelling is dark, the staff middle-aged & the food prepared on the spot. It is provincial in the best sense of the word, being one of the very few cafés in Tallinn that are spared piped music. Prices also stay 2 or 3 years behind those charged elsewhere, particularly surprising given its location on the tourist beat in the centre of the Old Town. There is a separate entrance to the restaurant, which consists of small dining rooms on the 1st floor that can be booked for private groups of 8 to 10. Choose the view carefully: one overlooks the balcony of the Russian Embassy from which the occupation of Estonia was proclaimed in 1940. In summer 2004 the Kalev Chocolate Museum moved to the top floor of the restaurant but still had not opened in spring 2008, although a small exhibition on the history of marzipan is open on the ground floor.

🍴 **Meistrite Hoov** (Masters' Courtyard) Vene 6. Whilst gentrification continues apace throughout most of Tallinn's Old Town, it is pleasant still to find a quarter that remains genuinely bohemian. Lavish chocolates are usually expected in boutiques or at least in department stores, but they are available here, too, & in fact are the main attraction. In the café, officially called Chocolaterie, wearing a suit is unheard of, self-service is the norm & soft cushions cover the chairs. Expect to be surrounded by modern art, both in painting & in ceramics. The size of the exhibition depends on the weather; it rapidly expands outdoors whenever it can. Several rooms above the café are now let out for 800–1,500EEK to non-smokers only. They have kitchen facilities so are useful for visitors wanting to stay longer than a few days in the town centre (see *www.jpgoldart.ee*).

Mocha Vene 1. Return visitors to Tallinn will remember this as the Mary & there seems little need for a name change. The selection of teas remains as extensive as that of the coffees & for those who would be happier in Austria or Germany, the Mocha provides perfect solace. After a cake or 2 here there is no need for lunch or supper. Papers to read abound, there is no rush & the music is much quieter than elsewhere. The neighbouring shops change frequently; let us hope that Mocha sees no need to follow suit. The Irish & Italian embassies share a building over the road so their flags plus the EU one make the café easy to find.

Moskva Vabaduse Väljak 10; 640 4694; www.moskva.ee. Some cafés survive in Tallinn on sheer cheek & this must be one of them. The name is as risky as ever given the poisonous level of relations with Russia & the location of this café on Freedom Square (Victory Square in Soviet times). The décor remains gloomy & the website is in dark brown, with no foreign-language translations. Yet local expats & Estonians return again & again. Perhaps it is for a sense of security as much as for the 1990s prices. The food is dependable, as is the company, & during the day, the music, if noticeable at all, will not intrude. The website gives details of live music that intrudes each w/end.

Musi (Kiss) Niguliste 6; 644 3100; www.musi.ee. This wine bar opened almost without anybody noticing in spring 2005. It has to be said that the chipped stairs & the formidable wooden door (always closed) are hardly an encouragement. As Musi is situated on one of the main tourist routes, this scenario is perhaps just as well, so tourists who do track it down will be rewarded with suburban prices & an almost homely feel, so small are the rooms. The abstemious will be able to have a meal here from the salads & pies on offer & nobody need worry about being over 25. It is probably a good sign, if a surprising one, that 3 years after opening, the menu & the website are still only in Estonian, but the website is in any case a visual & aural attraction in its own right. Do not ask for a wine list as what is offered changes frequently, but positively; just ask the staff for current offerings & prices. However high or low the bill, it will come in a jewellery box. Foreigners are welcome, but they must fit in.

Narva Kohvik Narva 10. Don't come here unless you are over 50 & want for a few minutes to go 'back in the USSR'. Presumably EU regulators have kept the hygiene up to scratch here but no modern designer has followed them. There is an explanation for the 'no cars' sign in the door. Apparently a wild youngster wanted to convert the café instantly into a drive-in, with grim consequences; it is thought, probably with a degree of humour, that this sign will deter any potential successors.

Park Weizenbergi, Kadriorg Park, on junction with Poska. Tumbling off the tram *en route* to the palace, the park or to KUMU, it is very tempting to stop *en route* here, given the thorough German influence on both the baking & the coffee. In winter hot wine is an added incentive for lingering. In good weather, buy a picnic to enjoy in the park.

Pollu Rävala 8. The headquarters of the Estonian Civil Aviation Administration, close to the Radisson & Viru hotels, is an unusual place to look for coffee but for those on a tight budget & not the least interested in atmosphere, the public café in the basement rewards those who track it down, with coffee for 8EEK, light snacks for 15EEK & hot meals for around 25EEK. The hot dishes come straight from the freezer & the flowers on the tables are guaranteed to be artificial, but at these prices who should care?

Scotland Yard Mere pst 6e; 653 5190; www.scotlandyard.ee. Many British antique shops must have been plundered to recreate the 1890s here, though whether gunsmiths needed to relinquish so much of their old stock is a moot point. The guns worn by the staff are fortunately fakes. Proximity to the port attracts the wilder, rougher crowd on Fri & Sat nights, but more conventional guests will feel happy here during the day & might even want to stay for a meal. Despite the old-fashioned décor, it is very much a young set who come here.

Stereo Lounge Harju 6; 631 0549; www.stereolounge.ee. Older visitors will remember George Browne's that used to be at this address. While pubs remained a novelty in Tallinn, its formula worked, but Stereo has shown that by 2004 a change was very necessary. The décor is totally white, in contrast to the staff who are in easyJet orange & the bottles which have stayed as their manufacturers produced them. There is no longer any need to battle to the bar for a drink; it & a healthy range of light dishes can quickly be brought to any table, but for those able to support themselves on a bar stool, the array of drinks served & the breadth of the TV screen will provide an enticing vista.

Tristan ja Isolde Raekoja Plats 1. Although part of the Town Hall, its entrance is so well concealed that, even at the height of the tourist season, space is often available. However, the most enticing time to come here is in midwinter, late in the evening. Stride across the deserted snow-covered square, pull open the squeaking door & enjoy glühwein in what looks like a Swiss country inn. Follow this with Irish coffee & chocolate cake & hopefully the warmth will last until you get back to your hotel.

ENTERTAINMENT AND NIGHTLIFE

On regaining independence, Tallinn immediately rebelled against the limited and formal entertainment that had previously been available. Out went dance bands, string quartets and folk dancing; in came discos, striptease and jazz. Private enterprise immediately seized the Finnish market that came every weekend laden with money and determined to spend it – not necessarily in the most sensible of ways; vodka at a quarter of the price it is at home is bound to lead to grief. Above all, the night went on until breakfast. No club now dares to close before 02.00. Admission fees are rare so it is common to sample quite a few different places in one evening. Now that Tallinn has a large middle class, the clientele is very mixed in most clubs as Estonians no longer feel excluded from them. None are yet typecast but go for smart-casual dress. Anything torn or ill-fitting is frowned on in Estonia. Better to be out of date than out of figure.

Before the clubs open, rock and pop concerts draw large crowds to Linnahall, near the harbour. It has performances most evenings.

OPERA AND CONCERTS The Estonian National Opera (*www.opera.ee*) has performances three or four times a week. Specialist tour operators can pre-book tickets as the programme is fixed about six months in advance. Given the inevitable government cutbacks in this field, it is remarkable how up to date the building now is following its 1998–2005 reconstruction, with the stage lighting being particularly impressive. Unlike Riga, Estonia's opera rarely attracts world-famous performers – and indeed some Estonian performers, especially in this field, have been attracted abroad by the much higher fees paid there. The fact that about 30% of the opera's tickets year-round are sold to non-Estonians shows the high standard that it offers, as well as the very reasonable prices charged. Even after the Opera House reopened in 2005 following its restoration, the highest ticket price was usually 350EEK, about £16/US$32, and many cost much less. Performances are always in the original language; 20% or so are of contemporary Estonian works, the remainder are popular classics. The opera is closed in July and August.

Classical concerts are held in the Old Town Hall, the Estonia Concert Hall, the House of Blackheads and in St Nicholas' Church, all of these venues being in the Old Town. In most cases tickets are sold only on the day or the day before the concert so there is no need (or possibility) to pre-book from abroad. Whilst some performances take place in midsummer, music-lovers are well advised to come at other times of year when the choice is wider and the standard higher.

Young people congregate at Linnahall, the concert hall beside the heliport near the harbour, where live music is staged most evenings. Performers are always local. Sometimes this is replaced by family shows and sometimes by raucous Russian plays not genteel enough for the main Russian Theatre. The website (*www.linnahall.ee*) is only in Estonian (*Pileti hind* are the ticket prices and Jäähalli is the ice-skating rink).

Films are always subtitled and never dubbed so tourists can see films missed at home without any problem. The Sõprus Cinema (*www.kino.ee*) in the Old Town at Vana-Posti 8 is easily accessible from many hotels. It is now part of a Baltic chain called Cinamon which is the name used for the complexes that have opened in Vilnius and Kaunas. Younger people flock to Coca-Cola Plaza (*www.superkinod.ee*), a combination of 11 separate cinemas and a shopping mall. It is situated behind the central post office on Viru Square so is close to many hotels.

NIGHTLIFE Tallinn prides itself on its nightlife and some tour operators promote it extensively. It has tended to attract some people who should really have kept their vomiting and urinating back home in Britain and Finland. However there has been a pleasant tendency since the autumn of 2007: the drop in the number of stag groups plaguing the Old Town.

Fortunately, nightclubs do not go in and out of favour as quickly in Tallinn as they do elsewhere and many clubs that were thriving six or seven years ago still do so now. Many do not charge an entrance fee, particularly midweek, so if you find you have stumbled into somewhere not to your taste, it won't cost much to move on.

The clubs listed below are all totally different, and this is deliberate. *Tallinn In Your Pocket (www.inyourpocket.com)* keeps very up to date on this topic as it is published six times a year and not being dependent on advertising can be objective. To whet your appetite, check their website before leaving home.

☆ **Astoria Palace** Vabaduse väljak 5 (Freedom Square); www.astoria.ee. It is rare for a nightclub to boast that it opened in 1926 rather than in 2006, but the Astoria rightly does so & is happy to promote its link with dance-hall days. The music played does not usually go back that far, but do not be surprised to relive the '60s & '70s here, in both Soviet & Western styles. The website warns visitors that it has no weapons deposit, so guns must presumably be left at home. With luck this deters the sort of guest who might otherwise have brought one.

☆ **Bonnie & Clyde** Olümpia Hotel, Liivalaia 33. As this club is safely ensconced in a 4-star hotel, it is never a mistake to suggest a date here. Do, however, dress up properly, first to get in & second not to lower the tone. If you are under 25, you may well not want to try unless you can be sure of being taken for at least 30. If you are 45, do not worry; nearly everybody else is too.

☆ **La Casa del Habano** Dunkri 2; www.havanas.ee. For those who hate nightlife but for business reasons have to pretend otherwise, Tallinn's first cigar lounge provided the perfect answer. La Casa has a licensed smoking room so there's no need to stand outside on the street before lighting up. To impress, insist on a Cuban cigar, but the miserly can also order Danish & Dutch ones. Sit at the window during the evening & see all of single Tallinn go by, some to the deluxe St Petersbourg Hotel & some to the Harley Davidson described below. As the lounge is also open during the day, come back then for a different view of families & cruise passengers.

☆ **Harley Davidson** Dunkri 11. This club must clearly be a rebellion against the deluxe St Petersbourg Hotel on the other side of the road. Nobody here has any dress sense at all & if they cannot arrive on a motorbike, will certainly choose a taxi instead. Pretend to be under 25 to be comfortable here &, yes, a leather jacket is the common currency. Probably to stop endless protests from hotel grandees, the club closes at midnight during the week & at the comparatively early time of 02.00 on Fri & Sat nights.

☆ **Marat (T)ooklubi** Tartu mnt 63; www.klubimarat.ee. Clubs, like restaurants, are now moving away from the Old Town to offer space as well as lower prices. The bland Soviet exterior here must put off some, but those who go in will find the surprising interior of an Estonian country cottage & will hear quite a lot of Estonian music as well. The name is a combination of the word *öö* that means 'night' & *töö* that means 'work'. The premises can be let for seminars during the day, before they are converted for pleasure in the evenings.

☆ **Molly Malone's** Mündi 2. www.baarid.ee. Yes, the old aluminium Guinness advertisements are corny, yes the music can be dated & yes, because of the location on Town Hall Square it can get very crowded in summer, but nonetheless a visit to Tallinn is not complete without a look-in at Molly's. Expats regularly congregated here, even before fish & chips came onto the menu. In the summer, spilling onto the square is normal so relative peace can alternate with Irish liveliness. The club is rightly sensible to advertise its prices on the website; even humdrum cafés nearby tend to charge a lot more.

GAY TALLINN Visitors to Tallinn may be surprised at how limited the gay scene is. Whilst the legal restraints faced by the gay community in Soviet times have all of course been abolished, the hostility has still not been eradicated. As a result, open affection outside the few gay clubs is very unusual and visitors are advised to avoid this. Some clubs even function behind closed doors and it is necessary to ring a bell to gain admission. Opening hours can often change, as can nights on which women

Lennart Meri

Old Tallinn... It looks at us in the morning when we are hurrying to work and in the evening as we return home, always with the same good-natured glance of a friendly old man. But we scarcely notice it. We scarcely notice the thousand-year history of these streets. Why should we? These ancient stones are a part of ourselves, flesh of our flesh. We were born and grew up among them. We fell in love, fought, dreamed, took part in strikes, died, built monuments to ourselves and never lost heart. Yes, we have always been rather cramped for space. But it is of course a joy to us to see how every year the cloud of romantic legend thickens over our city and it is an even greater joy to tourists. Some of these legends are not totally devoid of truth. It is quite true for instance that kings and princes, admirals and pirates once galloped along these uneven cobbles, that swords clashed in knightly tournaments and the sweet wine of Portugal flowed plentifully. Kings, rulers... Where are they now? But we remain, we with our thousand-year-old town, its legends, secrets, subterranean passages, walled-up windows, enchanted doors. So pause for a while before them, feel their surfaces that the centuries have polished smooth. Perhaps they have something to tell you? Perhaps you will be able to hear the clatter of hooves at midnight, the clash of swords, the stifled sighs, the grim song of troops on the march? Then hold your breath and listen, for these stones speak of our distant childhood.

Lennart Meri was President of Estonia 1992–2001 and died in March 2006

are admitted. This should be checked on their websites. Three well-established clubs are:

☆ **Angel** Sauna 1; www.clubangel.ee. Probably 'sauna' is the perfect description here, at least at w/ends when it gets packed. It is a fortunate comment on contemporary Estonia that this club can function so openly. Should you want a lesson in biblical history about the origin of heavenly angels, look at the website.

☆ **Ring Club** Juhkentali 11; www.ringclub.ee. Women & striptease are strictly segregated here but do check the explicit & detailed English-language website before setting off. Juhkentali is close to the bus station & is hardly the most salubrious road in Tallinn, which perhaps suits the risqué approach of this club & the gloomy underground surroundings in which its activities take place.

☆ **X-Baar** Sauna 1; www.zone.ee/xbaar. With its central location, comparatively long history & small size, this is probably the place to go first in Tallinn. The jazz & the pink décor will provide reassuring surroundings.

SHOPPING

From Monday to Friday most shops open 10.00–18.00 and on Saturday they close earlier, usually around 16.00. On Sundays they stay closed. However those in the Old Town of interest to tourists open in the summer 10.00–19.00 seven days a week. Supermarkets open every day, usually 09.00–21.00. Only the smallest shops now refuse credit cards. Some may take euros or dollars, even though this is technically illegal. However the exchange rate is likely to be very poor so local currency should always be used for small items where credit cards are not applicable.

BOOKS AND POSTCARDS Postcards are best bought at the **post office** at the top of the Old Town (*Lossi Plats 4, beside the Alexander Nevsky Cathedral*), although sadly it is closed at weekends. Here they tend to cost about half the price charged by the sellers on the street. This post office also sells a wide selection of stamps for collectors.

Raamatukoi (*Harju 1, opposite the tourist office*) and **Apollo** (*Viru 23*) are the best sources for travel books in English on Tallinn, Estonia and the neighbouring Baltic countries. They usually stock a wide selection of Bradt guides and also paperback fiction in English. As with the post office, their charges for postcards are much lower than those of street-sellers. In 2007, the **Estonian History Museum** opened a shop not in the museum itself, but behind it on the corner of Börsi Käik and Lai. It sells souvenirs based on its collections and also probably every book published in English about any aspect of Estonian history.

OTHER PURCHASES It is hard to support ethnic cleansing, but with the purchase of souvenirs it can probably be justified at **Meistrite Hoov** (Masters' Courtyard) at Vene 6 where a condition of trading is that anything sold is produced in Estonia. There is nothing wrong with Russian wooden dolls, Lithuanian amber and Chinese paper-cuts, but Tallinn Old Town is not the place where they should be promoted, as they all too often are. Come here for a range of small outlets selling locally produced beeswax candles, honey, woollen sweaters, juniper butter knives, hand-painted ceramics and glass. Renovation, which started in 2002, was largely complete by 2008.

For chocolate it is important to go to the **Kalev** shop at Lai 1, rather than to their other shops in the Old Town since prices here are much lower.

Those who shop for necessity rather than for pleasure usually call in at the hypermarket **Ulemiste**, beside the hotel of the same name a few hundred yards from the airport. It sells a wide range of souvenirs, cheap household goods, black bread and vodka which can be picked up just before checking in for a flight. Shopaholics, however, should go instead to the **Viru Centre**, a shopping complex beside the hotel of the same name and now linked to Tallinn's largest department store, **Kaubamaja**. Its multilingual website (*www.virukeskus.com*) gives full details of all the shops it includes. Being completely enclosed, and with the bus station in the basement, the outside weather is irrelevant year-round.

WALKING TOUR

Tourists tend to concentrate on the Old Town but many modern buildings are of interest, too. While the main sights in the Old Town can be covered in one day, more time is needed for others. A route for a day-long walking tour is suggested.

Start at the final Soviet architectural legacy to Estonia, the **National Library** (Eesti Rahvusraamatukogu), begun in 1986 and completed in 1993 (page 52). It is situated on the intersection of Endla and Tõnismägi close to the Mihkli and Santa Barbara hotels.

Opposite is a nondescript traffic island with some flower beds, but it used to be the site of the Bronze Soldier. For details of what happened there on 26 April 2007, see page 19 in the *History* section.

Cross the road to **Charles's Church** (Kaarlikirik). With its almost Episcopalian simplicity it is the perfect antidote to what is to come later in the walk (page 55). On leaving the church, turn right into Kaarli and then take the first road on the left, Toompea. The **Occupation Museum**, on the corner of Kaarli and Toompea, opened here in summer 2003 (page 53). The first building just on Toompea is the headquarters of the Estonian Defence League, which dates from 1918 when most of Estonia's forces were volunteers.

The plaque on the wall is to its founder Johannes Orasmaa who died in Kirov Prison in 1943, having been arrested in Tallinn on the same day in 1940 as General Laidoner. Orasmaa was a great skier, and encouraged his troops to take up this sport, so that they could be equally agile militarily when the need came.

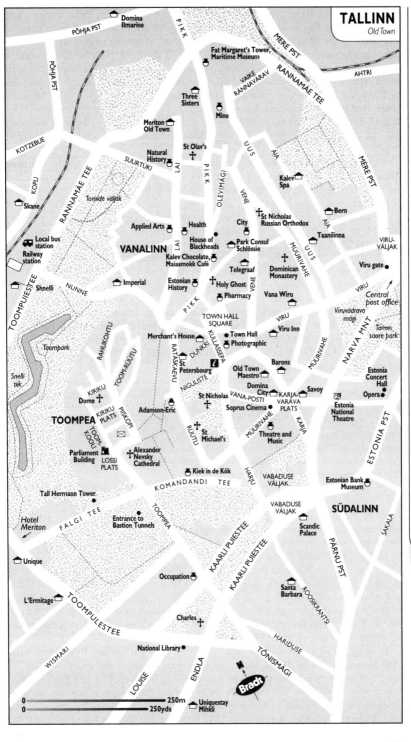

TALLINN
Old Town

PÕHJA PST
Domina
Ilmarine
PIKK
MERE PST
AHTRI

Fat Margaret's Tower,
Maritime Museum
VAIKE
RANNAVARAV
RANNAMÄE TEE
MERE PST

PÕHJA PST

KOTZEBUE

Three
Sisters
Mine
UUS
AIA

Meriton
Old Town
Kalev
Spa

Skane
RANNAMÄE TEE
Natural
History
LAI
St Olav's
OLEVIMÄGI
PIKK
VENE
St Nicholas
Russian Orthodox
Bern
Taanilinna
AIA
VIRU-
VÄLJAK

KOPLI

Local bus
station
Railway
station
SUURTUKI
Tornide väljak

Applied Arts
Health
City

VANALINN
LAI
House of
Blackheads
Park Consul
Schlössie
Telegraaf
VENE
MUURIVAHE
UUS
MERE PST

Shnelli
NUNNE
Imperial
Kalev Chocolate,
Maiasmokk Café
Estonian
History
Holy Ghost
Pharmacy
Dominican
Monastery
Vana Wiru
Viru gate

TOOMPUIESTEE

PIKK
TOWN HALL
SQUARE
VIRU
Viru Inn
Viru
VIRU-
VÄLJAK
Central
post office
Viruvärava
mägi
Tamm
saare park

Toompark
Snelli
tiik
RAHUKOHTU
TOOM-RÜÜTLI
Merchant's House
KULLASSEPA
DUNKRI
RATASKAEVU
St
Petersburg
NIGULISTE
Town Hall
Photographic
Barons
Old Town
Maestro
MUURIVAHE
NARVA MNT
ESTONIA PST

KIRIKU
Dome
KIRIKU
PLATS
Adamson-Eric
TOOM-
KOOLI
PIISKOPI
St Nicholas
VANA-POSTI
Domina
City
Soprus Cinema
KARJA-
VARAVA
PLATS
Savoy
KARJA
Estonia
Concert
Hall
Opera

TOOMPEA
Parliament
Building
LOSSI
PLATS
RÜÜTLI
St Michael's
Alexander
Nevsky
Cathedral
MUURIVAHE
Theatre and
Music
Estonia
National
Theatre

Tall Hermann Tower
Kiek in de Kök
KOMANDANDI TEE
HARJU
VABADUSE
VÄLJAK
Estonian Bank
Museum

Hotel
Meriton
FALGI TEE
Entrance to
Bastion Tunnels
TOOMPEA
VABADUSE
VÄLJAK
SÜDALINN
SAKALA

Unique
KAARLI PUIESTEE
Scandic
Palace
PÄRNU PST

L'Ermitage
TOOMPULESTEE
Occupation
KAARLI PUIESTEE
Santa
Barbara
ROOSIKRANTSI

Charles
HARIDUSE

WISMARI
National Library
ENDLA
TÕNISMÄGI
N
Bradt

LOUISE
0   250m
0   250yds
Uniquestay
Mihkli

Continuing up the hill, the statue on the left is to Admiral Johan Pitka, who worked actively with the British navy in 1918–20. As with General Laidoner, he was awarded a KCMG by the British. In 1940 he fled to Finland, returning to Estonia in 1944 to fight the Russians, even though he was by then 72 years old. How he died remains a mystery but it was probably in fighting, although he may have committed suicide to avoid capture by the Soviet forces. At the first crossroads, note the simple monument to 20 August 1991, the date Estonia declared independence during the failed Moscow coup. Had it been necessary, Estonians were ready to use the walls and towers to defend the Old Town from possible Soviet attack but the quick collapse of the coup and the immediate recognition by the USSR of Estonian independence prevented this.

To the left of the monument just below the hill is the entrance to the **Bastion Tunnels.** Tours do not start here but at Kiek in de Kök (see page 52), where tickets are bought. The public were first admitted in March 2007 and entry is only possible as part of a group tour. Individuals can join one, which at the time of writing starts at 13.00 and lasts for about an hour. However current arrangements should be checked in Kiek in de Kök as they may well change, given that further tunnels might be opened in 2008.

The tunnels date from the 17th century and were built in the expectation of a long Russian siege. Their construction lasted several decades and even now, not all the tunnels have been explored or even located. They were never used for fighting in the Northern War as the Swedes were finally defeated in 1709 by Peter the Great several hundred miles away at Poltava, now in Ukraine, and the other battles all took place a long distance from Tallinn. The Russians never needed them either, and they were handed over to the municipality of Tallinn in 1857. They were in fact only of real use for two days, 9 and 10 March 1944, when local people used them as air-raid shelters during the Soviet bombing campaign.

The Soviets in turn prepared them for further invasions, in this case nuclear ones, which again never materialised, and they installed the thick metal doors as protection against chemical attacks. They also installed electricity, a water supply and a telephone system, much of which remains. There is no artificial ventilation, with all the air coming from ducts leading to the surface. In the 1980s the tunnels were a sculpture warehouse and the homeless made considerable use of them in the 1990s. Much of the equipment abandoned by the Soviets in 1991 was stolen in a still unsolved robbery that took place on Christmas Day in 2004.

Up the small hill is a bronze statue of **Linda**, mother of the mythological Estonian hero Kalevipoeg, whose tears in theory formed Lake Ülemiste. It was produced in 1880 by August Weizenberg (1837–1921), who maintained close links with the Estonian nationalist movement, even though he lived for 18 years in Rome and then for 14 years in St Petersburg. A marble bust of this statue, also by Weizenberg (which he made in Italy using Carrara marble), is in KUMU.

A plaque on the house to the right, on the corner of Komandandi, commemorates its use by Gannibal, the black slave who rose to be a senior adviser to Peter the Great and who was briefly in charge of the Reval (Tallinn) garrison. He is perhaps better remembered as the great-grandfather of the poet Alexander Pushkin. Gannibal did not stay in Reval long, finding its racism towards him an unwelcome contrast to his treatment in cosmopolitan St Petersburg.

Looking ahead is a monument that dates from the 15th century, **Pikk Hermann** (Tall Hermann Tower). It has withstood numerous invasions and remains intact. Its height of nearly 50m is supported by foundations 15m deep. The first Estonian flag was flown from here in 1884, 34 years before the country was to become independent. Subsequent conquerors always marked their success by raising a flag here. A German guidebook printed in 1942 lists 12 major dates in Tallinn's history, the last being 28 August 1941, when the German flag was raised over Pikk Hermann. During the Soviet occupation, the Estonian SSR flag was flown, but the Estonian national flag returned in 1989. It is raised at sunrise and lowered at sunset, except at midsummer when it is not lowered at all on the night of 23/24 June. The blue in the flag represents the sky, black the soil, and white the aspirations of the Estonian people. It is open to the public just one day a year, 23 April, the day in 1919 when the first session of the Estonian Constituent Assembly took place.

Turn right down the hill (Komandandi) to **Kiek in de Kök** ('Peep in the Kitchen', page 52). The reason for the name becomes obvious as one climbs the 45m tower to the sixth floor and peers into more and more houses; only the steeples of St Nicholas and St Olav are higher. Kiek in de Kök does not have any catering but the nearest tower to it, Megedi, can be recommended in this respect. This tower, like most in the city wall, dates from the late 14th century and was continually enlarged during the 15th century. From around 1800 when its defensive potential declined, it was converted into a barracks. On leaving Kiek in de Kök turn back up the hill and turn right into Toompea, which ends in the square between **Parliament** (Riigikogu, page 53) and the **Alexander Nevsky Cathedral** (page 55). The juxtaposition of these two buildings appropriately contrasts official Estonian and Russian architecture. The one is simple, small and functional, the other elaborate and deliberately powerful, a completely Russian architectural outpost dominating the Tallinn skyline. The Parliament building, the interior of which dates from 1921, is one of very few in the Old Town to have seen frequent reconstruction, the last one resulting from a fire in 1917 which may have been started by the Bolsheviks.

Continue up the hill along Toomkooli with the post office on your right. By the end of 2008, this street should be completely restored, the first one to be back to its 1920s glory. Straight ahead, on Kiriku Square, is the Dome Church (Toomkirik), sometimes called St Mary's Cathedral (page 56).

As you turn left out of the church, the **Estonian Knighthood Building** dominates the opposite side of Kiriku Square. From 1992 until 2006 it provided temporary shelter for the Estonia Art Museum that now has its own building (KUMU) in Kadriorg. During the first independence period it was the Foreign Ministry and for much of the Soviet period served as the national library. Turning left from the former museum along Toom Rüütli leads, after 150m, to the main viewpoint across Tallinn. It is inevitably crowded during the tourist season so an alternative can be recommended along Rahukohtu, which also starts in Kiriku Square behind the church.

To reach the lower town, it is necessary in either case to return along Piiskopi towards the Russian cathedral and then to walk down the steps of Lühike Jalg ('Short Leg'), rather a misnomer as there are in fact about 100 steps. At the top, though, are several tempting cafés, souvenir shops and well-maintained toilets which can provide a respite before continuing the walk. Before starting the descent, look to the left along Pikk Jalg ('Long Leg'). The façade which commands one of the best views over Tallinn is modelled on the main building of Tartu University. Perhaps appropriately, in view of the current strength of the Estonian economy, this imposing building houses the Ministry of Finance. On the right at the end of Lühike Jalg is the **Adamson-Eric Museum** (page 49).

Continuing down the hill, the steps become a road which continues to a junction. To the left is Rataskaevu and to the right, Rüütli, both roads which house some of Tallinn's most famous restaurants. Ahead is **Niguliste** (St Nicholas' Church, page 57), which, like many other early churches in Tallinn, was a military installation as well as a church, with ample hiding places and secret exits to the city walls. Coming out of the church and turning left along Rüütli, the next building on the left is the **Swedish Church of St Michael** (page 57).

On leaving the church, turn right to the memorial to the writer **Eduard Vilde** (1865–1933). The illustrations depict scenes from his novels and plays, and the two stones represent an open book. Between 1918 and 1920 he served as Estonian ambassador in Copenhagen and Berlin, convincing both governments that an independent Estonia was here to stay. The **Tallinn Tourist Information Centre** is on the other side of the road and ahead is the bookshop Raamatukoi. On the corner of Harju and Kuninga note the plaque on the wall to the writer Juhan Smuul (1922–71) who lived here because the building belongs to the Writers' Union. Despite winning both Stalin and Lenin prizes and being chairman of the Writers' Union, he was a genuinely popular writer at the time which is why the plaque has not been removed. Hopefully, his works will soon be republished. **Jaan Kross** (1920–2007), Estonia's most famous 20th-century writer, lived in this building until a few months before his death, remaining fit enough to reach his fourth-floor flat without a lift. (In Soviet times, only buildings with five floors or more had lifts installed.)

Turn into Harju. The bombed site on the right has deliberately been left as it was, following the bombing raid of 9 March 1944. The inscription commemorates the 463 people killed that night. In June 2002 a referendum was held in Tallinn about the future of this site. Only 2% of the population turned out to vote, but 87% of them wanted to keep the site as a memorial and not let it fall into the hands of developers. Returning along Harju and then Kullassepa brings one into Raekoja Plats, or Town Hall Square. Just before reaching the square, it is worth turning right for a few minutes into the small alley, Raekoja. The building on the right, which now houses the **Photographic Museum** (page 54), was the town's main prison until the early 19th century.

The **Town Hall Square** is similar to many in northern Germany as it was the commercial centre for the Baltic Germans. In the 16th century, the Germans accounted for about 1,500 of Tallinn's total population of around 5,000. They maintained all positions of authority, ruling from the Town Hall and the surrounding buildings. The square was the centre for all major events in the town, happy and tragic. Carnivals, weddings and Christmas have all been regularly celebrated here and the Tallinn Old Days Festival, held each year in, early June, recreates the carnival atmosphere with its musical and artistic events. What was probably the world's first Christmas tree was displayed here in 1441. Yet the square was also the site for frequent executions and floggings, its grimmest day being in 1806 when 72 peasants were executed following a failed uprising. Nowadays it is hard to imagine such a background as work and punishment have given way to total relaxation. Cafés surround the square and spread into it during the summer. From 2001, a Christmas market has taken place here throughout December. One of the few buildings on the square that has kept its original function is the **pharmacy** (page 54), which dates from 1422. The Town Hall (page 54) is the only late Gothic building still intact in Estonia, dating largely from the 15th century.

Across the square, opposite the Town Hall, are several short streets which lead to Pikk. On the corner of Mündi and Town Hall Square is a millennium clock which counted down the seconds until midnight on 31 December 1999. Saiakäik is the smallest street in Tallinn. Take either Mündi or Saiakäik and turn right to the junction of Pikk and Pühavaimu for the **Holy Ghost Church** (Pühavaimu, page 56). Cross Pikk for the **Estonian History Museum** (Ajaloomuuseum, page 51), whose building is as impressive as any of the contents, perhaps more so. As you turn left into Pikk, the new Russian Embassy is on the left and on the right is Maiasmokk, a café that has deliberately stayed old-fashioned both in décor and in prices. The name translates appropriately as 'sweet tooth'. In summer 2004 the Kalev Chocolate Museum moved here too (page 51). Pikk has two of the few notable *Jugendstil* or Art Nouveau buildings in Tallinn, both designed by Jacques Rosenbaum. Number 18, next to Maiasmokk, has a flamboyant Egyptian theme; number 25 on the corner of

Hobusepea is more modest. Number 61, built across Pagari, and probably the blandest building in the Old Town, was the KGB headquarters in Soviet times and now houses the Interior Ministry. Unlike its opposite number in Vilnius, it has not been opened to the public.

Pikk 26, the **House of Blackheads**, is very far from being bland, dating as we see it now from 1597, although an earlier building on this site was rented by the Brotherhood of Blackheads from 1406. They kept the building until 1940, when the Soviet authorities banned the few still remaining members from gathering here. The Brotherhood was a self-elected group of successful merchants trading across the Baltic Sea. When winter conditions prevented boats from leaving Tallinn harbour, they would spend many days socialising here. Some of the silver, tapestries and portraits that they collected and exhibited here until 1940 survived the Soviet occupation and are now exhibited at the City Museum (see page 49) or in the Town Hall (see page 54).

The black head which can be seen above the façade is that of St Maurice, their patron saint. The façade is an early work of Arent Passer from Antwerp, who lived in Tallinn for about 50 years from 1590 until his death in 1637. He may well have modelled his design on Antwerp Town Hall which had been completed a few years earlier. He also modelled the tomb of Pontius de la Gardie in the Dome Church. Little else of his work has survived intact, although fragments from other carvings can be seen in the City Museum.

The Swedes took great care of the building in the 17th century and in 1663 started organising concerts there. This tradition has continued to this day and in fact access to the building is normally only possible when attending a concert. It is also used for formal banquets, such as the one held when Queen Elizabeth II came to Tallinn in October 2006.

Next on the left is **St Olav's Church** (Oleviste, page 57), named after the King of Norway and now a Baptist church. A few yards further down on the right is Fat Margaret's Tower which houses the **Maritime Museum** (Meremuuseum, page 52). Outside is a plaque unveiled by Prince Andrew in May 1998 which commemorates British naval involvement in the battles between Estonian forces and the Bolsheviks from 1918 to 1920. The other plaque, in Estonian and Polish, commemorates the escape of the Polish submarine *Orzel* from Tallinn harbour on 18 September 1939, when it managed to reach Rosyth in Scotland without being intercepted by the German navy.

Turn right out of the museum and leave the Old Town on Suur Rannavärara, the continuation of Pikk. On the right is the monument to those who died in the *Estonia* tragedy in 1994. It can be interpreted in a number of ways, perhaps symbolising the boat breaking into two or the total divide between life and death. Cross Põhja puiestee to the disused power station, now the **Science and Technology Centre**, where families take their children for hands-on experience with most fields of physics and electricity. Built originally in the late 1920s, it then had some claim to Art Nouveau influence but many subsequent alterations have completely removed any hint of beauty and style.

Return into the Old Town and walk behind Fat Margaret's Tower along Uus. Number 37 is the **Marine Mine Museum** (⊕ *10.00–18.00 Wed–Sun, admission 25EEK*). The mines displayed here (and the objects made out of them) all come from Naissaar Island off the coast from Tallinn (see page 66), which was the centre of production for the whole of the Soviet Union. This collection dates back to 1914, although the use of mines in the Baltic dates back to the Crimean War in the 1850s. One exhibit is of a mine sold by the British to the USSR in July 1941, another of a listening station built in 1980 to track down submarines should any have attempted to disrupt the Olympic sailing events taking place in Tallinn harbour.

Number 31 is the Scottish Club, in fact a restaurant open to all. It has the best-maintained lawn in Estonia. Next door is a whisky shop, a clear testimony to Tallinn's affluence and passion for Western consumer goods. It is hard to believe that until 1989 whisky was available only in foreign-currency shops. Turn right into Olevimägi and then left into Vene. On the left is a smaller, but no less Russian version of the Alexander Nevsky Cathedral, St Nicholas' Russian Orthodox Church. Again no concessions are made to Estonia; everything is written, spoken and sung in Russian. It dates from the early 19th century. On the right at number 17 is the **City Museum** (Linnamuuseum, page 49). As with the History Museum, the building is of as much interest as the contents. Having escaped the fires that ravaged so many buildings in the Old Town, this 14th-century merchant's house still has examples of 16th-century wooden panelling, windows and furniture.

On the right are the ruins of the **Dominican Monastery**, founded in 1246 but destroyed during the Reformation in 1524 when the monks were forced to flee. Extensive archaeological excavations were carried out between 1954 and 1968 when the ruins were first opened to the public. Take a torch and wear sturdy shoes as the surviving ambulatories are poorly lit. Of most interest are the stone carvings by the 16th-century Dutch sculptor Arent Passer. Chamber music concerts take place here during the summer. On leaving the monastery, turn left into Vene and left again into Katariina Käik. Gravestones from the monastery are lined up along the left-hand wall. This tiny alleyway is where local expats buy their souvenirs of Tallinn, as few tourists find it, unless they are taken as a group there. It is also used as a film set. Turn right at the end into Müürivahe, which runs below the city walls. Elderly Russians have stalls here, selling woollen sweaters, gloves and socks both in midsummer and in midwinter. The walk ends at the junction with Viru Street. To the left is the 15th-century Viru Gate, as formidable as the fortifications seen at the start of the walk. To the right is McDonald's; will it also last five centuries?

Visitors with more time can see many museums in addition to those mentioned in the walk. Back in the Old Town, in Lai, are the **Applied Arts Museum** (opposite) at number 17 and the **Health Museum** (page 51) at numbers 28–30.

Next to the **Applied Arts Museum** is the **Natural History Museum** (page 53) at Lai 29, and then the **Theatre and Music Museum** (page 54) at Müürivahe 12. Just outside the Old Town, behind the railway station at Kotzebue 16, is the **Dolls' Museum** (page 50).

WHAT TO SEE AND DO

MUSEUMS Most museums close at least one day a week – usually Monday or Tuesday – and some for two days; they also close on public holidays. Many do not open until 11.00 and only one, the Architecture Museum, stays open until 20.00 and this is only in the summer. Churches are open every day from around 09.00.

The most popular ones for foreign visitors, such as the City Museum, Kadriorg Palace and KUMU, charge around £2.50/US$5 for adults. Others charge around £1.50/US$3. Most museums give reductions for children and for senior citizens. There is no charge on 21 February (International Guides Day) and 18 May (International Museums Day) for many of the museums listed. There is also often one day a month when admission is free, although the day in question varies from museum to museum. Several state museums share the website www.ekm.ee, and several city ones www.linnamuuseum.ee. All the museums on this city website have free admission on the last Friday of the month. These and the individual sites listed below give current information on opening hours and on charges. The **Tallinn Card** gives free admission to all the museums listed.

Adamson-Eric Museum (*Lühike Jalg 3; www.ekm.ee;* 🕐 *11.00–18.00 Wed–Sun; admission 30EEK*) Adamson-Eric (1902–68) was without doubt the most famous Estonian artist who worked during both the independence period and the Soviet era. This house has no links with him, although before being used as a museum it did have workshops for coppersmiths. The museum opened in 1983 and the collection is based on around 1,000 works bequeathed by his widow. These cover his whole life in both painting and applied art. Gifts from abroad have recently been added to the collection. Labels are in English. Adamson-Eric's parents were able to pay for long periods of study during the 1920s in both Paris and Berlin. Elements of Fauvism and Cubism can be seen in many of his pictures but he was equally drawn to the Bauhaus and worked closely with Walter Gropius, George Grosz and Otto Dix. On his return to Estonia he first specialised in portraits, then added landscapes and broadened into applied arts. In this field, his work became as diverse as his painting. Around 1930 he began with tapestries and textiles and then added ceramics and metalwork to his range. Shortly before the war he diversified even more, starting to work with leather and to design stage sets. He retreated with the Soviet army in 1941 and managed to maintain his artistic integrity despite the stringent demands of Soviet officialdom. With the inevitable lack of materials for applied art at this time, he concentrated again on painting. In 1949, the political tide finally turned against him and he was expelled from the Communist Party, forced to give up his posts and sent into factory work. Although released in 1953 on Stalin's death, his health had deteriorated and he suffered a stroke in 1955. His reaction was simply to learn to paint as well with his left hand as he had previously done with his right! His health slowly improved and he was able to add porcelain painting and tile design to his work in the field of applied art. He remained active until shortly before his death in 1968.

Applied Arts Museum (*Lai 17; www.etdm.ee;* 🕐 *11.00–18.00 Wed–Sun; admission 40EEK*) The ticket desk still sells the Soviet guidebook which boasts that the exhibits 'are really wonderful, conspicuous in their originality and can bear comparison with the best items of the world'. The third floor (second to British visitors) exhibits work up to 1970 so concentrates on wood and textiles. The second floor continues from then until the present day, so unlike with many other creative fields, there was no sudden change in 1991. Here there is much more work in glass and china. In all fields the collections are extensive and show the Estonian dedication to pottery, weaving, glassmaking and woodwork that has surmounted all political regimes. The ground floor tends now to be used for temporary exhibitions so it is worth checking the website before going to see what is currently on show.

City Museum (*Vene 17; www.linnamuuseum.ee;* 🕐 *Mar–Sep 10.30–18.00 Mon, Wed–Sun; Oct–Feb 10.30–17.00; admission 35EEK*) The ground floor is taken up with a model of the Old Town in 1825 and it is remarkable how close this is to the town today. The Alexander Nevsky Cathedral is the only major addition and there is the section of Harju Street destroyed by Russian bombing in 1944. Note the burnt-out steeple of St Olav which was destroyed by fire in 1820 but had not yet been rebuilt in 1825.

Many of the exhibits on the upper floors here would now be regarded as politically incorrect in the West as they concentrate on the accoutrements of the rich; life below stairs and outside the guilds and churches is ignored. Part of the museum is quite understandably called the 'Treasury', given the quantity of tapestries, silverware, pewter and porcelain displayed there. Nonetheless, the collection shows the breadth of industry and culture that developed in Tallinn from 1860 onwards. The arrival in 1870 of the railway from St Petersburg led to an increase in the population from 30,000 to 160,000 by 1917. One anniversary the Estonians were forced to celebrate in 1910 was the 200th anniversary of the Russian conquest. The museum was closed in 2000 for extensive renovations which included proper lighting and the addition of considerable visual material. It now shows videos of pre-war and Soviet Estonia, of the 1944 bombing, the 1980 Olympics and the 1989 demonstrations that would in due course lead to independence. Allow at least an hour to see these properly. A room of Soviet and Nazi posters has also been added. The café on the top floor is unusual in offering only homemade food. This museum is well labelled in English and the postcard sets they sell are excellent value.

Dolls' Museum (*Kotzebue 16; www.linnamuuseum.ee;* ⊕ *Mar–Oct 10.30–17.30 Wed–Sun, Nov–Feb 10.30–16.30; admission 10EEK*) Opened in 1985 as a memorial to one of Lenin's closest colleagues, Mikhail Kalinin, the Dolls' Museum nonetheless even then had a small collection of toys. Kalinin is now completely forgotten (in Tallinn at least, if not in Kaliningrad!) and toys have taken over completely. The collection of dolls and doll's houses goes back as far as the 18th century, but there are also board games, teddy bears and general toys from 1900 onwards since this is one of the few elements of Estonian life unaffected by the changing political environment. The Teletubbies are a recent addition. The walk from the Old Town behind the Hotel Skane offers a completely changed architectural environment; Tallinn on the wrong side of the tracks becomes a town of poorly maintained wooden houses and an abandoned factory. The market beside the station is worth a stop of a few minutes. Excellent light refreshments are available at prices well below those elsewhere in the town and the choice of clothes, CDs and gadgets is a good reflection of mass Estonian taste.

Estonian Art Museum (KUMU Eesti Kunstimuuseum) (*Weizenbergi 34/Valge 1;* ☎ *602 6001; www.kumu.ee & www.ekm.ee;* ⊕ *May–Sep 11.00–18.00 Tue–Sun; Oct–Apr 11.00–18.00 Wed–Sun; admission 80EEK*) Having searched for a home since 1919, the collection now finally has one, purpose-built and opened with appropriate fanfare in February 2006. In size and scope, it dwarfs any other museum in Estonia and perhaps any elsewhere in the Baltic countries as well. Some of the pictures displayed here were in its last temporary home, the Estonian Knighthood building beside the Dome Church in the Old Town. Many are on show for the first time, including a large collection from the Soviet period (1944–91). The names of the 19th- and 20th-century artists displayed here are sadly unknown outside Estonia, but many styles will be recognised by visitors. Both in the Tsarist period and under independence, most Estonian artists of note studied in Paris so the prevalent style there is reflected in their pictures. Konrad Mägi (1878–1925) is the country's most famous landscape artist and his pictures here are of many regions in Estonia. It is hard to overstate the importance of this building to Estonian culture. Given the struggle for survival Estonians so often had to endure in the 20th century, it is not surprising that museums and galleries had a low priority under all regimes, whether Estonian or under a foreign power. Collections tended to be placed in buildings that happened to be available or which were seized from an ancient regime. The country can now afford to look after its history and its modern artists. Hopefully KUMU is seen as a model to be copied around Estonia. Vilnius is planning to follow suit with its modern art gallery in 2009, when it is European Capital of Culture, which will in turn force Riga to offer something similar.

Estonian Bank Museum (*Estonia pst 11;* ☎ *668 0760; www.eestipank.info;* ⊕ *12.00–17.00 Wed–Fri, 11.00-16.00 Sat; admission free*) The political history of the country is mirrored in this museum through its currency. In 1928 the kroon was tied to the British pound but it floated after 1933 when Britain left the Gold Standard. The current building dates from 1935 and manages to combine elements of neo-Gothic, neo-Renaissance and functionalism. In its predecessor, Estonian independence was proclaimed on 24 February 1918 and in this one a temporary Estonian government was formed in September 1944 between the German and the Russian occupations. The collections here are always bang up to date, so include not only the bank notes issued since 1992, but also designs for recent credit cards and even those for Estonian euro coins unlikely to be introduced until 2012. Quite a large number of commemorative coins are produced by the bank and are on sale here.

Estonian History Museum (*Pikk 17;* ✎ *641 1630; www.earn.ee;* ✆ *11.00–18.00 daily; admission 25EEK*) Dating from 1410, it was the headquarters of the Great Guild and has changed little since. Visitors who arrive when the museum is shut can at least be consoled by the sight of the 15th-century door knockers, but it is worth going indoors for the woodwork alone. The building has served many functions: after the fire at St Olav's in 1820, the congregation met here for 20 years. In 1896, it was the venue for the first film show in Estonia. Exhibits inside are well labelled in English and concentrate on archaeology and costumes. Of more contemporary interest is the Tsarist banknote and coin collection and a section on the founding of the local freemasons in the late 1770s. They were later banned by Alexander I in 1822. It has to be admitted however, that Estonian history is better covered in Tartu than in Tallinn. The museum shop is in a separate building on the corner of Börsi käik and Lai, about 100m away. It has an extensive range of English-language books on Tallinn and Estonia and also small souvenirs at prices usually lower than elsewhere.

Health Museum (*Lai 28–30;* ✎ *641 1732; www.tervishoiumuuseum.ee;* ✆ *11.00–18.00 Tue–Sat; admission 25EEK*) The building here dates from 1377 and a spiral stone staircase dates from that time. The Health Museum is one of the few totally contemporary museums in Tallinn and uses a range of models, toys, visual aids and colourful charts to show both adults and children the importance of healthy living. One cabinet shows the ideal weekly diet for a ten-year-old child, and in another, a virtual human being plays the violin continuously, to show all the muscles being used and the input of the brain. Some visitors may find the explicit illustrations of the effects of syphilis disturbing. Overall it is a brightly lit and well-thought-out display, a vivid contrast to many other museums. The mummified remains of an alcoholic chain-smoking 54-year-old are compared with the healthy organs of a car-crash victim and if this is not warning enough, the lungs of active and passive smokers are shown, together with a cirrhosis-ridden liver. It is one of the few museums in the country with a hands-on element – two exercise bicycles are available for visitors. More conventional museum exhibits include medical equipment from a hundred years or so ago.

Kalev Chocolate Museum (*Pikk 16;* ✎ *628 3811; www.kalev.ee;* ✆ *09.30–18.30 Mon–Sat, 10.00–17.30 Sun; admission free*) Now based at Pikk 16, above Maiasmokk café, the Kalev Chocolate Museum originally opened in 2000 beside the Kalev factory on the Pärnu road to the south of Tallinn, near the tram terminus. An extensive (and cheap) Kalev shop still remains there. In 2003 the factory moved out of Tallinn and that part of the building was taken over by the police, although the amount of computer theft that accompanied this move caused them considerable embarrassment and the local population considerable amusement. Whilst the museum gives a thorough coverage of the different production techniques used in its 200-year history and visitors have the chance to smell eight different flavours, the real interest is in the political history revealed in the designs on the boxes issued during the Soviet period. In 1950, the tenth anniversary of Estonia 'joining' the USSR warranted a special box-top, even though three of those years had been spent under German occupation. Later in the 1950s, pre-war pictures of Narva were used, even though it was the Soviet army that destroyed the city in 1944. By the 1980s the authorities became aware of the

knowledge Estonians now had of the West, so Mickey Mouse and Finnish television characters were allowed to join traditional Russian role models.

The history of chewing-gum in the former USSR deserves a book to itself since different politburos all devoted endless sessions to this topic. Puritans wanted it banned but the realists wanted to prove that whatever the USA could do, the USSR could do better. Production was first authorised in 1968, banned again and then reintroduced for the Olympics. Only the Kalev factory ever received the necessary authorisation to produce it.

The factory is proud that following independence in 1991 it has been able to re-establish export markets, even as far away as the United States. Perhaps a few elderly consumers there remember the Shirley Temple portrait used on boxes produced in the 1930s. Not even famous German factories are likely to be able to match the 237 varieties of marzipan produced by Kalev now. Prices in this new museum are a little higher than in most local shops, but of course the choice available is greater. At the time of writing in early 2008, some of the museum had still not reopened on the new site, but now that the restaurant above it has closed, this situation should soon be remedied.

Kiek in de Kök (*Komandandi 2;* ☏ *644 6686; www.linnamuuseum.ee/kiekindekok;* ⏲ *10.30–18.00 Tue–Sun; admission 25EEK*)

From its initial construction in the 15th century until its completion in the late 17th century, the tower grew in height and width with walls and floors as thick as 4m, but ironically, after a Russian attack in 1577, it never saw military action again. The last time it was prepared for war was in the 1850s when the Russians feared a British invasion during the Crimean War. On the top floor, note the model of the 'plague doctor' with a waxed tunic and cape impregnated with herbs. He carries a cane with which to touch patients to avoid any risk of infection. The main exhibition on the top three floors covers Tallinn's military history. The lower floors are now used as an art gallery.

Maritime Museum (*Pikk 70;* ☏ *641 1408; www.tallinn.ee/meremuuseum;* ⏲ *10.00–18.00 Wed–Sun; admission 40EEK*)

Fat Margaret, the tower which holds this museum, was built between 1510 and 1529. Some walls are as much as 6m thick. In 1830 it became a prison but after being stormed in 1917 it was left as a ruin for the next 60 years. Polish restorers, famous throughout the former Soviet block, finally came to the rescue in 1978. Climb to the roof for very photogenic views of St Olav's and the town gates. The museum covers shipbuilding, cartography, port construction and fish breeding. There is a recent exhibit on the *Estonia* which sank off the Finnish coast on 28 September 1994 with the loss of 850 lives. A model of one of the boats has political interest. It was originally named after Viktor Kingissepp, leader of the underground Estonian Communist Party in the early 1920s, who was executed in 1922 after leading a failed attempt to overthrow the government. In 1990 it was renamed after Gustav Sule, who was Estonian javelin champion in the 1930s.

National Library (*Tõnismägi 2;* ☏ *630 7611; www.nlib.ee;* ⏲ *10.00–20.00 Mon–Fri, 12.00–19.00 Sat, closed Sat in Jul & Aug; admission 10EEK*)

Day tickets for the National Library may be bought in the entrance hall, a section of which is decorated with prints by one of Estonia's most famous contemporary artists, Eduard Wiiralt. Sadly these are not lit as well as they should be. To encourage regular use, the library has several music rooms, antiquarian and modern bookshops, a café and even piped music. On a bitter winter's day tourists may wish to await a change in the weather amongst the many English-language books and journals now available there. As one of Estonia's many preparations for entry into the EU, there are also large French, German and Scandinavian reading rooms. Normally, however, visitors should head straight for the eighth floor to view two contrasting Tallinns. To the north and east is the Tallinn of the travel posters – the spires, turrets and golden domes. In the other direction is a part of the town best seen at this distance, consisting of abandoned factories and fading tower blocks, with minimal intrusion of any colour. This area is still changing too slowly.

The predecessor to this library was opened in 1918 in the Parliament building on Toompea and had 2,000 books, a number that only increased to 6,000 during the 1930s. After World War II, the history of the library mirrored that of the country as a whole. Its bleakest period was until 1953 when most of the collection was of Russian books translated into Estonian. On Stalin's death the library was renamed after one of Estonia's most famous authors, Friedrich Reinhold Kreutzwald, a clear sign of a more liberal climate. By 1967 funds were specifically allocated for books in the Estonian language and in 1988, shortly before this new building was supposed to open, it was renamed the National Library and the formerly restricted sections were opened to all. The design seems to symbolise *glasnost* ('openness'): light streams in through many massive windows and large open shelves display a wide cross-section of the two million books stored there. It will remain a grandiose memorial to massive public sector investment. Yet it was almost not completed. The fading Soviet government was not eager to continue funding projects outside Russia and the new Estonian one was faced with bills it could not pay. On 28 June 1989, between four and five thousand volunteers joined the building works under the slogan 'Dig a grave for Stalinism'. The director, Ivi Eenmaa, later to become mayor of Tallinn, single-handedly fought Moscow and then each new Estonian government for adequate funds and was finally able to open the library on 22 February 1993, two days before National Day.

Natural History Museum (*Lai 29a;* ☏ *641 1738; www.loodusmuuseum.ee;* ⊕ *10.00–17.00 Wed–Sun; admission 30EEK*) The surprise here is that most of the exhibits are contemporary rather than historical. Whilst there is an impressive array of stuffed animals, of far greater interest is the collection of photographs of the Estonian countryside, all well lit and well labelled. The standard of English is particularly high here.

Occupation Museum (*Toompea 8;* ☏ *650 5281; www.okupatsioon.ee;* ⊕ *11.00–18.00 Tue–Sun; admission 20EEK*) This museum could only be opened thanks to funds provided by an Estonian-American, Olga Ritso, who fled abroad in 1944 after both her father and her uncle had been killed by the Soviets. When the museum was formally opened by her and Prime Minister Juhan Parts, they cut not a ribbon but barbed wire. The pathetically inadequate clothing of the prison camps is perhaps the most moving exhibit though the sight of small cases into which thousands of Estonians had to pack belongings for their Siberian exile must run a close second. The red star and a swastika are always shown side by side. To the Estonians, the Russians and the Germans are equally guilty. There are also display cases showing day-to-day life in Estonia under Soviet rule. It seems hard to believe that these items were all most Estonians knew until 1991. The cellars are now being used to display statues from Soviet times, which had all been pulled down when Estonian independence was restored in 1991. One earlier one is however missing. A statue of Stalin which had survived since 1956 could not be included; being 4m high there was no way it could be brought into the museum for display. The entrance to the museum is on Toompea, not on Pärnu.

Parliament (*Lossi plats 1a;* ☏ *631 6331; www.riigikogu.ee;* ⊕ *when parliament is in session; admission free*) The façade is a simple Classicist one, and all the stone and wooden materials are local. Earlier buildings on this site had usually served as a governor's residence although, in the late 19th century, the building became a prison. The earliest fort was built on this site in 1227 and the northern and western walls date from this time.

The most famous room within the building is the White Hall, with its balcony overlooking the square. The current décor, with white cornices and a yellow ceiling, dates from 1935. From 1922 there had been a more elaborate neo-Classicist design, including ceiling mirrors and elaborate panelling. The current parliamentary chamber was rebuilt in 1998 and members of the public can attend debates there, but no interpretation from Estonian is provided. There are 101 members of parliament, representing ten parties, and around 20% of its members are women. Visitors are forbidden to enter 'with cold steel, firearms and pungent-smelling substances'.

Pharmacy (*Raekoja plats 11;* ☎ *631 4860;* ☉ *10.00–18.00 daily; admission free*) Tour guides often like to point out that this business opened 70 years before Columbus discovered America. The coat of arms of the Burchart family, who ran the pharmacy for 400 years, can be seen over the entrance. Amongst the medicines they dispensed which are unlikely to find contemporary favour were fishes' eyes, lambswool and ground rubies, but patients were at least offered these potions with a glass of hot wine to help digestion. In 1725 Peter the Great summoned Burchart to St Petersburg, but he died before Burchart could reach him. In 2000 the pharmacy was extensively refurbished. Part of it is a museum and part a modern chemist's shop.

Photographic Museum (*Raekoja tn 4–6;* ☎ *644 8767; www.linnamuuseum.ee;* ☉ *10.30–18.00 Thu–Tue; admission 15EEK*) Estonia has always had a strong photographic tradition and this museum displays not only cameras produced in the country but photographs from the 19th and early 20th centuries. The earliest date from 1840. We tend to think of business cards with photos as fairly new but the museum displays one printed in 1859. April fools with cameras started a little later, in the 1890s, so canals in Pisa and leaning towers in Venice date from then. The Minox camera was produced commercially in Riga from 1938, but the first ones to be made came from Tallinn in 1936, with several prototypes being displayed here. It is fortunate that many pictures from the first independence period have survived. One British custom has been taken over by Estonian photographers: everybody says 'cheese' in English and it is also the name of the local photographic journal. The basement is a gallery for the display and sale of contemporary photographs.

Theatre and Music Museum (*Müürivahe 12; www.tmm.ee;* ☉ *10.00–17.30 Wed–Sun; admission 20EEK*) Despite its name, this museum in fact covers only music. A violin-maker's workshop has been reconstructed and the display features most instruments of the orchestra, all of which have at some time been made in Estonia. The production of violins and pianos has a long and distinguished history in Tallinn. Very few labels are in English but, fortunately, this does not matter too much given the self-explanatory nature of the exhibits. Estonians are often accused of taking themselves too seriously; from the cartoons on the stairs, it is clear that Estonian musicians, at least, do not. No famous 20th-century conductor is spared portrayal in irreverent clothes. One violinist, Hugo Schuts, is even drawn in a bathing costume.

Town Hall (*Raekoja plats 1; www.tallinn.ee/raekoda;* ☉ *15 May–15 Sep 11.00–18.00, closed in winter; admission 40EEK*) The exterior and the interior are equally impressive. It was the administrative and judicial centre of the town and the extensive range of woodwork and paintings in the council chamber mainly reflect judicial themes. Six centuries of Tallinn's history have been determined in this room and, with the restoration of independence, its role will now increase. For much of this time there were clearly ample funds in the public treasury, as is shown by the opulence of the candelabra, the money-chests and the size of the wine cellars. One of the carvings on the magistrates' bench, of David and Goliath, is often taken to symbolise the relationship between Tallinn Council and its nominal masters on Toompea in the Old Town. The council chamber has always been heated, unlike the neighbouring Citizens' Hall. Dancing, eating and drinking at winter receptions tend to be particularly vigorous to compensate for this. The original weathervane on the top of the spire, known as Old Thomas, was destroyed in the 1944 raid but the rest of the building was spared. German architects, artists and craftsmen were employed for the Town Hall and all documents were written only in German, even during the long periods of Swedish and Russian rule. Only the tapestries have a non-German origin, being Flemish. The originals are not in fact displayed any more, because of their fragile condition, but two exact copies woven over a six-month period in 2003 by the British company Hines of Oxford now hang in the Citizens' Hall. Both are over 8m long and show scenes from the legend of King Solomon.

The tower is open daily 1 June to 31 August (admission 40EEK). The view from the top offers excellent shots of the Old Town for photographers but the stairs are steep so this is only recommended for the fit and determined. A large exhibition opened in the basement in summer 2003 and it is worth braving the extremely narrow staircase down to it. Plans and photographs of the square are shown as it has been, as it might have been and as it may be, together with many fragments unearthed in recent excavations. Do not forget to use the toilets here as they have been skilfully placed within the foundations.

Another exhibition opened in summer 2004 in the attic behind the clock. Its main exhibit is a model of Tallinn as it was in 1825, but more important is the fact that this attic has been cleared. Restoration that started in 1952 finally came to an end 52 years later. It generated 273 tonnes of debris, much of which had been stored here. Some of the smaller, more valuable finds in wood, earthenware and textiles are now on display beside the model.

CHURCHES

Alexander Nevsky Cathedral (⊕ 08.00–19.00 daily) The cathedral was built in 1900 on a former garden which had housed a statue of Martin Luther. It was Alexander Nevsky who defeated the Teutonic Knights in 1242 so the building had a dual role in pretending to show Russian superiority over both the Baltic Germans and the local Estonians. It was hoped that it would help to stifle the burgeoning nationalistic movements in Estonia, too. Ironically, the Tsarist power that it represented was to last only a further 17 years. Entering the cathedral represents a symbolic departure from Estonia. No-one speaks Estonian and no Estonian-language books are sold. The icons, the mosaics and the 15-tonne bell were all imported from St Petersburg. Occasionally plans are discussed, as they were in the 1930s, for the removal of the cathedral as it is so architecturally and politically incompatible with everything else in Toompea, but it is unlikely that any government would risk the inevitable hostility that would arise amongst the Russian-speaking population of Tallinn.

Charles's Church (*www.eelk.ee/tallinna.kaarli*; ⊕ 10.00–17.00 daily) This massive and austere late 19th-century limestone building seats 1,500 people and is the centre of the Estonian Lutheran Church. At a time when Russian rule was becoming more oppressive, its size discreetly symbolised Estonian nationalism. The name comes from an original wooden church built in the late 17th century during the reign of the Swedish King Charles XI, but which was then burnt down by Russian troops as they took over Tallinn in 1710. Only the tower bells were saved, and they are still in use. It was 150 years before rebuilding started. Otto Pius Hippius from St Petersburg was the architect, who also designed the Alexander Church in Narva and Sangaste Manor in southern Estonia. Although the new church took 20 years to build, the large altar fresco was completed in ten days in 1879 by the well-known artist Johann Köler. There are many of his paintings in KUMU (see page 50) and another famous altarpiece of his is in the church in Cēsis, northern Latvia. On the other hand, the church interior still looks incomplete, which it is, given the lack of paintings or sculptures on the side walls. Every generation has come with different names of people who should be honoured with a panel there. The latest proposal, still unactioned in 2008, was from the sculptor Tauno Kangro who suggested representations of the four evangelists.

The church is now used for the funerals of famous Estonians. In 2006 there was one for Lennart Meri, the former president, and then in January 2008 for Estonia's most famous contemporary writer, Jaan Kross.

Dome Church (*www.eelk.ee/tallinna.toom;* ⊕ *09.00–17.00 daily*) Work started on the Dome Church soon after the Danish invasion in the early 13th century and the first church was consecrated by King Waldemar II in 1240. It was slowly enlarged over the next four centuries as funds became available but much of the interior was destroyed in the fire of 1684 which devastated the whole of the Old Town. The Swedish King Charles XI imposed a special tax for the rebuilding of Tallinn and within two years the church had been largely restored. The Baroque spire was added in 1778 so in all the church has an architectural history of over 600 years. The altarpiece, painted in 1866, is the work of the Baltic-German artist Eduard von Gebhardt. The organ, probably the most powerful in Estonia, was made in Frankfurt an der Oder in 1913 and is the last to have been imported from Germany before World War I.

The Dome Church was the religious centre for the main families of the Tallinn Baltic-German community; their coats of arms cover the church walls and their tombstones cover the floor, although a few are of Swedish origin. At the back of the church are two tombstones commemorating the butchers' and the shoemakers' guilds. The most impressive tomb, which is beside the altar, is that of the French mercenary Pontus de la Gardie who served in the Swedish army in many battles with the Russians. In the north aisle is a monument to Samuel Greig, a Scottish admiral who served in the Tsarist navy from 1763 until his death in 1788. The inscription expresses the sorrow of Catherine II at his death. Like many Scottish predecessors and successors, he had a distinguished career in this navy. He helped to destroy the Turkish fleet at the battle of Chesme in 1770 and to build up Kronstadt into a major naval base. Next to this monument is one to Adam von Krusenstern, the Baltic German who led the first Russian expedition to sail around the world, in 1803. Note the two globes, both of which omit New Zealand.

Holy Ghost Church (*www.eelk.ee/tallinna.puhavaimu;* ⊕ *10.00–16.00 daily; admission 15EEK*) That this church does not face due east suggests that there was already a complex street layout by 1300 when building began. It was the first church to hold services in Estonian and the first extracts from the catechism in the Estonian language were printed for use here in 1535. The 1684 fire destroyed much of the interior and the original spire but the next spire was for many years the oldest in Tallinn, dating from 1688. It was badly damaged in a fire in 2002 but was quickly replaced.

The pulpit is the original one dating from this time. Some of the panels along the balcony, which were restored between 1998 and 2004 thanks to a donation by the British Hedley Trust, depict Old and New Testament themes, others the life of St Elizabeth of Thuringen, the patron saint of beggars and orphans. No specific artist has yet been identified for them and it is thought that several painters were probably involved. A booklet published to commemorate Queen Elizabeth II's visit in 2006 is on sale at the entrance; it illustrates each of the 50 panels and links them to the relevant biblical quotations. No full Bible was published in Estonian until 1739 which is probably why no text was given with the pictures; stories would be told and taught on the basis of these pictures alone.

Of the same age inside the church is the large wooden clock on the north wall, carved by Christian Ackermann from Königsberg. Spared from the fire was the folding altar carved in 1483 by the Lübeck artist Bernt Notke, whose *Dance Macabre* at St Nicholas' is noted below. Only the organ is modern, dating from 1929; it is one of the few in Tallinn's churches built by an Estonian and not imported from Germany. To the left of the altar, the White Ensign and the plaque below it commemorate the British sailors who gave their lives between 1918 and 1920 fighting the Bolsheviks. A replica of this plaque was unveiled at Portsmouth Cathedral by Prince Andrew in December 2005.

St Michael's Swedish Church (✆ 644 1938; *www.eelk.ee/tallinna.rootsi;* ☺ 10.00–18.00 daily)

St Michael's does not have a tower as it was first built in the early 16th century as an almshouse and hospital. Only in the 18th century was it consecrated. The Swedish community all fled in 1944 which gave the Soviet authorities a pretext for converting the building into a sports centre, mainly used for boxing and wrestling. Generous support from the Swedish Lutheran community enabled it to be reconsecrated in 1993.

St Nicholas' Church (Niguliste) (*www.ekm.ee;* ☺ 10.00–18.00 Wed–Sun; admission 35EEK)

In common with many other Tallinn churches, St Nicholas' was first built in the 13th century and then expanded over the next 400 years. The original spire dated from 1696 and, being outside the town walls, the church was spared from the 1684 fire. It was, however, badly damaged during the Soviet air raid on Tallinn of 9 March 1944, having had its last service the day before. The spire was firmly restored only in 1984. An earlier replacement collapsed in 1982 and the Soviet authorities flooded the streets with police to stop photographs being taken of this humiliation. (They did not completely succeed.) The carvings, chandeliers and pictures, many dating from the 16th century, had fortunately been removed before the bombing. They are all now on display again and are particularly valuable given that so much similar work in Tallinn was either destroyed in the 1684 fire or suffered from neglect in more recent times. The silver collection suffered a more precarious fate, with much being looted during World War II, but with the addition of some donations, the current exhibition is a very representative collection of Estonian work in this field from the 15th century onwards.

The interior of the church was slowly restored during the Soviet period from 1953. A new exhibition was opened in 2005 which describes this work and captions are in English. Before entering the main church, note the altar screen displayed just after the exhibition. It was made in the late 17th century for a church patron to have in his private chapel. The artist probably studied in Antwerp as there are similarities with work from there at the same period. St Nicholas' has kept its role as a museum and concert hall so has not been reconsecrated. The life of St Nicholas is portrayed in the altarpiece, over 6m wide and painted in Lübeck by Hermen Rode between 1478 and 1482. The *Dance Macabre* by Bernt Notke, another Lübeck artist, was painted a decade or so earlier and shows how nobody escapes death, whatever their powers when alive. Note the one very modern addition – a stained-glass window by the contemporary artist, Rait Prääts, whose glass can also be seen at the National Library.

St Olav's Church (*www.oleviste.ee; church* ☺ 10.00–14.00 daily. Tower ☺ Apr–Oct 10.00–18.00; admission 30EEK)

When first built in 1267, St Olav's 140m-high steeple made it one of the tallest buildings in the world. This steeple caught fire in 1820, having been struck by lightning, and its replacement reaches 'only' 120m. It is still, however, a major feature of the Tallinn skyline and since the summer of 2002 has been open to the public. Much of the interior of the church was destroyed in the 1820 fire, as it had been in an earlier one in 1625. The rebuilding, completed in 1840, provides a contrast to most other churches in Tallinn for its plain interior. Tsar Nicholas I donated a large bell in 1850 and his generosity is noted in an inscription written, with no trace of irony, in German. The organ dates from this time but the chandeliers are earlier and have been donated from other buildings.

EXCURSIONS FROM TALLINN

Where Tallinn is keen to show either how medieval or how modern it is, trips outside will reveal an Estonia either still trapped in the Soviet period or much more content to return to nature. Ideally, add an extra day to a Tallinn visit to allow time for some of these very different experiences.

The island Aegna, described on page 60, can be visited only in the summer, but Rocca al Mare, Kadriorg and Pirita are equally attractive under snow. The former Soviet naval base at Paldiski is macabre all year round.

ROCCA AL MARE OPEN AIR MUSEUM (*Vabaõhumuuseumi tee 12; www.evm.ee;* ⊕ *May–Oct 10.00–18.00 daily; admission 80EEK; Nov–Apr 10.00–17.00 daily, but buildings closed; admission 35EEK*) This museum deserves a half-day to itself, ideally in balmy summer weather or after a heavy fall of snow. Take the 21 or 21b bus from the railway station and also take a sweater as protection against the wind on the many non-balmy days. A winter excursion on a sunny day is worthwhile to get some impression of what most Estonians used to endure month in, month out, every winter. Visitors at midsummer on 23 June can enjoy the all-night celebrations held here. The name in Italian means 'cliff beside the sea' and was given by the original owner of the estate when it was bought in 1863.

The museum was founded in 1957 and first opened to the public in 1964. The descriptive panels throughout are in English. It now consists of around 70 buildings and when complete should have a hundred. The aim is to show all aspects of Estonian rural architecture, with houses of both rich and poor, and ash trees planted a short distance from dwelling-houses, to attract lightning away from where it could cause serious damage.

Most of the buildings date from the 19th century but one of the chapels was built in 1699. Note the lack of chimneys and the almost total use of wood. Metal nails were only common from the late 19th century. Glass windows started a little earlier in private dwellings, except on Saaremaa Island where examples from the 18th century are found.

The whole of Estonia is represented – windmills are, of course, from the island of Saaremaa but in contrast there are fishermen's cottages from Lake Peipsi on the Russian border. Even the poorest families managed to afford a sauna which to Estonians is as crucial to living as a cooking pot. The interiors have all been appropriately furnished with kitchen utensils, weaving looms and chests of drawers. The only regular import over the centuries was sharpening stones from Gotland, treasured in Soviet times when this source of supply, like so much else, was cut off from Estonia. Recent additions are houses built in the last century: tiled roofs and verandas are a clear sign of the 1920s.

Amongst the more unusual buildings is a tabernacle from the Herrnhut movement, a strict offshoot of the Lutheran Church. Future plans include the restoration of a Swedish cottage – about 8,000 Swedes lived in Estonia before World War II. There is already a Swedish church here, brought from the formerly Swedish-speaking village of Sutlepa. The exterior is 17th century and the interior 19th century. Inside there is a permanent exhibition of drawings from all the other Swedish churches in Estonia. In bad weather, finish your tour at the Kolu Tavern. Kolu is a village between Tallinn and Tartu, and the tavern here still has two separate bars, one originally for the gentry and one for the peasants. It serves filling, hot food such as pea soup and mashed potatoes with bacon, but do not expect any concessions to the 21st century; it remains firmly in the 19th, although a more conventional restaurant will in due course be built for more fastidious diners.

PALDISKI Since independence, an uneasy quiet has descended on this former Soviet naval base situated 40km west of Tallinn. Unusually for Estonia, a regular train service operates from here to Tallinn, with eight services a day, the journey lasting a little over one hour. However, individual tourists would be well advised to take a car and guide for a half-day excursion as several *en-route* stops can be made. Estonians are more than happy to see the back of the Russian sailors but have yet to find a new role for this harbour. A daily car-ferry service to Kappelskär in Sweden started in summer 2000 which provided much-needed employment and the switching of cargo services from Tallinn soon followed, which is helping to bring a sense of hope back into the town.

Peter the Great inspected the site personally in 1715 before authorising the building of a harbour which was originally planned as the largest in the Russian Empire and for defending the country against the Swedes. It was better protected than Tallinn and ice-free for much longer. This first point was brought home to Peter very forcefully in 1717 when two boats sank in a storm whilst moored in Tallinn harbour. From then until his death in 1725 he became obsessed with this project; the workforce was around 2,500 men supported by around 300 horses. A dam over 300m long was built. The harbour would never in fact be completed although innumerable attempts were made in the 18th century. Much of the labour was supplied by prisoners; so many died of ill-treatment that Paldiski became known as the 'second Siberia'. The final straw came in 1757 when the workers' pay was reduced from two kopeks to one kopek a day and over 200 died of starvation in the months of March and April 1758 alone. The dam soon collapsed and what remained of the harbour was destroyed in a storm in 1818. Now only some of the fort remains.

In September 1939 the USSR imposed a mutual assistance pact on Estonia under which Paldiski was seized as a naval base. In May 1940, shortly before the full occupation of the country, all Estonians were expelled from the town, a practice that would be repeated all too often from 1945 in many other towns and villages along the coast. Paldiski is now the largest Soviet blot on the Estonian landscape; only the dustbins, brightly coloured and modelled on penguins with their beaks open, provide relief from piles of rubble, barbed wire and ransacked blocks of flats. Improvements are very slow to come here.

The first building to be seen on the way into the town is the former prison, but it can hardly be distinguished from much of what follows. When the Russian forces finally left in September 1995, having been granted dispensation to stay after independence, a population of around 4,000 was left with only 10% of them speaking Estonian; the remainder were Russian-speaking civilians. A curtain behind a window, an irregular light or even the sight of an occasional human being, shows that life has not totally died out here but the slogan in the town's English-language brochure, *A Town with a Future*, seemed at the time to be a joke in particularly bad taste. However, in 2000 a new hotel was opened, the **White Ship** (Valge Laev; *Rae 32; 674 2095; www.weekends.ee*). 'Welcome aboard' mats are behind each entrance, a porthole is on the door of every room and maritime memorabilia cover all the walls. It would be possible to commute into Tallinn from here, and when Tallinn hotels are full, late bookers will have no choice.

Returning to Tallinn, two very contrasting stops can be made. Shortly after independence, a monument was erected in the forest at Klooga to commemorate the massacre of 2,000 Jews there on 19 September 1944, just before the German withdrawal. The small Estonian-Jewish community had already been killed by then; these victims were largely from other eastern European countries. The former village of Tabasalu is now the first of Tallinn's suburbs, most of whose inhabitants have much more money than sense or taste. The money stands out, but it is well protected by high walls and Rottweilers. A few poultry farmers remain on the outskirts of the village but it cannot be long before they are bought out.

AROUND TALLINN BAY Allow a full day to visit the island of Aegna, the yacht harbour at Pirita and the park at Kadriorg. Several buses serve Pirita from the town centre and the journey takes about ten minutes. The relevant bus stop is one beyond that for the hotel.

Aegna Boats to and from Aegna operate out of Pirita harbour from a small jetty beside the café, not from the larger jetty beside the hotel and yacht club. Boats leave for the island around 09.00, at 12.00 and in the early evening. Check timings at the tourist office or via a hotel reception before setting off and do not forget an umbrella in case the weather suddenly changes. Tickets cost 80EEK for the round trip.

Aegna is so quiet that even Estonians are prepared to turn off their mobile phones, and neither the Germans nor the Russians were able to leave their mark. Conifer trees abound, as do minute beaches, and the few open areas have been made available for camping. Much of the island can be seen in the three hours allowed by the morning boat schedule though a full day of peace and quiet is what most local visitors seek. Paths are clearly marked and a detailed map is displayed at the harbour.

Pirita, Viimsi and Kadriorg Palace Pirita was built as the Olympic village for the yachting and sailing events of the 1980 Olympics. For a precious three weeks Tallinn briefly returned to being an international city. An array of consumer goods, Western newspapers and direct international telephone dialling suddenly came to Tallinn and left equally suddenly when the games were over. Only the buildings have remained and they are so obviously of Soviet design that the harbour hardly seems to belong to modern Estonia. On returning to Pirita, visitors of Estonian origin may wish to take the 34 bus for 2km inland to **Metsakalmistu,** the Forest Cemetery. Most famous Estonians are buried in this pine forest, including the writer A H Tammsaare, the poetess Lydia Koidula, the chess player Paul Keres and more recently Lennart Meri, the president from 1992 to 2001. Since independence, the body of Konstantin Päts, president until the Soviet occupation, has been returned and he is now buried here together with his immediate family. He died in a Soviet psychiatric hospital in 1956.

The body of General Laidoner, however, still lies in 2001 in a communal grave in Vladimir Prison where he died in March 1953, despite strong pressure from the Estonian government for it to be formally identified and returned. His wife was released from prison in 1954 after his death but was only allowed to return to Estonia after her 70th birthday. She had been a pianist and took some music with her to Siberia, practising on walls and tables to keep her fingers fit. Johan Laidoner was commander-in-chief for much of the pre-war period and his former summer house on the Viimsi Peninsula, about 5km from Pirita, is now the **Laidoner Museum** (*Mõisa tee 1;* ✆ *621 7410; www.laidoner.ee;* ✆ *11.00–18.00 Wed–Sun; admission 25EEK*). The most moving exhibit is a French–Russian dictionary given to him during his imprisonment in 1944; he used several pages of it to compose his political testament. It ends, in English, with the words 'Estonia, with all thy faults, I love thee still. Johan Laidoner'. Considering how jealous Stalin was of his reputation, it is remarkable how many items associated with him and with this house have survived. During Soviet times the KGB had taken it over in order to break completely the links with Estonian independence. Estonians are pleased to point out that Laidoner did in the end outlive Stalin, even if only by a few days in March 1953.

The museum is constantly being expanded, with several additions dating only from early 2008 so that they could be ready for the 90th-anniversary celebrations of Estonia's declaration of independence. With the help of the Imperial War Museum in London there is now a British room, covering the navy's role in helping to establish Estonian independence in 1918–20. (There are two memorials to this, one in the Holy Ghost Church in Tallinn, see page 46, and one in Portsmouth Cathedral. Both were unveiled by Prince Andrew.) It is expected that many more exhibits will soon come from Britain. This would be appropriate in view of Laidoner's often quoted remark, 'Without the arrival of the British fleet in Tallinn in December 1918, Estonia and the other Baltic countries would have found themselves in the hands of the Bolsheviks.' Laidoner was given the KCMG award by the British government for his success and bravery in driving the Bolsheviks out of Estonia and his medal is exhibited here, together with many others that he was given. Fortunately they could all be removed from the house before his arrest by the Soviet authorities in July 1940. One of them has a swastika on it; it was presented to him in 1936 in his capacity as head of the Estonian Olympic organising committee. A few hours before he and his wife were deported, they were visited by the American Consul John Wiley and his wife Irena; she describes the meeting in her book *Around the Globe in 20 Years.* Mrs Laidoner told her: 'This house and garden are already our prison. Any minute we will be deported. However I have had such a full and happy life; I am so thankful for the past that I have to accept any future that is my lot.'

Laidoner kept in close touch with Britain, coming for instance to the funeral of George V and the coronation of George VI. In 1926, he fixed the Iraqi–Turkish border in the Mosul under the auspices of the League of Nations. Iraq was at that time a British mandate and although Laidoner accepted many of the Turkish claims, he never lost the respect of the British for undertaking the task in a totally neutral manner.

Other rooms in the museum cover Estonia's participation in both sides during the Cold War, since those who stayed in 1944 and their heirs were conscripted into the Soviet army, whereas those who left for Australia, Canada and the United States often signed up there. An equal number of medals from both sides are displayed here. The army is shown as it was between 1920 and 1940 and then from 1991 when it could again serve an independent Estonia. Linked specifically with the 90th-anniversary celebrations mentioned above is a room devoted to the Independence War that took place between 1918 and 1920, ending when the USSR was forced to recognise Estonia under the Tartu Treaty.

The series of Cold War cartoons on display are by Edmund Valtman (1914–2005), who left Estonia in 1944 when he was 30 years old. In 1949 he settled in the United States where he was for many years cartoonist for the *Hartford Times* in Connecticut, but his fame was nationwide. Many American cartoonists of course also covered these themes, but those of Valtman have a particular poignancy, given that he experienced Soviet rule in 1940–41 and lost his home country to it three years later.

The Poles have likewise opened a room in honour of Marshal Pilsudski who played a similar role to Laidoner in ensuring his country's independence from Russia.

The walk back to the centre of Tallinn is two or three miles. Cross the main road from the harbour to the site of **St Birgitta's Convent**. Although the convent is included in most sightseeing tours, walking here can be a precarious experience as the surroundings of the ruin are so badly maintained. The convent lasted intact for only 170 years, from 1407 until the siege of 1577 when it was largely destroyed by troops of Ivan IV in the Livonian Wars. The outline of the main body of the church is clear; the western gable together with the vestry, cloister and refectories can be identified. Minor restoration and excavation work started in 1960 and was brought to a close only in 2001. The new convent on the north side was completed in 2000 and part of the building is used as a hotel (see page 30).

Staying on the land side of the main road, after half a mile is the **Soviet War Memorial**. It could hardly be anything else, given its size and the military themes of the bronze statues. The Estonians carry out minimal maintenance here, and some elderly Russians congregate on the days of the old Soviet holidays such as May Day and 7 November. The text is particularly offensive to Estonians as the monument – completed only in 1975 – is dedicated to 'Fighters for Soviet Power'. A Soviet guidebook excuses this long delay by claiming 'at last Estonian artists had enough skill and adequate economic means to complete such an ensemble'. The obelisk dates from 1960 and commemorates the hurried departure from Tallinn of the Bolshevik fleet in 1918 when German forces occupied the town.

An even more dominant landmark from the Soviet era is the **TV Tower** (*www.teletorn.ee*), about a mile inland from Pirita on Kloostrimetsa. Going there by bus, expect to be surrounded by elderly Russians with flowers since the Russian cemetery and crematorium are nearby. The few tourists who now visit the tower also seem to be Russian. This is a pity as it does provide an extensive view of the town and port not available elsewhere. The entrance is as flamboyant as one would expect: the windows are of stained glass, with portraits of valiant industrial workers; covered aisles surround basins of fountains which in turn are surrounded by lawns. However, nothing has been maintained properly (except for the lifts inside) so moss and weeds become ever more prominent. Nobody has bothered to put Estonian signs in the lift or change the menu in the revolving-tower restaurant from smoked fish and chicken Kiev. The tower was closed in early 2008 and at the time of writing it was not clear when it will reopen and what changes will be made.

A few hundred yards further along this road is **Maarjamäe Palace** (*www.eam.ee;* ⊕ *11.00–18.00 Wed–Sun; admission 25EEK*), which has probably had one of the most turbulent ownership histories of any site in Tallinn. Maarjamäe means 'Mary's Hill' but the German name, Streitberg ('Hill of Strife'), was for many centuries more appropriate. The only consolation is that the blood shed here spared Tallinn itself from many battles. The final one took place in the early 18th century as Russia seized the Baltics from the Swedes during the Northern Wars. To set the seal on his conquest, Peter the Great established Kadriorg Park as a summer residence, so many of the St Petersburg nobility felt obliged to followed suit. Those who could not immediately afford the luxury of a suitable building subsidised it with a factory, so lime kilns and sugar refineries adjoined the manor houses. The sugar was sold in Riga and St Petersburg and the plant was run on British coal. A fire in 1868 destroyed much of the factory and it was never rebuilt. In the 1870s, when the estate was bought by Count Anatoli Orlov-Davydov from St Petersburg, the rebuilding he ordered came to deserve the title 'palace'. Terraces, a gateway decorated with copper eagles and the Gothic tower gave it an almost regal air. The Dutch Consulate bought it in the 1920s when the Orlov-Davydovs emigrated to France and continued its use as a summer residence. It was to lose its appeal in this role when in 1926 the road to Pirita was built across the grounds, cutting off the manor house from direct and private access to the sea. However, the road brought with it commercial potential which was eventually realised in a hotel and restaurant called the Riviera Palace. In 1937 the Estonian air force took it over as a training school and they are sadly responsible for the dreary façade. From 1940 until 1975, when Maarjamäe became a museum, the Soviet military used but did not abuse it. During the 1980s, Polish restorers finally brought the building back to its turn-of-the-century glory, turning their attention to the chandeliers, fireplaces, parquet floors and ceilings. It is ironic that one of the last Soviet legacies to Tallinn should be the perfect surroundings for a museum which chronicles Estonian independence.

Although few labels are in English and the one available guidebook is now badly out of date, this is without doubt the best museum in Tallinn. New rooms are constantly being added, exhibits are generously displayed, the layout is sensibly planned and there is the complete absence of benign neglect that seems to permeate so many other Tallinn museums. It covers Estonian history from the mid 19th century until the present day. It amply contrasts the lifestyles of rich and poor and shows the diversity of industrial products and international contacts that the country enjoyed during the first period of independence between the two world wars. It even had a thriving tourist board whose brochures displayed here sold Estonia as 'The Cheapest and Most Interesting Country in Europe'.

One room opened in the summer of 1998 is devoted to the life of Konstantin Päts, Estonia's president between the two world wars. It features portraits both of his close political associates and of his main opponents, all the work of Ants Laikmaa, the most famous Estonian artist in the late 1930s. That their dates of death are nearly all 1940 or 1941 shows the brutality of the Soviet occupation. A room dedicated to the Forest Brothers, the guerrilla organisation that fought the Soviet occupation in the late 1940s, covers this theme movingly but not bombastically. The significance of Estonians living in St Petersburg is often forgotten but the museum covers a demonstration held there by 40,000 of them in March 1917; it played a crucial role in the build-up to independence.

In 2006 a gallery was added explaining the campaigns of the mid 1980s against the commercial exploitation of phosphate. By mid 1987 the Estonian press was openly expressing opposition to this, on obvious environmental grounds. There were public demonstrations on 1 May at Tartu University, knowledge of which would reach the world through Radio Free Europe, thanks to a broadcast by Toomas Hendrik Ilves who was working there at the time. He is of course now President of Estonia. The next stage was to carry posters in English, with the slogan 'Phosphate, No Thanks', so that photographs could be taken abroad. The success of these demonstrations would in the next year lead to open defiance of Moscow on many more issues.

What to do with the conference room at the museum is clearly a source of embarrassment. Its wall mural 'Peoples' Friendship' was completed in 1987 by one of the most famous artists of the Soviet era, Evald Okas, so it just preceded *perestroika* ('reform') and then independence. Visitors who wander into the room will find the mural totally covered by curtains, but there will be no objection from the staff to drawing them back to see the mural.

At the back of the palace are some Soviet statues too big (and too boring) to drag to the Occupation Museum in the town centre. It is perhaps a pity that they cannot be lifted so that visitors fortunate enough not to have known that era can at least have an idea of its constant physical domination.

Continuing towards the town centre is one of the few late 1950s constructions of which Estonians can be fiercely proud – the **Song Festival Amphitheatre.** It replaced a smaller arena that had been built in 1928, and has the massive grandeur to be expected from that time, but is not wasteful of materials and does not dominate the surrounding area. The parabola provides cover for 5,000 singers and up to 20,000 more have often taken part. The most famous recent festival took place in 1989, when the previously banned national anthem, 'My Native Land', was sung by an audience of around 300,000 people, 20% of the entire population of the country. In winter, the steep slope at the back of the parabola provides Tallinn's only ski- and toboggan-run. Note the plaques at the top of the slope which commemorate each of the Song Festivals held every five years since 1869. The 2004 Festival was commemorated by a statue at the top of the auditorium to Gustav Ernesaks (1908–93), who did more than anyone else to keep the Estonian element alive in the Song Festivals held during Soviet times. Whatever boundaries the Soviet authorities set, he would push them further. In 1960 he was notionally banned, but just conducted some songs anyway.

The **tower** (⊕ *times vary so check www. lauluvaljak.ee; admission usually free*), although also built in 1960, was not opened to the public until 2000, and gives photographers good shots of the Old Town and the port combined. It has an exhibition covering many of the festivals held here so to some extent duplicates what is now shown at the Tartu Song Festival Museum (see page 86). In 1910, with the majority of representatives on Tallinn City Council now ethnic Estonians, attempts to 'celebrate' the 200th anniversary of Peter the Great conquering the Baltic countries were quashed. The most unpleasant year was in 1950, with frequent changes in the programme, the addition of Russian songs and the arrest of several senior participants. The dullest was undoubtedly 1985, reflecting the stagnation of the USSR at that time. Few can have foreseen how different the 1989 one would be.

Returning to the shoreline, at the junction of the roads to Pirita and to Narva, note the **Russalka (Mermaid) Memorial**, which commemorates the sinking of a battleship with this name in 1893. It depicts an angel looking out to sea. In 2005 replica gas lamps were installed around the monument. Do not be surprised to see Russian-speaking wedding couples laying flowers here on a Saturday. The sculptor, Amandus Adamson, is one of Estonia's most famous, and perhaps because of this monument he was granted official respect in the Soviet period and a memorial bronze bust of him stands in Kadriorg Park.

Inland, the vista is now dominated by KUMU which well deserves all four capital letters, given the size of the building. It looks down from the hill at the eastern end of Kadriorg Park. This is the **Eesti Kunstimuuseum** (see page 50), the Estonian Art Museum, which opened in February 2006. Everything is 'big' about it; even the lifts will hold 122 people. A small selection of the art shown here came from the Knighthood Building where it had been on temporary display since 1992 but much will be seen for the first time, including a collection dedicated to the Soviet period. The atmosphere is totally different from that in the cramped buildings of the Old Town; there should finally be some outreach to the many people who feel intimidated from entering other museums in Estonia. Cafés, a children's centre and an auditorium will all help in this endeavour, as will regular temporary exhibitions by contemporary artists.

The park is the next stage of the walk, with one corner is just behind the Russalka Memorial. The park, and **Kadriorg Palace** (*www.ekm.ee;* ⊕ *10.00–17.00 Tue–Sun; admission 55EEK*) which forms its centrepiece, was built immediately following Peter the Great's first visit to Tallinn in 1718 with his Italian architect Niccolo Michetti. The triumphal decoration of the ceiling in the Great Hall celebrates his defeat of the Swedes in the Northern War and is loosely based on Rembrandt's *Diana and Actaeon*. The hunter being torn apart by his dogs can be seen to symbolise the Swedish King Charles XII being let down by his army. Sadly the building was not completed by 1725 when Peter the Great died and no subsequent Tsar ever showed the commitment that he did. In fact Catherine I never came to Tallinn again after his death. Perhaps the description often given of the palace as a 'mini-Versailles' is fair, as what was carried out does show some French and Italian influence. A fire destroyed much of the interior in 1750 and it was subsequently never again used by the Russian royal family. In 1930 Kadriorg Palace became the official residence of the Estonian president but now houses the Foreign Art Museum, the collection being mainly Flemish and Baltic German.

None of the furniture was originally here. The Russian royal family took furniture with them as they travelled between their palaces and also 'borrowed' extensively from the local nobility. Much of this collection is what the Baltic Germans had to leave in their manor houses when Hitler 'called them home' in October 1939. Despite the cool personal and state relations with the Russians, a lot of furniture was still ordered from St Petersburg during the first independence period (1920–40). However, the room devoted to Soviet art from the 1920s is likely to be of most interest to visitors. The designs on the porcelain show the most immediate break with the past as all the themes are 100% political. It would take another ten years before painting was similarly controlled. Some of this porcelain was prepared for the first Soviet Art Exhibition held in St Petersburg in 1923, by which time the St Petersburg Imperial Porcelain Factory had become the State Porcelain Factory. It came to be known as 'agitation porcelain'. Many rooms have been restored to their original 1930s layout, when President Päts lived here. The Danzig-Baroque library is the most elaborate room and was completed only in 1939, a year before the Soviet takeover. The salon has a wooden drinks cabinet with panels portraying scenes from *Kalevipoeg*, the 19th-century Estonian national epic. The palace reopened in 2000 and then work started on re-landscaping the surrounding gardens. Much of this exterior work was completed in 2005.

Kadriorg Park is a year-round joy for local people and tourists alike. In winter the combination of sun and snow amidst the trees and sculptures offers a peaceful contrast to the hectic commercial life of Tallinn just a few hundred metres away. Spring brings out the blossom of the cherry and ash trees, summer the swans, the squirrels and the fountains and autumn the blends of gold and red as the trees shed their leaves. A cottage in the park used by Peter the Great during the construction of the palace has housed the small **Peter I House Museum** (*www.linnamuuseum.ee/peetrimaja*; ⊕ *Sep–Apr 10.00–17.00 Wed–Sun; admission 15EEK*) since the early 19th century. Although none of the furniture is original, the layout is as Peter would have known it. It is easy to forget, in the context of St Petersburg, how modestly Peter himself lived, despite the number of palaces that he built. It was Emperor Alexander I who saw the house in 1804 and then had it opened as a museum in 1806. The basement exhibition covers Peter's 11 visits to Tallinn and his most famous comment on the town: 'If Tallinn had been mine in 1702, I would have established my capital here and not on the Neva.'

A hundred metres back towards town, on Weizenbergi opposite the main entrance to Kadriorg Palace, is the **Mikkeli Museum** (*www.ekm.ee*; ⊕ *10.00–17.00 Tue–Sun; admission 25EEK*). This building was the palace kitchen but in 1997 was opened to house the collection of Estonia's most fortunate private art collector, Johannes Mikkel. Born in 1907, he was able to start buying during the first independence period when departing Baltic Germans and Russian nobles abandoned enormous quantities of paintings, porcelain and prints. He was allowed to trade during the Soviet period and enhanced his collection with items bought in the Caucasus and central Asia. There is no predominant theme, but the quality and taste of every item stands out, be it a piece of Kangxi or Meissen porcelain, a Dürer woodcut, a Rembrandt etching or any one of his 20 Flemish paintings. Folders in English are available in every room with descriptions of all major exhibits and modern lighting ensures that each item is viewed as well as possible. Mikkeli died in January 2006 so perhaps the museum will soon be enhanced with further pieces from his private collection.

On leaving the museum and turning left, a slight detour can first be made to the far side of the lake behind the Mikkeli building. The splendidly isolated house at Roheline 3 is the **Eduard Vilde House Museum** (*www.linnamuuseum.ee/vilde*; ⊕ *11.00–18.00 Wed–Sun; admission 10EEK*) where Estonia's most prolific writer, both at home and in exile all over Europe, spent the final six years of his life between 1927 and 1933. Typically for most established Estonians at that time, the furnishings are simple and there are many empty spaces. Return to Weizenbergi to continue back into town. At the corner of Poska on the left, house number 20a has some Baroque imitation of the palace although it was built only in 1939. Weizenbergi lasts a further 300m or so before joining Narva mnt. Every house is probably now owned, or was before World War II, by a famous Estonian. Small, modest cars may be parked in the street, but considerable wealth is discreetly hidden behind the lace curtains. The turn-of-the-century, four-storey houses display hints of Art Nouveau, whilst the wooden ones are characteristic of middle-class suburbs throughout Estonia. On a neighbouring street, Koidula, one of the largest wooden houses belonged to Estonia's most famous author, A H Tammsaare (1878–1940), who died in March 1940. In his honour it is now the **Tammsaare Museum** (*Koidula 12a; www.linnamuuseum.ee/tammsaare*; ⊕ *10.00–17.00 Wed–Mon; admission 20EEK*) and after years of neglect through the 1990s was finally, and very successfully, redesigned in 2006. He spent the last eight years of his life here and, given that he never earned much money from his books, the house shows how a middle-class Estonian, rather than a rich one, would have lived at the time. Tammsaare is depicted on the 25EEK note and it is perhaps significant that it is his farm that is pictured on the reverse, not this townhouse. His most famous work, the five-volume *Truth and Justice*, is set in the 19th-century Estonian countryside. It is sadly not currently available in English although a translation was in hand in 2008. This is a sensible place to look for tasteful souvenirs at prices often a quarter of what is now charged in the Old Town. Some downstairs rooms are now used for modern art exhibitions, which provide a much-needed splash of colour in contrast to the gloom upstairs.

At the junction of Weizenbergi and Narva mnt there is a taxi rank and bus stop. A large Methodist church has recently been built on the far side; otherwise Narva mnt from here back to the Viru Gate is totally devoted to Mammon. There is no point in describing any of the buildings since they are mainly being pulled down to give way to glass skyscrapers. This area will soon be Tallinn's Wall Street or Square Mile, with only Tallinn University, which opened in 2005 in the building of the former Pedagogical Institute, offering a contrast.

NAISSAAR If Tallinn is cutting edge, dynamic and every other cliché associated with the capitals of the EU accession countries, the island of Naissaar is the complete opposite. Most of its website is only in Estonian and its boat schedules remain a state secret until the start of services in the early summer. The electricity supply, usually limited to two hours in the morning and a further two in the evening, impose a firm schedule for getting up and going to bed. However it is worth making sacrifices, at least for a day trip, to see the legacies of not only those who lived there but also those who succeeded in occupying the island for several years or those who, like the British, just stayed a few months. It is advisable to pre-book a guide, if only to be sure of avoiding areas where there could still be unexploded mines, the worst of several Soviet legacies.

History Naissaar has had to reinvent itself several times during the 250 years since it began to be regularly inhabited. The name means 'women's island' but there is no clear origin for this name, only fanciful and largely unprintable legends. Ironically, it has in fact been male dominated for most of its occupation, with women having far less importance than on the mainland. The early Swedish-speaking settlers who came in the mid 18th century were fishermen who traded their catches and spruce in Tallinn for the agricultural goods that the sandy windswept terrain on the island did not allow them to grow. Many had in fact lived in Finland and they came to escape the Tsarist seizure of Finland from the Swedes, even though Estonia was of course also in the Russian Empire by then. However neither the Russians nor any Baltic-German landlords attempted to exert any control over the island and it was also spared the plague. These factors encouraged a community to settle there and a population of 200–300 did so then; the number of inhabitants was to stay at this figure until the start of World War II. A Swedish primary school was established in 1874 and an Estonian one in 1925.

The island was always cut off for several weeks at a time in winter, when the ice was too thick for boats to secure a passage but too thin for horses, and later cars, to cross it. The few affluent islanders were invariably pilots who guided foreign trading ships into Tallinn harbour. Captains unwilling to pay the fees could find their boats shipwrecked around Naissaar and the cargoes that were salvaged could provide more income than the pilot's fee would have done. Piracy was certainly more lucrative than fishing, the main occupation on the island.

The British navy occupied the island for a few months in 1854 as part of its attempt to prevent supplies reaching Russia during the Crimean War. This was only partially successful, as Königsberg being a German port was able to profit greatly from this situation. The naval personnel, being on the island for several months, taught the local people how to play cricket, but the game did not catch on.

If you were asked where in the world has the densest railway network, Naissaar is hardly going to spring to mind as the answer, but it might well be correct in view of the activity in this field shown between 1910 and 1913. In that short time, the island was criss-crossed with narrow-gauge railways to move timber and peat. The Soviet authorities used most of these and recently several have been restored; some lines are pulled by a steam engine and on others, visitors propel themselves on a draisine, a type of bicycle fixed to the tracks. As more of the network is restored, this will become the best way to see the island, as it is just too large for walking to be realistic.

Each Russian regime was marked with deportations. The first took place in 1730, when the Russians built a fort on the island to defend the island from possible Swedish attacks. This made sense at the time, in the wake of the Northern War which the Russians had recently won after 20 years of battles. In fact, the Swedes would never attempt to invade again. The next deportation came towards the end of the Tsarist regime, in 1914, as part of the defence against the Germans. This excuse was to be used twice again, in 1940 and then in 1944. However from 1944 onwards, it became clear that Estonians would never be allowed to return to Naissaar, and with the danger of unexploded mines they could not even do so in 1991 in the aftermath of independence being restored. It was not until 1994 that Naissaar became Estonian again. In the meantime it had been home to 3,000 Soviet soldiers who laid 10,000 mines to protect the USSR from a NATO invasion that never came. Ice floes often moved these mines and set them off.

Naissar today The port where boats arrive has the railway going in several different directions, the island administrative centre and a café. Visitors are likely to stay in the village of **Männiku,** about 2km from the port. The houses look reasonably modern but very un-Soviet with the use of light woods and extensive glass. This is because they were all prefabricated in Finland and were part of the reparations demanded by the Soviet Union at the end of World War II. The larger Soviet buildings, including the factory that produced the mines, have all been abandoned now, but a schoolroom has been converted into an amusing museum. Much has been left as the Russians abandoned it, with posters proclaiming *perestroika*, unread books by Lenin, enormous radiograms and even some ballot boxes. Two waxworks of Soviet marines have been added, one asleep and one on the toilet. In 2006 some photographs were added of the German occupation here between 1942 and 1944.

In the 1990s the village of **Lõunaküla** at the southern end of the island was completely abandoned, although it had been the administration centre in the 1930s. Not a single house remains from that time, as Soviet soldiers destroyed the last one – for firewood – in 1978. The shell of the church, built in 1934 by the Swedish Lutherans, has remained, since the building was used firstly for storing hay and then as a sports hall. Proper restoration was under way in 2008.

The memorial in the cemetery to the British soldiers who gave their lives in this area during the Crimean War was first erected in 1927 but was of course destroyed in Soviet times. Many of those buried here in fact died at sea. The cemetery was built near the shore and away from the church in deference to the French Catholics, who could not be buried on Lutheran ground.

Lõunaküla suddenly sprang to life in 2006 when Estonia's most famous conductor, Tõnu Kaljuste, started to sponsor a series of concerts here during July and August. These were a great success and so was the 2007 session, so clearly they will now become an annual event. The website www.nargenopera.ee gives full details of the programmes as they are ready. A package is offered including the connecting ferry each way and a ride on the narrow-gauge railway.

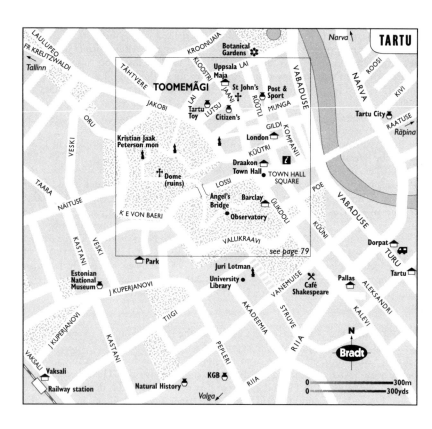

see page 79

3

Tartu ESTONIA

Telephone code 7

Unlike Tallinn or Pärnu, Tartu is not a town of instant charm. Arriving by any of the dreary approach roads does not suggest the imminence of a famous university town or of one where Estonia gained its statehood. Yet intellectually and architecturally it is the centre of Estonia. Its university cultivates an Oxbridge/Ivy League tradition but has combined it with the radicalism of Berkeley or the London School of Economics. Estonia's most famous scientists studied and taught here and its most famous patriots, whether in opposition to the Tsar, the pre-war President Konstantin Päts or the Soviet regime, likewise spent their formative years in Tartu. The 200km distance from Tallinn suited both sides. Political activists could be more daring and the government could feign liberalism, safe in the knowledge that its detractors would not be a threat to the capital. With independence and democracy now safe in Estonia, Tartu will have to take up new causes. It introduced parking meters to the country in 1992 but a more lasting testimony to the first period of renewed independence must be in the offing.

It is only since about 2000 that Tartu started to take tourism seriously. Museums were moved from gloomy suburban locations to properly adapted buildings in the town centre. In contrast, the National Museum will leave Tartu altogether in 2010 for a new purpose-built site at Raadi Manor House, 3km away, but this is understandable given the breadth of the collection. Hotels also started to open in the town and to promote themselves vigorously. Pedestrian precincts appeared and so did signs in English. More recently, in 2003, the squalid bus station and the equally rundown Hotel Tartu beside it were modernised. A new railway station will open in summer 2009.

Tartu can therefore now offer a more savoury arrival and departure. First-class rail travel from Tallinn started in 2005. Air services to Stockholm from the local airport are due to start in autumn 2008 and a convention centre opened in summer 2008, built as part of the Dorpat Hotel, which itself only opened in 2007. The celebration in October 2007 of the 375th anniversary of the founding of the university, which was attended by Queen Silvia of Sweden, was a great incentive for renovation in the Old Town. To be a successful second city, Tartu will clearly need to be a business centre as well as an academic one and must compete with Tallinn as a centre for Estonian and international companies. This is hardly unfair, as Tallinn opened its own fully fledged university in 2006. In tourism it will need to operate seven days a week during the summer. For many shops to close early on Saturday and all day on Sunday, and then for the museums to close all day Monday and Tuesday, sends out a disturbing message of indifference to Tartu's increasing number of visitors.

Tartu now has a diverse programme of festivals that take place all year round except in July and August (when the hotels fill up anyway). If it matters whether you turn up for the cross-country ski marathon, the break-dancing finals or student rag week, check their dates on www.kultuuriaken.tartu.ee before contacting your tour operator. This site also gives the programme at the Vanemuine Theatre, which spills out onto the Town Hall Square (weather permitting) during the summer. One thing unites all

Tartu

3

these programmes: even if they were not designed as such, they are a perfect deterrent to stag parties, which stay firmly in Tallinn as a result.

HISTORY

The university was founded in 1632 but the town dates back much further than this. Its location at the crossroads of the north–south link from St Petersburg to Riga and the east–west one from Tallinn to Pskov has given it written records since 1030. Until recently the Emajõgi River also had a serious role in trade. The town's future outside the university will depend largely on relations with Latvia and Russia. If trade continues to decrease with these two countries and EU membership stimulates more contact with the West, Tartu's location to the east will make it less competitive than towns along the coast.

Although Tallinn was always spared fighting within the city, Tartu sadly was not, and during the 16th century it was the constant battleground between the Russians, the Baltic Germans, the Poles and the Swedes. Three more recent calamities hit the town – its destruction by Peter the Great's armies in 1708, a fire in 1775, and then World War II, when both the Russian retreat in 1941 and their return in 1944 caused considerable damage.

As the earlier town was largely built of wood, what the visitor now sees dates only from the late 18th century onwards. The major buildings, such as the Town Hall and the Stone Bridge, were built specifically on the instructions of Catherine the Great. The bridge was destroyed by Soviet bombing in 1944, but it is hoped that in due course funds can be raised to rebuild it.

In the small streets around the Town Hall Square, the 20th century is not obtrusive. The 21st is only allowed to develop at a distance, largely over the river. It is easy to visualise a thriving market town, which was its role for many centuries. A full day is needed to cover the town centre and the university, and a further half-day to visit a selection of the museums. The parks beside the river offer relaxing walks and concerts in the summer.

TARTU UNIVERSITY

The importance of the university can be seen in the determination of each new conqueror to make their mark on it immediately. Conversely, bands of lecturers sometimes moved the university to temporary safety when the town of Tartu was threatened.

When it first opened in 1632, it was the second university in the Swedish Empire, Uppsala being the first. It is thought that there was only one ethnically Estonian student in the university at that time. Twenty years later, because of the Russo–Swedish War, it moved to Tallinn for ten years and when the Russians attacked again in 1700, it moved to Pärnu. Most of the faculties were housed in Pärnu fortress, just above the gunpowder cellar. Before Pärnu fell to the Russian armies, the archives for these turbulent 70 years were taken to Stockholm and many of the academic staff, being Swedish, returned with them. The issues these archives cover have a very modern ring to them. The possibility of war with Russia is mentioned, as is the constant need to remind students to be loyal to the Swedish king. There are also concerns that scientific discoveries should not threaten theological teaching. Far more worrying for many of the staff, however, were the lack of pay, difficult landladies, leaking roofs and disputes with the military over room allocations.

Peter the Great had originally planned to reopen the university either in Pärnu or in Tartu but the founding of the Academy of Science in St Petersburg in 1724 put paid to this. Both Pärnu and Tartu submitted plans to refound the university on various occasions during the 18th century, but these were unsuccessful; it would only reopen

Ants Oras

The Red Soldiers marching in the streets to the tune of one of the four or five songs they seemed to know were a very neglected, listless lot. A large proportion of them were illiterate. Soon after the occupation, delousing stations were set up for them, an establishment with which we were made familiar for the first time. The Red Commanders, as the officers were still called, dressed more smartly but they were obviously unaccustomed to living in a 'bourgeois' environment, even after its Sovietisation. Having been assigned some of the best living quarters in our town, they found themselves out of their depth in dealing with such gadgets as bath taps, lavatory chains or electric lights. In one flat, a Soviet officer used his bathroom as a pigsty in which he reared a large sow. In spite of protests from inmates of the floor below, he refused to see the inappropriateness of his conduct. The Red wives adapted themselves more easily to their new surroundings, however. Being well provided with money, they stormed our shops, always buying the most expensive articles, although their taste was more gaudy than ours. Though they generally avoided red, of which they must have had a surfeit at home, their dresses looked exotic in their many-coloured richness. Their make-up was very marked and most of our perfumes were too subtle for them. An unexpected feature was their religiousness. The Orthodox churches were crowded with women fresh from Soviet Russia, whereas the men stayed away.

Ants Oras was a lecturer at Tartu University who fled to Sweden in 1944

nearly a hundred years later in 1802, as a reaction to the French Revolution. The Tsarist authorities panicked at the ideas that students sent to study in western Europe were bringing back with them and from 1798 such studies were banned. In the best Tartu tradition, however, the result was that such ideas simply reached Estonian students more quickly than they otherwise would have done as the teaching staff were unwilling to acquiesce in the reverent approach that the Russians and the Baltic Germans had wanted.

The university now had a comparatively stable century ahead of it. Funding from the state was adequate and provided for all the main buildings that were needed on its reopening. Even a botanical garden was included. It was lucky that the Napoleonic Wars started only after the completion of Tartu University otherwise funds would never have been found for it. The town was to grow with the university, the population increasing from 3,500 in 1802 to 8,500 in 1826. The teaching staff were drawn from all over Europe, with the majority having a German background as this was to be the language of instruction. If one member of the faculty deserves special mention, it must be Karl Morgenstern who ran the library for 37 years from 1802 until 1839. By joining the book exchange association of the major German universities, he ensured that Tartu became a mainstream European university. He also collected toys and until 2003 his former house was the Toy Museum now on Lutsu (see page 71). His successors, German and Russian, expanded this work so that by 1917 there were 180 exchange partners including several in Japan and the United States. Morgenstern was also accomplished at what would now be called public relations and persuaded many wealthy patrons to donate books and antiquities to the library and to the classical museum that he founded.

The period of peace between the Napoleonic Wars and the Crimean War again ensured immense financial support for the university, equalling that given to Moscow. The building of the railway links to Tallinn and St Petersburg in the 1870s

Tina Tamman

I was a university student in Soviet Estonia for five years, which was then the standard length of studies. I was offered no choice of subjects, but I was happy at the time and remember this period fondly. In independent Estonia it is no longer fashionable or even acceptable to praise the Soviet period but I certainly benefited from the system.

The university had an excellent library which opened at 08.00 and closed at 22.00, seven days a week. When I came to write a thesis in my final year on the American writer William Saroyan, there was nothing available in Estonia and all the books and reviews had to be ordered from a library in Moscow. This service was quick, efficient and free of charge.

I benefited, too, from sharing a room at the university hostel, at first with ten other girls but after a few months I managed to transfer to a smaller room which I shared with only three others. Inevitably this brought the four of us very close, and we liked this. We learnt to be considerate. We had lots of parties with loud singing when there was something to celebrate and quiet periods when one of us had to study. From those parties, I still remember the Armenian brandy and the enormous piles of aubergine sandwiches: Bulgarian tinned aubergine paté was the cheapest sandwich filler in those days.

Bedclothes in the hostel were changed once a fortnight. This did not, however, get rid of the bedbugs, which were widely believed to have been brought in by some Russians. I remember once waking up in the morning to see a dead bedbug on my pillow; I had apparently squashed it in my sleep. There was warm water in the showers, which worked most evenings, and there were lockable shower cubicles. In the communal washrooms, the water was icy cold, particularly in winter, and everybody washed in full view of each other. The toilets were often blocked and the communal kitchens filthy. Everyone took turns to clean the kitchens – some better than others! Quite a lot of cooking and eating was done in groups. The most popular dish was sautéed potatoes, which required only potatoes and cooking fat. Meat was beyond the reach of most students.

We did not pay for the hostel and most students received a grant of 35 roubles a month, which just about paid for the food; help was needed from parents for anything beyond this basic level. In contemporary Estonia the grant system has been largely abolished, and student loans introduced.

Although I was reading English, this involved studying Marxism–Leninism and a host

and then to Riga in 1887 brought considerable expansion to the university, the number of students increasing from 600 in 1865 to 1,700 in 1889. The year 1889 also marked the start of greater control from St Petersburg and, with the use of Russian as the language of instruction, the Russian name for Tartu, Jurjev, replaced the German name of Dorpat at the university. The Estonian name Tartu was used only after independence in 1919, when Estonian also became the language of instruction. The Ministry of Education took direct control of academic appointments, so much of the autonomy previously enjoyed by the university was withdrawn and many of the German-speaking staff left. One embittered historian wrote that 'the bright flame of German science went out because it was smothered by barbaric Slavic hands'. The two protagonists for the soul of Tartu University during the 19th century, the Baltic Germans and the Russians, clearly saw the battleground as simply between themselves. The occasional Estonians who managed to enter were expected to integrate and put their peasant background behind them.

of related subjects. Even physical education was compulsory. I was excused from Russian as I had done very well in it at secondary school. The strangest subject was 'safety in factory work', although none of us was expected to work in a factory. About a hundred of us would dutifully copy down what the lecturer told us; I remember him particularly drawing a lathe on the blackboard. I had never seen one in real life and have not done so since.

English studies were arranged in small groups of around 12 students. It was very formal, with an awesome English grammar book written by a Russian and published in Russia. All our language teachers were Estonians who had never been to England. Our literature teacher was an English communist who emigrated to the USSR, and then married an Estonian poetess. Literature for him ended before World War II and we were never taught anything about post-war writing.

There was no shortage of activities in Tartu. The town had an excellent theatre, as it still does, combining drama, opera and ballet. There were coffee-shops of the German and Austrian kind where we could linger. We could not afford butter on bread or sugar in coffee but we would talk long into the night, sometimes able to stretch to a glass of Hungarian wine.

By contrast in the autumn we would be sent to a collective farm to work. This was hardly fun as it rained often, the potato fields became soggy and the potatoes heavy. The work was at the expense of our university studies and may well account for the fact that I never really mastered the basics of Latin.

We were guaranteed a job at the end of our university course regardless of our exam results. Since I had been reading English, I was offered a job as an English teacher, as were the other 25 of us. Take it or leave it, but sign on the dotted line for the minimum of two years – that was the principle. It is a day I still remember well. It was well organised and, with hindsight, even reassuring, but so demoralising at the time. I refused to sign at first but was told that I had no option, although I was not interested in a teaching career.

It has been reassuring in the years since that many of the students with whom I read English and shared accommodation have had very satisfactory careers as teachers after all. They did not seem enthusiastic at the time but later grew to like their teaching jobs.

Independence has changed a lot in people's attitudes; present-day pupils are willing to learn and their parents are even willing to pay for extra lessons. It is a far cry from the days when nobody in Estonia wanted to learn English because there was nothing one could do with one's language skills.

The German army seized Tartu on 24 February 1918, and on 7 March decreed that tuition in German instead of Russian would be instituted with effect from 20 March. After protest, this deadline was extended by a further two weeks. The university reopened in full at the end of April 1918 with a complement of 60 staff, 30 of whom had been recruited from German universities. This would however be the shortest 'interregnum' in the history of the university. Following the armistice of November 1918, the German military had to withdraw. In the meantime, many academics left with the retreating Bolshevik forces to found a university in exile at Voronezh. Most of the artefacts and books they took with them have remained there, even though the Soviet government agreed their return under the Tartu Treaty of 1920.

The new Estonian government wisely took its time before reopening the university in December 1919, with Prime Minister Jaan Tönisson carrying out the formal ceremony. To begin with, about half the lectures were given in Russian and half in Estonian, but Estonian quickly became the predominant language. The new country immediately had at its service an internationally respected university. Former staff members happily came back from exile to work there and were soon joined by many foreign experts; by 1930, the teaching staff had reached 400. For 20 years, the university was pleasantly normal, teaching local students in their national language.

From 1940 to 1945 the situation became vicious. The Russians dismissed and deported many of the leading faculty members; the Germans treated the replacements they appointed even worse in 1941, when several were sent to concentration camps. In 1944, most senior members not sympathetic to the Russians had just enough time to flee to Sweden. Only 22% of the staff en poste in early 1940 were still there in the autumn of 1944. On all three occasions, the occupiers had detailed plans for running the university, cynically realising that it had to be neutered if they were to control Estonia effectively. The Soviet regime did make large funds available immediately on their re-occupation to rebuild the university, following the destruction much of the town had suffered during the war. Constant expansion was planned throughout the Soviet era with student numbers doubling from 3,500 in 1950 to 7,000 in 1978. A computer centre was established in 1976 and a history of the university printed in 1982 talked proudly of 'modern methods of management' being used in the running of the university. The 350th anniversary in 1982 was fervently and formally celebrated with a massive budget provided for further new buildings.

Anyone now prominent in Estonian public life was educated at Tartu under the Soviet system but the academic rigour of the courses and the subtlety of the teaching in most cases made the political background irrelevant. What was missing was contact outside the USSR; Tartu was a closed city so initially Westerners could not travel there at all and later only for the day from Tallinn.

Undergraduates had no chance to be taught languages by native speakers or to keep up to date with Western research. One of the first tasks of the new administration since 1989 has been to 'internationalise' the university again without allowing its Estonian identity to suffer. Lecturers from many EU countries, rather than from just one, ensure this necessary diversity. Wandering amongst the students and perusing the noticeboards, it is hard to realise that the current transformation took less than eight years. Reading the English-language brochures or browsing the website (*www.ut.ee*) shows immediately what has been achieved. However the years from 2009 onwards will be more difficult for the university. The drop in the Estonian birth rate from 1990 may lead to lower standards, if the same number of students is recruited as before. The new university in Tallinn may well appeal to those wanting to combine their studies with life in a large town. More vocational courses will have to be offered, and there are also plans to widen the range of courses taught in English so that the university can draw students from outside Estonia.

PRACTICALITIES

The **Tavid** currency exchange office at Rüütli 2 is open every day and offers competitive rates for over 50 currencies, and their list shows how extensively Estonians now travel on their holidays. Their website, www.tavid.ee, gives the exchange rates offered in their Tallinn offices, but usually the Tartu ones are the same or very similar.

The **telephone** code for Tartu is 7, which should be used for all calls from overseas, as well as those from a mobile or from outside the city.

Tartu is very child-friendly with many hotels having family rooms. The Toy Museum has a playroom and the Sports Museum several activities.

TRANSPORT

GETTING THERE AND AWAY

By bus Tartu is well served by buses to all major towns in Estonia. They run every half-hour to Tallinn and most are non-stop, taking about two and a half hours. Buses operate several times a day to Rakvere, Narva, Võru, Valga, Viljandi and Pärnu. An increasing number of these can be booked online on www.busireisid.ee. Fares to Tallinn can vary quite considerably according to the company operating the bus, but there is usually only one operator, so only one fare, on other routes. Expect to pay 130–150EEK for Tallinn. Eurolines have daily morning and evening buses to and from Valmiera and Riga, which stop at Valga. They also operate a daily service to St Petersburg via Narva.

By train The large wooden railway station appropriate to Estonia's second city was allowed to decay to such an extent in the 1990s that it had to be closed. In 2008 this wooden building was being renovated into a restaurant, and a new station was being constructed next to it, which should open in 2009. Whatever mess currently greets a traveller here, compensation lies in the first-class carriages that run to Tallinn three times a day. This is undoubtedly the most comfortable way to travel between the two cities, and the most dependable. The journey takes a little over two hours. There is a dedicated first-class coach where tea and coffee are served free of charge, and further refreshments can be purchased. The fare is only 140EEK, as opposed to 90EEK in the rest of the train. Discussions began with the Latvian authorities in 2006 about restarting a service to Riga through Valga and, with the abolition of border controls in December 2007, this seemed likely to go live in 2008.

By air Scheduled air services to Stockholm were due to start in autumn 2008, with perhaps others being added in 2009. For further details, see www.hot.ee/tartuairport.

By ferry, boat and barge Sightseeing boat trips operate along the Emajõgi River in the summer, as do ferry services to Piirissaar Island in Lake Peipsi. Sometimes there are services to Värska as well. Full details of all boat and ferry services are on www.transcom.ee. Negotiations started with the Russians in 2001 to resume what had been a very popular trip in Soviet times – a boat from Tartu to Pskov – but even now, the Russians have still not provided the visa exemption which is needed for such trips to be viable. The Estonians have no plans to attempt future negotiations unless there is clear evidence of a Russian volte-face.

In 2006 the first rebuilt Peipsi barge took to the river again from a landing stage on the east side of the river at Ujula 96. In the 19th century, hundreds of these barges linked the rivers and lakes of Estonia and inland Russia and were easily identifiable with their large square sails. None survived World War II, but a sufficient number of plans and drawings were left to enable modern craftsmen to start building them again. When not in use, the barges can be visited at their landing stage. The website www.historicships.ee gives a full history of these boats and details of services being planned with those now being built.

LOCAL TRANSPORT There is an extensive **bus** network within Tartu and to the suburbs. Locally produced city maps show the routes, but these maps are also displayed, together with timetables, at most bus stops. Visitors staying several days might want to buy a copy of the timetable – Tartu Linnaliinibusside Sõidugraafik. A day ticket available from kiosks costs 40EEK. Individual tickets bought there cost 13EEK and if bought on the bus cost 16EEK.

There is a **taxi** rank beside the bus station and another on the river at the end of Town Hall Square. Most journeys are likely to cost 60–100EEK.

3

⌂ **Barclay** (49 rooms) Ulikooli 8; ✆ 7 447100;
e barclay@barclay.ee; www.barclay.ee. When it opened
in 1996, it was undoubtedly the best hotel in Tartu, &
the only one in the town centre, but complacency set in
& 10 years later it gives the feeling that the façade, the
interior & the staff could all do with a facelift. The
wooden panelling is bland & there are no pictures in
the restaurant. However, prices have now dropped
dramatically, so its regular business visitors are likely to
stay loyal & will appreciate the very quiet yet central
location. Its restaurant became specifically Estonian in
2007, perhaps in answer to the very Russian Rasputin
(see page 79) just a few doors away. The building was
previously the Soviet military headquarters, under the
command of Dzhokhar Dudayev, who would later
become president of the breakaway republic of
Chechnya. As he was very sympathetic towards the
Baltic independence movements, a plaque at the
entrance commemorates him. This was placed here
after he was assassinated by the Russians in 1996.
$$$

⌂ **Draakon** (41 rooms) Raekoja Plats 2; ✆ 7
442045; e tonyas@solo.delfi.ee; www.draakon.ee. With
BBC TV, & a location beside the Town Hall, this hotel
soon became popular with British visitors when it
opened in summer 2000. It was also famous for making
a serious effort to cater for those with disabilities,
when other hotels did not, with no narrow staircases &
all facilities being wheelchair accessible. However, since
2006 service standards appear to have fallen greatly, so
it is to be hoped that these can soon be restored to
their former levels. $$$

⌂ **London** (60 rooms) Rüütli 9; ✆ 7 305555; e
london@londonhotel.ee; www.londonhotel.ee. This very
conventional, in the best sense of the word, business
hotel in the town centre opened in 2002. Rooms are
large & the reception staff consistently helpful. It
provides an excellent location in winter, with everything
else on the doorstep, but in the summer, life on the
streets might last a bit too long for comfort. AC arrived
in the top floor rooms in 2007, which is an essential
adjunct in hot weather. The hotel should not be judged
by the appalling standard of English in its brochures or
on its website. Its Kokoko café adopts the pleasant
American custom of charging for only one cup of coffee
with no charge for refills. A computer, free of charge to
guests, is conveniently located in the generous lobby
area. $$$

⌂ **Dorpat** (200 rooms) Soola 8; ✆ 7 337180;
e info@dorpat.ee; www.dorpat.ee. The opening of
this enormous hotel in 2007, followed by a

conference building in 2008, shows Tartu's confidence
in a future as a year-round business centre. Its 3-star
rating, plus its location directly beside the bus station,
will certainly ensure a stream of tourists through the
summer. Many rooms have views & the whole 3rd
floor is dedicated to those allergic to carpets, with
rooms & corridors furnished entirely in wood. The
spa centre visitors will now take for granted in a
hotel of this size, but probably not the salt chamber
there which can cater for eight people at once. For
those unwilling to travel by bus, parking space for 400
cars will be provided in the conference centre. Prices
are so reasonable that visitors are unlikely to
complain about the poor soundproofing & curtains
not quite thick enough to keep out the summer light.
The buffet lunch for 75EEK will amaze visitors from
Tallinn used to paying more than this just for a starter
or a sweet. $$

⌂ **Kantri** (27 rooms) Riia 195; ✆ 7 383044;
e info@kantri.ee; www.kantri.ee. Located 5km south
of the town centre, this hotel cultivates a manor-
house feel with its small number of rooms & ample
surroundings, although it is in fact a completely new
building. It was the first hotel in Tartu to take groups
when foreigners started to arrive in the early 1990s &
its attractive prices still entice them. However a
coach or a car is essential for anyone staying here as
there is minimal public transport in the vicinity. $$

⌂ **Pallas** (61 rooms) Riia 4; ✆ 7 301200;
e pallas@pallas.ee; www.pallas.ee. Pallas is the name
of a famous art college that was located on this site
before the war, but which was destroyed in 1944. The
hotel is a completely new building, above a
department store but worth the ascent to the 2nd
floor. The lobby & several rooms are all decorated
with paintings from its former pupils. Eduard Ole,
Eduard Wirralt & Konrad Mägi are the painters
mainly represented here & originals of their work
can be seen in the Art Museum (see page 81). The
suites have painted walls & ceilings. All rooms have
AC but vary greatly in size. Those looking towards
the town are probably the nicest, but traffic noise
can be heard in them. It is a short walk to the old
town, but close to the bus station & a number of
specialist shops. $$

⌂ **Park** (19 rooms) Vallikraavi 23; ✆ 7 427000; f 7
434382; e info@parkhotell.ee; www.parkhotell.ee.
Situated in University Park, this 2/3-star hotel attracts
regular visitors with its quiet location & a real fire in the
b/fast room. It had the misfortune to open in 1940 but in
March 1964 welcomed a guest whose visit to Tartu will

never be forgotten by those old enough to remember it. Finnish President Kekkonen was the first Westerner to see Tartu after the war & he spoke Estonian throughout his stay, to the consternation of his hosts – most of whom spoke very little, or none. (His skiing was equally proficient & therefore alarming to his local minders.) He formulated a speech that did not directly offend the Russians, but with its many references to Estonia & its minimal ones to the USSR, made clear where his sympathies lay. Many Estonian exiles felt he had sold out to the USSR, but an equal number of others, & certainly Estonians who had stayed in the country, were pleased to see any possible links with the outside world, however controlled they would be from Moscow. Less welcome guests at the hotel 2 years later were Jean-Paul Sartre & Simone de Beauvoir, rewarded for their loyalty to the USSR by a trip to Estonia & to Lithuania, an unheard-of privilege for Westerners at the time. She found the hotel 'très elegant', & the rooms 'modernes et gaies', & was relieved at the absence of a minder at the end of the corridor, highly unusual in the USSR. The best suite in the new hotel, renovated in 2000, is named after President Kekkonen & at only 1,800EEK is luxury at a bargain price. Regular visitors like the quiet location & the lack of any evening entertainment. It is a hilly walk of 15mins to the town centre but after a snowfall or during a long summer evening, this can be very congenial. In Soviet times of course it was a way of ensuring no casual contact took place between any visitors to the university & local students. $$

🏠 **Raadimoisa** (40 rooms) Mõisavärava 1; ↘ 7 338050; f 7 338051; e info@raadihotell.ee; www.raadihotell.ee. In a sense, this hotel opened 3 years too early, as its location will only be convenient when the National Museum opens over the road in the former Raadi manor house in 2010. It is just on the edge of the city, about 2.5km from the centre. However its rooms are all spacious, several have parquet floors for those allergic to carpets, & access by coach is easy, which certainly doesn't apply to any of the hotels in the Old Town. $$

🏠 **Tartu** (62 rooms) Soola 1; ↘ 7 314300; e info@tartuhotell.ee; www.tartuhotell.ee. Many hotels in Estonia still have a Soviet exterior, but this one still had a Soviet interior in 2000. Restoration of this archetypal Soviet hotel began in 2001 & was fortunately completed in 2003. It then became, by one room, the largest hotel in Tartu, having one more room than the Pallas, but in 2007 was dwarfed by the Dorpat, which has 200. It is basic, but does not pretend to be anything else, & is within 10mins' walk of the town centre. There are several family rooms & a number of hostel rooms with bunk beds for backpackers. The location beside the bus station is convenient on arrival & departure. $$

🏠 **Uppsala Maja Guesthouse** (5 rooms) Jaani 7; ↘ 7 361535; e uppsala@uppsalamaja.ee; www.uppsalamaja.ee. This is a little corner of Sweden, installed in central Tartu by its Swedish twin city (of Uppsala) in 1996, although the house dates from the 18th century & may in fact be the oldest existing house in Tartu. It has had a series of owners, including a butcher whose hooks are still on display. The bedrooms share facilities, & there's a kitchen & library, stocked with books on Uppsala & Swedish newspapers. It can be recommended for long-stay visitors. Quiet is assured here, as it is located just outside the club/restaurant area of the town. $$

🏠 **Aleksandri** (38 rooms) Aleksandri 42; ↘ 7 366659; e aleksandri@aleksandri.ee; www.aleksandri.ee. This guesthouse about 15mins' walk from the town centre opened in 2002. Bathrooms, toilets & a kitchen are shared between 2 rooms; otherwise it could be classed as a hotel. Rooms are large & the road is quiet, even if some of the guests are not. Unusually for Estonia, b/fast is not included in the room price, but is available next door in the rather incongruous surroundings of the Õlle Tare beer hall. $

🏠 **Vaksali 4 Hostel** (27 rooms) Vaksali 4; ↘ 7 441610; e info@hostel4.ee; www.hostel4.ee. Built in 2007, this currently puts its neighbour, the former station, to shame but hopefully the station will in due course catch up. Rooms here are small, facilities are shared & no b/fast is served, with guests making their own in the kitchen, but given the prices charged, this is no cause for complaint. As several buses serve the station, the hostel too is well connected to different parts of the town. $

WHERE TO EAT

In the 1990s people ate out in Tartu because they did not want to cook at home. From 2000, they went out to eat food they could not cook at home or at least could not obtain in the shops. In other words, eating out here finally became a pleasure. This it has remained, and more so as the number of restaurants increases each year and the price gap with Tallinn widens at a similar pace, always of course in favour of Tartu.

The most unexpected place to find cheap drinks is at the café in the foyer of the National Museum (see page 85) where in 2007 a wide range of beers and liqueurs were available at EEK8–12, although they have to be drunk between 11.00 and 18.00 Wednesday to Sunday, when the museum is open. Otherwise expect cafés to be open 10.00–18.00 and bars until midnight.

✕ **Bagua** Pikk 40; ✆ 7 402509. It is not necessary to cross the river to find Chinese food, but when the Old Town is packed either with tourists or with students, it may make sense to take the 15min walk to get here. Prices are of course lower than in the town centre & with portions about double, this is the place to make savings but to eat well at the same time. The staff are willing to turn off the music when asked, which is a frequent request. 100EEK

▭ **Café Shakespeare** Vanemuise 6; ✆ 7 440140; www.shakespeare.ee. Not surprisingly, this is situated in the Vanemuise Theatre. Following the Western pattern, theatres are now eager to encourage visitors to come at times when there are no performances, just as much as when there are. The exterior is drab, but the surroundings have recently been enhanced by the landscaping of the area between the theatre & Ülikooli. The statue immediately outside the restaurant is of Karl Menning, the first director of the theatre on this site. It commemorates the centenary of its opening which took place in 1906. The interior however offers varying poster exhibitions & an equally varied menu. Quite a lot of ad hoc entertainment is provided by the actors who double as waiters here – Vanemuise was, after all, the god of song in Estonian mythology. Being in 'theatreland', the restaurant/café is open until midnight during the week & 02.00 on Fri & Sat, but is just as popular at lunchtime. Tell the staff if you are in a rush, otherwise they will assume you want a leisurely meal, in line with most students & artists. 200EEK

▭ **Café Wilde** Vallikraavi 4; ✆ 7 309765; www.wilde.ee. You do not have to be under 30 to be admitted here, but it probably helps! There's an excellent range of cakes & open sandwiches, unusually fresh coffee, gentle service & academic décor as well as loud music. Note the griffin logo around the walls, this mythological winged lion being the protector of publishers. The terrace seems to be the refuge of every chain-smoker in Tartu, so avoid this if it bothers you, or escape to the English-language section of the bookshop beside the café when you're done eating & drinking. The café is named after Peter Ernst Wilde (1732–85), a doctor, veterinary surgeon & publisher who printed the first medical textbooks in Estonian here & won the rare privilege of being allowed to publish uncensored. There's a restaurant upstairs, & literary pundits can test their

wits by trying to identify all the Irish & Estonian writers portrayed on the walls. Groups can book, at no extra cost, a side-room to the restaurant which is music-free. At the front of the building, a bronze sculpture pictures an imagined meeting between Oscar Wilde & a contemporary Estonian author Eduard Vilde (1865–1933), a similar enfant terrible. This was unveiled in 1999 to commemorate the centenary of Oscar Wilde's death in 1900. In 2004, the Tartu city government presented a copy of this statue to Galway, in Ireland. 220EEK.

✕ **Crepp** Rüütli 16; ✆ 7 422133; www.crepp.ee. France finally came to Tartu in 2005. All the pictures on the wall are of France & even French newspapers are available. It almost seems a surprise that the French spelling 'crêpe' is not used in the name. The menu is in fact more extensive than the name suggests, but always with a French bias, so expect a baguette rather than black bread. 150EEK.

✕ **Gruusiasaatkond** (Georgian Embassy) Rüütli 8; ✆ 7 441386; www.gruusiasaatkond.ee. Like the Contravento in Tallinn, this restaurant has built up a regular clientele who it is hoped will safeguard it from change. The Georgian menu is sufficiently extensive to warrant several visits, particularly by vegetarians, & the décor sufficiently bohemian to ensure that prices stay low & that Tartu's small financial community stays away. They will also not like the dark mahogany tables, or shashlik cooked on an open fire. Help Georgians by drinking their wine here. The import ban imposed by Russia in 2006 seems to have enhanced the choice now available in Estonia. 180EEK.

✕ **Italia Kook** Gildi 1; ✆ 7 423747. Follow the smell of garlic which wafts up to Rüütli & do not be intimidated by the closed door on the ground floor & the long flight of stairs up to the 1st floor. The reward will be cheap but varied Italian food & an unexpected Art Nouveau décor in the chairs. Model bunches of grapes & garlic cover the walls, should anyone still be in doubt as to where they are meant to be. 170EEK.

✕ **Neljas Aste** (The Fourth Instance) Lossi 17; ✆ 7 441264; www.neljasaste.ee. It is an encouraging comment on the lack of crime in Estonia that space could be found in the law courts to open a restaurant. It is one of many setting up just outside the Old Town, so within easy reach of hotels & offices but able to offer much lower prices. Before entering, note the monument

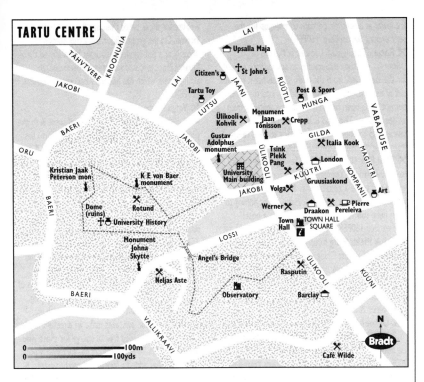

TARTU CENTRE

on the opposite side of the road to Johan Skytte, who established the university. Queen Silvia of Sweden unveiled it in October 2007, on the 375th anniversary of the founding. The dishes here have provocative names but innocent ingredients: 'Dictatorship of the Proletariat' is simply a herring salad. 160EEK.

⊡ **Pagari** Raekoja plats 2. An ideal fast-food outlet, being right in the town centre, but with ultra-provincial prices & a sufficient range of pies & cakes to satisfy the tourist desperate not to waste a lunch hour with leisurely eating. 100EEK.

⊡ **Pereleiva** Rüütli 5. Probably the most central coffee house in Tartu, & certainly the one with the best baking. It stays open until 19.00 during the week but on Sat & Sun follows the irritating Tartu habit, shared by all shops, of closing at 16.00, even in the height of the tourist season. 140EEK.

Pierre Chocolaterie Raekoja Plats 12; ☏ 7 304680; www.pierre.ee. Spacious coffee houses, which one has taken for granted in Tallinn for several years now, finally reached Tartu in 2007 with the opening of this one on the main square. It has a broader menu than its counterpart in Tallinn (page 37) which really just concentrates on chocolates, & being open to midnight, is convenient for light meals at any time of day. Perhaps it is at its best outside the summer season, when it is

necessary to linger amongst the drapes & old furniture indoors. 150EEK

✗ **Pussirohukelder** (Gunpowder Cellar) Lossi 28; ☏ 7 303555; www.pyss.ee. For much of the 1990s this was a grand, medieval restaurant built sufficiently deeply below the city walls to ensure that mobile phones would not work there. Although it made no attempt to hide the brickwork when it reopened in 2001 as a very lively pub & discotheque, the age range of the clientele has dropped at least one generation. Its publicity material proclaims that 'it always survives wild party nights'. It is also proud of its 11m-high roof, which perhaps makes it the tallest pub in the world, & so perhaps the most expensive to heat as well. The menu is limited, though reasonably priced, & vegetarians are as unwanted as ever, but who need worry about food in such surroundings? The website address says it all. 210EEK.

✗ **Rasputin** Ülikooli 10; ☏ 7 305996; www.rasputin.ee. Deep red is obviously the predominant colour here, rather than the crimson of later Soviet times. The menu must be one of the longest in Tartu but it is rare to find anything unavailable. As every dish is prepared individually, don't come in a rush, but to enjoy a whole evening, sometimes to the background of live Russian folk music. Forget milk with tea & drink it with honey or jam plus sultanas. Prices are lower at lunchtime, perhaps to make up for the very evening atmosphere. 160EEK.

✗ **Rotund** Toomemagi. Located at the top of University Hill, the restaurant is an appropriate reward for the steep walk from the town. In summer it spreads out of its tight, octagonal surroundings into the park, but not being open late in the evenings spares it from wilder students. The food is basic but cheap & elaborate sauces help to enliven it. A good place to seek refuge from a sudden Baltic storm. 120EEK.

✗ **Thai** Pikk 40; ↘ 7 402509. Several restaurants have now had the courage to open across the river in what used to be a gastronomic & architectural wasteland. It is now neither, & clubs are beginning to open here too. It cannot be long before a hotel follows suit. 160EEK.

✗ **Tsink Plekk Pang** Küütri 6; ↘ 7 303411; www.pang.ee. Whilst Chinese food in Tallinn still has to make its mark, it came instantly at a high level when this restaurant opened in 2002. It has all the qualities that in the context of Chinese food assure quality – noise, a bland décor & brusque service. 150EEK.

◻ **Ülikooli Kohvik** (University Café) Ülikooli 20; ↘ 7 375405; www.kohvik.ut.ee. Gentrification hit the 1st floor of this former student dive with a bang in 2005. Out went the local students & prices geared to them & in came a genteel café with an English-language

website for those twice their age & with 4 times their income. On the ground floor, the 2 mix somewhat uneasily as a self-service restaurant has survived there. Quality, if not prices, does stretch downstairs, an arrangement which has hopefully become permanent. 170EEK.

✗ **Volga** Küütri 1; ↘ 7 305440; www.restaurantvolga.ee. To the relief of some & to the surprise of many, since the autumn of 2007 Tartu has had a luxury restaurant. It seats 120 downstairs & on a mezzanine floor, but has a private room for small groups on the 3rd floor, which overlooks the main university building. It has an Art Deco 1920s flavour reflecting when it first opened. A band is perhaps surprising for a restaurant in this category but it is only scheduled to play at w/ends. 400EEK.

◻ **Werner** Ülikooli 11; ↘ 7 441274; www.werner.ee. Although located in the heart of the student area, this is a café where nobody need be ashamed to admit their age. The 19th-century prints of Tartu on the walls provide an ambience for looking backwards rather than forwards. Bouillon with pie followed by salmon pancakes make an excellent lunch. Chess sets are provided free of charge for those who wish to linger. A 2006 renovation has fortunately not spoilt it but has added a formal restaurant upstairs, & the 2 parts of the business are kept well apart. 150EEK.

TOURIST INFORMATION

The tourist board have an office/shop conveniently located in the Town Hall (Raekoja) building (↘ 7 442111; e tartu@visitestonia.com; www.tartu.ee). It sells a wide range of postcards, small souvenirs and maps for the whole of Estonia as well as on Tartu specifically. Their website is in fact more comprehensive than the national tourist ones. Their office also has a computer which visitors can use free of charge. *Tartu In Your Pocket* is published every six months and is the best source of information on opening hours, exhibitions and new restaurants. It can also be consulted online at www.inyourpocket.com. A local site with some English on it, www.kultuuriaken.tartu.ee, is the best source for concert and theatre programmes. The word in the address means 'cultural window'. The most detailed history in English of Tartu and its buildings, to which the author of this book was a contributor, is *Millenary Tartu* which was published in 2006.

Daily walking tours start in front of the Town Hall at 17.00 and participants just turn up and pay on the spot. See www.beneficium.ee for further information, and also details of tours available to Lake Peipsi and other places within easy access of Tartu.

SHOPPING

Tartu prices have to be geared to academics rather than to the business community so are considerably cheaper than those in Tallinn or Pärnu. Most of its tourists are still domestic which is another reason for this difference. Most souvenir shops are along Rüütli or on Town Hall Square. A craft centre, St Anthony's Guild, opened behind Lutsu Str in 2006, so it is possible to see everything sold there being made.

BOOKS The bookshop **Apollo** (*Kaubamaja shopping centre, Riia 1;* ☉ *09.00–21.00 Mon–Sat, 09.00–18.00 Sun*) has a wide selection of travel books in foreign languages. The University Bookshop (**Ülikooli Raamatupood**) at Ülikooli 11, between Town Hall Square and the main university building, also has travel books and a wide selection of other books about Estonia published in English. It however closes at 16.00 on Saturday and does not open at all on Sunday. Two secondhand bookshops with quite a range of material in English are next door to each other on Riia. They are **Sõna** at Riia 5 and **Antikvariaat** at Riia 7; both are open 10.00–18.00 Monday to Saturday.

WHAT TO SEE

A WALK AROUND TARTU A tour should start at the **Town Hall Square**. This north side of the square has a number of well-preserved, late 18th-century buildings whereas those on the south side are largely 20th century. Number 18 is famous on two counts: it belonged to the family of General Barclay who successfully repulsed Napoleon, and it leans to one side because it was built on swampy foundations. It is now the **Art Museum** for Tartu artists who made their name during the first independence period, when, thanks to the local Pallas Art College, Tartu was the national centre for painting. A remarkably large number of women attended the college at that time, including Karin Luts (1904–93), Estonia's most famous woman artist, whose work reflects the time she spent in France and Italy. She went to Sweden in exile in 1944 but somehow never managed to regain her fame there. Several paintings by Konrad Magi (1878–1925) are exhibited here, although there are now more in KUMU in Tallinn. He is probably Estonia's most famous painter and prices for his work are certainly higher than for anyone else's.

The work of an earlier artist displayed here, Georg Friedrich Schlater (1804–70), should also be noted. He was born in Tilsit, now Sovietsk, and grew up in Riga but spent his entire adult life in Tartu. He concentrated on lithographs of the city in the era just before photography took over, so has left an extensive architectural record of Tartu before the arrival of industry and railways. Later he would turn to portraits and photography.

Although the **Town Hall** gives the impression of careful planning and its façade has survived in total from its construction in 1789, there was much dispute about its size, use and layout. A suitable design for the fountains at the front of the Town Hall was resolved only in October 1998. The one chosen, of an embracing young couple, clearly breaks with the more staid tradition of earlier Estonian sculpture (which is why it was used as the cover picture for the fifth edition of *Estonia: The Bradt Travel Guide*). Town Hall Square stretches from here to the river and was formerly a market. The first stone bridge in the Baltics, a gift to the town from Catherine II following the fire of 1775, used to cross the river here. It was destroyed in World War II by the Russians as they advanced on the town in 1944, but an appeal launched in 1992 hopes eventually to raise sufficient funds to rebuild it.

Leave the square behind the Town Hall to the right, noting the large wall painting on the building at the corner of Lossi and Ülikooli; this pictures the university in the 1860s. A short walk along Ülikooli brings the **main university building** into view. Look first however to the left, at the building on the corner of Jacobi and Ülikooli which displays a modern montage – photographs of staff members in 2007. The façade may well seem familiar after a few days in Estonia; it is depicted on the back of the 2EEK note and was copied in Tallinn Old Town by the main building overlooking Pikk Jalg ('Long Leg'). The architect, **Johann Wilhelm Krause** (1757–1828), later became famous throughout Estonia, but this was his first major work, completed in 1809. He had previously enjoyed a very varied career. From 1778 to 1781 he studied theology in Leipzig but failed to graduate. He then spent a year as a British mercenary in the USA. It would be the late 1790s before he settled down in the Baltics to art and architecture. The building now houses the main student assembly hall, the administration, and the **Museum of Classical Antiquities** (⏲ *11.00–17.00 Mon–Fri; admission 25EEK for museum, assembly hall & lock-up*). Posters in the entrance hall advertise all the concerts and plays taking place in the university. The collection in the museum is far more extensive than its name suggests. Whilst there are original Greek works and many plaster cast copies as well, the museum also has on display two Egyptian mummies and several hundred Russian icons, many recently seized from smugglers. There is one of four death masks of the German philosopher Immanuel Kant, which was presented to Karl Morgenstern, the founder of the collection. The museum first opened in 1803, just a year after tuition began again at the university. The **Assembly Hall** is acoustically one of the best concert halls in Estonia; Liszt and Schumann performed here in the 19th century and were followed more recently by every favourite Soviet pianist and violinist. It had to be rebuilt following a fire in 1965 which was caused by badly maintained electric wiring. Any important event in the university takes place here but the one that deserves particular mention was its reopening in December 1919 in Estonian hands and with Estonian established as the language of tuition, replacing German and Russian.

In the attic above the Assembly Hall, one of five original **student lockups** remains. These were based on models from Göttingen and Heidelberg and date from the early 19th century when German influence was at its strongest. Specific sentences were laid down for any of the misdemeanours students were likely to commit. Insulting a cloakroom attendant warranted five days, insulting a woman only four. (Female students were not accepted at the university until 1915.) Smoking on university premises and returning library books late were regarded equally, both leading to a two-day sentence, but swearing was four times as evil since it carried an eight-day sentence. The austere furniture and surroundings are no worse than many students at liberty would have endured in their lodgings. The graffiti on the walls testifies to the wide range of talent amongst those detained here. The incorrect Latin, however, was bequeathed by Soviet restorers after the 1965 fire.

Coming out of the university building and turning left along Jaani, look out for the statue of **Jaan Tõnisson** at the junction with Gildi, erected in 2001. Tõnisson had many senior political posts in the 1920s and was also editor of Estonia's most famous newspaper, *Postimees*. The local offices of the newspaper are opposite the statue. A hundred metres further down Jaani is **St John's Church** (Jaani Kirk) where restoration was completed in summer 2005. Visitors in the early 1990s found it difficult to imagine that it had once been one of the most imposing Gothic buildings in the Baltics, with 2,000 terracotta statues adorning both the inside and outside walls. The building was badly damaged in August 1944 as the Germans retreated in the face of the Soviet armies. The church was neglected for most of the Soviet era, with much of the nave collapsing in 1952. There was even a threat to tear it down but then it was realised that the Niguliste Church in Tallinn might provide a suitable model, so the plan was to reopen it as a concert hall. Rebuilding work for this project finally started in 1989 under Polish supervision. Polish restorers had a worldwide reputation at the time in view of what they had achieved in Warsaw. Estonians took over in 1991 with the aim of restoring the church to its original state with about half of the original 2,000 terracotta statues on display. In 1997, when the roof was completed, a Christmas service was celebrated for the first time since World War II; the copper steeple and the bells followed in 1999. A single window was commissioned in 2000 from Urmo Raus, an Estonian stained-glass designer who was then settled in France (and today lives and works in the Netherlands). This window has now been withdrawn; some people disliked the abstract design, others the fact that the artist no longer lived in Estonia and they wanted the work to be done locally. Visitors will therefore now see totally plain glass with frames of stainless steel.

Opposite the church on Jaani there was for many years a nondescript office building with a warning sign in Estonian and English – Varise Misohtlik, 'Liable to Fall Down'. This was a transit prison in 1941 and 1949 for those due to be transported to Siberia, and about a hundred executions took place here in each of those years. In Soviet times it became a sobering-up station but as independent Estonia did not believe in such institutions, it again became a prison, but one from which it was all too easy to escape. It closed in 1999 and the building has now been transformed into luxury flats. In the neighbouring small streets are several stone and wooden houses that survive from the 19th century; fortunately these are being restored and not torn down. Crossing Lutsu the next building of note on the left-hand side is number 16, the **Town Citizen's Museum** (*www.linnamuuseum.tartu.ee; admission 10EEK*), a recreation of every room in a townhouse from 1830, where a middle-class family would have lived. At that time they would have been German, or possibly Russian, but certainly not Estonian.

A detour is possible here to the **Botanical Gardens** (*www.ut.ee/boated;* ☉ *May–Sep 07.00–21.00; rest of year 07.00–19.00; greenhouse 10.00–17.00 year-round; admission to gardens free, greenhouse 25EEK*) by continuing along Jaani and turning right along Lai. The gardens are then on the left hand side of Lai, stretching down towards the river. With their summer opening hours, they can be visited before or after the museums and shops. Booklets with details of the collection are sold at the entrance.

The basic layout here has hardly changed since the gardens opened in 1811. The collection outside is of species from all over the Russian Empire as it was then, and which subsequently became the Soviet Union. Recent additions are the clematis and rose gardens. The greenhouse displays tropical plants from America and Australia which could not of course endure the Estonian climate outside. Non-botanists should still come here to climb to the top level of the greenhouse which gives the best view in Tartu over St John's Church.

To continue the tour, return to the back of the university building where there is a new statue of the Swedish King **Gustav Adolphus**, the founder of the university in 1632. The statue is new because the earlier one was removed during the Soviet era. This one was unveiled in 1992, during the first royal visit to Estonia following the restoration of independence, by King Carl Gustav of Sweden. The Swedish royal family offered to replace the statue in 1982 for the 350th anniversary celebrations but the offer was rejected. This did not prevent rebellious students from restoring the king in snow each subsequent winter. A stiff ten-minute walk now follows to reach the monuments at the top of the hill behind the university. A walk in this area shows the university at its most serious and at its most carefree.

Three memorial statues immediately stand out, one of **Karl Ernst von Baer** (1792–1876) who is seated with a book open in his lap. As the founder of embryology, he is Tartu's most famous scientist and also equally famous as an explorer. He was one of very few Baltic Germans to integrate with Estonians and to learn the language. A rather sour portrait of him adorns the 2EEK note. This seriousness does not prevent students using his statue as a site for wild fraternity and sorority parties, with dancing and bonfires. Those who can afford it wash him with champagne. Because he also taught in St Petersburg and Königsberg, his work was praised in Soviet times, and now the Russians claim him and refer to him frequently in histories of 'Kaliningrad'.

The second statue is of Estonia's first poet, **Kristian Jaak Peterson** (1801–22), who is standing, clasping a stick. It is claimed that he walked from Riga to Tartu to study here, such was his enthusiasm. He died of tuberculosis at the age of 21, but despite hardly reaching adulthood, he proved that poetry and serious prose need not be written only in German. His work covers a wide range of topics, including religion, music and the natural world, but he was sadly ahead of his time. Ironically, one year after his death, some poetry he wrote in German was published in Leipzig, but it was another hundred years before his poems in Estonian appeared. Since 1995, his birthday, 14 March, has been celebrated as 'Mother Tongue Day' and on this day in 2006 President Meri died; he was a great supporter of this cause.

Next to Peterson is a statue of **Willem Reiman** (1861–1917) who was to Estonian history what Peterson was to the language. He was the first lecturer at the university to give history an Estonian, rather than a German or a Russian, perspective. Later he would be well known for his work in the temperance movement and had he lived into the independence era, he would undoubtedly have campaigned for Estonian prohibition, following the American and Finnish examples of the time.

Behind the Peterson statue is Kissing Hill, a surprisingly open area for lovers to congregate; the tougher male students traditionally show their affection by carrying their girlfriends here from Angel's Bridge, a distance of about 200m. This bridge was built as a memorial to **Georg Friedrich Parrot**, the first chancellor of the university when it reopened in 1802.

The hill is dominated by **Tartu University History Museum** (*www.ut.ee/ajaloomuuseum; admission 25EEK*), housed in the shell of the former St Peter and St Paul Cathedral which had been originally built in the 13th century. When completed it was the tallest church in Estonia and, from pictures that survive, one of the most imposing Gothic ones in the Baltics. Wars and fires soon took their toll, and by the early 17th century the entire interior had been destroyed. Much of what remained was looted and the site even degenerated into a rubbish dump. In 1807 the choir was restored and rebuilt as the university library, a role it would maintain until 1985 when the present museum opened. Extensive renovation was carried out both in the independence period and during the Soviet occupation and has continued more recently. In 2005 the tower was opened to visitors ready for a stiff climb. In the summer the view is restricted to that of church steeples rising through the trees, which block the view of anything else.

The museum was established here in 1982, when the library moved out. The top floor is still called Morgenstern Hall after Karl Morgenstern, the first university librarian. The collections now cover all the scientific and medical fields in which Tartu showed particular expertise and most rooms have labels in English. A range of artists have painted all the highlights of the 19th century, while photographers have played the same role in this century. Perhaps the most interesting person covered is Ernst von Bergmann (1836–1907) who was Professor of Surgery here during the 1870s. He was the first medic to wash his hands before operating, rather than just afterwards, and was also the first one to wear a white coat in the theatre. One large map shows the worldwide extent of the Tartu diaspora. The role of the Jewish community is documented in a chart which covers the period from 1865, when Jews were first allowed to live in Tartu, through to the 1890s, during which time the quota system which restricted the number of Jewish students rose from 5% to 20%. This quota was abolished only in 1916. Jewish studies were banned by the Russians in 1940 and the few Jewish staff that remained at the time of the German invasion the following year were all arrested and murdered.

The **Observatory** was built shortly after the reopening of the university in the early 19th century and was designed by Johann Wilhelm Krause, the architect of the main university building. Until World War I it was probably the best in Europe, having registered 120,000 different stars. A small exhibition inside covers the history of the observatory and displays several telescopes. This exhibition has hardly changed since it first opened in the 1890s, so shows the best of 19th-century astronomy and telescopes which were actually used then. Several came from England and Germany. The exhibition was formally closed to the public in 1993, pending a planned restoration, but can be visited on request. An English-language catalogue of the telescopes can be consulted on www.obs.ee. The observatory had remained in use until 1964, when a new one opened outside Tartu at Toravere. The view from the roof is the best over Tartu but admission to it is not always possible. The Estonian flag flies from this roof 24 hours a day; unlike the flag on Hermann Tower in Tallinn, it is not lowered at sunset.

There are several routes back to the town from the university. The quickest is along Lossi to the back of the Town Hall. The nearby Barclay Plats should not be missed. In its centre is the statue of General Barclay de Tolly, who successfully fought Napoleon. The statue was paid for by his troops. A longer route goes along Vallikravi, Struve and Vanemuise and passes the University Library. In front of the library is a fountain/sculpture completed in 2007 in memory of **Juri Lotman**, probably the most famous academic based in Tartu during the Soviet period. Semiotics was his field and probably only those who understand its meaning will be able to understand this work of art. As a Jew, Lotman could not pursue his studies in Leningrad in the early 1950s, when Stalin had launched his anti-Semitic campaign of 'cosmopolitanism', so he came to Tartu and stayed there until his death in 1993. Although respected worldwide, he was not allowed to travel to the West until the late 1980s.

MUSEUMS Two museums, of Classical Antiquities and of University History, have been described in the walk above. Eight others of interest to foreign visitors are described here. Unless otherwise stated, all are usually open from 11.00 to 18.00, Wednesday to Sunday, although they close on 23 and 24 June, and 20 August. That said, tour operators can make arrangements for group visits on closed days. As opening hours can be changed at short notice, it is advisable to check the relevant website first. Admission is normally 10–20EEK, but free on the last Friday of the month. Tartu does not have an equivalent to the Tallinn Card to cover admission fees and public transport.

Estonian Agricultural Museum (☎ 7 412397; www.epm.ee; ⊕ Apr–Oct 09.00–17.00 daily; rest of year 10.00–16.00; admission 35EEK) is at Ülemurme, 6km south of Tartu, but buses going to Põlva and Võru all stop there. As its name implies, it is by far the largest museum in the country on this theme and even determined city-dwellers should be interested by the diversity of its collection. It is far from being a collection of rusty tools, an all-too-common occurrence in this field. It has machinery, models, space, diagrams and effective lighting to show what has and what has not succeeded in Estonia over the last 200 years. It is fortunate that so much survived the war, including tractors imported from America in the 1930s. Visitors are welcome to picnic in the grounds and admission is free of charge on the first Sunday of the month.

Estonian National Museum (Kuperjanovi 9; ☎ 7 421311; e erm@erm.ee; www.erm.ee; 11.00–18.00 Wed–Sun; admission 10EEK) This should serve as a model for others in Estonia; it is sad that more foreign tourists do not visit. Layout, lighting and description have all been properly thought out and, given the paucity of English-language books about Estonia, this is the best introduction to take their place. The 19th century is particularly well documented and temporary exhibitions enhance what is shown in the main collections. The museum covers not only Estonians, but other nationals who have lived there such as the Baltic Germans, the Russians and the Swedes. Recent additions include a room on the Soviet period and photographs of many of the country's manor houses. Note in particular the pictures of bomb damage of 1941, of the final shopping queues in 1991 at the end of the Soviet era and the montage of Stalin on a gallows daringly put together in 1941. Do open the drawers upstairs to see the displays of gloves woven in all areas of the country. The total collection of beer tankards made from birch wood amounts to 3,000 but of course only a few can be exhibited at any one time.

The museum has a café in the entrance with some of the cheapest prices in Estonia. Fortunately stag groups from Tallinn are unlikely to discover it. Take the stairs at the back of the café up one floor to an exhibition of dolls. These were all made in the US by the exile community during the Soviet era and represent the costumes of each region in Estonia, the idea being that future generations should have this bond with their parents' homeland.

Opposite the museum is the largest fraternity house of the university; such organisations were banned in the Soviet period but have enjoyed a revival since then. The university assures visitors that in this building 'old strict discipline has given way to modern liberty and the best man is not one who drinks most beer but the one who does it best and shows most sociability'. The railway station is a walk of around 300m from the museum so visitors coming for the day from Tallinn can end their tour at the museum. (Sadly they cannot start here as the train arrives at 10.00 and the museum opens only at 11.00.) In 2010 the museum will move to new larger premises at Raadi Manor House, on the outskirts of the town to the east.

Estonian Postal Museum (*Rüütli 15; ☎ 7 300775; ⊕ 11.00–18.00 Wed–Sun; admission free*) does not just limit itself to stamps. Postmarks are of equal significance in the political history of Estonia, as were the interventions of censors for almost all previous regimes. It also shows the postal routes taken by carriages before the start of rail services. Note the stamps issued in Otepää from 22 July to 12 August 1941, when the Russians had fled and the Germans had not yet had time to impose their own postal system. Sadly the Communications Museum in Leningrad took much of the collection which had been assembled for this museum before it opened in 1938. The shop here has a varied selection of postcards for sale at prices lower than elsewhere in Tartu, plus of course sets of stamps.

KGB Museum (*Riia 15b; ☎ 7 461717; www.tartu.ee/linnamuuseum.tartu.ee; ⊕ 11.00–16.00 Tue–Sun; admission 12EEK*) The museum opened in 2003 in its former local headquarters, although the entrance is in fact on Pepleri. The exhibition has really come about through the efforts of Enn Tarto who as a dissident had three different spells in prison during the Soviet era, totalling 15 years in all. Despite this, he was fortunately able to be an active parliamentarian during the 1990s. Visitors can see the cells as victims knew them and also an exhibition of Estonian resistance during the Soviet era.

Song Festival Museum (*Jaama 14; ☎ 7 461021; www.tartu.ee/linnamuuseum.ee; ⊕ 11.00–18.00 Tue–Sun; admission 20EEK*) This building is as important as its contents, since it was the headquarters of the Vanemuine Society from 1870 to 1903. The society was founded in 1865 to promote performances by choirs in Estonian and this led to the first song festival in 1869, which was held in Tartu. From 1896 they would all be held in Tallinn. In 1870 the open-air stage at the back of the building hosted the first performance of a play in Estonian – *The Cousin from Saaremaa*, written by Lydia Koidula, which was particularly well received since the audience had expected it to be in German, as all previous plays had been, and were delighted with the change. Another change would take a further six years, as it was 1876 before women actors were allowed on stage. A major female role in the 1870 production was therefore taken by Harry Jannsen, Lydia Koidula's brother.

The museum has pictures and mementoes from each festival, but the 20th century ones are of most interest, since it is possible to hear recordings and see films from each one. Those in the 1950s and 1970s suffered most from Soviet interference. The 1960 one is best remembered for the courageous impromptu singing of 'My Country is My Pride and Joy'; given the enthusiasm that this raised, the Soviets did not dare to ban it again. The song festivals held in exile at that time are also covered.

Sport Museum (*Rüütli 15;* ☎ *7 300750; www.spordimuuseum.ee;* ⊕ *11.00–18.00 Tue–Sun; admission 25EEK*) This museum opened in 1963 and, given Soviet support for this activity, much of the material was collected then. The current building opened in 2001, and also houses the Postal Museum. A collection had in fact been started in 1934 so photos, medals and sportswear go back to the beginning of the 20th century. Many of the early posters are in German. Understandably the exhibition concentrates on Estonian Olympic champions, in their own right from 1920 to 1936 and again from 1992, and under Soviet auspices from 1948 to 1988. Teams trained very hard for the 1940 games, scheduled to take place in Helsinki. Paul Keres, on the 5EEK note and best remembered as a chess player, is seen here playing tennis in Vancouver in 1975, just a few days before he died.

There are short films with highlights from all the Olympic Games and exercise bicycles for those who feel the need to emulate those shown in these films and in the exhibits. Unlinked with sport, there are some display cabinets of jewellery here, with exhibits dating back to the first millennium BC.

Tartu City Museum (*Narva mnt 23;* ☎ *7 461911; www.tartu.ee/linnamuuseum;* ⊕ *11.00–18.00 Tue–Sun; admission 20EEK*) The building that now houses the museum dates from 1790 when Tartu's architecture was at its height; after the fire of 1775 buildings were in stone, and were made to last and to impress. The architect Johann Walter, who also designed the Town Hall, was clearly briefed to make this the most lavish private residence in Tartu and to base the design on the contemporary French style of Louis XVI. However, it did not stay long in private hands and the next two centuries would see it being used as a printing press, a school, a hostel and then finally a cultural centre during the Soviet period. For the first ten years after the restoration of Estonian independence, this museum was housed in totally inadequate premises near to the university, but in 2001 it finally moved here, to a building that can do justice to the collection. The museum is fully equipped for those with disabilities.

The highpoints here are the model of Tartu in 1940, before any bombing, and the actual table at which the Tartu Treaty was signed. It was by this treaty, signed in 1920, that the Soviet Union recognised Estonian independence and its borders. Earlier exhibits cover 14th-century painted glass cups, and clocks, silver and textiles from the Swedish period in the 17th century, and the coin collection – around 7,000 coins in all – is the most extensive in Estonia. Films from the first period of independence and from the Soviet era are shown regularly.

Tartu Toy Museum (*Lutsu 8;* ☎ *7 461777; www.mm.ee;* ⊕ *11.00–18.00 Wed–Sun; admission 25EEK*) This opened in 1994 although the building now occupied dates from 1770. Its collection, based entirely on voluntary donations, is mainly traditional, but modern toys are being added. In political terms, this is a classless museum with the porcelain dolls of the rich claiming the same space as the rag dolls and wooden horses of the peasants. The products of craftsmen and of the large factories are given equal space. It is hoped to extend the collection of board games and mechanical toys as more gifts are received. Some board games continued in the Soviet era but with different names and flags. That era also had the sexual divisions of the West with cars, trains and weapons for boys and dolls for girls. The dolls and their 'houses' come from all over the world. In 2007 an extension opened covering puppet theatres and animation films, for which Estonia was already famous in Soviet times. Tasteful wooden toys are sold in the museum shop and a playroom is available for children, although it closes at 16.00.

Natural History Museum (*Vanemuise 46;* ☎ *7 375839; www.ut.ee/natmuseum;* ⊕ *10.00–16.00 Wed–Sun; admission 25EEK*) Perhaps because of its size alone, this museum needs an entry here, but as its botanical, geological and zoological collections are similar to those that can be seen in any major city, they are probably only of interest to specialists. However it is worth coming to admire the vast mural in the entrance hall. Its coverage of nature makes sense, but the intrusion of an enormous space rocket shows firm intervention from Moscow in the late 1960s when the space race was at its most fervent.

4

Riga LATVIA

Riga is the largest and most cosmopolitan of all the Baltic capitals and is by a long way the most interesting town or city in Latvia. It is located on the Daugava River about 15km from the point where the Daugava meets the Baltic Sea in the southeastern corner of the Gulf of Riga. Riga can trace its history to the beginning of the 13th century, but it was in the course of the Middle Ages that it developed into a Hanseatic city, and by the 18th and 19th centuries it had grown into one of Europe's leading ports and industrial centres. By the late 19th/early 20th century it had also become a cultural centre, famous for its opera, theatre and music.

Renovation of the city and new building started immediately after Latvian independence was re-established in 1991. A particular spurt for this, including the rebuilding of the House of Blackheads, was provided by the 800th anniversary of the founding of Riga in 1201. Another was the Ice Hockey Championships held in 2006.

THE CITY

The modern city is divided into two parts by the city canal which flows through the elegant parks that separate the historic Old Town from most of the New Town, with its shops, offices and suburbs. The air of elegance and spaciousness created by the area of open space in what is otherwise the centre of a busy capital has led to Riga being compared to Paris by a number of guidebooks and travel writers. There is some justification in the comparison. Even when Latvia was part of the Soviet Union, Riga was more sophisticated than Russian Soviet cities and towns, since it had better shops and the odd decent restaurant and café. Now its medieval and Art Nouveau architecture and well-kept parks allow the comparison to continue. There are modern international hotels, many good cafés and restaurants, and small and pleasant shops stocking local art and international brands. In 1992–93 the local authority privatised about 90% of Riga's shops, from the old GUM (State Universal Store) in the Old Town, to the small bookshops and tobacconists.

Between 1945 and 1991 Riga grew enormously, largely as a result of Soviet expansion which generally took the form of building large, drab, low-quality blocks of flats in the suburbs. One of the first, called Kengarags, can be seen along the Daugava and plenty can also be seen on the trip from the airport to the city centre.

The present population is estimated at just under 800,000, but even now about 42% is Latvian and about the same percentage is Russian (the balance is made up of Poles, Belarussians and Ukrainians). Over half the population (about 54%) is female.

Until Latvia's independence from the Soviet Union in 1991 Russian was the predominant language heard in Riga. Now, as can be seen from the signposts, Latvian has regained ground, but Russian is still widely spoken (as are English and German, as second languages).

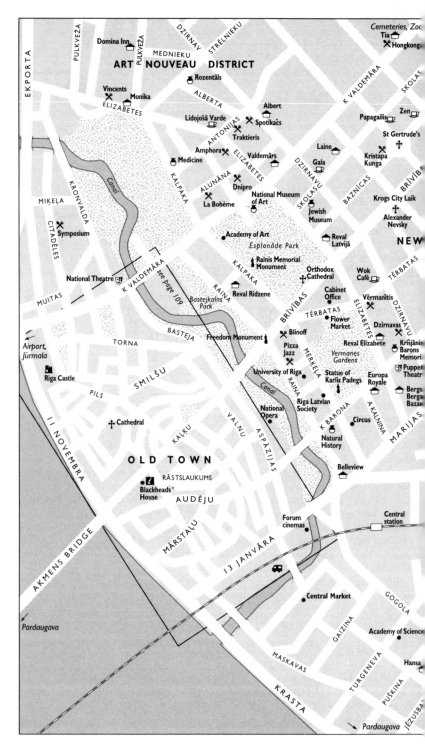

Cemeteries, Zoo
Tia
Hongkong

EKPORTA

PULKVEŽA

Domina Inn

DZIRNAV

STRĒLNIEKU

MEDNIEKU

ART NOUVEAU DISTRICT

Rozentāls

Vincents
Monika

ĒLIZABETES

ALBERTA

K VALDEMĀRA

SKOLAS

Zen

Papagailis

St Gertrude's

Lidojošā Varde

ANTONIJAS

Albert
Spotikačs

Traktieris

Amphora
Medicine

ĒLIZABETES

Valdemārs

Laine

DZIRNAVU

Gala

Kristapa
Kunga

BAZNĪCAS

BRĪVĪB

Krogs City Laik

KALPAKA

ALUNĀNA

Dnipro
La Bohème

National Museum
of Art

SKOLAS

Jewish
Museum

Alexander
Nevsky

MIKEĻA

KRONVALDA

Canal

CITADELES

Symposium

Academy of Art

Esplanāde Park

Reval
Latvijā

NEW

Rainis Memorial
Monument

KALPAKA

Orthodox
Cathedral

Wok
Café

National Theatre

K VALDEMĀRA

see page 109

RAINA

Reval Ridzene

BRĪVĪBAS

Cabinet
Office

Vērmanītis

TĒRBATAS

MUITAS

Bastejkalns
Park

TĒRBATAS

Flower
Market

ĒLIZABETES

DZIRNAVU

Airport,
Jūrmala

TORNA

BASTEJA

Freedom Monument

Blinoff

Dzirnavas

Reval Elizabete

Krišjānis
Barons
Memori

Riga Castle

SMILŠU

Pizza
Jazz

MERKELA

Vermanes
Gardens

Puppet
Theatr

PILS

University of Riga

RAINA

Statue of
Karlis Padegs

Europa
Royale

Bergs
Berga
Bazaı

Cathedral

KALĶU

VALNU

Canal

National
Opera

Riga Latvian
Society

K BARONA

Circus

A KALNINA

MARIJAS

II NOVEMBRA

OLD TOWN

ASPĀZIJAS

Natural
History

Belleview

RĀSTSLAUKUMS

Blackheads'
House

AUDĒJU

Forum
cinemas

Central
station

MĀRSTAĻU

13 JANVĀRA

Pardaugava

Central Market

GOGOLA

GAIZINA

Academy of Science

AKMENS BRIDGE

MASKAVAS

TURGENEVA

Hansa

PUŠKINA

KRASTA

Pardaugava

JEZUSBA

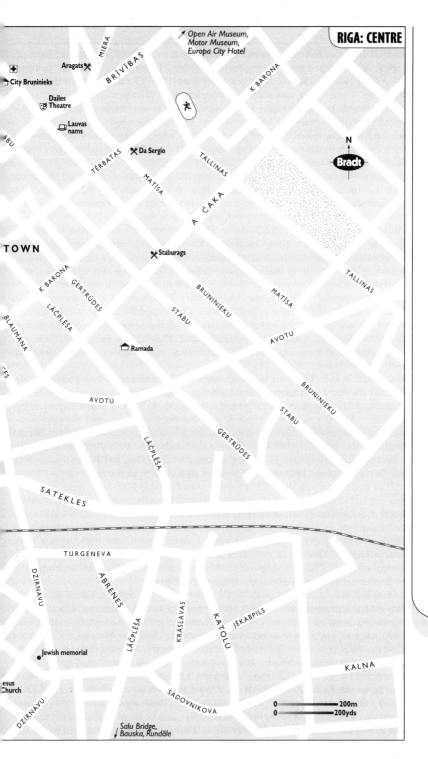

RIGA: CENTRE

↗ Open Air Museum,
Motor Museum,
Europa City Hotel

MIERA

BRĪVĪBAS

Aragats ✕

City Bruninieks

Dailes
Theatre

Lauvas
nams

ĀBU

TĒRBATAS

✕ Da Sergio

MATĪSA

K BARONA

TALLINAS

A ĊAKA

Bradt

N

TOWN

✕ Staburags

K BARONA

GERTRŪDES

LĀČPLĒŠA

BLAUMAŅA

ĒS

BRUNINIEKU

STABU

Ramada

MATĪSA

AVOTU

TALLINAS

AVOTU

LĀČPLĒŠA

GERTRŪDES

BRUNINIEKU

STABU

SATEKLES

TURGENEVA

DZIRNAVU

ABRENES

LĀČPLĒŠA

KRĀSLAVAS

KATOĻU

JĒKABPILS

KALNA

Jewish memorial

esus
Church

DZIRNAVU

SADOVNIKOVA

0 ━━━ 200m
0 ━━━ 200yds

Salu Bridge,
Bauska, Rundāle

In 2001 Riga celebrated 800 years of recorded history. By 2008, the city had been the capital of an independent country, presided over by Latvians, for a mere 37 years: for 20 years between 1920 and 1940 and again since 1991. The remainder of the time it had been fought over and ruled by peoples from all over northern Europe, but predominantly by the Germans and Russians. What is remarkable is that while other peoples have disappeared or been swallowed up into larger states, a people known as the Latvians have survived to establish themselves with a distinct national identity and their own government and to emerge into the 21st century as an independent nation with Riga as its capital.

Archaeological excavations indicate that the area now occupied by Riga was probably inhabited and operated as a trading centre as early as the 2nd century BC or even well before: it is thought that the name Riga may originate from a local word 'ringa', meaning a winding river, and it is clear that well before 1201 Riga was already developing as a small harbour. The first mention of the modern city can however be traced to 1201 when Bishop Albert von Buxhoevden (or Buksherden) of Bremen established the first German fortress here as part of his crusade to introduce Christianity to the local Livs. Religious life was quickly established, with several churches, including the Dome Cathedral, founded in the early years of German domination. During the 13th century Riga suffered from no fewer than five major fires, which eventually gave rise to a law prohibiting the construction of wooden houses inside the town walls, but overall the town prospered as a trading centre, joining the Hanseatic League in 1282. Despite the prosperity, there was constant tension between the citizens and their rulers, giving rise to numerous battles and reprisals.

In 1521 St Peter's Church began to operate as a centre for Reformation doctrine; in 1524 the first Latvian Evangelical Lutheran congregation was formed at St James's Church. As Lutheran teachings gained a foothold in Riga, Catholicism retreated: Catholic churches were demolished, and religious paintings and carvings were destroyed. Lutheranism has been the dominant religion ever since. Teutonic influence gradually waned and in 1561 Riga fell into the hands of the Polish/Lithuanian Empire. The end of the 16th century marked a period of instability, and Russia (under Ivan the Terrible), Poland, Denmark and Sweden all laid claim to the city.

The Polish–Swedish War of 1599–1629 ended as far as Riga was concerned when the city fell to Gustav Adolf II in 1621. Following the Peace of Oliva of 1660, Riga became the second capital of Sweden. Again there was a period of commercial success and prosperity. In 1663 a water supply was established using wooden pipes. In 1681 Riga's first newspaper, the *Rigische Nouvellen*, was established. In 1685 the first Bible was printed in Latvian. In the same year a number of large rocks that blocked navigation of the Daugava were removed by explosion. In 1701 a pontoon bridge was built over the Daugava – it was the longest in the world.

Swedish rule continued until 1710, when after an eight-month siege by the Russians, Riga surrendered to the Russian general, Count Sheremetyer. This siege was begun in person by Peter the Great, who launched the first three shells of the attack and then noted in a letter to his close companion, Alexander Menshikov, 'The Lord God has enabled us to see the start of our revenge on this accursed place.' For the next 200 years Riga remained under Russian control, although it continued to be heavily dominated by the Baltic Germans who lived throughout most of Latvia. This period was by no means a bad one for Riga. Peter I married the fourth daughter of Ernst Glück, the Lutheran pastor who translated the Bible into Latvian. She became Catherine I of Russia. Writing in German of the time he spent in Riga between 1764 and 1789 **Johann Gottfried Herder** wrote 'I lived, taught and behaved in such a free and such an unrestrained way in Livonia such that I can hardly imagine living and behaving again.' In 1743 street lighting was introduced. In 1782 a theatre was established (where Wagner conducted from 1837–39). Riga was also a place of intellectual and scientific enlightenment in the 18th century. In 1798 Dr Otto Herr introduced vaccination against smallpox, and in 1802 the Latvian pharmacist Grindels founded the Society of Pharmacy, which started a trend for the formation of a whole range of medical and scientific associations. In 1801 torture was abolished as part of the legal process, as was public execution.

The 18th century also saw a growth of Latvian cultural awareness. Whilst Herder wrote his *Fragmente über die neuere deutsche Literatur* ('Fragments Concerning Recent German Literature') in Riga, in 1774 he published a number of Latvian folk songs in German translation.

Riga avoided the effects of the Napoleonic Wars; although Napoleon had threatened to attack 'this suburb of London', he never reached it. As Napoleon's troops approached Riga in 1812, the governor-general of Riga set the wooden houses of the Riga suburbs on fire to deflect the invaders. In the wake of the French Revolution, the wave of liberation that swept across Europe made itself felt in Riga too, and in 1817 serfs were emancipated, 40 years before those in Russia. In 1830 farmers gained the right to live in the cities. In 1840 a rural education law was passed. Soon an educated rural class grew up, starting up trade in Riga and other towns. Jews were given residency rights in Riga only in the mid 19th century, before which most were itinerant traders. By the outbreak of World War I in 1914, their numbers in Riga had reached about 100,000 and they were active both in commerce and in the academic world.

In 1857–58 the town walls were dismantled to allow expansion. In 1861 the railway came and the postal service was expanded. Riga gradually developed into a major industrial centre and the first shipyard opened in 1869. Telephones arrived in 1877; horse-drawn trams appeared, and a major bicycle factory was established. In 1887 an electric power generation station was built. This industrialisation also brought a huge increase in the population of Riga: in 1767 the town had 16,300 inhabitants; a hundred years later the population had grown to 102,590 (of whom about 20–25% were Latvian). By 1897 the population more than doubled to 255,879, but the Latvian population now accounted for almost 50%. A prosperous Latvian working class and middle class began to emerge.

Parallel to this industrial expansion came a growth in Latvian nationalism. Latvian newspapers, notably *Tas Latviešu Ļaužu Draugs* ('The Friend of the Latvian People'), had appeared since the 1820s and 1830s, but Russian remained the language of education, government and the legal system. However, Krišjānis Barons' work in collecting Latvia's *dainas*, traditional four-line folk songs, and the establishment of a folk song festival in Riga in 1873, gave impetus to the movement called the Latvian Awakening, which grew out of the Riga Latvian Association. The Latvian Association published a Latvian encyclopaedia, founded a national opera and a national theatre. The folk song festival gave birth to a national anthem, 'Dievs Svēti Latviju' ('God Bless Latvia').

The end of the 19th century was also a time of growing working-class political awareness. In 1899 women workers at the Dēuta textile mill went on strike. The police intervened, and before long demonstrations began in the course of which five workers were shot dead and 31 wounded. A full-scale riot soon ensued. In 1904 the Latvian Social Democratic Party was formed, the most significant movement of its kind in imperial Russia.

On 13 January 1905 a demonstration of the poor and working classes was put down with force in Moscow. The demonstrators had wanted to show solidarity with demonstrators who had gathered four days earlier in front of the tsar's palace in St Petersburg to hand in a petition seeking political reform. A demonstration in support also began in Riga, but again it was put down by force of arms and over 70 people were killed. The Social Democratic Party began to organise resistance, and by October Riga was in the grip of a general strike. Armed peasants attacked German landowners, and other strikers attacked the prison, aiming to free a number of political prisoners.

Before the end of the year Russian troops moved to regain control, putting the revolution down with particular brutality in which over 900 peasants and teachers were executed under martial law, and thousands were exiled to Siberia. The Russian authorities aimed their vengeance especially at teachers who were known for their social-democratic leanings. Many Latvian intellectuals escaped only by fleeing to the West. The writer, Jānis Rainis, fled to Switzerland; **Kārlis Ulmanis**, the chairman of the Peasants' Party, who was later to become president of Latvia, sought refuge in the United States.

The outbreak of World War I drove Latvia into the arms of the Russians with whom they allied themselves against the German foe. In 1915 German forces were approaching Riga. In a manic evacuation, the Russians moved Riga's industry and about 96,000 workers to Russia. Even the power station was dismantled and moved. In all, about one-third of the total population of Latvia was forced to leave the country. In 1917 German troops crossed the Daugava, and the capital surrendered to them.

In the same year, however, the Russian Revolution was making its consequences felt. Whilst some political elements in Riga sought the annexation of Latvia to the German Empire, others were looking to Soviet power to free their country from the Germans. In spring 1918 Latvia was split into three: Kurzeme and Riga went to Germany, Latgale to Russia, and the rest of Vidzeme was left unmolested. However, following the defeat of Germany, on 18 November 1918, in the Riga national theatre an independent republic of Latvia was proclaimed, and Kārlis Ulmanis was given the task of forming a provisional government. A period of what amounted to civil war ensued, the Russians supporting Latvia against the persistent exercise of German military force. Only on 11 August 1920 was a peace treaty signed between Latvia and the Soviet Union following the final expulsion of German troops from Latvia in December 1919.

The period between the two world wars is often referred to as the first period of Latvian independence. The 1920 treaty provided for the Soviet Union and Latvia to recognise each other as states. In 1922 Latvia adopted its own constitution and issued its own currency. Jānis Čakste was elected as the first president of the republic.

Riga was not immune to the Depression that gripped most of Europe during the 1930s and unemployment rose to high levels. On 15 May 1934 Ulmanis mounted a coup and formed an authoritarian administration. Democratic socialists were imprisoned, political parties of both left and right were banned, and freedom of the press was curtailed. In 1935, the Freedom Monument was erected in the centre of Riga (see page 143).

Under the terms of the pact between Hitler and Stalin of 23 August 1939 it was agreed that the Baltic countries would fall under the sphere of influence of the Soviet Union. By the end of that year the Soviet Union had already begun to establish a military presence in Latvia. On 17 June 1940 Soviet troops marched in to take over the country and establish a pro-Soviet regime. On 21 July 'elections' were held under Soviet auspices and a new government and parliament declared Latvia to be a republic of the USSR. Ulmanis was deported, as were thousands of citizens from Riga and elsewhere in Latvia, many of them to Siberia or central Asia.

In June 1941 the USSR was forced to join in the war when attacked by Germany. Latvia was unprepared, and on 1 July 1941 Hitler's troops arrived in Riga to 'liberate' it from Stalin's USSR, causing the Soviets to retreat, leaving devastation in their wake. Stalin had murdered or deported a substantial proportion of the Jewish population in Riga as enemies of the people; Hitler imposed his anti-Semitic policies, massacring

Jews at Rumbula and Biķernieki, and establishing concentration camps. Riga was 'liberated' on 13 October 1944. The German occupation of Kurzeme continued until May 1945 when the Red Army arrived again to 'liberate' Riga from the Germans. The retreating Germans destroyed houses, factories, roads and bridges, and thousands of Latvians fled to the West.

After the end of World War II the USSR provided economic assistance to Latvia, and Russian immigrants took the places left by the fleeing or slaughtered native Latvian population. However, the Soviet 'liberators' were not welcomed: many Latvians formed resistance groups and fighting ensued until Stalin intervened with his usual brutality, ordering mass deportations to Siberia in 1949 and acts of destruction including the blowing up of the Blackheads' House (see page 131) in May 1948.

However, Latvian nationalism whilst repressed was not extinguished. When foreign tourists were allowed back to Riga from 1959, they immediately noted the differences from Russia. Bernard Newman, taking one of these first tours wrote: 'I found real waiters and quick service and the best meals I had encountered in the USSR. At the opera, I saw hairstyles and dresses years ahead of those worn in Moscow.' Clearly the Latvians, called by some visitors at the time 'The Welsh of the Baltic', were making the most of the 'Khrushchev thaw', which allowed a degree of local autonomy.

In 1988 5,000 demonstrators gathered in Riga on 14 June to commemorate the deportations, and on 23 August 10,000 demonstrators gathered to mark the anniversary of the Hitler–Stalin pact. In the meantime in June at a meeting of the Latvian Writers' Union a resolution was passed that led to the founding of the Popular Front of Latvia in October 1988 that was to campaign for political, cultural and economic independence.

In 1989 Latvia experienced its first free elections of deputies to the Supreme Soviet of the USSR. This event was followed by the passing of laws in the Latvian Supreme Soviet proclaiming the sovereignty of the Latvian Soviet Socialist Republic and declaring Latvian the official language of the country. Latvia was again on the road to independence. On 18 November 1989 over 500,000 people gathered on the banks of the Daugava in Riga to mark the 71st anniversary of Latvia's independence.

On 4 May 1990 the Supreme Soviet of Latvia met in the pre-war Saeima building and passed a resolution on 'the renewal of Independence of the Republic of Latvia'.

A period of instability followed as the Latvian Communist Party endeavoured to take back the helm of government, staging a failed coup in January 1991 in which five people were killed. A plebiscite held in March 1991 resulted in three-quarters of the population voting to secede from the Soviet Union. On 19 and 20 August Soviet troops blocked roads leading to Riga and seized the Interior Ministry building. The Moscow coup failed, however, and on 21 August the Latvian parliament voted to restore independence. On 25 August 1991 Iceland became the first country to recognise the new independent Baltic state, but others soon followed, and by the end of the year the Republic of Latvia had been granted admission to the UN. A new constitution proclaiming Latvia as an independent democratic republic was adopted in 1992. Riga was once more the capital of an independent democratic state.

Since then Riga has made huge efforts to establish itself not only as a vibrant capital of Latvia but also as the major city in the Baltics. Activity at the airport has certainly helped with this aim. Although in terms of size it is the largest of the Baltic capitals, in terms of influence it faces tough competition from the others. Even within Latvia, its trading status is frequently under threat from the port of Ventspils. Major strides have however been made in improving the city. Many buildings have been restored or rebuilt (most notably the Blackheads' House), infrastructure has been improved and the economy expanded. Since the country's accession to NATO and the European Union in 2004, the city has looked forward to consolidating this progress and establishing itself as a major European capital. Although worries about an economic downturn filled the Latvian press in late 2007, visitors in early 2008 saw as much construction activity as at any time since 1991.

SUGGESTED ITINERARIES

DAY ONE The Old Town warrants a day to itself and the two walks described on pages 117 and 121 will take about a day, whilst still allowing time for some visits. Riga Cathedral (page 137) should be one of these as it covers all of Riga's history, and the Barricades Museum (page 130) should be another, given its coverage of the battles that took place in the town in January 1991. The Museum of Decorative and Applied Art (page 131) will then provide a pleasant contrast, showing what the artists of Riga could achieve when left in peace. Finish the day at the National Opera (page 113), having remembered to change clothes first.

DAY TWO The Art Nouveau district (page 122) warrants a full morning to itself, such is the range and number of buildings there that need to be admired. It is now well supplied with cafés so a break is always possible. The walk up five flights to the Jānis Rozentāls and Rūdolfs Blaumanis Memorial Museum (page 136) is well worthwhile for the decoration along the staircase and on the ceiling, and then for the photographs that can be taken from the museum of the buildings on Alberta.

The afternoon can be spent at the Open Air Ethnographic Museum (page 135), seeing how most Latvians lived until the early 20th century. In the summer, return to enjoy the setting sun from either the 26th floor of the Hotel Latvija or the 11th floor of the Hotel Albert. In the winter, enjoy instead the Old Town illuminated.

DAY THREE It seems a pity to suggest leaving Riga after only two days there, but on a tour limited to three days, one should be spent visiting Rundāle Palace (page 149) and its gardens, which shows the Tsarist empire at its best in the 18th and 19th centuries. In the summer, a more leisurely day could instead be spent at Jūrmala (page 148), where any Rigan who could afford it spent their summers in the early 20th century. Take a boat in one direction and a train in the other.

PRACTICALITIES

MONEY AND BANKING

Currency In July 2008, exchange rates were £1 = Ls0.90, US$1 = Ls0.45, and €1 = Ls0.70 – the latter being a fixed rate. See page 3 for further information on the currency.

Changing money You can change money easily: there is a bureau de change at Riga Airport, which is always open for flight arrivals, but slightly better exchange rates are available in the town. The bureaux de change at the railway station and the bus station are open every day, but not late in the evening. Banks are always dependable for reasonable exchange rates. The bureaux de change in the town vary enormously in the rates they offer. Some are more competitive than the banks but others may charge up to 20% commission; rates are consistently poor at Valutas Maina. A nasty trick amongst many exchange bureaux that became prevalent in 2005 and which has continued since was to advertise the selling (*pārdošana*) rates for foreign currencies but not the buying (*pirkšana*) rate. It is therefore always important to check the buying rates before making any commitment. In 2008 the shop Latvijas Balzāms at Vaļņu 21, behind the Riga Hotel, consistently offered good rates and also good prices for alcohol. The exchange bureau there is open seven days a week, 10.00–19.00, but the shop stays open until 22.00.

Try to carry most cash in small change since museum entrance charges are low (usually no more than Ls1), as are most things you are likely to need on a day-to-day basis (drinks, bus fares and so on); large denomination notes are rarely welcome. Therefore when changing money, always ask for Ls5 notes and for coins. As prices are low, avoid changing large sums. Street crime is rare in Latvia, and the atmosphere is generally relaxed. However, you should avoid carrying large sums in cash, and it is wise to leave money and valuables in a hotel safe; carry some cash in a money belt.

LOCAL MEDIA Riga is extremely well provided with up-to-date English-language information for visitors. However, visitors should treat warily the listings magazines often distributed in hotels, of which there are now a large number. In some cases, being totally dependent on advertising, much of it from nightclubs, their coverage of the city is inevitably biased. It is often better to pay the moderate costs for the *Baltic Times, Riga In Your Pocket* and the *City Paper* for a detached view and a much higher standard of writing. Two free magazines, the *Baltic Guide* and *Riga Now*, do however offer several background articles in each issue which are not simply advertorials and which provide a useful update on Riga at the time of publication. (Note that the *Baltic Guide*, despite its title, covers only Riga.) It is worth reading the website for *Riga In Your Pocket* (*www.inyourpocket.com/city/riga*) before arriving, since the whole current edition is published on line.

European editions of British and American newspapers are on sale in Riga at the larger hotels on the day of publication.

Although there are no local radio or television stations that transmit in English, if you have access to FM radio you may be interested in:

96.2	**Radio Naba** A student station playing all types of non-classical music
99.5	**Russkoje Radio** Easy listening Russian channel
100.5	**BBC World Service**
103.7	**Klassika** Classical music
105.2	**Radio SWH** Popular Latvian music

COMMUNICATIONS

Telephones The country code for Latvia, for calls from outside the country, is 371. To call Riga from abroad therefore dial 371, and then the eight-digit number. All landlines throughout the country now start with the figure six, and mobile numbers with the figure two.

To use a public payphone in Riga you need a phonecard (Telekarte). These can be bought at kiosks, stores, post offices, etc, wherever you see the sign Telekarte, and are available for Ls2, 3 or 5. The post office at 1 Stacijas laukums and Plus Punkts kiosks also sell Interkarte, an international prepaid calling card that can also be used with mobile phones (6787 0123; *www.baltia.net*).

Mobile phones Latvians now have more mobile phones than landline ones. To call mobile phones in Riga, just dial the eight-digit code. Contact your service provider before leaving in order to set up international roaming. If your own mobile phone does not operate in Latvia, it is possible to rent one from many shops in the centre of the town or from the better hotels. For further information on telephoning contact Lattelkom (6700 0177; *www.lattelkom.lv*).

Useful telephone numbers

Fire	01	**Directory enquiries**	118 or 117
Police	02	**Tourist information**	6703 7900
Ambulance	03		

Post The most convenient post office (Latvijas Pasts) for most tourists in the Old Town is at Grēcinieku 1 (*www.pasts.lv;* ⊕ *07.00–22.00 Mon–Fri, 09.00–18.00 Sat*). It sells phonecards and postcards, and can help with international calls. Other post offices are at Stacijas laukums (Station Square) and 41–43 Elizabetes. Postage prices are similar to those charged in western Europe, but as they change frequently, they should be checked at a post office on arrival or on the website.

Internet All major hotels have a business centre offering a full range of services including internet access, but the charges are high. Some hotels, such as the Latvia and the Gutenbergs have a computer in reception which guests can use free of charge. An alternative is internet cafés, of which Riga has a generous sprinkling, including the sample listed below. Most offer internet access for Ls0.60–0.80 per hour.

In the Old Town
🖳 **Dualnet Café** 17 Peldu (next to the Ainavas Hotel); ☎ 6781 4440; ⊕ 24hr

🖳 **Planeta** 14 Pils; ☎ 6722 6673; ⊕ 24hr

🖳 **Vecais Kvakers** 10 Kaļķu; ☎ 6750 3594

In the New Town
🖳 **DR Centrs** 75 Elizabetes iela; ☎ 728 2876; ⊕ 09.30–22.00 Mon–Fri, 10.00–21.00 Sat & Sun

🖳 **Ultra LV** 123 Čaka; ☎ 6727 2262

WiFi The number of wireless hotspots in Riga is growing all the time. If your laptop is equipped with a Wireless LAN card, you should be able to go online at all the larger hotels free of charge. The Radisson was one of the first to offer this service, so others quickly followed. By the end of 2007 most cafés in the Old Town were providing this service as well.

EMBASSIES
🄴 **Canada** Baznīcas 20–22; 6781 3945; www.dfait-maeci.gc.ca

🄴 **Germany** Raiņa 13; 6708 5100; e info@riga.diplo.de; www.riga.diplo.de

🄴 **Russia** Antonijas 2; ☎ 6733 2151; e rusembas@delfi.lv; www.Latvia.mid.ru

🄴 **UK** Alunāna 5; ☎ 6777 4700; e british.embassy @apollo.lv; www.Britain.lv

🄴 **US** Raiņa 7; 6703 6200; e 7pas@usembassy.lv; www.usembassy.lv

HOSPITALS AND PHARMACIES
✚ **Hospital** Gaiļezeva; Hipokrāta iela 2

✚ **Dentist** Elladent; Vilandes iela 18; ⊕ 09.00–23.00 Mon–Fri, 09.00–14.00 Sat–Sun

Pharmacy (aptiek)
✚ **Rudens Aptieka** Gertrūdes iela 105; ⊕ 24hr

✚ **Vecpilsētas Aptieka** Audēju iela 20; ⊕ 24hr

✚ **Drogas** Numerous branches across the city.

RELIGIOUS SERVICES The majority of churches are Lutheran, with Orthodox churches coming in second place. Few offer services in languages other than Latvian or Russian. There is currently no mosque in Riga.

✝ **Church of England** St Saviour's, 2a Anglikāņu (service in English 11.00 Sun)

✝ **Lutheran** The Cathedral (Sun 12.00); St John's (08.00, 09.00, 11.00 Sun); and many others.

✝ **Old Believers** Grebenščikova Church, 73 Krasta (services in Church Slavonic at 08.00 & 17.00 Sun)

✝ **Orthodox** Orthodox Cathedral, 23 Brīvības (services in Church Slavonic at 08.00 & 17.00 Mon–Fri, 07.00, 09.30 & 17.00 Sat, & 08.00, 10.00 & 17.00 Sun)

✝ **Roman Catholic** St Jacob's/St James' (page 139), 7 Jāņa (the Roman Catholic Cathedral – service in English 10.00 Sun); Our Lady of Sorrows, Lielā Pils

✝ **Synagogue** 6–8 Peitavas (Hebrew service 09.30 Sat)

TOILETS
Men's toilets are often marked ▼, women's ▲ V (*vīrieši*) or K (*kungi*) are also used for men, and S (*sievietes*) or D (*dāmas*) for women.

TOURIST INFORMATION
If you need detailed information, suggestions for particular trips or other specialist information, the staff at tourist offices will be pleased to help. They can also arrange guides. The main office is located in the Old Town in the Blackheads' House at 7 Rātslaukums (✆ *704 4377;* e *tourinfo@rcc.lv; www.rigatourism.com;* ☉ *10.00–18.00*). Other offices are at the railway and at the bus stations.

Riga In Your Pocket and the *City Paper* have detailed coverage of forthcoming events.

The Riga Card
The Riga Card (*www.rigacard.lv*) provides access without further charge to trams, buses and trains in Riga and Jūrmala, as well as entitling the holder to free admission or a discount at certain museums. It also includes a free walking tour of the Old Town and a free copy of *Riga In Your Pocket*. The card costs Ls10 for 24 hours, Ls12 for 48 hours and Ls16 for 72 hours (half-price for children under 16). It can be purchased from most hotels, the airport (arrivals hall) and tourist information offices. Although it is convenient, most tourists do not spend this amount of money per day if they pay for individual journeys and tickets as they go. It can only be recommended for the days when all museums are open and to those likely to travel quite extensively on public transport.

TRANSPORT

RIGA AIRPORT
The airport (Lidosta Riga) is about 8km from Riga and since 2006 has been subject to a massive expansion and rebuilding programme. That year, and in 2007, it increased its passenger numbers by half a million to reach three million a year and doubtless this rate will continue. In 2008 it will become a serious transit airport between western Europe and the former CIS, perhaps to Asia as well, as Air Baltic launch overnight services to places such as Tbilisi and Tashkent.

The journey from the airport to the centre of Riga should take no more than about 20 minutes by taxi, and about 30 minutes by bus. Allow longer in the rush hour. A taxi from the airport to the capital should cost a maximum of Ls10 and all taxis operating there have to be metered. There is also a bus service, the A22, between the airport and Abrene in the Moscow district with several stops *en route*, including one outside the Avalon Hotel, useful for those staying in the Old Town, and another close to the bus and railway stations. The bus leaves from a stop in front of the terminal slightly to the right and on the far side of the airport car park. In 2007 it ran every 20 minutes from 05.30 to 24.00, but the frequency is likely to be extended in 2008, given the enormous increase in flights now operating from the airport. Buy your ticket (Ls0.40) on board. There is also a charge of Ls0.60 for cases, payable on board.

In January 2008 Air Baltic started a non-stop coach service between the airport and the Hotel Lātvija. It operates every 30 minutes from 05.00 to 24.00 and costs Ls3 per person.

TAXIS
Taxis are plentiful. You can flag them down anywhere in Riga but in the Old Town there are normally several waiting at both ends of Kaļķu, just near the Hotel de Rome and just beyond the Riflemen's Monument. Licensed cabs (these all have yellow licence plates) are fairly reliable provided you check that the meter is on. Rates

are 50 santīmi per kilometre during the day, rising to 70 santīmi per kilometre between 22.00 and 6.00. If you want to save money, avoid using taxis waiting outside hotels, as these tend to charge above average rates. To book a taxi, use one of the following free 24-hour numbers:

🚕 **Bona Taxi** ↘ 800 5050   🚕 **Vudi** ↘ 800 3535
🚕 **Rigas Taksometru parks** ↘ 800 1313

DRIVING IN RIGA

It is best to see Riga on foot. The Old Town is a relatively small area and most places you are likely to want to visit in the New Town are also most easily reached on foot. A car is therefore not much use for short stays in the city. Note too that access to the Old Town is restricted for cars. To enter the Old Town you need a special pass which costs Ls5 per hour, plus an Ls5 deposit. You can buy the pass at Statoil (1c Eksporta) or at Marika Exchange (14 Basteja bulvāris). Note too that on-street parking in the New Town can be hard to find. There are some multi-storey/underground car parks, including 50 K Valdemāra (entrance opposite Antonijas) and the Ģertrūdes Centrs near St Gertrude's Church.

If you do drive, be aware that the maximum speed in Riga is 50km/h, seatbelts are compulsory, you must always drive with headlights on, various on-the-spot fines are imposed for traffic violations, and that road markings, traffic signs and other drivers' behaviour are not always of the same standard you would expect at home.

CAR HIRE

For visiting areas outside Riga a car is useful, although public transport and organised tours are usually available. Car hire is relatively easy to organise but is quite expensive, as it is in the other Baltic countries.

🚕 **Avis** 92 Lāčplēša; ↘ 6722 5876;
e avis@avis.lv; www.avis.lv; Riga Airport ↘ 6720 7353
🚕 **Baltic Car Lease – Sixt franchisee** 28 Kaļķu (Hotel de Rome); ↘ 6722 4022; Riga Airport ↘ 6720 7121; e rent@sixt.lv; www.sixt.lv
🚕 **Budget Rent A Car** Riga Airport; ↘ 6720 7327; e budget@budget.lv; www.budget.lv

🚕 **Easyrent** 52 Daugavpils; ↘ 6919 3198; e office@easyrent.lv; www.easyrent.lv
🚕 **Europcar** 10 Tērbatas; ↘ 6721 2652; e europcar@europcar.lv; www.europcar.lv; Riga Airport ↘ 6720 7825
🚕 **Hertz** 24 Ernestines; ↘ 722 4223; Riga Airport ↘ 6720 7980; www.hertz.lv
🚕 **National Car Rental** Riga Airport ↘ 6720 7710

BUSES AND TRAMS

Riga has a well-developed transport system of eight tram lines, 24 trolleybus lines and 39 bus lines. The fare is the same on all three: Ls0.50 for tickets bought on board, or Ls0.40 for tickets bought in advance at kiosks. Unlike in Tallinn, there is no discount for buying tickets in booklets, and there are no timed tickets for say eight hours or one day. In addition to the bus, tram and trolleybus, there is another form of transport, the *taksobuss* or *mikroautobuss*, which covers longer distances and costs more, depending on the length of the journey.

The maps in *Riga In Your Pocket* and the yellow Jāņa Sēta *Riga* map contain information showing public transport routes. There are no route maps at bus/tram stops or inside the buses and trams, but the driver normally announces the name of the approaching stop and other passengers are generally helpful if you ask for directions.

The bus station (*autoosta*) is in Prāgas, close to the main market and on the other side of the railway station (under the bridge) away from the city centre. You can telephone for information (↘ 900 0009), but may find it advisable to attend in person. Timetables are on display; otherwise apply to window 1 for information. Some ticket sellers also speak English. The convenient self-service cafeteria on the first floor here is excellent value for both snacks and hot meals. Next to it is a small hotel which sells rooms for about Ls30 a night. Probably of more use to passing travellers could be the showers here which cost Ls2.50 to use, including soap and a towel.

TRAINS Riga has a modern railway station (*Stacijas laukums;* \ *6723 1181*), where trains are an increasing irrelevance. It is an enormous specialist shopping centre; one outlet sells 30 different swords, another 50 different teas. Of most interest to passing foreigners will be Sopranos, the ice-cream shop, with probably about 30–40 different varieties to choose from. Whilst its ice creams are not particularly cheap (a cornet costs around Ls1), they do tea or coffee for Ls0.25, a price now unheard of elsewhere in Riga.

Trains come in ones and twos rather than in 40 different varieties. For those who insist on tracking them down, look for the Biļešu kases, or ticket offices, where most staff speak English. Counters 7–12 sell tickets for local trains. Fares are cheaper when tickets are bought here rather than on the train itself. The timetables show the track (*ceļš*) the train leaves from. When you go to your train, you will also see the word *perons* (platform) with a number. Ignore this and look for the right track. Timetables and other information are available in English on the Latvian Railways website (*www.ldz.lv*).

For changing money at the station, the **Hansabank** (⊕ *08.00–20.00 daily*) offers good rates. As elsewhere in Riga, avoid the exchange bureau Valutas Maina, where rates are poor.

TOUR BUSES A number of firms offer city tours by coach. It is probably best to organise these through your hotel if you are staying in one that offers this facility. Otherwise you can contact one of the agencies below:

Latvia Tours 8 Kaļķu; \ 6708 5057, & 13 Marijas; \ 6724 3391; www.latviatours.lv. A dependable operator since 1991, this does city tours May–Sep 10.00–13.00 Mon & Sat; It also offers regular trips to the Open Air Museum (see page 135) & Motor Museum (see page 133), Rundāle (see page 149), & Sigulda, & trips to Cēsis, Jūrmala & Liepaja can also be arranged.
Riga Out There Hospitalu 8–49; \ 6735 0227; e info@rigaoutthere.com. A joint British–Latvian company giving an unusual edge to tourism in Riga & throughout Latvia. British tourists can phone them in London on \ 020 8123 2077.

Riga Sightseeing Amber Way Stabu 19–206; \ 6727 1915; e info@sightseeing.lv; www.sightseeing.lv. Daily departures from the Opera House & individual sightseeing around Latvia & the Baltic countries. Walking tours as well as tours by bus.
Balticgen m 2641 6972; e aleksgen@balticgen.com; www.balticgen.com. Specialises in tours for groups & individuals interested in Jewish history who want to combine a specialist itinerary in this field with general visits.

BOATS In summer you can take boat trips on the Daugava departing from 11. Novembra krastmala, close to Akmens Bridge. Departures are at 11.00, 13.00, 15.00, 17.00 and 19.00, and each trip lasts an hour. A longer trip to Mežaparks and back takes about two hours and costs Ls2. It is possible to take this trip one-way and then to return by tram (\ 6953 9184). There is no convenient website with details of the services so it is best to check first at the pier or at the tourist office.

CYCLING Sharing Riga's roads with their notoriously aggressive car drivers is only an activity for the brave, although a growing number of people seem to be cycling in areas away from the city centre. If you do want to hire a bike you can do so from:

☏ Gandrs 28 Kalnciema; \ 6761 4775; e gandrs@gandrslv; www.gandrs.lv (in Pārdaugava; cross the Vanšu Bridge on foot or take bus number

22). Bikes costs Ls1 per hour or Ls5 for the day, plus a deposit of Ls20.

Riga offers a wide choice of accommodation. If money is no object, you can choose from an ever-growing number of luxury hotels, many conveniently situated in the Old Town. For budget travellers there are some very acceptable options, too: some of these are located away from the centre but most are on tram routes, which makes getting into the Old Town an easy and relatively quick matter.

Hotel building started on a large scale in 2005 and continued until spring 2008. Despite inflation in many other fields, this is likely to lead to lower hotel rates for several years ahead, particularly in winter. The price codes given below should be taken only as an indication of what visitors may end up paying. Hotels give much lower rates to tour operators who support them regularly and to those who book early. Last-minute bargains are rare in Riga. In newer hotels air conditioning can be taken for granted. It is rarely needed, but on Riga's few really hot days during the summer, it is a great asset. Free-of-charge WiFi access can also be taken for granted in most four–five-star hotels and in many three-star ones too. Riga has become very successful at hosting large conferences and when these take place, hotel rates of course increase.

An alternative to staying in Riga, particularly in summer, is to book a hotel in nearby Jūrmala, Riga's seaside resort. Jūrmala is about 20 minutes from Riga by car and about 40 minutes by train (see page 148). Jūrmala has some attractive and recently restored small hotels, as well as larger hotels with views over the Gulf of Riga. However, if you have only a few days in Riga, you probably won't want to travel backwards and forwards every day. Other possibilities are to stay in Bauska, Jelgava or Sigulda, all about an hour from Riga but pleasant towns in their own right, too.

At the time of writing there was no tourist information service at the airport, although there are plenty of telephones if you want to find a hotel yourself before going into town. Prices of Riga hotels are often quoted in euros on websites and in brochures but you will always need to make payment in lats. The rates quoted by hotels always include a buffet breakfast and VAT, unless otherwise specified.

All the quality hotels take credit cards. In practice, there tends to be little difference between prices for single rooms and prices for doubles, and single travellers will often be given a double room anyway.

LUXURY $$$$

⌂ **Hotel Bergs** (38 apartments) In the Berga Bazārs, 83–85 Elizabetes; ☏ 6777 0900; e reservation@hotelbergs.lv; www.hotelbergs.lv. The Hotel Bergs is in the Berga Bazārs shopping area on the edge of the New Town. The hotel & surrounding area is named after the Bergs family who lived in Riga before World War II & whose descendants now run the hotel. The monumental exterior is in contrast to the subtler interior décor. Most of the apartments have kitchenettes; all are spacious & tastefully decorated. The hotel is suitable for tourists, many of whom will also enjoy the handmade chocolates & other exclusive products on sale in the adjoining shopping area, but it also has some of Riga's most comprehensive business facilities, as well as an elegant & acclaimed restaurant.
$$$$

⌂ **Europa Royal** (60 rooms) Kr Barona 12; ☏ 6707 9444; e riga@europaroyale.com;

www.europaroyale.com. After years of uncertainty, this hotel finally opened in 2006 in a building as interesting for its political history as for its architecture. In 1919 the occupying German army used what is now the car park as an execution ground. It was a newspaper publishing house between the World Wars, with an interior designed by one of the most famous architects of the time, Eižens Laube. His quarrels with the owners were so bitter that Laube continued to write about them in exile in the US until his death there in 1967. In the 1980s the building housed the Latvian Writers' Union, a major force behind the burgeoning independence movement. Its opening has been delayed for so long to ensure that as much of the late 19th-century Renaissance exterior is preserved as possible. Rooms at the front are grander but noisier because of the constant traffic on Barona;

those at the back are quieter but much smaller. The Europa group also run two similar hotels in Lithuania, one near the Gates of Dawn in Vilnius & the other in Klaipeda. $$$

⌂ **Grand Palace Hotel** (56 rooms) 12 Pils; ☎ 704 4000; e grandpalace@schlossle-hotels.com; www.schlossle-hotels.com. Superbly located near the cathedral, this luxury hotel opened in 2001 & is probably the most expensive in the Old Town. Although the building is old, the hotel has all modern facilities, including a fitness centre, sauna & steam room. Each room has a gold, white & blue decorative scheme & antique-style furniture but also satellite TV & internet access. There are 2 restaurants, the light & airy Orangerie & the velvet-curtained Seasons. Considerable price reductions are usually available here in Jul & Aug, when loyal business customers are away. $$$$$

⌂ **Hotel de Rome** (90 rooms) 28 Kaļķu; ☎ 708 7600; e reservation@derome.lv; www.derome.lv. At the edge of the Old Town, this German-run 4-star hotel is one of the best in Riga. The location, overlooking the Freedom Monument & surrounding parks – of which there is a terrific view from the restaurant – on the edge of the Old Town but within easy reach of the New, is ideal for the tourist. But it is also within easy reach of all the government offices, ministries & many company headquarters, so is suitable for anyone visiting Riga on business. The standard of accommodation & of the common parts is high. The German Otto Schwarz restaurant offers an excellent b/fast & first-class meals at other times of day. Latvian politicians come & go rapidly, but whoever is in power always eats here. Tourists who would like to enjoy its view towards the

FIRST CLASS $$$–$$$$

⌂ **Ainavas** (22 rooms) Peldu 23; ☎ 6781 4316; e reservations@ainavas.lv; www.ainavas.lv. In this hotel, opened in 2001, each room has a different colour scheme & décor based on the browns or greens of Latvia's countryside ('*ainavas*' means landscape). The tone is set in the lobby bar, which is decorated with wood & flowers & where a welcoming fire burns in the hearth. Located in a quiet street in the south of the Old Town, the hotel is suitable for both tourists & businesspeople: each room has a TV with email connection & a dataport. $$$$

⌂ **Bellevue** (112 rooms) Raina bd 33; ☎ 6706 3400; e bellevue@nordichotels.eu; www.nordichotels.eu. Opened in March 2008, this hotel is on an appropriate site, as the original hotel with this name opened here in the 1870s. The architect, Jānis Baumanis, was responsible for many of the buildings in the immediate vicinity & can perhaps be described as Riga's most prolific

Freedom Monument should take advantage of the lower meal prices offered at lunchtime. $$$$

⌂ **Reval Hotel Ridzene** (95 rooms) 1 Reimersa; ☎ 732 4433; e ridzene@revalhotels.com; www.revalhotels.com. Formerly a Soviet hotel, the Ridzene has been elegantly refurbished several times since independence & is now part of the Reval group. It is located opposite the Esplanade Park in the New Town, & beside the American Embassy, which probably makes it the safest address in Riga. From the sauna you can enjoy superb views over the New Town. The Piramida restaurant in the glass pyramid is amongst the best in Riga. $$$

⌂ **Radisson SAS Daugava Hotel** (361 rooms) 24 Kuģu; ☎ 706 1111; e info.riga@radissonsas.com; www.radissonsas.com. The Radisson is very much a business hotel – one of the leading business hotels in the Baltics. It is a rather unimaginative white block of a building & is on 'the wrong side' of the Daugava away from the main part of the city, but is quiet & has good views over the river. It is an international-standard establishment with both rooms & suites, including 2 floors of 'business-class' rooms which have their own lounge for drinks & are fully equipped for business needs, including 2 telephone lines for internet access. There is security parking, 24hr room service & cable TV. With 10 air-conditioned conference rooms the hotel can lay on conferences for up to 360 delegates. A business service offers translation, secretarial & other commercial services. The Grill Room restaurant is highly recommended. There is a modern fitness centre, sauna, swimming pool & shops. It offers free transfers from the airport, albeit at fixed times, & an hourly shuttle bus to the Old Town. $$$$

architect. He was without doubt the first famous one of ethnic Latvian origin, resisting attempts by his father to use the German name Baumann. $$$$

⌂ **Centra Hotel** (27 rooms) Audēju 1; ☎ 6722 6441; e hotel@centra.lv; www.centra.lv. The hotel opened in 2000 & is wonderfully situated near St Peter's. It is decorated in a minimalist style with furniture & fabrics which all come from Latvia. Although the area nearby can be noisy at night over the w/end, being the centre for stag parties, the rooms are well soundproofed. Rooms on the higher floors offer unusual views of the Old Town. The hotel is excellent value, with rooms at prices below those in similar hotels in the same area. $$$

⌂ **Domina Inn Riga** (100 rooms) Pulkveža Brieža 11; ☎ 6763 1800; e info@dominahotels.lv; www.dominahotels.com. Near Albert, & close to several museums, this hotel clearly set a trend when it opened here in 2005 as several others have since opened nearby. With standard rooms & little sense of design anywhere, it is clearly planned for groups, but AC & under-floor heating in the bathrooms add a welcome luxury touch. Domina, an Italian company, already run 2 successful hotels in Tallinn & hopefully the artistic taste shown there will soon spread south. $$$

⌂ **Garden Palace** (66 rooms) Grēcinieku 28; ✆ 6722 4650; e info@hotelgardenpalace.lv; www.hotelgardenpalace.lv. One of many hotels that opened in 2007, but few can match its location on Town Hall Square or the antique furnishings that it has managed to acquire, even including tiled stoves that would seem to belong to Rundāle Palace. Its rooms are surprisingly large for an Old Town building, as is its lobby. It is fortunately just outside the area frequented by stag groups so can be recommended all week. $$$

⌂ **Hotel Gutenbergs** (38 rooms) Doma laukums 1; ✆ 6721 1776; e hotel@gutenbergs.lv; www.gutenbergs.lv. Located in one of the Baltic countries' first publishing houses, hence the name, in a quiet street next to the cathedral, this hotel has proved very popular since its opening in 2001, & often needs to be booked well in advance. It consists of 2 connected 4-storey buildings, one built in the 17th century & one in the 19th, & has a rich, 19th-century décor throughout. Walk along every corridor to see the exhibits brought together from 19th-century Riga. An attraction in summer (which the hotel thinks begins in April) is the rooftop terrace, where you can eat, drink & count the 17 churches visible from this wonderful vantage point. It is completely covered, so do not be deterred by rain from visiting it. Avoid the small ground-floor sgl rooms in the summer & at w/ends, since they overlook a rowdy bar on the other side of the road. $$$

⌂ **Islande** (205 rooms) Ķīpsalas 20; ✆ 6760 8000; e reception@islandehotel.lv; www.islandehotel.lv. Opening on Ķīpsala Island was a brave decision in 2006 but with each passing year it makes more sense. The Exhibition Centre is close by & in the rush hour, walking over the bridge over the Daugava River is quicker than attempting to drive. Wandering amongst the wooden houses nearby is a peaceful alternative to more conventional sightseeing in the town centre; another is looking at all the pictures of Iceland displayed in the corridors. Being on the route to the airport is another bonus. The hotel structure takes advantage of its location with a large lobby, ample parking space & bigger rooms than is usual in the price range. Fit visitors can take advantage of the bowling alley & the gym, both free of charge to guests. There is also a wide range of spa treatments offered.

The 9th-floor restaurant is a good vantage point for viewing Riga at its best (the Old Town) & at its worst (beside the harbour). As an alternative, the hotel also has a restaurant on the ground floor, called as might be expected, The Iceland. $$$

⌂ **Konventenhof** or **Konventa Sēta** (80 rooms, 61 apartments) Kalēju 9–11; ✆ 6708 7501–5; e reservation@konventa.lv; www.konventa.lv. The Konventa Sēta stands out from other hotels in Old Riga in that it is housed on the site of the old city walls in a complex of restored buildings, some dating back to the 13th century; guests can look at the covered foundations. The complex includes a good restaurant, Raibais Balodis, & a bar, Melnais Balodis. Although the hotel's position next to St John's Church could hardly be more central, on occasions it can be noisy at night on the Kalēju side. $$$

⌂ **Maritim Park** (240 rooms) Slokas 1; ✆ 6706 9000; e info.rig@maritim.lv; www.maritim.lv. A large hotel across the river from the Old Town. The location may put off some people, but it is quiet & you can reach the Old Town in about half an hour on foot or by taking tram number 2, 4 or 5. On the positive side, the rooms & the Bellevue restaurant on the 11th floor have wonderful views of the Old Town. If walking into town isn't enough exercise, you can use the hotel's gym. Incidentals are quite pricy, perhaps taking advantage of the fact that there are few cafés or shops in the immediate vicinity. $$$

⌂ **Metropole** (80 rooms) Aspāzijas bulvāris 36–38; ✆ 6722 5411; e metropole@brovi.lv; www.metropole.lv. The Metropole is suitable for both tourists & business travellers. Built in 1871 it is the oldest hotel in Riga & has been completely refurbished in an attractive Scandinavian style. It is conveniently located on the edge of the Old Town & only a short walk away from the New Town. All rooms are equipped with satellite phone & cable TV but rooms at the front are still rather noisy. $$$

⌂ **Monika** (80 rooms) Elizabetes 21; ✆ 6703 1900; f 703 1901; e monika@centrumhotels.com; www.centrumhotels.com. This 4-star hotel was opened in January 2006 by the Lithuanian Centrum group, who run the Artis & Ratonda hotels in Vilnius. As with the Artis, a solid 19th-century building has been taken over & the interior completely modernised. This building is one of the early works of Edmund von Trompowsky (1851–1918), probably Riga's most prolific eclectic architect from that time. Several of his other works are within walking distance of the hotel. The restaurant Sokrats is decorated with quotations, & not only from Socrates, which ensures a sedate air missing in so many Riga restaurants. Many of the rooms have a bath, &

some have a balcony offering views across Elizabetes to Kronvalda Park. Sgls however are small. All have AC. $$$$

🏠 **Reval Hotel Lātvija** (600 rooms) Elizabetes 55; ☎ 6777 2222; e latvija.sales@revalhotels.com; www.revalhotels.com. This was the hotel in which Intourist put up its customers in the days of the USSR, but it was totally renovated & reopened in 2001 as a high-quality international-style hotel. It was closed in 2005 for further renovation & for the building of an extension & conference centre. When it opened again in 2006, it was with the aim of being *the* Baltics venue for major conferences & in this it has undoubtedly succeeded. Two advantages are its location in the New Town but just 5mins from the Old Town, & the views from its upper storeys, its 2 glass-sided lifts & the Skyline Bar on the 26th floor. All rooms include satellite TV with games & email possibilities, & minibars with drinks, chocolate & condoms. Underground parking is available, & on the 27th floor there is a sports & leisure club, equipped with a weight room & sauna. $$$

🏠 **Riga Hotel** (280 rooms) Aspāzijas bulvāris 22; ☎ 6704 4222; e info@hotelriga.lv; www.hotelriga.com. On the edge of the Old Town, directly opposite the Opera House, the Riga is one of the largest & oldest hotels in central Riga. Fully refurbished in 2002–03, all the rooms are pleasantly decorated & spacious. Some have internet dataports. The hotel offers a sauna, bar, conference facilities & a casino. To see what the staff got up to before 1991, visit the Occupation Museum which displays the bugging devices they used to monitor phone calls. More recently, the hotel was used in the TV series *Archangel*, starring Daniel Craig. $$$

🏠 **Vecrīga** (14 rooms) Gleznotāju 12–14; ☎ 6721 6037; e vecriga@vecriga.lv; www.vecriga.lv. A small hotel in a renovated 18th-century house in what is now a rarity, a quiet street in the Old Town, next to the Palete restaurant. Some parts of the building even date from the 15th century. Spacious bedrooms are fitted out with comfortable antique-style furniture, although the bathrooms tend to be small. The hotel has an intimate atmosphere but all modern facilities, & an elegant restaurant. $$$

TOURIST CLASS $$

🏠 **Albert** (250 rooms) Dzirnavu 33; ☎ 6733 1717; e info@alberthotel.lv; www.alberthotel.lv. This 11-storey hotel opened in December 2005. Do not be deterred by the stark exterior. The inside is well designed & full of references to Albert Einstein. The Bestsellers restaurant is in fact lined by books: hardly in the Einstein category, but which add an unexpected intellectual air. All rooms have AC & many enjoy good views towards the Old Town. Its Star Lounge bar on the top floor will clearly aim to compete with that at the Reval Lātvija for offering the best Old Town view. Tourists interested in Art Nouveau will appreciate the location close to Albert. $$

🏠 **Avalon** (111 rooms) Kalēju 70; ☎ 6716 9999; e reservations@avalon.eu; www.hotelavalon.eu. One of several hotels to open in summer 2007, it had no difficulty in quickly finding groups to fill it. Its location is practical rather than aesthetic, overlooking the busy road 13. Janvāra & the railway, but this does mean the airport bus stops outside the entrance & both the bus & railway stations are within walking distance. Excellent soundproofing keeps out the inevitable noise. The back overlooks the Old Town & some rooms on the higher floors have good views. Being a new building, all rooms have AC, & many have baths. Seven rooms overlook the atrium so do not have outside windows. The large entrance foyer, the good number of lifts & the pull-in for buses & taxis directly in front of the hotel are all very welcoming, particularly for groups. $$

🏠 **City Hotel Bruņinieks** (The Knight) (70 rooms) Bruņinieku 6; ☎ 6731 5140; e info@cityhotel.lv. Originally known just as Bruņinieks, the hotel changed its name to City in 2003 as no foreigner could pronounce the name. A suit of armour is displayed in the foyer, but otherwise this is a perfectly normal 3-star hotel. The façade is 1905, & has rightly been left as such, but renovation regularly takes place indoors. Some may find the location near the theatre of help & it is sufficiently far from the town centre for the neighbouring shops all to offer Latvian rather than Western prices & for peace & quiet to be assured in the evenings. The hotel caters in particular for families, with adjoining rooms available & – for those with smaller children – trpl rooms with a roll-up bed. Being just off Brīvības, the main road leading to the Freedom Monument, the hotel has a wide range of buses within walking distance. $$

🏠 **Europa City** (150 rooms) Brīvības 199; ☎ 6716 6000; e riga@europacity.lv; www.europacity.lv. As with the Vilnius Hotel in the same group, the location is dreary but in this case it is at least convenient. Being on 2 tram routes into the centre gives a guaranteed & regular service taking 15mins each way. Brīvības is the main road to the north so is constantly busy with traffic, but the hotel is well soundproofed. However there is the advantage that a lot of time is saved when leaving for or arriving from Tallinn as most of the Riga traffic is avoided. Businesses are beginning to move to this area, so shops & cafés are following suit. The view from the top-floor restaurant will become more attractive each year. $$

⌂ **Forums** (32 rooms) Vaļņu 45; ✎ 6781 4680; e reservation@hotelforums.lv; www.hotelforums.lv. On the edge of the Old Town, near the train station, the hotel has large rooms, with a bath & satellite TV. Despite the modest 19th century exterior, it offers elegantly decorated accommodation. Some of the rooms on the upper floors have good views. Expect most other visitors to be Russian. B/fast is served, but there is no bar or restaurant, so evenings are quiet. $$

⌂ **Hanza** (80 rooms) Elijas 7; ✎ 6779 6040; e reservations@hanzahotel.lv; www.hanzahotel.lv. In the 1990s it would have seemed like madness to open a hotel in the Moskva district, such was its reputation for crime & decay. By 2007, when the Hanza opened, the turnaround was nearly complete & gentrification is hurriedly under way. As neighbours the hotel has the Jesus Church & the Belarussian Embassy, so little risk of any wild Saturday nights here. The market, bus & railway station are each about 10 mins' walk away; closer are the Academy of Science, with its roof-top views, & the airport bus, about 400m from the hotel. A wide lobby & 2 large lifts ensure that check-in, even for groups, is very quick. Most rooms have good views towards the river, but are wisely provided with thick wooden shutters, rather than curtains to keep out the bright light on summer mornings. $$

⌂ **Kolonna** Tirgoņu 9 (40 rooms) ✎ 6735 8254; e reservationriga@kolonna.com; www.hotelkolonna.com. When this hotel opened in the Old Town in 2005, it seemed surprising that it had not done so 10 years earlier. It fills a need for a tourist-class hotel right in the centre & the 18th-century woodwork left intact in many rooms is an added bonus. It is well worth paying extra for rooms on the 6th floor which have AC & views. Good soundproofing offers protection from liveliness outside. The Kolonna group runs similar hotels in 5 other Latvian towns. $$

⌂ **Laine Hotel** (28 rooms) 11 Skolas; ✎ 6728 8816 or 728 9823; e info@laine.lv; www.laine.lv. In the 1990s, this was hardly more than a hostel so return visitors are now greatly surprised at the transformation since then. The entrance through a dismal courtyard has not changed, but all the facilities within certainly have done, AC & a terrace being the latest additions in 2007 & bathrooms down the corridor long gone. $$

⌂ **Best Western Hotel Mara** (24 rooms) Kalnciema 186; ✎ 6770 2710;

e hotel@hotelmara.lv; www.hotelmara.lv. With so many flights now arriving late in Riga or leaving early, a quiet hotel near the airport has considerable appeal, particularly to those who do not need to travel in or out of town during the rush hour. The hotel has its own shuttle bus to the airport & the local town bus stops nearby. A large patio offers added appeal during the summer & the low prices will for many be an added incentive for not staying further in. $$

⌂ **OK Hotel** (34 rooms) Slokas 12; ✎ 6786 0050; e service@okhotel.lv; www.okhotel.lv. The OK opened in 2001 & is modest but good value. Rooms are adequately furnished & include telephone & cable TV. The disadvantage is its location, over the river from the Old Town. On the other hand, it does have a garden & open-air bar. The restaurant has AC but the rooms do not. It is a 30min walk from the Old Town, but the hotel can also be reached quickly by taking tram no 4 or 5 from the Grēcinieku stop to the Kalnciema stop, just over the river. $$

⌂ **Radi un Draugi** (Relatives & Friends) (76 rooms) Mārstaļu 1–3; ✎ 782 0200; e radi.reservations@draugi.lv; www.draugi.lv. This hotel, right in the centre of the Old Town, is comfortable & affordable, as well as being in a superb location. It is used extensively by the British-Latvian community when they return 'home'. The British link is shown in the tea- & coffee-making equipment provided in each room. Recently modernised & extended, the hotel has only 1 major drawback, its location on Grēcinieku, the street most popular with stag groups, so insufferable at w/ends to anybody else. On Mon to Thu nights, whilst not completely stag-free, others can enjoy themselves in the vicinity. $$

⌂ **Tia** (50 rooms) Kr Valdemāra 63; ✎ 6733 3918; e tia@tia.lv; www.hoteltia.lv. A clean, basic but comfortable hotel near the centre, about 15mins' walk to the Old Town but on the doorstop of a wide range of Art Nouveau architecture. $$

⌂ **Valdemārs** (85 rooms) Kr Valdemāra 23; ✎ 6733 4462; e reservations@valdemars.lv; www.valdemars.lv. This hotel was completely renovated during 2005 & upgraded from a hostel to a serious hotel, although its elegant, centrally located Art Nouveau façade, dating from 1901, makes it look grander than it really is. It is now the centre for the Scandinavian community in Riga as its owners spent the Soviet period in exile in Sweden. $$

✖ EATING AND DRINKING

Riga has certainly been an international city for cuisine since at least 2000. In both the Old Town and the New Town Japanese and Chinese restaurants compete for custom with Italian, Russian, Ukrainian and, of course, Latvian restaurants. As renovation spreads to the New Town, so restaurants follow. Tourist traps are few and obvious to anyone remotely sober. Whilst many prices increased by 10% during 2007, restaurants and cafés had to be careful to keep their clientele, so often had to absorb increases they were paying for food and salaries. It is reassuring that most of the restaurants recommended in this book's predecessor, *Baltic Capitals*, are still here and that others can be added. Cafés and bars inevitably have a more precarious existence but their numbers ensure that this does not matter too much.

Wine is widely available in restaurants but is imported and therefore not cheap. Beer is good quality and good value for money. Local spirits are of course also much cheaper than imported ones.

In general you don't need to book in advance, although if you want to make absolutely certain of a table in a particular restaurant at peak times you could do so. Menus are nearly always available in English, so don't be afraid to ask if one doesn't appear automatically. Prices given below provide a rough indication of what you can expect to pay for a three-course meal excluding wine. Latvian cuisine, if eaten regularly, is not for the weight-conscious. Once or twice on a weekend trip to Riga, however, it is an enjoyable and fun thing to try. Restaurants are open from at least 12.00 until 23.00, and many stay open until midnight.

RESTAURANTS

✗ **1739** Skārņu 6; ✆ 6721 1398; www.hbv.lv/1739/. Quiet is very rare in the Old Town, but upstairs here it is assured, except on Fri when live music intrudes. The restaurant is named after the date of the building. It is best known for its extensive Italian menu & for the fact that vegetarians are offered more than 1 dish. Some Latvian food is available too. Unusually for Riga, a cheaper menu is available at lunchtime. Prices however remain reasonable, & for wine too, during the evening. Ls18.

✗ **Arbat** (named after an area in Moscow) Vāgnera 3; ✆ 6721 4056. This is probably the most upmarket Russian restaurant in Riga, although the prices, for the quality of the food, are not at all unreasonable. Caviar, sturgeon & vodka feature prominently on the menu & blend well with the richly ornate interior. The dishes are attractively presented by staff who are unusually keen to please. If you have always wanted to know what it would feel like to be a character in *War and Peace*, a visit here will help you imagine it. Ls40.

✗ **Bellevue Maritim Park Hotel** Slokas 1, ✆ 6706 9000; www.maritim.com. The 11th-floor restaurant looks out over the river onto the Old Town & is an ideal place for a sunset dinner in summer. The menu changes every month, so it is difficult to make recommendations. Fish & seafood are often among the highlights, & there are frequently local game dishes, too. The décor, like everything else in this hotel, is modern, airy & elegant. Ls40.

✗ **Bergs Hotel Bergs** in Berga Bazārs, Elizabetes 83–85; ✆ 6777 0957; www.hotelbergs.lv. Since the opening of the hotel, this restaurant has established itself as one of the best places to eat in Riga. The atmosphere is relaxed & the food includes a wide range of original dishes. The chef used to work at Vincents restaurant, where he achieved the high recognition he has now brought to Bergs. The Bergs serves lunch & dinner, & a b/fast buffet from 07.00–11.00; in the afternoon you can drop in for tea & cakes on the terrace. Ls35.

✗ **La Boheme** Alunāna iele 2a; ✆ 6732 1938; www.laboheme.lv. This restaurant is run by Via Hansa, one of the most successful local tour operators, so the expected mix of professionalism & commercial success is immediately evident. Being opposite the British Embassy, Angus beef is one of the regular highlights of the menu, but as the chef has come from Vincents, their menu is similarly wide & they clearly expect to woo Vincents' normally very loyal clientele. Prices are lower & La Boheme has no celebrity obsessions so quite a range of normal people eat here. The liberal use of alcohol in the cooking is most welcome. Jerusalem artichokes are amongst the more unusual vegetables served. Ls25.

✗ **Da Sergio** Tērbatas 65 (entrance from Matīsa); ✆ 6731 2777; www.dasergio.lv. A very Italian Italian restaurant, with a chef from Venice, many ingredients imported directly from Italy, Italian music & Italian food & wine. The atmosphere is warm & welcoming & puts you in the mood to enjoy everything from the bread, baked daily on the premises, to the excellent desserts, via an interesting range of pizza, pasta, meat & fish main courses. Prices are very accessible. Ls18.

✗ **Dzirnavas** (The Mill) Dzirnavu 76; ✆ 6728 6204; www.lido.lv. One of the most popular of Riga's restaurants among locals, this Latvian farmhouse-style restaurant is not the place for a quiet tête-à-tête. The service is buffet style: choose from a vast array of food laid out in several rooms, take it back to your table, across the stream in the centre, & enjoy it to the strains of Latvian country music. The food is decent, the atmosphere fun, & the prices very affordable. If you want a quick initiation into Latvian food & at the same time to observe local life, this is a good place to start. Ls8.

✕ **Fabrikas** Balasta dambis 70; ✆ 6787 3804. After its opening in summer 2006, Fabrikas' publicity machine stayed in top gear well into 2007, partly as so few other places opened that year. If it does not quite deserve all the accolades the freebie magazines showered on it, it can certainly be recommended, above all for its quirky location in a former factory, which has given it its name. It is on Ķīpsala Island, beside the river & opposite the ferry terminal. It takes about 10mins to walk from the Exhibition Centre & about 15mins from the Islande Hotel & so from the nearest bus stop. Many descriptions claim that it offers views of the Old Town, but from most tables it is the harbour, a Soviet tower block & abandoned warehouses that will be seen. It is however surrounded by wooden buildings which have now mostly been restored as the area is becoming an elegant residential district. Most main dishes are Thai or Chinese, but with a 7-page menu of hors d'oeuvres it is possible to make up a full meal from any nationality. At Ls20–50 a bottle, wine is absurdly expensive, but beer is cheap at Ls3 for half a litre. Ls15.

✕ **Honkonga** 61 Valdemāra 61; ✆ 6781 2292. What a relief to find a Chinese restaurant in the Baltics where what you see is what you get. The ambience is straightforward but the cooking more elaborate. It is clear that Chinese are in control of the whole operation & are catering for their colleagues; if others wish to come, they are welcome to have a meal that makes no concessions to so-called Western tastes. Ls13.

✕ **Indian Raja** Vecpilsētas 3; ✆ 6721 2614; www.indianraja.lv. This is one of Riga's few Indian restaurants, but would be likely to be one of the best even if it had lots more competitors. The food is authentically Indian & includes tandoori & tikka dishes as well as curries. Thai dishes are also available. The camel images that feature on the door are possibly a reference to the fact that Indian spices, transported by camel on part of their journey, used to be stored in a warehouse here. Prices are not low, but the quality of food & service is worth paying for. There is also a branch of the restaurant in Jūrmala. Ls12.

✕ **Kamāla** Jauniela 14; ✆ 6721 1332. An Indian ambience suffuses the restaurant: you'll notice the incense before you enter, & once inside, the colourful table & wall decorations will transport you beyond Riga, partly because the restaurant is vegetarian, still a very un-Latvian concept. The menu too features Indian food fairly strongly, but a range of other dishes is also available. Recommendations are difficult as the menu changes from day to day but you will always find a number of very appealing, & rather different, options, including perhaps tofu shashlik (bean-curd kebab). Ls13.

✕ **Krievu Sēta/Russkij Dvor** (The Russian Courtyard) 3 Ķengaraga; ✆ 6713 4930; www.lido.lv. This is the Russian equivalent of the Latvian-food Lido restaurant, & owned by the same group. A huge building in an unfashionable part of the city, off Maskavas (Moscow St), the interior resembles a theme park, with its painted wood & traditional matroshka dolls. Like the Lido it offers a self-service restaurant with a massive choice of dishes & a recreational area outside. The food includes Russian favourites such as borscht, blini, solyanka & pork, all at low prices. Tram no 7 or 9 from opposite the Opera will take you there. Alight at the Ķengaraga stop. Ls7.

✕ **Lido Atpūtas Centrs** (Lido Recreation Centre) Krasta 76; ✆ 6750 4420; www.lido.lv. This is undoubtedly one of Riga's recent success stories in the restaurant world. To take over an out-of-town estate rather than a house, in an area barely accessible by public transport, required considerable daring but the gamble has paid off as the crowded car park proves every evening. Family groups are the main target, as large play areas are available, & service is cafeteria-style with trays along the counter. More & more foreigners are now coming, too; they enjoy, as the Latvians do, the space, the light & the wooden tables, not to mention the variety & quality of food available in the bistro, express restaurant or beer cellar with its own micro-brewery. They enjoy the broad clientele, too; Latvia mixes here in a way it hardly does elsewhere, except in other restaurants run by this chain. The centre also has the largest skating rink in the Baltics. To get there take tram 7 or 9 to the Dzērvju stop. It's then a 10min walk towards the windmill. Alternatively take a short taxi ride (Ls5–6). Ls9.

✕ **Livonija** 21 Meistaru; ✆ 6722 7824. There are few restaurants in Riga where an identical review could be written year after year. For the Livonija, this is the case & it has always been positive. Nothing changes, & why should it? A broad international menu, with a wine list to match, is offered, although there is a good choice of Latvian dishes. Acclaimed dishes include local venison, pork knuckle, smoked eel & lamprey. The service remains unobtrusive & the Art Nouveau chairs will

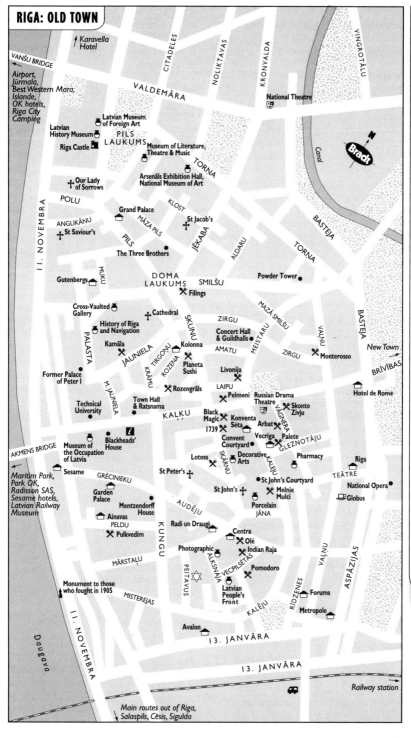

RIGA: OLD TOWN

VANŠU BRIDGE

↑ Karavella Hotel

Airport,
Jūrmala,
Best Western Mara,
Islande,
OK hotels,
Riga City
Camping

CITADELES

NOLIKTAVAS

KRONVALDA

VINGROTĀLU

VALDEMĀRA

National Theatre

Canal

Latvian Museum
of Foreign Art

Latvian
History Museum
Riga Castle

PILS
LAUKUMS

Museum of Literature,
Theatre & Music

TORNA

Arsenāls Exhibition Hall,
National Museum of Art

† Our Lady
of Sorrows

POLU

KLOST

Grand Palace

St Jacob's

ANGLIKĀNU

MĀŽA PILS

JĒKABA

ALDARU

TORNA

BASTEJA

† St Saviour's

PILS

The Three Brothers

11. NOVEMBRA

MUKU

Gutenbergs

DOMA
LAUKUMS

SMILŠU

Powder Tower ●

Cross-Vaulted
Gallery

† Cathedral

MAŽĀ SMILŠU

✕ Filings

History of Riga
and Navigation

SKUNU

ZIRGU

PALASTA

Kamāla

Kolonna

Concert Hall
& Guildhalls

MEISTARU

VALNU

BASTEJA

JAUNIELA

TIRGOŅU

ROZENA

AMATU

ZIRGU

✕ Monterosso

New Town

Former Palace
of Peter I

M. JAUNIELA

KRĀMU

Planeta
Sushi

Livonija
✕

BRĪVĪBAS

✕ Rozengrāls

LAIPU

Technical
University

Town Hall
& Ratsnama

✕ Pelmeni

Russian Drama
Theatre

Hotel de Rome

KALKU

Black
Magic

Konventa
Sēta

Skonto
Zivju

AKMENS BRIDGE

Museum of
the Occupation
of Latvia

Blackheads'
House

1739 ✕

VAGNERA

Arbat ✕

Vecriga

Palete

GLEZNOTĀJU

KALEJU

Maritim Park,
Park OK,
Radisson SAS,
Sesame hotels,
Latvian Railway
Museum

Sesame

GRĒCINIEKU

Lotoss

Convent
Courtyard

SKĀRNU

Decorative
Arts

Pharmacy

Riga

TEĀTRE

St Peter's †

St John's Courtyard

National Opera ●

Garden
Palace

AUDĒJU

St John's †

✕ Melnie
Mulci

Globus

Mentzendorff
House

KUNGU

Porcelain

JĀNA

Ainavas

PELDU

Radi un Draugi

✕ Pulkvedim

MĀRSTAĻU

Photographic

Centra

✕ Olé

Indian Raja

ALKSNAJA

VECPILSETAS

Pomodoro

RIDZENES

✕ Forums

ASPĀZIJAS

Monument to those
who fought in 1905

MISTEREJAS

PEITAVUS

Latvian
People's
Front

VALNU

11. NOVEMBRA

Avalon

KALEJU

Metropole

Daugava

13. JANVĀRA

13. JANVĀRA

Railway station

Main routes out of Riga,
Salaspils, Cēsis, Sigulda

never be forgotten. The restaurant is in a cellar well underneath the hurly-burly of Livu laukums; this position shelters it not only from noise but also from the climate: it stays cool in summer & warm in winter. Ls18.

✕ **Melnie Mūki** (The Black Monks) 1–2 Jāņa Sēta; ☎ 6721 5006. Dark & rather formal, this highly respected restaurant in what used to be a cloister in the Old Town is rapidly gaining popularity for international food at prices that, if high for Riga, are by no means off the scale for the overseas visitor. The cuisine is genuinely international; Turkish kebabs alongside dishes with Asian influences. Ls15.

✕ **Monterosso** 9 Vaļņu; ☎ 6722 2017. Perhaps the display of the menus just in Italian puts off the stag groups who otherwise might take advantage of this very central location. Visitors will be pleasantly surprised at the diversity of the menu & the resulting range of ingredients given that 'Italian' is all too often a debased term now. Italian speakers get served best, followed by those who dress up somewhat. Wine is pricy, despite its good quality, so consider beer or a soft drink instead. Ls20.

✕ **Otto Schwarz** Hotel de Rome, 28 Kaļķu; ☎ 6708 7623; www.derome.lv. Located on the top floor of the hotel, this is an international restaurant with an emphasis on German cuisine, including even a special asparagus menu in season. It is one of Riga's most established restaurants, but has lost none of its prestige as the number of competing restaurants has grown. A major advantage is the excellent views over the Freedom Monument & the parks. A good choice of vegetarian dishes is always available. Prices are international, but at lunchtime there is a business menu for Ls8 (2 courses) or Ls10 (3 courses); these must be the only prices in Riga which did not change between 2005 & 2007. Ls30.

✕ **Palete** Gleznotāju 12–14; ☎ 6721 6037; www.palete.lv. Located in an elegant building in a narrow street in the Old Town, the Palete is worth a visit. Despite its central location, it is often missed by tourists, so even in summer it tends to be uncrowded. Good value, atmospheric & elegant with unobtrusive piano music. Dishes range from pasta to fried shellfish, chicken fillet with fried cheese & melon, & sometimes even rarer finds such as ostrich. The name means 'palette' & comes from its location in Painter St. Ls15.

✕ **Pizza Jazz** Raiņa 15; ☎ 6721 1237. The pizzas offered by this Lithuanian chain may not be the best you've ever tasted, but they are highly acceptable & eminently affordable. The menu has a large choice of pizzas, available in large or small size (& small really is

quite small), as well as pasta & salad. Even large pizzas are only a little over Ls2. The main menu is in English as well as Latvian & Russian. The dessert menu isn't in English but there are enticing pictures. Try the *biezpiena štūdele*, cottage-cheese strudel, if you fancy something with a Latvian flavour. Other branches are at 76 Brīvības, 19 Šķūņu & at the railway station. Ls7.

✕ **Planeta Sushi** Šķūņu 16; ☎ 6722 385; www. rrg.lv. Owned by the Russian Rostik restaurants group, like TGI Friday & Patio Pizza, & with branches in Moscow & other Russian cities, the pedigree for serving authentic Japanese food may not sound too promising. The quality of the vast range of Japanese dishes, however, comes as a very pleasant surprise. From *miso* soup to sushi (Japanese & Californian), *teppan* steaks or *shabu shabu*, the taste is first rate, & the prices quite reasonable too, with shrimp or squid sushi at only Ls1.20 per portion & teppan steaks at Ls5. The paintings of cherry trees on the wall & the Westernised kimonos worn by the waitresses are definitely less authentic, but the overall ambience is pleasant, unhassled & comfortable, & the location, close to Cathedral Square, makes this a convenient & highly recommendable spot. Ls18.

✕ **Pomodoro** Vecpilsēta 81; ☎ 6721 1044; www.pomodoro.lv. Turn off Audēju with its crowds of shoppers into the peace of Vecpilsēta & you will shortly find yourself at Pomodoro: a bar, café & restaurant. The restaurant is on the ground floor of a 17th-century warehouse, & the décor is a mixture of traditional & modern, but the mood is definitely contemporary. Pizza & homemade pasta are the specialities, & the Italian owners ensure authenticity. Prices are very reasonable, & a special children's menu is also available. Another branch has recently opened at the Domina shopping centre (2 Ieriķu; ☎ 787 3648). Ls18.

✕ **Raibais Balodis** (Colourful Dove) Konventa Sēta, Kalēju 9–11; ☎ 708 7580. Part of Konventenhof Hotel. Although the name may suggest a Latvian restaurant, the food here is definitely international. Menus change to make use of seasonal produce such as asparagus. The setting in the 13th-century convent is a definite plus, as are the fresh flowers & helpful service. Try for a window table overlooking Kalēju. Ls20.

✕ **Rozengrāls** Rozena 1; ☎ 6722 0356; www.rozengrals.lv. Given the success of medieval restaurants in Tallinn, it is perhaps surprising that it took until summer 2005 for a similar one to open in Riga. Abandon any thoughts of electric lighting, cutlery or quick service & descend into the cellar for a long carnivorous lunch or dinner. The long tables here lend themselves to group celebrations, not for quiet dinners *à deux*. Ls16.

✗ **Spotikačs** Antonijas 12; ✎ 6750 5955. Unless you visit Ukraine there are not many opportunities to sample the cuisine. This restaurant will give you a good idea of what's eaten in Kiev: straightforward, tasty dishes, with plenty of meat, potatoes & *vareniki* (dumplings). The floral friezes & puppets give the décor a childish feel &, added to the friendly service, should make your visit here a happy experience. If you need any further help, try the chilled homemade vodka. A branch has also opened in Jūrmala. Ls10.

✗ **Traktieris** Antonijas 8; ✎ 6733 2455. Hearing Russian & Ukrainian spoken here by other diners is clearly a good sign. The Russia to which this restaurant wants to link is of course the one that died in 1917, not the later variant that died in 1991. Although in the heart of the Art Nouveau area, the décor is from rural Russia, as are the costumes worn by the staff. The menu is from aristocratic St Petersburg & includes staples such as blini & borscht as well as more unusual dishes, but the prices appeal to quite a range of classes. In 2002, a buffet was opened, presumably for architecture fanatics determined to miss nothing in the surrounding neighbourhood, but a stay of at least 2hrs is recommended in the main restaurant. Ls12.

✗ **Vērmanītis** Elizabetes 65; ✎ 6728 6289. If Latvians meet each other, this is often the place they will choose, but foreigners rarely seem to do so. Prices are certainly not 'Old Town' & it manages to bridge the generation gap better than many other restaurants. Probably the self-service elements & the wooden dance floor help to do this, as does the music, which is softer than elsewhere. Older folk will be soothed by the stained glass & stone in much of the decoration. It is supposed to recall the first independence period from 1920 to 1940. Pizza & salad are always popular dishes here amongst foreigners but Latvians stick to the dependable local meat dishes. Ls8.

CHEAP AND FILLING

✗ **Blinoff** Brīvības bulvāris 30. If you want to replenish your energy between the Old Town & the New Town, call in at Blinoff. This small but welcoming café offers a long list of blini for Ls1–2. Choose from sweet or savoury blini, with coffee or a soft drink.

✗ **Dnipro** Alunāna 6. That a new café should open in the sparsely served diplomatic quarter is no surprise, but that it is Ukrainian probably is. Perhaps it is an indication of how respectable Ukraine has become the more it distances itself from Russia. For some it will be a home from home, with the language spoken by the staff, the décor & the food. For others it will be a conveniently quick place to get a pasty or some chicken Kiev.

✗ **Vincents** Elizabetes 19; ✎ 6733 2634 or 6733 2830; www.vincents.lv. Vincents (the name comes from the van Gogh reproductions which decorate it) is one of Riga's best-known restaurants. Situated in the New Town, it offers a wide variety of dishes based on cuisines from around the world. Like many restaurants it is making increasing use of high-quality local products, for example farm chicken from the Dobele region in western Latvia, but also has an impressive range of meat & fish dishes based on the best imported ingredients. A fairly recent addition is a sushi menu. It also has an attractive terrace for open-air eating in summer. Its reputation as a place where the 'stars' dine, not to mention American presidents, has led to very high prices by Riga standards, although good reductions are offered for groups having the same menu. If you can't afford to go there, you can always try the menus on the website yourself. Ls30.

✗ **Wok Café** Dzirnavu 60; ✎ 6728 2878; www.vairaksaules. The opening of this restaurant in 2007 is part of the trend to experiment outside the Old Town. 'Café' is rather a misnomer as a full range of Asian dishes is offered & on Tue–Sat they are all available until 06.00 for those who need a break from nightlife. Whilst meat is of course on the menu, there are plenty of vegetable & noodle dishes that exclude it. Ls10.

✗ **Zivju Restorāns** (Fish Restaurant) Vāgnera 4; ✎ 6721 6713; www.zivjurestorans.lv. There are 4 separate dining rooms, so wherever you are sitting the atmosphere is quiet & intimate. Fish is a mixture of local catch (try, for example, the Baltic pike perch rolls as a starter) & of more exotic origins, & is always a pleasure to look at as well as to eat. A harpist plays the only musical accompaniment & she fits the sedate décor & time-scale for eating. This is an environment strictly for pleasure, not for business. Ls25.

✗ **Lotoss** Skārņu 7. It is surprising to find good value on the route along which all cruise passengers are frog-marched through Riga, but here it is certainly provided & lucky patrons (or those who come in the off-season) can take advantage of the window seats overlooking St Peter's. Brunch is the speciality here but plenty of visitors are just as happy with eggs & filling soups in the early evening as at midday.

✗ **Olé** Audēju 1. Another buffet-style café, which, despite the name, serves international, not Spanish, food. Take as much as you can eat & you should still have change from Ls3. Catering really for locals, it closes Sat & Sun.

✕ Pelmeņi XL 7 Kaļķu 7. It's not sophisticated, but it certainly won't leave you either hungry or bankrupt. *Pelmeņi* are rather like ravioli, but their Russian origin means they're more substantial. You can fill up your plate with an XL portion from a choice of 6 different types (chicken, pork, vegetarian, etc), & accompany the main dish (Ls1.50) with soup & salad. There is a similar ambience, but bigger choice, at Pelmeņi, 38a Čaka.

✕ Pīrādziņi K Barona 14. A *pīrāgi* (Latvian pasty) shop offering pasties with a wide range of fillings from cabbage to meat. An excellent snack if you're in a hurry in the New Town.

Town Hall (Ratsnama Kafejnica) At the back of the Town Hall is a small shopping arcade, but it is easy to see the entrance to the staff restaurant (🕒 to the public 08.00–11.00 & 13.00–16.00 Mon–Fri), behind the oak trunk which is allegedly 3,500 years old. There is always plenty of room & a good selection of filling dishes, & prices are wonderfully 1990s.

CAFÉS For internet cafés, see *Internet*, page 98.

💻 Café Opera Aspāzijas bulvāris. A suitably ornate café has been inside the Opera House since it opened in 1995, with plenty of marble & wood. It never advertises, which suits the regulars who prefer the peace & quiet & the absence of tourists even in Jul & Aug. A thick soup followed by a light salad makes a good lunch here. The café has an outside terrace, too – with parasols which appear at the first drop of rain.

💻 Lidojošā Varde Elizabetes 31a, cnr Antonijas; www.flying-frog.lv. 'The Flying Frog' serves simple food (omelettes, pasta, salad, hamburgers) at very affordable prices, as well as drink. Popular both in summer, when you can sit on the terrace, & in winter, when a fire glows in the hearth. Handy when exploring Riga's Art Nouveau buildings. If you want to get into the mood for a visit, listen, yes listen, to the website, which has its theme song as a background to the menus. Ls12.

COFFEE AND TEA A new generation of coffee and tea houses has arrived in Riga in the last few years. Gone are many of the traditional Viennese-style cafés, to be replaced by an ever-growing choice of international chains, which are very popular locally, probably because of the consistent quality of the products served. However. some old-style ones remain and these are listed. The chains have so many branches now that there is no point in listing them. They have become unavoidable! If there is an economic downturn in Latvia in 2008, perhaps some of the boutiques that have recently raided the Old Town will be replaced by the cafés whose premises they usurped.

💻 Aspara Tea Rooms Skārņu 22. In the historic Ekke's convent built in 1435 as a guesthouse for travellers (page 122), this tea house offers a relaxing ambience in the heart of the Old Town. In the basement you can sit on cushions & choose from a vast array of Japanese, Chinese & Indian teas, while upstairs the décor is European medieval. Another branch is located in a small wooden house in the Vermānes Garden (opposite house no 75 on Elizabetes). Other branches also at 10 Škūnu, 77 Valdemāra & 2 Tērbatas. Don't ask for coffee here; they simply never serve it!

💻 Charlestons Cappuccino Bar Blaumaņa 38–40; www.charlestons.lv. A popular café with locals, who enjoy the coffee & the range of sandwiches, cakes & salads. If you're in Riga long enough, a loyalty card will make your 7th cup of coffee free. It stays open in the evening so is useful for those not feeling obliged to drink alcohol then.

💻 Emihla Gustava Shokolahde Marijas 13/VI (in Berga Bazārs); www.sokolade.lv. Also at 24 Aspāzijas bulvāris (in Valters un Rapa bookstore); check the website for other branches likely to open soon. Essentially handmade chocolate shops, but you can also have coffee, or chocolate, watch Belgian-style chocolates being made (at the Berga Bazārs) & enjoy a chocolate or 2 with your coffee. Those who frequent Pierre in Tallinn & Tartu will be equally happy here.

💻 Franču Maiznīca (French Bakery) Basteja bulvāris 8. It would have been easy for standards to slip here, once the novelty of real France penetrating Riga had worn off. Fortunately this is not the case, even 3 years after the opening in 2004. The croissants & baguettes remain as fresh as ever & nobody will mind French liqueurs rather than wine being a major ingredient in winter warmers or summer coolers. New clients are reassured by *le patron* looking in on most days to check on standards & to greet his regulars. A second café opened in 2006 at 30 Gertrūdes.

💻 Kapučino Bārs Torņa 4. Decaf coffee has not caught on in Latvia yet, although the larger restaurants can usually supply it if needed. Here however it is guaranteed, but is only optional as the real thing can be provided without difficulty. Sandwiches, another rarity in Latvia, are in plentiful supply here too. Not surprisingly, the quota of expats is high.

⊑ **Konditoreja Vecriga** Vāgnera 5; www.konditoreja.lv. It is very clever of this café to have a website as tourists abroad can already have a visual treat before they even leave home. Partly, it has to be said, this promotes the full-size cakes that the bakery sells to take away. Its selection of what to eat on the premises is probably the largest in the Old Town & its dead central location makes frequent stops here an obvious temptation.

⊑ **Monte Kristo** 27 Gertrūdes; also at 10 Elizabetes. At once spacious but cosy, this high-class coffee house offers a very wide choice not only of coffee but also of tea. Cakes include an enticing berry tart, excellent warm & with cream.

✕ **Zen** Stabu 6; www.zen.lv. This will definitely not be your cup of tea if you are just looking for a refuelling stop. Enter Zen & you enter a slow-motion world which you will need some time to enjoy. Chinese tea is prepared in ceremonial style &, authentically, takes at least 20mins. The décor is oriental too: tatami, cushions, candles & lanterns, though – slightly out of kilter with the rest of the place – waterpipes are also available.

ENTERTAINMENT AND NIGHTLIFE

OPERA AND CONCERTS The Latvia National Opera (*3 Aspāzijas bulvāris;* ↘ *722 5803;* f *722 8240;* e *boxoffice@opera.lv; www.opera.lv*) has an extensive programme of opera, ballet and recitals. Ticket prices are extremely reasonable by international standards, tending to range from Ls2 to Ls30, although international stars may sometimes dictate higher prices. Tickets can easily be booked from outside Latvia via email, and then collected at the ticket office (slightly behind the main building, towards the park) on arrival in Riga. Even if you do not book in advance, it is often possible to buy tickets once you are in Riga. Performances are normally in the original language but subtitled in English and Latvian where necessary. Programmes are in Latvian and English. An opera festival is held every year in June. This can be booked directly or as part of an opera tour (see page 7). Unfortunately the opera is closed in July but now has a summer season for a week in August. Inside the Opera House is Café Opera, a peaceful haven of wood and marble, which offers a pleasant venue for a snack and is open even in July and August when the theatre is closed.

The Latvia National Opera has an extremely high reputation and over the years has attracted a wide variety of well-known musicians and designers. Richard Wagner conducted over 40 operas during his time in Riga (1837–39), although in the forerunner to the current building, which was not built until 1863. He also wrote a large part of *Rienzi* while he was here, and it is said that he conceived some of the motifs for *The Flying Dutchman* on a journey from Riga to Copenhagen. More recently Bruno Walter spent several years conducting at the Opera House. Although many performances are of the classical repertoire, there is a strong tradition of contemporary dance, and the choice of operas is often bold, including for example in 2004 a revival of Anton Rubinstein's little-known *Demons*.

Classical concerts are held in a variety of venues, including the **Wagner Hall** (Vāgnera Zale, *4 R Vāgnera;* ↘ *6721 0817*), the **Great Guildhall** (Lielā Ģilde, *6 Amatu;* ↘ *6721 3798*) and the **Small Guildhall** (Mazā Ģilde, *3–5 Amatu;* ↘ *6722 3772*). Organ and other chamber recitals are given regularly at the **Cathedral** (Doma laukums), usually on Wednesdays and Fridays. Tickets can be purchased just inside the porch of the main entrance. In all these cases, there is generally no need to pre-book, unless the artist is extremely well known. Other venues also host occasional performances: if you keep your eyes open when walking around Riga you will see adverts for upcoming events. The *Baltic Times* also gives a selection of concerts with details of time and place. Information on music in Riga generally can be found at www.lmic.lv.

Venues for non-classical music are more varied. For blues, one of the most highly recommended places is **Bites Blūzs Klubs** (*34a Dzirnavu;* ☏ *6733 3125*), which frequently attracts singers from the USA and elsewhere. **Sapņu Fabrika** (Dream Factory, *101 Lāčplēša;* ☏ *6729 1701;* e *info@sapnufabrik.com*) is a large hall which puts on a variety of world music, jazz and rock concerts. The **Hamlet Club** (*5 Jāņa Sēta;* ☏ *6722 8838*) hosts jazz concerts, and also serves as a small theatre, putting on plays which often have a strong political content. For a genuine Latvian experience, try **Četri Balti Krekli** (Four White Shirts, *12 Vecpilsētas;* ☏ *6721 3885; www.krekli.lv*), which specialises in Latvian musicians, including for example Ainars Mielavs.

Every summer the **Rigas Ritmi Festival** (*www.rigasritmi.lv*) is held in Riga in June/July. It attracts well-known musicians from around the world, who not only perform but also give masterclasses. The music is wide-ranging, including reggae, world music, bossa nova, jazz'n'soul and Caribbean. Venues include open-air performances in parks and squares in Riga and even on cruise ships on the Daugava.

FILMS AND THEATRE Riga offers a number of state-of-the-art cinemas, all of which show films in the original, rather than dubbed, so visitors will have no problems viewing missed Hollywood films. Seat prices are low by international standards at an average of Ls3–4, but even so discounts are offered on weekday showings before 17.00.

With 14 screens, **Forum Cinemas** (*www.forumcinemas.lv*) is the largest cinema in Riga and the second-largest cinema complex in the whole of northern Europe. It is situated on Janvāra, between the bus and railway stations, opposite the end of Aspāzijas bulvāris, and has all the modern facilities you would expect. The website is in English and tickets can be bought from it. Other possibilities include **Daile** (*31 Barona;* ☏ *6728 3843; www.baltcinema.lv*), which shows older films for just Ls1.50 per person; **K Suns** (*83/85 Elizabetes;* ☏ *6 728 5411*), which tends to show European, rather than Hollywood films; **Kinogalerija** (*24 Jauniela;* ☏ *6722 9030*) which specialises in classics; and **Riga** (*61 Elizabetes;* ☏ *6 728 11 95*), the first cinema to open in Riga and recently renovated in its original style but with modern equipment.

Riga has a number of theatres but most of these are inaccessible to visitors who do not speak Latvian or Russian. For those who do, the **New Riga Theatre** (*25 Lāčplēša;* ☏ *6728 0765; www.jrt.lv*) tends to perform avant-garde plays in Latvian, while the **Russian Drama Theatre** (*16 Kaļķu;* ☏ *6722 4660*) does what it says. The **National Theatre** (*2 Kronvalda bulvāris;* ☏ *6732 2759; www.teatris.lv – Latvian only*), housed in a classical building close to the canal, performs a primarily classical repertoire. It was here that Latvia declared independence on 18 November 1918. A concert is held here every year to commemorate the event. For more information, see www.theatre.lv, which gives information in English as well as Latvian.

Of possible interest is the **State Puppet Theatre** (*16 Kr Barona;* ☏ *6728 5418;* e *info@puppet.lv; www.puppet.lv*). The puppet theatre is a strong Latvian tradition and performances are generally well acclaimed. They are in Latvian or Russian, but visitors with a particular interest may appreciate the artistry.

BARS AND CLUBS Riga's night scene has blossomed in the last few years. It now offers a huge variety of venues and entertainments to suit all tastes and most pockets. The venues below are only a very small selection of what is on offer. Most are conventional bars through the day and are closed only between 03.00 and 11.00. Given the sordid reputation of some Old Town establishments, it is worth considering a tour as an introduction to this highly fraught area. Dependable ones are operated by the British–Latvian organisation Riga Out There (☏ *6748 2443; www.out-there-eu*) who make clear exact costs in every club before entry. They have a London phone number too

(☏ *020 8123 2077*). For up-to-date listings in this rapidly changing area, consult *Riga In Your Pocket*.

☆ **Pulkvedim Neviens Neraksta** (Nobody Writes to the Colonel) Peldu 26–28; ☏ 6721 3886. One of the longest-established clubs in Riga, this is also one of the city's trendiest venues, regularly crowded with young locals & visitors – but seems to have no connection with the Márquez novel of the same name. The food is generally well liked, although the service can be slow. If you like sitting in a warehouse listening to alternative music, this is for you. If you prefer something more colourful, go down to the Baccardi Lounge in the basement of the same building, & enjoy cocktails to the accompaniment of disco house, but be warned that if you're over 20 you may well be the oldest there.

🏳 **Rigas Balzāms** (Black Balsam) Bdg 1b at Torņa 4 in the Jēkaba Kazarmas row of shops near the Powder Tower; ☏ 6721 4494. If you'd like to try Riga's distinctive alcoholic drink then the bar named after the drink, Rigas Melnais Balzāms, is a good bar to visit. It is recommended trying it first in a fruit cocktail or poured liberally over ice cream. Very few non-Latvians can take it neat. In the winter, it goes well with hot tea or hot blackberry juice. The faint-hearted can choose from many better-known drinks. The bar also serves pub-type food, & the pleasant ambience makes it a popular place for Rigans relaxing after work – & well into the evening. The same management have now opened a 2nd bar, Jaunais Rigas Balzāms at 2 Doma Laukums (Cathedral Square).

🏳 **Skyline Bar** In Reval Hotel Lātvija, Elizabetes 55; ☏ 6777 2222. One of the best views in Riga is to be had from the Skyline Bar on the 26th floor of the Reval Hotel Lāvija. Take one of the 2 glass-sided lifts up to the top & enjoy a beer or a cocktail with all Riga spread below you. It opens at 15.00 so depending on when the sun sets, a pleasant couple of hours can be spent here seeing first this & then the Old Town illuminated. Equally this is an ideal venue for enjoying a thunderstorm.

♀ **Vairāk Saules Cocktail Bar** (More Sun) Dzirnavua 60; ☏ 6728 2878. One of the longest cocktail menus in Riga (around 90) won't prevent you being stunned by the brightness of the décor in this trendy bar. The music is mostly R&B & the service better than in many bars. It is a popular venue with locals, so make sure you arrive early if you want a seat.

🏳 **Paldies Dievam Piektdiena Ir Klāt** (Thank God it's Friday) 11. Novembra 9 (Note the road is called 11. Novembra & the address is number 9); ☏ 6750 3964. Closed on w/days until the eponymous Fri, this w/end bar offers a taste of the Caribbean on the banks of the Daugava River. Everything about the bar transports you across the Atlantic: the food, including Cuban black bean soup, the reggae music, the barman in shorts, the flamboyant cocktails &, on Fri & Sat, women dancing on the bar.

☆ **La Habana** Kungu 1 (entrance from Rātslaukums, Town Hall Square); ☏ 6722 6014. On the upper floor this is a quiet restaurant serving Tex-Mex dishes. The basement is quite different. From Thu to Sat, it turns into a popular disco hosted by local DJs. The rest of the week Latin music predominates, as you'd guess from the decoration – pictures of Che Guevara, Fidel Castro et al.

☆ **Voodoo** Part of Reval Hotel Lātvija, Elizabetes 55; ☏ 6777 2355; www.voodoo.lv. Newly revamped club offering several dance floors, quieter areas for drinking & a lively atmosphere. It attracts many Russians, partying in Riga, as well as locals. Admission at Ls3–5 good value.

GAY RIGA Although the legal restrictions which the Soviet authorities imposed have long since disappeared, the gay scene is not yet well developed in Riga. Open affection in public is rarely seen and may attract hostility. The first gay pride march in Riga took place in July 2005, with many more protesters than participants and with the prime minister expressing open hostility to it. Subsequent marches needed enormous police protection. It is necessary to register before being able to use the local website www.gay.lv but it is in English (and Spanish) The phone number is ☏ 6727 3890 and email address gay@gay.lv. Only two gay clubs are widely advertised:

☆ **Purvs** (The Swamp) 60–62 Matīsa; ☏ 6731 1717; www.purvs.lv; ⏰ 22.00–24.00 Mon, Wed, Thu, 22.00–06.00 Fri & Sat; closed Tue & Sun. Generally well reviewed, if you can find it – there is no sign. It offers dance performances, sometimes including transvestite shows. Admission Ls2–4.

☆ **XXL** 4 A Kalniņa; ☏ 728 2276; e xxl@xxl.lv; www.xxl.lv; ⏰ 18.00–07.00 daily, but men only on Sun. XXL started life as a small bar but has now expanded into a larger club & restaurant, with shows on Fri & Sat at 03.00. Video cabins & dark rooms are also available. Admission Ls1–10.

Amber is formed from the resin which oozed from pine trees some 30 to 90 million years ago and gradually fossilised. It is found in several parts of the world, but the oldest source, some 40–50 million years old, is in countries around the Baltic Sea, including Latvia. The use of Baltic amber goes back a very long way: amber of Baltic origin has been found in Egyptian tombs from around 3200BC, and Baltic amber was regularly traded in Greek and Roman times. Animal figurines made of amber have also been found in Latvia dating back to the 4th millennium BC. After the Teutonic Order conquered Latvian territory, local people were forbidden to collect it on pain of hanging and only in the 19th century could inhabitants of the coast once again begin amber-working.

Traditionally Latvian folk costumes made use of three items made from amber: beads, brooches and *kniepkeni* (fastenings for women's blouses). All of these items, and many others, can be found in shops in Riga. Are they all real natural amber? Definitely not. Unfortunately the only recommended test to establish authenticity is hardly a practical shopping tip: make a solution of water and salt and drop in your amber. Only real amber will float.

Dzintars, the Latvian word for amber, can be seen and heard all over Riga. It is the name of Latvia's main perfume company, a brand name for a cheese spread, the name of a well-known choir, a children's dance group, and is also a common first name (*Dzintars* for men and *Dzintra* for women).

SHOPPING

Riga is the most expensive of the three capitals for shopping, probably because of the larger base of local and expat ostentatious consumers there than in Tallinn or Vilnius. It is also becoming increasingly favoured by rich Russians, who have happy memories of earlier stays during Soviet times. To some extent this is reflected in the higher quality of goods sold and in the type of items offered. Forget the small items of linen or wood that adorn the markets elsewhere and think in terms of amber or silver.

During the summer, shops open every day from 10.00–19.00, sometimes closing a little earlier on Saturday and Sunday. In the winter, some will close on Sundays. Credit cards are widely accepted and bargaining is usually futile.

Unlike in Tallinn, there is no need to avoid the centre to get cheaper prices. There is sufficient competition in the Old Town, and fewer set routes for the cruise groups, so prices are not so varied. There are also fewer street traders.

SOUVENIRS For jewellery **A & E** at Jauniela 17 (note that in this case the suffix 'iela' for street is part of the name whereas normally it is written as a separate word) has reigned supreme ever since Hillary Clinton graced the shop with her presence during her husband's presidential visit in July 1994. Other spouses of world leaders have followed in her footsteps. For tasteful souvenirs in china and glass, **Laipa** (Laipu 2–4) can be recommended. They also stock woollen goods, wooden toys and some paintings. Those who take an excursion to the **Open Air Museum** on the outskirts of Riga will find an extensive selection of crafts for sale there, with prices set for Latvians rather than for foreign visitors.

BOOKS Books are an excellent memory from Riga, given the number of English-language ones that have excellent photographs of the architecture. They range in size from pocket-size booklets to massive coffee-table volumes. Prices are usually lower at the tourist office on Town Hall Square or at the bookshop in the same complex behind the office and which faces onto Grēcinieku. It is called **Ratslaukums Grāmatnīca** (Town Hall Bookshop). The ranges at **Valters un Rapa** (*Aspazijas 24*) opposite the Riga Hotel and at **Globuss** (*Vaļņu 26*) just around the corner are however more extensive. Globuss has a congenial café on its first floor. An extensive selection of secondhand books about Latvia and the Baltics, in English and in German, is always available at **Jumava** (*Vāgnera 12*). The **Occupation Museum** on Town Hall Square has the best selection of books about World War II and the Soviet era. Again, most of these are in English.

OTHER PURCHASES Alcohol is of course easily purchased all over the town, at least until 22.00 when sales in shops have to stop. **Latvijas Balzāms** produce most of the local spirits, so not only Riga Balzāms but also gin and vodka. They have several shops in the Old Town but the largest selection is available at Vaļņu 21. The exchange office in this shop usually gives good rates for sterling and US dollars. Prices for alcohol at the airport are close enough to those in town for it not to be worthwhile dragging bottles there, but cigarettes are much cheaper in town so should be bought in advance. British visitors should note that whilst the import of alcohol for personal use has been unrestricted since Latvia joined the EU, there is still a restriction of 200 cigarettes per person.

The **Centrs** supermarket (*Audēju 16*) which dates from the 1930s has gone through several metamorphoses since 1991; the latest was in 2006. It has now become a series of franchised outlets. Few are particularly imaginative, but it still has the advantage of being a one-stop shop, heated or airconditioned as necessary, where the maximum amount of varied goods can be bought at reasonable prices within the shortest amount of time.

WALKING TOURS

The majority of sights are in the Old Town (Vecrīga), the area of the city located between the Daugava River and the city canal (pilsētas kanāls). If your time is limited, this is the place to start. If you have more time, you could include a look at the Art Nouveau area. For visitors with still more time or other interests, a number of other walks in and around the centre are also described.

The Old Town contains a wealth of historic buildings, from the medieval town walls dating back to the 13th century to the grey modernity of the flats and offices built when Latvia was part of the Soviet Union. Between the two extremes there are buildings of almost every period and style, including Classical, Gothic, Art Nouveau and modern. Much of the Old Town suffered neglect when Latvia was part of the USSR, but a great deal of restoration and reconstruction has now been undertaken (the reconstruction of the Blackheads' House and surrounding area being one of the most striking examples).

The best way to see the Old Town is on foot: the area is relatively small, but in any event, large parts of the Old Town have been made traffic-free zones (there is access for vehicles, but you have to buy a pass), while other parts consist of narrow streets, making vehicle access impractical. Many of the streets are cobbled and others suffer from lack of maintenance, so you have to keep your eyes open for holes and uneven road and pavement surfaces. Wear sensible walking shoes.

The main sights of the Old Town are described below by reference to two suggested walking routes covering the Old Town sights on either side of Kaļķu.

OLD TOWN WALK 1 Our first walk starts from the Hotel de Rome at the corner of Kaļķu and Aspazijas bulvāris, not far from the Freedom Monument. Walk down Kaļķu away from the Freedom Monument and the parks along the side of the hotel and you will find yourself almost immediately at Vaļņu, a pedestrianised street of shops, bars and cafés. Turn right into Vaļņu. At the end of the street you will see one of the major landmarks of the Old Town, the **Powder Tower** (page 141). This sturdy tower is all that remains of the 18 towers which once formed part of the city walls. You may wish to visit the **War Museum** (page 137), which the Tower now houses. If not, stand on Smilšu (Sand Street), one of Riga's oldest streets, with your back to the Powder Tower and look across Basteja bulvāris where you can see the remains of Bastion Hill (Basteja kalns), one of the fortification towers dating back to the 17th century.

Behind the Powder Tower is Torņa (Tower Street), a well-restored, traffic-free street. Walk along this street and you come to part of the city wall (best seen from the parallel Trokšņu). Riga was protected by a wall from the early 13th century. Eventually it extended to a length of over a mile. By the 14th century the walls were 1.83m thick. The arches between the pillars would be filled with stones and sandbags to provide reinforcement when the city was under siege; in peacetime they were emptied again and used for storage or as stables or even accommodation. The income derived from letting the arches was used to raise money to pay for the upkeep of the city's defences.

At the corner of Torņa and Aldaru (Brewer Street) is the **Swedish Gate** (Zviedru Vārti), so called because it was built when Riga was under Swedish rule and because it was the gate through which the Swedish king, Gustavus Adolphus, entered the city in 1621 (a stained-glass window in the Dome commemorates this). It is the only city gate still left intact. According to legend, the citizens of Riga abducted a young Latvian woman who had unwisely fallen in love with a Swedish soldier and was meeting him secretly near the gate, and walled her up in the gate as a warning to others. The Swedish Gate is unusual in that it passes through a whole house, number 11 Torņa: the first recorded house in private ownership in Riga.

Although it is not possible to visit them, there are several attractively restored historic houses on Torņa of which the most notorious is the one now at number 7, a large pink house that was once occupied by the city executioner until the position was abolished in 1863. Number 5 Torņa was the site of the prison built in 1685 by Rupert Bindenschu, the architect who also worked on the reconstruction of St Peter's Church.

At the end of Torņa you come to Jēkaba (Jacob's or James's Street) and to the right **Jēkaba laukums** (Jacob's or James's Square), where concrete barricades were erected during the struggles of January 1991. The square, which was first laid out in the 18th century, was once used for military parades and exercises. On the side of the square closest to Jēkaba is a row of low buildings. The middle building, taller than the others, is the former arsenal. Built between 1828–32 to designs by I Lukini and A Nellinger on the site of what was once part of the town wall, the arsenal that stood here was replaced by a customs house. Now the building is a gallery (the **Arsenal Museum of Fine Arts**, Mākslas Muzejs or 'Arsenals') where modern painters exhibit (page 129).

Close to the end of Torņa is a green which forms part of **Pils laukums** (Castle Square). The large building on the corner on your right is the Bank of Latvia, built in 1905 to designs by the Latvian architect, Reinbergs. Number 2 Pils laukums was formerly a Red Army museum but is now the **Museum of Literature, Theatre and Music** (Rakstniecibas, Teatra un Muzikas Muzejs, page 133). The main building on Pils laukums, at the other side of the square, is **Riga Castle** (Rigas pils), a large cream building with a red roof (page 141), where the President of Latvia now lives.

The castle also houses two museums, the **Latvian History Museum** (Latvijas Vēstures Muzejs, page 132), which traces the course of Latvian history from 9000BC to the 20th century; and the **Latvian Museum of Foreign Art**, Latvijas Ārzemju Mākslas Muzejs (page 132), the biggest collection of foreign art in Latvia. To the right of the castle, in the direction of Kr Valdemāra, is the old stable block, recognisable by horse-head designs on the wall.

Leaving Castle Square (Pils laukums) and crossing the cobbled area of the square (the opposite end to the one at which the stables are located, in the direction of Lielā pils) you come to a church, the Roman Catholic church of **Our Lady of Sorrows** (Sāpju Dievmātes baznīca, page 139). Just beyond the Catholic church is Riga's only Anglican church, **St Saviour's** (page 140), which stands in Anglikāņu, just off Lielā pils. The church was built for the British community in 1859 and became a discotheque during the Soviet occupation, but is now restored and holds regular Sunday services. On a fine day the outdoor café at the end of Anglikāņu offers views over the river and the imposing Vanšu Bridge, and makes a pleasant stop. The tall building on the far bank is the Hansapank 26-storey office building.

Returning to Pils, go back to the corner of the square and turn right into Mazā pils, heading away from the tower of Riga Castle. The three houses at numbers 17, 19 and 21 Mazā pils are known collectively as '**the three brothers**' (Trīs brāļi, page 142). Note also the house at 4 Mazā pils where the Baltic historian Johans Kristofs Broce worked from 1742–1823 as rector of what was then Riga's imperial lycée.

Opposite 'the three brothers' is Klostera (Monastery Street) which leads to **St Jacob's**, or **St James's**, Church (page 139), the Roman Catholic Cathedral of Riga, and the church with the lowest of the three spires which dominate the Old Town.

At the corner of Jēkaba baznīca, if you turn right, you come to a formidable brown building with a coat of arms and a balcony over the main entrance. This is the building where the Supreme Soviet of Latvia used to sit. Between 1919 and 1934 it was the seat of the **Latvian National Parliament**. Now it functions once again as the parliament building, the seat of the Saeima. It was here on 4 May 1989 that parliament passed a resolution on the independence of Latvia. The building itself is in the style of a Florentine palace. Note the decoratively carved double doors and heavy lanterns. In the outbreak of crime which followed independence in the early 1990s, the bronze plaque on the front of the building was stolen. On 20 January 2007 the triangular monument opposite the Saeima in the garden beside the cathedral was unveiled. The date was the 16th anniversary of the attack by Soviet forces on central Riga which led to the erection of the concrete barricades in this area to protect Parliament and other crucial buildings. The eight names engraved on it are of those unarmed Latvians who died resisting the Russians.

Turn right into Jēkaba and walk along the back of the cathedral. Numbers 6–8 Jēkaba form a substantial stone building which houses the **Latvian National Library**. Designs by the Riga-born architect Gunars Birkerts for a new national library, to be known as Gaišmaspils (the 'Castle of Light'), remained for years on the drawing board. However, by late 2007 there seemed to be a genuine determination on the part of the government to start the building, perhaps because the Bill Gates Foundation expressed an interest in August 2005 in providing some of the necessary funds. The new site is clearly marked over the Daugava River. Turning left back into Smilšu, the house at number 6 has a modern front and is now a bank. The upper storeys are good examples of the Art Nouveau style of architecture for which Riga is so famous. The buildings at number 2 and number 8 are also worth a look. Next to number 6 is Aldaru (Brewer Street) with its view back to the Swedish Gate. The large brown building that dominates the rest of Smilšu is occupied by ministries and government offices.

Here the road forks. Take Mazā Smilšu (Little Sand Street) and turn right into Meistaru (Master Street). On your left is a large yellow building called the **House of the Cat**: perched on each of the building's two pointed towers is an arched cat looking down on the city. The origins of this piece of architectural caprice are uncertain but inevitably there is a story. Apparently a Latvian businessman sought admission to the city guild but was refused. To spite the guild he bought the nearest land he could find to the guildhall, built the house that still stands and had two cats put on top so that each directed its backside towards the guildhall. According to the same story the spurned merchant was eventually forced to move them, hence their present position.

If you continue down Meistaru you come to what used to be the Guild Square but is now known as the **Philharmonic Park** (Filharmonijas Parks). On a wet day it can look fairly grim but in better weather it is enlivened by kiosks selling ice cream and drinks, and by pavement artists, and sometimes also by stag parties. The **Great Guildhall** (page 120) is the large, dull yellow building at one edge of the square, at the corner of Meistaru and Amatu (Commercial Street). The **Small Guildhall** is right next to it on Amatu itself. These buildings represent the centres of Riga's former glory as a Hanseatic City. Continue along Amatu to Šķūņu (Barn Street). On your right there is a camel-coloured building with white decoration, an excellent example of Riga's Art Nouveau. Note the sculptures of a boy reading (at roof level) and of frogs (by the entrance).

If you turn right out of Amatu, past Zirgu, you come to the Cathedral Square, Doma laukums. The square is dominated by **Riga Cathedral**, or the Dome Church (Rīgas Dom – the word comes from the German *Dom*, meaning 'cathedral'; see page 137) or St Mary's Cathedral, as it is sometimes referred to, the largest church in the Baltic countries. The church opens from 10.00 to 18.00 daily (*www.doms.lv* has full information), but there are also opportunities to attend concerts there on Wednesdays and Fridays, frequently featuring the cathedral's splendid organ, and services are held (in Latvian) at 08.00 every day and at noon on Sundays. Close to the main entrance and away from the main square is the **Cathedral Cloister** and courtyard (page 138) which was finally restored in 2005. This can be visited daily and has good views of the cathedral exterior.

Just off Doma laukums, Tirgoņu (Traders' Street) has a number of bars and restaurants. Both these streets have a variety of cafés, bars and restaurants which are preferable to those on the square itself.

The building at 8 Doma laukums is the **Latvia Radio Building**. It and the nearby Finance Ministry recall the architectural style of Nazi Germany and were built during the 1930s at the time of the Latvian president, Kārlis Ulmanis. The Radio Building was one of the buildings that was barricaded in 1991 by demonstrators resisting communist sympathisers; bullet holes in the building offer a grim reminder of the fighting. Doma laukums was heavily guarded and occupied by people lighting bonfires and erecting tents. From time to time radio staff would appear on the balcony of the Radio Building to announce the news to the people gathered in the square below. It was from the same balcony that President Gorbunovs proclaimed independence in August 1991. Opposite the Radio Building is Rigas Fondu Birēa, the **Riga Stock Exchange**, a green and brown building with ornate statues. It was built in 1852–55 in Venetian style to a design by the architect Harald Bose, but fell into disuse during the Soviet occupation; during the 1990s it was again occupied by a bank.

If you leave Doma laukums passing the main door of the cathedral with the Radio Building behind you, you come into Herdera laukums, **Herder Square**. This small square is dominated by the statue of the German critic, writer and theologian, Johann Herder, who lived in Riga from 1764–89. It was unveiled originally in 1864 to celebrate the 100th anniversary of his arrival in Riga from Königsberg and unlike many other German monuments, it survived World War II. The statue was removed early in the Soviet period, but fortunately not destroyed then. It was returned to this site, but with a new base, in 1959 when the East German leader Walter Ulbricht visited Riga. The earlier inscription had referred to Herder's work as a theologian but the new one simply gave his name and dates of birth and death. Turning out of Herdera laukums you come to Palasta (Palace Street). The building that was once the clergy enclosure of the abbey attached to the cathedral is now the **Museum of History and Navigation of the City of Riga** (Rīgas Vēstures un Kuģniecības Muzejs, page 132). Further on in Palasta at number 6 stands a tiny building in which the Russian tsar, Peter I, kept his personal carriage when he visited Riga. Just beyond it at number 9 is what used to be **Peter I's palace**, from which Palasta derives its name. In 1745 the palace was rebuilt to designs by Rastrelli, the architect better known in Latvia for his work on the Rundāle Palace (page 149).

OLD TOWN WALK 2 Our second walk in the Old Town starts from the beautifully restored **Rātslaukums** (Town Hall Square) towards the end of Kaļķu near the river.

The distinguished building dominating the square is the **Blackheads' House** (Melngalvju nams, page 121), rebuilt in 1999. Although the ornate exterior is the most stunning aspect, the interior can also be visited. Particularly impressive is the assembly hall on the first floor. If you have any questions about Riga, you can visit the Riga tourist information office housed in part of the Blackheads' House. Next to the museum entrance there is a small café, where the brave can sample Vecriga coffee (coffee with Balzāms). While on the square, have a look at the statue of **Roland** (page 144) and also at the newly restored Town Hall (Rātsnams) opposite the Blackheads' House.

After the medieval atmosphere of the Town Hall Square, the aggressively 20th-century atmosphere of the **Riflemen's Square** (Strēnieku laukums) next to it towards the river comes as something of a shock. The large statue is the Riflemen's Memorial (page 142) which was erected in 1970 to commemorate the valour of the Latvian Rifle Regiment during the civil war. The ugly black cuboid building behind the memorial was also built in 1970 and used to be a museum devoted to the exploits of the regiment. Now it is the **Museum of the Occupation of Latvia** (Okupācijas Muzejs, page 134). The museum offers a detailed and poignant account, with many personal histories, of the various occupations Latvia was subjected to during the 20th century.

The traditional bridge with the large lantern-like lights is the **Akmens tilts** (Stone Bridge) which replaced the long pontoon bridge that spanned the river before World War II. A more elegant example of 20th-century architecture is the dramatic modern bridge, the harp-like Vanšu tilts, which crosses the river to the north.

Leave the square by turning into Grēcinieku (Sinner's Street) and taking Kungu (Gentleman's Street). On the corner of Grēcnieku and Kungu is the **Mentzendorff House** (Mencendorfa nams, page 133). The house once belonged to a rich Riga merchant family and is now a museum of life in the 17th and 18th centuries. Walk down Kungu past the Mentzendorff House to Mārstaļu. Number 21 Mārstaļu is (or will be, once restored) a fine example of Baroque domestic architecture and was built in 1696 for another wealthy citizen of Riga, Dannenstern and his family. Nearby at number 19 is a plaque to George Armisted (see page 124), a Scot who was lord mayor of Riga city. A statue to Armisted stands near to the Opera House. (If you are travelling more widely in Latvia, you can see the manor house built by Armisted, Jaunmoku Pils, just outside Tukums.) The red house at number 2 Mārstaļu is the Reiter House (Reitera nams), built in 1682 for another wealthy Riga merchant, Johann von Reiter, and now used for conferences and exhibitions. At the time of writing, it was undergoing extensive restoration.

Turn right into Audēju (Weaver Street) and then right again into Vecpilsētas (Old Town Street). The buildings at numbers 10 and 11–17 are good examples of some of the 20 or so medieval warehouses of the Old Town. On the corner opposite the Italian restaurant is the house from which the Latvian Popular Front operated in the late 1980s and which is now a small museum (page 135). Return to Audēju and continue walking away from Mārstaļu. The street is normally packed with shoppers, but if you have chance glance up over the door of number 3. Next to the German motto 'God protect our going in and going out' you will see storks on a nest. Storks are a striking feature of rural Latvia, where the 6,000 or 7,000 pairs which arrive annually are welcomed by local people as bringers of good luck. Throughout Latvia, including in the ballroom decoration at Rundāle (page 149), you will find the stork motif.

Turn left into Rīdzene, alongside the Centrs shopping centre, then left again into Teātra (Theatre Street), which brings you to Kalēju. Just off Kalēju is a passage leading to the **Konventa Sēta**, an area of beautifully restored historic buildings between Kalēju and Skārņu. The area, which dates back to the 13th century, now contains a hotel, shops and the **Porcelain Museum** (Rigas Porcelāna Muzejs, page 136). Close to the Konventa Sēta at the end of Teātra there is a part of the city wall. An archway in Kalēju leads to Jāņa Sēta (John's Courtyard), a cobbled courtyard with the city wall on one side and a bar, café and restaurant forming the other sides of the quadrangle.

A second arch leads out of the courtyard to **St John's Church** (Jāņa baznīca, page 139), with its wonderful vaulted ceiling inside and intriguing stone faces outside.

Skārņu (Butchers' Street) got its name from the shops that were located in this part of Riga in medieval times. Number 22, next door to St John's Church, is a house known as Ekes konvents (Ekke's Convent). The building is currently a tea house. Further along Skārņu, next to number 10, the old white building with brick-lined windows is **St George's Church** (Jura baznīca), possibly the oldest building in Riga and generally dated at 1202 or 1204. In 1989 it became part of the **Museum of Decorative and Applied Arts** (Dekoratīvi Lietišķās Mākslas Muzejs, page 131), which specialises in applied art from Latvia and abroad from the 19th century onwards. Opposite Ekke's Convent in the shadow of St Peter's there is a modern statue of some animals called **The Town Musicians of Bremen**. Based on an old German tale by the Brothers Grimm, it was a gift from the city of Bremen to the people of Riga and marks a long association between the two cities. The original was unveiled in Bremen in 1953 but this adaptation, cast in late 1989, shows the symbolic breakthrough of an iron curtain, as happened at that time when the Berlin Wall came down.

On the other side of Skārņu stands one of Riga's most famous and distinctive churches, **St Peter's** (Pētera baznīca, page 140), a large red-brick church with a simple, light interior decorated by coats of arms. St Peter's is the tallest spire in Riga. Except on Mondays you can take a lift up to the viewing platform and have a spectacular view of Riga. On leaving St Peter's, return to Skārņu and then turn right into Kaļķu. This last part of our walking tour of Old Riga will take you past some of Riga's newest shops and bring you back to the Hotel de Rome and a sign that Riga is now a thoroughly 21st-century consumer-oriented city: opposite the hotel and almost in the shadow of the Freedom Monument is what was Riga's first McDonald's (and was previously the site of the university bookshop).

ART NOUVEAU WALK

ART NOUVEAU WALK Riga has one of the largest collections of Art Nouveau buildings in the whole of Europe. Around one-third of all the buildings in central Riga were built in this style between around 1896 and 1913. Even if you did not think you were interested in architecture, it is worth having a look at a few of the most striking examples – which may make you change your mind. In this case, you can integrate a quick tour of the Art Nouveau area within the New Town walk (see page 124). Visitors more interested in buildings could easily spend a half-day exploring the area in more detail and visiting the Jāņis Rozentāls and Rūdolfs Blaumanis Memorial Museum (see page 136).

Although Art Nouveau buildings are to be found throughout the New Town, as well as in certain parts of the Old Town, the area with the most striking buildings is the rectangle bounded by Elizabetes, Antonijas, Alberta and Strēnieku. Also of interest are many of the buildings along Brīvības, Lāčplēša, Ģertrūdes, A Čaka and Tērbatas, all in the main New Town shopping area.

Wandering around these areas, and remembering to look up to the very top of the buildings, gives an idea of the range of styles and the sheer inventiveness of many of the architects. Some of the most memorable buildings are the work of Mikhail

top left   **Cosmonaut Memorial, Kaliningrad** (JS) page 280

top right   **Freedom Monument, Riga** (CN) page 124

right   **Sculpture of kissing students outside Town Hall, Tartu** (CN) page 81

below   **Detail of building on Liepų, Klaipeda** (JS) page 242

above **Orthodox church, Kaliningrad** (HE) page 278

left **Detail of Alexander Nevsky Cathedral, Tallinn** (JS) page 55

below **St Anne's Church, Vilnius** (GT) page 210

top **Amber Museum, Kaliningrad**
(JS) page 277

above **Blackheads' House, Riga**
(CN) page 131

left **Water spout on Town Hall, Tallinn**
(TV/TCTO) page 54

top **Kaunas from the Nemunas River** (JS) page 217

above **Turn-of-the-century house, Liepaja** (AWB) page 160

below **'Fishing Village', Kaliningrad** (HE) page 271

above   **Aerial view of Tallinn Old Town**   (TV/TCTO) page 42

below   **Vilnius Old Town in winter** (AA/TLT) page 196

Within the relatively short time when Art Nouveau flourished in Riga various sub-styles can be distinguished: eclectic Art Nouveau, perpendicular Art Nouveau and from 1905 the distinctively Latvian National Romanticism.

Art Nouveau (or *Jugendstil* as it is known in German) originally developed in Germany and Belgium towards the end of the 19th century and spread rapidly throughout Europe as far as Spain and Hungary. Its original decorative elements – birds, animals, shells and elaborate flower motifs are typical – were in stark contrast to the academic styles of the late 19th century. Philosophically, Art Nouveau introduced the concept that everything useful should be beautiful; the outside of a building for example should be suited to the function of the building. As the style spread throughout Europe individual countries developed their own variations.

The style which developed in Riga was influenced mainly by German, Austrian and Finnish architects, but the approach also has distinctive elements drawn from Latvian cultural traditions and construction techniques. Most of the architects who designed Riga's Art Nouveau buildings were trained at the Riga Polytechnical Institute; almost 90% were Baltic Germans, but the 10% or so of native Latvian architects built about 40% of the new buildings.

The most extravagant Art Nouveau buildings are in Alberta. Five of the apartment blocks here (numbers 2, 2a, 4, 6, 8) were designed by Mikhail Eisenstein. Close by, Elizabetes is also rich in Art Nouveau buildings, including the former studio of the painter Jānis Rozentāls, now a museum. The building was designed in 1904 by Konstantīns Pēkšēns (one of the most prolific Art Nouveau architects, responsible for over 250 buildings). The spectacular murals lining the circular staircase inside the building bear witness to the fact that Art Nouveau was not limited to building exteriors, but also included interior design, furniture, china, glassware and book design.

After the revolution of 1905 a distinctively Latvian variation of Art Nouveau developed, known as National Romanticism. Keen to promote national awareness at a time of oppression, architects sought to use traditional Latvian folk art elements and to use the language of the indigenous art of wooden construction. Natural building materials were used, and typical elements were steep roofs, heavy structures and the use of ethnographic ornamental motifs. Some examples include Brīvības 47, Terbātas 15–17 and Kr Valdemāra 67, all built by Eiž ens Laube (together with K Pēkšēns in the case of the school building at Tērbatas 15–17).

Eisenstein (1867–1921), father of film director Sergei of *Battleship Potemkin* fame. These include 10b Elizabetes, with its monumental faces, and the well-restored building at 41 Strēnieku, now occupied by the School of Economics. Numbers 2, 2a, 4, 6 and 8 and 13 Alberta are also his work. Number 4 is of particular interest. With lions dramatically astride the turrets, it was for several years the home of Eisenstein himself. At number 12 Alberta, designed by Konstantīns Pēkšēns, is the **Jānis Rozentāls and Rūdolfs Blaumanis Memorial Museum** (Jāņa Rozentāla un Rūdolfa Blaumaņa Memoriālis Muzejs, page 123). The museum is an interesting record of the lives of the painter and the writer, but even if you do not visit the museum, it is worth looking into the entrance and admiring the elaborate staircase. It is hoped in 2008 to open a museum on Alberta dedicated to Art Nouveau.

Other buildings of note in this area include the block at the corner of Strēlnieku and Elizabetes (21a) which has a plaque to commemorate the architect and diplomat

Mārtiņš Nukša (1878–1942), 23 Elizabetes, with the motto 'Labor vinvit omnia' ('Work conquers all'), numbers 3 and 14 Ausekļa, and numbers 3 and 4 Vidus.

While Eisenstein's buildings are in the eclectic Art Nouveau style, the buildings in the New Town shopping area reflect a greater diversity of styles. Examples of perpendicular Art Nouveau can be seen at 49–51 Terbātas, the work of Eižens Laube, and at 61 Lāčplēša (architect Rudolf Dohnberg). One of the first National Romanticism buildings is at 4 Lāčplēša, an apartment block designed by Pēkšēns and built in 1905.

Although the majority of Art Nouveau buildings are in the New Town, there are some in the Old Town as well. There are examples at Smilšu (number 8, the cake shop; number 6, a bank; and number 2, designed by Pēkšēns); Sķūņu (number 4 and 12–14); there is an imposing doorway opposite the Pūt, Vējiņ! restaurant at 25–29 Jauniela (architect Wilhelm Bockslaff); and a more colourful example at 23 Kalēju, the work of Paul Mandelstamm. The attractive Flower House, with paintings of pharmaceutical plants on the outside walls, is at the corner of Mazā Monētu and Mazā Jaunava, just behind the Rolands Hotel.

NEW TOWN WALK The Old Town and New Town are separated by the city canal (pilsētas kanāls) which runs through a series of parks and gardens. The canal follows the line of part of the old city wall which was demolished in the 19th century. Through the centre of the parks, separating the Old Town from the New Town, is **Brīvības bulvāris** (Freedom Boulevard), here a pedestrianised street that is also the site of the Freedom Monument. This is where the New Town Walk starts.

The **Freedom Monument** (Brīvības piemineklis, page 143) dominates the centre of Riga and has played a central and symbolic role in Latvia's chequered history. Close to the Freedom Monument (on the Old Town side of the park) stands the **Laima Clock**, another landmark and a popular meeting point. Laima is the name of a well-known chocolate manufacturer and the Latvian word for happiness or good luck (there was an ancient deity of that name).

Southwest of the Laima Clock is a fountain, the Nymph of Riga, which dates back to 1888. Close by is the statue of **George Armisted** (1847–1912) and his wife, strolling with their dog. This was unveiled by Queen Elizabeth II during her state visit to Riga in October 2006. Of British origin, Armisted was one of Riga's most successful and most long-serving mayors, being in office from 1901 to 1912. (His contemporary successors, lucky to be in office for as long as two years, must be very envious.) The buildings visible in all directions from here are testimony to the wealth of the town under his stewardship. These stand in front of the stately **National Opera,** the home of Riga's opera and ballet companies. Originally built as a German theatre, this impressive building (Classical on the outside, Baroque on the inside) can be seen from anywhere in this central parkland area. Founded in 1919, the National Opera was the focus of Latvian cultural life during the first independence and has resumed an important role in recent years (page 113).

The Opera House is a good starting point for strolls through the parks in the centre of Riga: through Bastejkalns Park (page 144) with its memorial to five victims of the events of 1991, through Kronvalda Park (page 145) with its monuments to Latvian writers, Riga Congress House (Rigas kongresu nams) and the Riga Council Building (Rīgas Dome), or beyond the Freedom Monument towards the New Town, through Vermānes Park (page 145) or the Esplanade Park. This is a moment to recall **Georg Kuphaldt** (1853–1938), who is hardly known now but who fully deserves a reputation similar to that enjoyed by Armisted. He was chief landscape gardener in Riga from 1880 until 1915, when he was expelled as a German spy, simply because he had a telescope in his garden. Whilst the Esplanade parks and gardens are a constant reminder of his talent, so are other gardens throughout the former Russian Empire. Kadriorg Park in Tallinn and the park beside the sea in Liepaja both owe their current designs to him, as do the Winter Palace Gardens in St Petersburg. Although he lived for another 20 years in Berlin, he was sadly not able to use his talent effectively there.

A number of interesting buildings are scattered in or around the parks. These include Riga University on Raiņa bulvāris, a Gothic building with elements of the Romanesque. It stands on the site of the ancient Rīdzene River, long since channelled underground, and was originally used by the Riga Polytechnical Institute. It features a stone staircase divided into three parts, the centre section of which is traditionally used only by graduates. On Merķeļa, the street behind the university and alongside Vermānes Park, is the impressive **House of the Riga Latvian Society** (Rīgas Latviešu Biedrība). The society was founded in 1868 at a time when Latvian was fighting to become a widely acknowledged language but the current building, with paintings on the façade by Jānis Rozentāls, dates from 1910. Just opposite, say hello to the engaging statue of **Kārlis Padegs**, an artist whose scandalous paintings were the talk of Riga in the 1930s (page 143). Think of him talking about his pictures just here, since it was in Vērmanis Park that they were exhibited. The statue was a private donation to the city as it would probably be hard to justify one from public funds. At the north end of the Esplanade Park on K Valdemāra stands the Academy of Art (Mākslas akademija), a fine example of neo-Gothic architecture. In front of it there is a statue by Burkards Dzenis (1936) of Jānis Rozentāls, the founder of the Latvian Realist school of painting, with a brush and palette in his hands. Note some motifs from his paintings at the base of the pedestal. Next to the Academy is the **National Museum of Art** (Nacionālais Mākslas Muzejs, page 129), built in 1905 by Wilhelm Neumann in German Baroque style, which houses a collection of 17,000 paintings. If you are not making a separate trip to examine the Art Nouveau area (page 123) in detail, here would be a good point to make a quick foray into the area. From the State Museum of Art return to Elizabetes and proceed a little way north away from the park. Quite soon you will come to 10b Elizabetes, a highlight among Mikhail Eisenstein's Art Nouveau buildings. Make sure you cross the road to look up at it or you will miss the impressive details at the top.

At the south end of the Esplanade Park on Brīvības bulvāris is the **Russian Orthodox Cathedral** (page 139), with its distinctive domes surmounted by Orthodox crosses, built in 1876–84 to designs by Roberts Pflugs. During the Soviet years it was used as a planetarium and for scientific lectures. Now it has been handed back to the Orthodox Church, and has been magnificently restored. On the north side, note the statue to **Barclay de Tolly**, the most famous Russian general in the battles with Napoleon in 1812. The original was meant to be ready for the 100th anniversary of his victories in 1912 but was in fact only unveiled late in 1913. Two years later, when the Germans were a likely threat to Riga, it was removed inland and disappeared. The first Latvian government and then the Soviet one were both of course equally uninterested in its restoration but an ethnic Russian paid for this copy, which was unveiled in July 2002.

Opposite the cathedral, the large government building is the Ministru kabinets, the Cabinet Office.

If you are interested in churches, it is worth continuing up Brīvības for two blocks beyond the Hotel Lātvija, where you will come to another Russian Orthodox building, the **Alexander Nevsky Church** on the corner of Brīvības and Lāčplēša. It is named after the 13th-century Russian prince who was canonised by the Russian Orthodox Church in 1547 for his efforts to preserve Orthodoxy in Russia against the **Teutonic Knights** whom he defeated at Lake Peipus (now in Estonia) in 1242, a story immortalised in Eisenstein's 1938 film *Alexander Nevsky*. A little further on, down Ģertrūdes on the left of Brīvības, is **St Gertrude's Church**, a large red-brick church built in 1863–67 to designs by Johann Daniel Felsko (1813–1902). Felsko was

Riga's chief architect from 1844 to 1879 and introduced the boulevards to the New Town and then the railway system. The plain interior, pleasing woodwork and gallery are typical of many Latvian churches.

Wander back towards the parks through the boulevards lined with shops and, increasingly, cafés and restaurants, and admire the many different styles of Art Nouveau buildings on Tērbatas, Lāčplēša and the surrounding streets.

MOSCOW DISTRICT WALK Depending on how energetic you are feeling, you can either walk to the Maskavas district or take tram number 7 from the stop opposite the National Opera on Aspāzijas bulvāris. Either way, you will start off going round or through the **Central Market** (Centrāltirgus). In the 19th century this area was full of what used to be called 'red warehouses' (some still stand), so called after the colour of the bricks used to build them. The modern market buildings consist of five large pavilions, each one originally designed to deal with a different product. Each one is 12m high and covers an area of 75,000m², and was built in 1930 to a design intended for Zeppelin hangars. Apart from the formal market, the area around the hangars is full of stalls selling all manner of food, clothing and other goods. Maskavas starts at the end of the market, close to the river. Whether on foot or by tram, follow this road away from central Riga, and very shortly you will see on your left an excellent example of Soviet architecture of the Stalin era in the form of the **Academy of Sciences** building. Constructed in 1957, its nickname, 'Stalin's birthday cake', reflects its ornateness. Similar buildings can be found in Moscow and Warsaw. Though they are now faded and difficult to see, sharp eyes may spot the communist hammer and sickle motifs close to the top. Since 2006 it has been possible to ascend the tower. Tickets for the lift cost Ls1 and are available at the reception desk, normally seven days a week and even after dark. Sometimes a guide is on duty to point out the main sights. This is a much less crowded viewpoint than St Peter's (or the Skyline Bar at the Lātvija Hotel) and is the best way to judge Riga's current urban development.

Continuing westwards along Elijas is the **Evangelical Lutheran Church of Jesus** in the centre of a square bordered to the north by the Hanza Hotel and then by the Belarussian Embassy. A Lutheran church has stood on this site since the 17th century, and one with the current design in wood since the 19th century. It has always been open for worship, even during the German and Soviet occupations. Only the limestone foundations remain from the 17th-century building, which was blown up by the Swedes to prevent it from being seized by the Russians in 1656. One built in the 1680s was again destroyed by the Swedes as they were forced to surrender Riga to the Russians in 1710. The next church was consecrated in 1733 and Johann Gottfried Herder (see page 120) preached here during his stay in Riga between 1764 and 1769. This church was burnt down in 1812 as part of Riga's defences against Napoleon, in case he attempted to invade the city. Its successor was built in the 1830s, when it was the largest wooden church in Latvia, which it still is. It survived both world wars, although the church was extensively restored in 1938 on its 300th anniversary. The booklet sold at the church for Ls1 is written in excellent English and fully describes all the architectural changes and the various organs that the church has had.

Continue east to the junction of Gogoļa and Dzirnavu, where the **Great Synagogue** once stood. It was built between 1868 and 1871 and was burnt down on 4 July 1941 just as the Germans arrived in Riga. The number of people inside who were deliberately massacred remains uncertain but is probably about 600. The site was ignored during the Soviet era, until 1989 when a small memorial was erected. Excavations of the foundations slowly started in the late 1990s and have now been opened. On 4 July 2007, a few days before she retired, President Vīķe-Freiberga unveiled a monument to commemorate 400 Latvians who were active in protecting members of the Jewish community from the Holocaust.

Strūgu (between Gogoļa and Maskavas, just before the elevated Lāčplēša) reflects the area's Russian past: the name means 'Barge Street' and recalls the days when barges and rafts sailed along the Daugava between Riga and ports in Russia.

Before long the road passes under the elevated approach to Salu Bridge and you find yourself in **Maskavas district** (Maskavas Forštate), so called because it was a Russian area in earlier times (Maskva is Moscow in Russian) and the road to Moscow passed through it. For many years it was inhabited mainly by Russians and Jews and, although this is no longer the case, it continues to attract a high proportion of people of non-Latvian origin. The area is a quiet haven where it is easy to imagine yourself back a hundred years: the streets are still cobbled, many of the houses wooden, trees and parks plentiful and the number of cars typically very low.

If you have come by tram, get off at Mazā Kalna (two stops after coming under the elevated road). The area near the junction of Maskavas and Mazā Kalna used to be known as Krasnaja Gorka (Red Hill) and was where the Russian population of Riga came to celebrate the first Sunday after Easter, a traditional Orthodox feast day. The traditional Russian name is barely remembered now, but the tradition remains alive in the name of the nearby street, Sarkanā (Red Street). Walk up Mazā Kalna as far as you can go, noting the traditional 'shops' on the left (holes in the wall), and you will come to the **Russian Orthodox Church of St John the Baptist** at the edge of the **Ivan Cemetery** (Ivana Kapi). If you are interested in trains, you can turn left when leaving the church and walk along Lielā Kalna. Where the road turns you will find a footbridge across a huge swathe of railway lines. From the centre of the bridge is a good view of Riga New Town, including the dominant Reval Hotel Lātvija. If trains are of little interest, turn right out of the church and then right along Daugavpils. A left turn along Jēkabpils leads through two parks, formerly cemeteries, **Klusais dārzs** (Quiet Garden) to the left and **Miera dārzs** (Peace Garden) to the right. Each has a church in its ground: St Francis, a Catholic church in the latter, and All Saints, a Russian Orthodox church in the former. At the edge of the park turn left down Katoļu as far as Maskavas.

It was in this area that the **Jewish ghetto** was established in 1941. In August 1941 the Riga citizens who lived in the district were moved to locations closer to the centre of the city, and by October an area of about 750m² had been formed taking in Lāčplēša, Maskavas, Ebreju (Jews' Street) and Daugavpils. The total Jewish population of the ghetto was about 30,000. The men in the ghetto who were fit to work were put to forced labour; the others were taken to Rumbula Forest on 30 November 1941 and systematically murdered by German guards with the assistance of a significant number of Latvian collaborators. Other Jews were brought in to replace those murdered, only to suffer the same fate in the forests of Biķernieki or in Dreiliņi. The total number of people killed in this way has never been finally ascertained, but estimates indicate it to be around 50,000. On 2 November 1943 the Riga ghetto was closed following the Warsaw ghetto uprising, and the few remaining inhabitants were shot or transported to concentration camps. No trace of the ghetto remains today, although there is a Jewish cemetery (Ebreju kapi) not far away between Tējas and Lauvas.

A left turn along Maskavas, followed by a right turn into Grebenščikova leads to the **Church of the Old Believers** (page 138), the glittering dome of which you can see from a distance. The area beyond the church and close to the river has seen considerable development in recent years. The large Mols shopping centre now stands on the river bank and its buildings dominate the environs. Before crossing to it, you may like to visit the **Armenian Apostolic Church** (at the time of writing being restored) on Kojusalas. From in front of the shopping centre you can take a shuttle bus back to the station, close to the Central Market.

MEŽAPARKS WALK

The Mežaparks area in the northeast of Riga lies on Ķīšezers (lake) and includes a park, which houses Riga Zoo as well as the immensely large Lielā

The only synagogue that now operates in Riga is in Peitavas. The site of what used to be the main synagogue (the Choral Synagogue) on the corner of Dzirnavu and Gogoļa is marked by a memorial (not a very impressive one) consisting of parts of the old synagogue set in a sort of park. A plaque records the destruction of the synagogue on 4 July 1941. Number 29 Dzirnavu was also the site of a Jewish school until 1940. It opened again in 1989 as the only recognised Jewish school in the country.

There is a Jewish Museum and community centre (page 133) at 6 Skolas, a short walk from the Reval Hotel Latvijā, which deals with the history of Jewish life in Latvia since the 18th century and the revival of Jewish life in the country since independence.

A number of plaques in Riga commemorate influential Jews in Latvia. At 2a Alberta a plaque marks the house where Sir Isaiah Berlin, 'the British philosopher', lived between 1909–15. At 6 Blaumaņa there is a plaque for Marks Razumnijs (1896–1988), a Jewish poet and playwright.

On Ķīpsala (Kip island) is the house of Jānis Lipke (1900–87), who sheltered 53 Riga Jews in his house on the island during World War II. As their number grew, two large cellars were dug to conceal them, and 43 survived the war.

On the outskirts of Riga are also a number of sites which may be of interest. Rumbala, 10km outside Riga off Maskavas, is a site where some 25,000 Jews from the Riga ghetto were murdered in 1941. Biķernieku mežs, also close to Riga, is a similar site. A memorial was recently dedicated to the victims here by the Latvian president. To get there take bus number 14 from Brīvības to Biķernieku mežs. Finally, Salaspils, 20km south of Riga, was a Nazi camp where many thousands of people, including Jews, were killed (page 151).

For information on the Jewish ghetto, see page 127.

Estrāde (large stage), a stadium which can hold up to 20,000 singers and 30,000 spectators and is used for the annual Song Festival. The area also includes a spacious residential sector, which claims to be Europe's first garden city. To visit Mežaparks, take tram number 11 from Kr Barona to the Zooloģiskais dārzs (Zoological Park) stop, a trip of around 20 minutes. The route takes you past Meža Kapi (Woodlands Cemetery, page 147).

The first houses and streets here were built in Kaiser's Park, as it was then called, in 1902 but the area was gradually extended over the next 30 or so years. In its heyday it included Art Nouveau, functionalist and Art Deco family houses, all individually designed and all set in spacious green gardens. Between them, the individual gardens boasted around 100 species of trees and shrubs, many of them rare. The majority of owners were Baltic Germans, most of whom left Latvia from 1939 onwards. Under the Soviet occupation the houses, originally intended for one family, were turned into multi-occupancy dwellings and gradually fell into disrepair due to lack of money. Over the last few years, many of the properties have been restored, although some are still in various stages of neglect, and the area is now once again one of the most sought after in terms of real estate in Riga.

The best way to see the area is just to wander along some of the streets to the east of Kokneses prospekts. An interesting circular route would take you from the tram stop along Ezermalas, right into E Dārziņa, right again into V Olava, left down Jāņa Poruka, right into Vēlmas, left into Sigulda, left along Kokneses prospekts, a short detour into Visbijas prospekts, returning again to Kokneses prospekts, left along Pēterupes, continuing into Hamburgas and finally back along Ezermalas to the tram stop.

Some houses which may be of interest include the richly decorated Villa Adele at Hamburgas 9, now the residence of the German ambassador; the plain house at Jāņa Poruka 14, an attempt to create a distinctly Latvian style of functionalism; Hamburgas 25, a decorated Art Nouveau mansion built on top of what used to be a sand dune; and the mansard roofs, verandas and terraces of houses designed around 1911 by architect Gerhard von Tiesenhausen at 2, 4, 6–8 Visbijas prospekts.

WHAT TO SEE AND DO

MUSEUMS Riga has a huge number of museums, most of them of a high standard. They tend to be closed on Mondays and sometimes Tuesdays, so if you have a particular interest you should plan your trip carefully. From 2007, some of the larger museums started to open daily in the summer. This is noted below, and hopefully the trend will extend to others. The website of the Latvian Association of Museums (*www.muzeji.lv*) is usually fairly up to date on museum opening times but it does not help with information for national holidays.

The only museums open on Monday throughout the year are the State Museum of Art, the Motor Museum, the Open Air Ethnographic Museum, 'Jews in Latvia' and the Sports Museum. In general museums open at 10.00 or 11.00 and close at 17.00. In summer, a few of the museums stay open until 19.00, usually on Wednesday or Thursday. These include the State Museum of Art, the Arsenal Museum of Art, the Museum of Decorative and Applied Art, the Museum of Natural History, the History Museum and the Photographic Museum.

Which, if any, museums you visit, obviously depends on your personal interests. The most commonly visited museums include the Barricades Museum, the Open Air Ethnographic Museum, the Museum of the Occupation, the Motor Museum, the State Museum of Art, the Jānis Rozentāls and Rūdolfs Blaumanis Memorial Museum and the adjacent Art Nouveau houses, and the Blackheads' House.

Jāņa Akurāters Museum (*O Vāciesa 6a, Pārdaugava;* ✆ *6761 9934;* ☺ *11.00–17.00 Wed–Sat*) Across the Daugava River from the Old Town, this wooden house was the home of Jānis Akurāters (1876–1937), the popular Latvian writer, rifleman and later director of the Radio Service in Riga. Right up to his death, he wrote poetry and novels, his best known being *Kalpa zena vasara* ('The Young Farmhand's Summer') and *Degosa sala* ('The Burning Island'). The fact that the house was not large meant it was not nationalised under the Soviet occupation, and Akurāters' family continued to live there, with his original furniture and other belongings, until 1987.

Arsenal Museum of Art (*1 Torņa;* ✆ *6721 3695;* ☺ *11.00–17.00 Tue–Sun; May–Sep until 19.00 Thu*) This gallery is used for temporary exhibitions of modern art, photography and architecture. Its bookshop is the best source of foreign-language material on the contemporary Latvian arts.

National Museum of Art (*Kr Valdemāra 10a;* ✆ *6732 4461; www.lnmm.lv;* ☺ *11.00–17.00 Wed–Mon; May–Sep also Thu 11.00–19.00; admission Ls 1*) The museum, built in 1905 by Wilhelm Neumann in German Baroque style, houses a collection of 32,000 works of art and is a must for anyone interested in 19th- and early 20th-century Latvian art. Inevitably, there is a great deal of work by Rozentāls (his portrait of the singer Malvīne Vīgnere-Grīnberga painted in the last year of his life is particularly well known). Other names, less well known outside Latvia, are also of interest: Vilhelms Purvītis (1872–1945), whose Impressionist landscapes depict Latvia's forest and lakes; Jūlijs Feders (1838–1909), who painted a vast and imposing landscape of the Gauja valley north of Riga; and many others. Also of interest may be a portrait of the Russian writer Turgenev (painted in 1869) by A Gruzdins (1825–91), a bust of the Russian composer Mussorgsky by Teodors Zaļnkalns (1876–1928), a portrait of Kārlis Zāle (the designer of the Freedom Monument) by Ludolfs Liberits (1895–1959) painted in 1934 and showing a relaxed Zāle smoking a cigarette, and a picture of the old harbour when it was located closer to the Old Town, by Jāņis Roberts Tilbergs (1880–1972). Latvia's best-known woman painter is Alexandra Belcova (1892–1981). Several of her portraits are on show. Art by non-Latvian artists is less prominent, but the museum does have a notable collection of paintings of the Himalayas by the Russian artist and explorer Nicholas Roerich (1874–1947). In addition to the permanent collection, the museum also holds frequent exhibitions of works by early 20th-century artists. At the entrance is a small area selling postcards of some of the paintings and greetings cards of Old Riga.

The museum is beautifully located in the Esplanade Park. When leaving have a look at the sculpture of Jāņis Rainis, one of Latvia's most famous writers and translators, and admire too the building next door, the Latvian Academy of Art, a fine example of neo-Gothic brickwork. The totally incongruous 8m-high steel tower in front of the Academy was a gift in 1993 from Riga's twin city in Japan, Kobe. The two clocks show the different times in each city.

Aviation Museum (*Riga Airport – to the right of the terminal;* ☎ *6720 7482; www.avia.ak22.net;* ⊕ *in theory 08.00–17.00, but closed Mon and Sun Dec–Mar; admission Ls2–5*) The museum is not well known by the general public but has achieved cult status among people interested in the Soviet era. The museum contains Soviet helicopters and planes of various ages, including almost all the models of the Soviet MiGs, which can be viewed in detail when the museum is open, or over the wall if it is closed. The planes are ones that were used for training, but none is now airworthy. Access is dependent on the attendant being around, and the charge is Ls5 for foreigners and Ls2 for locals, but Russian speakers should have no problem in paying Ls2 and it is worth others trying as well. Such discrimination is now illegal within the EU but visitors to St Petersburg will be well aware of such dual pricing.

Barricades Museum (*Krāmu 3;* ☎ *6721 3525; www.barikades.lv;* ⊕ *10.00–17.00 Mon–Fri, 11.00–17.00 Sat; admission Ls1*) Strolling across Cathedral Square, it is hard to believe that it was a battleground in January 1991. A large model here shows how the Latvians defended themselves at the time and film commentaries bring the noise, fear and drama to life, not to mention the bitter cold. This was the sequel to the storming of the Television Tower in Vilnius. Most of the exhibits are described in English but the staff are very helpful at providing further background.

Krisjāņis Barons Memorial Museum (*Kr Barona 3–5;* ☎ *6728 4265;* ⊕ *11.00–18.00 Wed–Sun; admission Ls0.40*) The museum is the flat (number 5) occupied by Krisjāņis Barons (1835–1923), the Latvian poet and folklorist who is best remembered as the collector of Latvian oral literature: *dainas*, traditional four-line songs. The entrance is via a filthy staircase with loose wires hanging out of the wall and abandoned bottles in the corridor, hardly appropriate for someone to whom Latvia owes so much. Fearing that traditional Latvian culture would be lost, Barons travelled around the country collecting songs. He also advertised in newspapers and was sent tens of thousands of examples of dainas which he then catalogued. He began to publish his collections of dainas in 1894 and the project eventually ran to six large volumes containing around one and a half million songs. The museum recreates his life and work through documents and photographs. Information is available in English; examples of folk music and videos can also be purchased.

The Blackheads' House (*Rātslaukums 7;* ✆ *6704 4300; www.nami.riga.lv;* ⊕ *10.00–17.00 Tue–Sun; admission Ls1.50*) The Blackheads' House, one of Riga's most important monuments, was restored in 1999. The wonderful façade is one of Riga's highlights, both during the day and when floodlit at night. This magnificent house (really a building made up of two houses connected by an enclosed courtyard), with its Dutch Renaissance façade (1620), dated back to 1334 but was badly damaged in World War II and finally destroyed by the Soviets in 1948. The 'Blackheads', first mentioned in 1413, were an association of unmarried merchants who lived in Riga and Reval (Tallinn). Originally a loose association, they grew to become a powerful force. It is believed that they got their unusual name from their black patron saint, St Maurice. The first floor of the building was used for shops and businesses; the guildhall of the association occupied the second floor; the upper floors were used for storage and warehousing.

The huge step-gable is 28m high and highly decorated with statues of people and other animals. The building is topped by a large figure of St George which acts as a weathervane. A statue of Roland stands in front of the building. A popular figure in the Middle Ages, and especially in Germany, the Roland statue was originally erected in 1897 but damaged in World War II. A replica has now replaced it (see page 144).

The interior is now a museum. Particularly impressive is the assembly hall on the first floor. Although none of the paintings here are original, they are faithful copies. Note the Swedish and Russian royal families looking across the floor at each other. Much of the silver collection which used to be here is now in Bremen, taken by Baltic Germans who left Riga in the 1930s, and some in St Petersburg, although some families have been helping to rebuild the collection in Riga. You can also visit restored rooms on the ground floor and tour the old foundations in the basement. As with the Stadtsschloss in Königsberg, the Russians left the foundations intact, only needing to remove the areas above ground from view.

The Cathedral Cloister (see page 138)

'Dauderi' Latvian Cultural Museum (*Sarkandaugavas 30;* ✆ *6739 2229; www.dauderi.lv; take tram 9 from the centre north to Aldaris;* ⊕ *11.00–17.00 Wed–Sun; admission Ls1*) This museum is housed in an elegant red-brick house and was built between 1897–98. During the first independence period, it was the summer residence of the Latvian president, Kārlis Ulmanis, before he was deported. It contains a vast collection of memorabilia related to the recent history of the country brought together by Gaidis Graundiņš, a Latvian living in Germany. There are also mementoes of Latvia's first period of independence, such as banknotes, stamps, photographs and so on, all collected from Latvian exiles.

Museum of Decorative and Applied Art (*Skārņu 10–20;* ✆ *6722 2235; www.dlmm.lv;* ⊕ *11.00–17.00 Tue–Sun; 11.00–19.00 Wed; admission Ls2*) The Museum of Decorative and Applied Art opened in 1989 in the restored Jura baznīca (St George's Church) in the Old Town, generally acknowledged as the oldest stone-built religious building surviving in Riga. The exhibition hall still has a church-like feel about it, although it has not been used for church services for almost five hundred years. The exhibits include tapestries, pottery, glasswork and sculpture, and the old churchyard has been transformed into a sculpture garden. The building itself has been very well restored, and is sometimes used for state occasions: in 1998 a summit of European prime ministers was held here.

Museum of Fire-Fighting (*Hanzas 5;* ✆ *6733 1334;* ⊕ *10.00–16.30 Wed–Sun; admission Ls0.20*) This unusual museum is housed in an Art Nouveau fire station built in 1912 just north of the Art Nouveau district and contains displays depicting the history of

fire-fighting in Riga. The engines displayed go back to 1899 and include a Chevrolet from America. Whatever the nature of the regime, many fire crews in Latvia have been voluntary, and there are photographs of them in action and posing formally. Foreign fires are covered too, from Moscow in 1812 to New York in 2001. A major feature is a fire engine built during the first period of independence.

Latvian Museum of Foreign Art (*Pils laukums 3;* ↘ *6722 6467; www.amm.lv;* ⊕ *11.00–17.00 Tue–Sun; admission L1.20*) Housed in part of Riga Castle, the museum consists of three floors of paintings, sculptures, drawings and ceramics by artists from Germany, Holland, France and Belgium. It is a rather odd museum: many of the oldest exhibits (sculptures from Greece and Rome and artefacts from ancient Egypt) are mixed up with modern works; the more conventional galleries exhibit paintings by 17th-century Dutch artists, German works dating from the 16th–19th century and Belgian painting of the 20th century. There are almost no works of great distinction.

Latvian History Museum (*Pils laukums 3;* ↘ *6722 1357; www. history-museum.lv;* ⊕ *11.00–17.00 Wed–Sun; 11.00–19.00 Thu; admission Ls0.70, free on Wed*) This museum, part of the castle complex, traces the history of Latvia and Latvian culture from 9000BC to the present. Each room takes a different and unrelated theme. It is good to see a museum in Latvia that is keeping up to date and where care is taken over presentation and lighting. Do not judge the museum by the gloomy entrance to the building or by the torn signs on the stairs. One room concentrates on archaeology but sadly the labels are only in Latvian; another covers religious statues in both stone and wood which have been rescued from churches all over the country. Turning to more modern history, there are models and original tools to display 19th-century farming, a school room from the 1930s and a costume room from the same period. When the EBRD (European Bank for Reconstruction and Development) met in Riga in May 2000, a permanent coin room was set up in the museum. The coins on display go back to the 9th century but of most interest, perhaps, are those from the 1914–20 period when German and Russian ones circulated side by side. A hat exhibition opened in 2002.

Museum of Riga's History and Navigation (*Palasta 4;* ↘ *6735 66 76; www.rigamuz.lv;* ⊕ *10.00–17.00 daily, & to 19.00 on Wed in summer; closed Mon & Tue 16 Oct–30 Apr; admission Ls2.50*) Founded in 1773, this is the oldest museum in Latvia. It was originally set up to house items from the private collection of Nicolaus von Himsel (1729–64) whose portrait by an unknown artist hangs in the ground-floor exhibition hall. The main permanent exhibition traces the development of Riga from its beginnings to 1940. It does so by reference to maps, plans, pictures and objects of all kinds from the everyday life of the city's inhabitants.

The collection is weak on the medieval period but particularly strong on 1920–40, showing how affluent and diverse life was for a reasonable number of people at that time. The display covers magazines published in several languages, fans, pottery, glasswork and clothes. In 2002 the impressive Colonnade Hall reopened; it was originally built between 1778 and 1783 from designs by Christoph Haberland, the architect who designed Riga Town Hall. It was closed for renovation in 1984 and this has only now been completed. Some of the original brickwork can be seen. It houses a large portrait of Peter the Great arriving in Riga in 1710.

The second main permanent exhibition is devoted to the history of navigation from ancient times to the present day. One room is dedicated to the work of Krišjānis Valdemārs (1825–91), a pioneer in naval education in Latvia. What is displayed here would be more than enough work for most people, but Valdemārs was also active as a short-story writer, a newspaper editor and as a constant political campaigner in the

National Awakening Movement. The exhibition includes many models of ships which have been connected with Riga from the 10th century to the present day.

'Jews in Latvia' Museum (*3rd floor, Skolas 6;* ☎ *6738 3484;* ⏲ *12.00–17.00 Sun–Thu; admission free, donation requested*) The museum is in the New Town in a street close to the Reval Hotel Lātvija. This small but moving museum is devoted to the history of Jews in Latvia, from the first records of Jewish families living with full civil rights in Piltene in the mid 16th century, through growing discrimination in the 19th and early 20th centuries to the destruction of the synagogues in Riga, Jelgava and Liepaja in 1941 and the terrible sufferings subsequently imposed by both the Nazis and the Soviets. The exhibits, in English as well as Latvian, illustrate the many fields in which Jews contributed to Latvian life in the past, and continue to do so today. On the staircase going up to the museum are photographs and descriptions of some of the Latvians who saved Jews from persecution during World War II, sometimes at the cost of their own lives. Their work is also described in the museum itself.

Literature, Theatre and Music Museum (*2 Pils laukums;* ☎ *721 1956;* ⏲ *10.00–17.00 Wed–Sun; admission Ls0.40*) The former Rainis Museum, founded in 1925 and devoted to Latvian literature, has recently been rebranded as the Museum of Literature, Theatre and Music. Permanent exhibits include photographs, manuscripts and texts relating to the history of Latvian literature from its earliest times right up to the 20th century. Recent additions are two exhibitions devoted to Gunārs Freimanis (1927–93) and Voldemārs Zariņš (1917–81), both of whom were persecuted by the Soviet authorities. Freimanis spent ten years in the Russian gulags; Zariņš was sent to forced labour in the coal mines of Tula. Other exhibitions are changed periodically. Unfortunately, all the information (except for a short pamphlet) is in Latvian.

Mentzendorff House (*Grēcinieku 18;* ☎ *6721 2951; www.mencendorfanams.com;* ⏲ *10.00–17.00 daily but closed Mon & Tue 16 Oct–30 Apr; admission Ls1.20*) The former residence of a wealthy Riga merchant family, this house is now a museum devoted to life in Riga in the 17th and 18th centuries. The building dates from the 1720s when it replaced an earlier one destroyed in the Riga fire of 1677. Wall paintings from that time have only recently been discovered; in some rooms there were as many as five layers of paintings and then 20 layers of wallpaper from the 19th and 20th centuries. Some of the early paintings were modelled on the work of the French artist Antoine Watteau (1684–1721). The house now carries the name of the last Baltic-German family to live here until 1940, though it is sometimes still called the 'Merchant's House' in view of the number of trades carried out here. The outlines of the grocery store that the Mentzendorff family ran can be seen on the ground floor, although not all the articles displayed are originals from this house. Note the raised edge of the long wooden table, which prevented coins slipping to the floor. In winter, the kitchen stove was the centre of the household: it was used to cook the food, smoke the meat and heat the whole house. The basement is used for temporary art exhibitions, but the higher floors display furniture, clothes, clocks, playing cards and musical instruments which the Baltic Germans would have enjoyed in the 18th and 19th centuries. In Soviet times 15 different families lived in the building and they were only moved out in 1981 for restoration to begin. It was completed in 1992.

Motor Museum (*Eizenšteina 6;* ☎ *6709 7170; www. motormuzejs.lv;* ⏲ *10.00–18.00 daily; admission Ls1*) The museum is around 8km from the Old Town. The best way to go by public transport is to take a number 14 trolleybus from Brīvības or a number 18 from Čaka and get off at Gaiļezers Hospital, about 500m from the museum. The museum is not easy to spot: look out for what appears to be a large Audi dealership and showroom; it is a modern red-brick and glass building. The entrance is reached via a bridge from the car park.

The collection was started by enthusiasts for old cars in 1972 and the museum opened in 1989 at the end of the Soviet era. It houses an acclaimed collection of over 100 motor vehicles, including cars which once belonged to the Soviet leaders, Stalin, Khrushchev and Brezhnev, and Erich Honecker, the leader of the former German Democratic Republic. Wax figures of some of these former politicians and motor enthusiasts help to liven up the displays: Stalin sits in his armoured ZIS 115 (said to have done 2.5km to the litre), Brezhnev at the wheel of his crashed Rolls-Royce; Gorky stands next to his 1934 Lincoln.

The first car assembly plant in Tsarist Russia was established in Riga in 1909 and this was followed by no fewer than 30 bicycle factories during the first independence period. Their products are also exhibited here, as are later Soviet motorbikes. A lot of the cars that form the backbone of the collection were abandoned in 1939–40, firstly by the Baltic Germans recalled 'home' by Hitler, and secondly by the embassies closed after the Soviet occupation. Others are German cars abandoned during the long retreat towards the end of World War II. One is a Rolls-Royce which had been built under licence in Germany. Although the museum is famous for displaying the car that Brezhnev crashed, another one of the 40 or so that he owned is also on display – a 1974 Continental presented by the American government.

Latvian Museum of Natural History (*Kr Barona 4;* ✆ *6722 6078; www.dabasmuzejs.gov.lv;* ✵ *10.00–17.00 Wed–Sun; admission Ls0.60*) The museum is strongest in palaeontology but also has permanent exhibitions of geology, zoology, entomology, anthropology and environmental protection. More recently it has added an exhibition concentrating on the Daugava River and the effect of the construction of the hydro-electric power station on the river basin. Note the herbarium display, the work of the botanist J Ilsters. Most information is in Latvian and Russian only but an interactive computer programme for children on the top floor is in English.

Museum of the Occupation of Latvia (*1 Strēlnieku laukums;* ✆ *6721 2715; www.occupationmuseum.lv;* ✵ *11.00–18.00, closed Mon Oct–Apr; admission free*) This museum, housed in an exceptionally ugly cuboid building, contains a permanent exhibition devoted to the history of Latvia during the Soviet and Nazi occupations of 1940–91. The displays are on the first floor and exhibit photographs and documents, maps and artefacts dealing with the period and also contain a replica of a barracks room from a Soviet gulag. One display covers the life Latvians led in Siberia after release from the camps but while they were still exiled. Another shows the struggle of Latvians in the West to keep the memory of their country alive during the Soviet occupation. Extensive collections of letters, photographs and everyday articles depict the horror of life for those jailed or deported. The renovation of the Hotel Riga provided a new exhibit for the museum – the bugging equipment with which the hotel staff monitored phone calls during the Soviet era. There is excellent background material in English to all the exhibits and a bookshop which sells most of the publications available in English on the two occupations.

The long-term future of the building is a subject of great controversy. Some Latvians feel that the theme of the museum is so important that even if another building were found elsewhere (unlikely under current financial circumstances) it would suggest a loss of interest in the topic on the part of the city administration. Others feel that a Soviet building, whatever its current contents, should no longer be allowed to disfigure the heart of Latvia's capital. The Latvian-born architect Gunars Birkerts, who now practises in America, has suggested alterations to the building which might provide an appropriate compromise and which would certainly make it aesthetically acceptable. No decision has yet (in 2008) been made. However, the plans to build a new national library, concert hall and art gallery are likely to take priority over the next ten years.

Open Air Ethnographic Museum (*Brīvības gatve 440;* ✆ *6799 4515; www.virmus.com;* ⊕ *10.00–17.00 daily, but buildings closed Nov–Mar; admission Ls1*) On the northeastern outskirts of the city close to Lake Jugla, about half an hour by bus number 1. Get on at the corner of Merķeļa and Tērbatas and get off at the Brīvdabas Muzejs stop.

Although modern Riga has much in common with other European capitals, a visit to the beautifully constructed Open Air Ethnographic Museum will help you understand some of the more distinctive elements of Latvian history and tradition. It will certainly make you appreciate too how close nature lies to the heart of every Latvian and just how attractive Latvian nature can be.

'Museum' is something of a misnomer for this 100ha site, which contains farms, churches, windmills, houses, fishermen's villages and many other buildings, set in a huge pine forest next to Lake Jugla. Brought together from all parts of Latvia, some buildings date back to the 16th century. Most constructions are wooden and blend beautifully with the surrounding trees. It is a pleasure just to walk among them, as well as to learn more about traditional Latvian life from the many exhibits. At the weekends it is usually possible to watch craftsmen at work: a blacksmith forging a hunting knife, a woman weaving traditional clothes.

Some favourites are the strange traditional *dore*, hollowed tree trunks standing on stone bases and used for beekeeping; wooden *pirts*, traditional baths; the wooden Usma church, which is still used for church services and weddings; and the 18th-century *krogs* (pub) which serves traditional food and drinks including barley beer. It is also a good source of Latvian handmade souvenirs, with prices much lower than those in the town centre. You should allow at least two hours for a visit, and you could easily spend a half or even a whole day here. The museum website offers a virtual tour of all the buildings for those without the time or energy to make a personal visit.

Pharmaceutical Museum (*13–15 Riharda Vāgnera;* ✆ *6721 6828; www.mvm.lv;* ⊕ *10.00–17.00 Tue–Sat; admission Ls0.20*) Part of the Paul Stradin Museum of the History of Medicine, this branch is housed in a beautifully renovated 18th-century house in the Old Town. It has an extensive collection of documents, samples of medicine manufactured in Latvia and many other pharmacy-related items which non-visitors would be hard-pushed to imagine. The interior of a 19th-century chemist's brings it all to life.

Latvian Photographic Museum (*8 Mārstaļu;* ✆ *6722 7231 www.fotomuzejs.lv;* ⊕ *10.00–17.00 Tue, Fri, Sat, 12.00–19.00 Wed & Thu, closed Sun, Mon; admission Ls1*) The basic exhibition is of cameras and pictures from 1839 to 1941, including many of historic events such as the 1905 Revolution and World War I. A studio from 1900 has also been set up, where it is possible for visitors to take a photo using the technology of that time. An interesting exhibit is dedicated to the Minox 'spy camera', invented by Walter Zapp, who was born in Riga in 1905. The cameras were made in Riga between 1938 and 1943 and have been used ever since. The museum is now gradually being extended to cover World War II.

Museum of the Popular Front (*Vecpilsētas 13–15;* ✆ *6722 4502;* ⊕ *14.00–19.00 Tue, 12.00–17.00 Wed–Fri, 12.00–16.00 Sat; admission free*) This is a small, recently opened museum in the former offices of the popular movement which contributed so much to the regaining of Latvian independence. It displays pictures of the movement's leaders and the demonstrations leading up to independence and also shows how the

office looked in its period of struggle. The planning for what is described at the Barricades Museum (see page 130) took place here.

Rigas Porcelain Museum
(Kalēju 9–11, in Konventa Sēta courtyard; ℡ *6750 3769;* ☉ *11.00–18.00, closed Mon; admission Ls0.50)* The museum opened to acclaim in 2001 and is the only porcelain museum in the Baltic countries. Riga has a long history of making porcelain, starting with the opening of the Kuznetzov factory in the first half of the 19th century, and the 6,000 exhibits reflect the many types of porcelain, from prestigious tea sets to crockery for everyday use, which have been made in the city from the mid 19th century to the present day. One room is devoted to items from the Soviet era, including vases and statues of Lenin, Stalin and other leaders. By far the most dominant item is a 2m-high red and gold vase made to celebrate Riga's 700th anniversary in 1901. Visitors can see demonstrations of porcelain manufacturing and for Ls3 can take part and decorate mugs themselves.

Latvian Railway Museum
(2–4 Uzvaras bulvāris; ℡ *6583 2849; www.railwaymuseum.lv;* ☉ *10.00–17.00 Wed–Sat; admission Ls0.50)* Just across the river from the Old Town, five minutes beyond the Akmens Bridge, the museum dates from 1994 and is run by Latvian Railways. The building was previously an engine repair shop. During its short life it has accumulated a wide range of materials going back about 100 years, including signals, timetables, track and, above all, steam engines. There are constant additions to the collection. One German engine from World War II is fitted out as a snowplough. As late as April 1944, the Germans produced a timetable for the whole Baltics area. It is displayed here and it remains the last one to have appeared. The Soviets regarded such information as too dangerous to impart and the three Baltic railway administrations have been unable to co-ordinate a similar publication. Railway enthusiasts may be interested to know there is another branch of the museum at Jelgava (one hour by bus from Riga), which concentrates on railway safety and training.

Jāņis Rozentāls and Rūdolfs Blaumanis Memorial Museum
(12–19 Alberta; ℡ *6733 1641;* ☉ *11.00–18.00, closed Mon & Tue; admission Ls0.60)* The entrance to this museum is on Strēlnieku. It commemorates the life and work of two well-known Latvians: Rozentāls, the painter, lived here between 1904 and 1915; Blaumanis only for two years. Take the elaborate staircase in the rather neglected hallway to the top floor and ring to gain admission. The ironwork, the tiling and the paintings on the ceiling are all original but the windows are of a later date. The architect for the building was Konstantīns Pēkšēns (1859–1928). He designed it for his own use, but then gave the top floor to Jāņis Rozentāls in 1904.

Rozentāls and his wife Elija, a renowned mezzo-soprano, lived here with their three children. The writer Rūdolfs Blaumanis rented a room in the flat and lived here in 1906–08. The living rooms contain pictures, photographs and artefacts connected with the life of the artists. The studio and other rooms on the top floor are an art school and are used to exhibit works by the students who range from young children to mature painters. Good photographs of Alberta can be taken from the top floor. Extensive renovation of the building was under way in 2008.

Latvian Sport Museum
(9 Alksnāja; ℡ *6721 5127;* ☉ *11.00–17.00 Mon–Fri, 11.00–17.00 Sat; admission Ls0.50)* The collection was brought together by a sports fanatic who devoted his life to it, and on his death in 1975 bequeathed it to Riga. It has a unique range of bicycles, including a collapsible Peugeot built in 1915 and used during World War I and an English Raleigh lady's bicycle dating from 1895, as well as more conventional exhibits. It is housed in an attractive 17th-century warehouse.

Paul Stradin Museum of the History of Medicine (*1 Antonijas;* ☎ *6722 2656;* *www.mvm.lv;* ✆ *11.00–17.00 Tue–Sat except last Fri of each month; admission Ls1*) Located in the New Town on the corner of Antonijas and Kalpaka. This museum is the creation of the Latvian doctor and surgeon, Paul Stradin (1896–1958), who collected the majority of the exhibits over a period of 30 years and presented them to the city of Riga. The exhibits, which include medical instruments, books and papers, cover a wide range of topics, from Riga during successive plague epidemics to how the human body copes with eating in outer space. Space exploration was a source of great pride to the USSR so any museum that could cover the topic was obliged to do so.

Theatre Museum (*37–39 Smiļģis, in Pārdaugava;* ☎ *611893;* ✆ *11.00–18.00 Thu–Sun;* *12.00–19.00 Wed; admission Ls0.50*) This museum is housed in the building where theatre director and actor Eduards Smiļģis (1886–1966) lived for all but five years of his life. It was empty for five years after his death before being converted into a museum that opened in 1974. Although his personal theatre here could have accommodated an audience, he always rehearsed in strict privacy, totally on his own. This theatre was modelled on the Daile Theatre in central Riga. He played every major role in the plays of Jānis Rainis and of Shakespeare, and when he gave up acting in 1940, he continued to direct. Both his sons were killed fighting, one in the German army and one in the Russian army. The collections comprehensively cover the history of the Latvian theatre, not only in Riga but also in Ventspils and in Liepaja. No famous actor is missed, nor any famous stage-set. The private rooms and offices have been left just as Smiļģis would have known and used them.

Latvian War Museum (*20 Smilšu (in the Powder Tower);* ☎ *722 8147; www.karamuzejs.lv;* ✆ *May–Sep 10.00–18.00 Wed–Sun; Oct–Apr 10.00–17.00; admission free*) During the Soviet occupation this museum was devoted to demonstrating how Latvia became a revolutionary Soviet state. Now it is a mainstream war museum with collections of army uniforms and other exhibits devoted to the military history of Latvia. Exhibits cover the period from the 15th to the 20th century but the main part of the collection focuses on the traumatic events of the 20th century. Of particular interest are the exhibitions devoted to the Latvian Riflemen's Regiment, and a recent addition, the development of the Latvian army from World War I to 1940.

CHURCHES Churches are one of the highlights of a visit to Riga. Three spires dominate the Old Town skyline – St Peter's, the highest, the Dome and St Jakob's – but other churches are also well worth a visit, including St John's, the Orthodox Cathedral and the Grebenshchikova Church of the Old Believers.

Like museums, several churches close on Mondays and/or at weekends, including the cathedral, St John's, and St Peter's, so check opening hours when planning your visit.

Riga Cathedral (*Doma laukums (Dome Square);* ☎ *6721 34 98; www.doms.lv;* ✆ *10.00–18.00 daily; groups can book from 09.00; admission Ls0.50*) The website was still only in Latvian in 2007 but should be in English by the summer of 2008. Although size alone does not justify a visit, there is no denying the huge dimensions of this, the largest church in the Baltics. The solid brick walls and 90m tower dominate not only the Cathedral Square but much of the Old Town, and have done so for almost 800 years. Sometimes known as the Dome Cathedral (a tautology, as 'Dome' comes from the German *Dom* meaning 'cathedral'), the church was built at the instigation of Albert, Bishop of Riga, now buried in the cathedral. The foundations of the church were laid in 1211 and the building consecrated in 1226. Over the years, the church has been modified and reconstructed a number of times, with the result that it is now a mixture of various styles, although it retains a strong Teutonic flavour.

Originally the church was built on a hill but today visitors walk downhill from Cathedral Square to enter via the main door. This is because earth has gradually been built up around the cathedral to try and avoid the floods which used to occur frequently in Riga. On one occasion in 1709 it is even reported that fish were caught inside the church.

After it became a Protestant church in the Reformation, much of the cathedral's elaborate interior decoration was destroyed. A striking feature which remains is the large number of coats of arms of merchants from Riga fixed on the sides of the immense pillars, all of which were donated by rich mercantile families in search of immortality. Of interest too are the stained-glass windows. Two towards the front on the north side illustrate important moments in Riga's history: one depicts Walter von Plettenberg reading the edict proclaiming religious freedom and pledging protection from the Catholic bishops (1525) and another the welcome of the Swedish king, Gustavus Adolphus, in Riga on 25 September 1621. As these do not look obviously evangelical, they were not covered during the Soviet occupation. The impressive wooden pulpit, in the middle of the church in accordance with Lutheran tradition, dates from 1641. Pēteris Stučka, a leading Latvian Bolshevik, gave a speech from it in 1918, which meant that it was very well preserved during Soviet times. Services were forbidden here from 1959 until 1989 during which time it was used only for concerts. Now of course it is used for both.

What the cathedral is most famous for, however, is its organ, a huge instrument with four manuals and a pedal board, 124 stops and 6,718 pipes. When it was built in 1884 by the firm of Walcker & Co of Ludwigsburg it was the largest organ in the world. The Walcker family website www.walckerorgel.de gives a summary of its construction and how it relates to others built around the same time.

The Cathedral Cloister (*next to the main cathedral entrance;* ☉ *10.00–17.00 daily in summer; small admission charge*) The cloister is itself a remarkable Romanesque masterpiece, with impressive ornamentation of twining flowers and leaves. Restoration has been in progress since the mid 1980s but is not yet complete. Displayed within the cloister is an assortment of items, including the original weathervane from the cathedral spire, a cockerel some 6ft tall, originally constructed in 1595 but replaced by a replica in December 1985; a plaster copy of the statue of Peter I, the original of which stood between 1910 and 1914 where the Freedom Monument now is; and a 3ft-high stone head, unearthed in the cloister in 2000. This last exhibit is still something of a mystery. Originally found in 1851 near Salaspils (just outside Riga), the stone was then lost for almost 150 years. It is possible that the head served as an idol for the Livs, the group of people who have lived on what is now Latvian territory for over 20 centuries. Records exist of the worship and making of idols in Latvia as late as the 16th to 18th centuries, but to date no other idol has been found with such strange and expressive features.

Church of the Old Believers (*Krasta 72 at the end of Grebenščikova; tram 7 or 9 from opposite the National Opera to the Daugavpils stop, approx 10 mins;* ☏ *6711 3083*) This is a church used by Orthodox Old Believers, a sect which fled from persecution in Russia in the 18th century. Their first church was erected on this site in 1760 but was burnt down and replaced by the current one in 1814. The steeple was added later, in 1906, and has traces of Art Nouveau in its design. It is surmounted by the only golden dome in Riga and can easily be spotted from any high building in the city centre. The interior contains icons dating back to the 15th century.

Orthodox Cathedral (*Brīvības bulvāris, in the Esplanade Park;* ↘ *6721 1216*) The Russian Orthodox Cathedral with its five imposing cupolas offers an insight into another aspect of multi-sided Riga: traditional Russian culture. Built between 1876 and 1884 to designs by Roberts Pflugs, the cathedral was used as a lecture hall and then as a planetarium in Soviet times, and even today Rigans often refer to it as the planetārijs – the planetarium. It now functions again as a place of worship and has been beautifully restored. The final touches were in 2008 still being made, and there are plenty of opportunities to donate to the restoration fund. The interior now sparkles with newly gilded coffins, iconostases (screens containing icons) and wall and ceiling paintings. During the Soviet occupation the crosses were removed from the building. Those now in the cathedral were made in Würzburg in Germany, consecrated in 1990 and given to the cathedral by a Latvian living in Germany.

Our Lady of Sorrows (*Lielā pils;* ◷ *06.00–13.00 & 14.00–19.00 daily*) The Roman Catholic Church of Our Lady of Sorrows dates from 1784–85, although a humbler church was located on the site before the Russian Tsar Paul I and the King of Poland, Stanislav August, were persuaded by the Austrian emperor, Joseph II, to donate money for the construction of the present church. For many years it was the only Roman Catholic church in Riga and the surrounding area. The statue of the Sorrowful Virgin above the outside door originally belonged in St Jacob's Church, but was left there by the Jesuits, later found by the Lutherans and given to this congregation.

St Jacob's or St James' (*Klostera 2;* ↘ *6732 6419;* ◷ *for visits 07.00–20.00 Sun–Fri*) Note: Jacob and James are alternative translations of the Latvian Jēkabs. Now the Roman Catholic Cathedral of Riga, the church was originally built in 1225–26. It has subsequently been rebuilt several times, although the sanctuary and the tall, whitewashed brick naves are original. The 73m spire is the lowest of the three spires which dominate the Old Town. The church has changed hands on several occasions: in 1522 it was the first church in Latvia to hold a Lutheran service, but only 60 years later it was handed over to the Jesuits. In 1621 it became a Swedish garrison church before finally returning to the Roman Catholic Church in 1922.

The brick walls have held a number of unexpected items. In 1656 the Russian Tsar Alexis Mikhailovich was attacking Riga. During the battle, several grenades hit the church and two of them were later immured above the altar. Then in 1774, during renovation work, the body of a man was found immured in the north wall. His silk garments indicated he was a man of some wealth, but his identity has never been discovered.

St John's (*Jāņa 7;* ↘ *6722 4028;* ◷ *11.00–17.00 Tue–Sun*) St John's Church was built for the Dominicans in 1234 but has since been much extended. The stunning high nave with a meshed vaulted ceiling dates from the 15th century and the ornate Baroque altar, with sculptures depicting the crucifixion and SS Peter and Paul, from the 18th. The altar painting, *The Resurrection*, is by the 18th-century Rigan artist August Stiling, while the painting *Christ on the Cross* in the sacristy is by one of Latvia's best-known artists, Jānis Rozentāls (page 136).

The history of the church again reflects Riga's turbulent past. The Dominicans were ousted in the Reformation, and for some time after 1523 the church was used as stables by the mayor of Riga, then as an arsenal, until in 1582 the Polish king, Stephen Batory, seized it and handed it over to the Jesuits. In due course it was returned to the Lutheran Church.

The outside of the church is also worth a good look. Behind the church on Jāņa are two life-sized statues, one of St John the Baptist, the patron saint of the church, and the other of Salome, who persuaded Herodias to give her John's head on a platter as a reward for her dancing. Round the corner, on the wall facing Skārņu, are two stone faces with open mouths. Some sources say they were an early elocution aid – to show monks how to open their mouths to project their voices. Others say they were used to somehow indicate that a sermon was about to begin inside the church. Also on that wall is a covered cross-shaped opening. Legend suggests that in the 15th century two monks voluntarily immured themselves in the wall in the hope of becoming saints. Until their death, passers-by gave them food and water through this hole. Unfortunately their plan did not succeed, as the pope refused to canonise them on the grounds that their motives were callow.

St Peter's Church (19 Skārņu; ✆ 6735 6699; ⊕ 10.00–17.00; 10.00–18.00 in summer, Tue–Sun)

St Peter's tower is the tallest and arguably the most beautiful church tower in Riga. The gracefully tiered steeple rises to a height of 123.5m and, along with the plainer and shorter towers of the cathedral and St Jacob's, dominates the Old City skyline. If you like bird's-eye views of cities, you can buy a ticket in the church entrance (Ls1.50) and take the lift up to the observation platform.

As you ascend, you may like to consider the tower's rather chequered career. A wooden tower was originally erected in 1491 but collapsed in 1666, killing the inhabitants of a neighbouring building. The replacement tower, completed in 1690, was badly damaged by lightning in 1721 and had to be reconstructed. When reconstruction was completed in 1746, it is said that the builder climbed to the top, drank a goblet of wine and then threw down the goblet: the number of pieces it shattered into would indicate the number of years the building would stand. Unfortunately, the goblet fell into a passing hay cart and suffered only a minor crack, as you can see for yourself if you visit the Museum of History and Navigation. Disaster struck for the third time, ironically on the feast of St Peter (29 June), in 1941 when German mortar fire destroyed both the tower and most of the church. Rebuilding took until 1973. Again a glass was thrown down from the top, but this time it shattered into many pieces. Since then, the only threat to the tower occurred in 2000, when a group of National Bolsheviks from Moscow took over the tower in a bid to reassert Soviet dominance after Latvia had regained its independence. Bearing the good omen in mind, visitors can ascend the tower with complete confidence and enjoy a 360° view from the recently renovated observation platform.

The church itself is an excellent example of Gothic architecture. Although first mentioned in records in 1209, only a few sections of the outer walls and some inside pillars remain from the 13th century. The interior style dates mainly from the 15th century, and is impressive in its sheer size and clarity of line. Before 1941 the church housed many religious and art treasures, including a marble pulpit, an oak altar and a magnificent organ. All were destroyed during the war. To commemorate Riga's 800th anniversary in 2001, seven local students made a reconstruction of the oak altar, based on old photographs, and presented it to the church.

St Saviour's (Anglikāņu 21; ✆/f 6722 2259; ⊕ for services & concerts only)

St Saviour's is Riga's only Anglican church and was built in 1857–59 to serve the English seamen and merchants who came to Riga. The bricks used to build the church were imported from England, as was the layer of soil on which the church was built, although a Riga architect, Johann Felsko, supervised the construction. During Soviet times, the church was used as a discotheque, but was given back to the Church of England when the Archbishop of Canterbury visited Riga in 1994 (see page 143 for a first-hand account of the church in the early days of independence).

BUILDINGS

Guildhalls

At the end of Meistaru is what used to be the Guild Square but is now known as the Philharmonic Park (Filharmonijas Parks). The Great Guildhall (Lielā Ģilde) is the large, dull yellow building at one edge of the square, at the corner of Meistaru and Amatu (Commercial Street). The Small Guildhall (Mazā Ģilde) is right next to it on Amatu itself. These buildings represent the centres of Riga's former glory as a Hanseatic City. The Great Guildhall was the council chamber of the merchants; the smaller one housed the council of the less influential craftsmen's guilds. The Great Guildhall was originally established in the 14th century, but has undergone substantial changes over the years. Between 1853–60 it was reconstructed in English Tudor style. The Old Guild Chamber dates back to the 16th century and is decorated with the emblems of the 45 Hanseatic towns. The so-called 'Brides' Chamber' dates back to 1521: until the 19th century it was still used on the wedding night of children of members of the guild or members themselves. However, a great deal of damage was done by a fire in 1963. Now the building is used as a concert hall. The smaller hall was built (in its present form) between 1864–66. It is also sometimes called the St John's Guildhall – notice the statue of St John with a lamb in one corner of the façade under the tower. Now it is used as offices.

Powder Tower

The Powder Tower is one of the oldest buildings in Riga. Its name is derived from the fact that it was once used to store gunpowder, although at times it was also referred to as the Sand Tower after Smilšu (Sand Street), the road that leads past the tower and which was once the main road to Pskov in Russia. Records of the tower can be traced back to 1330. The tower is the sole survivor of what used to be 18 towers that formed part of the city fortifications. Because it was used to store gunpowder it had to be dry, well ventilated and secure, hence the walls which are 2.5m thick. They were relatively effective: nine cannonballs are said to be embedded in the walls, relics of the Russian invasions of 1656 and 1710. Only the lower parts of the tower are original. The tower was substantially destroyed by Swedish forces in 1621 and restored in 1650.

Since it ceased to have any military significance, the Powder Tower has been put to various uses. In 1892 it was used as the headquarters of a German student fraternity called Rubonia. After World War I it was turned into a war museum. In 1957 it became the Latvian Museum of the Revolution and functioned as such until independence. Now it houses the War Museum (see page 137)

Reiter House

The house at number 2 Mārstaļu is the Reiter House, a building that derives its name from another wealthy Riga merchant, Johann von Reiter. The house was built in 1682. Note the six pillars that decorate what appears to be the front of the house but is, in fact, the side. As with the Mentzendorff House, restoration that started around 1980 revealed a large number of wall and ceiling paintings. It is now mainly used for lectures and conferences, but the public are able to see the entrance hall and the balustrade leading to the first floor. Extensive restoration was under way during 2008.

Riga Castle

The main building on Pils laukums is Riga Castle, a large cream building with a red roof. The present structure is the last of three which have stood here. Its predecessors were two Livonian castles, the first of which was built in 1330, the second in 1515. The leader of the Livonian Order lived in Riga Castle up to 1470 when his residence was moved, eventually to Cēsis. The people of Riga destroyed the castle in 1487 but were forced to build a replacement by Walter von Plettenberg, the last head of the Livonian Order. It was completed in 1515 and included the so-called Lead Tower (Svina tornis) which still stands. The castle was extended in the 18th century by the addition of a new wing which became the residence of the Russian governor, and

4

between 1918–40 that of the President of Latvia. It also underwent substantial restoration in 1938 which included construction of the 'three stars tower', easily recognised by the three stars on its top. In the early part of the 19th century Wilhelm von Kester built an observatory on the main tower from which Alexander I of Russia observed the solar eclipse of 23 April 1818. Today the castle is once again the residence of the president. It also houses the Literature and the History museums described above.

The Three Brothers The three houses at numbers 17, 19 and 21 Mazā pils are known collectively as 'the three brothers' (Trīs brāļi). The oldest is the right-hand house with the Germanic step-gable and dates back to the 15th century. It is claimed that it is the oldest domestic building in Riga. Little is known about its history except that in 1687 it is recorded that it was used as a bakery. Numbers 19 and 21 were built later in the 17th and 18th centuries respectively. In 1966 repair work began with a view to restoring the buildings after years of neglect. Number 17 is set back from the street: when it was built there was less pressure on building land in Riga so a small area was left for stone benches to be installed by the main entrance; but by the time the other houses were built land had become more expensive, so they were built closer to the road and with more storeys so as to maximise land use.

MONUMENTS AND STATUES
Riflemen's Memorial The Memorial to the Latvian Riflemen was erected in 1971 to commemorate the valour of the Latvian Rifle Regiment during the civil war. The Riflemen were first known for their courage in fighting on the front near Riga in 1915. Some of the Riflemen also formed Lenin's bodyguard during the 1917 Revolution. During 1917 the Riflemen split into white and red divisions and were caught up on different sides in the struggles of 1918–19: some reds later rejoined the whites and fought against the Germans, but a Latvian Rifleman became the first commander of the Red Army and some reds stayed in Russia and were eventually shot on Stalin's orders in the purges of 1937–38. The statue has long been a subject of strong disagreement. Some see it as an acknowledgement of the bravery of Latvians at the beginning of the civil war, 'a monument to the beginning of the Latvian nation'. Others feel it is too closely allied to the Soviet era and would like it removed and replaced by something more politically neutral. The Soviet text has been removed, but was replaced by a surprising date given for the riflemen of 1915–20, whereas the unit was only formed in 1917. Probably in the wake of the 'Bronze Soldier' incident in Tallinn in April 2007, it will be allowed to stay here so that the Russian government are not given a pretext for interfering in Latvian affairs.

Monument to the Deported The work of Latvian sculptor Pēteris Jaunzems and the architect Juris Poga, this monument was unveiled on 14 June 2001 to commemorate the 60th anniversary of one of the largest deportations of Latvians to Siberia. It had originally been planned to consecrate a memorial ten years earlier on the 50th anniversary, but such was the intensity of the arguments about it that it took a further ten years before sufficient consensus could be formed. Maybe there will be further changes. The jagged stones that represent the current memorial are symbols of the shattered lives of those who were deported. In 1941, over 14,000 Latvians were rounded up and loaded into trains at stations around Latvia, including Torņakalns. Families were split up. Women and children were mainly sent to camps in Siberia, men as slave labour to coal mines in the Arctic Circle or uranium mines in Turkmenistan. The modern monument, which has received criticism as well as praise, stands just outside Torņakalns railway station, south of Uzvaras Park, and can be reached by taking a train heading for Jūrmala or Jelgava from the central station; Torņakalns is the first stop.

Frances Samuel

The English Church of St Saviour's, built for the British community in Riga in 1859, had been used in Soviet times as a disco, painted a depressing purple, and was now closed up and empty. A visiting Anglican clergyman, a friend of the then US Ambassador in Riga, offered to hold a communion service in the derelict building. Ten or so of us joined in the first such celebration for 50 years or more, standing in a semicircle in front of a plain wooden table which served as an altar, with a cross made from two wooden poles tied together propped up in a camera tripod, and bread from a local baker's shop. The chalice was an ordinary wine glass we borrowed from the hotel bar. Our vicar had a fine actor's voice, which swept us along as we gave our hesitant and emotional responses; it was an extremely moving experience. Some months later a young American Lutheran minister began to hold regular services. The church in those early days was a lifeline for the tiny group of foreign diplomats, traders, students and others, as well as a few brave Latvians, and one splendid old Russian lady. We would gather after a stressful week, stand in a comforting circle for communion and say the Lord's Prayer together, each in her or his own language. Before we left Riga we got a young Latvian silversmith to put a silver collar on the humble wine glass. It is still sometimes used by the now thriving congregation of the fully re-established Anglican church.

Richard and Frances Samuel reopened the British Embassy in Riga in 1991.

Statue of Kārlis Padegs As you walk along Merķeļa opposite the House of the Riga Latvian Society, have a look at the artist who will be lolling stylishly against a railing, most probably adorned by flowers from his admirers. The work of Andris Vārpa, this delightfully informal statue, unusual in Riga, commemorates Kārlis Padegs (born in 1911 and died in 1940 in Riga), an idiosyncratic personality in Riga in the 1930s. Padegs broke with the traditional themes of Latvian painting of his time, preferring instead shocking topics, freely expressed. His anti-war paintings and frequently ironic approach were frowned on during the Soviet occupation and his work was rarely seen. The monument was presented as a gift in 1998 by Rita Červenaka-Virkavs, a Latvian artist living in Germany. It has been erected on the spot where Padegs once held an open-air exhibition of his works (see page 125).

Freedom Monument The Freedom Monument dominates the centre of Riga. Known locally as 'Milda', it was erected in 1935 and paid for by public subscription. It stands over 35m and is the tallest monument of its kind in Europe. It was designed by the Latvian architect Kārlis Zāle and consists of a tall granite column surmounted by a 9m-high figure of a woman holding three golden stars above her head. The three stars represent the three cultural regions of Latvia – Kurzeme, Vidzeme and Latgale. Engraved in gold letters on the base are the words 'Tevzēmei un brīvībai' ('for fatherland and freedom'). Also decorating the monument is a sculpture of Lāčplēsis, the legendary Latvian bear-slayer, who has long been a symbol of freedom in the country. The monument was dedicated on 18 November 1935, the 17th anniversary of the declaration of independence. The statue replaced one of Peter the Great on horseback that had been unveiled in 1910 on the 200th anniversary of the surrender of Riga by the Swedes to the Russians.

Nowadays the base is often surrounded by flowers, frequently red and white, the colours of the Latvian national flag. Flowers were forbidden during the Soviet era, as was any access at all to what they had made into a traffic island. Indeed the Soviet authorities had contemplated removing the monument altogether, since it served as a focus of Latvian nationalistic aspirations, but thought better of the idea, fearing demonstrations and reprisals. Instead they erected a statue of Lenin about 200m to the north. The two monuments stood back to back for decades, Lenin facing east towards Moscow, the Freedom Monument facing west. Lenin has now disappeared, but the Freedom Monument remains. The guards who now stand at the monument change every hour on the hour between 9.00 and 18.00.

Monument to the 1905 Demonstrators
In the 1905 park in Grīziņkalns, northeast of the New Town, is a monument to commemorate the meeting place on 20 October 1905 of about 100,000 strikers who rallied here against the Tsarist government. It was erected in 1975 in a park which also includes a stage for musical shows built in 1911. Trolleybus 13 takes you to Pērnavas in front of the park.

Statue of Roland
Statues of the knight Roland appeared in Hanseatic towns during the 14th and 15th centuries. Erected as symbols of liberty and independence, they were normally displayed prominently in the main square. Riga was no exception: a wooden statue was made and frequently used as a target during jousting matches and tournaments. Not surprisingly, the wooden statue was frequently damaged and then repaired, so in 1896 a stone statue, designed by Wilhelm Neumann and August Volz, replaced it. Neumann had recently come to Riga having totally rebuilt Daugavpils. His most famous works in Riga are the National Museum of Art and the surviving synagogue in Peitavas Street.

The knight rests his left hand on a shield bearing the coat of arms of Riga, while in his right hand he holds a sword. It was from the point of this sword that distances from Riga to other places in Latvia were traditionally measured. The statue was damaged in World War II and for many years was not seen in Riga. The original can now be seen in St Peter's Church, while this replica was placed in the Town Hall Square outside the Blackheads' House in 2000.

PARKS AND GARDENS
One of the most attractive aspects of Riga is the large amount of green space in the centre. Almost the whole of the area separating the Old Town and the New Town consists of well-tended parks and gardens which are a delight to stroll through whatever the season. In Riga as a whole, parks make up 19% of the total city area, and lake, rivers and canals a further 16%. This is largely due to one man, Georg Kuphaldt, who came to Riga in 1880 from Germany and stayed until his explusion as a spy in 1915 (see page 124).

Bastejkalns Park
The parks on either side of the Freedom Monument were laid out in 1853–63. The one through which Brīvības bulvāris runs is the Bastejkalns Park, named after the 17th-century bastion that once stood here and formed a vital part of Riga's defences. If you walk through Bastejkalns Park you will come across a set of engraved stones near the bridge that crosses the canal (most are on the New Town side, one is on the Old Town side of the canal). On the night of 20 January 1991 Black Beret forces loyal to Moscow attempted to capture a number of government buildings including the Ministry of the Interior on Raiņa bulvāris, the street running alongside the canal on the New Town side. Several Latvians were shot, some say by sniper fire from the rooftops. The stones preserve the memory of five victims: Gvīdo Zvaigne, a cameraman who was filming events; Andris Slapiņš, a cinema director and cameraman; two militiamen, Sergejs Kononenko and Vladimirs Gomanovics; and Edijs Riekstiņš, a student.

On the corner of Raina Boulevard and Valdemāra is a statue of **Kārlis Ulmanis**, the pre-war president, deliberately looking benevolent and therefore in total contrast to his Soviet successors. It was unveiled on 22 July 2003, to commemorate the date in 1940 when he was deported to Russia, although at the time he was told he would simply visit Moscow *en route* to exile in Switzerland. The statue is 2.5m high, so that he can look down on his people, but not aggressively so. This is again a deliberate contrast with statues cast in Soviet times.

At the opposite end of the park, in front of the Opera House, is a statue of **George Armisted** with his wife and dog (see page 124).

Kronvalda Park Next to Bastejkalns Park is Kronvalda Park with its monuments to the Latvian writers Edēus and Upīts. Also set in this park are the Riga Congress House and a monument to Rūdolfs Blaumanis (see page 136). A canal runs all the way through Kronvalda Park and behind the National Opera, extending in total for 3km, both starting and finishing in the Daugava, thus ensuring a steady flow of water. In summer a popular pastime is hiring pedal boats and drifting along the canal.

Vērmanes Gardens Bounded by Elizabetes, Kr Barona, Merķeļa and Tērbatas, the Vērmanes dārzs (as the gardens are called in Latvian) is the most popular of Riga's central parks. Opened in 1817, it was named in honour of the woman who donated the land to the city. Originally it was a refuge for residents of Riga who could not get out to the countryside. It soon acquired attractions, including a bronze fountain cast in Berlin, a playground, an ice rink, a sundial and the first rose garden in Riga. It has an open-air theatre and a statue of Krišjānis Barons, the writer and poet.

Uzvaras Park (*Walk across Akmens Bridge (Akmens tilts) or take the number 2, 4 or 5 tram from 11. Novembra krastmala to the second stop after the bridge across the river*) Uzvaras bulvāris (Victory Boulevard), which leads on from the bridge, heads directly to Uzvaras Park (Victory Park), the largest park in Riga. The plan for the park was made by Georg Kuphaldt in 1909 and, to commemorate 200 years since the incorporation of Riga into the Russian Empire in 1710, the park was called after Tsar Peter I. In 1915, while the park was still being completed, Kuphaldt, a German, was expelled from the country along with all his compatriots. A few years later, in 1923, the park was renamed Victory Park (Uzvaras Parks) to commemorate Latvia's liberation from German occupation – somewhat ironically given the fact that the park was so much the work of a German. Today the park is dominated by the Soviet War Memorial, more correctly the monument to the Fallen Soldiers of the Army of the USSR, Liberators of Riga, and the Latvian SSR from the German Fascist Conquerors. Erected in 1985, the monument was paid for by contributions automatically deducted from the pay packets of workers in Riga. Since the restoration of independence, the monument has become something of a rallying point for communists who meet here on former Soviet holidays. In 1996 some men from an extreme right-wing group tried to retaliate by blowing up the monument but succeeded only in killing themselves.

Arcadia Park The smaller Arkādijas Parks, which directly adjoins Victory Park to the south, was created in 1852 by the Prussian consul general, Wehrmann (Vērmans), and acquired by the city in 1896. Next to it, Māras dīķis (Mary's Pond) is a popular place of recreation. It derives its name from the mill attached to St Mary's Church which was acquired by the city of Riga in 1573. The pond is probably the old millpond and is sometimes referred to as Mary's millpond (Māras sudmalu dīķis).

Riga National Zoo (*Meža prospekts 1;* ↘ *6751 8669; www.rigazoo.lv; take tram no 11 from Barona to the Zooloģiskais dārzs (Zoological Park), taking around 20mins;* ☉ *Apr–Oct 10.00–18.00 daily; Nov–Mar 10.00–16.00*) The zoo, the Baltics' oldest and largest though by no means one of the world's largest, has expanded and improved greatly in recent years and makes a pleasant visit, particularly on a summer day. It is set in the pine forest of the Mežaparks, close to the Ķīšezers Lake and next to the Mežaparks garden city. Allow at least two hours to see some of the almost 500 species and over 3,000 animals. Attractions include elephants, camels, bears and ostriches. There are pony rides and other entertainment for children too.

Song Festival Park (Viestura dārzs) (*North of the Old Town, on the corner of Eksporta and Hanzas*) This was once a much larger park owned by Tsar Peter I and containing plants brought from all parts of Europe. Although it has been remodelled since then, it is a scenic and well-maintained park with the attraction of being well off the beaten track. It has a playground for children and also a decorative feature to commemorate the centenary of the first Latvian Song Festival which was held here in 1873. The memorial consists of several fountains, a wall with portraits of seven Latvian composers and a large memorial stone. The annual Song Festival is no longer held here, but in the large open-air auditorium in the Mežaparks (the Mežaparka estrade).

CEMETERIES Riga has a number of cemeteries that are worth visiting, if time permits, since they reflect something of the history of Latvia and present a number of architectural styles. Three (the Brothers' Cemetery, Rainis Cemetery and Woodlands Cemetery) are close together in an area directly south of Mežaparks. Another two are next to each other, in the same direction but closer to the town centre (the Great Cemetery and Pokrov Cemetery). All can be reached by taking tram number 11 from Barona towards Mežaparks. For the Brothers' Cemetery, Rainis Cemetery and Woodland Cemetery alight at the Brāļu Kapi stop. For the Great Cemetery get off at Kazarmu. For Pokrov Cemetery alight at the Mēness stop.

The Brothers' Cemetery (Brāļu Kapi) (*Aizsaules*) The Brothers' Cemetery or the Cemetery of Heroes is a fascinating ensemble of architecture and sculpture in attractive natural surroundings. It was planned in 1915 when thousands of Latvians were dying in the fight against the Germans in Kurzeme, and the same year the first fallen soldiers were buried here. It took 12 years to complete the cemetery, the overwhelming part of the work being done between 1924 and 1936. There are approximately 2,000 graves in Brāļu Kapi, 300 of them simply marked 'nezinams' ('unknown'). On 25 March 1988 a memorial service for the victims of the years of the Stalin terror was held here, organised by the Latvian Writers' Association, and 10,000 people attended.

In Latvian folklore the oak symbolises masculine strength, while the lime tree symbolises feminine love; both of these powerful symbols are used extensively in the cemetery. The Latvian coat of arms appears over the entrance gate, while on both sides there are sculpted groups of cavalrymen. An avenue of lime trees leads to the main terrace. In the centre an eternal flame burns, flanked by oak trees. Beyond it is the cemetery itself, bordered by trees, shrubs, bushes and walls decorated with the coats of arms of all the Latvian regions and towns.

Especially moving are the *Levainotais Jatnieks* ('The Wounded Horseman') and *Divi brāļi* ('Two Brothers') sculptures. At one end of the cemetery stands the figure of *Māte Latvijā* ('Mother Latvia') who looks down in sorrow at her dead, a wreath to honour her fallen sons in one hand, in the other the national flag. The sculptures are the work of Kārlis Zāle who is himself buried here.

The cemetery was allowed to fall into neglect during the Soviet period, but was restored in 1993 and has since then become a focus of Latvian national feeling.

Rainis Cemetery (Raiņa Kapi) (*Aizsaules*) Latvia's best-loved writer, Jānis Rainis, died on 12 September 1929 and was buried here three days later. The cemetery was renamed in his honour. An avenue of silver birch leads to his grave which is marked by a red granite sculpture. Around the monument there is a semicircular colonnade entwined with ivy.

Alongside Rainis lies his wife, the poet Aspāzija (Elza Rozenberg), who died in 1943. The cemetery is also the resting place for a great number of Latvian writers, artists and musicians, many of whose graves are decorated with a creativity to match the lives they were designed to commemorate.

Woodlands Cemetery (Meža Kapi) (*Aizsaules*) Woodlands Cemetery was designed by Georg Kuphaldt, the director of Riga's parks, in 1913. Numerous political and government figures from the period of Latvia's first independence are buried here, including the former president, Jānis Čakste, and the government ministers, Zigfrids Meierovics and Vilhelms Munters. In addition, a number of Latvian artists, writers, poets and scientists lie here, among them Jānis Rozentāls, Anna Brigadere and Paul Stradin. In April 1988 Latvia's leading human rights activist, Gunārs Astra, was buried here. Astra was sentenced to seven years' imprisonment followed by five years' internal exile by the Soviet regime in December 1983 for the crimes of possessing recordings of radio programmes, photo negatives and subversive books and for writing a manuscript of a personal nature. In his final words to the court he delivered an impassioned speech against the Soviet regime including these words: 'I fervently believe that these nightmare times will end one day. This belief gives me the strength to stand before you. Our people have suffered a great deal but have learned to survive. They will outlive this dark period in their history.'

The Great Cemetery (Lielie Kapi) (*Miera and Senču*) The cemetery has lost much of its former glory, many monuments having been removed or badly vandalised in the Soviet era and also in the early 1990s, but it still contains the graves of many of Latvia's best-known citizens, including artists, politicians, scientists and businesspeople. Close to the entrance near Klusā is the Green Chapel, the oldest building in the cemetery (1776). Confusingly, it is now a red-brick building, although originally it was a wooden construction painted green and the name has stuck. Graves which may be of interest include a monument to Andrejs Pumpurs (1841–1902), author of the *Lāčplēsis*, the epic poem of Latvia's hero bear-slayer; a large granite pyramid to Patrick Cumming, a Scot who came to Riga in 1777 and later became president of the Riga Stock Exchange; the graves of Krisjānis Barons and Krisjānis Valdemārs; and a memorial, erected in 2001 as part of Riga's 800 years' anniversary celebrations, to the Scot who was mayor of Riga from 1901 to 1912, George Armisted.

Pokrov Cemetery (Pokrova Kapi) (*Mēness, Miera and Senču*) Across the road from the Great Cemetery, this Russian cemetery is in even greater need of care and attention. Many of the gravestones are from the 19th century and commemorate Russians who died in Riga while working for the Tsarist government. There is also a large monument dedicated to communist soldiers who fell during and after World War II.

EXCURSIONS FROM RIGA

If you are in Riga for only two days, you probably will not want to leave the city itself unless you have a particular interest in other parts of Latvia. If you are there for three days or longer, however, you may well like to take one or more half-day trips, enjoy some of the other attractions of Latvia and gain a broader perspective of the country. Latvia is a small country: everywhere can be reached within a few hours, so in a sense the whole of Latvia is your oyster. The most obvious choices, depending on your interests, are Jūrmala (the seaside area close to Riga), Rundāle (a beautifully restored

18th-century palace close to the Lithuanian border), and a visit to the memorial site of the Salaspils concentration camp.

JŪRMALA Jūrmala is not really a place at all but a name: *Jūrmala* is the Latvian for 'seaside' or 'by the sea' and is in reality the collective name given to a number of small towns and villages along the Baltic coast about 25km from Riga. The beautiful 30-odd kilometre stretch of beach is virtually unspoilt and is the major attraction of Jūrmala. The Gulf waters are clean enough to swim in (the EU blue flag was awarded in 2000), though not always warm enough, and the beaches and woods are ideal for long walks. Sometimes pieces of amber are washed up on the beach, particularly after a storm. Eating and drinking possibilities are good, and if you don't feel healthy enough to enjoy all this, many of the hotels offer spa treatments and massages. Only one word of warning: in hot weather there are often mosquitoes so be sure to carry around a good insect repellent.

The Jūrmala area first became popular in the late 18th and early 19th centuries, when families began to leave Riga for the summer in search of fresh sea air. Wooden summer houses quickly began to appear just behind the coastline. The first hotel in the area was built in 1834 in Dubulti; in 1870 the first sanatorium (the Marienbāde in Majori) was constructed; and in 1877 the railway line to Tukums was completed, opening the area up to greater numbers than ever. Mixed bathing was permitted in 1881. The sea air, mild climate, spa water and medicinal mud also made the small, growing towns along the coast a favourite with convalescents, so Jūrmala also gained a reputation as a health resort. The resort was developed even further under the Soviet occupation: hotels, convalescent homes, sanatoria and pioneer camps were built from 1945 onwards, transforming Jūrmala into one of the most important holiday resorts in the Soviet Union, attracting over 250,000 visitors a year. Since the restoration of independence, much work has been done to redecorate the many summer houses that give the place its distinctive feel. In 1997 the government declared the area around Ķemeri, at the far end of Jūrmala, to be a national park. The most popular spots are Lielupe (named after the river which in turn means 'big river'), Dzintari ('pieces of amber') and Majori.

Getting there and away You can get to Jūrmala from Riga by train, bus, taxi or car. On summer weekends it can also be reached by boat.

Frequent trains depart from platforms 3 and 4 of the central railway station in Riga. It takes about 20 minutes from Riga to the first stop at Lielupe, although not all trains stop there. However, all trains do stop at Majori (about 40 minutes from Riga). Trains are most frequent between May and October (one every 10–20 minutes) and run from about 05.00–23.00. The price is Ls0.64 each way. Note that there is no one station called Jūrmala – it is probably best (unless you have a specific goal) to get out at Majori.

During the summer there are frequent buses from the bus station. Taxis leave Riga from a special taxi rank just outside the station. There is also a comfortable minibus connection between Jūrmala and Riga, running every 20–30 minutes, also from outside the railway station.

Jūrmala is only a 20–30-minute drive from Riga. However, as you approach Jūrmala you must pull into the lay-by at the toll point and buy a special ticket to gain access to the area by car. Tickets cost Ls1 a day.

The boat trip takes two hours and costs Ls3 one-way for adults and Ls1 one-way for children between six and 12 years old. On Saturdays and Sundays in summer the *Jūrmala* leaves from 11. Novembra krastmala, just next to Vanšu Bridge, at 11.00, arriving in Jūrmala at 13.00. The return trip leaves Majori at 17.00, arriving in Riga two hours later. (For further information, ☏ 6957 8329.)

Museums, churches and buildings The most popular museum in Jūrmala is probably the **Rainis and Aspāzijas Memorial Summer House** (☎ *6776 4295;* ⏰ *11.00–18.00 Wed–Sun; admission Ls0.50*) in Majori. It was here that the writer, Jānis Rainis (1865–1929) had his summer house (at 5–7 J Pliekšāna) in which he lived with his wife, the poet Aspāzija, from 1927 until his death on 12 September 1929. The room in which Rainis worked has been left intact: his books, papers and even the woven blanket which his mother made for him all remain; a similar room contains the remaining effects of his wife. The third room was used by their housekeeper. Note too the monument to Rainis and Aspāzija on Jomas next to the Jūrmala culture centre; erected in 1990 it is the work of the sculptors Z Fernava-Tiščenko and J Tiščenko.

Also nearby is the **Aspāzija House** (*18/20 Meierovica prospekts, Dubulti;* ☎ *6776 9445;* ⏰ *14.00–19.00 Mon, 11.00–16.00 Tue–Sat; admission Ls0.30*), where Aspāzija (1865–1943) lived the last ten years of her life. It is a small summer cottage, typical of wooden seaside architecture of the early 20th century.

If you are interested in traditional Latvian life, you can visit the **Jūraslīcis Open Air Fishery Museum** (*1 Tīklu;* ☎ *6775 1121;* ⏰ *10.00–18.00; admission Ls0.50*) at Buļļuciems, a modest complex of 19th-century wooden buildings. To find the museum watch out for the black anchor on a small pillar of stones, just beyond the Kulturnams in the centre of the village. Tīklu takes you to the museum.

The Lutheran church at Dubulti, with its Art Nouveau elements, plain interior and wooden gallery, used as the Jūrmala Museum of History and Art during the Soviet era, is one of the largest churches in Latvia and its spire is a well-known landmark, visible from the Daugava River. The Orthodox church (Sv Kņaza Vladimira pareizticiga baznīca) at 26 Strēlnieku prospekts dates back to 1896 and contains some pleasing icons.

In the early 20th century, Ķemeri was famous for its medicinal mud cures and attracted people from many parts of northern Europe. Like the spa building itself, the Ķemeri Hotel is in the Classical style. Built between 1933 and 1936 it is known as the 'white castle' or the 'white ship'. The interior is elegant and spacious, the exterior simple yet imposing. The work of E Laube, it ranks as one of the finest examples of architecture from the first period of Latvian independence. The hotel is due to reopen in mid 2009 as the Kempinski Ķemeri Palace.

Ķemeri National Park

Ķemeri was established as a national park only in 1997. It covers an area of some 40,000ha, about 50% of it forest, 30% bog or marshland, 10% water and 10% agricultural land. About a quarter of all recorded fauna in Latvia can be found here and over half of Latvia's bird species, including the rare sea eagle and black stork. Also to be found here are beavers, which play an important part in the ecology of the area. The park is accessible to the public only by personal application. For further information contact the Information Centre of Ķemeri National Park (*Meža Maja, Ķemeri;* ☎ *773 0078;* e *nationalparks@kemeri.gov.lv; www.kemeri.gov.lv*). To get there take a train to Ķemeri station (see page 101). Alternatively you can take bus number 6 from Sloka or bus number 11 from Lielupe. If you go by car, follow the signs to Jūrmala and continue on the A10 towards Ķemeri.

RUNDĀLE PALACE

(☎ *6396 2197;* e *rpm@eila.lv; www.rundale.net;* ⏰ *Nov–Apr 10.00–17.00 daily; May–Sep 10.00–18.00; Jun–Aug 10.00–19.00, closes 13.00 1 Jan, 24 Jun, 25 Dec; admission Ls2.50*) Unique for a cultural institution in the Baltics, the palace really is open every day, including national holidays. It lies about 77km south of Riga to the west of Bauska and can easily be visited by car, coach or local bus. There are no direct buses from Riga, but very regular services to Bauska where it is necessary to change to a bus going to Eleja or to Dobele. The website gives timetables for all of these. Consult your hotel or one of the tour organisers mentioned on page 101 for details of coach trips. If you are travelling by car, the road to Rundāle and Pilsrundāle

(P103) is signposted on the right after you cross the bridge travelling south over the River Mūsa, leaving Bauska Castle behind you.

If you visit only the palace, a long half-day (four or five hours) would be sufficient. However a full day can be enjoyed here, particularly in fine weather when the gardens are at their best. If you combine it with a visit to Mežotne and/or Jelgava, you would need more or less a full day. There is no need to stay in the area, as you can return to Riga easily. If you wanted to sample life in a Latvian manor house, however, you could overnight at Mežotne. There are hotels at Bauska – cheaper of course than those in Riga – and it is logical to overnight there *en route* to Vilnius. For information on Bauska, take a look at *Latvia: The Bradt Travel Guide* (see *Further Information*, page 292).

Rundāle is often billed as the most significant palace in the Baltics. Certainly most visitors will be impressed by its grand exterior, dominating the surrounding flat farmland leading down to the Lielupe River, and the 50 or so sumptuously decorated rooms which have been restored. This restoration will continue for several more years.

Rundāle Palace (Rundāles Pils) was built in the 18th century as a summer palace for Ernst Johann von Bühren (Biron in Latvian) by the Italian architect Francesco Bartolomeo Rastrelli. Rastrelli, already established as the architect of the Winter Palace in St Petersburg, began work in 1736 and took five years to finish the task. The interiors were mostly completed later, between 1763 and 1768. Among those who worked on them were Italian painters from St Petersburg and Johann Michael Graff from Berlin, whose work includes the artificial marble wall panelling and the decorative moulding in many rooms.

Why was such a lavish palace built by Rastrelli beyond the Russian borders? The link with Russia was Anna Ioannovna, a niece of Tsar Peter I who, in 1710, married Frederick, Duke of Kurland. During the 1720s Ernst Johann von Bühren, a Baltic-German baron, became her chief adviser, and some say lover also. In 1730, on the death of Peter, Anna became Empress of Russia and delegated much of the management of the empire to a group of German advisers, von Bühren among them. When von Bühren expressed the wish for a summer palace, Anna complied by sending Rastrelli to Kurland and providing all the necessary money and craftsmen, too; nearly everyone involved in the construction – a total of 1,500 craftsmen, artists and labourers – was sent from St Petersburg. Before the palace could be finished, however, Rastrelli began work on another major project, a palace at Jelgava, seat of the Duchy of Kurland. Many of the workmen and the materials needed for Rundāle were transported to Jelgava instead. In 1740, just before Rundāle was completed, Anna died, von Bühren was forced into exile, and the building of the palaces halted. Only in 1763 when the Russian Empress Catherine II restored von Bühren to favour, did he return to Kurland and finish the work on Rundāle. The palace was finally completed in 1767, but von Bühren was able to enjoy it for only a short time until his death in 1772. When Russia annexed the Duchy of Kurland in 1795, von Bühren's son, Peter, agreed to leave, taking with him some of the splendid interior items from Rundāle and installing them instead in his properties in Germany. Rundāle itself was given to another favourite of Catherine II, Subov.

Since the incorporation of Kurland into Russia in 1795, the palace has had many uses and owners. Although damaged in the Napoleonic Wars and again during World War II, the exterior has been repaired and remains fundamentally unaltered from its original design. The interior has not survived so well. Parts of the castle were used as a granary after 1945, and other areas fell into severe disrepair. In 1972, however, the Rundāle Palace Museum was established and major restoration work began. Artists in Leningrad began the restoration of works of art, and they were subsequently joined by experts from Riga, Moscow and Belarus. As a result the 50 or so rooms (out of 138) restored contain many impressive, but few original, works of art. Particularly interesting are the Golden Hall (the throne room), with beautiful ceiling decoration and chandeliers, the Grand Gallery (the banquet room) and the aptly named White Hall (the ballroom), with its intricate stucco. Look out here for the storks!

The palace also houses some permanent exhibitions (additional admission charge payable): 'Treasures of the Rundāle Palace', with furniture, porcelain, silverware and paintings, and 'The Time of Misery', an exhibition about Lutheran churches in Latvia during the years of Soviet power. The 'Time of Misery' exhibition, beside the ticket office at the entrance to the palace, is closed in the winter between October and March.

Behind the palace, the French-style formal garden has been largely reconstructed. It is surrounded by a canal, beyond which are hunting grounds.

On the south side of the palace is a formal Baroque garden; visitors to the palace in the 1990s who return now are amazed at the restoration which was completed in 2006. A restaurant in the palace is used for formal receptions, and is a favourite place for weddings.

SALASPILS To reach Salaspils by car take the A6 south towards Ogre and look out for the large granite sign 'Salaspils 1941–44'. Take a train heading southeast for Ogre, Lielvārde or Aizkraukle and alight at the Dārziņa stop. A single ticket costs Ls0.50. Then follow the footpath for about 15 minutes. The tourist office advises that visitors should not walk this footpath alone.

First mentioned as a settlement in 1186 it is a place associated with war, death and destruction. The Battle of Salaspils of 1605 delayed the Swedes from gaining a foothold in Latvia. Some 12,000 Swedes under the leadership of Charles IX attacked a Lithuanian unit of about 4,000 men but were repulsed: only about a quarter of the Swedish army managed to retreat to their ships in Riga.

Now, however, it is remembered largely as the site of the Nazi concentration camp, Kurtenhof. Built in 1941 during the Nazi occupation of Latvia in World War II, the camp operated for three years. In 1944, as the Red Army approached Riga, the camp guards and administrators ordered the inmates to exhume and burn the thousands of bodies buried at the camp; it then was burnt to the ground by the retreating Nazis in an attempt to hide the atrocities committed there. Over 100,000 men, women and children, most of them Jews, were put to death here, among them Austrian, Belgian, Czech, Dutch, French, Latvian, Polish and Soviet citizens. Today, lines of white stones mark the perimeter of the camp.

The Salaspils memorial, which now dominates the site of the former camp, was erected in 1967 to honour those who died there. It was designed by Ernst Neizvestny, at the time one of the most famous sculptors in the Soviet Union, who later became well known as the sculptor employed for Khrushchev's tomb. However, as he was driven into exile in 1976, all references to him here were removed and a local Latvian collective was given credit for the memorial. Now living in the USA, he is still active. A huge concrete wall in the shape of a long beam marks the position of the former entrance; symbolising the border between life and death, it bears the words of the Latvian writer, Eižēns Vēveris (a prisoner at Salaspils): 'Aiz šiem vārtiem vaid zeme' ('Beyond these gates the earth moans'). You can actually walk the length of the wall inside it – there is a door at each end. A series of steps takes you through a number of gloomy rooms, giving the impression of a mausoleum. There is also a small exhibition with photographs of the camp. The seven sculptures which stand in the grounds behind the wall evoke the suffering but also the spirit of defiance and resistance of those imprisoned and killed.

The stillness of Salaspils is broken only by the ticking of an underground metronome beneath the altar-like structure located to the left as you enter the grounds. The noise of the ticking is a reminder of the lives spent and ended here. A narrow path leads through the woods to the place where the prisoners were executed.

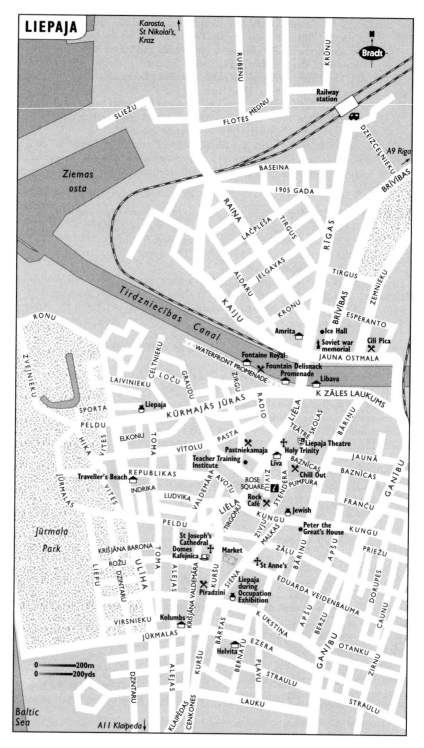

LIEPAJA

Karosta,
St Nikolai's,
Kraz

Bradt

RUBEŅU

KRŪNU

Railway
station

SLIEŽU

FLOTES

MEDNU

DZEICEĻNIEKU

A9 Riga

BRĪVĪBAS

Ziemas
osta

BASEINA

1905 GADA

RAIŅA

LĀCPLĒŠA

TIRGUS

RĪGAS

ALDARU

JELGAVAS

TIRGUS

ZEMNIEKU

KAIJU

KRONU

BRĪVĪBAS

ESPERANTO

Tirdzniecības Canal

RONU

ZVEJNIEKU

WATERFRONT PROMENADE

Amrita
Ice Hall
Soviet war
memorial
Cili Pica

JAUNA OSTMALA

CELTNIEKU

LOČU

GRAUDU

ZIRGU

Fontaine Royal
Fountain Delisnack
Promenade
Libava

LAIVINIEKU

RADIO

K ZĀLES LAUKUMS

SPORTA

Liepaja

KŪRMAJĀS JŪRAS

LIĒLA

TEĀTRE

SKOLAS

BARINU

PELDU

ELKONU

TOMA

VĪTOLU

PASTA

Pastniekamaja

Holy Trinity

Liepaja Theatre

JAUNĀ

HIKA

VITES

VĪTES

Teacher Training
Institute

Liva

BAZNĪCAS

BAZNĪCAS

Traveller's Beach

REPUBLIKAS

VALDEMĀRA

AVOTU

Chill Out

JŪRMALAS

INDRIKA

ROSE
SQUARE

STENDERA

PUMPURA

FRANČU

LUDVIKA

Rock
Café

Jewish

Jūrmala
Park

PELDU

LIĒLA

TIRGOŅU

ZIVJU

KUNGU

Peter the
Great's House

KUNGU

KRIŠJĀŅA BARONA

TOMA

ULĪHA

St Joseph's
Cathedral
Domes
Kafejnica

Market

KURŠU

MALKAS

BARINU

ZĀĻU

APSU

PRIEŽU

ROŽU

LIEPU

DZINTARU

ALEJAS

KRIŠJĀŅA VALDEMĀRA

St Anne's

Pirandini

SIENA

Liepaja
during
Occupation
Exhibition

EDUARDA VEIDENBAUMA

APSU

DORUPES

CAUNU

VIRSNIEKU

Kolumbs

JŪRMALAS

BĀRTAS

K UKSTIŅA

BERŽU

GANĪBU

OTANKU

0 —— 200m
0 —— 200yds

KURŠU

ALEJAS

KLAIPĒDAS

CENKONES

Helvita

BERNATU

EZERA

PĻAVU

STRAULU

ZIRNU

STRAULU

Baltic
Sea

A11 Klaipeda

LAUKU

DZINTARU

152

5

Liepaja LATVIA

The two names under which this town has been known both have appropriate origins, Liepaja meaning 'lime tree' and Libau, the German name, meaning 'sand'. Both apply equally today and, indeed, the lime tree forms part of the city's coat of arms. Sand, though, is the obvious image that springs to mind for a town on this flat coastline, particularly in contrast to the other Baltic ports which are either based away from the sea, such as Riga and Kaliningrad, or which grew up around a rocky promontory, such as Tallinn.

HISTORY

THE GERMAN BACKGROUND Documentary references to the town date from 1253, but the recent discovery of Roman coins in the area shows that commercial activity around a port was clearly taking place at least a thousand years earlier. As so often in the Baltic region, we are dependent on German written sources for background, and these are reluctant to admit to civilisation before the arrival of the Teutonic Knights in the 13th century. However, once the Germans did come, they would be the de facto rulers of the town until 1918 and it might even be argued until 1939. Russians, Swedes and Poles all incorporated Liepaja into their empires, but they were happy to delegate the running of the town to the German merchants. Only since 1991 have all crucial decisions in the town been taken by Latvians for Latvians.

The land to the east of Liepaja was known for many centuries as Courland, with usually a duke in charge. Duke Jakob Kettler was the most famous one, and he ruled between 1642 and 1682. This was a relatively quiet time for the area, with most of the great powers involved in the Thirty Years War, which was taking place further west. Trade could continue unhindered through the port, with salt, herrings and iron being imported and leather, amber and wax being exported. This pattern had been set in the 14th century and would last until industrialisation in the 19th. The duke was able to some extent to turn the tables on his larger neighbours by purchasing two colonies, the islands of Tobago in the Caribbean and Fort James in the mouth of the Gambia River in west Africa. The street layout as seen today around the market dates from this time. In 1697, shortly before war broke out between them, Peter the Great stayed in Liepaja *en route* to Britain, and a year later Karl XII of Sweden would also pay a visit. Peter stayed at Kungu 24 and Karl at Kungu 26. The Swedes surrendered Liepaja to the Russians in 1710 (it would be another ten years before Riga fell) during the Northern War and the end of this war meant that they would have no future role in Liepaja, or anywhere else in the Baltics. The plague hit Liepaja as savagely as it did many other Baltic cities during the fighting. It is sadly characteristic of German historical records from the time that the death of 700 Germans is reported, with simply a note to the effect that a higher number of Latvians also died.

The surfacing of the roads in Liepaja, which started in 1700, was thanks to the Swedes; when stones were no longer available from Sweden they came from Prussia

THE FUTURE LATVIAN PRESIDENT

Colonel Stephen Tallents, sent in 1919 by Prime Minister David Lloyd George to the Baltics to represent British interests, had his first meeting with the Latvian Prime Minister Kārlis Ulmanis in Liepaja. Ulmanis was later to become president until he was arrested by the Soviet authorities in 1940. Tallents was clearly not impressed by him, as he wrote:

Ulmanis was a tall stout man of peasant extraction, who had spent some of his earlier years in America and spoke English fluently, if with a debased accent. He might have been the chairman of a remote Rural District Council and had in fact been, I believe, the manager of a co-operative society. He had at one time lectured on dairying up and down the Latvian countryside, and had thus acquired a close familiarity with peasant affairs. In January he had left for Copenhagen, nominally for diplomatic purposes but actually, it was widely believed, through fear of the Bolshevik advance. His seat of government at the moment was in a couple of small Libau flats whilst some of his ministers were living with a company of refugees in an old steamer which was lying in the harbour.

instead. Shipbuilding started around 1780, followed by an iron foundry in 1802 and a printworks in 1823. In the field of crime, Liepaja made a remarkably progressive decision in 1792 to ban executions in public.

Liepaja's success as a port meant that visitors in the 18th century expected more than it could give. Johann Wilhelm Krause, architect of Tartu University's main building (see page 81), visited in 1784 and wrote that not a single building gave him pleasure. He was reminded of towns on the Hudson River. He complained both about the number of wooden buildings and their poor designs, but outside a capital city at that time it was hard to expect much stone or brick. In 1844, J G Kohl wrote in his *Travels in Russia* that

The environs of Libau are the most dreary and melancholy that can be imagined – wide, flat naked sandy wastes stretch on every side as far as the eye can reach.

This would soon change, thanks not to an industrialist or to a politician, but to an architect.

BERTSCHI TIMES At least by the late 19th century anybody with the determination to get into the town itself would be amply rewarded in an architectural sense. By then the architect Max Paul Bertschi (sometimes written Bertschy or Bertchy or in the Latvian transliteration as Berči) had firmly made his mark. He was born in Berlin in 1840 where he studied in the 1860s under the most famous architect there, Karl Friedrich Schinkel. After further studies in St Petersburg and then work in Daugavpils, he came to Liepaja in 1871 and devoted the rest of his life to the town. As with Schinkel, it is his diversity which gives him his justified fame. He worked in neo-Gothic, Classical and the eclectic styles. His most famous building is St Anne's Church but he was equally at home designing schools, wooden houses and a linoleum factory. If Berlin had its Schinkel times, or *Schinkelzeit*, Liepaja certainly had its *Bertschizeit* a few decades later. Bertschi died in 1911 but his son continued the architectural practice after World War I.

BRITAIN IN LIEPAJA Britain has a good reputation in the Baltics as one of the few imperial powers not to occupy the area. It is forgiven a minor exception when Liepaja was occupied for two days in May 1854, as a warning to the Russians during the

Crimean War. The British were not interested in action in the Baltic Sea; they simply wanted to blockade the Russian navy there so that it could take no part in the war in southern Russia or attack the British coast. They taunted the Russians outside several of their well-defended harbours but wisely did not attempt to attack them. British raids along the Baltic coast were therefore restricted to ports such as Liepaja which had few land defences.

Half a century later, Britain can claim a role in Latvia's independence. Within days of the armistice being signed in November 1918 on the Western front, naval forces returned to the Baltics to help prevent Bolshevik expansion and so indirectly helped Estonia and Latvia towards their independence. At that time, Latvia could have become a German colony, or part of the Bolshevik Empire or independent. It would be late 1919 before Latvia was secure, with Riga as its capital, in Latvian, rather than in German or in Russian hands. Earlier that year, Liepaja played a temporary role as capital when forces under Kārlis Ulmanis, who later became president of Latvia, had to flee there. In fact, for a few days in late May, he would have to flee further, onto the *Dunois*, part of the British fleet.

FROM THE CRIMEAN TO WORLD WAR I The Russian surrender in 1856 brought an end to the Crimean War and so to military activity in the Baltics. However the ease with which Liepaja fell into British hands was a warning. Whilst peace in the area seemed assured in the immediate aftermath of the war, this would clearly not last for long. Alexander III ordered the building of fortifications beside the coast at the area now known as Karosta (see page 163) and these were completed under Nicholas II in 1904. Karosta was also one of Russia's first submarine bases. Ironically much would be dismantled only four years later in 1908 following an improvement in the relationship between Nicholas II and Kaiser Wilhelm II of Germany. This did not in fact make any difference to the conduct of World War I in the area, as Liepaja's control was decided by land battles, not by sea ones. It was, however, from the sea that the Germans launched the war in the area. On 2 August 1914 their cruiser *Magdeburg* shelled the port, but no Russian ships of any significance remained at that time. They had all already withdrawn to St Petersburg. The Germans occupied Liepeja by land on 8 May 1915 and Tsarist Russian forces would never return.

In the civilian area, the late 19th century was a very prosperous time for Liepaja, with the population growing tenfold between 1863, when it was 10,000, and 1914, when it was 130,000. Similar, although not such spectacular growth was taking place at many Baltic ports, but Liepaja had the advantage of being ice-free for nearly all the winter and of having had several centuries of trading links well beyond Europe, so it could take this expansion in its stride. It developed at the same pace as many American ports and for the same reasons. The railways, combined with ever-larger ships using the port, could supply the raw materials needed outside Russia and import the consumer goods which the expanding middle class in Russia could by then afford. In percentage terms the number of Germans would decrease, but their power remained the same. Unlike Riga, Liepaja had strong trading links with what is now Ukraine.

BETWEEN THE TWO WORLD WARS The armistice at the end of World War I covered only the Western front, not the Eastern one, where the Treaty of Brest-Litovsk in March 1918 was the complete reverse, with the Russians surrendering to the Germans. British naval intervention and a strong independence movement in Latvia prevented Liepaja from remaining under German military control, but the Germans certainly had not been deposed commercially, and by 1921 all the main German businesses had reopened. It was no longer formalised, but Latvians still played a minor role. They had wooden houses with thatched roofs, the Germans stone houses with tiled ones. Formal segregation and discrimination were not allowed but in practice the

German private clubs and spas remained. The Germans owned and managed business, whilst Latvians remained as workers. The Jewish community was to some extent a balance between them, operating many of the independent shops.

The population of the town halved from 130,000 in 1914 to 57,000 in 1939. There were several causes for this: Russian transit business through the harbour largely disappeared and conversely the Soviet regime had little need for the goods which could be imported through Liepaja. Many markets enjoyed by the factories before the war disappeared during it and could not be revived. The Russian military of course had to withdraw. Travel writers and economists both ignored the town. One English-language guidebook to Latvia of 250 pages published in 1937 gives just two paragraphs to Liepaja in the whole book. Others are scarely more generous.

WORLD WAR II The signing of the Molotov–Ribbentrop Pact between Germany and the USSR in August 1939 enabled Soviet forces to be based in Liepaja from that time. Full occupation came in June 1940. The summer and autumn of 1941 are the most tragic months in the town's whole history. Soviet deportations started, as elsewhere in the Baltics, on 14 June. Ten days later, the town would be a battleground between the advancing Germans and the rapidly retreating Soviet forces. As soon as the Germans were settled, they established several local execution centres along the beach and in the harbour for the murder of the Jewish population of 9,000, a task which was completed by the end of the year. Three thousand people were killed in one day at the lighthouse. Western Latvia was not in the end spared the renewed Soviet occupation, but at least it was spared street-by-street fighting in 1944–45. The Germans remained in occupation there right up to the final surrender on 8 May 1945, having repulsed early Soviet attempts to dislodge them. Hitler ignored many requests from his generals for these troops to be withdrawn to fight in Germany itself.

THE SOVIET ERA A history of the Soviet period in Liepaja has yet to be written. Maybe its absence so far should be taken as a sign of minimal activity outside the Soviet bases. Much of the town was off-limits to local people, quite apart from outsiders, and of course foreigners had no chance to visit. Many Russian speakers moved in, some as part of the military and some into the factories. For the first time in its history, Liepaja had no role in its own fate. Some buildings from that time still disfigure the landscape but what Bertschi built previously was so sturdy that there was no pretext for large-scale development in the town centre. Nowadays most people link the regime with the prison at Karosta (page 163), which has been opened as a tourist attraction.

Unlike in Kaliningrad, the Soviets saw no need in Liepaja to remove the German architectural and ecclesiastical heritage. It was of course neglected but not to a degree which could prevent restoration. Liepaja is the only town of any size in the Baltics where the Soviet legacy does not still intrude.

RENEWED INDEPENDENCE It has to be admitted that in the 1990s, Liepaja did not present a happy picture to the few tourists or business visitors who happened to turn up there. With foreigners having been banned for so long, it was difficult suddenly to welcome them and to provide the minimal facilities that even adventurous ones would need. The second edition of *Latvia: The Bradt Travel Guide,* published in 1999, warned readers that the town centre was 'fairly run down' and most of the historical buildings 'were in need of repair'. In the main hotel hot water was 'still irregular' and 'strange smells have been known to pervade the ground floor'. This is all now in the past. Perhaps to make up for lack of foreign contact for 50 years, Liepaja now has twinning links with 14 cities around the world, some such as Klaipeda on the doorstep, and some far away such as Bellevue in Washington State, USA, close to Seattle. Staff exchanges have enabled administrative experience to develop at a quicker pace than might otherwise have happened.

The new century seemed suddenly to present a new challenge, and one that has been vigorously taken on board. Liepaja is finally a thriving Latvian city, owing its success to Latvians promoting it across Europe and lobbying successfully for it in Riga. In public relations, its obvious rival to the north, Ventspils, has undoubtedly done better, but in actual results Liepaja wins hands down. It is Liepaja, rather than Ventspils, that has well-designed hotels, and air links to Riga and abroad, and that is reviving its railways and its trams. Few must be the towns in Europe that organise both an organ festival and a rock one, but Liepaja does. For accommodation it is possible to stay in a warehouse or a prison, to have Egyptian or French furniture or to see the best of modern local painting in reception. Its former colonial masters would be shocked at this diversity and sense of fun; visitors will without doubt enjoy it.

PRACTICALITIES

Liepaja is a tough city for individual tourists as so little information is available in print, although the tourist-office website offers plenty of help. There are no bus maps, no listings magazines and few local publications in either English or German, so a lot of research for a trip that can normally be done online can only be done on arrival. The **Tourist Office** (*5/6 Rožu laukums;* ✆ *6348 0808;* e *info@liepajaturisms.lv; www.liepaja.lv/turism*) opens daily from May to October. As most museums close on Monday and Tuesday, it is best to visit Liepaja between Wednesday and Sunday. Churches are however open daily and in good weather it is a pleasure just to stroll in the streets taking in the architecture and then to relax on the coast. The tourist office organises a two-hour walking tour every day from June to September which leaves from outside the office at 14.00 and which costs 2.50Ls.

See the Riga chapter, pages 96–7, for information on currency and **telephones**. All Liepaja phone numbers start with the digits 634, which has to be dialled for local calls as well as from elsewhere in Latvia. The **post office** in Liepaja is at Graudu iela 45 (⏰ *08.00–19.00 Mon–Fri, 09.00–16.00 Sat*). As in other countries, the postal service has had to diversify to survive, so this is also the best place to buy chewing gum in Liepaja. Several hotels provide a computer free of charge to their guests but the main public **internet** cafés in the town centre are:

🖥 **Balta Data** Jaunā Ostmala 3.5; www.netlogs.lv
🖥 **Netlogs** Peldu 16; www.netlogs.lv
🖥 **Sapņu Sala** Lielā 12
🖥 **Tilks** Peldu 32; www.gandat.lv

TRANSPORT

Air Baltic (*www.airbaltic.com*) fly to Liepaja from Riga five times a day Monday–Friday and twice on Saturdays and Sundays, and bargain fares are often available on this route. If the pleasure of obtaining a Ls1 ticket is somewhat muted by the tax of Ls9, this fare of £10/US$20 is still a bargain. The route is in any case subsidised by Liepaja Town Council to encourage its use. Using public buses to the airport at both ends, the total journey time should be not more than two hours. It is of course possible to combine this Air Baltic domestic flight with their international network from Riga. In 2007 Air Baltic also operated daily direct services from Liepaja to Copenhagen and to Hamburg. Others may well follow.

The airport is about 6km from the city. Full timetables for flights, and also details of pleasure trips over Liepaja and of the public buses serving the airport are on the airport website (*www.liepaja-airport.lv*).

Buses operate to all major towns in western Latvia from Liepaja and also along the coast to Palanga and Klaipeda in Lithuania. Some of these buses continue to Kaliningrad. For other places it is necessary to change buses in Riga, which is a journey of about four hours, although some express services reduce this time to around three hours. The bus station's website (*www.aslap.lv*) gives all services out of Liepaja, but is only in Latvian.

Trains started operating again to Liepaja in 2006 after a gap of several years, albeit only once a day to Riga. This service leaves Liepaja around 06.00 so that local people can have a full business day in Riga; the return train leaves Riga at 18.00. The journey takes three hours and costs 4Ls. A choice is offered of one coach without a video and the others with one. There is a small surcharge for buying the ticket on the train rather than at the ticket office. Schedules and fares can be checked on www.ldz.lv.

Buses leave from the forecourt of the railway station and the ticket office inside handles tickets for both rail and bus services. It can also sell onward rail tickets to Russia from Riga.

The **tram** service that operates every ten minutes passes the station and is the best way into the town centre, given the distance of three kilometres or so. It follows Riga iela to the Amritsa Hotel where it crosses the canal past the Promenade Hotel and continues along Lielā iela through the town. Tickets if bought at kiosks cost Ls0.20, but on the tram Ls0.24 is charged and Ls0.25 on the bus. It is appropriate that the station was built by Max Paul Bertschi (see page 154), who has so many other buildings to his name in Liepaja.

In the town, international and cross-country buses can be pre-booked at a ticket office at Peldu 5 (⊕ *08.30–12.30 & 13.30–18.00 Tue–Fri, 08.30–14.30 Sat, closed Sun & Mon*). International ones only are sold at the Latvia Tours office in the Līva Hotel building; the entrance is on the street, not via the hotel entrance.

LOCAL TRANSPORT There are several bus routes within Liepaja, but no map which shows them. The one **tram** route (see above), which dates from 1899, runs for 13km from north to south.

ACCOMMODATION

Given that Liepaja had been a military city, it is not surprising that for many years tourists were restricted to a few guesthouses or the Līva Hotel. The opening of the Amrita in 1997 was the first break with the past, and then the large number of hotels that opened in 2007 suddenly gave visitors a wide choice. This applies just as much to the disabled for whom provision is now automatic in newly built hotels.

At the time of writing, there was little difference in prices throughout the year, but competition for the inevitably smaller number of visitors coming out of the summer season is bound to change this situation.

FIRST CLASS $$$

⌂ **Europa City Amrita** (83 rooms) Rīgas 7–9; ☎ 6340 3434; Skype hotelamrita; e info@hotelamrita.lv; www.amrita.lv. For 10 years from 1997, when the hotel had the monopoly on good accommodation in Liepaja, it did not take advantage of this situation & standards were always high. Doubtless they will remain so, & regular clients will certainly stay loyal. The location on the main road to airport, railway & bus station makes access by public transport very easy. $$$

⌂ **Libava** (7 rooms) Vecā Ostmala 29; ☎ 6342 4543; e info@libava.lv; www.libava.lv. Ideal for small conferences or a close circle of friends wanting luxury at prices that only buy normality in Riga. Four rooms have a jacuzzi, but all have individual AC, baths & skylight windows. The very light colours contrast with what is on offer elsewhere in Liepaja. The winter garden, full of flowers year round, tempts vistors to stretch b/fast into lunch & then into dinner,but for the more active, the hotel hires out pedaloes for use on the canal. $$$

🏠 **Promenade** (42 rooms) Vecā Ostmala 40;
📞 6348 8288; e info@promenadehotel.lv;
www.promenadehotel.lv. Liepaja really arrived as a
tourism destination with the opening of this 4-star
hotel in the summer of 2007. Being converted from a
warehouse beside the river, it is not short of space so
guests benefit in their rooms, as do local artists whose
work converts the reception area into a gallery. Ample

TOURIST CLASS $$

🏠 **Fontaine** (19 rooms) Jūras 24; 📞 6342 0956;
e info@fontaine.lvt; www.fontaine.lv. The reception
here is an antique shop & its ambience carries
throughout the hotel. Expect narrow & wooden
staircases & little space, which is what 19th-century
Liepaja was about. All the rooms are dbl &, with the
communal kitchen area, this is certainly the place to
be sociable rather than sgl. Do not take room names
too seriously; there is little to choose between the
Wedding Suite, Grandma Suite or Arab Suite. $$
🏠 **Fontaine Royal** (51 rooms) Stūrmaņu 1; 📞 6348
9777; e royal@fontaine.lv; www.fontaineroyal.lv.
Although under the same ownership as the Fontaine,
this hotel could not be more different, except in the
sense that they are both deliberately unconventional.
This one is obsessed with gold, on the furniture, the
ceiling, the blankets & even on the chandeliers. It is so
gaudy that it suddenly becomes acceptable (as a joke).
In some rooms, the ceiling paintings add a little taste, in
others it takes it further away. If forced to characterise
the décor, 'Egyptian' is probably the nearest adjective
that is fair. A concert hall attracts a wide variety of
musicians but again, do not expect the conventional. Do
not expect a lift either. $$

BUDGET $

🏠 **Helvita** (13 rooms) Bernātu 11; 📞 2633 3332;
e hotelhelvita@inbox.lv; www.helvita.viss.lv. This hotel,
which opened in 2005, is best known for its garden,
with its very English lawn, extensive patio & rock
garden. Three of the rooms are suites, surprising given
its size & general clientele, but perhaps not given that
the prices are still a lot lower than those charged for a
basic room in Riga. The indulgence of breakfast in bed
costs Ls1 pp. $
🏠 **Karosta Prison** (10 rooms) Invalīdu 4; m 2636
9470; e info@karostascietums.lv;
www.karostascietums.lv. Those who have witnessed
the transformation of the prison in Oxford, England,
to a boutique hotel should probably keep well away
from Karosta. This hotel prides itself on the changes it
has not made, rather than on those which it has.

sofas are provided for those who want to study this art
at leisure. Those who cannot afford a room with a
balcony overlooking the river should make sure they
walk up & down the fire escape to get a similar view.
The dining-room menu is more comprehensive &
cheaper than one would expect in a hotel of this size &
standard. Soundproofing throughout is of a very high
standard. $$$

🏠 **Kolumbs** (26 rooms) Kuršu 32; 📞 6342 5577;
e info@hotelkolumbs.lv; www.hotelkolumbs.lv. Smoking
is banned in all rooms here, & of course in the
communal areas too. The only exception is the top-
floor balcony. Rooms are divided into 'standard' &
'comfort', the latter being larger & with AC. It is a pity
that the rooms facing the front have not been properly
soundproofed, & there are no sgls. The Skybar is an
excellent vantage point for comparing the unbombed
parts of the town with those rebuilt since the war. The
basement offers a selection of billiard tables. $$
🏠 **Līva** (111 rooms) Lielā 11; 📞 6342 0102;
e info@liva.lv; www.liva.lv. With each renovation, this
hotel gets further from its Soviet past, although some
hints of this still linger, particularly in the wide lobby.
However its location on Rose Square & its prices
provide ample compensation & its size is very useful for
large groups wanting to stay together. $$
🏠 **Roze** (18 rooms) Rožu 37; 📞 6342 1155;
e info@ parkhotel-roze.lv; www.parkhotel-roze.lv. This
hotel has been converted from a large private house,
built in wood around 1900. Its big garden & location
near to the beach are positive features, but the lack of a
dining room, in an area with no restaurants, is a
disadvantage. $$

However, for those wanting a night of Soviet hardship
at minimal cost, it will provide satisfaction. $
🏠 **Travellers Beach Hostel** Republikas 25, cnr of
Uliha; m 2869 0106; e liepaja@hostel.lv; www.
liepajahostel.lv. The hostel prides itself on being 'Aussie
owned' & this is certainly reflected in the lively English
on the website. Accommodation varies widely from a
bed in a dormitory for Ls10 to a normal twin hotel
room for 30Ls. Ample kitchen facilities are available, as
well as a sitting room, & free transfers are provided on
departure to the bus/train station. The website shows a
video of the journey by tram from the station to near
the hostel. $

✖ EATING AND DRINKING

Liepaja does not yet offer gastronomic experiences and is unlikely to do so in the near future. The larger hotels offer the best choice of menu, and certainly of drinks, so many tourists just circulate between them; one Liepaja hotel claims that 'even the most refined gourmand will be satisfied with the variety of meals in the restaurant'. This is an exaggeration, and tourists for whom food is a major element of a holiday should stay in Riga. There are however a number of restaurants and cafés in the town that should be noted. Prices given below are an indication of the cost of three courses without wine.

☆ **Chill Out** Baznīcas 14–16; ✆ 6342 7318; ⏰ 12.00–06.00. No visit to Liepaja is complete without hearing some dance music. The advantage of listening to it in a club of this size is that there is plenty of entertainment (and even some quiet) elsewhere in the building, when boredom sets in. 10Ls.

✖ **Čili Pica** Jaunā Ostmala 3–5 (also at Klaipēdas 62); ✆ 6340 7500; www.cili.lv. Lithuania, rather than Italy, is responsible through this chain for the now passionate addiction amongst young Latvians for pizza. They were probably surprised that an item previously only found in deep freezers could & should in fact be made just before consumption. This has been the secret of the chain's success, plus the variety of sizes & flavours offered. Try to save room for their fruit salad, again made freshly on the premises & not from a tin. 9Ls.

✖ **Domes Kafejnīca** Rožu 6; ✆ 6342 2160; ⏰ 09.30–18.00. Observant passers-by beside the Town Hall will notice the window of this café but access is through the main entrance of the Town Hall. Join civil servants here for an inevitably quiet snack or midday meal. What is now the restaurant were cells for the court that sat in this building until 1945. As the building dates from 1889, it hardly need be said that it was built by Max Paul Bertschi. 8Ls.

🎸 **First Rock Café** Stendera 18–20 (entrance from Zivju); www.rockcafe.lv (in Latvian only); ⏰ 09.00–22.00 Sun–Thu, 09.00–06.00 Fri–Sat. For many local tourists, this is Liepaja's main draw & their only port of call. Others, who think they are decades past any interest in rock, are advised at least to have a drink here. In the summer, with so much taking place out of doors, it is in any case difficult to avoid. In the unlikely event that any passer-by does not know what is going on here, an enormous guitar dominates the

junction of Zivju & Stendera where the café is situated. Inside are instruments, clothes & music donated by players who have made their name here, & outside along Zivju is the **Musician's Walk of Fame**, 2 rows of bronze plaques commemorating both the currently active & the departured in this field. 15Ls.

✖ **Fontaine Delisnack** Dzirnavu 4; ✆ 6348 8523; ⏰ 24hrs. Come here not particularly for the food, but for the cross-section of Liepaja society. The young party-goers of course tend to dominate later in the evening, but through the day the mixture of Thai, American & Italian food brings in many local people wanting a quick snack instead of the more formal meals served in the Fontaine Royal or the Promenade, the hotels on either side. 6Ls.

✖ **Pastnieka Māja** Brīvzemnieka 53; ✆ 6340 7521; ⏰ 11.00–23.00. Probably the largest restaurant in Liepaja not linked to a hotel. The name means Postman's House but it cannot be identified with any particular person who lived there. Much of its former totally wooden décor remains, but some has inevitably given way to glass & modern paintings. Some regulars just drink beer, others have a full formal meal. There is a good wine list, but it seems a pity to request it when Liepaja has so much good local beer. The location is just sufficiently far from the town centre to avoid any extraneous noise, even the passing of the tram. 14Ls.

✖ **Pīrādziņi** Kuršu 7; ✆ 6342 5481; ⏰ 07.30–20.00. Latvians are no longer ashamed of their food, as they were in the 1990s, & are happy to promote it, now that clients always have the choice of something else. This café is 100% Latvian, so come here for pasties & ample servings of potatoes & cabbage, all preceded by a thick vegetable soup. Forget any ideas of diet or vegetarianism. 7Ls.

WALKING TOURS

Most suggested tours start at Rose Square, Rožu laukums, but it is worth beginning over the canal on Rīga iela opposite the Amrita Hotel. Whilst most of the walk will be set in the 18th and 19th centuries, it is important to see Liepaja's best modern building, the **Ice Hall,** which dates only from 1998 and is devoted to Latvia's passion for (and success in) ice hockey. Sometimes the ice is well covered and the hall is used for pop concerts. Note the Soviet war memorial on the canal side of the building with the dates 23–29 June 1941, which was when the Soviet army nominally defended Liepaja against the invading Germans. These dates are used to conceal the fact that the town was never 'liberated' in 1945, so strong was the German and Latvian resistance in this area. Liepaja only fell into Soviet hands with the overall German surrender on 8 May 1945.

Cross the canal onto **Lielā**, the main road through the town. This is the Latvian translation of the German name Gross Strasse (Large Street) and in Soviet times it was inevitably renamed after Lenin. The tram stop immediately ahead is the one to use for the Libava, Promenade and Fortune Royal hotels. The block of flats at Liela 4 on the western side of the road looks as though it was designed by Bertschi but in fact were designed by his son, who closely followed his father's ideas.

Lielā 5, on the opposite side of the road, looks as though it is another Bertschi building, but it is one of the very few in the town dating from the late 19th century designed by another architect.

A brief diversion is worthwhile along Teātra to see what was originally meant to be the German Theatre but is now the **Liepaja Theatre.** Building began in 1912 but continued during the early part of World War I, so confident were the Germans of long-term victory. Performances in Latvian started in 1918 and in fact none ever took place in German. Opposite the theatre at Teātra 3 is the former local branch of the National Bank of Russia, designed by Bertschi in 1898. Continuing south along Skolas and then back along Baznīcas to Lielā, the walk passes several more Bertschi buildings as well as some smaller wooden ones. The bank at Baznīcas 4, on the corner with Lielā, is one of the few buildings of note in Liepaja which date from the 1930s and so is in the functionalist style, very common in Latvia at that time.

Cross **Rose Square** (see page 164) and continue along Tirgoņu, now a pedestrian street. It is worth retracing one's steps at the end of this road, turning into Peldu and then back to Rose Square along another pedestrian precinct, Zivju. It is best to ignore the contents of the shops along here, largely a bland mixture of trainers, Chinese toys and garish tea mugs. However walking down the middle of both Tirgoņu or Zivju and looking at everything above the ground floor is a highly rewarding experience. Some of the buildings are wooden, some granite and some brick, but all are architecturally diverse. Most date from the late 19th century.

The continuation of Tirgoņu is Kuršu which has some similar buildings and also others from the 1920s and 1930s. Siena, the continuation of Zivju, is blighted with the 'Khrushchev'-style blocks of flats found all over the former USSR. A detour is worth making eastwards on Kungu, a road that crosses both Tirgoņu and Zivju. Number 24 is **Peter's House** (see page 164) and number 26 is the building Charles XII of Sweden used on his visits to what was still then his empire in 1698. It is now the **House of Craftsmen**, best known for an amber necklace displayed here which, at 123m long, is probably the longest one in the world. A lot of more modest work is also on display.

Proceeding south from Zivju, the road broadens into a square, Kuršu laukums, with **St Anne's Church** (see page 162) on the eastern side. Until the early 20th century, the square had been an open market, and until 1792, the site for public executions. Lesser criminals were also chained outside the church for public ridicule. In 1907, the **indoor market** now seen here was built with the aim of bringing together all the smaller markets scattered around the town. It has kept the name Peter's Market which was given to commemorate the 200th anniversary of his conquest of Liepaja in 1710. The interior and exterior of the building were sadly allowed to decay in the Soviet period, but both were fully restored between 2000 and 2002. Potential EU entry in 2004 was a major encouragement to ensure that a fully hygienic environment was restored.

A walk westwards of about 500m from St Joseph's along Peldu across Valdemāra (the tram route) leads to Jūrmala Park which, like Rose Square, was a creation of Georg Kuphaldt (see page 124). The end of Peldu is marked by the open stage used in the annual rock festival held in August. The park is 3km long and notable for the large number of trees planted there, some brought from abroad, and all integrated into a landscape which also includes plenty of flowers, lawns and sporting facilities. Further west is the sea.

Return from Jūrmala Park along Kūrmājas which leads back to Lielā and to the walkway beside the canal. The **Liepaja Museum** (see page 163) at number 16 is equally impressive from the outside as it is from the inside. It was originally built by Bertschi as a private residence but was acquired by the town for the museum in 1935. However, the best preserved building in Liepaja is numbers 2–6 Kūrmājas, a Art Nouveau masterpiece that matches anything in Riga. When first built, it belonged to the shipping line that took emigrants and cargo to the United States. Early in the 20th century, about 15,000 people a year would have passed through this building to buy their tickets. This figure reached 70,000 in 1913, the year before World War I broke out. During the first period of Latvian independence, from 1920 to 1940, there was minimal emigration. This area close to and beside the canal was totally closed when the Soviet military were here. Now it is one of the most open, with its hotels, clubs and 24-hour shops, and much more activity is bound to come to the canal shore over the next few years.

WHAT TO SEE

CHURCHES

Holy Trinity Church It is not hard to visualise what impression this church made when first consecrated in 1758 for use by the German community. It dominated the then small wooden buildings which were all around it, even though its tower would only be built a hundred years later. For the tough, it is worth climbing the steep and sometimes narrow steps in this tower that lead up to the clock and to the outside viewing platform. The exterior of the church still needs a lot of work, but the Rococo interior and the organ are now both in fine shape. The church is proud of its statistics: the altar-stone with its height of 13m is the largest in Latvia and when the organ had 7,000 pipes installed in 1885, it became until 1912 the largest in the world. An international festival of organ music takes place here each September.

St Anne's Church A church has been on this site since the late 16th century, but the current one was designed by Bertschi in a very roundabout manner. The tower, which had been struck by lightning in 1798, was slowly rebuilt in the early 19th century but then Bertschi was asked to improve it, and make it match the older church building. In a sense he failed, as he was asked next to rebuild the church in line with the tower. By the end of the century the church as we see it now was complete and a clear unity. The altarpiece is much earlier than the church, dating from 1697, and was carved in Ventspils. It shows both Old and New Testament scenes.

St Joseph's Cathedral As Liepaja leapt in size during the late 19th century, so the need grew for a Catholic church, and St Joseph's was, in 1900, the result. There had been an earlier church on this site and the side chapel is to some extent built from what was left of it. This chapel now houses a model of a ship built by some 19th-century sailors to celebrate their return home in a storm. Both the bricks and the slates used in the construction of the building were imported from Germany. Size here goes in the opposite direction from that prevalent in the Holy Trinity or St Anne's. Both the altar and the organ are tiny in comparison with those in the other two churches.

St Nicholas' Marine Cathedral Tsar Nicholas II was keen to stamp the Russian language and the Russian Orthodox faith far more firmly on the Baltic countries than his predecessors had thought necessary. The Alexander Nevsky Cathedral in Tallinn is the most prominent example of the policy, but this church must come a close second. Built in 1900 and consecrated in the presence of the tsar, it was in fact used very little during the 20th century. Its name is conveniently that both of the tsar and of the patron saint of seamen. Its shape, that of the bow of a ship, reflects its original purpose of serving the Russian naval forces based in Liepaja. The port of Karosta, which means 'port for war', was being constructed at the same time as the church.

The German army used the building for storage in World War I and the Soviet authorities used it likewise, and also as a sailors' club after their conquest of Latvia in 1945. Luckily the icons and bells were safely stored away during this period and with the most impressive artistic element being the painted ceiling, the church has suffered more from neglect than from wanton destruction. Only since 1997 has it again been fully functional as a church, but restoration was still slowly continuing ten years after that.

OTHER SITES

Jewish Museum (*Kungu 21; www.liepajajews.org;* ⊕ *11.00–15.00 Mon, Wed, Fri, other times by prior arrangement; admission free, but donations welcome*) This museum opened in 2007 and is currently divided into three sections. The first shows Jewish life both in Liepaja and in the Courland countryside until 1941. The second details the mass murder of the community at the end of that year, but also commemorates Germans and non-Jewish Latvians who gave their lives in their attempts to resist Nazi genocide policies. The third room covers the attempts to rebuild the tiny community left after the war, and those who joined it from elsewhere in the USSR.

Karosta Prison (*Invalīdu 4; www.karostascietums.lv;* ⊕ *1 May–30 Sep 10.00–18.00 daily; pre-booked groups also welcome other times of year; admission Ls2*) A prison was of course as important as a church when the harbour was built around 1900, but unlike the church the function of this building never changed; only the owners did, and very frequently until 1945. It was even in use for a few years after Latvia's return to independence in 1991. Whatever the regime, nobody ever escaped. It is now open for conventional tours or as what its detractors would call a theme park offering 'prison experiences', where visitors can be shouted at and even shaken somewhat by 'guards', and be slammed into a dark, damp cell. Perhaps this may be extended in the future to mock executions, as about 150 real ones took place here during the 20th century. Whatever choice is taken, the prison stands as a damning indictment of Soviet rule. The really tough can overnight here (see page 159). The prison is about 6km from the town centre but can be reached by minibus 1, 3 or 6, or bus 4 or 7 that leave from the stop by the Hotel Līva in Rose Square.

Liepaja Museum (*Kūrmājas prospekts 16; www.liepajamuzejs.lv;* ⊕ *10.00–18.00 Wed–Sun, with extension on Fri to 19.00; admisson free*) The major collection here covers the 19th century, so shows the rapid expansion of the town then. Fortunately, given that this was a pre-photography era, several local painters bequeathed to the museum for exhibition the pictures of the town they produced at the time. As the tsars came often, and usually left gifts, there is much Russian material here too. Conversely, several examples of the work of local artists who impressed the royal family sufficiently to have their work taken to St Petersburg are also exhibited here. One gallery is devoted to Mikelis Pankoks (1894–1983), the most famous local sculptor. He left Latvia in 1944 and as people did not hear from him, it was assumed that he had died, as so many did, in trying to escape from the oncoming Russians. In fact he managed to reach

Switzerland but soon suffered from a breakdown and would spend the rest of his life in a mental hospital, although this did not mean he gave up his art. It was only in 1994 that his story was published in the West and Latvians became aware of the work he had continued to produce in Switzerland.

The **Liepaja Occupation Museum** (*7–9 Ukstiņa*) is under the same administration but in a different building. It keeps the same opening hours as the main museum and admission is also free of charge. It has a somewhat broader remit than the Occupation Museum in Riga, covering day-to-day life from 1940 to 1991 as well as the horrors of military activity and deportations carried out by the Soviet and German authorities.

Northern Fort

Situated about 1.6km to the north of Karosta Prison, the remains of the short-lived defences built in the 1890s can still be seen straddled along the coast. As previously mentioned, these were regarded as redundant after Tsar Nicholas II met Kaiser Wilhelm II in 1908. Although the Soviets sealed off the area by land from the rest of Latvia, they never bothered to restore these defences on the assumption that any future war would be nuclear. A torch is needed for exploring inside and care should be taken since the ruins are not being maintained.

Peter's House

(*Kungu 24*) Peter the Great stayed in this building in 1697, *en route* to studying naval technology in England and in Holland. His week in Liepaja showed him the potential for an ice-free port on the Baltic coast, even though the harbour here was still very rudimentary when he saw it. He must already have had thoughts of conquering it for the Russian Empire. Nominally Peter travelled in disguise, using a pseudonym, so that he could experience day-to-day life, but as he came with a large entourage, and was 2m tall, many people must have known who he was.

The building was originally all in wood; the extensive plaster was added in the 19th century, when it became a private residence. Steep roofs were favoured by the rich at that time. It is possible that Peter planted the willow tree in the garden.

Rožu laukums

(Rose Square) Only one name mattered throughout the Russian Empire between 1890 and 1915 if a prestigious landscape garden was required, and it was that of Georg Kuphaldt (see page 124). Riga is where Kuphaldt did most of his work but he was also engaged in St Petersburg, Sochi and Tallinn. He worked on Rose Square between 1911 and 1913 and wisely his design was subsequently left intact, although few of the surrounding buildings date from that time. The 14 plaques in the centre represent each of the towns with which Liepaja is twinned.

The square is now dominated by the **Teachers' Academy**, built in 1954. Its neo-Classicist façade is an obvious indication of its date and it was clearly not meant originally to be a college but rather the local Communist Party headquarters.

6

Vilnius LITHUANIA

Telephone code 5

Lithuania is a Baltic state and Vilnius is its capital. Yet Vilnius is unlike the other 'Baltic capitals' in a number of ways. It is 200 miles from the Baltic Sea and its true links have always been south and west. Links to the north and east have always been imposed, and never voluntarily undertaken. It has in its past been the capital of much more than what is now Lithuania; in the 15th century its boundaries stretched to the Black Sea and the country was 18 times as large as that within its current borders. In later centuries it has suffered as much as Riga and Tallinn, but usually under different occupiers and at different times. Only World War II and the subsequent occupation forced an artificial bond over the three capitals.

If you catch Vilnius on a hot summer's day, you may feel as though you are in southern Europe rather than in the north, with light pastel colours on most façades in the Old Town and an exuberant Baroque church staring out from every corner. Shade can be as important as sunshine. Wine is as perfectly natural to drink here as beer, and it is not essential to race back to work after lunch.

The Tsarist and then Soviet rulers from Russia have left an architectural legacy, but it is fortunately far less obvious in the town centre than in Warsaw, Riga, Tallinn or in the other major Lithuanian cities. Like the people, the architecture is sedate.

The 19th- and 20th-century political, religious and military history of Vilnius has been well concealed and perhaps this is just as well; only since 1990 have the population been aware of it. In 1985 three researchers rediscovered the Vilnius Cathedral Treasury that had been hidden since 1939. So frightened were they that the treasures would be taken to Moscow, that only in 1998, when they felt absolutely certain of Lithuanian independence, did they reveal their discovery.

Preliminary work for a new bridge across the Neris, which was started in 2000, revealed a hoard of coins that had been hidden from the Swedes before their occupation of Vilnius in 1702. In 2001 two different mounds of bones were discovered: one was from the French soldiers who died in Vilnius during the retreat from Moscow in 1812 and the other from Russian soldiers killed in the recapture of the city from the Germans in 1944. By 2003, excavations revealed the execution chambers at the KGB headquarters where hundreds of Lithuanian patriots were secretly killed in the late 1940s. A few years earlier the Nazis had carried out their executions in the forest at Paneriai, sufficiently far from the town not to be seen and where the evidence could be more easily concealed.

The most recent tragedy to take place in Vilnius was on 13 January 1991 when the Soviet army killed unarmed civilians guarding the Television Tower. This was in front of the world's media and the exposure has probably ensured that Lithuanian independence will never be threatened again. Contemporary Vilnius fights its internal political battles through the media and no longer on the streets. A whole generation has now grown up with no recollection of this past, or of queues, censorship or military service in distant parts of the USSR. Tourists can ignore this past if they wish, but will probably be able to appreciate the present more if they realise the background against which it has arisen.

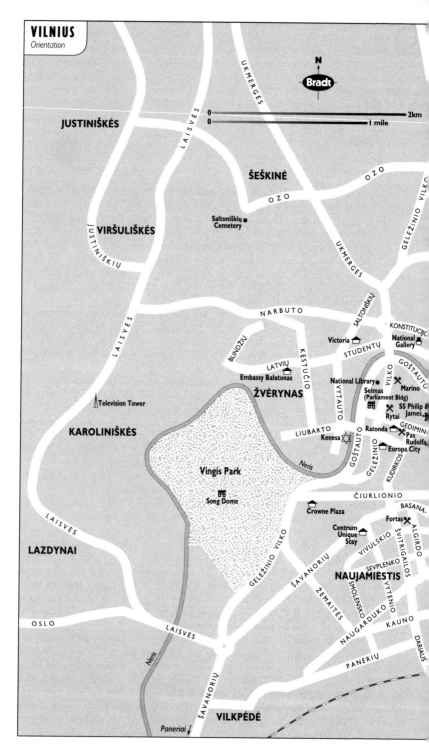

VILNIUS
Orientation

N

Bradt

0 ——————————————————— 2km
0 ——————————————————— 1 mile

JUSTINIŠKĖS

ŠEŠKINĖ

VIRŠULIŠKĖS

Saltoniškių
Cemetery

NARBUTO

Victoria   National
                Gallery

KONSTITUCIJO

STUDENTŲ

Embassy Balatonas   National Library   Marino

ŽVĖRYNAS   Seimas
                     (Parliament Bldg)   SS Philip &
                                          James
                     Rytai

LIUBARTO   Ratonda   GEDIMIN
                     Kenesa   Pas
                                        Rudolfa
                                        Europa City

Television Tower

KAROLINIŠKĖS

Vingis Park

Neris

Song Dome   ČIURLIONIO

                     Crowne Plaza   BASANA.

                     Centrum   Fortas
                     Unique
                     Stay

LAZDYNAI   NAUJAMIESTIS

OSLO   LAISVĖS

Neris

PANERIŲ

VILKPĖDĖ

Paneriai

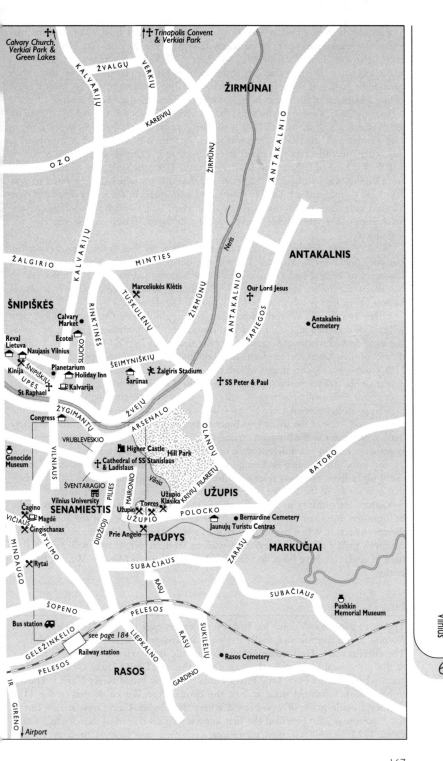

Fortunately contemporary Vilnius now shows off rather than hides. Tourists may wear torn jeans at an opera or be happy to drive a car 20 years old. Do not expect such behaviour from local people. Whether at 15.00 in an office or at 03.00 in a nightclub, expect them to take care about their appearance and similar care about their surroundings. If you witness raucous behaviour late at night, it will be from tourists taking advantage of the cheap beer, not locals on a regular weekend binge.

In early 2005, Vilnius was awarded the accolade of European Capital of Culture for 2009, which it will share with Linz as the designation is now shared between a city in 'old' Europe and one in the 'accession' states. Yet Vilnius is as 'old' and as 'European' as any other contenders for this award; in fact, more so in many respects. Younger visitors will find it hard to believe that from 1945 until 1990, the only way to travel abroad from Vilnius was by plane via Moscow and that this was a privilege granted to very few local people indeed. The few foreigners who came in the other direction were allowed only three nights there, in case they stayed long enough to 'contaminate' the local population with counter-revolutionary thoughts. Travel outside the city was forbidden.

Now Vilnius is firmly back where it belongs. There are four flights a day to London, but only one a day to Moscow. Dozens of coaches a day drive tourists, students and labourers to Poland and Germany. Very few bother to drive the 100 miles east to Minsk, or the rather longer distances to Kaliningrad or St Petersburg. It is almost impossible to find goods produced in Russia in the shops.

Other aspects of a Western lifestyle are coming to Vilnius. On the outskirts, 'new villages' of detached and semi-detached houses are slowly replacing blocks of flats as the most desired modes of housing. Over the river from the Old Town, a new business district of skyscrapers and modern office buildings is rising around the lofty new Town Hall, completely regenerating a suburb that was once a no-go area for tourists. Within a year or so, stricter parking regulations in the Old Town will give more space to pedestrians. Eventually, commuters will come in on smooth-running trams rather than on bumpy trolleybuses. A town bypass will have removed unnecessary lorries from the suburbs and some of the smart Old Town restaurants will have moved to the shopping malls which cater to the burgeoning middle classes. What visitors really want, however, is going to remain – a different walk on their doorstep whenever they leave a hotel, cuisine from any country in Europe that can claim to have one, a choice of music every night from the most reverential to the most outrageous, and an artistic legacy that is as strong in the façades of the city's buildings as in the displays inside.

Visitors are unlikely to see any signs in Polish or Russian. Lithuanian has finally become the dominant language, which shows how far in the past the role of these former masters is. When the local shops start to take the euro, likely to be in 2013, the country's policy of closer integration with its Western neighbours will, for the first time in centuries, have been decided in Vilnius, and not in Moscow, Warsaw, Paris or Berlin.

HISTORY

The main avenue in Vilnius has had several names over the past 100 years – Stalin Avenue, Lenin Avenue and, under the tsars, St George's Avenue, to name but three. The current name, **Gedimino** Avenue, is the only appropriate one, being in honour of the man considered to be the founder of the city, Grand Duke Gediminas. The place where the bubbling little River Vilnia meets the broad River Neris is known to have been inhabited since at least the Bronze Age. We know that in the 11th century a castle made of wood stood where the Higher Castle now stands. But it was Gediminas who provided the first known written record of the city, in a letter dated 1323 inviting German merchants, craftsmen and farmers to settle in and around his city, which he had raised to the status of capital, offering them exemption from taxes and freedom of worship.

A popular local legend about the birth of Vilnius tells how Gediminas was on a hunting trip with his entourage around these heavily wooded hills when he decided to set up camp rather than return to his castle at Trakai. During the night he dreamed of a huge iron wolf standing on the hill, howling the howl of a hundred wolves. He consulted a pagan priest about the dream, who told him that it was a sign to build a great fortress and city there. The howling meant that the future city's fame would spread far and wide.

In truth, it was certainly Gediminas who transferred the court from Trakai to Vilnius around the year 1320. At the time Vilnius was already a bustling trading centre with German and Russian communities who had their own churches, even though the country itself remained pagan. The Teutonic Order made frequent and bloody raids on the country, but Gediminas managed to put off any major incursions by promising repeatedly to convert to Christianity – which he never did. While he procrastinated with the West, he expanded the emerging Lithuanian Empire to the south and east as far as Ukraine.

In time the threat from the Crusaders became more acute: Vilnius was attacked seven times between 1365 and 1402. More protective fortifications and two more castles were built. The pagan state finally succumbed to Christian conversion when Grand Duke Jogaila initiated a 400-year common history between Lithuania and Poland through marriage. This failed to stop the relentless assaults of Teutonic Knights, however, and it was not until the Battle of Žalgiris in 1410 that Grand Duke Vytautas dealt them a blow from which they never recovered. Vytautas also annexed many Ukrainian and Russian lands, pushing the Lithuanian Empire all the way to shores of the Black Sea.

Vilnius flourished for the next 200 years, in a period of growth and prosperity it has never seen since. New roads extended the city in all directions, while Slavs, Jews and Tatars settled in large numbers. The city's first synagogue was built in the 16th century. The Union of Lublin in 1569 further strengthened the bond with Poland, creating a huge unified state, or commonwealth. Vilnius lost its administrative role and Polish dominated as the official language, but the arrival of the Jesuits that same year resulted in a construction boom in the new Baroque style of architecture, much of it sponsored by a small number of powerful noble families. A college that the Jesuits founded became a university in 1579, which soon earned itself a reputation as one of Europe's great academic institutions. Meanwhile, the role played by the Roman Catholic Church in the life of the city strengthened.

War and plague followed, however, bringing destruction and decline to this city of 30,000. As the might of Muscovy grew, the commonwealth failed to hold off a powerful invasion in 1655. Cossacks plundered Vilnius for weeks, destroying Catholic and Jewish buildings, wreaking anarchy and terrorising inhabitants. Almost half of the city's population was lost to plague which hit the city in 1657–58, while the rampaging Russians were not driven out until 1660. But, surprisingly, Vilnius recovered quickly. Magnificent Baroque churches, chapels, mansions and palaces were built over the coming decades and, despite the city being attacked and occupied by both Russian and Swedish armies in the early 18th century, as well as being devastated by more fires and plague, many have survived to this day.

The long, steady decline of the Polish–Lithuanian Commonwealth resulted in a third and final partition in 1795, in which Vilnius, now a city of 20,000, and most of Lithuania became part of Tsarist Russia. Hopes for independence were briefly revived when Napoleon stormed through Europe and captured Vilnius in 1812 and in the 19 days he spent in the city he set up a provisional national government. But, six months later, a decrepit Grand Armée, beaten at Berezina and frozen by the Russian

A MacCullum Scott

Late in the evening of 21 June 1924 I arrived in Vilna. It was the eve of St John's Day, the great pagan midsummer festival throughout the Baltics. Fires were lit beside the river, small boats decorated with lanterns and bearing festive parties were rowed up and down stream. The sound of music and singing floated over the water. From the midst of the city, outlined against the pale northern sky, rose abruptly the Hill of Gedimin like an altar to the ancient gods of the Lithuanian race.

Vilna is now, by the turn of the international kaleidoscope, part of the Republic of Poland, but there has been no revolutionary change in social manners. The old formalities of address still continue. The hotel porter and the barefooted chambermaid both addressed me as 'Barin' or lord. 'Would the Barin like some hot water? Will the Barin be wearing his coat?' It is an old, old work in Vilna.

My hotel was in Adam Michevicius Street, named after the national poet of Poland who was a native of Lithuania and a student at the University of Vilna. The next street on the right was Jagellon Street, named after the Grand Duke who united the thrones of Lithuania and Poland. I passed a 'Kultur' shop, in the window of which was displayed a large map showing the extent of the former territories of Poland and Lithuania, stretching from the Baltic to the Black Sea. The new generation in Vilna feeds its soul upon dreams of the past.

Some day Europe will rediscover Vilna. At present few people in western Europe know that this is a bone of contention between Poland and Lithuania and that it is impossible to make out whether it is inhabited by Poles, Lithuanians, Russians or Jews. To discover Vilna is to revisit an ancient civilisation which has for centuries been buried under the debris of later and barbarous regimes. However, the Vilna that now emerges is no city of the dead. It fills its lungs with the exhilarating air of freedom. It is full of energy, zeal and effort as if it were determined to make up for the years which have been lost. Europe must learn that Vilna has a personality and that it is a very vivid one.

From Beyond the Baltic *by A MacCullum Scott, published in 1925*

---

winter, staggered back to Vilnius with mounted Cossacks hot on their heels. Some 40,000 of Napoleon's soldiers died in Vilnius from starvation, cold or under the Cossacks' swords, most of them bundled into mass graves and church crypts.

The people of Vilnius continued to struggle for independence. Resistance was especially rife at Vilnius University, which paid a harsh penalty for its participation in a rebellion in 1831. It was closed the following year, a measure that would stay in effect right up until Lithuania finally won back its freedom 90 years later. Catholic churches were closed or converted to the Russian Orthodox faith. The Russian authorities even considered changing the name of the city to Chortovgorod ('city of devils'). After hanging the rebels of a second rebellion in 1864 on Lukiškių Square, a ban was imposed on written Lithuanian and street names were changed to Russian ones.

Like other European cities, Vilnius now thrived as a zone of industry. Its population swelled to more than 150,000 by the end of the 19th century, with Russians arriving in large numbers. The city also thrived as a centre of Jewish culture and learning in Yiddish, becoming known as the 'Jerusalem of the North', though the community remained very much cut off from the rest of society. The proportion of Lithuanians shrank, so that by 1904 the authorities could see no danger in lifting the ban on their language. Books, newspapers and cultural organisations quickly encouraged national awareness at a time when feelings of national identity were on the rise throughout Europe. In December 1905, a 'Great Seimas' of 2,000 Lithuanians demanded greater autonomy and the use of Lithuanian in schools. The latter demand was granted.

Nine years later war was once again unleashed on Europe. The mighty German army stormed eastwards and in late 1915 the Russians abandoned Vilnius, which now had a population of 235,000. A new Lithuanian Council was formed, which began negotiations with the Germans for full independence, a goal that was reached in a declaration on 16 February 1918. Chaos reigned, however, and in the scuffles at the end of the war the Bolshevik army and the Polish army each held the city twice and Lithuania once. Lithuania's possession of the city was agreed to on all sides on 7 October 1920, but two days later the Polish army marched north and retook it, an action secretly backed by the Polish leader Jozef Pilsudski, who had been born near Vilnius. When Pilsudski died 15 years later, his wishes were that his body should be buried in Warsaw, but that his heart should be cut out and buried in Vilnius. His heart lies today encased in his mother's tomb in Rasų Cemetery.

After a period of lacklustre international mediation, the League of Nations put Vilnius on the Polish side of a demarcation line in 1922. Lithuania protested by stressing the city's historic role as its former capital, but its appeals fell on deaf ears. In a characteristic display of persistence, the newly independent nation retaliated early in 1923 by seizing Memel (Klaipeda), then under League of Nations supervision, giving it a vitally needed port on the Baltic Sea. Under Polish control, Vilnius's economy and importance declined while Kanuas developed quickly as the new Lithuanian capital. Lithuanian cultural activities in Vilnius were curbed, mass was allowed only in Polish and many ethnic Lithuanians moved to Kaunas.

In March 1939, Hitler was given his last bloodless conquest when Nazi Germany took Klaipeda. The carve-up of eastern Europe that resulted from the Molotov–Ribbentrop Pact of 23 August 1939 initially consigned a helpless Lithuania to the German sphere of influence. But when Lithuania refused to attack Poland as a German ally, a second secret pact signed in Moscow on 27 September transferred it to the Soviet sphere. On 10 October, while Soviet military bases were being established within the country, Vilnius was returned to Lithuania. Occupation, then annexation, followed in June 1940. On 14 June 1941 the first Soviet deportations were carried out and 35,000 people were sent to the frozen wastes of Siberia. Most did not survive the first winter.

On 22 June the Nazis surprised Stalin by launching Operation Barbarossa. Within two days they were in Vilnius. With the Nazi occupation of 1941–44 came the murder of 95% of the country's pre-war Jewish population of 300,000 people. Since Jews made up 40% of the population of Vilnius, this meant that virtually half the city was systematically eliminated, mostly in the Paneriai Forest close to the city. Only one German officer rebelled against this policy, Major Karl Plagge, who probably saved about 1,000 Jews during this time. In April 2005 he was posthumously awarded Israel's 'Righteous Amongst the Nations' honour for his courage.

The war ended with a second Soviet occupation of Vilnius, one that was to last almost 50 years. Demographic changes continued. Tens of thousands of Lithuanians had fled westwards to escape the clutches of the Soviets. With Vilnius now in the Soviet Union, many Poles moved west and there were further deportations to Siberia – about 130,000 between 1944 and 1953, including a third of the clergy. Armed resistance and guerilla warfare took place against Soviet rule throughout the Baltic countries, but by Stalin's death in 1953 this had been brutally crushed. However, as more Russians and migrant Lithuanians arrived in Vilnius, the city's population started to grow again.

Vilnius remained the capital of occupied Lithuania. Churches were closed to become warehouses and car repair garages, then later, during the Khrushchev era, some became art galleries and museums. Grey suburbs of factory-made housing blocks

Vytautas Landsbergis

The Soviets had decided to act without delay, and a terrible slaughter took place on the streets of Vilnius that night. The disturbance began just after midnight when Soviet tanks and armoured troop carriers loaded with special KGB riot troops came roaring through our streets. They drove straight to predetermined destinations; their orders were to seize the radio and television studios as well as the television tower which stands on the outskirts of Vilnius. As they followed their instructions, the people responded to their manoeuvres and a sequence of events followed which stirred the conscience of the world. Some people had already kept vigil at the television facilities for several days and nights, and now others hurried through darkened streets, often passing the cumbersome tanks as they lurched slowly forward. When they reached the threatened buildings, they linked hands and began to sing the old folk songs of Lithuania or shouted slogans such as 'Lithuania will be free'. Soon they heard bullets passing over their heads as automatic rifles and machine guns swung into action. According to standard Soviet calculations, the crowd should have been scattered under this onslaught, but they did not move and so the strategy was changed with shots being direct at people's legs and then at their bodies. Back at the Supreme Council, I learned what was going on and immediately summoned the deputies to a rally in Parliament. Most responded without delay, and as they assembled, they witnessed the volunteer defenders inside the building gathering together to take the oath of allegiance afresh. Many of them went on to make their confessions, in grim recognition of what we might all soon be facing. Our defenders had no other weapons than a few pistols and rifles, sticks and petrol bombs.

The most difficult hours still lay ahead of us. Long before dawn on 13 January, the local hospitals began to overflow with the dead and injured. Because Vilnius TV was now in Soviet hands, the Kaunas station replaced it as our chief means of disseminating information. We remained in Parliament awaiting an onslaught. I asked the women to leave us, but they all refused. I then addressed the crowd surrounding the Parliament buildings, imploring them to move away to avoid casualties, but I received the same response. Everyone then knew exactly what to expect, but they all refused to move. Their heroism was unflinching, and later I was told that some had even been angry that I had urged them to leave. I had prepared a videoed speech, which could be transmitted if we were killed. In it, I gave careful directions for a campaign of passive resistance and suggestions about how life could be made difficult for our enemy under a new occupation. Fortunately this did not come about, because the assault ended at daybreak, and although the threat was not over, it was never repeated on that scale. It was a people's victory in the best sense. Indeed, a cynical KGB officer was later overheard to say: 'We did not attack the Parliament because of the excess flesh surrounding it.'

From Lithuania, Independent Again *by Vytautas Landsbergis. The author, who would subsequently become President and then Speaker, describes the night of 12–13 January 1991 in Vilnius*

were constructed for the growing numbers of workers. Most Lithuanians managed to find work within the system, whether in collective farming on nationalised land or in the industrialised city. Initially, the institutions of power such as the Communist Party, the government and the KGB were in Russian hands, but gradually, as the years passed, more and more college graduates joined the Party knowing that this would further their careers. However, underground publications also began to appear, particularly in the 1970s, the most significant being the Chronicle of the Catholic Church in Lithuania. It was smuggled abroad under the noses of the KGB for 20 years and was never discovered.

When Mikhail Gorbachev tried to stop the stagnation of the Brezhnev years by introducing greater openness, a group of Lithuanian cultural figures and academics set up the Sajūdis national movement in 1988 to push for further discussion about the past. As popular support quickly grew, its leaders began to speak of independence, a full declaration of which came on 11 March 1990. Lithuania was the first Soviet republic to do so.

The move was met by Moscow imposing a tense economic blockade. Then, while the attention of the world was focused on the Gulf, came a night of orchestrated violence as Soviet tanks ran through a crowd of unarmed Lithuanian civilians protecting the Vilnius Television Tower on 13 January 1991, resulting in 14 deaths.

Three weeks later, Iceland became the first country of many to recognise Lithuanian independence. The crumbling Soviet Empire fell that August.

Once again Vilnius is the proud capital of an independent country that is today part of the European Union and NATO. Since independence, a succession of dynamic, at times controversial mayors has generated local, national and international funds to restore the Old Town, which was declared a UNESCO World Heritage Site in 1994. Since 2003 a new city of glass-fronted skyscrapers has risen over the river. Whilst friends of Vilnius would argue that the city's selection for the coveted European Capital of Culture award for 2009 was an obvious choice, this did not come about without the serious and long-term planning put into the town's submission by the municipal authorities. The private sector too has shown its confidence in Vilnius. Hardly any major Western company does not have representation there and the number of outside investors in the hotel and construction businesses shows a long-term worldwide commitment to its continuing success.

SUGGESTED ITINERARIES

DAY ONE Start with half a day beside the cathedral (page 208). A visit here, and then to the National Museum (page 207) and the Applied Arts Museum (page 204), will immediately show how close the town's links have been with cultures to the south rather than with those to the north, above all with the Catholic Church. By 2009, there will be another attraction here, immediately behind the cathedral, and this is the rebuilt Royal Palace where work started in 2003. Weather permitting, the journey on the funicular railway to the top of the castle will give a view of Vilnius that reflects each of its conquerors and now the planning policies of a totally independent Lithuania. Note Gedimino Avenue which starts at the cathedral and which is now a pedestrian precinct during the evening. Perhaps take lunch on the corner at Literata, no longer a dissident intellectual café, but more a substantial Nordic restaurant.

After lunch, walk along Universiteto to, of course, the university (page 169) and wander in its courtyards and St John's Church (page 212), now fully recovered from its 40 years of Soviet desecration. Do not forget to visit the bookshop, Littera. The book selection (in English) is fine but even finer is the artistry on its ceiling. Finish at the Picture Gallery (page 208) and see how extensively Lithuanian artists were able to travel in the 19th century and also how they portrayed Vilnius itself. Many of the local buildings shown are still perfectly recognisable today.

Be sure to take in an early evening concert (page 192), preferably in a church so that the music can be enjoyed in the environment for which it was probably written.

DAY TWO The KGB Museum (page 206) probably deserves a half-day to itself, as some time is needed for reflection afterwards. Perhaps it is just as well that it is situated

A colourful, mysterious, exotic figure in the Vilnius literary landscape, Jurga Ivanauskaitė was at the forefront of Vilnius's new generation of independent-minded novelists and artists for 20 years until her tragic early death from cancer in 2007. Her first books established her reputation as an unconventional writer. The easy style and contemporary characters of her first short stories, published when she was 24, were an immediate popular success. Making good use of her family's unusually rich library – her grandfather was Kostas Korsakas, one of Lithuania's Marxist literary critics – she popularised non-Marxist ideas. Her youthful characters played Beatles songs, enthused about Surrealist painters, wore leather jackets and contemplated the exciting mysticism of Carlos Castaneda. They were misunderstood, frequently depressed and disappointed with life.

Partly, it was Ivanauskaitė's family background that helped her publish her books through Vaga, which until 1990 was the only outlet for fiction in Lithuania. It could also be said that in her favour was the fact that she was regarded as less of a threat by the Soviet authorities because she was female. That a young woman could be a literary rebel was unheard of in both Soviet and pre-Soviet Lithuania. Critics ignored her books, as they did anything they disapproved of.

Her 1993 novel *Ragana ir lietus* ('The Witch and the Rain') caused a national scandal. A love story told by three women – a modern-day bohemian outsider, a medieval witch and Mary Magdalene – it was immediately condemned in official circles as common pornography. But it sold 20,000 copies in two weeks.

In the mid-1990s, Ivanauskaitė's books, as well as her ethereal paintings, underwent a complete transformation after she travelled to India and Tibet. Three groundbreaking non-fiction books on Tibetan life and religion were the remarkable result. A collection of travellers' tales and insights into the religion, political situation and everyday reality of Tibetans living in exile in northern India, *Tibet in Exile* has a personal foreword by the Dalai Lama, whom Ivanauskaitė met on several occasions.

In *Journey to Shambhala* the author describes many of her personal experiences and experiments with Buddhism. The book is beautifully illustrated with mandalas, painted at moments of intense inner conflict between her Western background and her new experiences of living and being instructed by lamas in Ladakh and Nepal. *Lost Promised Land* recounts her incredible journey to occupied Tibet. For some time before her departure in June 1998, her name had been on a Chinese blacklist as the leader of a Tibet support group in Lithuania. On reaching the sacred land by 'a secret route via Hong Kong suggested by friends,' she discovers the ruinous 'lost promised land' of Tibet.

Jurga always saw herself as working towards her best book. A second collection of poetry, *Ode džiaugsmui* ('Ode to Joy', 2007), dramatically existential, was published on the day of her funeral. Even when she was too ill to write, she felt compelled to continue with her mother's help.

There have been 13 translations of Jurga Ivanauskaitė's books, six into Latvian and one into Estonian, but sadly none into English. Perhaps it is only a matter of time before the work of this most colourful and intriguing of Lithuanian authors is fully appreciated by an international audience.

a few hundred yards from anywhere else likely to be of interest. Since 2006 it has expanded to exhibit all facets of life during the Soviet era.

Town Hall Square is the base for enjoying several of Vilnius's best-known churches and is also where the Kazys Varnelis House Museum (page 208) is situated. Varnelis is probably Lithuania's most generous benefactor, having returned from his US exile not only with a wide variety of his own paintings but also with an even more valuable collection of maps, first editions, furniture and china. Do not forget to leave the square for a short walk into the former Jewish quarter where each passing year brings further restoration and colour.

DAY THREE It is time now to be outdoors some more. See why Napoleon fell for St Anne's Church (page 210) on his hurried forays through Vilnius in 1812. Cross the bubbling River Vilnia into Užupis (page 202) where the poor have been replaced by the capital's most successful people and also by its most amusing (1 April is the day to see it at its best, when the 'republic' flamboyantly celebrates its 'independence'). Read the Užupis constitution nailed to the wall on Paupio Street, then visit some of the 'republic's' little galleries, where contemporary artists all like to their work to be displayed. Finish the morning at the Amber Museum (page 204) and perhaps be tempted to do some shopping there, before relaxing over lunch at one of the many tasteful cafés along Pilies.

In the afternoon, walk along the river to the Applied Arts Museum before continuing to St Peter and St Paul (page 212), undoubtedly the most flamboyant of all the churches in Vilnius. Return along the other bank to see New Vilnius arising, literally, given the number of skyscrapers either complete or being built. See how the river so rigidly divides Old from New Vilnius.

PRACTICALITIES

MONEY
Currency In 1993 Lithuania reintroduced its pre-war currency, the litas (abbreviated throughout this book as Lt), which is divided into 100 centas.

On the reintroduction of the currency, the exchange rate was fixed at 4Lt to US$1, and remained pegged at that level until 2002, when it was replaced by a similar fixed link, that of 3.45Lt to €1. In July 2008 the UK pound was worth around 4.35Lt and the US dollar around 2.20Lt. This fixed exchange rate to the euro is scheduled to remain in place until Lithuania formally joins the single European currency, possibly in 2013.

Banks Banks throughout Estonia and Latvia, and also those in Poland near to the border, also sell litas. An exchange office, with good rates, is always open at Vilnius Airport when flights arrive and the one situated between the bus and railway stations is open 24 hours a day. Those in the town centre tend to keep to office hours, although a couple do open on Saturdays and Sundays, for example the Parex Bank branch next to the railway station. Unlike in Estonia and Latvia, rates vary very little between the different banks and exchange offices, no matter which currency is exchanged.

LOCAL MEDIA Visitors interested in recent political news from the Baltic area should buy *The Baltic Times*, which is published in Riga every Thursday and is usually on sale in Vilnius the same afternoon. It also lists concerts and films for that week. *Vilnius Now* started publication in 2005, following the success of a similar monthly magazine in Riga. It is distributed in all the major four- and five-star hotels and concentrates on dining and entertainment. It also has informative historical and business features.

The bi-monthly *Vilnius In Your Pocket* has built up for itself a legendary status since it started in 1992; it became immediately notorious for the sharpness of its pen in the face of bland service, unimaginative décor and tepid food. As standards have improved so much since then, it can usually adopt a more positive tone, but it remains as harsh as ever about the places that still deserve it. Some hotels provide it free of charge; otherwise it can be bought in kiosks for 5Lt. *Exploring Vilnius* comes out twice a year and is free of charge. It has very useful snippets on all the main sights, and details of public transport, but does not describe restaurants or hotels.

Travellers also planning to visit Riga or Tallinn should try to find the bi-monthly *City Paper*. Its reviews of hotels and restaurants are detailed and in a part of the world not known for lively political and artistic writing, it provides the perfect one-stop shop for English-speaking readers wanting an instant briefing on all the major local issues and attractions.

A few copies of the European editions of British and American daily newspapers are on sale in hotels that cater for business travellers but visitors should not rely on this. No local daily newspaper appears in English nor do local television stations transmit in English but hotel televisions can nearly always receive BBC World and CNN.

COMMUNICATIONS

Telephone To reach a landline within Vilnius, just dial the seven-digit number. If phoning from elsewhere in Lithuania, use first the prefix 8 which is used for all out-of-town numbers and then the Vilnius code 5 before the seven-digit number. All mobile numbers have nine digits and these are prefixed with 8, wherever the call is made. Phoning Lithuania from abroad, remember the country prefix of 370 which is followed by the city code and then the local number. For mobiles, the 370 country prefix is followed by 8.

Costs for phone calls made from hotel rooms vary enormously. Some hotels have deliberately reduced their charges to try to persuade guests not to use their mobiles. Others have left them at the absurdly high rates of the 1990s. Phone boxes take only cards which can be bought at any kiosk. They are issued in sums of 9Lt, 13Lt and 30Lt. Expect to pay about 3Lt a minute to phone Britain or the USA from these boxes, which are increasingly rare in Vilnius as mobiles take over the communications market.

Mobile phone users wanting to avoid roaming costs can of course buy a SIM card for use within their phone. Prices change in this field all the time but local calls should cost only the equivalent of a few pence and international ones about 50p/US$1 a minute, so similar to the charges payable in a public phone box.

Useful telephone numbers

Fire	01	Directory enquiries	118
Police	02	International calls	1573
Ambulance	03		

Post The main post office is at Gedimino 7 (⏰ *07.00–19.00 Mon–Fri, 09.00–16.00 Sat*). It sells a wide range of postcards and packing materials for those who need to send parcels. It also sells sets of all the stamps that have been issued in Lithuania since the re-establishment of independence in 1991. Its website (*www.post.lt*) gives full information on current tariffs.

Internet At the time of writing only one hotel, the Centrum Uniquestay, provided computers free of charge in each room. Most others provide connections for those who wish to use their laptops, but do check charges before settling down to a few hours of emailing. Some provide computers in a business centre for guests, which may be free of charge (as at the Novotel) or may have a cost. With WiFi spreading so quickly, it is impossible to give up-to-date guidance for reception, except to say that all hotels with conference facilities are bound to have it. To check the current situation, refer to www.wifi.lt.

There are not many internet cafés in Vilnius, perhaps because so many local people can now afford to have computers at home, or can use them in their offices. As the Reval Hotel Lietuva charges 20Lt an hour for its computers, some guests walk across the river to the Old Town where Collegium at Pilies 22 (⊕ *08.00–20.00 daily*) offers congenial surroundings and internet access for 8Lt an hour. Unlike the city's other internet cafés, there might even be people as old as 25 working there. Much cheaper is one that opened in 2007 behind the Radisson Astoria in the Russian bookshop, Russkaja Knyga, Rudininku 8, which charges 3Lt an hour but is only open 09.00–18.00 Mon-Sat.

EMBASSIES The number of foreign embassies in Vilnius increases every year, as more countries feel the need for direct representation there rather than treating Lithuania as a sideline from an embassy in Riga, Stockholm or Warsaw. The website of the Lithuanian Foreign Ministry (*www.urm.lt*) gives a full list together with all contact details. The main ones likely to be of interest to readers of this book are listed below. Whilst the phone numbers given will probably be answered in office hours only, there will be a recorded message at other times with the mobile phone number of the duty officer should urgent contact be needed.

🅔 **Belarus** Muitinės 41; ✆ 5 213 2255;
e lithuania@belembassy.org; www.belarus.lt
🅔 **Canada** Jogailos 4; ✆ 5 249 0950;
e vilnius@canada.lt; www.canada.lt
🅔 **France** Švarco 1; ✆ 5 212 2979;
e ambafrance.vilnius@diplomatie.gouv.fr;
www.ambafrance-lit.org

🅔 **Russia** Latvių 53/54; ✆ 5 272 1763;
e post@rusemb.lt; www.rusemb.lt
🅔 **UK** Antakalnio 2; ✆ 5 246 2900;
e be-vilnius@britain.lt; www.britain.lt
🅔 **USA** Akmenų 6; ✆ 5 266 5500;
e mail@usembassy.lt; www.usembassy.lt

HOSPITALS AND PHARMACIES You can find a pharmacy (*vaistinė*) on virtually every street in Vilnius, but only one is open 24 hours:

✚ **Gedimino Vaistinė** Gedimino 27; ✆ 5 261 0135

Professional medical care that reaches the sort of standards found in private hospitals in Western countries is available at two locations. If you have private health insurance in your home country you may be exempt from payment, so if possible ask about this beforehand.

✚ **Baltic-American Medical & Surgical Clinic**
Nemenčinės pl 54a; ✆ 5 234 2020; e info@bak.lt;
www.bak.lt

✚ **Medical Diagnostic Centre** Grybo 32/10; ✆ 5 270 9120; e mdc@medcentras.lt; www.medcentras.lt

Professional medical check-ups in English are also provided by appointment at a small clinic right next door to the cathedral: Medicine General Private Clinic (*Gedimino 1a, 2nd floor;* ✆ *5 261 3534;* e *medgen@takas.lt; www.clinic.lt;* ⊕ *09.00–17.00 Mon–Fri*).

ENGLISH-LANGUAGE CHURCH SERVICES
✝ **Grace International Baptist Church** Verkių 22;
www.church.lt. Services every Sun at 11.00.
✝ **International Church of Vilnius** Vokiečių 20;
www.icvilnius.org. An ecumenical service is held in the

Lutheran church every Sun at 09.30.
✝ **SS Philip and James** Lukiškių aikštė 10; Roman
Catholic mass every Sun at 09.00 with confessions
beforehand on request.

TOURIST INFORMATION There are two offices in the Old Town (*at Vilniaus 22 & at Didžioji 31;* ✆ *5 262 9660;* e *tic@vilnius.lt; www.vilnius-tourism.lt*) and one at the railway station, which therefore also serves the bus station, as they are side by side. There isn't one at the airport. Although they are called 'Municipal Tourist Offices', all three can also provide information on other places in Lithuania. The one with the address in Didžioji is in fact in the Old Town Hall in the centre of the square.

Opening hours vary on a seasonal basis but they are all open at weekends during the summer and sometimes on Saturdays during the winter. Minimum hours at all offices during the week in winter are 10.00–17.00.

TRANSPORT

AIRPORT TRANSFER Two buses and several minibuses operate from the airport into town. Bus tickets should be bought on arrival from the kiosk at the airport where they cost 1.10Lt, or 1.40Lt if bought from the driver. The number 1 runs to the bus/train station and the number 2 runs along Švitrigailos across Gedimino and then crosses the river to the Lietuva and Holiday Inn hotels. Unfortunately no buses pass any of the hotels in the Old Town but none is more than a few hundred yards from a bus stop.

Microbuses operate along these routes as well and also on others. They usually charge 3.00Lt and payment is always made to the driver. They stop at all bus stops but will also stop elsewhere. They do not operate within the Old Town. Services by both means of transport operate from early in the morning until fairly late at night so there is almost always public transport, no matter when a flight leaves or arrives.

TAXIS Vilnius taxi drivers had a very bad reputation amongst foreigners in the early '90s, but now problems are few and far between. As anywhere else, enter only a clearly marked car, and check that the meter is turned on immediately. On this basis a journey within the city should not cost more than about £3/US$6 and one to the airport about £9/US$18. At the airport, charges are clearly marked in English on a board beside the taxi rank outside the terminal.

Taxis ordered by phone are a little cheaper than those hailed on the street so if you can get a Lithuanian speaker to do this, take advantage of it. Tip 10% if the driver is polite, does not smoke and turns the radio off when you enter. Reputable companies of several years' standing include:

🚗 **Denvila** ➘ 5 244 4444   🚗 **Martonas** ➘ 5 240 0004
🚗 **Ekipažas** ➘ 5 239 5540   🚗 **Vilniaus** ➘ 5 212 8888

BUSES AND TROLLEYBUSES There are a wide number of routes except into the Old Town, where only one bus, the number 11, operates and that only on a half-hourly basis. However a bus stop is never far away wherever you are in the Old Town. Some bus stops have maps showing all the routes and all buses have the main streets along which they travel marked on a side window. Stotis is the railway/bus station where many routes start and finish. Tickets cost 1.10Lt if bought in a kiosk and 1.40Lt if bought from the driver on the bus. In either case, remember to punch them at the start of your journey. There is no reducton for buying a larger quantity as there is in Tallinn.

Full timetables and routes are given on www.vilnius.transport.lt. Much of the fleet, it has to be admitted, is quite elderly but since 2004 serious efforts have been made to replace the entire rolling stock so travellers should be sure of a comfortable ride on many routes.

CAR HIRE There is no point in hiring a car within Vilnius but there are several places on the outskirts of the town for which it would be useful, such as the Television Tower, Europe Park and the Antakalnis Cemetery. It could also be useful for visiting Kaunas and Trakai where some of the sites are a distance from public transport. In the summer, cars are often booked well in advance so this should be arranged through travel agents abroad at the same time as hotels and flights are booked. However, the firms listed below may be able to help at short notice. Apart from Aunela, they all have offices at the airport and can deliver cars there or to a hotel in town.

🚗 **Aunela** ╲ 8 686 63444; e aunela@takas.lt; www.aunela.lt

🚗 **Avis** ╲/f 5 232 9316; e apo@avis.lt; www.avis.lt

🚗 **Budget** ╲ 5 230 6708; e budget@budget.lt; www.budget.lt

🚗 **Hertz** ╲ 5 272 6940; e reservations@hertz.lt; www.hertz.lt

🚗 **Litinterp** ╲ 5 212 3850; e vilnius@litinterp.com

🚗 **Sixt** ╲ 5 239 5636; e rent@sixt.lt; www.sixt.lt

CYCLING The streets of Vilnius are a little more cyclist-friendly than other eastern European cities, but drivers can be aggressive and impatient, especially at peak hours. So nobody's going to stop you if you cycle your velocipede on the pavements.

In summer 2001, the former mayor Artūras Zuokas introduced 1,000 distinctive orange bikes to Vilnius for public use. Cycle paths were painted and metal racks installed at strategic points throughout the city centre, the idea being that you could jump on a bike and cycle to your chosen destination for free, leaving the bicycle at the nearest rack. Needless to say, every single bike was stolen within hours. But the cycle paths still exist, making pedalling through the Old Town a pleasurable experience.

You can rent a bicycle, and also find out more about biking through the Baltics, at Lithuanian Cyclists Community (m *8 699 56009;* e *BaltiCCycle@bicycle.lt; www.bicycle.lt*).

⊢ ACCOMMODATION

There is a wide choice of accommodation in Vilnius, ranging from dorm beds in hostels to luxury hotels. Prices are similarly variable, and are usually a fairly reliable indicator of the quality of any particular establishment.

Since a sudden burst of activity in hotel construction in 2003–04, there have been no major new projects, although several hotels have been enlarged. In 2009 a Kempinski will open opposite the cathedral. The deluxe traveller can now rely on the chains that prevail elsewhere, whilst budget travellers are no longer dependent on a haphazard range of guesthouses. Many tourists automatically choose the Old Town but regular visitors to Vilnius are now increasingly turning to the larger hotels over the river and in the New Town where rooms are bigger, views more extensive and driving less problematical. Short periods of intense heat in the summers of 2002 and 2003 persuaded most hotels in the four- and five-star category to install air conditioning, even though it only needs to be used for about four to five weeks in most years. Because supply nearly always exceeds demand in Vilnius (unlike in Riga and Tallinn), hotel prices are reasonable on a year-round basis and many agents can offer considerable reductions on the rates advertised by the hotels directly. Independent travellers, however, are unlikely to be offered discounts in summer, even if they stay for several nights, but do ask about weekend rates, which some hotels provide. Prices are generally lower in winter, when you are likely to find a room in most hotels just by turning up on the day. In summer, independent travellers are advised to book ahead. Breakfast is frequently included in the price.

Although the hotels at the airport have recently renovated and upgraded their rooms, the drive from town takes only 20 minutes by bus or 15 minutes by car, so these hotels have not been included here.

What an overwhelming feeling of change there is in the Lithuanian capital these days. The Old Town, once notable for its elegant ruins, left to gently crumble during decades of neglect in the Soviet era, is now the eye of a storm of activity. On the other side of the river, a series of brand-new, shiny skyscrapers stand above a broad boulevard known as the local Champs-Elysées. Vilnius is suddenly looking like a modern European capital you can do business in.

It would be a mistake to suggest that all these developments are down to one man's will. But the youthful, energetic former mayor of Vilnius, Artūras Zuokas, who served two terms between 2000 and 2007, was especially keen on raising the city's profile. He saw it as his mission to transform the sleepy Lithuanian capital into the Baltic region's most technologically advanced financial, business and cultural centre.

That dream took some persistence and a little controversy. Like a good many of Lithuania's leading politicians, Mr Zuokas was accused of corruption. But he brushes off accusations of bribery and alleged attempts to influence the outcome of his re-election in 2003 as being politically motivated. It has always been easy to make enemies in Lithuania's shady world of politics and business.

With a background in television journalism – he was a war correspondent in the 1990s in Iraq, Iran and Chechnya – Artūras Zuokas could see how easy it was to lobby the world's big television networks to get his city on the weather maps. It was, for a while, until the mayors and authorities of other neighbouring capitals got the same idea. As head of the Liberal-Centrist Union, one of the country's biggest political parties, he set up business breakfasts that became forums for discussing problems facing businesspeople from all walks of life.

Away from the new skyscrapers, the Old Town has been quietly and elegantly patched up. The splashes of pastel colours began before Mr Zuokas's tenure, but are now adorning the once rundown buildings of Užupis, the atmospheric district that the former mayor has made his home.

But taking into account the various patches of wasteland in and around the Old Town that could be regenerated into prime real estate, Mr Zuokas thinks that even this peaceful haven of the city needs a more dynamic edge. Controversially, he gave the go-ahead to plans to build a business centre on top of the cellars of what used to be a bustling row of houses in the old Jewish quarter. UNESCO, which eagerly awarded the Old Town World Heritage Site status ten years ago, threatened to withdraw that decision.

Any attempts to balance the quaintly old-fashioned with glass-fronted modernity are bound to lead to arguments. Sympathisers with the mayor claim that at least he comes up with original ideas and tries them out rather than resorting to endless debates. His influence has undoubtedly helped to shake Vilnius up and pull it into the 21st century.

LUXURY HOTELS $$$$-$$$$$

🏠 **Crowne Plaza** (108 rooms) Čiurlionio 84; 🔌 5 274 3400; e reservation@cpvilnius.com; www.cpvilnius.com. This huge tower block is a longish walk from the Old Town, though it profits from a pleasantly leafy location at the edge of Vingis Park. It is one of the very few hotels that functioned in communist times, but it was completely rebuilt in 2003; all the bedrooms are now equipped to state-of-the-art business & conference standards. In the basement are a swimming pool, sauna & gym. Fine views over the city can be enjoyed from the 16th-floor Horizon bar, while the restaurant, The Seasons, presents an international menu, including a choice of vegetarian dishes. $$$$

🏠 **Grotthuss** (20 rooms) Ligoninės 7; 🔌 5 266 0322; e info@grotthusshotel.com; www.grotthusshotel.com. The hotel advertises that it is a 5min walk from the

President's Office, which suggests the sort of clientele to which it aims to appeal. Although situated on a small street in the Old Town, the rooms are all large enough to work in & the choice of flowers & pictures that abound make work here much more congenial than it otherwise might be. Hopefully its neighbours around the rear courtyard will gradually adopt its aesthetic sense as well. An atrium in this courtyard is the location for its well-known restaurant La Pergola. Exclusivity here is ensured by restricting the number of tables to 5, but somehow the dishes on its extensive menu always seem to be available. $$$$

⌂ **Kempinski Hotel AAA** (107 rooms) Šventaragio; e info.project.vilnius@kempinski.com. Due to open in 2009, the Kempinski will be on the edge of the Old Town directly facing the castle, cathedral & bell tower. The 19th-century façade of this former telegraph building is being preserved while the interior will be renovated to offer elegant facilities, such as international restaurants, business centre & health club. Two extension wings are being built. $$$$$

⌂ **Le Meridien Villon** (189 rooms) A2 highway; ☏ 5 273 9700; e info@lemeridien.lt; www.lemeridien.lt. This is a huge motel & conference centre, located 19km from the centre of Vilnius, beside the main highway to Panevėžys & Riga. It lays on free shuttle buses to the city, & offers the services of a full holiday complex, including tennis courts, a fitness club, swimming pool & 3 saunas. Despite its distance from town the restaurant, Le Paysage, specialising in Gallic-influenced cuisine, has such a reputation that many people are happy to make the journey. $$$$

⌂ **Narutis** (50 rooms) Pilies 24; ☏ 5 212 2894; e info@narutis.com; www.narutis.com. With tasteful

French furniture & even frescoes in some of the rooms, the elegant Narutis is set in a 16th-century building on the Old Town's partly pedestrianised main street. Guests reach their rooms from a central plush lounge with its own glass elevator. Ask for the upper floors where the views of the Pilies Street market are best. The cosy Kristupo Café serves excellent food on the ground floor & dining is available in an atmospheric vaulted cellar. Now a member of the Summit Hotels & Resorts chain, the Narutis retains its own unique charm. $$$$

⌂ **Radisson SAS Astorija** (119 rooms) Didžioji 35/2; ☏ 5 212 0110; e reservations.vilnius@ radissonsas.com; www.radissonsas.com. This grand early 20th-century hotel in the heart of the Old Town has been refurbished by the Radisson SAS chain, but its lounge beside the lobby brings back the aura of its early days. All rooms have hairdryer, trouser press, telephone, cable TV, safe. Business-class rooms are larger, have tea/coffee/kettle in them & guests have free access to the health centre. A 'grab & run' b/fast is available in the lobby, but it is a great pity to take it when the alternative is to enjoy a leisurely & lavish buffet b/fast overlooking part of Town Hall Square. $$$$

⌂ **Stikliai** (43 rooms) Gaono 7; ☏ 5 264 9595; e sales@stikliaihotel.lt; www.stikliaihotel.lt. At an unbeatable location on a narrow cobblestone street in the Old Town, the richly decorated, 5-star Stikliai has stubbornly held on to its reputation as the city's most exclusive hotel since it opened shortly before Lithuania's independence. Royals & celebrities from western Europe have slept in its 4-poster beds, reclined on its sofas & dined in the restaurant on expensive French cuisine. They may also have used its sauna, swimming pool & fitness room. $$$$$

FIRST-CLASS HOTELS $$$–$$$$
⌂ **Artis Centrum** (65 rooms) Liejykos 11/23; ☏ 5 266 0363 or 266 0366; e artis@centrumhotels.com; www.centrumhotels.com. The latest addition to Vilnius's Centrum group of hotels occupies a refurbished Old Town mansion overlooking the President's Office garden, so in a very quiet location at the front. The street at the side, Liejykos, can be noisy in the evenings & in 2008 a conference centre was opened at the rear. All twin/dbl rooms have baths & fabric paintings on the walls. Sgls are on the small side & have conventional paintings. A recent expansion has seen the opening of a swimming pool & gym to which hotel guests have access free of charge. The restaurant is very reasonably priced for a hotel of this standard. $$$$

⌂ **Atrium** (29 rooms) Pilies 10; ☏ 5 210 7773; e hotel@atrim.lt; www.atrium.lt. Situated in a peaceful courtyard just off one of the busiest streets in the heart

of the Old Town, this hotel boasts large & well-appointed bedrooms. It has an excellent Argentinian restaurant, El Gaucho, which naturally specialises in steaks. $$$

⌂ **Barbacan Palace** (33 rooms) Bokšto 19; ☏ 5 266 0840; e barbacan@centrokubas.lt; www.barbacan.lt. The hotel is under the same management as the Centro Kubas listed below but they could not be more different. The Barbacan is larger, & is one of the many hotels that opened in 2003. It has conventional décor throughout & is on a quiet side street at the edge of the Old Town. Many rooms have a view of the Artillery Bastion & the restaurant/café has prices well below those normally to be expected in the Old Town. Its original features are a basement bowling alley & billiards table, with reduced prices for hotel guests. $$$

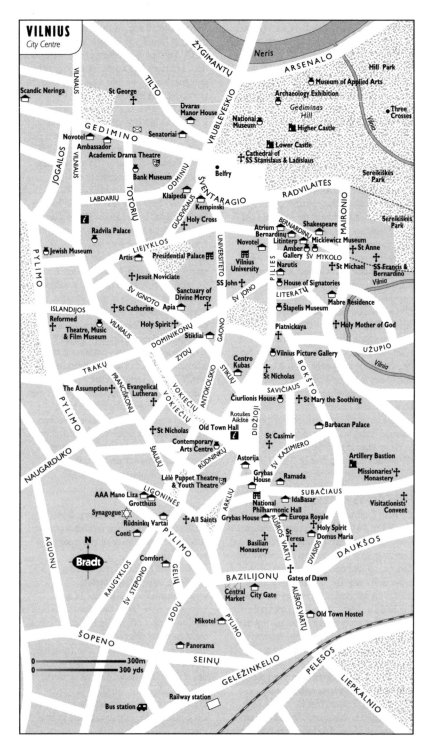

VILNIUS
City Centre

Best Western Naujasis Vilnius (114 rooms) Konstitucijos 14; ☎ 5 273 9595; e office@hotelnv.lt; www.hotelnv.lt. This hotel used to be considered large but, with the refurbished Reval Lietuva now towering over it, suddenly seems small. Every 2 years it is updated so perhaps is typical of any go-ahead Lithuanian organisation. Finally the surroundings are getting updated too, so there is no need to flee into the Old Town for shopping or different restaurants. Soon it should be an integral part of 'business Vilnius' which is taking over this side of the river. $$$

Centro Kubas (14 rooms) Kubas Stiklių 3; ☎ 5 266 0860; e hotel@centrokubas.lt; www.centrokubas.lt. A designer-style hotel decked out with old agricultural tools in all the public areas & in the rooms too. A windmill dominates the lobby. The rooms are spread across 4 floors & linked by a glass lift. A peephole in each room is part of the security arrangements. Use of laptop computers is free of charge. $$$

Congress (80 rooms) Vilniaus 2/15; ☎ 5 269 1919; f 5 251 4280; e info@congress.lt; www.congress.lt. Housed in a fine old building overlooking the River Neris, this used to be a budget hotel, but has been given a new name & totally refurbished to business-class standards, so has gone through a similar metamorphosis to the Grand in Tallinn. The name perhaps puts off tourists, which is a pity given its convenient location, but this greatly reduces prices at the w/end. Car parking & internet connections are free of charge. $$$

Conti (88 rooms) Raugyklos 7/2; ☎ 5 251 4111; e info@contihotel.lt; www.contihotel.lt. The opening of this hotel in 2003 marked the beginning of the regeneration of the rundown area to the rear of the synagogue. It incorporates a host of modern design features including full disabled access, a welcoming lobby with waterfall & well-appointed bedrooms with en-suite facilities & internet access. All bedrooms have prints showing Vilnius as it was about 100 years ago. Try to get rooms 506, 507 or 508 for the best views of contemporary Vilnius. The kitchens are equipped to allow Jewish groups to prepare kosher food. $$$

Dvaras Manor House (8 rooms) Tilto 3; ☎ 5 210 7370; e hotel@dvaras.lt; www.dvaras.lt. This is a very select hotel, & as its name & décor suggest, it is eager to promote its grand background. All rooms have AC, & internet access free of charge. There is a similarly classy restaurant, which serves a wide international menu & has a notable wine list. $$$$.

Europa Royale (39 rooms) Aušros Vartų 6; ☎ 5 266 0770; e vilnius@europaroyale.com; www.europaroyale.com. A stylish, modern, luxury hotel in a beautifully renovated Old Town building. Heated bathroom tiles are a novelty in the en suites & most have baths rather than just showers. The nicest rooms are on the 4th floor as they have a view over the Gates of Dawn as well as over the Old Town. The hotel is in the same group as the hotels with this name in Klaipeda & Riga. $$$

Grybas House (9 rooms) Aušros Vartų 3a; ☎ 5 261 9695, 264 7474; e info@grybashouse.com; www.grybashouse.com. A delightful small hotel in a refurbished Baroque house set in a quiet courtyard at the northern end of the Old Town. The décor includes sculptures from the Congo & the former pier in Palanga. Water filters in every room & heated floors are what all guests remember here, & the gratis airport transfer is a nice gesture too. The Grybas family have run this hotel since it opened in 1992, but have modernised it twice since then. There is a fine basement restaurant, with live classical music on Wed evenings. $$$

Holiday Inn (134 rooms) Šeimyniškių 1; ☎ 5 210 3000; e holiday-inn@ibc.lt; www.holidayinnvilnius.lt. Surprisingly, it took until 2002 for this well-known chain to open a hotel in Vilnius, its first venture into the Baltic countries, & in 2008 this was still its only property in the region. The location, immediately east of the new business district, was a gamble when they first arrived but it has certainly now paid off. Novel then were baths, AC & proper soundproofing in every room, & competitors took time to catch up. Every room has a computer, although there is a charge for using it. The easy walk over the river to the Old Town ensures that when business clients leave for the w/end or for the summer, tourists always replace them. $$$$

Klaipeda (formerly **City Park**) (78 rooms) Stuokos-Gucevičiaus 3; ☎ 5 210 7461; e vilnius@klapiedahotel.lt; www.klaipedahotel.lt. Architectural controversy surrounded the unabashedly modern extension added to the original hotel located in a refurbished building with a central courtyard diagonally opposite the cathedral. Rooms are larger than one would expect in a central hotel, & adjustable underfloor heating in the bathrooms is probably a unique feature. The hotel is under the same management as those with this name in Kaunas & Klaipeda but is as different again as these 2 are from each other. This is a medium-size hotel, larger & more comfortable than its Kaunas namesake, but much smaller than the Klaipeda one. The fountains & gardens that were added in front of the hotel have made its situation particularly attractive, & this has increased the popularity of its Italian restaurant, Sofi L. There is also the rare facility of its own underground car park. $$$

Mabre Residence (41 rooms) Residence Maironio 13; ☎ 5 212 2087 or 212 2195; ℯ mabre@mabre.lt; www.mabre.lt. The Mabre occupies the grand neo-Classical courtyard buildings of a former Russian Orthodox monastery in the quiet eastern part of the Old Town. High walls give it a very exclusive feel, perhaps rather necessary as it is so close to many of the tourist sites, such as St Anne's Church. Facilities for guests include a sauna & fitness centre & a small pool. There is no charge for internet access in the rooms. The hotel is well known to Vilnius residents for its Steakhouse Hazienda, one of the first to open & still one of the best known. $$$$

Novotel (159 rooms) Gedimino 16; ☎ 5 266 6200; ℯ H5209@accor.com; www.novotel.com. This tall hotel became so popular amongst tourists & business visitors as soon as it opened in 2003 that it is hard to believe that it has not always been part of the post-independence scene. It has had its fair (perhaps unfair) share of local critics who feel that such a tall new building has no place so near to the Old Town & that it should have been built on the other side of the river. Gedimino now being a pedestrian precinct for much of the day has made a formerly busy location a quieter one, despite all the attractions & offices nearby. All rooms have baths & these are so placed that the TV can be watched at the same time; there are also separate showers & tea/coffee-making facilities. As the gym is on the 7th floor, it is possible to keep fit here with a view. Even though the restaurant is on the 2nd floor, the view of the activity on Gedimino makes it an attractive location & its prices have been set to bring in local custom as well as hotel guests. Its choice of fish dishes is unusual for Vilnius & puts many port restaurants to shame. The hotel stresses its family orientation, organising amongst other things a supervised Sun brunch & offering a children's menu in the restaurant. $$$

Ramada (55 rooms) Subačiaus 2; ☎ 255 3355; ℯ hotel@ramadavilnius.lt; www.ramadavilnius.lt. Emerging late in 2005, the Ramada was the first hotel to open its doors in Vilnius in 2 years & an even longer gap would follow. It is comfortable enough, with the unusual feature of TV & DVD player in each of the rooms. It benefits from an Old Town location close to the Lithuanian Philharmonic – ask for a room at the front for a busy view, or the back if you want to sleep. There's wireless internet access in the lobby, but not in the rooms, which tend to be fairly small. No parking available. Lower prices are available for w/end stays. $$$

Ratonda (48 rooms) Gedimino 52/1; ☎ 5 212 0670; ℯ ratonda@centrum.lt; www.centrumhotels.com.

This hotel is under the management of the Centrum Company, which runs the Artis Hotel. It is not as grand, & the rooms are smaller, but it is convenient for Parliament & government ministries situated near to it. The use of glass in the roof & walls was very special in the mid 1990s when the hotel opened, although is more common now. A sauna & a fitness centre were added in 2005. $$$

Reval Hotel Lietuva (291 rooms) Konstitucijos 20; ☎ 5 272 6200; ℯ lietuva.sales@revalhotels.com; www.revalhotels.com. The former Intourist hotel is much the largest & most prominent in Vilnius, & is now the main conference centre in the city. It is quite common in winter for conference guests never to leave the building from one day to the next. In 2000 the hotel was acquired by the Reval chain, which eliminated all Soviet features in a radical Scandinavian-style makeover. The even-numbered rooms offer grandstand views over the Old Town, as does the bar on the 22nd floor, which is at its best around sunset. The no 2 bus from the airport passes the entrance & a pedestrian bridge is the best way to get to the Old Town over the river. The Reval chain runs the equally large Lātvija Hotel in Riga, the Ridzene & Elizabete there, 4 hotels in Tallinn & the Neris in Kaunas, which opened in spring 2008; more will probably follow. Travel agents can often obtain lower rates if clients book more than one Reval hotel on the same tour. $$$

Šarūnas (55 rooms) Raitininkų 4; ☎ 5 272 3888; ℯ info@hotelsarunas.lt; www.hotelsarunas.lt. Not Vilnius's best-located hotel, a good 20min walk from the Old Town past a football stadium, the Šarūnas is nevertheless a stylish, modern business hotel owned by NBA basketball star & local hero Šarūnas Marčiulionis. Airport transfer & 24hr laundry are among the services, together with a well-equipped fitness room & sauna. $$$

Scandic Neringa (60 rooms) Gedimino 23; ☎ 5 268 1910; ℯ neringa@scandic-hotels.com; www.scandic-hotels.com. Certainly the most pleasant of the Baltic countries' Scandic hotels, the Neringa benefited from a Scandinavian-style facelift that now perfectly complements Gedimino Avenue's recent overall makeover. Two original features stand out: first the library with its deep sofas & armchairs & current editions of foreign newspapers & magazines, & second the alcoves on every floor that overlooks Gedimino, each with armchairs & fresh flowers. The ground-floor Neringa restaurant, which used to hum with the city's artistic elite in the late Soviet years, is worth visiting for its bizarre Socialist Realist murals, though these days the pizza restaurant next door is far more popular. $$$

🏠 **Shakespeare** (31 rooms) Bernardinų 8/8; 📞 5 266 5885; e info@shakespeare.lt; www.shakespeare.lt. This English-style country hotel on an Old Town backstreet adopts a literary theme, with most of the rooms named after famous writers & containing reading material linked to each. Many offer imposing views of nearby landmarks, such as St Anne's Church; all have safes, internet connections & underfloor bathroom heating, while the more expensive have AC. The Sonnets restaurant is one of the classiest & most expensive in Vilnius. The bar is of course called The Globe, where the drinks are pricy but the sofas so soft you'll have to concentrate while in company to prevent yourself nodding off. Try one of the Gothic-style desserts on the opulent menu. $$$$

TOURIST CLASS $-$$$

🏠 **Ambassador** (18 rooms) Gedimino 12; 📞 5 261 5450; e info@ambassador.lt; www.ambassador.lt. Handily located on the city's main street, this hotel was completely modernised by 2004. Unusually for a hotel in this category, several rooms have baths, rather than just showers. Its location combined with its price make it very sought after in the summer, when it is often fully booked months in advance. The café/restaurant on the ground floor keeps busy throughout the day & evening. Like the hotel, it is straightforward & functional, without any pretensions. $$

🏠 **Apia** (12 rooms) Šv Ignoto 12; 📞 5 212 3426; e apia@apia.lt; www.apia.lt. Wafer-thin & reasonably priced, the Apia allows you to squeeze into the very centre of the Old Town at no great expense to your wallet. If you're not bothered about a minibar, but need the option of satellite TV, this is for you. $$

🏠 **Embassy Hotel Balatonas** (28 rooms) Latvių 38; 📞 5 272 2250; e info@embassyhotel.lt; www.embassyhotel.lt. A small, easy-going favourite with visiting middle-class eastern European businessmen, the Hungarian-owned Balatonas is a pearly white villa located in the leafy Žvėrynas district, close to several embassies. $$$

🏠 **Business Guest House** (30 rooms) Saltoniškių 44; 📞 5 272 2298; e info@bgh.lt; www.bgh.lt. Despite the setting on the bustling northern edge of Žvėrynas close to a main road, the atmosphere inside is Scandinavian & efficient, with business services, sauna, swimming pool, & even a commercial art gallery. $$

🏠 **Centrum Uniquestay** (100 rooms) Vytenio 9/24; 📞 5 268 3300; e hotel@centrum.lt; www.uniquestay.com. The Tallinn-based, British-run Uniquestay group took over the management of this hotel in 2003, so computers were placed in every room at once, as were tea- & coffee-making facilities. Being a 10min walk from the Old Town, it has taken advantage of the location to offer enormous space in the public areas & larger rooms than might otherwise be expected. Most of these therefore have baths, & not just showers. It used to be seen as purely a business hotel, but has recently been successful in attracting tourists. The 4th floor has cheaper, smaller rooms with showers only. Easy parking for coaches & cars obviously helps access & departures. The location beside the Belarus Embassy ensures peace & quiet around the clock. $$

🏠 **Comfort** (57 rooms) Gėlių 5; 📞 5 264 8833; e reservation@takas.lt; www.comfort.lt. With a location about a 10min walk from the Old Town, this hotel will suit groups & individuals wanting low prices but reasonable standards & location. The immediate vicinity is dull, but life & colour are not far away. $$

🏠 **Domus Maria** (39 rooms) Aušros Vartų 12; 📞 5 264 4880; e domusmaria@vilnensis.lt; www.domusmaria.lt. This is officially a guesthouse but feels like a hotel. Most of its rooms were formerly monastery cells but those days are long past, although its position on a courtyard immediately behind St Theresa's Church gives it a serenity which will appeal to those wanting a quiet central location. The lounge on the 5th floor has extensive views over the Old Town. The restaurant offers perhaps the closest link to the past with the only decoration on the walls being a crucifix, but it looks down on a well-stocked bar. $$

🏠 **Ecotel** (168 rooms) Slucko 8; 📞 5 210 2700; e hotel@ecotel.lt; www.ecotel.lt. Another example of a hotel aiming at a combination of modernity & economy. It occupies a former shoe factory between the new business district & the Žalgiris Stadium so a 10min walk is needed to reach anything of interest. Among its unusual features are special rooms for allergy sufferers & extra-long beds for tall people. Expect to see lots of sports groups here. $$

🏠 **Europa City** (128 rooms) Jasinskio 14; 📞 5 251 4477; e city@hoteleuropa.lt; www.hoteleuropa.lt. Although a sister hotel to Europa Royale, this newcomer is much larger & less exclusive & is bound to suffer in comparison. Nothing is wrong with it, but nothing entices either, & whatever the interior, the surroundings are so drab that it really can only suit business travellers rather than tourists. $$

🏠 **Mano Liza** (8 rooms) Ligoninės 5; 📞 5 212 2225; e hotel@aaa.lt; www.hotelinvilnius.lt. This hotel is next door to the grander Grotthuss & both share a passion for good art, but in other respects the Mano Liza is rather simpler. Many guests are regulars from North America. $$

Mikotel (26 rooms) Pylimo 63; ✆ 5 260 9626; e mikotel@takas.lt; www.mikotel.lt. When gentrification finally comes to Pylimo St & its market, this hotel will be a lovely place to stay. For the time being, it is still an outpost of cleanliness & taste in surroundings that are the complete opposite. The self-catering facilities are a great asset for those wishing to cook some of their own meals & its location halfway between the Old Town & the stations means that some tourists never use a bus or taxi during their entire stay here. $$

Panorama (200 rooms) Sodų 14; ✆ 5 273 8011; e reservation@hotelpanorama.lt; www.hotelpanorama.lt. For years this was the notorious Gintaras, which seemed oblivious to all the surrounding changes, so sensible travellers who had just come into the bus station rushed by on the way to something more salubrious in town. Now all has changed & one has to wonder why it could not have done so 10 years ago. Its rooms can now be recommended, particularly those on the top floor which have the best views over the Old Town. Photographers should ask to get onto the roof to record them. Others can simply stay in the bar to enjoy the scenery. There is a bank in the foyer so no need to go out to look for better exchange rates. $$

Reval Inn (83 rooms) Ukmergės 363; ✆ 5 238 800; e vilnius@revalinn.com; www.revalinn.com. You can't miss this bright blue building on the road to Riga that stands out against the surrounding Soviet-era high-rises. If you don't mind staying right at the far edge of the city, it boasts unpretentious, friendly service & spotlessly clean rooms. Most bizarre is the special 'Trio Lux' lighting in every room, which 'creates your own mood'. Choose from a combination of reds, greens & blues to make shades of calming colours.. $$

Senatoriai (11 rooms) Tilto 2; ✆ 5 212 6491 or 212 7056; e info@senatoriai.lt; www.senatoriai.lt. This small low-rise hotel profits from an excellent location, being discreetly tucked away down a side street immediately to the rear of Gedimino, just a stone's throw from the cathedral. $$$

BUDGET HOTELS AND GUESTHOUSES $-$$

Bernadinų (11 rooms) Bernardinų 5; ✆ 5 261 5134; e guesthouse@avevita.lt; www.avevita.lt/guesthouse. Offering peace & quiet in the Old Town at a very reasonable price, this is a new guesthouse close to St Anne's Church. Pay a little extra for b/fast & parking in the courtyard. Some rooms are bigger & come with small kitchens. $

Jeruzalė (10 rooms) Kalvarijų 209; ✆ 5 271 4040; e jeruzale@takas.lt; www.jeruzalehotel.com. Comfortable budget option 10mins' drive from the centre, not far from the Calvary Church & trails in the forest. The low price of the rooms means you can splash out on taxis every day – or catch buses 26, 35, 36 or 50. $

Victoria (42 rooms) Saltoniškių 56; ✆ 5 272 4013; e hotel@victoria.lt; www.victoria.lt. When this first opened in the mid 1990s it was a welcome & necessary addition to the Vilnius hotel scene with bright décor & friendly service. It now has price & car-parking space going for it, but not much else given that what was novel 10 years ago is now standard throughout Vilnius. Group rates however will appeal. $$

BED AND BREAKFAST

Litinterp (16 rooms) Bernardinų 7/2; ✆ 5 212 3850; e vilnius@litinterp.com; www.litinterp.com; ◷ 08.30–17.30 Mon–Fri, 09.00–15.30 Sat. This hostel became famous when it opened & has kept ahead of most attempts to compete with it. The location, price & self-catering facilities make it ideal for those wanting a basic but impeccably clean base in the Old Town, although some rooms are very possibly the tiniest in town. The company also offers rooms in private houses in central Vilnius & Trakai, & has some apartments for rent. Advance bookings for Kaunas, Klaipėda, Palanga & Nida can be made, & car hire, interpretation & translation services are available. $$

✖ EATING AND DRINKING

The pleasure of dining in Vilnius today is that there is such an unexpected wealth of different kinds of restaurants, all of them striving to be original. It's partly because of the amazing culinary revolution that has taken place since the dull Soviet years that it is so easy to be impressed when you go out for a meal. The art of providing a romantic or a lively evening meal, even the ideal business lunch, is being perfected right across the capital. European and broadly international cuisine dominates, so as not to upset local palates too much, and traditional Lithuanian dishes like the uniquely weighty *cepelinai* are available in an increasing number of rustic–style theme restaurants that are as popular with the locals as they are with visitors. There are some strange absences, however. Asian cuisine is almost exclusively taken up by an inexplicable number of Chinese restaurants, some of them better than others. There is nothing Malaysian or Thai apart from the odd dish on an international menu or rare bursts of 'fusion'. One brave retired Indian air force commander, Rajinder Chaudhary, has struggled with his excellent Indian restaurant, Sue's Indian Raja, in four different locations in the last ten years, and still attracts only expats and tourists. But Vilnius is not just meat and potatoes. Greater awareness about healthy eating ensures that tasty, attractively presented salads are especially easy to find. With one or two exceptions, such as the pricy La Provence, there is not a great deal of variation in what you can expect to pay at the restaurants listed. The price of a three-course meal for two, excluding wine, should come to around 120–180Lt, but more detailed information is given for each entry. For bars and clubs, see page 193. Restaurants normally open from 12.00 to 24.00 every day.

RESTAURANTS

✗ **Belmonto Kriokliai** Belmonto 17; ☎ 5 615 20220; www.belmontas.lt. An incredible amalgamation of both indoor & open-air folk-style theme eateries, refreshing waterfall, beautiful countryside & space for everything from conferences to weddings – all just a 15min taxi ride from the centre of Vilnius. 90Lt.

✗ **Bistro 18** Stiklių 18; ☎ 5 677 72091. It is perhaps a sad commentary on other restaurants in Vilnius that all the reviews of this one highlighted its good service as soon as it opened in autumn 2007. This was fortunately still in evidence early in 2008. Its menu too was more varied than might be expected in a restaurant of its small size. 90Lt.

✗ **Čagino** Basanavičiaus 11; ☎ 5 261 5555. For authentic Russian dishes &, on Fri & Sat, 'Russian romance' played by a solitary musician with a guitar & a portfolio of popular, singalong songs, venture a few mins' walk away from the Old Town to this atmospheric subterranean hideaway. 80Lt.

✗ **Čili Pica** Didžioji 5 & Gedimino 23; www.cili.lt. Wander into 1 of the 10 branches of the phenomenally successful local Čili chain & you'll quickly discover how pizza has become the Lithuanian fast food of choice. But not why. The service is quick & the salads adequate, but the pizzas are nothing really special. 50Lt.

✗ **Čili Kaimas** Vokiečių 8 & Gedimino 14; ☎ 5 231 2536. Two among a plethora of new theme restaurants offering traditional Lithuanian food, these boast live chickens, pitchforks & even a country-style granny employed full-time at the Gedimino outlet to knit in front of diners. Some people will love Čili Kaimas, run by the popular Lithuanian pizza chain, for its culinary authenticity & its prices. Others will call it village kitsch. 55Lt.

✗ **Da Antonio** Vilniaus 23 & Pilies 20; www.antonio.lt. Excellent Italian dishes served at tables in a pleasantly decorated yet secluded seating arrangement. Come to this quite authentic trattoria rather than the homegrown Čili outlets if you fancy a real pizza & bottle of good Italian wine. 80Lt.

✗ **El Gaucho Sano** Pilies 10; ☎ 5 210 7773. With an unbeatable combination of relaxing atmosphere, spacious seating, meaty food & reliable service, this restaurant set inside the atrium of the Atrium Hotel claims to be Argentinian. That's debatable. But it's certainly perfect for an evening meal with good wine. 115Lt.

✗ **Ephesus** Trakų 15; ☎ 5 260 8866. Although open until 06.00 every night except Sun, when it closes early at 01.00, this is in fact a conventional Turkish restaurant which has imported not only its menu but also its prices & its generous portions. Even water pipes are available to stress its difference from contemporary Lithuania. 60Lt.

✗ **Fortas** Algirdo 17; ☎ 5 212 2000; www.fortas.eu. If you need an easy bite that's not too challenging, the chain-pub-style Fortas offers an eclectic range of dishes, particularly welcome in this southern part of the town where there is little else of note. 60Lt.

✗ **Forto Dvaras** Pilies 16; ☎ 5 261 1070; www.fortas.eu. A warren of rooms under bustling Pilies St that offer traditional Lithuanian cuisine such as the famously stodgy *cepelinai* & also *vederai* – pig intestines stuffed with mashed potato. You might even learn what the difference is between Samogitian & Lithuanian food. 70Lt.

✗ **Ibish** Aušros Vartų 11; ☎ 5 260 9065. The name is Turkish, but there's little that is genuinely Turkish about this new restaurant close to the Gates of Dawn. Instead, this 'lounge restaurant' boasts more than 100 cocktails to accompany your meal. Try the grilled salmon, which is accentuated by smoky bacon on a bed of lentils & carrots, adorned with lime. 100Lt

✗ **IdaBasar** Subačiaus 3; ☎ 5 262 8484; www.idabazar.lt. Another of Vilnius's long-time survivors, IdaBasar relies on hearty German cuisine mainstays – &

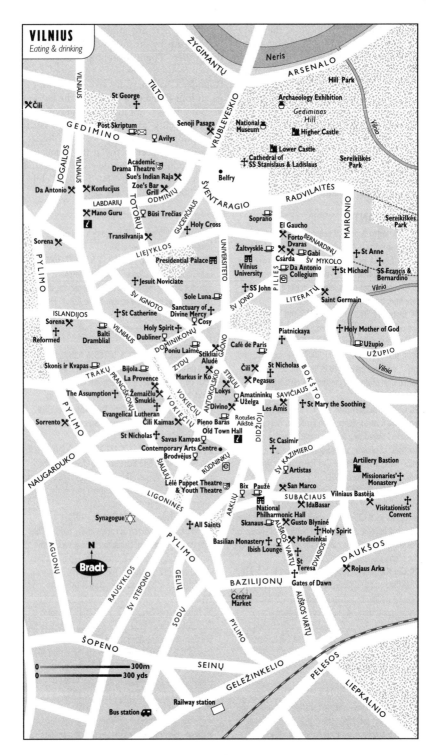

VILNIUS
Eating & drinking

ŽYGIMANTŲ
Neris
ARSENALO

Hill Park
✕Čili
St George ✝
Archaeology Exhibition
Gediminas Hill
Post Skriptum
GEDIMINO
Senoji Pasaga
National Museum
♀ Avilys
Higher Castle
Lower Castle
Cathedral of ✝ SS Stanislaus & Ladislaus
Serelkiškės Park
Academic Drama Theatre
Sue's Indian Raja ✕
Zoe's Bar ✕ Grill
● Belfry
RADVILAITĖS
Da Antonio ✕ ✕ Konfucijus
ODMINIŲ
Serelkiškės Park
LABDARIŲ
✕ Mano Guru
ᵢ
Būsi Trečias
Holy Cross
Soprano
El Gaucho
✕ Forto Dvaras
✝ St Anne
Sorena ✕
Transilvanija ✝
Žaltvysklė ⌑
Csárda ⌑ Gabi
Da Antonio Collegium
✝ St Michael
SS Francis & Bernardino
Presidential Palace ⌂
Vilnius University
Jesuit Noviciate ✝
SS John
Saint Germain
ISLANDIJOS
SV IGNOTO
Sole Luna
Sorena ✕
✝ St Catherine
Sanctuary of Divine Mercy ✝
♀ Cosy
Piatnickaya
✝ Holy Mother of God
Balti Dramblial
Holy Spirit ✝
Dubliner
Reformed
Užupio
Skonis ir Kvapas
Poniu Laime
Café de Paris
DOMINIKONŲ
Bijola
Stikliai Aludė
La Provence
✕ St Nicholas
Čili ✕
The Assumption ✝ Žemaičiu Smuklė
Markus ir Ko
✕ Pegasus
Lokys
Amatininkų Uželga
Les Amis
✝ St Mary the Soothing
Sorrento ✕
Divino
Evangelical Lutheran
Čili Kaimas ✕
Pieno Baras
Rotušes Aikštė
Old Town Hall
St Casimir ✝
St Nicholas ✝
Savas Kampas
Contemporary Arts Centre ●
Brodvėjus
Artillery Bastion
Missionaries' ✝ Monastery
Artistas
Lėlė Puppet Theatre & Youth Theatre
Bix Paužė
✕ San Marco
Vilnius Bastėja
LIGONINĖS
SUBAČIAUS
✝ Visitationists' Convent
Synagogue ✡
National Philharmonic Hall
IdaBasar
Skanaus ⌑ ✕ Gusto Blyninė
✝ All Saints
✝ Holy Spirit
Basilian Monastery ✝ Medininkai
Ibish Lounge
St Teresa ✝
✕ Rojaus Arka
Bradt
Gates of Dawn
BAZILIJONŲ
Central Market
0 ──────── 300m
0 ──────── 300 yds
ŠOPENO
SEINŲ
GELEŽINKELIO
PELESOS
LIEPKALNIO
Bus station 🚌
Railway station ☐

188

good German beer – to compete with the fresher newcomers. Not a bad option at the southern edge of the Old Town. 100Lt

✗ **Kinija** Konstitucijos 12; ☎ 5 263 6363; www.kinuvirtuve.lt. Possibly the best of Vilnius's countless Chinese restaurants, Kinija is located across the river from the Old Town, close to the landmark Reval Hotel Lietuva. The broccoli, aubergine & seafood dishes really stand out. Wash them down with a large bottle of gassy Tsingtao beer. 75Lt.

✗ **Kristupo Kavinė** Pilies 24; ☎ 5 261 7722; www.narutis.com. Though it is called 'Christopher's Café', this is really a classy restaurant next door to the Narutis Hotel on the Old Town's main drag. Rarely crowded, however, it offers beautifully presented dishes on rustic-style linen tablecloths, overlooked by framed sketches of sophisticated couples from the Roaring Twenties. 120Lt.

✗ **Les Amis** Savičiaus 9; ☎ 5 212 3738. The best of provincial France has finally reached Vilnius. The family do the cooking & waiting & the menu reflects what could be bought fresh during the day. It's a popular spot, so reserve ahead. 110Lt.

✗ **La Provence** Vokiečių 24; www.laprovence.lt. Advertising itself as '100% pure gourmet', this relatively pricy restaurant sandwiched between the 2 constituent parts of the far more informal Žemaičiai serves Provenal & other Mediterranean cuisines. The number of French-speakers regularly to be found here is proof of the high standards & extensive wine list. 160Lt.

✗ **Lokys** Stiklių 8; www.lokys.lt. One of the few survivors from Soviet times, 'The Bear' has updated its service standards but not its menu. It is a must for the enthusiastic carnivore. Boar, elk & even bear itself are on the menu. Eat in one of the tiny rooms carved out of the cellar, or on the ground floor in the shadow of a stuffed grizzly. The reasonably priced lunch menu is good quality, although a 20min wait is necessary. 130Lt.

✗ **Mano Guru** Vilniaus 22; ☎ 5 212 0126. This restaurant achieved instant success when it was revealed that all the staff were reformed drug addicts & that Mayor Zuokas had promoted this project having seen the success of the idea in Prague. The variety of food is such that one is willing to sacrifice alcohol & to leave by 20.30 which is the state of play here. Fresh fruit & vegetables which seem unavailable elsewhere all turn up with every dish & although meat & fish are served, they almost seem redundant. Puréed soup & the vegetarian main courses are more than enough. 65Lt.

✗ **Marceliukės Klėtis** Tuskulėnų 35; ☎ 5 272 508. Probably the most tongue-in-cheek of the traditional Lithuanian restaurants, & the longest running, this is off the beaten track in a bizarre setting of high-rises a short taxi ride from the centre. The hearty portions, merry atmosphere, live folk music & smiling service are worth the journey. 50Lt.

✗ **Markus ir Ko** Antokolskio 11; ☎ 5 262 3185. A relaxing, jazzy atmosphere, live piano music & succulent steaks on one of the Old Town's tiniest streets. 120Lt.

✗ **Medininkai** Aušros Vartų 8; ☎ 5 266 0771; www.medininkai.lt. The chefs here like to call the cuisine 'Lithuanian fusion', using imaginative ways to prepare & present traditional local food. With vaulted ceilings generously covered with frescoes, 18th-century Italian artwork & a peaceful red-brick courtyard open in summer, the Medininkai makes the most of its location in a former monastery near the Gates of Dawn. Another plus is that it is now under the reliable management of the adjoining Hotel Europa Royale. 120Lt.

✗ **Marino** Tumėno 4; ☎ 5 240 2677; www.marino-restaurant.lt. As the Vilnius elite spreads its business & residential neighbourhood further away from the Old Town, smart & shiny complexes such as Vilniaus Vartai (Vilnius Gates) with its class A offices & brand-heavy shopping mall, keep opening up. The exclusive Marino restaurant charms with its food & wine & fascinates with its views of local drivers in action as it is directly above one of the city's busiest roads. It justifies its high prices too. 260Lt.

✗ **Rojaus Arka** Daukšos 3; ☎ 5 212 0625. Often forgotten since it lies just beyond the tourist trail the other side of the Gates of Dawn, the 'Arch of Paradise' is easy to spot because of its ornately carved doorway. Inside, settle into the quiet, comfortable atmosphere & choose from a short menu of Lithuanian-style dishes. 60Lt.

✗ **Rytai** Naugarduko 22 & Gedimino 49a; ☎ 5 249 6655. Two of Vilnius's better Chinese restaurants, one near the Parliament, the other on the New Town's eastern edge. Inexpensive delights include a thick, rich chilli seafood soup & a squid dish that comes with oyster sauce & hot paprika. Ask for extra spice. 75Lt.

✗ **Saint Germain** Literatu 9; ☎ 5 262 1210. This charming little rustic French-style restaurant opened in spring 2005, promoting wine above all else, but also serving fabulous food. It has shelves haphazardly crammed with books & somehow managed immediately to appear old & settled. In the unlikely event that guests prefer to take away the wine rather than drink it on the premises, many varieties are sold by the bottle. 70Lt.

✗ **San Marco** Subačiaus 2; ☎ 5 264 6418. The new, elegant, centrally situated San Marco restaurant brings creative Italian cuisine to Vilnius in a Mediterranean setting. Opposite the National Philharmonic, it's an excellent choice for a first-class business lunch or evening dining. 90Lt.

✕ **Sofi L** Stuokos-Gucevičiaus 1; ☎ 5 210 7466. Adjoining the Hotel Klaipeda opposite the cathedral, but with its own separate entrance, Sofi L benefits enormously from having one of Vilnius's best-known chefs, Enzo Recupero, who regularly appears in the dining area to add an entertaining panache to the excellent Italian dishes being served. 110Lt.

✕ **Sorena** Islandijos 4; ☎ 5 262 7560. Vilnius's only restaurant featuring genuinely authentic cuisine from Azerbaijan, Sorena has slowly earned a reputation for its mouth-watering Caucasian food & friendly service. Named after a heroic army leader in the early history of Persia, there is also an Iranian element to the decoration & the food. Try the Tebriz, a tender roll of beef served on a skewer with a crisp green chilli pepper. 80Lt.

✕ **Sorrento** Pylimo 21; ☎ 5 264 4737; www.sorrentorestoranas.lt. A calm haven of refined Italian dining that is in strange contrast to the rest of busy, low-key Pylimo St. The wood-fired oven by the bar is responsible for some delicious pizzas. 110Lt.

✕ **Stiklių Aludė** Gaono 7; ☎ 5 262 4501; www.stikliaihotel.lt. Run by the plush Stikliai Hotel, the price difference between this beautifully decorated cellar-level tavern & the ultra-posh French restaurant next door seems to be getting wider all the time. The Aludė combines reasonably priced Lithuanian food with good service. 240Lt.

✕ **Sue's Indian Raja** Odminių 3; ☎ 8 600 27788; www.suesindianrestaurants.com.. Ideally situated opposite Vilnius Cathedral, Sue's offers authentic Indian cuisine that is ahead of its time in the Baltics. If you want hot spices, the Madras & Jhalfrezi dishes will not disappoint, but even for seasoned tastes there will be something special. Try the fish Amritsari, dipped in a masala of spices & herbs & deep fried. 85Lt.

✕ **Tores** Užupio 40; www.tores.lt. The website is so visually dramatic that it is worth watching in its own right. This restaurant manages to reinvent itself several times a day. At lunch during the week, visitors come for the fabulous terrace view; it is probably best to be over 40 & to have plenty of time. Early in the evening the clientele is there to be seen, so can drop in age to around 30. Later an even younger set take over & probably have to be asked to leave at 02.00, which is closing time. Generations do however mix over lunch at w/ends, particularly in the summer, when children can play outside. 110Lt.

✕ **Vandens Malūnas** Verkių 100; ☎ 5 271 1666. Occupying a converted 19th-century watermill in Verkiai Park, this is a popular excursion destination, particularly in summer, when 3 outdoor terraces are open. Traditional Lithuanian fare is served, & there is a good line in freshwater fish dishes. 90Lt.

✕ **Žaldokynė** Molėtai Rd; ☎ 8 655 09601. One of a growing number of out-of-town country inns serving traditional food served in a fun, barn-house atmosphere. This one is 17km north of Vilnius on the road to Molėtai, easily reached by taxi. Go for the Žaldoko appetiser, a clay dish of sausage, bacon, gherkins, salad & a shot of the house's very own homemade vodka. 60Lt

✕ **Žemaičiai** Vokiečių 24; ☎ 5 261 6573. Descend a hazardous flight of steps into a world of traditional food & furnishings from western Lithuania. The choice of seating ranges from throne-like chairs to country-home beds. Expect starchy food & good beer. 70Lt

✕ **Zoe's Bar Grill** Odminių 3; ☎ 5 212 3331; www.zoesbargrill.com. Chefs behind a lively open kitchen rustle up Caesar salads, delicious soups & a small selection of Thai dishes. This popular bar-restaurant opposite the cathedral also serves some innovative cocktails. 90Lt

CAFÉS

🍴 **Aula** Pilies 11; ☎ 5 268 7173. A long-time university café that has been smartened up & rebranded, Aula suits for an informal meal, offering a smattering of traditional Lithuanian fare & good old-fashioned Lithuanian beer. The streetside seating on pedestrian-only Pilies is popular in summer.

🍴 **Balti Drambliai** Vilniaus 41; ☎ 5 242 0875; www.baltidrambliai.lt Hard to define, 'White Elephants' is a cellar-level vegetarian café-restaurant with plenty to imbibe. There's also an Indian touch to the décor, which includes a magnificent bar with an elephant's head fashioned out of it.

🍷 **Bobo** Trakų 15; ☎ 677 77335. This tiny wine bar, perhaps the tiniest in the Old Town, has a dark soothing interior & a friendly knowledgeable staff. The music is soft enough for talking to be possible & the other clientele probably old enough to be worth talking to. The plasma-screen TV is signed by Ozzy Osborne & is consequently turned on only for special occasions.

🍴 **Café de Paris** Didžioji 1; ☎ 5 261 1021. The café-restaurant attached to the French Cultural Centre has a predictably good choice of crêpes & great coffee, but a totally un-French selection of loud background music which may drown out conversation. It's also getting a little worn at the seams.

Double Coffee Pilies 34, Gedimino 5 & 26; ☎ 5 261 4175; www.doublecoffee.lt. These are just 2 addresses as yet, but this chain is expanding rapidly across Vilnius; the website will always be up to date for fans. Prices are very non-Baltic, in fact rather too British, but clients probably accept this in return for the consistently high quality of the drinks & the service.

Gabi Šv Mykolo 6; ☎ 5 212 3643. A homely retreat on one of the Old Town's quietest streets offering unadventurous Lithuanian meals in a fireside atmosphere. Next door is the Amber Museum & St Anne's Church is a few steps away.

Pauzė Aušros Vartų 5; ☎ 5 212 2113. Point to whatever fresh cakes or buns you fancy & take them with coffee or tea. Savoury dishes are quickly microwaved. 'Pause' overlooks the busy square in front of the Filharmonija, so the window seats – & especially the balcony in summer – are pleasant for people-watching.

Pieno Baras Didžioji 21; ☎ 5 269 0991. It is amazing how this old café dating from the Soviet days keeps on running: probably because of its cheap prices & popularity with students. Line up for buns, coffee or cocoa & try to find a seat. Don't expect to find wireless internet here.

Ponių Laimė Stiklių 14; ☎ 5 264 9581. One of the best Old Town cafés for delicious cakes & biscuits with original recipes; 'Ladies' Happiness' is popular with men too. It's also good for lunch, with basic meals on display, weighed & microwaved.

Presto Pilies 24; ☎ 5 210 7779. With its prominent position on Pilies St, this is one of the more obvious, less atmospheric choices for freshly ground imported coffees & teas – & cakes, b/fast & beer too.

Prie Angelo Užupio 9; ☎ 5 215 3790. Once part of the arty Užupis district's enigmatic ruins, this is now a richly decorated café serving inexpensive lunches. Found next to the angel statue, it makes for a convenient break while exploring Užupis's oddities.

Skonis ir Kvapas Trakų 8; ☎ 5 212 2803. It feels like an upmarket tea room, tastefully decorated, with teas & coffees from around the world on display. Hidden in a courtyard, it's hugely popular, friendly & serves great meals too.

Soprano Pilies 2; ☎ 5 212 6042. For delightful ice cream on a hot day, Soprano is the best parlour in town. But if it's chilly, just take their excellent coffee.

Užupio Užupio 2; ☎ 5 212 2138. Predictably, the 'local' of Vilnius's bohemian quarter is a favourite with artists & students. Idyllically set by the River Vilnia, it has a spacious beer garden (the only one in Vilnius) & a contrastingly cosy interior, which makes the walk there in winter quite acceptable. Do not be surprised to see the former mayor of Vilnius, Artūras Zuokas, drop in from time to time, even though he could surely afford more lavish surroundings. Perhaps he likes the deliberately old-fashioned décor, which is such a contrast to the working environment he has established for the council & for the business community on the other side of the Neris River.

Užupio Klasika Užupio 28; ☎ 5 215 3677. With its top-quality Segafredo coffee & an assortment of homemade pancakes, salads & pasta dishes, this tiny, 5-table café is the perfect pause for breath on a daytime amble through the city. When more than 8 people are waiting for food, you may be there for a while. But the relaxed atmosphere & music are somehow conducive to conversation, or to reading the newspaper – or perusing your guidebook for that matter.

ENTERTAINMENT AND NIGHTLIFE

Vilnius at night is unrecognisable from the quiet backwater is was 15 years ago. Dozens of sweaty, pumping new nightspots and atmospheric watering holes seem to open every year, pushing the boundaries of the city centre westwards along Gedimino and eastwards into Užupis. For pre- or post-club relaxation, there is a greater choice of chillout zones, often off the beaten track. At weekends, opening hours extend beyond daylight. Clubbing is in; folk dancing is most definitely out.

There is still plenty of demand for chamber orchestras, contemporary dance, theatre, opera and ballet, however, and there is no more evocative city to combine a concert and an excellent evening meal than Vilnius.

Hardly a week passes in Vilnius without a cultural festival of one sort or another taking place. Unlike in many other capitals of eastern Europe, these continue through the summer and on into autumn. Whilst the occasional artist from abroad may be engaged to participate, such is the diversity of talent available in Lithuania itself, that even someone from Kaunas or Klaipeda might be seen as an outsider. *VilniusNOW!*, *Vilnius In Your Pocket* and *The Baltic Times* are the best local sources in print for information on events.

OPERA, BALLET AND CONCERTS Inside the colossal Lithuanian Opera and Ballet Theatre (*Vienuolio 1;* \ *5 262 0727; www.opera.lt*), three or four performances a week are held in a programme that is fixed about six months ahead. This extraordinary example of overblown Brezhnev-era architecture hasn't changed structurally, its huge chandeliers still glaring through monumental windows, but fortunately its productions have, with frequent new productions mingling with old favourites. Vilnius attracts some world-class performers, often Russian, though not quite as many as Riga.

Ticket prices are very reasonable, ranging from 10Lt to 120Lt. Operas and ballets are highly popular, but such is the size of the venue it is usually possible to buy tickets once you arrive in Vilnius. The ticket office can be found inside a door at the bottom of the building facing the river. Performances are normally in the original language, with some being contemporary Lithuanian works. The opera is closed in July and August.

The Opera and Ballet Theatre benefits from regular charitable donations from various countries and international corporations, enough to guarantee replacement of some outdated equipment every year. Plush new seats embossed with the opera logo were installed in summer 2005.

The best classical music concerts are held at the Congress Palace (*Vilniaus 6;* \ *5 261 8828*), where the Lithuanian State Symphony Orchestra teams up with local and international musical personages for concerts held throughout the year, except in summer, and the National Philharmonic Hall (*Aušros Vartų 5;* \ *5 266 5216*), the city's most impressive concert hall, which hosts everything from pianists and quartets by renowned foreign musicians to full-blown orchestral extravaganzas. On a smaller scale, the Music Academy (*Gedimino 42;* \ *5 261 2691*) students and professors give free-of-charge recitals on weekdays during term time.

Always look out for the St Christopher Chamber Orchestra, founded in 1994, which brings together several young chamber ensembles, string quartets and solo performers. Its brilliant concerts are performed at different venues in Vilnius as well as abroad.

In addition, concerts and organ recitals are held in several Old Town churches, especially the cathedral, St John's, St Catherine's and St Casimir's. At St Casimir's, live music is normally performed every Sunday immediately after the last morning mass ends at around 13.00. Open-air concerts – which take place in the courtyards of Vilnius University and the Chodkevičius Palace, among other venues – are a regular feature of the city's musical life in summertime.

The main venue for large-scale pop concerts is now the Siemens Arena (*Ozo 14; www.siemens-arena.com*), a new multi-purpose event and conference centre that opened in 2004 opposite the Akropolis shopping complex. In the Old Town, Tamsta (*Subačiaus 11a;* \ *5 212 4498*) has built up a reputation for great live blues, rock, hip hop and even gospel, its hip, bohemian and very friendly atmosphere open to any influences. Brodvėjus (*Mėsinių 4;* \ *5 210 7208*) is more of a beery pub venue, its younger fanbase bopping around to regular live concerts of local rock music, jazz and blues. The best venue for international and local DJs is Gravity (*Jasinskio 16; www.clubgravity.lt;* ⊕ *w/ends only*), famed for its location in a Soviet-era bomb shelter.

FILMS AND THEATRE State-of-the-art multiplexes now dominate the city's film-going scene. The last of the fondly remembered old Soviet-era cinemas are being sold and repackaged. The Lietuva on Pylimo is being turned into flats, the Pergalė on Pamėkalnio has become a new casino and restaurant and the Helios on Didžioji is now an entertainment complex of restaurants, nightclub and strip joint. The last non-multiplex survivor, the Skalvijos opposite the Green Bridge, lives under constant threat of closure but attracts an enthusiastic throng of art-house film lovers.

There are two multiplexes to choose from in Vilnius, both offering films in the original language with Lithuanian subtitles. An evening out at the cinema is therefore a good evening entertainment option for tourists, though the diet of big-budget Hollywood movies will not appeal to everyone. Check www.forumcinemas.lt or phone ↘ 1567 to find out what's on, where and when. Coca-Cola Plaza, also known by its old name the Vingis Cinema, has 12 screens and almost 2,000 seats (including a few dozen for the disabled) a short taxi ride from the Old Town at Savanorių 8. A little further away, Forum Cinemas has a second multiplex at the gigantic Akropolis shopping centre.

The Cinema Spring Festival is an increasingly interesting, week-long annual movie festival with films from around the world, usually taking place in April.

The language barrier should not be seen as a hindrance in the theatre. Many productions are, of course, of foreign classics which will be known to visitors, and in other cases the ticket prices are so low that it is worth staying for at least the first act simply to see Lithuanian drama in action. The National Drama Theatre (*Gedimino 4;* ↘ *5 262 9771*) is the city's biggest theatrical stage, used for plays, modern dance, avant-garde productions and festivals. A statue of three ghostly muses graces the entrance. New management at the Russian Drama Theatre (*Basanavičiaus 13;* ↘ *5 262 7133*) has brought in a more varied programme than just Russian-language performances, while the Small State Theatre of Vilnius (*Gedimino 22;* ↘ *5 261 3125; www.vmt.lt/en*) is a new stage with repertoire ranging from Chekhov to contemporary Lithuanian plays. The Youth Theatre (*Arklių 5;* ↘ *5 261 6126*) shows cutting-edge plays and innovative productions staged by some of Lithuania's best writers and directors.

Finally, the Lėlė Puppet Theatre (*Arklių 5;* ↘ *5 262 8678*) is a unique and entertaining festival of puppetry for children of all ages – and adults too. Located inside the Baroque Oginskis Palace, like the Youth Theatre, it has managed to stay open through good times and bad since it was founded in the 1950s.

BARS AND CLUBS

A revolution has taken place in the last seven years. Vilnius now offers a wide range of options for the evening and early-morning hours. It's no longer just boom-boom techno. DJs play as much cool jazz and lounge music as they do throbbing performances of light and noise. Bars, meanwhile, range from old-fashioned, fireside pubs like Transylvania and Prie Universiteto to more colourfully designed watering holes like Savas Kampas. Cozy, Paparazzi and Pabo Latino are more modern, club-style venues with tasteful, unintrusive chillout sounds, where you can mingle a little conversation with a little dancing and, in the case of the first two, extremely good food.

Bars and clubs tend to open at midday, but are more flexible about their closing times, which are often 02.00 midweek and even later at weekends.

◱ **Amatininkų Užeiga** Didžioji 19. A prominent location ensures that this tavern gets a tidy turnover, but the emphasis is on bar food & the beverage of choice is beer. If that's what you want, & you're quick enough to grab one of the tightly squeezed tables on the pavement out front in summer, then this may not quite fall under the label 'tourist trap'.

◱ **Artistai** Šv Kazimiero 3; www.artistai.lt. The large, buzzing courtyard is the reason to come to this bar & relax during summer sunsets. But a comfortable interior, friendly service & Elvis recurring in the rock 'n' roll music selection should be enough to push you to venture down atmospheric Šv Kazimiero St in winter too.

◱ **Avilys** Gedimino 5; www.avilys.lt. A popular microbrewery in a cellar close to the cathedral, the 'Beehive' is known for its honey-flavoured or ginseng-spiced beer. It certainly takes precedence over the food, which is tasty but hardly inspiring. The varied bar snacks, which include everything from garlic bread to prawns, may be a better bet to go with the drinks, while the hedonistic 1920s alcohol ads decorating the walls only encourage you to drink more.

◱ **Bix** Etmonų 6; www.bix.lt. More for those with alternative tastes, this Tarantino-style bar with rock music was founded over 10 years ago by the early-'90s Lithuanian group of the same name. Still an exciting venue for a beer, & perhaps even a lurch to the noisy drones on the cellar dance floor, Bix is a true, unpredictable original.

♪ **Brodvėjus** Mėsinių 4; www.brodvejus.lt. Attracting a youthful crowd of mostly raucous students, this informal, barn-style venue with regular shows of live music is a good option if you fancy a wild, spontaneous evening.

♪ **Cozy** Domininkonų 10; www.cozy.lt. As comfortable & relaxing by evening & into the early hours as it is during the day for its morning coffee & well-proportioned meals, Cozy is a warm, glowing chillout zone.

☆ **Entertainment Bank** Pamėnkalnio 7; www.pramogubankas.lt. The rather absurd name belies the fact that this flashy new one-stop entertainment centre in a previously undeveloped corner of the Old Town is popular with young locals with deep pockets. The developers have spared no expense (over 7.25 million Lt) in making this an extravagant venue, where fun-seekers can dine, drink, dance or gamble the day & night away in 2 restaurants, 2 clubs, 7 bars, & a casino without leaving the building.

☆ **Galaxy** Konstitucijos 26; www.forumpalace.lt. The largest nightclub in Vilnius, which can absorb 1,000 people or more, opens only on Fri & Sat when it can be sure of this turnout. A privilege card offers discounts once 5,000Lt (£1,000 or US$1,900) has been spent which perhaps indicates the clientele it attracts. The opening until 05.00 makes this financial barrier quite easy to reach. Seating is pretty sparse, so book a table or keep dancing.

☆ **GCW** Vienuolio 4; www.grandcasino.lt. The sophisticated side of Vilnius's new 21st-century casino scene, the Grand Casino World complex, promised big things for connoisseurs of gambling & non-gamblers alike when it opened in 2004. While the casino itself continues to house an attractive collection of card & dice games, the other constituent parts of the complex are just as much of an attraction. These include the excellent Tokyo sushi restaurant, the not-so-good Thai Gourmet restaurant, the meat-dish-and-beer-bar Grand Pub with its assortment of screens for watching sports events, & the fizzy lounge-style nightclub, the Champagne Bar.

☆ **Gravity** Jasinskio 16; www.clubgravity.lt. As famed for its location in a Soviet-era bomb shelter as it is for its international DJs, Gravity attracts young local celebs & a faithful crew of regular party-goers. Found down a 60m tunnel that raises the adrenalin with a thudding bass noise, Gravity is minimalistic & industrial in its décor & unrelenting in its clubbing energy.

♀ **In Vino** Aušros Vartų 7; www.invino.lt Strong on atmosphere, this wine bar close to the Gates of Dawn is full of non-attitude people whose playful chatting grows louder as the evening wears on. The bar is stocked with 'wines for the mind' & 'wines for the soul'.

☆ **Pabo Latino** Trakų 3; www.pabolatino.lt. Highly popular with stylish 20- & 30-somethings, this Old Town nightclub is sumptuously decorated, often more along the lines of an eastern harem than a Latino dance party, with billowing tents outside in summer & plush cushions & rugs inside. For interesting conversations with beautiful locals, head for the courtyard's wooden steps.

☆ **Pacha** Gynėjų 14; www.pachavilnius.lt. This club opened in 2008 & was determined at once to be the place to be seen after midnight. With its size & variety of entertainment it may well still be no 1 in several years' time.

♪ **Paparazzi** Totoriu 3; www.paparrazi.lt. Following a brilliantly publicised opening in early 2005, this bar certainly set itself up as the place for the pretentious under-30s to be seen. The bar area has conventional celebrity photos, though nobody seems to have thought about the irony of including Princess Diana in a bar of this name. Those, however, in the toilets will only 'appeal' to those with the most broad-minded of tastes.

♪ **Prie Universiteto** (also known as The Pub or the Pub'as) Domininkonų 9; www.pub.lt. A busy expat hangout with English-style bar-food during the 1990s, the Pub then changed hands & the food & the music went rapidly downhill. Things are improving, however, & it's still the best venue to watch a live football game on the big screen. It even had a recent evening of alternative music dedicated to the late John Peel.

♪ **Savas Kampas** Vokiečių 4; www.savaskampas.lt. This popular bar serves a wide range of food, including tasty lunchtime hotpots on w/days. Its cellar closed in early 2005, when the kitchen moved down there as Lithuanians are no longer so keen on eating in cellars. The décor in the expanded ground-floor dining area is as varied as the food.

♀ **Shooters** Totorių 3; ✆ 5 655 52518; www.shooters.lt. A novelty for Vilnius in 2008 in that it serves 300 different cocktails, but no beer. The website should in due course list them all, & in English too. It strikes a nice balance between cool elegance & frivolous unpretentiousness.

♀ **SkyBar** Konstitucijos 20 (inside the Reval Hotel Lietuva); www.revalhotels.com. Everybody's favourite cocktail-bar-with-a-view, SkyBar is located at the top of the towering, 22-floor Reval Hotel Lietuva. It opens only at 16.00, but it's where all tours of the city should start or end. Just make your way through the lobby to the speedy lifts on the right. As you enter the bar, seat yourself on the left-hand side for the best view of the neon-lit Vilnius panorama, gazed at through floor-to-ceiling windows.

📧 **Transylvania** Totorių 22; www.transylvania.lt
A friendly bar with a curious mix of rustic-style atmosphere, surprisingly authentic Romanian food & edgy rock music.

GAY VILNIUS

In most countries in central and eastern Europe gay scenes have been slow to emerge since the legal restraints of the Soviet era were abolished. In culturally conservative Vilnius, there is barely a scene at all. The hostility the gay community faced in earlier times has still not been eradicated. Gay marches in nearby Warsaw and Riga in 2005 attracted at least twice as many people hurling homophobic abuse at those brave enough to turn up and demand gay rights. Vilnius has never even had a gay march and the new mayor has said he will never allow one.

The press is hardly leading the way. Occasionally, the daily newspaper *Respublika*, the local equivalent of *The Sun*, runs hysterical anti-gay and anti-Semitic articles written by its editors. The fact that the publication is barely prosecuted and that statements from politicians criticising the articles are painfully slow in coming reveals the lack of understanding in society.

Fortunately, several websites, including www.gay.lt and www.gayline.lt, keep the community together. There is one gay club in Vilnius. Until very recently, its regularly alternating locations had to be kept a tightly guarded secret. Now, however, there is a permanent address.

☆ **Men's Factory** Ševčenkos 16; ☏ 8 699 85009; www.gayclub.lt; ⏰ Wed–Sat. Despite its rather seedy location down an inconspicuous back street a 10min hike from the Old Town, Men's Factory finally has a fixed abode. The club is modestly sized, but that means it gets tightly packed, especially on the regularly scheduled events nights. Also on the menu are lasers, DJs, stage shows, snow machines & 'sweet surprises'.

SHOPPING

Vilnius is in general the cheapest of the three Baltic capitals in which to shop, probably because, in both senses of the word, it cannot be spoilt by cruise passengers whose presence always increases prices. Kaliningrad is of course far cheaper still, particularly for amber, since fewer tourists go there and most of what is sold is to local people. Bookshops are usually closed on Sundays, even in midsummer, but other shops open around 10.00 and close around 19.00, although they will close an hour or two earlier at weekends in the winter. All take credit cards, but are unlikely to accept any currency apart from the local one.

SOUVENIRS Amber is the best buy from Vilnius. Market stalls with it line Pilies, the main street through the Old Town, but to ensure quality it is best for those without real knowledge of it to use the specialist shops. The **Amber Museum Gallery** (*Mykolo 8; www.ambergallery.lt*) is mainly a museum about the mining of amber but it also has a shop with an extensive collection of individual stones or amber set in jewellery. They have an informative website about the origins of amber and their displays. Almost next door is **Sauluva** (*Mykolo 4; www.sauluva.lt*) with a wide range of souvenirs. Look out in particular for beeswax candles and dried flowers.

BOOKS The **Librairie Française** (*Didžioji 1, opposite the Picture Gallery*) is a somewhat misleading name, since it in fact stocks a fair selection of books in English, but it is in a very French environment, in fact in the house where Stendhal stayed in 1812; on one side is a French café and on the other, the French Institute. It is part of a group of bookshops originally founded in 1905, when it became legal to sell books in the Lithuanian language using the Roman alphabet. They would face many different censors during the 20th century and only from 1991 have they been free to sell what they want. **Humanitas** (*Domininkonų 5*) is the best source for art books, of which there are now a large number in English. The university has its own bookshop, **Littera**, in the main courtyard, famous more for its elaborate frescoed interior than for what is sells, but it does have a wide range of postcards and books in English on Lithuanian history.

OTHER PURCHASES Shopping centres came somewhat later to Vilnius than they did to Tallinn and Riga but will doubtless be just as popular. In fact **Akropolis** (*www.akropolis.lt; ⊕ daily until midnight*), about 3km west from the town centre and which opened in 2002, prides itself on the number of Latvians and Belarusians it now attracts. Those who knew Vilnius in Soviet times will find it hard to believe that such a beautiful complex with space, air conditioning, and an ice rink could arise so quickly in its aftermath. Alcohol, clothes and fabrics are the best buys here and full details of all the shops and entertainment are on the website. Opposite the Reval Lietuva and the Best Western hotels, on Konstitucijos, is a somewhat smaller centre, **Europa** (⊕ *until 22.00 Mon–Fri, to 20.00 Sat/Sun*), but certainly large enough to stock anything a tourist may want to buy.

WALKING TOURS

Since the Old Town is one of the biggest and most beautiful in Europe, tourists tend to concentrate on the sights and attractions inside it. But the surrounding streets, hills and views offer a great deal, too. While the main sights in the Old Town can be covered in one day, more time is needed for venturing beyond it. A route for a day-long walking tour is suggested below, followed by a few shorter ones.

OLD TOWN WALK Start at **Vilnius Cathedral** (Arkikatedra Bazilika), a classical structure at the northern edge of the Old Town that was once the site of a revered pagan temple (page 208). The first Christian church was probably built here following the Grand Duchy's initial conversion to Christianity in the 13th century, but most of what you see today dates from around 200 years ago. After Lithuania was occupied by Soviet forces, the three statues of saints that tower over the façade were removed and destroyed, only to be replaced by reproductions of the originals in 1996.

Inside, the impression is of an ornate gallery with oil paintings hung on two tiers, so it should come as no surprise to learn that the building was given the function of art gallery and concert hall under the Soviets. In the first decade after the war it was even mooted as a garage for truck repairs.

One of the most resplendent of the 11 small chapels is also the oldest, the early 17th-century Baroque **Chapel of St Casimir**, patron saint of Vilnius. A visit to the vaults below reveals an altar once used for pagan rituals and the coffins of royal and noble family members whose lives have become romanticised among Lithuanians. Outside the cathedral, the Clock Tower (Arkikatedros varpinė), a favourite local rendezvous point, recently got a set of new bells that were blessed by Lithuania's Cardinal Bačkis before they were hung. The tower has a curious history. Its round lower storey, which is pierced by numerous gunports, dates back to the 14th century and belonged to the fortification system of the Lower Castle; it is the only part of it which survives to this day. It was converted into the cathedral's bell tower in the 1520s by the addition of two octagonal tiers. Later a fourth tier was added to house a clock, which still preserves its original mechanism. In 1893, it finally assumed its current appearance when it was crowned with a small steeple.

With your back to the cathedral doors, turn left and head across **Cathedral Square** (Katedros aikštė), a vast paved space to the side of the cathedral that makes an ideal starting or finishing point for parades and processions, towards the trees of Kalnų Park. But before you do so, search for the 'miracle stone'. It is said that here in Cathedral Square you can make your dreams come true by finding the slab marked *stebuklas* ('miracle'), then quickly making a wish while turning 360° clockwise. This paving stone marks the end of the human chain that linked Tallinn, Riga and Vilnius in 1989, formed by two million Lithuanians, Latvians and Estonians to protest against the Soviet occupation. However, you have to look for the mythical slab yourself, for superstition decrees that no-one is allowed to reveal its precise location.

Since 1996, Cathedral Square has been the setting for a monument to **Grand Duke Gediminas** – a particularly fitting location, as it must be close to the spot where he had his legendary dream about the iron wolf. The commission for the statue was entrusted to veteran sculptor Vytautas Kašuba, who had spent most of his career in America and died soon after the monument was erected. Gediminas is shown with his sword in his left hand, an allusion to his supposed preference for diplomacy over war – though in reality he most probably used both to achieve substantial territorial gains for the Grand Duchy.

With Vilnius being joint Capital of Culture in 2009 the amount of restoration work undertaken before that year is bound to increase. Immediately behind the cathedral is the most ambitious of these projects, the reconstruction of the Renaissance-style **Royal Palace**. A splendid medieval complex that fell into ruin and was finally destroyed by the Tsarist authorities in 1802, the aim is to complete the rebuilding by 2009 – also the date of Vilnius's momentous 1,000th anniversary.

Once inside tree-shaded Kalnų Park, keep left to find the path that winds upwards around the hill to the **Higher Castle** (Aukštutinės pilies bokštas), also known as Gedimino Castle, from which the best of the many views of Vilnius can be had (page 205). The viewing platform at the top is worth the struggle to climb steps that are unnervingly narrow at times. The castle also houses a small museum of armoury and a model of medieval Vilnius.

Opened in 2005, a funicular railway leads back down to city level and the spacious courtyard of the **Applied Arts Museum** (Taikomosios dailės muziejus, page 204). Enter either this or the **National Museum** (Lietuvos nacionalinis muziejus) from the front by first going through one of the gateways (page 207). A stylised statue of Mindaugas guarding the museum entrance was unveiled together with the King Mindaugas Bridge across the road to great fanfare and fireworks in July 2003, marking the 750th anniversary of the coronation that brought Christianity to Vilnius for the first time.

Head back past the front of the cathedral, diagonally across Cathedral Square, and find the northern end of Pilies, the Old Town's mainly pedestrian-only thoroughfare. A handful of cafés here make a convenient pause for breath and sell good coffee, cakes, lunches and ice cream. Take Bernadinų, the first narrow lane to the left, which snakes past the **Adam Mickiewicz Museum** (Mickevičiaus butas-muziejus, page 206) towards **St Anne's Church** (Šv Onos bažnyčia), the charming Gothic church that Napoleon famously said he would like to take back to Paris on the palm of his hand (page 210). The more imposing **Bernardine Church** (Bernadinų bažnyčia) stands immediately behind it (page 210).

Double back across busy Maironio Street to find **St Michael's Church** (Šv Mykolo bažnyčia), which since the Soviet period has housed the Museum of Architecture, interesting as a curiosity since it displays plans of buildings in Vilnius that were never approved. Built by the head of one of Vilnius's great noble families, Leonas Sapiega, as a personal mausoleum in the early 1600s, one or two of the church's lovely details, like the rosette ceiling, are also worth popping in for. Further along Šv Mykolo is the **Amber Museum-Gallery** (Gintaro muziejus-galerija), Vilnius's most illuminating museum (and shop) dedicated exclusively to Baltic Gold (page 204).

The street brings you back onto bustling Pilies. Turn left and walk up, pausing at Pilies 26. Known today as the **Signatories' House** (Signatarų namai), this was where the 20 members of the Council of Lithuania met in 1918 to sign a declaration on the nation's independence. There is not a great deal in this small museum to see – only to imagine. Even the declaration itself is not on show. It has disappeared, since in Polish and Soviet times it needed to be hidden, and there are various theories as to where it might be. One theory doing the rounds in 2007 was that it might be hidden in the walls of the Lithuanian Language Institute on Antakalnio, near SS Peter and Paul Church. In 1918 the house belonged to a rich architect, Petras Vileisis, whose brother Jonas was one of the signatories. Jonas may have taken the document to him and for safekeeping hidden it within a wall. The first and ground floors of the museum both have exhibition rooms where temporary artistic and photographic displays are held.

Stroll through the arcade over the road to browse through thousands of souvenirs, classier and pricier versions of which are on display in several amber and linen shops along this part of the street. At the top of the arcade, Pilies opens out onto more stalls selling everything from gimmicky ceramics to woolly socks. A lovely row of shops on the left includes a charity shop selling stuffed toys and knick-knacks handmade by the disabled, a tea shop, a gallery showcasing local artists and an irresistible attraction for choc-lovers – a shop with a bounteous display of chocolates of every size, shape and filling. Venture a little further into Bokšto to find the city's eclectic Russian and, round the corner, Polish art galleries.

The downstairs section of the **Šlapelis Museum** at Pilies 40 is a re-creation of the pioneering Lithuanian bookshop established in 1906 by Jurgis Šlapelis and his wife Marija. Displayed in the couple's flat above, which is entered from the courtyard, are books and other objects associated with the national cultural revival they did so much to promote, as well as exhibits from the little-documented inter-war Polish period.

Over the square, standing on a platform above an open-air art market, is **St Paraskeva Russian Orthodox Church** (Piatnickaya cerkvė), originally built in 1345, where Peter the Great of Russia supposedly stood as godfather to the christening of Hannibal, the great-grandfather of the Russian poet Alexander Pushkin in 1705. Hannibal was abducted from his home in Africa at the age of seven, rescued from his life as a slave in Istanbul by the Russian envoy and presented as a gift to Tsar Peter.

As the road upwards closes in to become Didžioji, **Vilnius Picture Gallery** (Vilniaus paveikslų galerija) lies beyond an unassuming gateway on the left that leads into a grand and elegant courtyard (page 208). Another of the city's Russian Orthodox churches, the Byzantine-style **St Nicolas** (Šv Mikalojaus cerkvė), an oasis of candlelit peace away from the bustle of the street, can be explored a short distance further up Didžioji on the left. As with all of Vilnius's Russian Orthodox churches, no concessions are made to Lithuania; everything is written, spoken and sung in Russian.

As Didžioji broadens enough to deserve its name ('great'), boutiques on both sides reveal how many of the Western world's fashion brands are on offer in today's transformed Vilnius. But to discover how most of the city's churches looked 20 years ago, forlorn, dilapidated and empty, take the first street left, Savičiaus. About 100m down on the right is **St Mary the Soothing** (Marijos Ramintojos bažnyčia), its courtyard locked and unkempt. The single tower of this late Baroque church dates from the mid 18th century and is still tall enough to feature as part of the Vilnius skyline.

Double back to Didžioji, passing the **M K Čiurlionis House** (M K Čiurlionio namai) dedicated to Lithuania's most beloved artist and composer (page 205). Another essential museum for art-lovers can be found at number 26. The astonishing legacy of an artist who returned to his home country from America in 1998, the **Kazys Varnelis House Museum** contains an astonishing personal collection of art (page 208). Cross the street to the grand, 18th-century **Town Hall** (Rotušė), which today has multiple uses, ranging from classical music venue to contemporary art gallery. The foyer makes an austere setting for often absorbing exhibitions of art and architecture.

Keep heading upwards, bearing left of the Town Hall, and after a few steps **St Casimir's** (Šv Kazimiero bažnyčia) comes into view. This was Vilnius's very first Baroque building, modelled on Rome's church of Il Gesu with the characteristically Lithuanian addition of twin spires (page 210). Occupying powers have done some odd things with St Casimir's. During the six months Napoleon was in control of Vilnius the church stored wine for the French army. It was during the Nazi occupation in 1942 that St Casimir's royal lineage was recognised by placing a gold-coloured crown above the central dome. Then, in 1976, during the Soviet period, St Casimir's became the city's museum of atheism. The instruments of torture used during the Inquisition, such as leg braces and a chair of nails, were displayed here as though they were part of 20th-century religious practice. Yet outside genuflecting women were praying towards the Gates of Dawn. One Intourist guide, when asked by an angry tourist what these women were doing, was told, 'They are probably tying their shoelaces.'

An intersection of streets appears further up the hill, with a small parking area in front of the **National Philharmonic** (Filharmonija). Take a peek down charmingly narrow Šv Kazimiero Street, which dips back to the left, before approaching Aušros Vartų with its myriad of churches, spires and souvenir shops (seek out the bizarre and cluttered workshop of local craftsman Jonas Bugailiškis at number 17). What immediately catches your eye is the stunning 18m-high Baroque **Basilian Gate** (Bazilijonų vartai). It leads to a monastery that is used by a small group of Uniate Basilian monks and its rundown **Church of the Holy Trinity** (Šv Trejybės cerkvė). Wander beyond the gateway to discover the church and the monastery's calm courtyard. The monastery served as a conveniently isolated prison in Tsarist times and the poet Adam Mickiewicz was held here for a while, a fact recorded on a plaque. Restoration of the church and its 16th-century frescoes is expected to take many years. Another peaceful, leafy courtyard next to the curious Arka Art Gallery (Arka galerija), immediately before the Basilian Gate, is a relaxing coffee stop served by the Arka café.

Aušros Vartų now takes in the **Orthodox Church of the Holy Spirit** (Šv Dvasios cerkvė), the most revered religious building of Lithuania's Russian-speaking community, found through another gateway (page 211). The forms of what are said to be the miraculously preserved bodies of saints Anthony, Ivan and Eustace, who died for their faith in 1347, can still be seen underneath their shrouds. They were murdered by militant pagans on the spot where the Church of the Holy Trinity now stands. At the far end of Aušros Vartų, beyond **St Teresa's Church** (Šv Teresės bažnyčia), lies the climax to this pilgrimage between the spires of Vilnius, the **Gates of Dawn** (Aušros Vartų koplytėlė), to which the most pious of worshippers crawl in veneration up steps from street level. The gates hold a gold-and-silver image of the Virgin Mary in a chapel that is a shrine for devout Catholics.

Backtrack down past the Philharmonic and take a left on Etmonų, at the end of which stand the Youth Theatre and Puppet Theatre. Both opened many years before independence but have found new audiences as Lithuanians keep up their passionate love of the stage (page 193). Take the passage right, which brings you alongside the Radisson SAS to the rear of the Town Hall. Head left and left again onto Rūdininkų for two sites that bring back the tragedy of the Holocaust in Vilnius. This was then part of the terror-stricken 'ghetto' where the city's large Jewish population were kept before being herded out for extermination. A map on the wall of Rūdininkų 18, where one of the **ghetto** gates stood, shows how the streets looked at that time. A courtyard at Rūdininkų 8 was where the cruel process of selection was made. Jewish families were permitted only two children in the ghetto. If there were more, the parents had to choose who was to be taken away and killed. The old and weak – those of no practical use to the Nazis – were also 'selected' here. A plaque on the wall marks this terrible place.

Back on Vokiečių, a broad avenue that is home to more fashionable independent shops and boutiques, the **Contemporary Art Centre** (Šiolaikinio meno centras) holds some of the city's most daring modern artwork (page 206). About 50m up Šv Mikalojaus, the second lane on the left, find the oldest Gothic building still standing in Vilnius, **St Nicholas's Church** (Šv Mikalojaus bažnyčia), built in 1320 to serve German merchants in the years before Lithuania itself widely adopted Christianity. When Lithuanians' cultural and religious activities were severely restricted during Poland's occupation of Vilnius between the wars, this was the only church where they were allowed to attend mass in their language.

In 2004, a new **Jewish Museum** was opened to the public at Naugarduko 10. Now called the Tolerance Centre (page 206), gradually the collections at the other Jewish museums, at Pylimo 4 and Pamėnkalnio 12, are being transferred here. Some exhibits are moved over each year. If you visit one of these museums, it should be the 'green house' at Pamėnkalnio 12, set back up a hill from the main street. Here you'll find a chilling photographic record of sites where massacres under the Nazis took place. But all three museums stand as a ghostly reminder of what was once a thriving Jewish community. About 200 Jewish communities existed in Lithuania before World War II. Vilnius, where 40% of the population was Jewish, had 105 synagogues and prayer houses and six daily Jewish newspapers, making Vilna, as it was known in Yiddish, the 'Jerusalem of the North'. About 300,000 Jews lived in Lithuania at the turn of the last century. More than 90% of this community was wiped out during the Nazi occupation.

An appropriate few hundred metres away from these memorials to tragedy is Vilnius's strangest statue. It is of the late Californian rock musician **Frank Zappa**, but was in fact unveiled in 1995, two years after his death. He had hoped to visit Lithuania to see it but his final illness prevented this. Find it by turning off Pylimo up Kalinausko; it is in a rather mediocre courtyard behind the first office block on the right. It is probably a suitable compromise for its location. Those who see statutes as a way of the establishment perpetuating itself for ever will probably not be aware of it, and those with a sense of humour will be relieved that the ultimate figure of anti-establishment behaviour will not be forgotten.

Return to Vokiečių via Vilniaus, passing the **Theatre, Music & Film Museum** on your right. The first courtyard on the right after Trakų reveals the location of one of Vilnius's newest and most colourful art shops, Rūta's Gallery (Rūtos galerija), whose imaginatively styled paintings, sculptures, dishes, handmade jewellery and other items are reasonably priced and not too bulky to take home. Another easily missed courtyard at Vokiečių 20 leads to a church that has served Vilnius's Lutheran community since 1555, known today as the **Evangelical Lutheran Church** (Evangelikų Liuteronų bažnyčia). The main point of interest here is the elaborate Rococo altar, built in 1741 by the same architect who designed the magnificent Basilian Gate and the **Orthodox Church of the Holy Spirit,** Jan Krzysztof Glaubitz. The stunning ornateness of the altar stands out boldly against the whitewashed interior.

Cross to the other side of Vokiečių, doubling back slightly, and dive through one of the archways beneath the residential buildings into a broad courtyard to find the tail-end of Žydų (Jews') Street. This is where the **Great Synagogue**, the centrepiece of Vilnius's thriving Jewish community, stood before it was badly bombed during the war and finally destroyed completely in the early years of the Soviet occupation to make way for a school. A small monument to the Talmudic scholar Rabbi Elijah, the Vilna Gaon, stands at the back of the school, solitarily lamenting a lost world of 300,000 Jews who lived and worked in confined, cobbled streets that stretched like a maze through this part the Old Town.

Žydų emerges onto the similarly narrow Stiklių, which has an array of poky gift and clothes shops both left and right. Pause for a well-deserved coffee, cake or lunch break at Ponių Laimė on the corner. The tour heads left from Žydų down Stiklių to reach Domininkonų. The focal point for the city's Polish faithful is the cavernous **Church of the Holy Spirit** (Šventosios Dvasios bažnyčia), a few steps to the left (page 211), while down the hill on the right, on Universiteto, lies the charming complex of courtyards that makes up **Vilnius University** (Vilniaus Universitetas). Before exploring this, however, pop into one of the city's most beautiful Baroque courtyards, at Universiteto 2. In summer this is often the gorgeous backdrop to a café and makes a wonderful location for a daytime coffee or an evening beer.

Vilnius University (page 169) dates back more than 400 years, although the city's history as victim of persecution and occupation ensured that it did not stay open all that time. The Russians closed it in 1832 and it wasn't until 1919, the year after Lithuania won its long-awaited independence, that it reopened. There are 12 courtyards to discover, some more tricky to find than others. Try to see the map at Universiteto 7 before entering. In the grand courtyard at the top of the steps is the monumental façade of St John's Church (Šv Jono bažnyčia), beyond which lies a magnificent interior and intimidating assemblage of ten altars (page 212).

Exit the university where you came in and, opposite, find the **President's Palace** (L R Prezidentūra), a building with a history dating back to the 14th century and where Napoleon slept in 1812 on his doomed march to Moscow. Today, after many renovations, it houses the busy offices of the Lithuanian president. It is open on Fridays and Saturdays for pre-booked groups. A tour showing the main reception rooms, the President's Office and the gardens takes about 45 minutes. The furnishings are entirely modern, much of them in oak and birch, but the designs are from the early 19th century. One room has four large portraits of the previous Lithuanian presidents, three from the 1920–40 period and one of Algirdas Brazauskas, in office 1993–98. An even larger painting shows Vytautas the Great riding into the Black Sea, recalling the time when the Polish–Lithuanian Commonwealth stretched that far in the mid-15th century.

FURTHER WALKS

Changing Vilnius walk Of course, there's more to Vilnius than the Old Town. **Gedimino Avenue** is the city's main drag, extending westwards from the cathedral. It is lined with ever-increasing numbers of classy shops, apartments and mini-malls. Real estate developers are sure that Gedimino will quickly become one long, highly attractive, open-air shopping centre to rival anything Copenhagen or London has to offer. That's ambitious. But with the avenue now physically transformed all the way to the Žvėrynas suburb in the west, the paving evened, underground parking installed and the groaning trolleybuses banished to just one intersection, they are not so far off the mark.

Changes are visible right the way along the street. The Vilnius municipality offices have moved from Gedimino 9 to a new skyscraper the other side of the river, leaving this neo-Baroque block to re-emerge as a swanky superstore; one of the city's grimy old cinemas has become a Benetton store; the towering Novotel is a brand-new building with fashion shops on the ground floor; and the 19th-century building at Gedimino 20, once the shabby Hotel Vilnius, shines like never before as a multi-million-pound commercial and residential Grand Duke Palace.

The most essential thing to see on Gedimino Avenue, however, has stayed structurally unchanged since it was built as a courthouse and prison in 1899. Now housing the vivid and shocking basement-level **KGB Museum** (Genocido aukų muziejus), the much-feared building facing Lukiškių Square was the Soviet secret service's Vilnius headquarters (page 206). Hundreds of people were imprisoned, tortured and executed in its cells and thousands more were sent to Siberia between the 1940s and the late 1980s.

In the middle of the square a giant statue of Lenin gestured with arm outstretched at the KGB building. It was pulled apart by a crane in front of cheering crowds in 1991 and now stands at the Grutas Park of Soviet Statues near Druskininkai.

Gedimino extends beyond the Lithuanian Music Academy, where free public concerts are frequently held in term time, to its westernmost section, which boasts even more boutiques and independent shops. Concealed from view, one of the country's biggest prisons lurks down Ankštoji, a narrow side street to the right, although developers may soon persuade the government to move the prison to a less exclusive area.

Before reaching the River Neris, the avenue opens out into **Independence Square** (Nepriklausomybės aikštė), bordered on one side by the 'Stalinist Baroque' **National Library** (Martynas Mažvydas biblioteka), built in the 1950s, and on the other by the late Soviet-era **Parliament** building (Seimas), which originally housed the Supreme Council of Lithuania. This is where the republic's leaders declared independence from Moscow on 11 March 1990. Barricades were erected to protect the Parliament from Soviet tanks. These giant cubes and slabs of crude concrete remained in place into the early 1990s. Today, a few can still be seen on the side of the building facing the river.

Stroll across the recently renovated old river-bridge into the leafy residential district of Žvėrynas to find the eye-catching onion domes of the **Russian Orthodox Church of the Apparition of the Holy Mother of God** (Znamenskaya cerkvė), one of the city's warmest and most appealing churches. As Žvėrynas quickly became the city's first garden suburb, divided into separate plots in the 1890s, this was the first church to be built here, in 1903. To the left, where Vytauto meets Liubarto, and a little to the right stands the tiny, Moorish-style Kenessa, built for the Karaite community in 1922, but used as a warehouse during the Soviet occupation.

Žvėrynas, a dense knit of streets, some of them almost rustic with quaint wooden houses, is arranged in a bend in the river. It is an increasingly chic place to live, no more than a square mile wide and very pleasant to stroll around. Find a pedestrian-only suspension bridge dramatically spanning the river from grassy banks into the tall pines of Vingis Park on the far side.

Bohemian Vilnius walk The Hill of Three Crosses (Trijų kryžių kalnas) is another of Vilnius's dramatic viewpoints, higher than the castle, from which the entire panorama of the Old Town is visible. Reach it via an open-air stadium from the southern end of T Kosciuškos, or cross a wooden bridge over the Vilnia from tennis courts in Sereikiškių Park and follow the river to the right before finding steep and rickety steps to the top.

The gleaming white crosses are a replacement for wooden crosses first raised here 350 years ago commemorating 14 monks who were dragged from a Vilnius monastery in the 14th century and murdered by pagans. Seven of them were butchered in cold blood, the rest tied to crosses and floated down the River Neris. The crosses were removed by the Soviets in 1950.

Sereikiškių Park borders **Užupis**, another quietly charming part of the city to stroll about. But it has a wacky side too. Užupis is the equivalent of Greenwich Village in New York or Montmartre in Paris, a place with unconventional ideals and creativity. It declared itself the 'breakaway republic of Užupis' in 1998, with its own independence day on 1 April, its own constitution, which is nailed to the wall on Paupio Street, and its own flag, president and customs officers – who always seem to be off duty. Its 'national symbol', an angel blowing her horn in celebration of freedom and independence, stands atop a column in the central square. The names of everyone who contributed the cash to make it are carved into the base.

Užupis literally means 'the other side of the river'. Up until a decade ago this was one of the most neglected and squalid areas in Vilnius, populated by drunks and criminal types. Today it is prime real estate. Parts are still ruinously rundown, but it is a fascinating place to wander. It might remind you of small towns in Italy, with its smattering of outdoor cafés and boys and girls roaring about on mopeds.

To enter Užupis, pass the white-box **Church of the Holy Mother of God** – a Russian Orthodox church that has over the years been a barracks, a library, a university department and a smithy – and cross the bubbling Vilnia into Užupio Street. The building with the welcoming terrace just across the water is the Užupio café, frequented by artists, poets and all manner of bohemians. As you cross the bridge, look down at the wall of the near bank to see the Užupis Mermaid, a beautiful little siren who bids adieu to visitors leaving the Old Town.

After the café, at the end of a little alley to the left, is the **Alternative Art Centre**, worth a look for its bizarre 'art' collection. Retrace your steps and just a little up the street at number 5 is the Užupio Gallery, a working gallery that features unique enamel items and jewellery.

Užupis is full of lovely courtyards. Don't be afraid to poke your head in and look around. As you face the angel from its front, enter the archway on the right and you will feel as if you've stepped back in time. Notice the water pump, which supplies water for washing dishes and clothes, and for drinking.

Climb the hill and bear right at the fork (bear left to find Tores, the bar and restaurant with the best terrace view in town). Pass the unmarked morgue on the left. When you reach a bus stop and an old payphone, turn right onto Žvirgždyno Street, marked by a small, rusty sign. Fifty metres ahead is the entrance to the **Bernardine Cemetery** (Bernardinų kapinės), one of the most serene and beautiful places in Vilnius. It was founded in 1810 by Bernardine monks and stands on the tall banks of the Vilnia, virtually undisturbed by visitors. University professors, artists and scientists are among the people laid to rest here.

21st-century Vilnius walk

Having had foreign monuments stamped all over its streets and squares in the past, Vilnius seems wary of erecting new ones to the grand dukes of its illustrious history or to the national heroes of its fight for survival. But monuments to capitalism, each more impressive than the last, are rising all the time. The riverbank between the southern end of A Goštauto and the precarious, two-lane Geležinio Vilko is known today as the Business Triangle, crammed with flashy new high-rise office buildings. Close by, the Vilnius Gates (Vilniaus vartai), opened in 2006, tower above the Geležinio Vilko underpass.

However, the most visually striking of all these post-millennium skyscraper projects is **Europa Square** (Europos aikštė) and the sleek, glass-fronted structures around it. The wall of windows facing recently renamed Konstitucijos (Constitution) Avenue is the new **City Hall,** inside which is an accessible ground-floor room displaying a fascinating model of all the future construction developments in Vilnius. Behind it, at 134m, the circular **Europa Tower** (Europos bokštas) is the Baltic countries' tallest building. Thirty-three floors up, the panorama of Vilnius from the viewing platform is unrivalled – and it's free to get to the top. Just enter the ground floor and ask the security guard. But attempt this only at weekends; the companies that rent these prestigious offices do not want nosy sightseers getting lost or clogging up the elevators.

Arguably the most comfortable view in Vilnius, however, is from one of the curvaceous, ocean-blue chairs of the 22nd-floor SkyBar in the Reval Hotel Lietuva, just across Konstitucijos Avenue from Europa Square. Sitting with cocktail in hand, this is a perfect spot to watch the sunset.

Before 2002, these streets north of the river were a no-go area for most tourists, a scruffy mess of Soviet-era concrete, home to a few straggly shops and a shopping centre that more resembled an indoor market selling clothes, watches and electrical gadgets that had fallen off the backs of trucks.

Much of the ugly concrete is still there. But squeaky clean, colourfully landscaped shopping centres filled with refreshing air conditioning and the sound of running water – in particular the Central Universal Store (VCUP) and the Europa shopping centre – are taking the attention away from the eyesores. The latter include the pedestrian precinct between the refurbished Reval and the Green Bridge, once a futuristic showpiece of the late communist years. Now it is crumbling and cracked and permeated by strip bars. Halfway down the precinct, the Planetarium is still operational, despite having a furniture showroom in the lobby.

The **Green Bridge** (Žaliasis tiltas) itself is firmly part of the old era, its comical Socialist Realist figures of grim workers and determined peasants a bizarre contrast to the skyscrapers behind it. Why they were not pulled down immediately after the collapse of the Soviet Union, along with Lenin, and deported to the Grutas Soviet theme park is a matter of intense speculation. The authorities say that they stand as a warning to future generations of the horrors (artistic and otherwise) of communist rule. But it is also true that many locals actually see them as genuine works of art, created by Lithuanian sculptors, not imported from Moscow. In a similar way, many residents are proud, not ashamed, of architectural monsters such as the gargantuan Opera and Ballet Theatre (Operos ir baletos teatras), which virtually overshadows the Green Bridge, or the Parliament building, or even the city's hideous high-rise suburbs, all of which were designed by Lithuanian architects.

The green swathe of riverbank west of the Green Bridge is gradually being put to use. Next to the pedestrian-only **White Bridge** (Baltasis tiltas), which daredevil stunt pilot Jurgis Kairys flew under in 1999, are skateboarding, basketball and volleyball courts for restless youths – and 'The Beach'. In summer, sip on a cold local draught beer under imported palm trees as the sand, brought here in trucks all the way from Lithuania's coastal dunes, tickles your toes.

WHAT TO SEE AND DO

MUSEUMS AND GALLERIES In an irritating overhang from earlier times, most museums are closed on at least one day a week – usually Sunday or Monday – and many for two days; they also close on public holidays. Most do not open until 10.00 and rare is the museum that closes as late as 18.00. Churches are open every day from around 09.00.

Admission prices here are given for adults. Most museums give reductions for children, senior citizens and, providing you have an international card, students and teachers. The websites www.muziejai.lt and www.lnm.lt provide further information.

Amber Museum-Gallery (*Šv Mykolo 8;* ✆ *5 262 3092;* ⊕ *10.00–19.00 daily; www.ambergallery.lt; admission free*) Privately run (it's a shop too), this gallery reveals the history of 'Baltic gold' in several cavernous cellar rooms. You can also find amber in blue, black, white, red and green. It has plenty of unusual, handmade items to choose from including exquisitely designed necklaces, miniature amber musical instruments, and even an amber-coloured liqueur in a flask with amber-topped stopper. Each piece comes with a certificate of authenticity.

Applied Arts Museum (*Arsenalo 3a;* ✆ *5 262 8080; www.ldm.lt;* ⊕ *11.00–17.30 Tue–Sat, 11.00–15.30 Sun; admission 6Lt*) Constructed as an arsenal in the 16th century by Sigismund the Old, the more decorative third floor being added by his son a few decades later, this was at the time the biggest building in the Polish–Lithuanian Commonwealth. It was virtually destroyed when the Russians invaded and pillaged the city in 1655, only to be rebuilt 150 years later.

These days it houses a rather austere collection of portraits, but also one or two paintings that are worth the price of admission alone, including canvases by Francisco

Ximenez, Luis Morales and the master of Austrian Baroque, Johann Michael Rottmayr. Don't miss also one of the best displays of folk art and Lithuanian wooden crosses. Many of these are by Vincas Svirkis (1835–1916), who spent his life roaming the countryside carving saints and religious scenes into the crosses he left behind as he moved from village to village.

Artillery Bastion (*Bokšto 20;* ✆ *5 261 2149;* ⊕ *10.00–18.00 Tue–Sat; admission 3Lt*)

In centuries past, this part of Vilnius was infamous for its prostitution and wild taverns. Witches were said to gather here for demonic orgies. The bastion, part of the city's 17th-century defence against invading armies of Russians and Swedes, quickly fell into ruin and was used in the 19th century as a windowless orphanage, then became a rat-infested rubbish dump and public lavatory. The Soviets used it to store vegetables until it was finally restored in 1967. Today, there is not a great deal to see beyond a handful of old cannons, but there is plenty of history to imagine in the darkness. The fat, round walls of the Subačiaus Gate, home to the Vilnius Executioner, used to stand adjacent to the Bastion. With his mask on, he would walk down Subačiaus to Town Hall Square where condemned prisoners awaited their fate. The Slavs who tended to live on Subačiaus said that they knew the executioner's identity, because their dogs would bark at him, mask on or off.

Higher Castle (*Arsenalo 5;* ✆ *5 261 7453;* *www.lnm.lt;* ⊕ *10.00–17.00 Tue–Sun; admission 4Lt*)

A climb via a cobbled path to the top of 50m-high Gediminas Hill rewards with a perfectly situated viewpoint across the rooftops and spires of the Old Town. A recently installed, super-smooth funicular railway, found in the courtyard of the Applied Arts Museum, makes the going easy up to this point. Take the natural next step and scramble to the summit – the viewing platform atop the Higher Castle – and the reward will be even greater.

In this 180° panorama it is possible to make out virtually every major landmark in Vilnius, from the Gothic spires of St Anne's Church in the east, to the new financial centre rising up from the grassy banks on the opposite side of the river. Vilnius's Soviet-era high-rise housing and Television Tower stand out among the trees on the horizon; if it were not for these, one would have the impression of a city surrounded on all sides by thick forest. As such, the Higher Castle makes an ideal place to begin or end a tour of the city. Normally, in summer, the best light for photography is in the later part of the day.

The museum housed in the castle shows models of the castles of Vilnius as they looked in the 14th and 17th centuries, as well as a display of weapons, armour and a few maps. Other than the tower, little remains of the castle save for the fragments of outer walls.

It can now be taken for granted that the Lithuanian flag will be raised on the castle tower every day. This first happened on 1 January 1919, but following the Polish seizure of Vilnius in 1920, it was not seen again here until 1939. The flag was banned again in 1944 when the Soviets established what seemed to be a permanent occupation, but was courageously raised once more on 7 October 1988, three years before their regime finally collapsed.

M K Čiurlionis Museum (*Savičiaus 11;* ✆ *5 262 2451;* ⊕ *10.00–16.00 Mon–Fri; admission free*)

The grand piano on which the gifted Lithuanian composer and painter wrote some of his best pieces is the main object of interest here. Prolific and yet at the same time a sufferer of depression and insomnia, M K Čiurlionis (1875–1911) lived in this small apartment in 1907–08. Fans of his paintings, like the cycle on the signs of the zodiac, will have to travel to the far more interesting Čiurlionis Museum in Kaunas.

Contemporary Art Centre (*Vokiečiu 2;* ✆ *5 262 3476; www.cac.lt;* ⊕ *12.00–21.00 Tue–Sun; admission 6Lt*) Right alongside the Town Hall stands the concrete-and-glass Contemporary Art Centre, which, although an ugly blot on the face of the Old Town, provides much-needed display space for exhibitions that are predominantly, but not exclusively, of the works of living artists. The shows here are usually highly original and often shocking. The gallery's single permanent display is on Fluxus, a bizarre experimental art movement led by the Lithuanian-born George Maciunas, friend of Yoko Ono and John Lennon, which thrived in the US in the 1960s.

Jewish Museum (*Pamenkalnio 12;* ✆ *5 262 0730; www.jmuseum.lt;* ⊕ *09.00–17.00 Mon–Thu, 09.00–16.00 Fri, 10.00–16.00 Sun; admission free*) The wooden 'green house' houses a documentary display focusing on Jewish culture and life in Vilnius and Lithuania immediately before World War II and its destruction during the Holocaust. Outside stands a monument entitled *Moonlight*, which commemorates Chiune Sugihara, the Kaunas-based Japanese diplomat who is credited with rescuing up to 6,000 Jews, by granting them transit visas through Japan and therefore the opportunity to leave Lithuania.

Housed in a tenement building at Pylimo 4 is the **Lithuanian State Jewish Museum**, on the first floor of which are displays of liturgical objects, dolls used for theatrical performances during the Feast of Purim, prints and drawings of Vilnius's Great Synagogue, and photographs, supplemented by a few tantalising fragments, of the wonderfully elaborate wooden synagogues, all now destroyed, which once graced several Lithuanian towns. Two rooms on the floor above are dedicated to a photographic record of memorial sites throughout Lithuania to victims of Nazism, and to a gallery honouring those who sheltered or otherwise saved Jews.

The Tolerance Centre (*Naugarduko 10*) opened in 2004 and the collections found at Pylimo 4 and Pamenkalnio 12 are being gradually transferred here.

KGB Museum (*Auku 2a;* ✆ *5 249 6264; www.genocide.lt/muziejus;* ⊕ *10.00–17.00 Tue–Sun; admission 4Lt*) The entrance to one of Vilnius's most essential sites is at the western side of the building, as the front on the square is now a memorial to the many people who died there. In Soviet guidebooks, the building is described simply as 'a municipal institution'. From the mid-1990s until 2005 the collection was constantly being expanded to give full details of Soviet repression against Lithuania (particularly the Siberian deportations), and on the resistance to it.

The cells in the basement, which were used for the imprisonment and torture of political opponents until 1991, can be visited. These include an isolation cell which has neither heating nor windows, a special padded and soundproofed cell for suicide risks, and two cells where water torture was administered in order to keep prisoners constantly awake.

There is documentary material on some of the most prominent victims, while sacks of incriminating documents shredded by the KGB in the final three years of Soviet rule are also on view. A former execution chamber opened to the public in 2003. Great efforts were made to conceal this activity from the other prisoners, including naming the area 'the kitchen' and delaying executions until the spring, when removal and burial of the bodies became easier.

There are short labels in good English throughout the museum, but it is certainly worth hiring the audio guide for a fuller explanation of the terrifying role this building played through the Soviet period in Lithuania. The ticket desk sells several books in English about repression at that time.

Adam Mickiewicz Museum (*Bernadinu 11;* ✆ *5 279 1879;* ⊕ *10.00–17.00 Tue–Fri, 10.00–14.00 Sat/Sun, closed Mon; admission 2Lt*) The famous Polish poet lived here for only two months, in 1822, but this apartment-museum provides the best insight into his life and creative mind to be found in Vilnius. It also shows paintings and engravings that reveal something of everyday life in the city at that time. Poland's greatest national poet is also one of Lithuania's national heroes, as the first words of his best-known epic *Pan Tadeusz* make perfectly clear: 'Lithuania, my homeland, you are like health. Only he who has lost you can know how much you are cherished.'

National Museum *(Arsenalo 1; ☎ 5 262 9426; ⊕ 10.00–18.00 Wed–Sun; admission 4Lt)*
Curios as diverse as a wonderfully ornate Baroque-style sledge from the 18th century, a handprint in iron of Peter the Great made at the opening of a smelting house in Belmontas, built to make guns for Russia's war against Sweden, and a Vilnius executioner's sword are just a few of the exhibits that brighten up the first hall. The sword, made in Germany in the early 17th century, is broken into two pieces, perhaps from a particularly tough neck. Exotic gifts from far and wide that have found their way here include a fan from the Emperor of Japan, presented to the officers of a Russian frigate in 1857, and an Egyptian sarcophagus that was a gift from the Museum of Prague in 1899.

Upstairs, a new exhibition celebrating Vilnius's millennial birthday in 2009 guides visitors through the history of Lithuania starting from 1,000 years ago. Fascinating maps, weapons, portraits, coins and other more unusual objects illustrate the battles against the Teutonic Order, the empire of the Grand Duchy, and everyday life in Vilnius in the centuries since then. The exhibition really emphasises the life of the citizens of Vilnius, the display showing satchels, plates, spoons, scarves and perfume bottles dating back to the 1600s. Another hall shows how rooms in typical Lithuanian farmsteads looked in centuries past. While large families often lived in cluttered surroundings, one room was always kept spotlessly clean in case visitors came to call unexpectedly. For an illuminating tour of the museum, ask for an English-speaking guide.

Pushkin Memorial Museum *(Subačiaus 124; ☎ 5 260 0080; ⊕ 10.00–17.00 Wed–Sun; admission 4Lt)*
A hike along Subačiaus out to Vilnius's farthest reaches, or a ride on bus number 10 southwards from the cathedral, will take you through the shadowy residential district of Markučiai to a park and a hilltop house. The great Russian poet never lived here, of course, but his son Grigorij (1835–1905) did, together with his wife Varvara (1855–1935). Today, this large, rather rickety wooden house is home to many volumes of Pushkin's works and other curios, the ground floor furnished in the style of the late 19th century. Stroll to the back of the house, past a statue of Pushkin, and the quiet grounds extend to steps leading down to a lake. Paths reach out from here into the surrounding countryside and are a delight to explore.

Radvila Palace *(Vilniaus 22; ☎ 5 262 0981; www.ldm.lt; ⊕ 12.00–17.00 Tue–Sun; admission 5Lt)*
A generally austere collection of art from the 16th century onwards. Built for Jonušas Radvila, Voivod of Vilnius and Grand Hetman of Lithuania, this 17th-century Renaissance-style palace is now used mainly for showcasing 165 portrait engravings of Radvila family members, and also for the odd music concert.

Theatre, Music and Film Museum *(Vilniaus 41; ☎ 5 262 2406; www.teatras.mch.mii.lt; ⊕ 12.00–18.00 Tue–Fri, 11.00–16.00 Sat; admission 4Lt)*
Despite its name, the 'display' on film is disappointingly cursory, with the briefest of looks at Lithuanian successes during the later Soviet years and virtually nothing on Lithuanian directors and actors since then. This history of the performing arts instead concentrates on the glory days before World War II, with keyboard instruments, still-working musical boxes and musty theatre costumes. One local theatre-turned-cinema director explains his request for subsidies from the Lithuanian government with his idea that, 'In future cultural life, films will take the place of the theatre.'

Kazys Varnelis House Museum (*Didžioji 26;* ☏ *5 279 1644; www.lnm.lt;* ⊕ *10.00–17.00 Tue–Sat; admission free but tours must be pre-booked*) It would almost be easier to describe what this eclectic art museum does not contain, rather than what it does. From his arrival in the USA in 1949, Kazys combined his work in op art with a passion for collecting just at the time when prices were low and quantities high. He had as much an eye for Chinese painting as he did for British first editions, Italian Renaissance furniture or Lithuanian cartography. Throughout the museum the best of old Europe combines with the best of modern America and the map collection has no equal anywhere. There are 170 maps in total, nearly all of them of Lithuania and the surrounding region. Ample space and light are provided for the fascinating collection of modern art. Although born in 1917, Kazys was still painting in the studio at the top of this house in 2007. The studio can usually be visited, as can the Gothic brick cellars, which date from the 15th century. The museum is open only by appointment so it is essential to email (*kvmuziejus@lnm.lt*) or phone ahead, or make arrangements through a travel agent who works with Lithuania.

Vilnius Picture Gallery (*Didžioji 4;* ☏ *5 212 4258; www.ldm.lt;* ⊕ *12.00–18.00 Tue–Sat, 12.00–17.00 Sun, closed Mon; admission 5Lt*) This state-run gallery shows in chronological order the development of painting in Lithuania and there are some real gems to discover, in particular where the main art movements of 19th-century Europe are reflected in Lithuanian art. The gallery's first rooms begin with portraits, some dating as far back as the 16th century. The portraits of former rulers give an insight into the colourful history of the Polish–Lithuanian state.

Artists to look out for include Jan Rustemas, who became head of the city's first department of painting at Vilnius University in 1819. Born in Turkey to Greek parents, he lived in Warsaw and Berlin before bringing influences from these cities to Lithuania. He is credited with steering students away from Classicism and towards Romanticism. Vincentas Dmachauskas's intense *Forest Fire* is a dramatic record of the destruction of the country's forests in the 19th century, monstrous fires that were also described by local writers and poets. There are also some evocative impressionist landscapes, such as Juozas Balzukevičius's *Across a Ryefield*.

CHURCHES
Vilnius Cathedral (*Katedros 1;* ☏ *5 261 1127;* ⊕ *09.00–20.00 daily*) There is more to this grandiose display of neo-Classicism than meets the eye. The Chapel of St Casimir inside is a flamboyant Baroque masterpiece with some breathtaking stucco work, while the cathedral's creepy crypt reaches into the bowels of the earth to reveal a fascinating cross-section of history, from the pagan to the present.

The cathedral occupies the site of what was once an ancient, open pagan temple revered by Lithuanians and dedicated to the worship of Perkūnas, god of thunder and fire. According to some accounts, toads, grass snakes and other sacred creatures were kept nearby, ready for sacrifice on an altar that stood about 5m high. A fire blazed in a hollow in the temple, kept alight day and night. Virgins chosen for their beauty had the task of keeping the temple flames burning. If they failed, they were drowned with a cat and a snake, or were buried alive.

Over the 800 years since these pagan times, five consecutive cathedral buildings have been built on the site, each in turn ravaged by fire, flood or war. Twelve different floors can be identified in the crypt, right down to the pagan altar itself. The earliest floor, dating from the 13th century, is now 3m deep. One or two glazed terracotta tiles that have survived from this time are on show by the entrance. You can also make out the top of the doorway of the very first cathedral, built by Mindaugas, the man who unified the Baltic tribes for the first time. He was baptised with his family around 1251, and erected a cathedral, a square building with a massive tower, shortly afterwards. The pagan lords and tribes were not happy with this sudden conversion, and when they killed Mindaugas ten years later, the building was converted for use as a temple.

Grand Duke Jogaila converted to Christianity in 1387, uniting Lithuania and Poland. He took the name Wladislaw (Ladislaus) and built a church here dedicated to St Ladislaus and Poland's patron saint Stanislaus. This stood until a fire in 1419. Grand Duke Vytautas rebuilt it as a huge, Gothic, red-brick cathedral full of expressive architectural detail. It stood almost 8m taller than the present cathedral, and was completed only in 1430, the year Vytautas died. It was damaged by fire on several occasions in the next 300 years, and was repeatedly rebuilt and restored. But this was marshy ground, and in the mid 1700s the foundations started sinking. Cracks appeared and in 1769 a severe storm blew down the south tower, killing six people.

Extensive reconstruction giving the cathedral its final shape started in 1783, according to a design by Laurynas Stuoka-Gucevičius. His idea, fashionable at the time, was to give the appearance, inside and out, of a real Greek temple. In fact, the neo-Classical style is very rare for a cathedral. Stuoka-Gucevičius also designed Vilnius Town Hall, the palace at Verkiai, and also the wonderful circular church in the village of Sudervė, 25km northwest of Vilnius. The cathedral was his last great work.

The great crypt was the final resting place for grand dukes, archbishops, noblemen and their families. There are about 20 vaults under the floor of the naves and chapels. Some have yet to be discovered, undisturbed behind thick walls. The remains of Alexander, Grand Duke of Lithuania and King of Poland at the turn of the 16th century, and the wives of Sigismund Augustus – Elzbieta and Barbora Radvilaitė – were discovered in 1931. They were moved through the crypt to a hauntingly lit mausoleum. Barbora has a special place in the nation's heart. She and Sigismund were married out of love and kept their union a secret from the scheming nobles of the Polish–Lithuanian Commonwealth until she died mysteriously in 1551.

Under the Soviets, Vilnius Cathedral was closed and the three huge statues of saints Helena, Casimir and Stanislaus on the pediment were hauled down and demolished. After Stalin's death in 1953, the building became an art gallery. Finally, during the first congress of national revival in 1988, it was declared that the cathedral would be returned to the Church. Eight years later, after independence, replicas of the saints' statues were returned to their place on the grand façade.

The curious cupola that conflicts with the cathedral's overall design stands out as the stunning Baroque Chapel of St Casimir, a survivor of the earlier cathedral building. With red marble from Galicia, black and brown marble from the Carpathian Mountains, lavish stucco and 17th-century frescoes, the chapel is a feast for the eyes. Exquisitely decorated by Italian masters over a period of 14 years from 1622, for the sum of 500,000 gold coins, it was built as a final resting place for the remains of St Casimir, the patron saint of Lithuania, who died in 1484.

Casimir was the youngest son of a wealthy family whose brothers and sisters became kings and queens of European states through lineage and marriage. The pious Casimir, however, was more interested in charity and would go to the cathedral to pray even at night. When he died from tuberculosis at the age of 25, it was rumoured that his coffin could cure illness and disease. A fresco on one side of the chapel shows the legend of Uršulė, a sick orphan who prayed beneath the coffin and found herself miraculously cured. The fresco on the wall opposite shows the moment when the coffin was opened by clergy to see if the body was still well preserved – the sign of a saint. It was, of course, and Casimir was canonised in 1602.

The chapel has some odd features. A 17th-century retable (a decorative panel at the back of an altar) shows a *Madonna and Child*. The Madonna has a surprisingly broad smile, very unusual for this kind of reverent artwork. In front of it, a silver-coated portrait shows St Casimir with three hands. Some say this was to emphasise his generosity – he gave as if from three hands. Look up into the cupola and you'll see beasts and objects finely moulded from stucco – an elephant for moderation (an elephant never eats more than his/her share), an elk to prevent rash decisions, and a mirror to see both sides of an argument.

The chapel nearest the entrance on the southern side is now known as the 'Deportees Chapel' because of the recent memorials that have been erected there to the many senior figures in the Church who were persecuted in Soviet times. One of the statues is of Mečislovas Reinys, who was Archbishop of Vilnius before his arrest in 1947. He died in 1953 in Vladimir Prison near Moscow. Another is of Vincentas Borisevičius, Bishop of Telšiai until he was executed in 1947 for the 'crime' of being a 'bourgeois leader'. His final words were: 'Your hour of victory is brief; the future is mine; Christ will be victorious, just as Lithuania will be victorious.' It would be 40 years before he was proved right.

Church of St Anne (*Maironio 8;* ℡ *5 261 4805;* ⊕ *08.30–18.00 daily*) A masterpiece of late Gothic, the enchanting façade features 33 shapes and sizes of red bricks arranged in flamboyant patterns. Its intricate towers, spires and narrow windows were enough to enchant Napoleon, who in an oft-quoted remark said that he wished he could carry it back to Paris on the palm of his hand. He is, in fact, unlikely to have said such a thing, since like the rest of Europe in 1812 he disliked Gothic intensely as an outmoded style. Lithuanians saw Napoleon as a liberator from the grip of Tsarist Russia and probably concocted this story themselves. The French leader stationed some of his cavalry in St Anne's and most of its stained glass was broken and the wax ceilings destroyed by the soldiers' campfires.

The mystery of who designed the church endures to this day. One tale tells of a talented young Lithuanian apprentice named Jonas who helped his master from Belarus in the initial stages of construction before going to study architecture abroad. On his return he mocked his old master's work and completed the church in a flourish while the offended master vanished for several years. During this time Jonas married the master's daughter and settled into the family home. Late one stormy night, the master returned and insisted on Jonas showing him the brickwork. On the scaffolding, the more Jonas enthusiastically explained his work, the more envy the master felt. Eventually he pushed Jonas over the edge. Jonas caught hold of a piece of overhanging wood, but the master took a brick and brought it crashing down on Jonas's head. This tale of the outré may be mere legend, but it is strange how the lower part of the façade appears so much more austere than the rest. It is also true that in written records there were two architects, one known simply as 'Johannes', the other not mentioned at all.

Bernardine Church/Church of SS Francis & Bernardino (*Maironio 10;* ℡ *5 260 9292;* ⊕ *08.30–18.00 daily*) More than just the Gothic backdrop to St Anne's, the Bernardine Church is impressive in its sheer size. The vaulting is wondrous, but tragically the rest of the interior did not escape the ravages of the centuries. Fire, war and neglect left it to rot until 1994 when it was returned to the brethren of St Francis. Students from Vilnius Art Academy have slowly been renovating it ever since. Mass in English is held here every Sunday at 17.00.

Church of St Casimir (*Didžioji 34;* ℡ *5 212 1715;* ⊕ *10.00–18.00 daily*) The oldest Baroque church in Vilnius, St Casimir's was founded by Jesuits in 1604. Named after Lithuania's patron saint, who had just been canonised, it's modelled on Il Gesu in Rome, the Jesuits' much-imitated mother church, but with characteristically Lithuanian twin spires set on top. St Casimir's has suffered many abuses through the centuries, including 20 years of humiliation as the Soviets' museum of atheism. Locals especially recall the prime exhibit – a re-creation of Inquisition torture implements,

displayed to show the cruelty of the medieval Catholic Church. Now it is back in the safe hands of the original owners. The glittering crown on the central dome symbolises the royal family that Casimir came from (see Vilnius Cathedral, page 208). It was placed there in 1942.

Church of St Catherine (*Vilniaus 30; closed to the public except during concerts*) This rather intimidating structure originally belonged to a Benedictine convent founded in 1618. Following a series of fires, it was rebuilt between 1741 and 1753 by the Vilnius-born Polish architect Jan Krzysztof Glaubitz, who also designed the extraordinary Basilian Gates. In order to overcome the restricted nature of the site, he adopted an audacious design based on a nave which is as high as it is long. The exterior features an elaborate rear-facing gable as a counterbalance to the majestic twin-towered façade. The interior is richly furnished, but has not been accessible for many years because of ongoing restoration work. Recently, however, the church has been opening on selected evenings as an evocative venue for chamber music concerts.

Church of the Holy Spirit (Catholic) (*Dominikonų 8;* \ *5 262 9595;* ⊕ *07.00–18.00 daily*) A Dominican friary established in Vilnius in 1501 gave Dominikonų Street its name. Its extravagant Church of the Holy Spirit, a lavish display of Baroque furnishings and decoration that are almost Rococo in appearance, is a suitable setting for several hauntings and unexplained events. The interior was ravaged by fire in the 18th century and almost completely remade. Its huge crypt, which extends underground even beyond the walls of the church, was used to bury corpses from the Napoleonic Wars and, before that, plague victims. The bodies remain incredibly well preserved, stacked up on top of each other. It is not possible to go down there.

Strangely, the church was not closed by the Soviets and remained a place of worship throughout the last century. Today it is the religious heart of Vilnius's Polish community. The eye of the visitor is drawn immediately to the altarpiece, which depicts a vision of Christ as he appeared in a miracle to a local nun in 1931. The painting, *Divine Mercy*, was completed by the Vilnius artist Eugenijus Kazimierovskis (1873–1939) in 1934 but only after ten attempts to portray the vision as accurately as possible. The inscription 'Jezu ufam tobie' means 'Jesus, I trust in thee'. To the Polish community, the wide rays of red and white light represent their flag. The painting was hidden in the countryside through most of the Soviet period, only being brought back to this church in 1986 at the beginning of the *perestroika* period. Its long-term location is a matter of considerable dispute, as a chapel over the road has been built to house it but the Polish community is eager to keep it where it now stands and where Pope Paul II saw it on his 1993 visit to Vilnius.

Statues of King David and angel musicians adorn the beautifully carved case that protects an organ made in 1776 by Adam Casparini. This is the oldest organ in Vilnius and a model of it is being built for Christ Church at the University of Rochester, New York. It should be finished in 2008.

Church of the Holy Spirit (Orthodox) (*Aušros Vartų 10;* \ *5 212 7765;* ⊕ *08.00–18.00 daily*) The most revered of the city's Russian Orthodox churches stands in a peaceful courtyard away from the bustle of Aušros Vartų Street. There is not actually a great deal to distinguish it from the surrounding Catholic churches, it having been rebuilt by the genius of the late Baroque period Jan Krzysztof Glaubitz after a fire in 1749. But the most important feature makes it a popular place of pilgrimage for Orthodox Christians – the well-preserved bodies of saints Anthony, Ivan and Eustace, killed by pagans in 1347 for not renouncing their faith. The three lie in a glass-topped case shrouded in red most of the year, in white during Christmas and black during Lent. Should you be in Vilnius on 26 June, however, visit this church to feel the healing spirit that is said to envelop it when the bodies are unveiled.

Church of St John (*Šv Jono 12;* ❧ *5 261 1795;* ⊕ *for services 11.00–13.00 Sun*)

Immediately after Grand Duke Jogaila shed his pagan beliefs to convert to Christianity in 1387, he commissioned this church, completed 40 years later. Originally Gothic, the awe-inspiring Baroque façade you see today was designed once again by Jan Krzysztof Glaubitz, in the 1740s. The interior, accessible from a university courtyard, boasts a high altar consisting of no fewer than ten interconnected altars. One of the many memorials inside is dedicated to the memory of Adam Mickiewicz.

Church of SS Peter and Paul (*Antakalnio 1;* ❧ *5 234 0229;* ⊕ *07.00–19.00 daily*)

One of Vilnius's most stunning Baroque churches, with twin-tower façade and a central dome, the magnificent Church of SS Peter and Paul was completed in 1685. It was built on the site of a wooden church that had been burned by pillaging Russians during their destructive invasion 30 years earlier. This was a time of almost constant war, but churches like this continued to rise up. The man who commissioned the Church of SS Peter and Paul was Mykolaj Casimir Pac, Field Hetman of the Grand Duchy of Lithuania. His appeal to the Mother of God above the church entrance is not for strength in war, but for an end to war: 'Regina pacis fundanos in pace' ('Queen of peace, protect us in peace'), although this could simply have been a playful pun on the patron's name.

Mythological scenes and strange creatures, flowers, trees, and over 2,000 human figures in stucco decorate the rich interior. Baroque also placed a lot of emphasis on death, which accounts for the array of skulls, skeletons, dragons and demons immediately on the left and right as you walk in. Criminals were not allowed to enter any further into the nave than this point and the ugly images were meant to remind them of the consequences of sin.

In the amazing figures and images in stucco, stories can be made out. Many relate to the sea, since Peter and Paul were both fishermen, and possibly the main curiosity in the entire church is an enormous, boat-shaped chandelier, hanging from the cupola like a grand cluster of jewels, magnificently catching the light.

If the bottom of the kettledrum close to the altar to Mary on the left appears blackened, this is because it also doubled in times of war as a cooking pot and a bath for the soldiers.

Gates of Dawn (*Aušros Vartų 12;* ❧ *5 212 3513;* ⊕ *09.00–17.00 daily*) One of the

essential sights on any trip to Vilnius, the 16th-century Gates of Dawn – originally part of the city's fortifications – now hold a small chapel housing a gold-and-silver holy image of the Virgin Mary, the Madonna of Mercy, which overlooks the street through open windows. Locals cross themselves every time they walk underneath it, while the most devout of worshippers crawl piously on their knees up steps from a doorway on the left. Unless you want to crawl too, climb past them to inspect the miracle-working icon up close. Afterwards, pass out of the gates to find part of the original city wall stretching down a dark back alley towards the Artillery Bastion.

LANDMARKS

Europa Tower (*Konstitucijos 7a;* ❧ *5 248 7171; www.europa.lt;* ⊕ *09.00–18.00 Sat/Sun only; admission free*) Thirty-three floors up in the Europa Tower, the tallest skyscraper in the Baltic countries, completed in 2004, the view of central Vilnius is unrivalled. It's perfect for a bird's-eye perspective on where the best vacant lots of real estate are hiding. And getting to the top is free. There is only one restriction: the Europa Tower is a caffeine-fuelled office building, which means that the resident companies do not want unruly groups of sightseers milling around, clogging up the lifts. So access to the public is only at the weekend. Otherwise, groups can call ahead to book visits on weekdays.

After an ear-popping elevator ride to the top, the open air is invigorating. The 33rd floor is an open terrace facing southwards, while the vista to the north is from office space that can be rented out for seminars or private parties, for which food and drink can be ordered from one of the eateries in the Europa shopping centre below. Both views stretch the full 180°.

It's the panorama to the south that grabs the attention, taking in the Old Town, the river and the brand-new smattering of nearby skyscrapers. From this height, however, some of the buildings become virtually indistinguishable and the tall glass barrier also slightly obscures the visibility. But it's the thrill of standing on one of the highest viewpoints for hundreds of kilometres around that you should come for.

Looking north, you can see Vilnius's ragbag of old and new suburbs – the tumbledown wooden shacks of Šnipiškės, which will soon disappear to make way for new buildings, and in the distance masses of identical Soviet-era residential blocks.

Gariūnai Market For years one of the biggest open-air markets in eastern Europe, Gariūnai these days is dominated by poor-quality products from China and Turkey. The sprawling market stands in the shadow of the city's water-heating plant, about 10km west of the city centre on the road to Kaunas. The stalls sell pushchairs, lightbulbs, pirate DVDs, hi-fis, bad coffee, you name it. Some of the clothes sellers have recently gone upmarket with permanent stalls that actually resemble small shops. The rest, though, is set up from scratch early in the morning, which explains why so many of the salespeople yawn at you. In the early 1990s it was rumoured you could buy weapons here by finding the man with the toy gun on his bonnet. The best times to go are weekend mornings; by noon the market is closing up. Watch your wallet/handbag.

Paneriai (*Agrastų 17;* ☎ *5 260 2001*) Out in the forests to the southwest of Vilnius lies the village of Paneriai, consisting mostly of close-knit wooden houses, unpaved streets, a railway track and stray dogs. Close by, about 100,000 people were murdered in a clearing, their bodies burned in pits. Most of them were Jews from Vilnius – a fact ignored in the wording on the memorials here until 1990. In fact, a dance hall was raised on the site in the early Soviet period. Today, the pits are displayed, the whole place eerily quiet except for the occasional passing train. It is notoriously hard to find due to the shameful lack of signposting. Take a train going to Trakai and get off at the Paneriai stop. Walk along the lane that runs more-or-less parallel to the tracks in the same direction the train is heading. The memorial lies at the end of the road, after about a kilometre. A small branch of the Lithuanian State Jewish Museum displays some photographs, but it has no set opening times and is closed in winter.

Television Tower (*Sausio 13-osios 10;* ☎ *5 252 5333;* ⏲ *12.00–21.00 daily; admission 15Lt, children 6Lt*) Venture out into the 'sleeping districts' of Vilnius's high-rise suburbs at least once during your stay and experience this Soviet vision of the 1970s space age, with an unequalled panorama from its 55th-floor restaurant. Christened Paukščių Takas, Lithuanian for 'Milky Way', when it opened in 1980, the restaurant is 165m up and rotates slowly so that a full circle is completed in 50 minutes. On a clear day you can see up to 70km in every direction (don't come if the sky is thick with cloud), when you will discover just how amazingly green Lithuania really is. Coniferous forests stretch out to the horizon. The Old Town and Vilnius's landmark buildings are clearly visible just to the east. Beyond, you can spy on Belarus, the last dictatorship in Europe, only 40km away.

6

Before you shoot up in the high-speed elevator, you have a choice at the reception of either paying the entry fee and then having the freedom of the menu, or taking one of four set meals for about double the price, which includes the entry fee. We recommend the former, since the set meals are more a convenient tool for the restaurant when coping with groups.

Before you leave, pay your respects to the 14 Lithuanian civilians who died here defending the Television Tower from Soviet tanks on the night of 13 January 1991. A small exhibition remembering this tragic event can be found on the ground floor. Outside, granite markers show the precise places where the victims were crushed beneath tanks or shot. Sadly, the surroundings look a little unkempt, weeds protruding through the concrete blocks.

However, the tower comes to life in December when it becomes what is claimed to be the tallest artificial Christmas tree in the world, with fairy lights stretching up its entire height.

Verkiai Palace (*Žaliujų ežerų 47;* ℡ *5 271 1618;* ⊕ *09.00–17.00 Mon–Fri; admission 3Lt*)

The remains of a superb Classical mansion stand on a hill just to the north of Vilnius. The land here belonged to grand dukes until 1387, when Jogaila, on his conversion to Christianity, granted it to the new diocese of Vilnius to be used by the bishops as a summer residence. In 1780, a huge palace was constructed here, but Napoleon's soldiers ravaged it in 1812. Soon after that the central part of the palace was pulled down.

Today, the rooms in the remaining wings of the palace contain a great deal of handsome, intricate woodwork and some attractive painted ceilings. There's also a lovely view of the forested River Neris valley below, and at the very end of the ridge is a fireplace surrounded by stones. A legend tells how a sacred fire was once tended on this spot by a pagan priest and beautiful virgins.

Walk down the long flight of steps to an old mill, recently renovated into a restaurant, named Verkių Vandens Malūnas. It serves delicious homemade meals and has peaceful outdoor seating overlooking the river in summer.

Vilnius University (*Universiteto 3;* ℡ *5 261 1795;* ⊕ *09.00–17.00 Mon–Sat*) The oldest

university in eastern Europe is a maze of 12 courtyards, corridors, halls and towers. It is a delight to explore and usually no-one will mind if you do. An absurd practice of selling tickets at the gate was recently established, but we recommend you walk directly through with a sense of purpose, pretending you're a visiting professor or a mature student. A basic map of the complicated layout is at Universiteto 7.

Founded by the Jesuits in 1570 and given university status in 1579, Vilnius University has not always been allowed to flourish and contribute to the cultural, social and political life of the city. Many of its students and professors have aided the resistance against virtually every occupation, often to find themselves persecuted, even executed. The entire university was closed by the Russian Tsarist authorities in 1832 for backing the failed rebellion the year before. It stayed closed until 1919, the year after Lithuanian independence was regained.

At the far end of the initial Sarbievijus Courtyard is the lovely Littera bookshop, whose walls and ceiling were painstakingly decorated by local painter Antanas Kmieliauskas in preparation for the university's 400th birthday in 1979. In fact, the university as a whole is in good condition because of the extensive renovations made in time for that event. Another artist, Petras Repšys, created the stunning fresco cycle in the Centre for Lithuanian Studies next door, working at it for nine years, finishing in 1985.

Up a flight of steps from the Sarbievijus Courtyard is the Great Courtyard, dominated on one side by the monumental Baroque façade of St John's Church. There is an almost Mediterranean flavour to the open arcades around the courtyard, while faded frescoes from the 18th century show figures who influenced the early part of the life of the university. An arch in the western side of the courtyard leads to a small but charmingly leafy courtyard beside the Observatory, the walls of which are decorated with the signs of the zodiac.

CEMETERIES Vilnius has a number of cemeteries set amid the hills around the city centre that are really worth visiting, if time permits, for they reflect aspects of the city's tumultuous history. Reach Antakalnis Cemetery by walking beyond the Church of SS Peter and Paul up busy Antakalnio Street, bearing right onto L Sapiegos then turning right onto progressively quieter Kuosų and Karių. The Bernadine Cemetery is found, eerie and cut off from the rest of the city, in Užupis, at the end of a little lane off Polocko Street. Rasa Cemetery is best reached by strolling up Rasų Street away from Subačiaus in the Old Town.

Antakalnis Cemetery (Antakalnio kapinės) A calm and peaceful place that brings together much of Vilnius's modern history, the biggest public cemetery in Vilnius has elegantly carved old memorial stones covering the rolling, tree-shaded landscape, the crosses and tombs adorned and inscribed in Lithuanian, Russian and Polish. Following the paved path into the cemetery, you find a series of identical stone crosses over to the left dedicated to Polish soldiers killed during World War I – as bloody and tragic a conflict in eastern Europe as it was in the West. By taking paths to the right, you'll find broadly chiselled Soviet-era statues in the Socialist Realist style, commemorating those poets and political leaders who toed the Party line. Cut into a hill at the cemetery's heart is a sweeping, semicircular memorial to the 14 people who died defending the Television Tower and the Parliament building in January 1991.

Bernardine Cemetery (Bernadinų kapinės) Beautifully perched on a high bank above the little River Vilnia, at the far end of the quaint suburb of Užupis, is this tranquil spot, tightly packed with lopsided metal crosses and tiny, uneven plots. Founded in 1810, this quiet retreat holds the last resting places of university academics and painters. Over the long years, trees have gently elbowed their way between the tombs, making them even more irregular, gradually spilling through railings that fence off the graves. Desolate and wonderfully gloomy, there's no calmer place in Vilnius.

Rasa Cemetery (Rasų kapinės) Deceptively isolated, this hill of crosses contains the graves of famous Lithuanians like Jonas Basanavičius, the founder at the end of the 19th century of the first Lithuanian-language newspaper *Aušra* (Dawn). He lies close to the chapel, while uphill from the main entrance lies the tombstone of revered painter and composer M K Čiurlionis. Right next to the entrance, however, is a more controversial site – the family plot of the Polish leader Josef Pilsudski, the man responsible for Poland's annexation of Vilnius in 1920. He was buried in Krakow, but his heart was cut out and buried here, in this tomb. Rasa Cemetery has been a place of spiritual reverence also during troubled times. In October 1956, a small crowd of daring Lithuanians gathered here to protest against the suppression of the Hungarian uprising.

EXCURSIONS FROM VILNIUS

Vilnius offers a wide choice of places to visit for a half- or full-day excursion and it is well worth extending a short break to allow time for these. Kaunas (see pages 217–30) definitely requires a full day and staying the night is also worthwhile to give more time to cover what it offers. A half-day in Trakai is enough for seeing the spectacular Island

Castle, but not for walking around the lake and the charming village. Details of Trakai and many other places near Vilnius can be found in *Lithuania: The Bradt Travel Guide* (see page 292). **Europos Parkas** can be covered in half a day; about two hours is probably sufficient to cover the array of sculptures, but in good weather a leisurely day could happily be spent there.

EUROPOS PARKAS (*10km north of Vilnius; follow the signs off the road that passes Verkai & the Green Lakes;* ⟍ *5 237 7077; www.europosparkas.lt;* ⊕ *09.00–sunset; admission 20Lt*) There's a lot of talk about the concept of Europe in Lithuania, just as there is in the other EU countries. Here, however, it is brought to life just a few kilometres from the 'centre of Europe' as defined in 1989 by the French National Geographic Institute. Although only about 10km north of Vilnius, access by public transport is very difficult, so it is worth joining a group tour or sharing a taxi with others. Europa Park is an open-air museum of mostly bizarre modern sculptures in a woodland and meadow setting (take insect repellent in July), with exhibits specially created for the site by around 100 different artists from 30 countries around the world.

Founded in 1991, it is the brainchild of the Lithuanian sculptor Gintaras Karosas who had conceived the idea a few years earlier while still a teenager and who did much of the preparatory work of clearing the site with his own hands. He created the pivotal Monument of the Centre of Europe which features a pyramid and indications of the direction and distances to a range of worldwide capitals, of which the furthest away is Wellington in New Zealand. Karosas was also responsible for the heavily symbolic *Infotree* by the park entrance, which gained an entry in the *Guinness World Records* for being the world's largest artwork of television sets. There are 3,000 in all, arranged (when viewed from above) in the shape of a tree, with a decaying statue of Lenin in the middle.

Chair Pool by the American Dennis Oppenheim is the most popular work, and also the most humorous, as its subject is exactly what the title suggests, a giant chair with a small pool instead of a seat. The success of this led to the commissioning of a second composition from Oppenheim, *Drinking Structure with Exposed Kidney Pool*, consisting of a hut dipping down towards the water. Other sculptures guaranteed to catch the eye are Magdalena Abakanowicz's *Space of Unknown Growth*, a group of 22 concrete boulders; Jon Barlow Hudson's *Cloud Hands*, which consists of four granite blocks seemingly suspended in the air; and the 6m-high *Woman Looking at the Moon* by the Mexican Javier Cruz.

Kaunas LITHUANIA

Telephone code 37

That Kaunas was a capital for 20 years, from 1920 to 1940, becomes quickly apparent when walking through the town from the bus or railway station into the town. Like Bonn for Germany in the post-war era, Kaunas was officially a 'provisional' capital, as the Lithuanian government was forced to flee there when the Poles were clearly not willing to give up Vilnius. If the former presidential palace now seems modest, this did not prevent the government from building ministries, museums and churches that over 60 years later have not lost any of their grandeur, even if they have now lost their original function. Other legacies from that era are two funicular railways and two large river bridges.

Two names which even today's local visitors remember are those of Darius and Girėnas, pilots who in 1933 almost succeeded in flying non-stop from New York to Kaunas but sadly crashed and were killed in East Prussia. A sports stadium and an airport are named after them, as is a major street. The wreck of their plane, together with their blood-stained shirts, is displayed in the War Museum. Their statues are amongst the largest in Kaunas and their portraits are on the 10Lt note.

HISTORY

Being a crossing on the Nemunas (Memel) River, and at the junction where the Neris River joins it, Kaunas has for centuries been a frequent battleground between all Lithuania's largest neighbours eager to subject it. Napoleon fought for the town in 1812 and the Russians then built a circle of fortresses to defend what was the westernmost outpost of their empire. The capture of these forts by the Germans in 1915 would lead to their victory over Tsarist Russia and then to Lithuanian independence. Throughout the 19th century the Russians banned building on the nearby hills and allowed none in the town to have more than two storeys, so concerned were they at the potential threat from the Germans. They took no interest in preserving the town's varied architectural legacy or in contributing to a new one.

When the German government was reluctantly forced to make Bonn a provisional capital in 1949, they at least had a serious cultural centre on which to base it. Kaunas by 1920 had declined to little more than a dilapidated village. One journalist described it as 'a cramped and exceedingly unhealthy town of mean streets and wretched wooden houses'. Another wrote of the open drains beside all the main roads and the tram-cars dragged along by a single horse. All visitors complained of the lack of hygiene in the one small hotel in the town but only one diplomat admitted to solving this problem by finding '*une petite amie*' who offered much more congenial accommodation.

It would be the 1930s before the government unofficially planned on the basis that Kaunas would be a permanent capital. Officially they used the 500th anniversary of the death in 1430 of Grand Duke Vytautas, when the Lithuanian Empire was at its largest, as a pretext for commemoration. Most of the majestic buildings along and

217

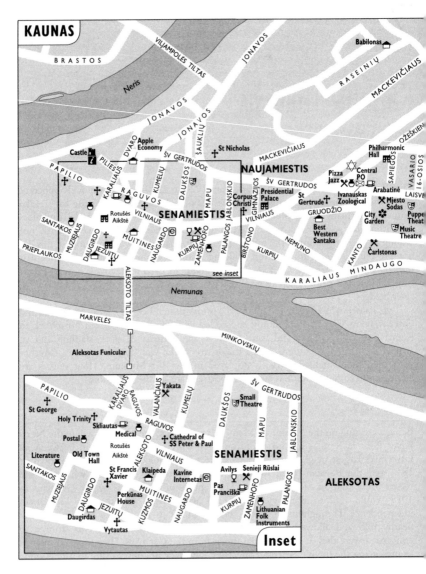

beside Laisvės Alėja reflect this change in policy. Vytautas Landsbergis, whose son of the same name led Lithuania to independence around 1990, was one of several architects involved in building a serious Kaunas at that time. By 1940, this development had become so extensive and so solid that it would survive 50 years of Soviet rule.

Kaunas was often at the forefront of Lithuanian resistance to Russia, whatever the nature of the St Petersburg or Moscow regime. Two uprisings took place in the 19th century, in 1831 and 1863; then in 1972 a 19-year-old student Romas Kalanta burning himself to death in public became the precursor of many other demonstrations against Moscow.

Since independence Kaunas has not really found a new role for itself as Vilnius is eager to make up for the 20 years it did not have as a capital. New political movements

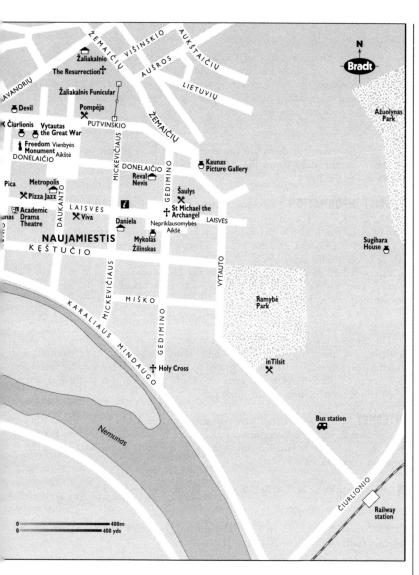

no longer start here and most of the 20 mayors the town had between 1991 and 2007 showed little sense of direction, a state of affairs Vilnius was happy to exploit. With Vilnius as European Capital of Culture in 2009, Kaunas has an even tougher task in presenting itself to the outside world as an independent entity. However a trebling of property prices between 2003 and 2006 shows that business is now keen to bring it to life again.

PRACTICALITIES

Kaunas is somewhat more demanding on tourists than the region's capitals in that it has no obvious centre. Using public transport is a must here and the erratic museum opening hours will give rise to some frustration. However minor effort

The most famous resident of Kaunas known worldwide was Dr Ludoviko Zamenhof, who invented Esperanto whilst still running his medical practice. A street is named after him, and a travel agency Bonvoje based there offers tours with Esperanto-speaking guides. The bookshop Septynios Vienatves on Daukšos 31 has a dedicated Esperanto section.

will be well rewarded; there are museums and buildings here with no parallel elsewhere in the Baltics and the two funicular railways add a further sense of quirkiness to the town.

TOURIST INFORMATION The main **Tourist Information Centre** is at Laisvės 36 (\ *37 323436;* e *info@kaunastic.lt; www.visit. kaunas.lt;* ⊕ *09.00–18.00 Mon–Sat*). It has a lot of useful free leaflets with basic information on the main attractions but there are no detailed guidebooks available in any foreign language, either on the town as a whole or on specific aspects of it.

The jewellery shop **Kauno Vartai** (*Rotušės 29; www.kaunovartai.lt*) on Town Hall Square, next to the Pharmacy Museum, acts as a branch of the main tourist information centre, holding its leaflets and selling useful maps and tasteful souvenirs. Its website is in fact a tourism one as well, and the office is also open on Sundays between May and September.

The *Survival Guide* published by the university lists every possible service that a student, and therefore a tourist. might want. Obviously its restaurant and entertainment recommendations are geared to younger people but they list prices and facilities in excellent English and costs are clearly spelt out. It is available online at www.vdu.lt/international/survival_guide.pdf.

INTERNET Most Kaunas hotels have computers in their lobby which guests can use free of charge, within reason. Internet cafés seem to come and go more frequently here than in other towns, but amongst those operating since 2003, so likely to continue doing so, are:

e Kavinė Internetas Vilniaus 24; ⊕ 09.00–22.00 daily

e Skylė Ožeškienės 5; ⊕ 24hr daily
e OK Maironio 13; ⊕ 09.00–24.00 daily

In 2007 they charged 3Lt an hour. The general post office at Laisvės 102 also has internet facilities (⊕ *0.00–20.00*), at 2Lt an hour.

TRANSPORT

BY AIR No-frills flights with Ryanair from London Stansted direct to Kaunas started in autumn 2005; they were followed by services to Dublin, Frankfurt and Liverpool. Wizzair operated from Warsaw in 2006/7 but currently (spring 2008) are not doing so. Whilst discussions for such flights had been going on intermittently for several years previously, it seemed that only in 2005 was Kaunas's Karmėlava Airport willing to accept the terms no-frills carriers dictate and it is ironic that at the time of writing the only carrier there is the most dominant one in this field. Ryanair's arrival should have led to a considerable increase in tourism to Kaunas but this has yet to happen. Many tourists travel directly to Vilnius or Klaipeda from the airport and the majority of travellers are still Lithuanians working abroad. Serious overseas promotion of Kaunas has yet to start.

The airport, sometimes known as **Karmėlava** after the suburb where it is situated, is 12km northeast of the town centre. (There is also a small private airport to the south of the town, called **Darius and Girėnas**.) The airport website www.kaunasair.lt gives full details of current air services. All facilities open and close around the flight timings so both departing and arriving visitors are assured of banking facilities and sensible exchange rates.

The airport is well served by public transport, with bus 29 and minibus 120 passing by regularly. The 29 crosses the town centre from the castle to the bus and railway station so passes close to most hotels. The 120 is quicker, but goes only to the castle. The website www.transportas.kaunas.lt gives bus timetables in English. For the 29 bus, buy a ticket at the kiosk in the airport for 1.20Lt or pay 1.50Lt on board. For the 120 pay 2Lt on board. Taxis are not properly regulated at the airport so are best avoided.

Getting to Vilnius from the airport
For travel to Vilnius, it is possible to take the 29 to the bus station and then another bus (or train) from there. The fare is likely to be between 11 and 15Lt. A little more expensive, but much more convenient, is the minibus (*www.airport-bus.lt*) that travels directly to Vilnius bus station from Kaunas Airport and which connects with each flight. It has a set fare for travel to Vilnius bus and train station (35Lt early in 2008) and then additional ones for continuing to a specific address in the town. They also arrange transfers to the coast. Full details are on the website.

BY BUS AND TROLLEYBUS
Tickets should always be bought in kiosks, where they cost 1.20Lt each, whereas paying the driver costs 1.50Lt. There are no day passes so a ticket has to be used for each journey. An excellent map can also be bought at kiosks with a title in English, *The Routes of Public Transport in Kaunas City: Sites of Interest to Tourists*, which clearly indicates the location of all major sites and the bus routes which serve them. As the major east–west streets in Kaunas are one-way, stops used in each direction will be in different places. The routes of most use to tourists are trolleybuses 1, 5, 7 and 13 which link the bus and railway station with both the new and old parts of the town and also with the castle. The castle is the terminus for many local bus routes.

Minibuses are more difficult to use because they do not have specific stops but are quicker than the trolleybuses; the flat-rate fare of 2Lt is payable to the driver. Hotel receptions should be able to advise on their routes when needed.

Getting to Vilnius and elsewhere from the bus station
Buses leave for Vilnius from the bus station about every half-hour and minibuses hover in Vytauto, the street outside. Prices are similar, between 11 and 15Lt. There are also less frequent, but direct, services to all other large towns in Lithuania. International services operate to Riga and Kaliningrad as well as to many places in Poland and Germany.

BY TRAIN
Perhaps during the lifetime of this book, trains will become an attractive option for travel to Vilnius. Given the grandeur of Kaunas station, they certainly should be, but it is a sadly deceptive introduction to the slow speed and lack of comfort on the train. About ten trains a day operate to Vilnius, taking 75 minutes – a similar journey time to that on the buses, which operate much more frequently. It is only in the rush hours that the trains might be quicker, when buses can be held up in the traffic. At 12Lt, the fare between Kaunas and Vilnius is usually a little cheaper than that charged on the bus.

ACCOMMODATION

Since spring 2008, visitors have had a wide choice of hotels in Kaunas, and should hopefully be paying less than they used to. During the Soviet period, foreign tourists were rarely allowed to overnight here and in the 1990s it was common to repeat the pattern established then of just visiting Kaunas for the day, or of stopping just for a few hours *en route* to the coast. The combination of poor accommodation and little promotion ensured the continuation of this practice well into the 2000s. By 2010, there could well be another international chain joining Reval here, and there is certainly scope for more individual hotels too.

⌂ **Kaunas** (85 rooms) Laisvės 79; ✆ 37 750850; ℮ kanuas@kaunashotel.lt; www.kaunashotel.lt. For visitors staying several days, this hotel has a perfect location on Laisvės from which no museum, church or restaurant is more than 10mins' walk, whether it is in the old or new part of the town. It is expanding all the time & by 2008 most rooms will have baths rather than just showers, & AC together with tea- & coffee-making facilities. Many have a view over Laisvės & therefore over town life, but double glazing ensures that the visual side of any outside activity reaches the rooms, but not the sound. It is worth paying more to guarantee a room with this view rather than having one facing the back. The cellar restaurant is built into a former brewery & the wall paintings enhance the country feel. However the portrait of Bishop Valanius over the stairs is surprisingly incongruous. The 19th-century bishop struggled to keep the Lithuanian language alive when it was under severe threat from the Tsarist authorities, but is in fact best remembered as a high-profile temperance campaigner. When the conference room is not booked, guests can watch films there about Kaunas & Lithuania. There is no charge for this & the website gives full details of the available titles. $$$$

⌂ **Reval Neris** (208 rooms) Donelaičio 27; ✆ 37 306100; ℮ neris.sales@revalhotels.com; www.revalhotels.com. Through much of the 1990s this hotel could not throw off its Soviet past & even a refurbishment in 1998 was insufficient to make staying here a pleasure. Sensibly Reval completely rebuilt it before reopening it in April 2008. In view of how they have transformed other basket cases into seriously professional hotels, they should have no problem here. With a big conference room accommodating 450 people, Kaunas can at last attract this business; the chain now needs to encourage tour operators to overnight in Kaunas & not just have a midday stop here. Buses & trolleybuses to the station & from the airport stop outside the door, but because Denelaičio is one-way eastwards, those arriving or leaving on public transport in the other direction have to walk about 400m to or from Kęstučio. $$$$

⌂ **Best Western Santaka** (92 rooms) Gruodžio 21; ✆ 37 302702; ℮ office@santankahotel.eu; www.santanka.lt. Those who knew Kaunas in the 1990s, & then stayed here because it was a new hotel, may be surprised that it is now an old one. Perhaps that

is its current appeal. The building was a warehouse that dates from around 1900, but only the outside gives away this former role. The interior layout is unduly complex, with rooms varying in size & shape, but the Best Western franchise guarantees necessary standards throughout. Complete peace is assured, as it is off the main street, & perhaps that is why its most famous guest has been the Dalai Lama. All attractions in the Old Town are within easy walking distance. $$$

⌂ **Daugirdas** (48 rooms) Daugirdo 4; ✆ 37 301561; ℮ hotel@daugirdas.lt; www.daugirdas.lt. This is under the same management as the Perkuno Namai but it is hard to find a common link, so different are they. This hotel is an amalgam of 2 buildings, 1 brand new & 1 between 200 & 400 years old. In between is a covered arcade which is the reception & bar area, even provided with replica gas lamps to link it with Kaunas a hundred years ago. The hotel was a success as soon as it opened in 2007, probably for its location 200m from Town Hall Square, its wine cellar & for its terrace bar on the 4th floor, complemented by particularly friendly staff. In early 2008 it was still let down by rundown surroundings, but hopefully these neighbouring blocks will soon be restored to the standard of the hotel & the view from the 4th floor will be correspondingly enhanced. $$$

⌂ **Klaipeda** (28 rooms) Rotušės 5/Kuzmos 8; ✆ 37 229981; ℮ kaunas@klaipedahotel.lt; www.klaipedahotel.lt. Previous visitors will remember this hotel as the Minotel, which has now been slightly extended from its previous 21 rooms. It has been taken over by the Klaipeda group that also runs hotels with this name in Vilnius & Klaipeda, but all 3 are completely different. This one is much smaller than the other 2 & still retains a family-run air about it. The location is quiet for now but it remains to be seen what restoration does to the surrounding streets. There is no lift, so those who cannot carry cases up stairs should be sure to book a ground-floor room. $$$

⌂ **Perkuno Namai** (30 rooms) Perkūno 61; ✆ 37 320230; ℮ hotel@perkuno-namai.lt; www.perkuno-namai.lt. The 'Thunder House' is hardly an appropriate name for somewhere so quiet, located in the most genteel & park-strewn suburb of Kaunas, & favoured in the 1930s by senior businessmen & politicians. Buses do not therefore come by here, but the large rooms, the extensive views & the balconies available with many rooms more than compensate for the extra cost of a taxi in & out of town. Given the diversity of the menu in the restaurant, for many guests there is no incentive to leave the hotel for dinner. The hotel rightly achieved immense publicity in the early 1990s when it was the first private hotel to open in Kaunas & reintroduced the concept of service which had been missing in the town for 50 years or so. The Daugirdas Hotel (see above) which opened in 2007 is under the same ownership. $$$

🏠 **Apple Economy** (14 rooms) Valančiaus 19; ☎ 37 321404; www.applehotel.lt. That this modest hotel has no real competitors in Kaunas says all too much about the lack of young tourists here. Its prices are about half those of other hotels, but it certainly does not offer half the value. It has a good location in the old town, brightness & efficient service. An unexpected extra is an African souvenir shop. $$

🏠 **Daniela** (75 rooms) Mickevičiaus 28; ☎ 37 321505; e daniela@danielahotel.lt; www.danielahotel.lt.

As at the Santaka, every room is different here but the contemporary art exhibited in the corridors & rooms compensate for the otherwise bland surroundings. The location is ideal for the larger museums in the New Town & being on a cross street ensures relative quiet. It advertises itself as 4-star, which is perhaps pretentious, but given the prices it charges, 3-star standards are quite acceptable. $$

🏠 **Žaliakalnio** (Green Hill) (29 rooms) Savanorių 66; ☎ 37 321412; e zaliakalnis@greenhillhotel.com; www.greenhillhotel.lt. Tourists happy to start their day with a funicular ride into town can take advantage of the lower prices & extensive town views from here; the hotel is close to the Resurrection Church. The other surroundings are dreary, but the facilities within the hotel & the diversity of paintings on the walls should compensate for this. Being a completely new building adds to its comfort. $$

✦ EATING AND DRINKING

For about the first ten years after the restoration of independence in 1991, Kaunas had a very poor choice of restaurants. This then suddenly changed and by 2005 about 30–40 could genuinely be recommended, many having websites as well. Doubtless this number will continue to increase. Many tourists never leave Laisvės Alėja for their meals, but a detour of just 200–300m is well worthwhile. As yet, there is no need to go further.

The prices given below for restaurants are a rough indication of the cost of a three-course meal without drink. Beer drinkers will save a lot over wine drinkers, and will fit in better locally.

✕ **Avilys** Vilniaus 34; ☎ 37 203476; www.avilys.lt. An enormous cellar where beer is as much part of the food as the drink, given the number of dishes cooked in it. It is brewed on site. Many locals just drink here as the food is pricier than elsewhere in Kaunas & the live entertainment is perhaps a tad too lively to have with dinner. 80Lt.

✕ **Čili Pica** Laisvės 76; ☎ 37 425134 www.cili.lt. Any list of restaurants in Lithuania must now pay respect to this pizza chain, of which this is just one outlet in Kaunas. It is one of the country's most successful businesses & expansion continues rapidly, recently into drive-in take-aways. Service is quick & friendly, sadly still an unusual combination in Lithuania. 45Lt.

✕ **Miesto Sodas** Laisvės 93; ☎ 37 424424; www.miestosodas.lt. Quite a contrast to many of the other restaurants listed here, it is brightly coloured, uses glass extensively & specialises in salads rather than hot meat dishes. During the evening, older people stay on the ground floor whereas the younger generation go down into the nightclub. Neither is then embarrassed by the other. 60Lt.

✕ **Pizza Jazz** Laisvės 68; ☎ 37 204335; www.pizzajazz.lt. This ultra-central location on the famous pedestrian precinct ensures a broad clientele both during the day & in the evening. There is a division between a café & a restaurant, the latter boasting pictures of Marilyn Monroe & excellent coffee. Lithuanians have become addicted to pizza, even when they eat formally; hence the success of this restaurant. 60Lt.

✕ **Pompeja** Putvinskio 38; ☎ 37 422055; www.pompeja.lt. Pompeja has fortunately not suffered as a result of the number of groups who now eat here, & a good English translator was clearly put to work on the website in 2007. The serious visitor will probably prefer the quieter environment at lunchtime whilst others will want to enjoy the lively musical evenings that are provided through much of the summer. 50Lt.

✕ **Šaulys** Nepriklausomybės 5; ☎ 37 42655. Relax here after being overawed by the Church of St Michael. As it is close to the university, its set lunch for 10Lt attracts both students & the business community. However Šaulys is at its best in the evening, when both Lithuanian & Italian cuisines are offered, plus more cocktails than any other bar in Kaunas can concoct. The décor reinforces the name: the walls are covered with stuffed animals, guns & horns. 70Lt.

✘ **Tado Blindos Smuklė** Kęstučio 93; ☎ 37 202993. This is not actually a cellar, but could be, given the dark décor. It's firmly Lithuanian, so beer rather than wine is the staple drink & meat should take priority over fish. 60Lt.

✘ **Viva** Laisvės 53; ☎ 37 40004. A self-service restaurant, centrally located & with a wide menu. Ideal for serious sightseers to whom lunch or dinner is a tiresome necessary interlude. 45Lt.

✘ **Yakata** Valančiaus 14; ☎ 37 204512 www.yakata.lt. Come here for a wide variety of fish dishes in an otherwise predominantly carnivore town. Being able to afford a Japanese meal will be a revelation for visitors from Britain, & finding such food down a side street in Kaunas will add to the pleasure of eating it. 60Lt.

SHOPPING

Apart from the **Čiurlionis Museum**, which offers a wide selection of books and CDs, there is little for sale at museums and galleries. The widest selection of foreign-language books, maps and postcards is at **Centrinis Knygynas** (*Laisvės 81, close to the Kaunas Hotel*). Prices here are usually 10% lower than those charged in Vilnius. The jewellery shop **Kauno Vartai** (*Rotušės 29; www.kaunovartai.lt*) on Town Hall Square is the most reliable source for jewellery and crafts, including some amber.

WALKING TOURS

KAUNAS OLD TOWN Architecturally, central Kaunas is divided into two areas: in the **Old Town** (Senamiestis), around the Castle and Town Hall Square, most buildings are from the 19th century or earlier; the **New Town** (Naujamiestis) is centred on the pedestrian precinct **Laisvės Alėja** which reflects a building frenzy in the 1930s when it was privately assumed that Kaunas would become Lithuania's permanent capital. However, the geometric layout of the New Town, with its long straight avenues, dates from 1871.

Kaunas Castle (*www.kaunopilis.lt; interior* ⊕ *Jun–Sep 11.00–18.00 daily, other times of year when exhibitions are open*) has clearly been the site of a fortification for at least a thousand years but the precursor to the stone and brick building now in ruins probably dates from the 13th century. Its 2m thick walls and the deep moat suggest centuries of bitter fighting but in fact none ever took place around Kaunas and the current neglected state of the castle results not from battles but from the Russians abandoning it in the 19th century and then from floods early in the 20th century. Now the castle has been modernised with sleek glass windows encasing the top, and it hosts regularly changing art exhibitions.

The **Church of St George** is so close to the castle and in similar brick that it seems part of the same complex but in fact is known to date from the early 15th century, when Christianity first came to Kaunas. The building was returned to the church in 2005, but given its neglect in Soviet times, when it was used as a warehouse, it will be many years before it can be restored. Between this church and the Town Hall Square is the **seminary**, remarkable for the fact that it was allowed to function throughout the Soviet era. It was of course subject to constant harassment but nevertheless 500 priests graduated during that time. The attached **Holy Trinity Church** was also used as a warehouse, but was however reconsecrated in 1982, eight years before the collapse of the Soviet Union. As a result, the interior was properly refurbished in time for the papal visit in 1993.

Rotušės aikštė (Town Hall Square) It is fortunate how little damage this square has suffered and much of it still looks as it would have done two hundred years ago. Strict controls now prevent developers from changing any of the façades. Because of the Tsarist ban on buildings of more than two storeys, the **Town Hall** with its six-storey tower dating from the late 16th century still dominates the square much as it did when it was first built. It is hard to believe that the tower is only 53m high. Fortunately each new ruler, including Soviet Russia, maintained it well and its nickname of the 'White Swan' has been passed down from regime to regime. Saturday is a good day to see the building in action, since most weddings still take place there. There is a **Ceramics Museum** (⊕ *11.00–17.00 Tue–Sun; admission 3Lt*) in the cellars; the entrance is precarious, down a narrow steep staircase with a ceiling not geared to anybody above average height. One cellar is a permanent exhibition of ceramics discovered in the city during archaeological excavations. Another is used for temporary exhibitions of works by local artists.

Fire, neglect and a constant change of ownership between various faiths, not to mention its use as a secondary school in the Soviet period, has left the **Church of St Francis** with a very bare interior. The exterior, built between 1666 and 1725, has kept its neo-Baroque façade and it is to be hoped that with the church now back in the hands of the Jesuits, a worthy interior can soon be built.

The statue which dominates the southwest corner of the square is of **Jonas Maciulis Maironis** (1862–1932), Lithuania's most famous poet who was also rector of the seminary from 1909 until his death. The face may seem familiar as it is on the 20Lt banknote. Wedding couples leaving the Town Hall often have their photograph taken here. Maironis lived in the building behind the statue which is now the **Literature Museum** (*Rotušés 13; www.maironiomuziejus.lt; ⊕ 09.00–17.00 Tue–Sat; admission 4Lt*) This covers not only his work but also that of many of his contemporaries. The collection was extended in 1999 to include literature produced from 1944 by the very large, and worldwide Lithuanian exile community. The museum website has extensive material in English about Lithuanian literature.

On the northwest side of the square are the 19th-century stables used by the postal service, which now house the **Communications History Museum** (⊕ *10.00–18.00 Wed, Thu, Sat, Sun; admission 2Lt*). The stress here is in fact on the postal side and exhibits cover sorting, route maps, transport and staff uniforms. Telegrams, telex and fax transmission are also covered. There is an extensive display of stamps from the pre-war republic and from the restoration of independence in 1991. Outside, a collection of horse-drawn carriages is being built up. Sadly despite extensive renovation in 2004, all the explanations are still only in Lithuanian.

The east side of the square used to consist of private houses, but these have been largely converted into shops and offices now, with number 28 being the **Museum of the History of Lithuanian Medicine and Pharmacy** (*Rotušés 28; ⊕ 11.00–17.00 Wed, Thu, Sat, Sun; admission 3Lt*), which has refitted a chemist's shop and dispensary as it would have looked in the 19th century. Some of the exhibits, however, date back to the 16th century and the shop could well have been functioning then. The origin of the equipment shows how international Kaunas had become during the 1800s. A pill-making machine is from Leipzig, an oil press from Luxembourg and a cash machine from the United States. A century before Viagra this pharmacy could offer its clients a herb called Erektosan. The museum also covers dentistry so has a drill operated by a foot pedal. The rooms on 18th-century medicine show a range of Lithuanian pharmaceuticals, laboratory gadgets and a place where different medications were mixed and boiled on the assumption that this would actually cure people. Much of the furniture and medical apparatus was assembled many years ago and presents some very strange and often stomach-churning sights for the modern eye.

The shelves are full of medications, such as the Venus Hair Potion, an elixir known for its powers to bring youth and beauty. A suspicious-looking powder named Caput Mortuum, made of dead people's heads, was recommended in the Middle Ages to keep up men's strength and vitality, and was also used to treat epilepsy.

The **cathedral**, on the corner of Vilniaus and Town Hall Square, is the largest Gothic building in Lithuania, although the interior is totally Baroque. The brickwork dates from the 15th century, with the woodwork and painting mainly from the 18th century. Its size is perhaps reflected in the fact that it has nine different altars. Being open in Soviet times, it was protected from the desecration that occurred then in so many other Kaunas churches. Two politically active and religious writers are also buried in the cathedral, the poet Maironis (see page 225) and Bishop Motiejus Valancius (1801–75), who is best remembered for his work printing and distributing books in the Lithuanian language in the middle of the 19th century. It was only legal to do so using the Cyrillic alphabet, but he persisted in using the Western alphabet.

Beyond the square Walking from Town Hall Square towards the Nemunas River along Aleksoto, another red-brick Gothic building stands out on the right-hand side. This is **Perkunas (Thunder) House.** Facts about its history and its use are distinctly lacking, but theories abound. Construction probably began in the 16th century and constant alterations were made until around 1800. The Hanseatic League may well have used it as their headquarters and in the 19th century a theatre operated here. The name comes from a figurine of the God of Thunder discovered in the 19th century. This highly original structure differed a great deal from the nearby wooden houses. The building is now in Jesuit hands and the interior can often be visited, even though it is not formally open.

Perilously close to the river is **Vytautas Church**, named after the Lithuanian duke who defeated the Teutonic Knights and extended the Lithuanian Empire to the Black Sea early in the 15th century. Beside the road leading down to the river is a marker showing how far and how often flood waters have risen. However, the church has survived well from the 14th century, despite floods, looting by Napoleon's army and constant changes in ownership between Orthodox and Catholic communities. It is now in Catholic hands.

About 200m along the river, the third turning on the left is Zamenhofo, where number 12 is the **Lithuanian Folk Instruments Museum** (⊕ *10.00–18.00 Tue–Sat; admission 2Lt*), a collection of small houses set around a courtyard. The museum was founded in 1983 by the father of the current director who took it upon himself to collect as many traditional instruments as he could whilst they were still in good condition. They are all constructed from very simple pieces of wood or metal, but nonetheless produce very acceptable music. The staff seem equally adept at demonstrating wind, brass or string instruments and tours can be accompanied by tapes playing in the background

KAUNAS NEW TOWN Vilniaus Street links the old and new parts of the town, which are divided by the wide road Gimnazijos. This is always very busy with traffic but fortunately there is an underpass, usually full of itinerant traders. Coming back into daylight, on the left is the former **Presidential Palace** (*Vilniaus 33; www.istorineprezidentura.lt;* ⊕ *11.00–17.00 Tue–Sun; admission 3Lt*), which opened in 2005 as a museum covering the 1920–40 period. It is remarkable how much worthwhile material has survived, given the speed of the Soviet takeover in 1940 and the danger for Lithuanians in keeping material away from this 'bourgeois' regime. A reasonable number of captions have been translated into English. In the gardens are statues of the three presidents who lived there: Antanas Smetona, Aleksandras Stulginskis and Kazys Grinius. Stulginskis has the most confident pose, even though he is portrayed with a stick. Grinius is seated with a look of exhaustion. Smetona has the detached look of an undertaker, perhaps suitable as he was the last president before the Soviet takeover in 1940. The palace is appropriately on the edge of the New Town, through which the walk now continues, and where this regime was to make such an architectural mark.

The New Town (Naujamiestis) is centred on the mile-long pedestrian precinct **Laisvės Alėja.** The precinct runs from the former Presidential Palace in the west to the Church of St Michael in the east. Visitors should however be careful at the cross

Owen Rutter

In Kaunas there is no traffic problem, for one rarely sees a motor-car; the clatter of hoofs and drosky wheels over the cobbles takes the place of humming engines and the only other public conveyances are dilapidated and overcrowded trams, each pulled by a single horse.

There are plenty of interesting types to be found on this Unter den Linden of Kaunas: barefooted peasant women, their hair hidden under white or coloured cloths, carrying baskets filled with fruit; priests, hideously shaven-headed like many others of the male community, in long black cassocks and bowlers or panama; then there are the sallow-faced Jews, the bearded Russians and the pretty girls with characteristic Lithuanian blue eyes and fair hair. Many look English and are well-dressed but sometimes they wear socks that leave an expanse of bare calf, a modern fashion that, who knows, may reach us yet.

The many Jews one passes are a strange contrast to the fair Lithuanians. The town has a large Jewish quarter; in fact, out of a population of 120,000, no less than half are Jews. Their restless energy has done much to help the trade revival of the Baltic countries. The Kaunas market is the meeting-place of Jew and Gentile and although there is no love lost between the two, trade bring them together.

The Town Museum is only open for four hours on two days a week. I found it closed, but discovered the curator sitting on a bench outside. He received the suggestion that he should open the Museum rather sourly until it transpired that I came from London, when his manner changed and he professed himself willing to show me anything I wished to see. The main exhibit is a picture of the Crucifixion, said to be an original Rubens. Fortunately it was not stolen in the War, either by the retreating Russians or by the invading Germans.

From The New Baltic States *by Owen Rutter, 1925*

---

streets which cars are allowed to use. There have been attempts to ban smoking as well as cars here but these have not been successful. However it is wide and windy enough for non-smokers not to be concerned over this and since 2007 smoking has at least been banned inside all buildings.

At Laisvės 106 is the **Tadas Ivanauskas Zoological Museum** (⏲ *11.00–19.00 Tue–Sun; admission 5Lt*), which claims to have 173,000 different items, although only 15,000 are on display. It is named after the founder, who managed to establish it in 1919, despite all the fighting going on around Kaunas at that time. A few labels are translated into English but most are still in just Russian and Lithuanian. Sadly little has been done here since the Soviet era, so whilst the building offers space, it does not have any sense of design and there are no new booklets or postcards for visitors to buy. The general visitor will find the gloomy environment oppressive but specialists interested in stuffed animals, butterflies or stamps with natural-history motifs should definitely come.

A little further along, at Laisvės 102, is the **main post office**, an enormous granite building dating from 1931 but with plenty of local wooden decoration as part of the interior. As mentioned earlier, by 1930 the government had accepted that Kaunas was likely to be the capital for many further years and a building of this stature reflects that view. The stamps exhibited cover such diverse themes as Lithuanian industrial products, medieval kings, flowers, fire engines and Chiune Sugihara, the Japanese Consul in Kaunas in 1940 who disobeyed his government by issuing visas which enabled several thousand local Jews to escape the Holocaust. Sets of stamps and first-day covers are also for sale here. The post office also has a large internet centre (⏲ *08.00–20.00 daily*).

Kaunas WALKING TOURS

7

Beside the building is a statue of **Vytautas the Great**, stamping on his enemies, which was unveiled on 23 August 1990, a year before Lithuania's most recent enemy, the USSR, collapsed. It was a copy of an original by the sculptor Vincas Grybas (1890–1941). He was in fact a communist and was murdered by the Germans as soon as they occupied Kaunas. Despite this, the Russians still removed the statue given its unacceptable theme. The open space on the other side of the road is a commemoration garden for Romas Kalanta, a student aged 19 who burnt himself to death here in 1972 as a protest against the Soviet occupation. Details of this quickly spread abroad, although nothing could be said about it publicly in Lithuania at the time. The memorial, made up of 19 stones to represent one for every year of his life, was carved in 2002 to commemorate the 30th anniversary of his death.

Laisvės Alėja comes to an end with a large square dominated from the centre by the **Church of St Michael the Archangel**. As in other major Baltic cities, the Tsarist regime built imposing Orthodox cathedrals in the late 19th century as part of their Russification campaigns. Ironically, by 1944, these churches were one of the few legacies that could not be destroyed by the new Soviet regime. During their occupation of Kaunas the building became a museum for stained glass and when independence was restored in 1990, the building was given to the Catholic Church, not to an Orthodox community. In the crypt the **Museum for the Blind** (☉ *08.00–16.00 daily; admission free*) opened in 2005. It is based solely on sound, smell and touch. The first exhibition, entitled 'Catacombs of the 21st Century', will stay until autumn 2008.

On the west side of the square is the **Mykolas Žilinskas Art Gallery** (☉ *Jun–Sep 10.00–17.00 Tue–Sun, Oct–May 11.00–17.00; admission 4Lt*). The building dates from 1989, the late Soviet period, when it was constructed to house the foreign art collection then held by the Čiurlionis Museum. However, Mykolas Žilinskas (1904–92) fled from Lithuania in 1940 to what would become West Berlin, where he assembled a large collection of 16th–20th century paintings and porcelain. Later, he kindly donated his personal collection to Kaunas. He insisted that he would only donate it to Kaunas, as it was the city where he was born. The collection was fortunately all taken there, although it was very risky and complicated to do so during Soviet times, and now forms the basis of the displays, supplemented by some Lithuanian paintings and by a Rubens picture of the Crucifixion. Of political interest are the Soviet items from the 1920s where designs from earlier periods are 'enhanced' with slogans. The tall statue of a male nude in front of the gallery continues to cause the controversy which was presumably its initial aim. It was unveiled in 1991; even under *perestroika* it could probably not have been shown in Soviet times.

Vienybės aikštė Vienybės aikštė (Unity Square) is to the north of **Laisvės**, at its eastern end, surrounded by two universities and the Military Museum. It is here that every 16 February Lithuania has commemorated its founding, surrounded by statues of those who were most active in the struggle for independence. Lenin of course took their place during the Soviet era but the originals were copied as closely as possible immediately independence was restored. Those less famous are commemorated with the eternal flame and with the inscription on the altar which translates as 'Give What You Must'.

When built in 1936, the **Military Museum** (*Donelaičio 64;* ☉ *11.00–18.00 Wed–Sun; admission 4Lt*), was the largest museum in Lithuania and it is pictured on the current 20Lt note. The architect Karolis Reisonas always built on a grand scale as is also clear from his Church of the Resurrection (see opposite). The collection covers all of the bitter wars fought on Lithuanian territory. For foreigners, the Napoleonic rooms are probably those of most interest since there is extensive coverage of his advance through, and then quick retreat from, Lithuania during his unsuccessful 1812 campaign against the Russians. For local people, greatest interest is shown in the wreck of the plane piloted across the Atlantic in July 1933 by Steponas Darius and Stasys

Girėnas, who just failed to reach Kaunas after a 37-hour flight. All sorts of memorabilia linked with them and with their fatal journey are also displayed.

Although almost totally unknown in the English-speaking world, Mikalojus Čiurlionis (1875–1911) would probably have become a world-famous figure had he lived longer or if Lithuanian independence had come about a few years earlier. He is both Lithuania's most famous composer and the country's most famous artist. He suffered all his life from physical and mental illness so viewing his painting and listening to his music is a melancholic but moving experience. Both are possible in the **Čiurlionis Art Museum** (*Putvinskio 55; www.ciurlionis.lt;* ⊕ *11.00–17.00 Tue–Sun; admission 5Lt*) which bears his name and which is situated just behind the Military Museum. It is hard to believe that all the paintings on display here date from the last ten years of his life. The part of the museum where his work is displayed dates from 2003, so is well lit and ventilated. It is however worth visiting the rest of the building which has an extensive collection of wooden carvings, mainly from the 17th–19th centuries.

On leaving these austere surroundings, the **Devils Museum** (*Putvinskio 64;* ⊕ *11.00–17.00 Tue–Sun; admission 5Lt*) over the road provides light relief, except perhaps in the depiction of Hitler and Stalin stamping over Lithuania. 'Devil' in the context of this museum could perhaps better be translated as 'joker' or 'trickster'. The original owner died in 1966, but his spirit of fun lived on and now more than 2,000 little devils are on display. Perhaps the museum proves that it was possible to survive with a sense of humour through the Soviet occupation.

One of the two funicular railways in the town goes up to the **Church of the Resurrection**, on Green Hill. It dominates Kaunas which was clearly the aim of the architect Karolis Reisonas, who won a competition for his design. Like so many other buildings that date from the 1930s, it reflects the need the town by then felt to operate on the basis of it being the permanent capital. Its size probably made it the largest building in the Baltics at the time: 3,000 people could stand indoors and another 2,000 on the roof. However it was never properly completed before the Soviet invasion in 1940 and was converted into a radio factory after their return in 1944. They obviously hoped that people would forget why it was originally built; that it was not mentioned in Soviet guidebooks is hardly surprising but it was still completely ignored during the early 1990s and only when fundraising started in earnest did it get noticed and visited again. Consecration was finally possible on 26 December 2004, when total emptiness greeted the visitor inside, with no woodwork, no seating and no stained glass. The thick whitewash covering the exterior gave a false impression of the work being complete, but it was not until 2008 that this was in fact the case.

There is a lift in the 70m tower to the roof which offers an extensive view over the whole town. It is one of the few places from which both the 19th-century town and the 1930s extensions can be clearly seen.

The walk down Žemaičių should be considered as an alternative to using the funicular again. At the foot of the hill, it becomes Vytauto, which finishes at the railway station. The **park** here was largely created out of two former cemeteries, a Tartar one and a Lithuanian one, both of which the Soviets cleared away in the 1960s. The park provided a backcloth for several revolutionary statues which are now in Grutas Park, the centre for Soviet sculpture near Druskininkai. The mosque built here in 1933 still exists although it was not of course allowed to function as such in Soviet times, when it was converted into a sports hall. The statue for the Unknown Soldier in the park commemorates soldiers who gave their lives fighting for Lithuanian independence in 1918–20. The **Deportation Museum** (*Vytauto 46;* ⊕ *10.00–16.00 Wed–Sat; admission free*) exhibits a collection of documents and photographs about the thousands of Lithuanians deported to Siberia. This took place in two main 'waves', one just before the German invasion in June 1941 and the other in March 1949. There were similar deportations at exactly the same time in Estonia and Latvia.

EXCURSIONS FROM KAUNAS

There are many worthwhile visits near to Kaunas which tourists staying longer than a day can make. Buses to most places leave from the main bus station, but quite a few buses also use the bus station beside the castle.

THE NINTH FORT (*www.9fmuziejus.ot.lt;* ⊕ *10.00–18.00 Wed–Mon; admission 4Lt*) This was the last of a ring of forts around Kaunas to be built and it was completed in 1902. During World War II it became a major site for Holocaust atrocities. Not only was the local Jewish community murdered here, but so were many prisoners brought from France. Some of the cells have been kept exactly as they were during the war, with even the graffiti still visible. One prisoner wrote: '*Nous sommes 5,000 Français* ('We are 5,000 French people'). In common with other camps in the Baltics, prisoners were shot rather than gassed and given the proximity of this fort to the town, knowledge of what was happening there must have been commonplace in the town. Amazingly in the early Soviet period, the fort remained in use as a prison and Lithuanian partisans were executed here. There is a bus to the fort from the bus station beside the castle.

PAŽAISLIS MONASTERY (⊕ *10.00–17.00 Mon–Sat*) The monastery is all the more imposing because it is so unexpected. A dreary journey on a trolleybus (number 9) through Soviet suburbs and alongside a small marina does not normally lead to an explosion of Baroque. Here it does, both inside and outside. No Lithuanian artist came near the building. Only Italians worked on it, hence the extensive use of black marble. It is fortunate that the centrepiece of the church, a tall hexagonal cupola, has meant that much of the original paintwork survived, however irreligious subsequent owners may have been. Building began in the late 17th century on behalf of the Camaldolese Order, an offshoot of the Benedictines who were accepted in the Polish–Lithuanian Commonwealth but hardly anywhere else outside Italy. The building was at peace through the 18th century but would then suffer nearly two hundred years of tragedy. Napoleon's troops looted it in 1812; in 1832 it was closed following the anti-Tsarist demonstrations of the previous year and then passed to Russian Orthodox monks who removed the altars and painted over some of the frescoes. As the Tsarist forces retreated in 1915, they took what they could to Russia. Whilst nuns were allowed to return between 1920 and 1940, during the wars and in the early Soviet period the building was a hospital, a store, a home for the elderly and finally an art museum. To be fair to the Soviets, restoration did start in 1967 but it was only completed in the mid 1990s, by which time the nuns had returned once more.

RUMŠIŠKĖS OPEN-AIR MUSEUM (*www.mmlab.ktu.lt/skansenas;* ⊕ *10.00–18.00 Tue–Sun; admission 8Lt*) Opened in 1974, this has brought together about 180 buildings from all over the Lithuanian countryside. The interiors are only open to individuals from 1 May 1 to 30 September, but special arrangements can be made for groups.

The buildings date from between 1750 and 1950, and – bearing in mind the 60,000 artefacts contained within them – there is no aspect of Lithuanian life which has not been covered. The museum is divided into four ethnographic areas and the inclusion of many farm animals, trees and plants ensures that the original settings are reproduced as accurately as possible. Demonstrations of handicrafts such as woodcarving, weaving, basket-making and pottery mirror activities throughout the Lithuanian countryside during the period covered. Three hours is the minimum time needed to get round and see the major exhibits, but a full day is well worthwhile in good weather. A few buses come directly here, but normally it is necessary to take the Vilnius bus to the nearest stop on the highway, called Rumšiškės, and then to walk for about 2km.

8

Klaipeda LITHUANIA

Telephone code 46

For many visitors with a knowledge of history, Klaipeda is still Memel. Unlike most of the other cities described in this book, it had centuries of uninterrupted German rule and only from the 1920s was this first threatened and later completely overturned. The border of the surrounding area, known as Memelland, was fixed in 1422 between the Teutonic Knights on the one hand and representatives of Polish and Lithuanian royal families on the other. These rulers would not last long, but the border they fixed certainly did. It would not be breached until 1923 and although it was briefly restored for a further six years from 1939 to 1945, it then disappeared for good and most traces of it were removed. With Lithuanian's borders now agreed with all its neighbours, and the country safely ensconced in NATO and the EU, it is impossible to visualise any further changes or this border ever returning.

That both London and Glasgow have Memel Streets, and are unlikely to change this name, shows the important trading link that the city provided. In the early 20th century, a Boer town in South Africa was also named Memel to show support for Germany in World War I. Modern Klaipeda, whilst keen to play a role as Lithuania's third-largest city, shows none of the nervousness of Kaliningrad in promoting its past. Former German residents, who were first allowed to return in 1987, four years before the collapse of the USSR, were happy to see the Old Town being restored and encouraged others to return as well. 'We really feel at home in Memel', and 'Our town has waited for us', were amongst their first reactions, in contrast to the disgust felt by those returning to Königsberg/Kaliningrad in 1991. As these Memelländer walked around, they would become a little more critical and point out the absence of life on the streets, of small businesses, of colour and of smells, but they would note the restoration of the Old Town that had begun in the 1970s. What they missed was soon remedied, entirely of course by Lithuanians. The city is now a powerful trading port, is becoming active in promoting cruise tourism, and can boast an international community, including twinning links with nine other ports.

Memel suffered, as Klaipeda did in Soviet times, through being seen as a means and not an end in itself, as a place to pass through but not somewhere to settle. For a year, in 1808, it was the Prussian capital, as King Frederick Wilhelm III had to flee from Berlin when it was occupied by Napoleon, but he left as soon as he could. Prussian rulers *en route* to St Petersburg, and Russian rulers *en route* to Berlin, always stopped in Memel, but after preening themselves once or twice in public, rapidly moved on. German civil servants hated a posting there, calling it 'Prussian Siberia'. Soviet tourists were eager to escape any urban environment for the sand dunes on the Curonian Spit or the beaches at Palanga.

Giving Klaipeda a chapter to itself in this book is hopefully an indication that the days of just passing through are now over and that the time to stay has definitely arrived. The number of hotels that have opened in the last couple of years is clear evidence of local trust in the city's future.

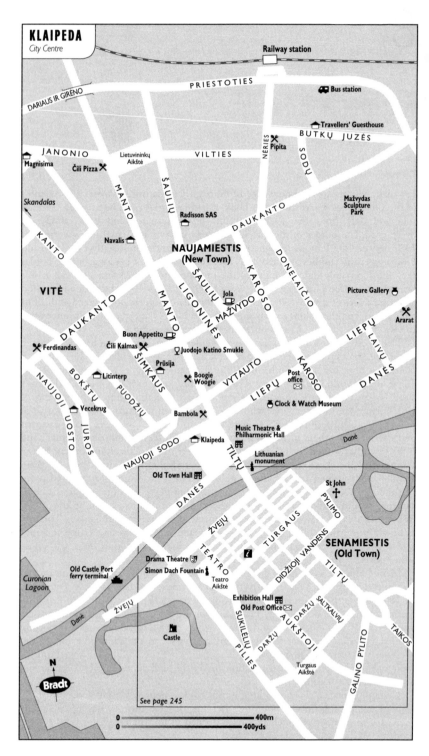

KLAIPEDA
City Centre

Railway station

PRIESTOTIES

DARIAUS IR GIRĖNO

Bus station

Travellers' Guesthouse

BUTKŲ JUZĖS

NĖRIES

Pipita

JANONIO

VILTIES

SODŲ

Magnisima

Lietuvininkų
Aikštė

Čili Pizza

ŠAULIŲ

MANTO

Skandalas

Radisson SAS

DAUKANTO

Mažvydas
Sculpture
Park

KANTO

Navalis

NAUJAMIESTIS
(New Town)

DONELAIČIO

ŠAULIŲ

LIGONINĖS

MAŽVYDO

Jola

KAROSO

Picture Gallery

VITĖ

DAUKANTO

MANTO

Ararat

LIEPŲ

LAIVŲ

Buon Appetito

Ferdinandas

Čili Kalmas

SIMKAUS

Joudojo Katino Smuklė

Prūsija

VYTAUTO

KAROSO

DANĖS

Litinterp

Boogie
Woogie

LIEPŲ

Post
office

BOKŠTŲ

NAUJOJI UOSTO

PUODŽIŲ

JŪROS

Vecekrug

Bambola

Clock & Watch Museum

Klaipeda

NAUJOJI SODO

**Music Theatre &
Philharmonic Hall**

TILTŲ

Danė

Lithuanian
monument

Old Town Hall

DANĖS

ŽVEJŲ

TEATRO

TURGAUS

St John

PYLIMO

SENAMIESTIS
(Old Town)

DIDŽIOJI VANDENS

TILTŲ

*Curonian
Lagoon*

Old Castle Port
ferry terminal

Drama Theatre

Simon Dach Fountain

Teatro
Aikštė

Exhibition Hall

Old Post Office

SUKILĖLIŲ

DARŽŲ

AUKŠTOJI

SALTKALVIŲ

TAIKOS

Danė

ŽVEJŲ

Castle

PILIES

Turgaus
Aikštė

GALINO PYLITO

N

Bradt

See page 245

0 _____ 400m
0 _____ 400yds

THE GERMAN ARRIVAL Less archaeological work has been done in this area than further north or south along the coast so it is difficult to judge the level of sophistication achieved before the Teutonic Knights established their first fortification here in 1252. There is evidence of settlements in the Stone Age (around 1000BC) and the Iron Age (from 300BC), but it remains unclear whether any trading was done from here across the Baltic Sea. The date of 1252 is close to those of the founding of Königsberg, Liepaja, Riga and Tallinn. Whilst Memel would be subject to attack from outsiders, they were never able to achieve long-term control as they did elsewhere. Fires in 1540 and 1854 and plagues in 1620 and 1709 caused much more damage.

Memel had a crucial role to play as a staging post for royal visits between Germany and Russia, so between Berlin or Königsberg and St Petersburg. Mostly these passed smoothly, with rulers and guests being deferentially welcomed by the local population. Catherine I however had cause to complain in 1712 that the other guests in her hotel were partying so intensively that she could get no sleep. The hotel owner was promptly arrested and imprisoned. Fortunately for him, Peter the Great would stay in the same hotel a few weeks later and ordered his immediate release. He probably made a substantial contribution to whatever noise there was on the nights that he stayed.

Memel's 'royal days' came to an abrupt end in 1833 when the new postal route to St Petersburg was opened via Tilsit, soon followed by the railway.

INDUSTRIALISATION The late 19th century saw strong nationalist movements against the Tsarist regime in most Baltic towns. In Memel local Lithuanians were far more concerned with their *Eindeutschung*, incorporation into the local German community. Being a part of Prussia, they were free to publish and circulate Lithuanian books, a right that had been withdrawn by the Tsarist government in 1863 in the territory they controlled to the east. There was also no basis for a religious divide as Germans and Lithuanians shared the Protestant faith. At governmental level, relations between the German and Russian empires remained cordial and lucrative for both sides. With the poisonous relations of the 20th century clouding contemporary views, it is easy to forget that for most of the previous 600 years, relations between Prussia and Russia were very good.

From 1867 until 1891 Memel could be sure of a high profile in the Reichstag as it was represented there by Field-Marshal von Moltke, the architect of Prussia's victory over France in 1870–71. Although major economic power would remain in German hands until World War I, Lithuanians were no longer seen as purely servants and played increasingly important roles in business and local government.

Much of the city's waterfront, where the warehouses were largely built of wood, was destroyed by fire in 1854. It was fortunate that this happened during such an affluent time for Memel so rebuilding could take place quickly and, in the long term, the city did not suffer. On this occasion, as both before and since, the basic layout of the Old Town was not changed, so what visitors now see is a street plan set in the early 15th century.

WORLD WAR I In late 1914 and early 1915, Russian forces overran large areas of German territory, including most of East Prussia. Memel was occupied only for a few days in March 1915. The Russians failed to cut the telephone links with Germany, so the local community was easily able to provide the necessary intelligence to the Wehrmacht which enabled them quickly to reconquer the city. The Russians were never a threat again, partly as the Germans were then able to occupy most of what is now the territory of Lithuania.

Bernard Newman

Memel, or Klaipeda to quote its Lithuanian name, is a very ordinary little town, clean and uninteresting. Its harbour is a second-class one. Before the War it was a sleepy timber port, doing but a trifling business, but then it became the port for the whole of Lithuania. Even so, if it were planted along the coast of England, it would attract little attention. Ships of any size find it impossible to enter the harbour.

Make no mistake about it, Memel is German. The population in the hinterland is mixed but in the town itself the German majority is overwhelming. An Englishman or a Frenchman can settle down in another country, become assimilated and within a few generations his descendants are indistinguishable from the local population. But Germans remain Germans. When I was last in Memel in 1934, the atmosphere was heavy with tension, but now in 1938 it was fully charged. Although German semi-military organisations were banned, I saw two columns of youths in plain clothes marching down the street. 'We will not rest until Memel returns to the Reich,' several Germans said to me on the slightest provocation. When I hinted that this might mean the end of Memel's prosperity as Lithuania's only port and a return to being a minor port in East Prussia, this argument had no meaning to them. Their Führer would ensure that they were compensated for all their trials and tribulations.. In any case, why should Lithuanian trade not continue to flow through Memel? The Führer was a reasonable man and would be willing to allow this. There was also a future for Memel as a naval port, being the nearest port to the Russian coast. When I pointed out that Memel was hardly equipped as a naval port, I was assured that the Führer would see to that, apparently coming to the port with a giant scoop to add another twenty feet to the depth of the harbour.

The swastika was forbidden in Memel but I saw it inside more than one house. I got the impression that it was almost worshipped in secret, hidden as Christian emblems used to be in the bad old days of persecution. In the harbour I witnessed striking scenes. There was a German ship tied alongside the quay and of course no Lithuanian regulations could prevent it flying its flag. Throughout the whole of the afternoon, small parties of pilgrims walked along the quay to gaze at the swastika, which they saluted with vigour and with feeling.

When I pursued my enquiries about the economic position of Memel, I made a discovery of considerable interest. Many of the industries in Memel are German owned. They are controlled by Germans who rushed their money out in difficult times. I had always understood from Nazi propaganda that such action was always the prerogative of the Jews!

From Baltic Roundabout *by Bernard Newman*

THE RELUCTANT FRENCH The Treaty of Versailles was vague as to the long-term future of Memel, except that the allies wanted it out of German hands. That a Lithuanian nation would survive was in serious doubt in 1919, but if it did, it would need access to a port, and ideally one in its own hands. The newly established nation of Poland could not claim it on ethnic grounds, but certainly had a case for guaranteed access to a large port. Once the Poles had seized Vilnius in late 1920, there was no way that any co-operation could take place with the Lithuanian government and in fact a state of war would exist between the two countries until 1937. Poland was therefore eager to keep Memel out of Lithuanian hands. As the British were committed in Danzig and also to the north in Estonia and Latvia, it fell to the French, on behalf of the League of Nations, to take over, at least nominally, from the Germans. The first

French governor arrived with a Polish interpreter, unaware that this language would be of no use in Memel; however it did at least show where his political sympathies lay.

Nobody is keen to dwell on this period of history so it is often ignored. The French surrendered without resistance to the Lithuanians, and left no tangible mark on their three-year period of rule. Their departure coincided with their occupation of the Ruhr, which was seen as a success, so failure in Memel could be concealed and forgotten. Not until 2003 did any book appear in French on this, and that book was published in Lithuania, not in France. The Lithuanian official line was always that their seizure of Memel resulted from an internal coup within the city, whereas it was in fact a straightforward invasion organised by the Kaunas government. It was only in the 1990s that even Lithuanian historians in exile would admit this. The British government gave active support to the independence movements in Estonia and Latvia whereas they were indifferent to Lithuania and would probably have been happy with a restored Polish-Lithuanian Commonwealth, with inevitably Poland playing the upper hand. This would have secured the bulwark against Soviet Russia, which was its prime concern. Individual members of the League were quickly reconciled to the Lithuanian seizure of Memel, wrongly hoping that the Lithuanians would see it as a consolation price for Vilnius staying under Polish control. In May 1924 the League formally gave up its claims on the area.

THE UNCERTAIN LITHUANIANS Although Lithuanians lived on both sides of the former Prussian–Russian border, there was little mutual interest or support. Those in Memel were urban, Protestant and well off. Those near the border in the new Lithuanian state were largely rural, Catholic and poor. The end of World War I had not changed this situation. Lithuanians living in Memel would probably have agreed with the many German writers at the time who compared crossing the border to going back a century. The more racist said it was like going from Europe into Asia. The British historian E H Carr, at the time working for the Foreign Office, noted 'the contrast between the well-tilled fields, the substantial brick buildings and the good roads in Memelland on the one side, and the tumble-down wooden hovels and mud tracks of Russian Lithuania on the other'. Successful Lithuanians ran their businesses or pursued their academic careers in Vilnius or Kaunas, not in Memel. If those in Memel had been given any say, they might well have chosen the free-state arrangement imposed on Danzig, which would have enabled them to trade more effectively with a wider range of countries than incorporation into Lithuania allowed. At that time, they were happy not to be part of Germany, where 1923 was the year of rampant inflation and it would be three to four more years before the Weimar Republic could be seen as truly stable. Probably the greatest support for the Lithuanian invasion came from Chicago, a major centre then (and still) of the 800,000 diaspora living at that time in the United States. This community sent a lot of money to help the incorporation of Memel but interestingly very few were willing to return 'home' where their commercial and administrative expertise could have been very helpful.

The Kaunas government did not approach the inhabitants of Klaipeda with any tact or even with common sense. Whilst imposing the Lithuanian language on court proceedings was logical in Kaunas, this was hardly the case in Klaipeda, where all the judiciary (and most of the criminals brought before them) were German speakers. Other over-rushed decisions concerned currency and passports, and the continuation of martial law. A demonstration which was part of a general strike in April 1923 was put down with six fatalities. A turning point came on 9 May when martial law was lifted, and further concessions to the German community soon had to be made. However the economic and political structure of the city made it inevitable that relations would remain poor. At the political top were Lithuanians sent from Kaunas and beneath them the economic German-speaking elite yearning for their previous autonomy. They however needed unskilled labour for their factories which only the more distant Lithuanian countryside could provide. In a cultural sense, too, Memel stayed German.

The arrival of the Nazi regime in Berlin was clearly an attraction to many Germans in Memel and its propaganda was very effective there, based around the slogan 'Heim in Reich'. This slogan is generally linked in the Baltics with the withdrawal of the Baltic-German community from Latvia and Estonia in the autumn of 1939, but in 1938 it referred to increasing pressure to reincorporate the territory of Memel back into Germany.

GERMAN AGAIN Hitler was already sailing to Memel when the Lithuanian Foreign Minister Juozas Urbsys was forced to agree to its surrender at a meeting in Berlin on 21 March 1939. His welcome was as ecstatic and as genuine as it had been a year earlier in Austria (even though seasickness on his part had delayed his arrival by several hours). Local elections in December 1938 had provided a warning of this, with overwhelming support for Nazi-supporting candidates. Many Jews left at that time, foreseeing the worst; those who left for Lithuania as the Germans took over found that they were already banned from local buses. As a result, they had to walk to the railway station with whatever possessions they could carry, facing constant abuse and ridicule as they did so.

There was little Western reaction to this German seizure, although it would be the last one with no resistance offered. Five months later, when Germany hoped to seize Danzig and the Polish corridor with similar ease, World War II broke out as the Western allies honoured commitments given to Poland. As with Königsberg, Memel was a very congenial environment in which to spend the first five years of the war, being spared any land fighting or air raids. Until late 1942, a final German victory seemed certain. Defeat would come to the area brutally and quickly at the end of 1944. Whilst there was little fighting in the countryside, Memel was bitterly defended by German forces so the combination of the Soviet bombardment and their destruction of the harbour shortly before the surrender of the city in January 1945 resulted in considerable damage. It is thought that about 40,000 people managed to leave the area by sea and across Poland before it fell.

THE SOVIET ERA Soviet policy in Klaipeda – the Russians adopted the Lithuanian name – became very different from that in former East Prussia to the south. There were never plans to expel the remaining German population and those who had left were encouraged to return. Some in fact who found themselves in what had by the summer of 1945 become the Soviet zone of Germany were actually repatriated. It is understandable why about 10,000 former Memelländer would want to take this opportunity. Despite 28% of the city being completely destroyed and 36% badly damaged, this still left 40% intact, and the percentage of usable housing in the surrounding countryside was much higher. Even if returnees were to find the contents totally looted, this could well seem more attractive than years in a refugee camp further west.

An economic regime typical of the rest of the USSR was soon established in the Klaipeda area. Whilst the larger economic concerns were quickly nationalised, local residents had to quickly turn to barter and the black market for day-to-day survival. Ironically, given its earlier role in Memel, there was a great shortage of wood, but agriculture quickly revived and those whose cars still worked could take cheese and meat to Latvia and bring back textiles. As manufacturing began in Kaliningrad, there would be similar 'exchanges' there. In the city, people not only kept chicken and rabbits, but even cattle, which they led into the countryside each day for grazing. It would be 1949 before Soviet collectivisation reduced but did not eliminate private trading. The speedy erection of five statues of Stalin, and the removal of any linked with Germany or independent Lithuania, certainly put the Soviet stamp on the city, but again in contrast with East Prussia, no attempt was made to pretend that life started only in 1945 and that nothing existed before then. Religious communities for instance, although drastically curtailed, could continue to operate in what was left of the damaged churches.

The Soviet military quickly seized the Curonian Spit and hunted to extinction the 1,200 elks that had led protected lives there under both the Germans and the Lithuanians. As fishing in the Baltic Sea might have been an easy escape route to the West, locals were not allowed to take part in it; instead, fishermen were brought from the Caspian and Black seas for five-year postings.

The German-speaking population faced an uncertain future in many ways. Soviet policy remained ambivalent for several years so some took on Soviet citizenship whereas others stayed stateless. The latter lost its appeal from 1950 when it no longer spared young men from conscription. Many had lost all forms of identification in the fighting in late 1944 and others had later destroyed them, not wanting to be linked with documents issued by the Nazi regime. The shrewdest move was to keep documentation issued by the Lithuanian government between 1923 and 1939. Those who returned in 1945–6 had obviously assumed that they would be able to change their minds and settle subsequently in Germany again. Even if the Soviets had ever thought this might be allowed, the increasing tension around the Cold War in the late 1940s prevented this.

It was not only the Western powers who presented a threat to the USSR at that time. The Forest Brothers, fervent Lithuanian independence fighters, were as active around Klaipeda as they were elsewhere in Lithuania. There was more fighting in the countryside around the city after World War II than had taken place during it. The Soviets therefore felt they had to tackle two enemies at once – Lithuanian 'bandits' and fascist 'remnants'. In the first case, by the mid 1950s they were able to muster sufficient military strength to eliminate the Forest Brothers but only after years of destruction wrought on their personnel and the humiliation of not being able to impose the Soviet system in any other way.

A political solution was then found for dealing with the German population who wanted to leave. The West German government reluctantly established diplomatic relations with the USSR in 1955 as the only way they could finally secure the release of prisoners of war still held there. Their embassy opened in Moscow in 1956 and by 1958 a formal agreement was concluded under which about 8,000 former German nationals were able to leave Klaipeda for West Germany (a further few hundred would leave instead for East Germany). The procedures were long-winded and, in the face of Soviet inertia and hostility, both considerable stamina and bribes were needed to acquire the necessary exit documents. Amber was a convenient bribe for Moscow officials unable to obtain it legitimately. Some Germans could not complete this obstacle course, and others stayed voluntarily; for those who survived, it would be 1990 before they could try again. The departure of so many Germans had a marked effect on the local free market which was by now tolerated once a week in Klaipeda. They dumped so much before they left that prices dropped drastically.

Klaipeda was very fortunate to have Alfonsas Zalys as its mayor from 1965 to 1990. He perfected the technique which the national Communist Party leader Antanas Snieckus had developed of acquiescing totally to many of Moscow's demands but fighting tooth and nail on others. The two of them probably worked together to keep Lithuanians as a large ethnic majority in Klaipeda, even if this meant not developing the port at a pace that it could otherwise have taken. In 1979, the percentage of Lithuanians in the city had reached its lowest point, 65%, but could easily have dropped well below 50% if Moscow's 'suggestions' about expansion had been heeded. In 1968, Zalys started restoring the old, and therefore very German, city centre. He could not prevent the destruction of the old cemeteries but he could at least ensure that they stayed as open spaces and that no objections would be made to flowers being taken there. He also helped to preserve many of the ornaments from these cemeteries, which are now kept in the Blacksmith Museum (see page 246). He was responsible for the opening of the Clock Museum (see page 246) in 1984, but his greatest achievement was the establishment of the university in 1990, just before he retired. He worked hard to give the harbour an international link, which was finally achieved in 1989 with the ferry to Mukran in East Germany. The two national governments concerned were not in the least interested in closer ties by then, but were worried that the political infection of Solidarity in Poland might affect workers involved in transit traffic by land.

INDEPENDENCE The city that Zalys bequeathed to an independent Lithuania was therefore far more ready for its sudden opening to a ruthless market economy than were many others, including Kaunas. The opening of the Curonian Spit at the same time was a great boost to tourism, and the 400-room Klaipeda Hotel, built for no real purpose in the early 1980s, was immediately able to receive coachloads of German *Heimkeher* who had not seen their former home since 1944. The airport close by at Palanga, which immediately became international, enabled the city to present itself effectively to the European business world several years before its immediate neighbours and competitors – Liepaja and Kaliningrad – were able to do so.

The next few years will provide more of a challenge to Klaipeda; industry has an ever-wider choice of transport outlets and manufacturing centres, whilst the novelty value to tourists has worn off. Nobody will simply come to Klaipeda just because it is there and because of its intriguing past. Klaipeda really has to sell itself. Serious promotion of the city to tourists abroad really dates only from 2006, although developments in the city itself started a few years earlier. It is therefore too early to judge the long-term results. However successful the city is, it will never again be just a transit stop. Lithuanians have achieved in 20 years what the Germans did not in 800 years; outsiders now stay in Klaipeda, deliberately and with pleasure.

PRACTICALITIES

TOURIST INFORMATION As with so many Baltic cities, do not expect any tourist facilities, or even a decent map, at the bus or railway station. Once in town however, the **Tourist Information Centre** (*Turgaus 7;* ☏ *46 412186;* e *tic@klaipedainfo.lt; www.klaipedainfo.lt;* ⊕ *Jun–Sep 09.00–19.00 Mon–Fri, 10.00–16.00 Sat–Sun; Oct–May 09.00–19.00 Mon–Fri only*) has an ample selection of leaflets and can also book hotels and car hire, etc. Not many books have been published on the area, but those available are all sold here, as is the excellent free guidebook *Explore Klaipeda*, which incorporates a useful public transport map. There are also computers which visitors can use free of charge for up to 15 minutes.

TELEPHONE The dialing code for Klaipeda is 46 so this prefix is required before the six-digit numbers given below when phoning from elsewhere in Lithuania or from a mobile.

TRANSPORT

Except when arriving and departing, visitors are unlikely to need local transport as most sites are within walking distance of the hotels where they are likely to stay. Those with little luggage can even consider walking from the bus and train stations as detailed below.

BY BUS Because of the almost non-existent train services, buses are the normal means of travelling around the country and into Kaliningrad or Latvia. Two websites (*www.autobusubilietai.lt* & *www.klap.lt*) give information on domestic buses. The journey to Kaunas takes less than three hours, and to Vilnius, four hours; on both routes there is a bus about every two hours between 05.00 and 19.00.

Eurolines (*www.eurolines.lt*) and Ecolines (*www.ecolines.lt*) both operate international services to Riga via Liepaja and to Kaliningrad along the Curonian Spit. The bus takes two hours to Liepaja, six hours to Riga and four hours to Kaliningrad.

Details of the local bus network are on www.klaipedatransport.lt. Tickets bought ahead in kiosks cost 1.50Lt; those bought on the bus cost 2Lt. There are no day tickets or discounts for buying booklets of tickets. The tourist office sells a public transport map, but the one included in *Explore Klaipeda* is probably sufficient for most visitors.

Minibuses, or microbuses as they are called locally, operate along similar routes to those of the large vehicles, but charge 2.50Lt, payable to the driver. Seats are always guaranteed and the buses can be stopped anywhere on their route.

The bus station (*www.klap.lt*) is opposite the railway station, about a kilometre from the city centre. It is currently very rundown but a thorough renovation was promised during 2008. It has a left-luggage office (⊕ *03.30–11.30 & 12.30–20.30 daily*), which is useful for passengers spending a short time in the city. Its website has an English section and lists both domestic and international buses.

BY BOAT Car/passenger ferries have been a regular feature of Klaipeda harbour since the early 1990s. The main operator is currently DFDS Lisco (*www.lisco.lt*) who have three separate services, each operating six times a week, to Kiel and Saasnitz in Germany and to Karlshamn in Sweden. The harbour is about 8km from the city centre, to the south. Car ferries to the Curonian Spit operate from what is known as the New Terminal, 2km south of the city centre. These carry the buses to Nida and Kaliningrad.

BY AIR The nearest airport to Klaipeda is at Palanga (*www.palanga-airport.lt*), 32km to the north along the coast. In summer 2008 FlyLAL started twice-weekly services to Palanga Airport from both London Stansted and Dublin. SAS operates twice-daily to Copenhagen, which then offers worldwide connections, and Norwegian Air Shuttle operates twice a week from Oslo. The airport website gives full details of services and also of connecting buses to Klaipeda, Liepaja and Palanga itself. (Although some buses are tied to specific flights, there are plenty of services in operation, so that those not wishing to take a taxi can wait for a bus.) In the course of 2008, it is likely that either Air Baltic or FlyLAL will operate a service to Vilnius. There is great local demand for this, given the successful service that now runs between Liepaja and Riga.

BY TRAIN There are two trains a day to Vilnius, which both take about five hours, one in the morning and one in the evening. They go via Šiauliai and not via Kaunas, which to some extent explains why they are so slow. Full details of the schedule are on the Lithuanian Railways (Lietuvos Geležinkeliai) website (*www.litrail.lt*).

ACCOMMODATION

Klaipeda has a short tourist season, really linked with that on the Curonian Spit, so hotels are heavily booked from mid-June to late August. The prices given below refer to that time, when most visitors are likely to be there. However those not tied to school holidays should certainly come in May or September and take advantage of lower prices then. For those prepared to endure the winter weather, even lower prices are available, or sweeteners such as a free transfer to Palanga Airport may be offered as an inducement.

⌂ **Radisson SAS** (74 rooms) Šaulių 28; ☏ 46 490800; e info.klaipeda@radissonsas.com. www.klaipeda.radissonsas.com. Regulars at the Radissons in the 3 capitals will initially be surprised at the small size of this hotel & its location a few hundred metres away from a any main road. However once inside, the service & facilities will put them at ease, given that the bathrooms all have underfloor heating & a telephone, not to mention an ever-increasing array of soaps & towels. The location in fact ensures complete peace & quiet & easy drop-offs outside the hotel for cars & coaches. $$$$

⌂ **Europa Royale** (50 rooms) Teatro 1; ☏ 46 404444; e klaipeda@europaroyale.com; www.groupeuropa.com. Although in the same group as the hotels with these names in Riga & Vilnius, this does not aim to equal them in any of the facilities it provides, Having said that, its prices are much lower too. Given that most visitors will be out for long days, the smallish rooms & cramped reception areas will not matter too much. B/fast is often a disappointment, but the dinner menu is extensive & the ambience pleasantly quiet. Its location in the Old Town is ideal, as walking to most of the sites is no problem. $$$

⌂ **Navalis** (28 rooms) Manto 23; ☏ 46 404200; e info@navalis.lt; www.navalis.lt. Old Germany & modern Lithuania blend well here. The façade is of a sombre 19th-century German red-brick building, but behind it modern Lithuania excels, as the hotel only opened in 2002. The rooms are spacious & well lit, & all have tea/coffee-making facilities, plus AC. Half of them have baths as well as showers. A glass lift is an unexpected modern feature; even more unexpected is the Turkish bath, free to guests for an hour every morning. $$$

⌂ **Vecekrug** (23 rooms) Jūros 23; ☏ 46 301002; e info@vecekrug.lt; www.vecekrug.lt. German speakers need not worry about the word krug (pub) in the name of this hotel, which in fact is very quiet & modern. It is impossible to describe the rooms as they are all totally different from each other, but AC is common to them all & half have baths, rather than just showers. The 5th-floor terrace is a definite summer attraction & further views are available from the 6th floor. The staff speak excellent English & the hotel is probably unique in Klaipeda in not really being geared to German visitors. $$$

⌂ **Klaipeda** (307 rooms) Naujoji Sodo 1; ☏ 46 404372; e hotel@klaipedahotel.lt; www.klaipedahotel.lt. Some hotels from the Soviet era have managed to put their past totally behind them, such as the Lietuva in Vilnius & the Lātvija in Riga. The Neris in Kaunas did the same in 2008. However this hotel, although renovated on several occasions since 1990, has never done anything sufficiently radical to assure visitors on this point. Many must come into the vast bare lobby, see the concrete staircase, the dark wood & the advertisement for the striptease club & then turn away immediately. Those with more determination will get a perfectly modern room, probably with a good view, & as the 'K' business complex arises around them, may well find it a convenient ghetto in which to stay & from which there will be no need to leave. $$

⌂ **Reval Inn** (84 rooms) Minijos 119; ☏ 46 380803; e klaipeda@revalinn.com; www.revalinn.com. Part of a chain that opened in both Tallinn & Riga during 2007, the Reval aims to provide basic but sufficient accommodation on the outskirts of the city. Largely geared to the needs of motorists, there are also able to offer much lower prices to those willing to bus into the city centre. The hotel is close to the ferry for the Curonian Spit. $$

✕ EATING AND DRINKING

RESTAURANTS Through the 1990s, tourists rarely left their hotels for meals, so poor was the choice of alternatives. From around 2000, this situation started to change and by 2006 a range of international cuisines was represented. Competition has done the hotel restaurants no harm; they have moved on from being safely predictable to being imaginatively fun.

Combined with the new restaurants, there must now be close on a hundred places in the city centre where visitors could happily eat. Those listed below are a mixture of the well established and those with a more unusual bent. Prices given here are the average cost of a three-course meal without wine.

✕ Ararat Liepų 48a; ☏ 46 410001; www.ararat.lt.
Although not right in the centre, the Ararat is a walk of just 10mins or so to the post office or Clock Museum. It could also provide an excellent welcome or farewell to the city, being close to the bus station. Whilst Armenia is well known for its grilled meat & game, this restaurant enlarges the menu to show all the varieties of dolmades available to vegetarians. Not being ultra-nationalist, it realises that a good meal is best complemented with Georgian wines, & then with Armenian liqueurs. 24Lt.

✕ Čili Pizza Manto 31; ☏ 46 315189; www.cili.lt. This is the most central of the 4 branches in Klaipeda of Lithuania's most successful chain. Rapid expansion has not reduced its appeal either to locals or to visitors, nor has it increased the size of the crusts at the expense of the toppings. 22Lt

✕ Kurpiai Kurpių 1a; ☏ 46 410555; www.jazz.lt. People come here for the jazz rather than for the food since, when music takes over, it really does so, which explains the little interest taken in the menu. The owner is Vytautas Grubliauskas, a Member of Parliament who, like the British MP Ken Clarke, happily combines politics with jazz. His website (*www.grubliauskas.lt*) explains how & why; the website

of the restaurant given above also has details of other jazz concerts which takes this music out of the building & all over the city. 30Lt.

✕ Memelis Žvejų 4; ☏ 46 403040; www.memelis.lt. This is the ideal venue for those who want to forget Klaipeda & relive Memel. The building is a former red-brick German warehouse which has been converted into a brewery & restaurant. Visitors are welcome to see the brewery in action & then to order the product by the litre, the jug or even the barrel. Food comes in similarly gargantuan portions. The ground floor is for individuals, the higher ones for private groups wanting karaoke, large TV screens &, at weekends, live music too. The website, as expected, details the menu & the entertainment, but surprisingly also provides a detailed history of the port. 35Lt.

✕ Stora Antis Tiltų 6; ☏ 46 493910; www.storaantis.lt. Regulars at the Livonia in Riga or Granma's in Tallinn will be very happy here, deep in a cellar & surrounded by memorabilia at least 80 years old. Allow the whole evening for dinner, given the size of the portions & the stress on meat or poultry for the main course, having begun with a full soup or a varied fish hors d'oeuvre. 40Lt.

CAFÉS

Klaipeda is best known locally for its bakery/café chain **Klaipedos Duona** (*www.duona.com;* ☉ *08.00–18.00 Mon–Fri, 08.00–15.00 Sat/Sun*), so synthetic bread or cakes from elsewhere are a rare lapse here. The branch at 10 Aukštoji is best known to tourists, being in the Old Town. To keep Klaipeda in mind when visitors have left, the company kindly provides many recipes on its website. There are many theories concerning the origin of the city's name but this company is happy to suggest the one that links the word '*klaip*' meaning 'bread' with '*eda*' meaning 'to eat', which makes the townspeople all 'bread-eaters'.

The city lacks the intimacy provided in the Old Town centres of other Baltic cities, but **Friedricho pasažas** (Friedrich's Passage) is being created as a pedestrian street to provide the nearest equivalent. With its cluster of cafés and small shops it offers both an obvious place for tourists to take a break from a walk and an area where local people can meet.

⊡ Čeburekinė Sido 10 Skerdėjų. A small café, with a run-down exterior, which deters many visitors. However those who ignore this will be rewarded with a wide range of home cooking, extending to light meals around lunchtime.

SHOPPING

The best bookshop in the town, **Knygų Klėtis** (*19a Aukštoji*), is the only one likely to have anything from Memel or Soviet days. Other shops, it has to be said, are disappointing for visitors. Perhaps the short peak season, plus the range of businesses that moved into out-of-town shopping centres, explains this. There are plenty of outlets for amber and ceramics in the Old and New towns, but none stands out.

In the 1990s, the city lacked charm and colour, and walking in Klaipeda was a chore. Walking is now a pleasure. There are of course the many restored buildings that help to recreate the atmosphere of the town before bombers and bulldozers were let loose on it. However visitors should perhaps be even more impressed by the artistic creations that hit them on every corner or in every square. The bronze cat and mouse are perhaps the most famous, but there are footprints, circular memorials, information towers, arches and monuments. Perhaps it is the intense pace of new creations that is preventing local writers and photographers from putting memories of them all between covers. So visitors should take a camera and thank the fact that, coming in a digital age, they can take innumerable photographs without counting the cost.

The walk starts at the bus or railway station, both close to the **Sculpture Park** (page 247), which is now the one large area of greenery in the town centre. In congenial weather, it is easy to wheel a case through the park and then on towards the hotels in the centre. Turn right at the far end of the park onto **Liepų**, the main street in the newer part of the town. This word means 'lime', although unlike its namesake in Berlin, Unter den Linden, it is not in fact tree-lined. In choosing it, the town council presumably hope that the name need never change again. In the past, the name of this street has always reflected the ruling power, so has been called Alexander after the Russian Tsar Alexander II, Smetona after the president in the 1930s, Hitler following the German occupation in 1939 and then Lenin in Soviet times.

The **Prano Domšaitis Art Gallery** (page 245) is on the right shortly after leaving the park. Some 300m further, on the left-hand side, is the **post office** ($\oplus$ *08.00–18.00 Mon–Fri*), which dates from 1893 and is the best of many neo-Gothic brick buildings on this street. It has a tower of 42m and a painted interior that has survived over a hundred years. It would be a pity to buy stamps anywhere else in Klaipeda, and for once a queue will not matter, given the beauty of the ceiling. At weekends, the business of selling stamps gives way to a carillon concert which emanates from the tower at 12.00 on both Saturday and Sunday. In 1987, during the early days of *perestroika*, a set of bells came from Germany to replace those destroyed in the war. These were in turn replaced in 2006 by a set from Holland which were played for the first time on Christmas Eve that year. The **Clock Museum** (page 246) is next to the post office and in the summer its courtyard is the best place to enjoy the carillon concerts.

It is now sensible to cross the river. Before the war it would have been more appropriate to stay on this side and admire the Stock Exchange, but this was completely destroyed during the fighting and the Klaipeda Hotel now stands on its site. The empty space between the hotel and the river was in Soviet times the setting for the compulsory Lenin statue which no town centre could avoid. Just before crossing the river, though, note the somewhat disjointed arch to the left which was built in 2003 to commemorate the 80th anniversary of Klaipeda joining Lithuania. The larger white section represents Lithuania Major, basically the territory of Lithuania now, but excluding the former 'Memelland', and the red stone represents Lithuania Minor, the areas of former East Prussia where much of the population spoke Lithuanian. The inscription reads: 'We are one nation, one land, one Lithuania'.

On the other side of the river, to the left of the bridge, is the sailing boat *Meridianas*, built in 1948 but lodged for many years here, first as a training vessel and now as a restaurant primarily used by tourist groups. The outline of the ship without its sails is often used as the logo for promoting Klaipeda, whereas the sails are the logo for Lithuania's most famous beer, Švyturys, which is brewed in Klaipeda. Three roads, Kalvių, Kurpių and Kepejų, lead off to the right from Tiltų towards Teatro aikštė (Theatre Square), and all have examples of *Fachwerk*, the style of building that uses

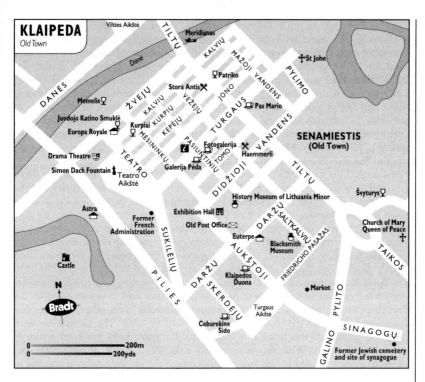

wooden frames reinforced with plaster and which is very appropriate for the soft foundations in this area. Extensive renovation of many of these buildings was under way between 2005 and 2008. If there is time it is worth walking along each of these three roads, but if not, take Kepėjų as far as the junction with Vežejų and note the *Tower* sculpture there. It dates from 1990 and set the trend for erecting in this area a wide number of works in marble or in bronze. It shows several of the architectural styles used in Klaipeda.

This is becoming quite an area for bronze sculptures. Some, such as the mouse outside the Kurpiai Jazz Club (page 241) or the cat firmly implanted a safe distance away on Kalvių, add frivolity to the area. Others, such as the footprints now being cast in memory of famous former residents of Klaipeda, have a more serious purpose. Klaipeda will soon deserve a history based purely on its new bronze monuments.

Theatre Square (Teatro aikštė), with its statue of **Ännchen von Tharau** (page 244), is the obvious tourist centre of Klaipeda, or perhaps one should say Memel given that the surroundings are so German. The current Classical building, which houses the theatre, dates from 1857, three years after the fire which destroyed so much in this vicinity. Sadly the building will always be remembered, not for any play performed here, but for the speech Hitler gave from the balcony when Germany seized Memelland in March 1939. Some reconstruction of the interior took place in the 1980s and more is under way in 2008.

The square can be left in any direction. Going westwards across the main road Pilies leads to the **castle** (page 246). Going south, on the western corner of the square where Sukilelių joins it, is the building used by the French for their military administration headquarters in the three years (1920–23) that they remained in Memel. Going east along Turgaus leads to the **tourist office** (page 238) at number 7; this road is in contrast to those between here and the river since buildings here are larger and of stone or brick. Following Sukileliu and then crossing a small park leads to Aukštoji, the street with the most impressive remaining examples of *Fachwerk*. Several of these buildings were warehouses and the locations of the hoists which were used for lifting goods to higher floors can still be seen. Number 7 is the **Art Exhibition Hall** (*www.parodurumai.lt;* ☉ *11.00–18.00 Mon–Fri, 11.00–16.00 Sat; admission free*), which takes art in a very broad sense of the term, often incorporating music and film as well. There is no regular exhibition here so check on the website to see what is currently showing. Quite often several different exhibitions run here concurrently and they will certainly be a total contrast to the formal exterior of the building. The **History Museum of Lithuanian Minor** (page 247) is almost next door to the Exhibition Hall, on Didžioji Vandens.

Number 13 is a post office which would normally be worth a visit, since its décor is so unlike what one would normally expect, but it cannot match the interior of the central post office (page 242). Number 19a is **Knygų Klėtis**, the best bookshop in the town and the only one likely to have anything from Memel or Soviet days. By now it may well be time for a pause, either in Klaipedos Duona bakery/café over the road, or at one of the restaurants in Friedricho pasažas, just coming up on the left-hand side.

Aukštoji leads to the market and then continues as **Sinagogų**. This area was a small Jewish quarter with about 1,000 Jews living here in the mid 19th century and by 1910 this figure had increased to 2,000. Restrictions on Jews settling here had for centuries been tougher than in other towns in Prussia or Russia and it was only under the French in 1920 that they were granted equal citizenship with other Germans and Lithuanians. By 1928 the community had increased to 4,500. The Lithuanians were happy to encourage this trend as a counter to the increasingly pro-Nazi nature of many local Germans. What was the cemetery until World War II, situated at the end of Sinagogu, was chosen by the Soviet authorities as the site for a radio aerial used to jam outside broadcasts. For many years bones were left where they had been dug up and some of the tombstones were built into the base of this aerial. The area has now been made into a park, with the few remaining tombstones being built into a surrounding wall. Nothing is left of the synagogue.

A quick return to the river can be made by walking along Tiltų but with more time allow a few minutes to turn right into **Turgaus**, Market Street or Marktstrasse in German times, and continue to the end where it forms a T-junction with Pylimo. Sadly it is only from old photos that visitors can see what used to dominate the view here, a 75m tower on a Gothic church designed by Friedrich August Stüler, one of Berlin's most famous 19th-century architects, who was also active in Königsberg (see page 274) and Rauschen. Not only was the church destroyed in Soviet times, but a public toilet was built in its place. Fortunately a Lutheran church was built here in the 1990s, but of course it is much smaller than the one it has replaced. Behind it are the town bastions, built at various times between 1780 and 1820 but never in the end used.

WHAT TO SEE

STATUE OF ÄNNCHEN VON THARAU This statue at the centre of Teatro aikštė (Theatre Square) was the symbol of Memel in the past, and was adopted by Klaipeda with equal enthusiasm as Soviet control lessened. The daughter of a country parson, von Tharau is known throughout Germany because the poet Simon Dach (1605–59) wrote passionately about her and his poem was put to music early in the 19th century; in the 20th century, his work was also translated into Lithuanian. Dach was born in Memel but spent most of his life teaching and writing in Königsberg. The original statue dated from 1912 but it disappeared during World War II. Some say that this was on Hitler's orders, as he was allegedly unhappy speaking to her back rather than her face when he addressed the local population from the theatre balcony behind the statue in March 1939, and proclaimed the incorporation of Memel into the German Reich. However, as the statue was still there in late 1939, this is unlikely and it was probably removed later to protect it from the Russians, although no original has ever been found.

The return of a statue to this site was the result of fortuitous timing and courageous co-operation in the late 1980s between Heinz Radziwill, a Baltic German whose family had lived in Memelland for generations, and Antanas Stanevičius, editor of the newspaper *Soviet Klaipeda*. Radziwell could provide the money and Stanevičius floated the idea in May 1988 in his paper. Inevitably there was still some Soviet opposition to a 'fascist' statue, but *perestroika* was sufficiently far advanced by then for the idea not to be dismissed out of hand. On 18 November 1989 the new statue was unveiled, after grandchildren of the original sculptor had tracked down models of the 1912 one. No statue was placed here in Soviet times, although there were plans for one dedicated to Martynas Mažvydas, author of the first book published in the Lithuanian language.

PRANAS DOMŠAITIS/FRANZ DOMSCHEIT ART GALLERY *(Liepų 33; ⊕ 12.00–18.00 Tue–Sun; admission 6Lt)* This is the Klaipeda branch of the Lithuania Art Museum. Half the gallery is devoted to a permanent collection of around 500 Domscheit's paintings, the other half to temporary exhibitions, usually of contemporary paintings and sculpture.

Few people in Memel happily crossed the racial divide between Germans and Lithuanians but Domscheit succeeded in doing so wherever he lived. He was born not far from Königsberg, East Prussia, in what is now Kaliningrad in 1880. As both parents were of racially mixed origins, he was happy to keep both his names – Domšaitis and Domscheit – throughout his life. He owes his start in the artistic world to Max Liebermann, one of Germany's most famous artists at the start of the 20th century, who persuaded a reluctant Art Academy in Königsberg to accept him as a student in 1907. From 1910 to 1914 he would be able to travel in a way that would never again be possible for him, to Paris, London, Florence and St Petersburg. On his deathbed he is alleged to have said '*Ich bin immer unterwegs*' ('I am always travelling'), which applied in particular to this time in his life. He fought on the Eastern front but was fortunately not injured and in the 1920s was largely based in Berlin, but rapidly became known all over Germany. Like Liebermann, he was hard to typecast, but perhaps *Neue Sachlichkeit*, 'new objectivity', is the most appropriate school with which his work can be linked. If not as politically intense as Käthe Kollwitz, he was never unwilling to shun sadness as a theme for his paintings.

Max Liebermann, being a prominent Jew with a brutal sense of humour, was one of the first artists to be banned under the Nazi regime. Domscheit, being so close to him, was bound to suffer soon afterwards and his art was exhibited by the Nazis in the celebrated 'Degenerate Art' exhibition in Munich in 1938. In the long term, this proved invaluable to him, as it made him famous outside Germany; most of the other artists whom the Nazis hoped to ridicule in this way likewise benefited from this worldwide exposure. From the 1930s he used only the Lithuanian form of his name on his paintings.

Domscheit sat out the war in Austria, painting trivial landscapes just to earn enough to survive. He was in 1949 pleased to leave Austria, together with many other Lithuanian exiles, for South Africa where he remained until his death in 1965. Although aged 70 when he arrived there, he stayed as active as ever and in many books is described as being South African. He took quite a number of his paintings with him from Europe, and after his death his widow took the collection with her to America. She put most of his pictures in the hands of the Lithuanian Foundation, the organisation that kept together the diaspora and made sure that Lithuania was never forgotten in the USA. They gave a few pictures to Klaipeda in 1989, during the *perestroika* period of Soviet Lithuania, and then the remaining 500 as soon as the country became independent in 1991. It was, however, ten years before this permanent home was found for them. Whilst individual paintings by Domscheit can still be seen in other galleries in Germany, the USA and in South Africa, this is appropriately a complete collection in the sense that each period of his life is extensively represented here.

BLACKSMITH MUSEUM (*Šaltkalvių 2;* ⊕ *10.00–18.00 Tue–Sun; admission 3Lt*) In its title, this museum is unduly modest. Whilst situated in a former smithy and showing the tools of this trade, what really makes it memorable are the variety of grave crosses collected at considerable personal danger by Dionyzas Varkalis throughout the Soviet period. Until 1974, there was an unwritten policy of benign neglect towards German cemeteries but from then on they were cleared and it was fortunate that Varkalis took the risk of protecting whatever he could find. There is some light relief here with door knobs and umbrella stands. It is important to go outside the museum into the back courtyard, where many railings and crosses, too big for the interior, are exhibited.

CASTLE (*www.mlimuziejus.lt;* ⊕ *10.00–18.00 Tue–Sat; admission 4Lt*) A wooden fortress was built here in the 13th century as soon as the Teutonic Knights conquered the area, and a brick one followed in the 17th century. It was however hardly used and was allowed to decline in the 18th and 19th centuries, when it was sometimes used as a prison. It played no role during any of the 20th-century battles, and restoration started only in 2002. Excavation had however started in 1968 and still continues to produce individually exciting finds, particularly of jewellery. One of the castle's tunnels is now a museum for these items; it also exhibits a model of how the 17th-century building looked.

CHURCH OF MARY QUEEN OF PEACE (*Rumpiškės 6a; admission free*). A Catholic church on this site was destroyed by the Germans shortly before their retreat in 1945. The large Lithuanian Catholic community that moved into Klaipeda after the war was keen to rebuild it, and permission for this was granted in 1955, a comparatively liberal time after the death of Stalin. The foundations were blessed in 1957 and the church, built entirely with private funds and private labour, was completed in 1960, with a tall steeple that could be seen from the sea (and thus portrayed an image of religious tolerance to foreign sailors whose boats were occasionally allowed to dock in Klaipeda). Many local residents recall the enthusiasm of the hundreds of people involved. Yet as soon as it was ready to open, instructions came from Moscow that the church was to be closed and it seems that this was a personal decision of Nikita Khrushchev. The steeple was removed and nominally the building was converted into a concert hall but it was well into the 1970s before the audience ever outnumbered the performers. After the arrest of many people who courageously demonstrated against the deconsecration and even prayed outside the building, the only other means of protest seemed to be to boycott any function that took place there. However a courageous new form of resistance was instigated in 1979 when a petition with 148,000 signatures was taken to Moscow. It would however only be in 1988 that the church was returned to the Catholic community, and reconstruction had to await independence in 1991. It is now possible to climb the tower, which is the best viewpoint for the Old Town.

Visits up the tower are not arranged at the church itself but at the tourist office in town (see page 238). They put together groups of five people or more so it is advisable to go there on arrival in Klaipeda to be sure of having a visit.

CLOCK MUSEUM (*Liepų 12; www.muziejai.lt/klaipeda;* ⊕ *12.00–18.00 Tue–Sun; admission 6Lt*) The opening of this museum in 1984 was the culmination of work that had started ten years earlier. Not surprisingly Alfonsas Žalys (see page 237) was a strong supporter of the idea and Dionyzas Varkalis, best known for his work in the Blacksmith Museum, was also active here. If the expression were not so cumbersome, the museum should be called one of 'time-measuring devices', given what is now on display. A modest collection was first shown in 1978 at the Art Gallery, before this dedicated site was made available.

The building had had many illustrious owners since it was constructed in 1820, but the best known was the first, John Simpson, one of several Scottish merchants from a family that lived in Memel for many generations.

There is little that links the museum specifically to Klaipeda; the collection of clocks comes from all over Europe and dates back to the 16th century. Models explain methods of time-keeping before it become mechanical, when it was dependent on sand and candles. Whilst the technical side is described in detail, for most visitors here the interest will be in seeing how clocks from each artistic era reflect it in the same way that the surrounding buildings do. This applies as much in the electronic era, covered here extensively, as it did in the Gothic one. There are sundials in the courtyard at the back of the museum, and also an increasing number of sculptures which enable local artists to interpret time in a far more abstract way than is possible indoors. The courtyard is also a convenient place to listen to the bells ringing from the post office tower.

HISTORY MUSEUM OF LITHUANIA MINOR (*Didžioji Vandens 6; www.mlimuziejus.lt;* ⏲ *10.00–18.00 Tue–Sun; admission 4Lt*) A museum with local material has been in Klaipeda since 1924 but only since 1988 has it been in this building and not subject to political pressures. Sadly, many previous occupiers either stole or destroyed much of the contents, but fortunately a great deal was kept by private individuals from the 1918–40 period and it is thanks to their generosity that the collection is now so extensive. These include a *Times Atlas* from 1920, unable to commit itself to any local border, the varied banknotes used around that time, and then French stamps overprinted with a price in German marks. Other displays cover the fall of Memel to Soviet forces in 1945 and the rebuilding of the city undertaken largely by German prisoners of war. Inevitably, the first new building was a Soviet war memorial unveiled on 28 June 1945. A model of the city as it was in the 1920s makes clear what has changed and what has remained to this day.

SCULPTURE PARK (*Liepų/Trilapio/Daukanto*) This was the main town cemetery until 1945, but was then deliberated left to decay until 1979 when the site was cleared. Fortunately brave local people were able to save some of the German crosses and headstones that are now in the Blacksmith Museum. Perhaps to appease the local population, a Soviet memorial to the 'Lithuanian Uprising' of 1923 was erected here, and then it became an exhibition centre for local sculptors, a role it still retains. The former chapel was converted into a Russian Orthodox church. The park carries the name of Martynas Mažvydas (1510–63) who published the first book (*The Catechism*) in Lithuanian. At the end of the Soviet era, there was a plan for a statue of him to be placed on the site where Ännchen von Tharau has now returned, but in the end he was only so honoured in 1997, the 450th anniversary of the publication of this book, when a statue was unveiled in Lietuvininku aikštė, about a kilometre to the northwest of this park.

LITHUANIAN SEA MUSEUM (*Smiltynė 3; www.juru.muziejus.lt;* ⏲ *normally Jun–Aug 10.30–18.00 Tue–Sun; Sep–May Sat/Sun only, but check website, which also gives details of performances*) The museum is at the northern end of the Curonian Spit, and is reached by ferry (pedestrians and bicycles only) from what is known as the Old Harbour, in

the town centre close to the castle. The museum is 1.5km from the terminal on the other side of the lagoon, but buses meet the ferries. Visitors wanting to drive have to take the ferry 2km to the south of this one which is also the one used by local buses.

Whilst other museums in Klaipeda retain a formal adult air, this one is definitely for families and its subsidiary name – Aquarium and Dolphinarium – will soon take over as its main one. There are tanks of fish here and even some static exhibits, but the real attraction is the display by the dolphins and the seals, sometimes joined by humans too.

The building, original a fortress, dates from the mid 19th century, but it soon became clear that it would have little use in military defence although in World War II it was used for storing armaments. The **aquarium** was founded in Soviet times, being built between 1973 and 1979. Like so much else in Klaipeda at that time, it resulted from the political skills of Alfonsas Žalys (see page 237), who told Moscow that the collection would be largely of Baltic seals caught locally but that he would call on resources elsewhere in the USSR. In fact he was slowly making contacts the world over to make sure this museum would be of an international standard. As foreign ships were from time to time allowed into Klaipeda, which was not the case with Liepaja or Kaliningrad, he could use these for regular contact with the outside world. By the time his Soviet masters discovered what he was doing, it was too late to stop the project. Given its location, it can draw on both fresh water from the lagoon and salt water from the sea on the other side of the spit.

The **dolphinarium** opened in 1994 although construction began in 1987. These were of course the most difficult financial years of all, covering the collapse of the USSR and Lithuania's attempt to establish its own hard currency. Cash was therefore of no use in buying the refrigeration plants needed from Ukraine, and these had to be bought with shoes, overcoats and television sets instead.

9

Kaliningrad RUSSIA

For 46 years between 1945 and 1991 the Soviet Union occupied the Baltic countries of Estonia, Latvia and Lithuania and also incorporated part of the former German province of East Prussia, renaming the town of Königsberg as Kaliningrad. Confusingly they used this name, too, for the surrounding region or oblast. A cultural and political uniformity was quickly imposed on all these territories and most former links with the outside world curtailed. Kaliningrad suffered most in this respect, with travel there even for Soviet citizens being difficult. Its history as a major German city was ignored; in the town centre British bombing in August 1944 and the final battle for the city in April 1945 left many buildings totally or largely destroyed. Much of what could have been restored was subsequently removed to make the break with the long German past even stronger. Tallinn, Riga and Vilnius were still granted a history, albeit a distorted one as the Soviet Union was unhappy to publicise the period between 1920 and 1940 when these towns were not part of it. Many of their pre-war inhabitants, however, were unable to enjoy it, having been murdered in the Holocaust, or deported to Siberia in 1941, or having fled west ahead of the Soviet army in 1944.

From around 1960, the Soviet authorities allowed travel to Tallinn, Riga and Vilnius but with a maximum stay of three nights. Travel between the cities was by air or on overnight trains. Longer stays were rarely granted to prevent serious contacts being established with the local populations. Tours always started and finished in Leningrad (now St Petersburg) or Moscow to stress the Soviet nature of the programme and to minimise the Baltic element. Travel outside the capitals only became possible in the 1980s towards the end of the Soviet period. Tourists first came to Kaliningrad from 1991 as the Soviet Union fell apart and the military were no longer able to prevent this. As Kaliningrad was a major naval base on the front line with NATO, admitting tourists was out of the question before then. The occasional visitor from Scandinavia came in the 1950s and 1960s but, in comparison, Tibet, North Korea or Albania seemed wide open in those days. Many former East Prussians were desperate to return and 64,000 Germans came to visit in 1992. Their largely hostile reports, and continued bitterness at what many regarded as an illegitimate occupation of their homeland, initially discouraged more general tourists. The expense and complications involved in obtaining full Russian visas for Kaliningrad was a further deterrent just when all its neighbours were abolishing visas and were actively promoting abroad.

However, from around 2005, there were clear public moves to encourage the study of German history and to welcome German participation in far more than charity projects and the restoration of the cathedral. In fact, the final project needed for the cathedral, the new organ, was paid for by the Russian government. Regular visitors noticed activity in the public sector all over the town. The two main lakes were cleared and paths started to be built around them. The Orthodox cathedral was completed, and Victory Square in front of it repaved. A German quarter, the Fishing Village, was started in 2006 along the river opposite the cathedral and this is being financed by Russia. Statues are being erected to famous Germans.

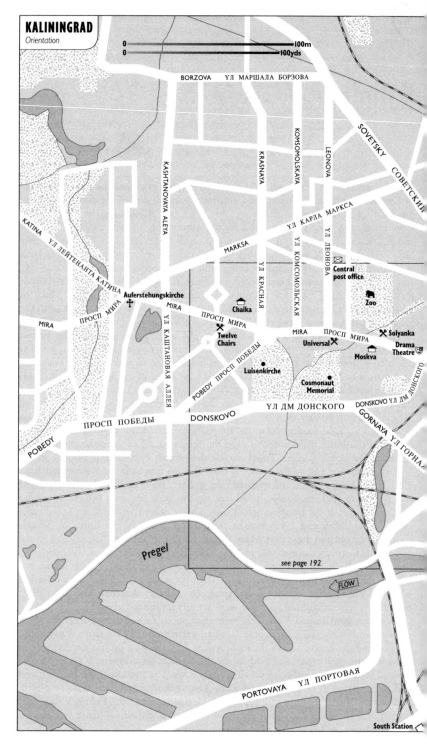

KALININGRAD
Orientation

0 ————————— 100m
0 ————————— 100yds

BORZOVA УЛ МАРШАЛА БОРЗОВА

KOMSOMOLSKAYA

KRASNAYA

LEONOVA

SOVETSKY СОВЕТСКИЙ

KASHTANOVAYA ALEYA

KATINA

УЛ ЛЕЙТЕНАНТА КАТИНА

УЛ КАРЛА МАРКСА

MARKSA

УЛ КОМСОМОЛЬСКАЯ

УЛ ЛЕОНОВА

Central post office

MIRA

ПРОСП МИРА

Auferstehungskirche

MIRA

ПРОСП МИРА

УЛ КАШТАНОВАЯ АЛЛЕЯ

УЛ КРАСНАЯ

Chaika

Zoo

Twelve Chairs

MIRA   ПРОСП МИРА

Solyanka

Universal

Drama Theatre

POBEDY ПРОСП ПОБЕДЫ

Moskva

Luisenkirche

Cosmonaut Memorial

УЛ ДМ ДОНСКОГО

DONSKOVO УЛ ДМ ДОНСКОГО

ПРОСП ПОБЕДЫ

DONSKOVO

GORNAYA УЛ ГОРНАЯ

POBEDY

Pregel

see page 192

FLOW

PORTOVAYA   УЛ ПОРТОВАЯ

South Station

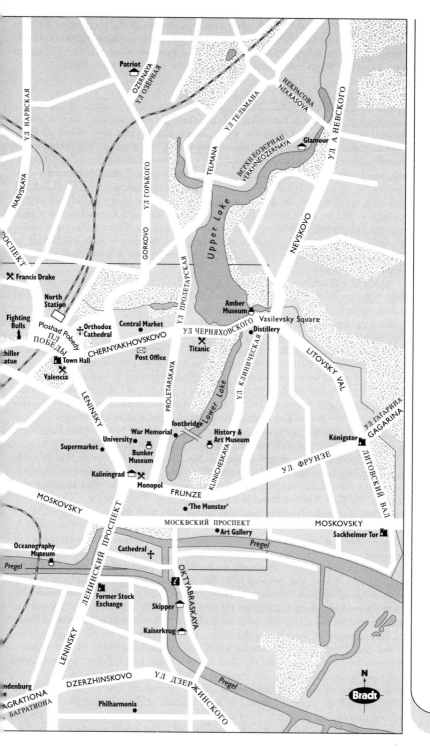

Patriot

ОЗЕРНАЯ
УЛ ОЗЕРНАЯ

НЕКРАСОВА
NEKRASOVA

УЛ ТЕЛЬМАНА

ВЕРХНЕОЗЕРНАU
VERKHNEOZERNAYA

Glamour

УЛ А НЕВСКОГО

УЛ НАРВСКАЯ

TELMANA

NARVSKAYA

ПРОСПЕКТ

УЛ ГОРЬКОГО
GORKOVO

Upper Lake

NEVSKOVO

✗ Francis Drake

North
Station

Fighting
Bulls

Ploshad Pobedy
ПЛ
ПОБЕДЫ

✝ Orthodox
Cathedral

Central Market

УЛ ПРОЛЕТАРСКАЯ

Amber
Museum

Vasilevsky Square

chiller
atue

CHERNYAKHOVSKOVO

УЛ ЧЕРНЯХОВСКОГО

Distillery

LITOVSKY VAL

Town Hall

Post Office

✗ Titanic

УЛ КЛИНИЧЕСКАЯ

✗ Valencia

LENINSKY

PROLETARSKAYA

Lower Lake

footbridge

War Memorial

University

Supermarket

Bunker
Museum

History &
Art Museum

Königstor

УЛ ГАГАРИНА
GAGARINA

ЛИТОВСКИЙ ВАЛ

Kaliningrad

Monopol

KLINICHESKAYA

FRUNZE

УЛ ФРУНЗЕ

MOSKOVSKY

'The Monster'

МОСКВСКИЙ ПРОСПЕКТ

MOSKOVSKY

Oceanography
Museum

ЛЕНИНСКИЙ ПРОСПЕКТ

Cathedral ✝

Art Gallery

Sackheimer Tor

Pregel

Pregel

Former Stock
Exchange

ОКТЯБРЬСКАЯ

Skipper

Kaiserkrug

LENINSKY

ndenburg
e

AGRATIONA
БАГРАТИОНА

DZERZHINSKOVO

УЛ ДЗЕРЖИНСКОГО

Pregel

N

Bradt

Philharmonia

Kaliningrad

9

The year 2007 saw the launch of international services by the local airline KD avia to Britain and Germany. Whilst the majority of passengers on these flights will simply change planes in Kaliningrad, *en route* to other destinations in Russia, this sudden introduction of direct links should encourage more tourists to pay a visit.

THE STATUS OF KALININGRAD

Independence in Estonia, Latvia and Lithuania brought an immediate influx of tourists to their capitals from all over the world, many taking tours that visited all three. Arrivals came to be counted in millions rather than in thousands. This added to the determination of the local town councils to eradicate the recent Soviet past. Cyrillic road signs were torn down, hard currencies introduced and visas abolished for most visitors. Active tourist boards were established, eager to work with the travel industry and with travel writers. In these capitals, the new private sector quickly adapted to tourism so that by 1994 visitors had no problem in finding a luxury hotel or a small two-star one, eating Chinese or Italian food, and reading a Western newspaper on the day of publication. Tourist visits are now similar to those in Stockholm, Lübeck or Kraków, with ample scope for specialist and general groups or individuals preferring to stay on their own.

World War II left savage human scars across the region but fortunately there was little fighting in the three other Baltic state capitals so an architectural heritage stretching back for eight centuries welcomes all visitors. Many of the sites are within walking distance of each other and of the hotels which visitors are likely to use. Others are cheaply and easily reached by public transport.

The transformation in Kaliningrad would be, and remains, more ambivalent. British bombing in August 1944 and bitter fighting in April 1945 left the town centre a shell. By the end of the Soviet period most of the inhabitants were from Russia, a few from the other Soviet republics. In 1991 they were suddenly cut off from home by three foreign countries – Lithuania, Poland and Belarus. Renewed contact from Germany with this former part of East Prussia was as much a threat as an opportunity. The year 1992 brought visions of Kaliningrad becoming the 'Hong Kong of the Baltics' but realism on the spot and indifference in Moscow soon put paid to this.

Until 2004, residents of Kaliningrad, unlike those from the rest of Russia, could travel visa-free to Lithuania and to Poland. Accession of these two countries to the EU put paid to this facility so they now face the same difficulty as other Russians with travel to the West. A new role was not found during the 1990s but there is now greater optimism as it becomes a pilot region in testing links with the surrounding EU. Local people tend to be more positive than their opposite numbers in St Petersburg or Moscow. There is less inequality and certainly much less crime. Those with reasonable qualifications can easily get worthwhile jobs.

Tourists will appreciate the massive grants the Germans have provided in the last ten years as they admire the restored cathedral, the enlarged History Museum, and the excavations of the castle foundations. They will enjoy the restaurants and the many 24-hour shops. Königsberg is methodically and aesthetically returning to many parts of Kaliningrad. Yet the abandoned fields in much of the countryside and the dismal blocks of flats in many of the suburbs show that little has changed for much of the local population. In some ways, Russia has left Kaliningrad behind. Those who never knew the Soviet Union can still take the chance to see Lenin looking down on most town hall squares, even though he was removed in 2005 from the Kaliningrad town centre where he otherwise would have obstructed the view of the new orthodox cathedral. They can still do serious shopping in local markets as peasants prefer to bypass the official distribution structures. They can wonder why the name of the town has not been changed, since Kalinin, as a close associate of Stalin, hardly inspires reverence any more. Kant would be the obvious person to choose in renaming the town as the philosopher is respected by both the Germans and the Russians, but some local residents claim that the town is not yet worthy of his name (see page 274). Others do not want to deny the Soviet past. Tourists need not worry whether it is or whether it is not, but for the sake of the local residents let us hope for not too long a delay. A move in this direction was taken in 2005 when his name was given to the university.

HISTORY

The history of the former German town of **Königsberg** began with bloodshed in 1255 and ended with bloodshed in 1945. The establishment of the first settlement by the Teutonic Knights was to lead by 1283 to the complete annihilation of the Prussian tribes. In 1945 the Germans would in turn be annihilated by Soviet troops at the end of World War II. In the intervening 700 years, war would generally pass the town by, its few temporary occupiers having established their authority in battles elsewhere. Membership of the Hanseatic League from 1340 ensured close relationships with all the other large ports along the Baltic coast and a common adherence to Lutheranism after the Reformation. It also ensured extensive trading links with Britain. During this long period of time, Germany and Russia would usually be friends, uniting just as easily against the French as against the Poles. Loyal former residents always refer to 700 years of German history, yet such rule can hardly be seen as continuous. For much of the 15th century, local rulers had to swear allegiance to the Polish crown. The Swedes followed in the 16th century and were only finally driven away in 1679. The first Russian occupation lasted four years, between 1758 and 1762. This was during the Seven Years War and a Baltic-German governor was appointed, so little resentment was felt. In 1807 Napoleon occupied the town for 39 days. Far worse than any occupation was the plague that killed a quarter of the population in 1709. In the mid 19th century, when most European cities had long since abandoned their city walls, Königsberg built one, together with impressive city gates on all the main roads. This was as much an artistic and architectural venture as a military one and in 1945 can only have delayed the Soviet advance by a few hours. It is now the most obvious German legacy in the town as it can be seen in so many different places.

LEARNING AND CULTURE Albertina University, founded in 1544, was a constant feature of the town's history. Foreign occupiers always respected it and eagerly encouraged its work. It was equally well known throughout Germany. It pioneered in many fields, being one of the first to lecture in German instead of Latin, to introduce science degrees and to admit women students. Throughout its 400-year history, any prominent writer, historian or scientist living in Königsberg had a post at Albertina. Its academic standards were only to slip twice during this time. An honorary degree was awarded to Napoleon's General Pierre Daru who led the forces that occupied Königsberg. In the university's final 12 years between 1933 and 1945, the teaching was as dominated by Nazi ideology as it was in all other German universities.

The original 16th-century buildings of the university were beside those of the cathedral in the heart of the old town. These were all destroyed during the fighting at the end of World War II, including a library of over half a million books. As part of the 300th anniversary celebrations in 1844, further faculties were built on the northern side of the Pregel River and some of the buildings survived the war and are still in use. These followed other institutions that had been founded earlier in the century, such as the botanical garden and the observatory built by Germany's most famous astronomer, Friedrich Wilhelm Bessel (1784–1846).

The philosopher **Immanuel Kant** (1724–1804) was undoubtedly Königsberg's most famous resident and probably the only one ever to achieve fame outside

Germany. He stayed loyal to the town throughout his life and never accepted posts elsewhere. In fact he went further than this and hardly left the town, indicating in many of his writings that travel would not have broadened his mind. Marxist philosophers see him as a precursor to Hegel and then to Marx himself. Because of the Russian occupation he was, like all other residents for that four-year period, a Russian citizen. One hundred and fifty years later these two factors would be crucial. During the Soviet period between 1945 and 1990, he was the one famous former resident who could officially be commemorated. His tomb outside the cathedral, erected in 1924 on the 200th anniversary of his birth, was not destroyed and his work continued to be published.

Kant was renowned for his rigid schedule and his regular companions. His butler always woke him at 04.45 each morning and he was always in bed by 22.00. He never married, to his regret, but he consoled himself with the thought that staying single kept his mind more alert. He held the Chair of Logic from 1770 until his death in 1804, the year of which he had actually predicted. He had a regular circle of friends whom he entertained each Sunday. Amongst these were two Englishmen, Joseph Green and Robert Motherby, whose shipping business, originally based in Hull, brought grain and herring to Britain. They had lunch with him every Sunday for about 20 years. In the 19th century their successors started a regular steamer service between Hull and Königsberg, profiting in particular during the Crimean War when Königsberg was the only source of Russian goods.

The second most famous resident of Königsberg was **Heinrich Schliemann**, who will always be associated with the discovery of Troy. He spent two crucial years there from 1853 to 1855, helping the Russian government break the British and French blockade of Russian ports during the Crimean War. Königsberg, being German, could not be cut off from trade in this way and he used it to import crucial war materials into Russia.

The most famous visitor to Königsberg was Peter the Great, who first came in 1697 *en route* to western Europe. A Russian trading community had already been settled in the town for over a hundred years and was sufficiently large to hold regular church services. Officially he came incognito, but being some 2m tall (well over 6ft) and bringing an entourage of 400, this pretence was impossible to maintain. He did enjoy disguising himself in a range of unlikely occupations but wildly drunken behaviour was on several occasions to let him down. On his visit to Königsberg the German court presented him with amber jewellery and horses from the famous breeding centre in East Prussia, Trakehnen. Later they would present him with the Amber Chamber, which would adorn the summer palace at Tsarkoye Selo for two centuries, before being brought back to Königsberg by German troops in 1942. After his 1697 visit, Peter the Great continued his journey to Holland and England, settling in Deptford for several months to study shipbuilding. He would send students from St Petersburg to study at Albertina University but this link was broken in 1720 as too few Russian students had sufficient knowledge of German to follow the courses. It was restored during the Tsarist occupation (1758–62) when Russian students attended Kant's lectures. It was probably Peter's the Great's envy of Königsberg as a successful ice-free port that encouraged Stalin to demand it as part of the post World War II settlement.

EXPANSION AND PROSPERITY Königsberg was under French occupation from 1807 to 1813 as Napoleon's power thrust eastwards. The remains of about 1,500 members of his retreating army were found at the back of the Town Hall in 2006. They were returned to France for burial, unlike in Vilnius where they were buried and commemorated locally (page 215). The 19th century was then one of fame in every commercial and intellectual field for Königsberg and the city enjoyed peace and prosperity throughout these hundred years. 'First' and 'largest' are adjectives that need to be used again and again. At the beginning of the century, in 1809, the famous

Königsberg marzipan was first produced. At the end of the century, in 1895, Germany's first electric trams operated here and then, two years later, the first 11 women graduated from Albertina. Well before the end of the century, the port handled more grain and wood than any other in Germany whilst at the same time 'Gräfe und Unzer' had become the country's largest bookshop. Shipbuilding, printing, railway engineering and textiles were the industries that enjoyed particular success. The opening of the railway link with Russia in 1861 greatly expanded the scope of the port, as did the construction of the canal to Pillau (Baltiysk) on the coast. Uniquely it could guarantee ice-free access throughout the winter. The first British steamer had in fact arrived seven years earlier in 1854 and trade with Russia through the port would greatly increase following the completion of the railway link.

Culturally, Wagner, Schumann and Liszt paid several visits for performances of their works; Bizet's *Carmen* was successfully performed in 1879 after its initial failure in Paris. In architecture, the Luisenkirche and the Stock Exchange are the most famous of a wide range of impressive 19th-century buildings that are still in use.

Königsberg remained untouched by World War I, although it was sufficiently close to several battles for it to be used as a military relief station and for its hospitals to be greatly expanded. Under the Versailles Treaty of 1919, independence was restored to Poland after over a century of German and Russian occupation. This led to the division of East Prussia and its capital Königsberg from the rest of Germany. Although links with the 'mainland' were assured, Königsberg was forced to look for closer trading links with the new Baltic countries of Lithuania, Latvia and Estonia and also with the Soviet Union. There are few realistic portrayals of the 26 years Königsberg was still to exist as a German city. The many memoirs that the exiles would produce after World War II present an idealised picture of a prosperous town with no crime, no tension and where the sun always shone. One writer does in fact admit that she cannot recall a rainy summer's day, so happy are her recollections of her childhood in Königsberg. There is no doubt that much was achieved there and evidence of this can still be seen in many parts of the town, despite the later bombing. One mayor, Hans Lohmeyer, was in office from 1919 to 1933 and he relentlessly drove the town forward. In Carl Gördeler, his deputy from 1922 to 1930, he had an equally active supporter. (Gördeler then became Mayor of Leipzig and, had the July 1944 plot to kill Hitler succeeded, he would have been nominated as German Chancellor. He and several other East Prussians were among the many executed for their role in the plot.)

Lohmeyer built a new main railway station, probably the first in Germany with non-smoking waiting rooms, and with a bowling alley. He foresaw the role air travel would play so gave his city a large airport. He realised the need for close links with the new Soviet government so helped to establish Deruluft, a joint venture with them which operated regular flights to Moscow. The two-storey road and rail bridge across the River Pregel, which is still in use, was built at his instigation. His most famous achievement was the annual Ostmesse, the export trade fair that dominated trade to and from the city throughout the inter-war period. First opened in 1920, by 1923 it was attracting 2,500 exhibitors and continued operating until the autumn of 1941.

Yet an honest portrayal of the city between 1919 and 1939 has to reflect the developments that hit the whole of Germany. The rampant inflation of 1923 destroyed many long-established businesses and then unemployment in the early 1930s provided the breeding ground for Nazism. The Nazis' main opponents both on the streets and in the ballot box were the Communists. None of the centre parties appeared to offer solutions to the ever-worsening crisis. At the Ostmesse in 1932, many stands were empty and an art exhibition had to fill up the empty space.

THE NAZI ERA In the last free election to be held in Königsberg the Nazis were elected on 5 March 1933, with 54% of the vote. Democracy and racial tolerance died that night throughout Germany. Opposition to the Nazis was dealt with as ruthlessly in Königsberg as elsewhere. Mayor Lohmeyer was sacked on 9 March. On 10 May a book burning was organised on the Trommelplatz, the main parade ground. Any books which could be stigmatized as 'Un-German, Jewish or Bolshevik' went up in flames. Sixteen staff at the university were immediately sacked on account of their political views or racial background.

The most famous Jew who left Königsberg in 1933 was the songwriter Max Colpet who wrote 'Where Have All the Flowers Gone' for Marlene Dietrich. In his American exile he went on to write for Charles Aznavour and to translate *West Side Story* into German. A five-year-old Jewish girl who also left in 1933 later achieved prominence as Lea Rabin, wife of the Israeli prime minister. By the end of the year, the Hansaring had been renamed Adolf Hitler Strasse, to mark the supposed permanence of the Nazi regime.

On 7 November 1938 a junior diplomat, Ernst von Rath, was shot in the Paris embassy and died two days later. He had joined the Nazi Party in 1932 whilst a student in Königsberg. His assassin, Herschel Grynzpan, was a young impoverished Polish-Jewish refugee who had just been expelled from Germany with all his family. This murder gave the Nazis a pretext for launching a new wave of attacks on all Jewish businesses and synagogues in Germany, on what later became known as Kristallnacht. The date of 9 November was already symbolic in German history since on that day the Kaiser had abdicated in 1918 and in 1923 Hitler had launched his unsuccessful 'Beer Hall Putsch'. Because of von Rath's links with East Prussia, these attacks were particularly brutal in Königsberg and the main synagogue was totally destroyed. Destroyed, too, were any hopes some maintained that Nazism could be tamed. For those happy to support the Nazi regime, Königsberg would survive for another six years. For anyone else, Königsberg as a cosmopolitan, racially diverse city, rightly proud of its past and present, died in November 1938.

Until 1944 one can almost say that Königsberg 'enjoyed' the fruits of World War II. The destruction of Poland reunited East Prussia with the Reich and the advance into Russia again brought the Baltic countries under German influence. 'Bombing' was what relatives in Hamburg or Berlin suffered, but it did not initially touch Königsberg. Food supplies were ample and prisoners provided cheap labour on the farms and in the factories. With most opponents of Nazism having been exiled by 1939, there could be no focus for any opposition and little need for it given the high standard of living enjoyed by most of the population. The year 1944, however, was a turning point. The defeat at Stalingrad in early 1943 and continuing German losses on all fronts after that could no longer be concealed from the population at large.

August 1944 presented the local authorities with an acute dilemma – how should the 400th anniversary of the founding of Albertina University be celebrated? In the past such celebrations had been particularly flamboyant and had been well documented for posterity. To continue in a similar vein might be seen as tasteless in the middle of an increasingly desperate war, yet to ignore the occasion could be termed defeatism. Gauleiter Erich Koch took the second option, even sanctioning new buildings for the university. He probably bore in mind Hitler's interest in Frederick the Great and the commitment the emperor had shown to the 200th anniversary in 1744. At one of the formal ceremonies, Koch presented three statues, of Kant, Copernicus and Hitler. In the British air raids that followed two weeks later, most of the university was destroyed, but two of these statues survived intact. Hitler did not.

The Royal Air Force launched two major bombing attacks, on the night of 26/27 August 1944 and again on 29/30 August. The desolation these caused can still be seen all too clearly in the former Old Town by the river. All the streets were destroyed and only the shells of the cathedral and the castle remained. The cathedral was rebuilt from

1991, but the castle was torn down in the late 1960s; none of the university buildings survived. Refugees from Lithuania started to come into East Prussia. Wild cattle, abandoned by their owners, drifted across the countryside. The Russians slowly encircled the town, the last train to Berlin leaving Königsberg on 22 January 1945. The next one would not leave until August 1991.

Even during the following two months, reality was evaded. Food and fuel supplies were adequate, the zoo sold annual season tickets valid until December 1945 and hairdressers required clients to make appointments two weeks in advance. Children, as normal for January, built snowmen at the side of the streets and passing soldiers handed out chocolate bars to them. Officially nobody could plan to escape, but 100,000 East Prussians did so via the port of Pillau which stayed in German hands until the end of the war.

The occupation of Königsberg came quickly and brutally; after a three-day siege the German commander, General Otto Lasch, formally surrendered to the Russians on 10 April 1945. He spent the next ten years in prison and then wrote his memoirs, which still remain contentious amongst the Vertriebene, the exile community who fled to West Germany. With 35,000 troops and no air cover against the 250,000 Russian force, the result of the battle could not be in doubt. Some argue that, with an earlier surrender, there would have been less suffering in the town as the Russians would not have felt so vengeful. Others argue that Lasch could have disobeyed Berlin earlier and arranged for a more orderly civil evacuation, as happened in other East Prussian towns. Cynics claim that he fought until his own life was in danger and then surrendered. Hitler had ordered him to fight to the last man, but he was one of many German commanders not to carry these orders out, even though he pursued such a policy further than was necessary.

The defence of Königsberg did not prevent war crimes being carried out to the last minute. In early April 1945, resources were still found to force-march 5,000 Hungarian prisoners from Königsberg to Pillau. Some 2,000 perished *en route* and most of the remaining 3,000 drowned in the sea or were murdered on the beach. Only 13 were rescued by extremely brave local villagers.

SOVIET RULE Although leaflets dropped by Russian aircraft before the final attack promised a quick and pleasant return to civilian life, the population of Königsberg was exposed to every possible form of human depravity as the Russian troops arrived. Women were 'lucky' if they were only raped by one soldier. Men forced into work brigades were similarly fortunate in that this ensured just enough rations to survive. Stalin is alleged to have encouraged his troops with the slogan, 'Take these blonde German women. They are all yours.' Soldiers could loot at will and understandably took the chance to do so. If there was one German word that they all learnt it was Uhr ('watch') but their interests could not be expected to stop there. Most had spent the last years seeing town after town destroyed by the German army and few would not have had many relatives killed. Despite the siege and the earlier bombing, Königsberg still had a modern vibrant feel to it. Russian troops expecting an impoverished German proletariat found thousands of townhouses full of clothes, china, furniture and jewellery. One soldier wrote home, 'It is hard to know where to look first when you enter a German house. Do you realise that they all have pianos the size of tables?' Some items were unknown to them, particularly to soldiers from central Asia. They had never seen bicycles or flushing toilets and were equally inept with both.

For about a week, Russian troops were allowed to rampage as the German army had done on their territory for the previous four years. Under the circumstances their behaviour was perfectly comprehensible, even though it can in no way be condoned. Königsberg was the first major German town to surrender. The soldiers knew that it was going to be incorporated into the USSR. Like Berlin and Dresden, in 1945 the town was to pay a particularly high price for its Nazi past. It would soon pay an even higher one.

If law and order were quickly restored, food supplies were certainly not and mere survival became a total preoccupation for the German population of around 100,000 who remained in May 1945. Survival was only possible through ingenuity and barter. Elderly relatives were abandoned so that their clothes could be sold and then their corpses would be cannibalised. (Only those who died of typhus could expect a burial.) Pets had to be eaten, as did any non-poisonous plants. Everyone turned their hands to thieving as honesty could only lead to starvation. The three letters LSR daubed across makeshift air-raid shelters were a familiar sight in the town since this was the German abbreviation for such cellars (*Luftschutzräume*). Under the occupation it soon came to mean *Lernt Schnell Russisch* ('quickly learn Russian').

In the early days of the occupation, it was assumed that the remaining German population would be allowed to stay. In fact, some German refugees who had reached what was now western Poland were returned. By 1946, though, the German population in the city had dropped to around 25,000. Relations between the Russians and the Germans became remarkably cordial and reminiscences from both sides dating from that time testify to this. The Russians needed the Germans for their skills and for their local knowledge. They admired their resilience and cleanliness. No Russian would regularly clean the doorstep and pavement outside their house, let alone outside a bombsite. Only the Germans could find the sewers, operate the drainage systems and restore production in the amber mines. When the Königsberg trams started to operate again in the summer of 1946, there were 400 German staff and only 70 Russians. The Germans needed the Russians for regular supplies of food and money, so became the workers, tradesmen and nannies that could ensure this.

The early Russian settlers had mixed backgrounds. Some soldiers simply stayed on, attracted by a potential lifestyle unlikely to greet them elsewhere in the Soviet Union. Those who had been imprisoned by the Germans, and could therefore be judged as traitors by the Red Army, felt less threatened here as their past could be more easily falsified or ignored. New settlers were positively encouraged from summer 1946. Those from a country background admired the asphalt and cobbles which were as novel to them as bicycles and flush toilets had been to the troops a year earlier.

The Germans still went to church, although the Russians by and large did not. There were of course no Orthodox churches and many Russians feared that expressions of religious belief might prejudice their future careers. A German club was founded in February 1946 and some Russians also attended. Genuine relationships between both communities started to be formed. There were again grounds for optimism. Such hopes were shattered in July 1946. Königsberg was renamed Kaliningrad (**Калининград**) in honour of Mikhail Kalinin who had just died (of natural causes). He had been a senior member of the Soviet Politburo, a man of little vision, but of great staying power. Confusingly, the same name was given to the new surrounding region (oblast in Russian). Although every other town and village in East Prussia, and all the streets, would now receive Russian names, many were better honoured. Insterburg, the second-largest town in the former East Prussia, was renamed Chernyakhovsk after a noted commander, Ivan Chernyakhovsky, who fought heroically in many battles on the Eastern front and died of his wounds in February 1945. Only the rivers and the town gates kept their German names after 1947 so the Pregel still ran through the town centre, overlooked by the Brandenburg Gate.

In the same month, the whole oblast of Kaliningrad was declared a military zone. A barbed-wire fence along the entire length of the new border with Poland went up in September 1946, dividing families and cutting the link with Germany. The following winter was, as elsewhere in Europe, a bitter one, and many were to suffer almost as badly as they had done in the summer of 1945. Many older people felt there was no alternative to suicide, particularly as rations were often restricted to 'specialists'. ('Parasites' were expected to fend for themselves.) In the countryside, conditions were worse as the months of hard frost and deep snow prevented any cultivation. Yet some Russians started to learn German and in June 1947 a German newspaper, *Neue Zeit* ('New Times'), was founded with six Russian staff and four Germans. Its contents were largely translations from Russian papers, but its publication did suggest a long-term future for the German community.

The complete opposite was made clear on 10 October when Stalin suddenly ordered what would now be called ethnic cleansing. On 22 October, the first special train left for Germany and many others were to follow. By March 1948, the policy had by and large been carried out, with only a few specialists allowed to stay a little longer because their expertise was still needed. Kaliningrad became a unique region of Europe in many ways. It had been ethnically cleansed with total success and with the full agreement of the wartime Allies. It became a community with no past and with minimal links to the outside world. Guidebooks and school textbooks would talk of Kant being born in Kaliningrad in 1724, but no other reference was made to the German era or even to the Seven Years War when the Russians previously occupied Königsberg. Lhasa, Pyongyang and Tirana suddenly appeared cosmopolitan in comparison as they did at least see regular delegations from abroad and occasional groups of tourists. Public displays of religion ceased as the German churches closed in 1948 and were restored only 40 years later when the Russian Orthodox Church took over some of the churches whose fabric could still be saved.

We must hope that those settlers who came in their twenties and are now retired will write up their experiences. For the time being, our knowledge of the next 40 years is restricted to the few official documents that have entered the public domain since the downfall of the USSR. Because of the military sensitivity of the area, minimal information was published during the Soviet era and there was no way in which it could be checked. We now know the background to the dynamiting of the castle ruins in 1969, which aimed to remove a clear visual link to the German past, but with the reopening of the university in 1967 skilful students would in due course track this history down. The Bunker Museum was also opened in 1969, at the site of the German surrender. It displayed large-scale models of the fighting in Königsberg. In 1974 came a museum dedicated to Immanuel Kant which could not conceal his German surroundings, although he was portrayed as a 'citizen of all Europe' because of his fame. In 1975 a second German was commemorated, the astronomer Friedrich Wilhelm Bessel (1784–1846), when a memorial plaque was erected on the site of his former observatory written in both Russian and German. (In 1989 Kaliningrad again had a Bessel Street, as it had before the war. A crater on the moon also bears Bessel's name.)

The destruction of churches continued until 1976. The last one to be blown up was the Lutherkirche, a beautiful neo-Renaissance building dating from 1907 which had not been seriously damaged during the war. The stagnation and inertia that took over during the later Brezhnev years in the USSR did not particularly affect Kaliningrad, any more than the earlier Khruschev thaw had done in the 1960s. The military maintained such a tight grip that political changes in Moscow were largely irrelevant. For the same reason, Kaliningrad was hardly to enjoy the *perestroika* and *glasnost* that characterised the final years of the Soviet Union in the late 1980s. Had visitors been allowed then, they would have found some lighter reading in the bookshops and a few Russian Orthodox services taking place in the former Lutheran churches. That tourists were still not allowed, under any circumstances, speaks volumes.

After the failed military coup in Moscow in 1991, Kaliningraders were polled by a local newspaper and asked for their views: 25% were saddened at its failure, 25% were glad and 50% did not care. An older generation had known political terror under Stalin and then years of political inertia following his death in 1953. Younger people had known only the inertia, being totally cut off from foreigners and the more radical outbursts that flowered from time to time elsewhere in the Soviet Union.

MODERN PROBLEMS The year 1991 should have forced a break with this tradition. With the formal demise of the USSR at the end of December and the establishment of the various independent republics, Kaliningrad was now cut off from the rest of the Russian Federation by three foreign countries: Lithuania, Belarus and Poland. It had to adapt to new circumstances in the same way that Königsberg/East Prussia had done in 1919. Yet no new Hans Lohmeyer was forthcoming who could successfully maintain links with Moscow whilst at the same time achieving the local economic autonomy needed to trade successfully with western Europe. There was talk of the town becoming the 'Hong Kong' of the Baltics but Moscow did not grant the full range of tax-free privileges that such a project needed.

Initially the sudden influx of high-spending nostalgic German tourists saved the town from making serious economic decisions. Some 64,000 came in 1992 and similar numbers continued for several more years. Many German charities became active and some businesses from Germany started to invest as low labour costs compensated for all the bureaucratic hurdles that still needed to be overcome. There are other resources, too. Amber is a unique and valuable local product and the legal sales abroad guarantee a regular income. Other export products such as timber have to compete against those from Poland and the Baltic countries where an efficient business ethos has quickly taken root. Income is clearly also derived from smuggling as local cigarettes are known to have worldwide distribution networks.

Ten years after the fall of communism, around 2000, there was still no alternative to take its place in Kaliningrad. The private sector, being so corrupt, did not contribute sufficiently to a tax base that could in turn drive the public sector out of its torpor. There was a general expectation that either Moscow or the EU would in due course bail out Kaliningrad; there was certainly no attempt to turn to self-reliance, nor were closer links established with other potential markets beyond Germany. The EU was seen as a threat, not as a possible stimulus.

However, as EU membership for its neighbours became more likely and then a fact in 2004, Kaliningrad began to reinvent itself. The awkward clash of two anniversaries in 2005 – the 750th anniversary of the founding of Königsberg and the 60th of its 'liberation' by Soviet forces – was a further stimulus for presenting a more attractive face to the outside world. Projects such as the building of the new Russian Orthodox cathedral beside Victory Square, which had hardly seen any activity for years, were suddenly completed. The opening of a truly five-star hotel on the coast at Svetlogorsk enabled foreign rulers to be entertained at the same level as their predecessors in the 19th century had been, and so presidents Chirac and Schröder attended a summit there in July 2005. Foreign investors, previously wary of the corrupt business environment, noted that this was being tackled and saw the advantages of a cheap labour force on the doorstep of the EU.

The year 2002 had brought Kaliningrad to the attention of the West in the context of imminent EU membership for its two neighbours Poland and Lithuania. Kaliningrad residents, unlike other Russian citizens, did not need visas to travel to either country and this enabled them to travel to other parts of Russia. EU policy, however, dictated that visas would be required in accordance with practice on other borders. By the autumn of 2003, a compromise was finally reached and transit arrangements through Lithuania were agreed. As long as they do not leave the train in Lithuania, residents of Kaliningrad are automatically issued transit visas free of charge. Germany remained the major trading partner in the West and the major supporter of any charity work. Whether for ringing bells in the cathedral or for ringing birds at the Rybachy Sanctuary, it is German money that is being provided.

Yet 'Königsberg' will never take over Kaliningrad as so few people on any side would wish for this. 'Königsberg' has returned and is making its presence felt where it is most welcome: in the churches, on the farms, in the factories and in museums. History begins again in 1255 and not in 1945. 'Königsberg' remains sensibly absent from the civil administration, from education and above all from the military. Agnes Miegel (1879–1964), Königsberg's most famous poet, wrote during her final years in exile: 'Königsberg, you are NOT mortal', and she has turned out to be right.

Königsberg and Kaliningrad began to co-operate in 1990. The commemorations in 2005 brought them closer than they had ever been during the previous 15 years. Exhibitions from Germany are now welcome in the main museums and galleries. Some Russian street names are being dropped in favour of German ones. Gorki Street is now Hoffman Street, named after the 19th-century poet Ernst Hoffman. On 28 December 2005 an air service, first started 85 years before, was restored to Berlin. Königsberg and Kaliningrad now happily coexist, as Russians and Germans have so often done in the past, but it is safe to predict that they will never embark on cohabitation.

PRACTICALITIES

Kaliningrad must now be unique in Europe in making so little provision for non-Russian speakers. They are even charged more in most of the local museums, a legacy of the dual-pricing system so common in Soviet times. There are many hotels, restaurants and shops where no or minimal knowledge of English or German must be accepted. The city website remains almost entirely in Russian only, as do street signs and most tourist publications. Thus, visitors wanting to spend time on their own without a guide will need to learn the Cyrillic alphabet before coming. The city and the coastal resorts are clearly eager to promote themselves within Russia, which can guarantee a large market. However this lack of provision for foreigners can rightly be seen as its attraction. 'Fit in or don't come' might well be its motto.

Smokers will like the lack of serious regulation, and the very cheap price for cigarettes, cartons of 200 costing less than packets of 20 in most other countries. Larger restaurants usually have a non-smoking section but bars and cafés do not.

MONEY AND BANKING Roubles can easily be obtained in the Baltic countries, in Poland and also through some banks in western Europe. At the Lithuanian and Polish borders, the local currencies can be exchanged into roubles, otherwise it is difficult in hotels to change anything apart from American dollars and euros. Most exchange bureaux will accept other currencies such as British pounds but rates are always most competitive for dollars or euros. As the dollar weakened during 2007, inevitably prices previously quoted in dollars were reassessed in euros. Travellers' cheques can only be exchanged at a few banks so are best avoided. Reliable ATM machines suddenly sprouted up across the city in 2005, and by 2008 were common in other places too, but of course instructions on how to use them are only in Russian. Credit cards are accepted by the main hotels and restaurants.

The rouble has been very stable since 1999. In July 2008, the euro was worth about R37, the pound R47 and the dollar, R23.50.

COMMUNICATIONS

Telephones Calls from Kaliningrad to foreign countries require an international access code of 810 and then the relevant country code and foreign number. Russian dialling codes all changed in late 2005. Calls made to Kaliningrad from abroad require the country code for Russia, which is still 7, then the Kaliningrad area code which is now 4012, followed by the local number.

Direct dial is available to countries abroad from some hotels but charges vary widely and should be checked before using the phone. There is often a three-minute minimum charge, even if the line is engaged or not answered. At telephone centres around the town, charges are lower and English or German are sometimes spoken. There are telephone centres in the main railway station, the Central Post Office (*Leonova 22*), and in the Kaliningrad Hotel. All have extensive opening hours. In 2008 they charged around 40p/US$0.80 per minute for calls to western Europe.

Useful telephone numbers

Fire	01	Ambulance	03	Police	02

Post The postal service out of Kaliningrad has greatly improved since 2000 even though everything until 2007 went via Moscow. Allow two weeks for cards to reach western Europe, slightly longer for elsewhere. As more post goes first to Warsaw, delivery times should become shorter. Charges are very low, even for air mail. Stamps are not sold at kiosks or hotel reception desks so have to be bought at post offices. The two main post offices in Kaliningrad are not in the town centre; the main one is near the zoo at Leonova 22 and another is in the main railway station to the south of the town centre. A third one is opposite the Central Market on Chernyakhovskovo.

INTERNET Internet cafés have not yet caught on in Kaliningrad but most telephone centres, such as those at the Kaliningrad and Moskva hotels, provide internet facilities. Expect to pay around 75p/US$1.50 an hour.

CONSULATES There is no British or American consulate in Kaliningrad so any emergency assistance has to be provided by the relevant embassy in Moscow. In 2007, there were German, Latvian, Lithuanian, Swedish and Polish consulates in Kaliningrad.

HOSPITAL AND PHARMACY
✚ **Klinicheskaya Hospital** Lower Lake, near Amber Museum; ☎ 43 4556   ✚ **Apteka Pharmacy** Mira 98; ☎ 21 7883

RELIGIOUS SERVICES There was no public worship in Kaliningrad from the expulsion of the Germans after World War II until the end of the Soviet era in the late 1980s, when some of the former German churches were taken over by the Russian Orthodox community. Some services are now held in German in the Lutheran chapel of the cathedral, but the regular church for Lutheran services is the restored **Church of the Resurrection** (Auferstehungskirche; see page 280).

TOURIST INFORMATION There are no tourist-information offices at the airport, or at the railway station. It is therefore advisable to pre-book a transfer on arrival and a guide for a day or two to get used to the town layout and public transport, and to be up to date on concerts. Kiosks sell town plans in Russian, but these can be several years out of date so may not show new hotels. They also sell reprints of German town plans from before the war. A local publication *Welcome to Kaliningrad* is distributed through the larger hotels. It consists mainly of advertisements in Russian but there are short descriptions in English of the major attractions. There are two tourist offices, one on the ground floor of the Kaliningrad Hotel and the other next to the Skipper Hotel in the 'Fishing Village', the new development on Oktyabraskaya beside the river opposite the cathedral.

TRANSPORT

AIRPORT A completely new airport terminal on the site of the former domestic terminal was opened early in 2007, in preparation for the widespread expansion of the local airline KD avia, which began in June 2007. Construction work will continue through 2008.

KD avia (*www.kdavia.eu*) now offers daily flights from London Gatwick and from several German airports, plus services several times a week from Paris, Rome and Barcelona. These form a 'hub and spoke' operation together with their onward flights to many airports in Russia. The airline is clearly not expecting a sudden influx of tourists to Kaliningrad as its sales activity is largely centred on promotion to the rest of Russia.

The former international terminal continues to be used by Air Baltic and LOT. Polish Airlines have a daily service to Warsaw which offers many European connections and Air Baltic flies daily between Monday and Friday from Riga via Kaliningrad to Copenhagen and back.

A local bus, number 138, leaves hourly from outside the terminal and stops at Vasilevsky Square (close to the Dona Hotel), Victory Square, at the Kaliningrad Hotel and then at the bus/railway station. It costs R25 and takes about 45 minutes. Fluent Russian speakers pay about R300 for a taxi, others R600 or more.

VISAS Visas valid for 72 hours are issued at the airport to all visitors who have pre-arranged this through a specialist tour operator in their home country. In early 2008, Kaliningrad was the only place in western Russia that had this facility for easier visas. Elsewhere, except for cruise passengers in St Petersburg, full visas issued by Russian embassies abroad are necessary. Before passing through passport control, look out for the representative of the MFA (Ministry of Foreign Affairs) who will stick the visa into the passport. Remember to bring a photo which is a necessary part of this, and to ensure that at least two free pages are available in your passport, one for the visa and one for stamps.

PUBLIC TRANSPORT An efficient and extensive network of buses, trams and trolleybuses covers the town with very low fares. A ticket costs 8R, the equivalent of £0.20/US$0.40, however long the journey. On minibuses within the city, the fare is 12R, but a seat is guaranteed. Tickets are bought on board, not beforehand in kiosks. The main bus station, beside the railway station, serves other towns and villages in the region. Timetables are clearly listed there, but only in the Cyrillic alphabet, as they are in the railway station; there is no written guide to these services. Do not expect English or German to be spoken either in the bus station or in the railway station. The rail fare to Svetlogorsk (Rauschen) is R45 and the bus fare to Baltisk is R50.

IMPORTANT NOTE ON TIMETABLES On international trains, Moscow time is used which is one hour ahead of local time. A train to Vilnius timetabled to leave at say 15.00 will therefore leave at 14.00. This does *not* apply to international buses, which use local time.

TAXIS These are now metered and are reasonably priced by Western standards. A short journey within the town centre should not cost more than R100 and one to the outskirts of the city will cost 200R. Unlike in the Baltic countries, most people get a taxi from a rank or on the street. It is not common to phone for them, except from the suburbs where they would otherwise be difficult to find.

ACCOMMODATION

HOTELS Russian visas are issued only with confirmed accommodation and approval from the Ministry of the Interior. Local agents arrange this through tour operators abroad who then in turn arrange for visas to be issued by the local Russian Embassy for stays of longer than 72 hours or on arrival at the airport for shorter stays. To avoid extra visa charges, bookings should be made at least six weeks before the planned date of arrival although about two weeks is long enough for visas on arrival. It is therefore not practical to book hotels directly since they cannot offer this visa service.

In 2006, there was a large increase in the number of new hotels available in all categories, all situated in the town centre. More are likely to open from 2009 onwards. Those who have used *Baltic Capitals* may be surprised to see the Hotel Comandor omitted. It closed in October 2007, given the new competition from several centrally located hotels able to offer the level of service that used to be unique to it.

During 2007 and 2008 there was a building boom in Svetlogorsk, where visitors keen to combine relaxation or spa treatment with some culture could consider staying, taking the train into Kaliningrad as necessary. Rooms in hotels there are much larger than in the town. There are plans to make the village of Yantarny a major gambling centre, with dedicated accommodation, but nothing has yet been finalised.

Visitors to Kaliningrad in 2009 may find two more hotels open. There are (controversial) plans to build one very close to the Orthodox cathedral on Victory Square and another on Frunze, fairly close to the Prussian Museum, behind a façade that has just about survived from German times, including the shop sign for the chemist that traded there, Kreuz Apotheke.

Modern hotels have air conditioning, but good soundproofing is still rare, as is cable or satellite television in the cheaper establishments. Be ready for a great variety in the standard of service, from outstanding to dire.

Prices
The price codes given indicate rates likely to be charged abroad by specialist travel agents who work with Kaliningrad. They usually include breakfast. Even small hotels often have quite a variety of rooms so visitors must expect a similar diversity in charges. There is little seasonal variation although hotels get very heavily booked from mid-June to mid-August, the German holiday season. The distinction between prices for foreigners and those charged to Russians was abolished in 2005.

🏨 **Glamour** (21 rooms) Verkneozhernaya 26; ☎ 34 0000; e info@glamour-hotel.ru; www.glamour-hotel.ru. The quiet location beside the Upper Lake is ample compensation for the 3km distance from the town centre, as are the larger-than-normal rooms & the views most of them have over the lake. Those coming for an appropriate occasion might want to splash out R10,000 for the Romance Room with its central circular bed, its skylight & its private jacuzzi. Although the hotel has 4 floors, there is no lift. Dark red drapes are to be expected in the restaurant, but Greek columns add a welcome touch of white, both there & on the outside of the building. At the time of writing, the lake was being landscaped so before too long visitors should be able to walk around it. $$$$

🏨 **Triumph Palace** (74 rooms) Bolshevistsky 3; ☎ 77 7733; e info@triumph-palace.ru; www.triumph-palace.ru. This hotel should really have been called the Palace of Glass, since this is its major claim to fame in a town where the effective use of this material is still all too rare. The hotel advertises itself (of course only in

Russian) as the best in town, which is somewhat of an exaggeration. Maybe the claim will be justified when the promised AC, sauna & gym appear. Rooms are small with no pictures: sad given the bleak environment in the immediate vicinity. $$$$

🏨 **Dona** (30 rooms) Vasilevski Sq 2; ☎ 35 1650; e dona@Kaliningrad.ru; www.dona.kaliningrad.ru. This hotel which opened in 2006 will probably set the pattern for many more in Kaliningrad; one has to wonder why it did not do so 10 years earlier. The only lapse is the lack of a lift. It is unashamedly elitist, with its Dolce Vita restaurant proud of its imported food & drink, a major incentive for Russian visitors. Only some of the vodkas are Russian. It is in a way surprising that it is situated on a very Soviet square, named after the general who defeated the Germans here at the end of World War II. Directions are given only for arrival by car as clearly anybody who has to travel by bus would not be welcome, even though the airport bus stops in this square. It even provides a fairly literate website in English. $$$

⌂ **Kaliningrad** (200 rooms) Leninsky 81; ✆ 35 0500; e rezerv@hotel.kaliningrad.ru; www.hotel.kaliningrad.ru. For the time being, this is by far the largest hotel in the whole region. All rooms are adequately furnished & reasonably soundproofed. Many have good views towards the cathedral. It is worth paying a little more for 'studio' rooms which have AC. Phones in the rooms each have separate numbers not linked to the main switchboard, so if calls are expected from abroad, these numbers should be passed to relevant contacts on arrival. The exchange bureau handles currencies other than dollars & euros at competitive rates. Avoid the computers in the tourism information office as they cost R180 an hour. Hotel staff & those in the shops speak adequate English or German. $$$

⌂ **Skipper** (18 rooms) Oktyabskaya 4; ✆ 59 2000; e info@skipperhotel.ru; www.skipperhotel.ru. The first hotel to open in 'Fishing Village' in 2007 immediately became popular, with its central location & views towards the cathedral. Fish tanks, full with potential fare for dinner & placed under the floor, add novelty to the dining. Nine rooms are standard, 9 superior; there are no sgls. A larger 4-star hotel, **Kaiserskrug**, will open in this complex during 2008. $$$

⌂ **Chaika** (25 rooms) Pugacheva 13; ✆ 35 2211; e rezerv@hotel.kaliningrad.ru; www.hotel.kaliningrad.ru. This was a hotel in German times & was renovated in 1995 to what must have been its former standards. Further renovation was undertaken in 2008. The surrounding area is a quiet, affluent suburb, largely untouched by bombing or fighting during the war. The décor remains German in all the rooms & German is the only foreign language spoken by the staff. B/fast is adequate, but not generous, & an extensive menu is available for other meals. The main road into town is a walk of 500m or so away, but then there are plenty of bus routes & passing taxis. It also has several 24hr shops. Nearer at hand are several bars & restaurants, all with a calm, elderly clientele. Visitors who want to turn the clock back to the Königsberg era will be very happy in this hotel. Although it is under the same management as the Kaliningrad & the Moskva hotels, & therefore shares their email & website addresses, the 3 hotels could not be more different. $$

⌂ **Moskva** (90 rooms) Mira 19; ✆ 35 2300; e rezerv @hotel.kaliningrad.ru; www.hotel.kaliningrad.ru. Tourists & business visitors were all greatly relieved when renovation here was finally completed in 2002. Twelve years after opening to the outside world, Kaliningrad finally had a normal hotel, with all the facilities that tourists & business travellers require, & perhaps even more important, staff who appear committed to their job. Perhaps the only surprise was to find it under the same management as the Kaliningrad Hotel, which was then still a Soviet remnant. Care too has been taken with the design of both the rooms & the public areas. The location, opposite the zoo is very convenient for many sites, as well as for public transport & shops. $$

⌂ **Patriot** (154 rooms) Ozernaya 25; ✆ 32 8707; f 27 5023. For visitors on a budget this hotel is ideal. It is clean, well maintained & adequately furnished. Most rooms have a fridge for families wishing to prepare picnics. It is a high-rise surrounded by others, about 2km to the north of the town centre. For many years, locals who could afford it came here for dental treatment as the surgery was regarded as one of the best in town but it moved out in 2003. The café has an unexpectedly wide menu with most main dishes costing around £0.75/US$1.20. $

⸙ EATING AND DRINKING

For ten years from 1991, when Kaliningrad first opened to the West, the food available was universally dull. In the last few years, however, it has undoubtedly improved, as local people demand the standards they find elsewhere and a higher standard of living enables them to afford variety. The return of German food is not surprising as part of the increasing interest in the city prior to 1945. What is sad is the lack of restaurants representing other parts of the former Soviet Union. Georgian or central Asian dishes would be a great bonus. Southern Europe is beginning to make its presence felt, and this trend is to be welcomed. Most of the irritants of eating in Soviet times have gone. Service is fairly quick, the menu does represent what is available and there will never be a problem finding a table. In most places, the menu will only be in Russian, but there will at least be the consolation that costs are so low that if a mistake is made, it will not be costly to order another dish. Many local people eat in hotel restaurants, given the wide menus they offer and the higher level of service. Tourists are more likely to find menus in English or German there, plus staff speaking a little of either language. These all open seven days a week from around 11.00 to 24.00.

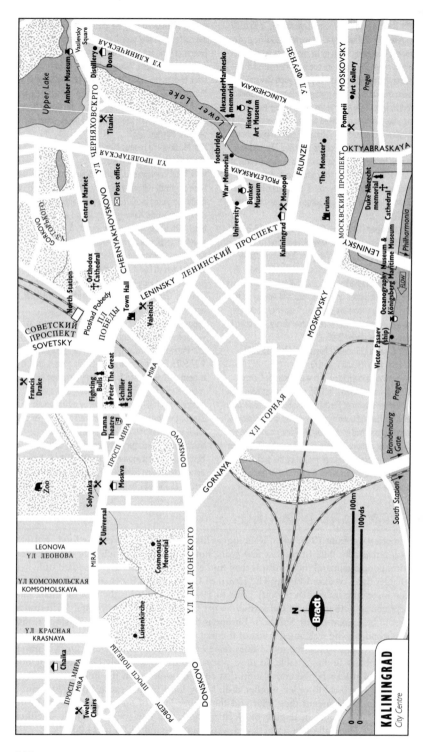

KALININGRAD
City Centre

RESTAURANTS

✘ **Francis Drake** Sovietsky 19; ✆ 21 8353. Only the names of the dishes here & the pictures on the walls have any link with Britain. A 'Sir Drake' salad for R120 is a mixture of meats, tomatoes & mayonnaise. A Manchester for a similar price is a fillet of pork, mushrooms, sour cream & garlic. The ice cream has fortunately no hint of Britain in it. Transportation problems have prevented the flow of British beer so far but hopefully this will be resolved before long.

✘ **Pompeii** (formerly Alina) Moskovsky 62; ✆ 45 2235. From the outside, this looks like an office block abandoned 20 years ago. However it is worth being brave, crossing the threshhold & going downstairs. This is Pompeii most definitely before the earthquake rather than after, with solid marble, individually woven cushions, & even crystal ashtrays. Although it's more expensive than most restaurants in Kaliningrad, few will begrudge paying R700–800 for an extensive meal here. Perhaps late-night visits should be avoided as the menu has a detailed price list for breakages caused by patrons.

✘ **Solyanka** Prospekt Mira 26; ✆ 27 9203. Self-service restaurants in Russia tend to be basic, but the Solyanka has definitely broken with this pattern. Cleanliness is taken to an obsession, in the toilets as much as in the restaurant itself. Menus are only in Russian, but with the clear displays, this hardly matters. A wide range of hot main courses is available for about US$3.50 each & there are also even cheaper snacks, while beer is around US$1.40 depending on the brand. Smokers are segregated into a glass-covered alcove. A board at the entrance invites job applications from potential waitresses & cooks. The salary offered of R12,000 a month, about €400, clearly gives the management a good choice as service always seems to be friendly & efficient.

✘ **Titanic** Chernyakhovskovo 74; ✆ 53 6768. The décor was meticulously planned before this restaurant opened in the summer of 2000. The designer clearly did more than see the film to have constructed the 'lifeboat alcoves', to have reprinted the old menus, & to have varnished the wood on the stairs. If the food is not quite first class, it is well above steerage. The veneer is almost April 1912 & when the restaurant opened it was a complete contrast to the rugged surroundings of the nearby market where the elderly attempted to supplement their minimal pensions by selling knitwear & vegetables. Like so much else in Kaliningrad, by 2005 the market had much less of a steerage feel to it. On the opposite side of the road are exchange bureaux with long opening hours & usually the best rates for dollars & euros.

✘ **12 Stuliev** (12 Chairs) Prospekt Mira 67; ✆ 21 09031. Named after one of the few satirical novels published in Soviet times, this small cellar-bar mixes the old & the young, locals & tourists. The menu is a mixture of German & Russian, the décor & music likewise, so perhaps this is a portent of continuing future collaboration. Whilst vodka is the usual R70 for a large measure, it is worth spending a little more on one of the 50 cocktails in which the restaurant specialises. Salmon salad accompanies them well. A bucolic evening here can happily be concluded with ice cream drenched in a liqueur.

✘ **Universal** Prospekt Mira 43; ✆ 21 6921. As this restaurant is part of a casino, smart dress is required & you can expect a search for weapons on entry. However it seems that the gamblers subsidise the food, which is extensive & freshly cooked. The restaurant is in fact a balcony overlooking the gamblers so the extravagance of new Russia can be safely viewed from a distance.

✘ **Valencia** Ploshad Pobedy 1; ✆ 43 3820. Most tourists visiting the Baltics want to forget previous holidays in Spain, but for those who cannot, southern warmth & a predictable menu of pancakes, paella & strong red wine is always on offer here. Their hours, too, are Spanish, as they close at 02.00 & happily serve both late lunches & late dinners. Local people always recommend it to Western visitors, on the assumption that they are looking for the familiar rather than the unusual.

ENTERTAINMENT AND NIGHTLIFE

There is no source in English or German for checking events in Kaliningrad but local guides can check Russian websites and the larger hotels keep up-to-date information in Russian.

MUSIC Most concerts take place at the Philharmonia, converted from the former Church of the Holy Family. Over the next few years, more will take place in the cathedral, now that the roof is complete and the interior has been completely restored. There are no plans to reconsecrate the cathedral.

THEATRE The Drama Theatre at Mira 4 performs only in Russian but its repertoire is international and with cheap tickets. An enjoyable evening can be spent there even without following all the dialogue.

CLUBS AND CASINOS As clubs and casinos are the centres for criminal activity, they are usually best avoided by visitors, except for those in hotels, which restrict entry to guests and carefully vetted local people. The Universal, mentioned above for its restaurant, checks all guests for weapons and is therefore secure. At the time of writing in early 2008, there were plans to build a gambling centre at Yantarny, deliberately away from population centres, but there was great opposition from many local groups and a doubt that – with the current visa stipulations – enough foreigners would come to make the exercise viable.

WALKING TOURS

A one-day walking tour is suggested and a day excursion to the coast is also outlined. About four or five days are needed to do justice to the town and the surrounding area but a lot can be done within the 72-hour stay allowed on visas issued on arrival. Tourists wanting to stay longer will need a full Russian visa obtained in the normal tedious and expensive manner through embassies abroad. Other places in the Kaliningrad region (oblast in Russian) are beyond the scope of this book but offer a worthwhile extension to visitors with the extra time. Several German guidebooks cover the region in great detail and they are regularly updated.

ONE-DAY WALKING TOUR A sightseeing tour of Kaliningrad has to start at the lobby of the Kaliningrad Hotel.

Those who came in the early 1990s, when the town was first open to tourists, might really have wondered whether such a visit was worthwhile. The hotel lobby could perhaps be passed off as mediocre. When they went outside, what stood before them and beside them was the Soviet Union at its very worst. Concrete was the sole building material and it was abused in many forms. To the left, the view was of an abandoned 16-storey tower block, an unfinished bridge and an enormous parking lot for trucks. Ahead was a wide straight road across a small island leading towards anonymous suburbs. To the Germans who had lived here before the war, sacrilege had been committed. This was their beloved Kneiphof, the island that had been the heart of Königsberg with the cathedral, castle, university and a cluster of surrounding lanes. Only the shell of the cathedral then remained, surrounded by an unkempt garden; its sole use was as a playground for local children, who could enjoy many variants of hide and seek. To the right a slightly less nondescript road offered a few shops with the relief of stone and granite. Few would imagine that it had once been the location of Germany's largest bookshop, Gräfe und Unzer.

The mood of the exiled Germans on their return – 64,000 came in 1992 – is perhaps best summarised by their most famous representative Marion Gräfin Dönhoff who became well known as the publisher of the weekly *Die Zeit*. After her visit in 1991, she wrote, 'If I had been parachuted into this town and asked where I was, I would have perhaps replied Irkutsk. Nothing, absolutely nothing, reminded me of old Königsberg.'

The contemporary visitor will be much happier, mainly thanks to the fund-raising and reconciliation initiated by Marion Dönhoff since that visit. Through her paper, and by lobbying the German government and private foundations, funds have been raised to rebuild the cathedral and many other former churches. The local administration started to make serious efforts at renovating this area in 2004 and doubtless this will continue for several more years. No longer does it shame

KÖNIGSBERG RAID OF 29–30 AUGUST 1944 1,900 miles, 176 aircraft, 485 tonnes of bombs, 16 minutes and 400 acres of devastation. This calls, and without apology, for yet another misquotation of the Prime Minister's famous epigram. Never has so much destruction been wrought by so few aircraft at so great a distance, in so short a time. Königsberg, the capital of East Prussia, the greatest port in eastern Germany, and the base for nearly 50 enemy divisions, is practically no more. Königsberg, the administrative centre of that province of Germany which has been the malignant breeding ground of the arrogant military caste, a town which has stood unchanged for 600 years, has to the benefit of mankind, been wiped out overnight.

The effects of this blow cannot be measured merely in acres, it is a pincer movement on the grand scale. Königsberg may have been just another strategical target to Bomber Command, though a large and important one at that, but it was also a tactical target for the Russians of absolutely first-class importance. The Russian victories of June and July brought them to within 100 miles of the town and within sight of the German frontiers; so did this great port with its ample dock facilities, miles of marshalling yards and modern factories, become of paramount importance to the armies desperately trying to stem the Russian advance.

With the few railways between Berlin and the front choked with supplies in one direction and the evacuation of such of the frightened populace as were allowed to go in the other, the port became the only means of relieving this bottleneck. Through its docks came the armour, the supplies and the reserves so urgently needed to re-equip the tattered divisions after their long retreat. Through its docks must go such of the much-needed agricultural produce as could be salved from this fertile but threatened area. Meanwhile the armament and engineering works were ideally situated for the maintenance and repair of unserviceable armour brought back from the front.

The Königsbergers, busily engaged in digging trenches, with their eyes turned fearfully towards the East, and the British heavily committed nearly a thousand miles away in the opposite direction, can have had little thought of danger from the West. The shock of discovering that Bomber Command could meet the needs of the Western armies, engage in the battle with the flying bombs and at the same time join in on the Russian front, will not have been confined to those who actually felt the blows.

Indeed to judge from the lack of comments in the press and on the wireless, it has left the enemy speechless.

Perhaps the best way of all of considering the effect of this raid is to ponder on what would have been the reactions of the Germans, and indeed of this country, had the Russians flown to Bremen before us and utterly destroyed it.

Kaliningrad. The **cathedral** (**Кафедрарный**, ☉ *09.00–17.00 daily; admission R70*) must be the first port of call on any tour as by 2005, in time for the 750th anniversary of the founding of Königsberg, it had been largely rebuilt to its pre-war format.

Construction of the cathedral started in 1333 and was completed in the comparatively short period of 50 years. The first organ was installed in 1535. The early site bore an uncanny resemblance to the vista that greeted tourists in the early 1990s – an austere stone building with little decoration surrounded by greenery. It had as much military as religious significance, proving the power of the Teutonic Knights over the Prussian heathens. The oak piles, topped with copper, which form the foundations, are a credit to the advance in civil engineering at that time. They continued to support the increasing weight of subsequent builds, although it has been calculated that the cathedral has sunk 1.7m over 700 years. Finance was soon a problem and had to be resolved by the sale of papal indulgences. In 1410 there was the first service of remembrance, to those who had died at the Battle of Grünewald, which saw the end of the Teutonic Knights as a major force in the area. The Reformation was eagerly taken up in the 1520s with Christmas 1523 being celebrated in German, a very popular move according to surviving reports. A second 58m tower was added in 1540.

Much of the interior was destroyed by fire in 1544 but it was again quickly rebuilt within six years and then expanded over the next century, when a larger organ was added and the clock built on the South Tower. It became the aim of every famous resident to be buried behind the gold altar.

However, Kant, as a non-believer, never entered the building and his funeral procession stayed outside. The last restoration of Kant's tomb was carried out in 1924 and it was little damaged during the war. It can be seen beside the cathedral wall. (The Nazis left it intact after exhuming his skull to check on Kant's Aryan origins.)

There was minor damage to the cathedral during the French occupation at the beginning of the 19th century, when it was variously used as a stable, a prison and a hospital. Whilst Königsberg expanded in every other field over the next 100 years, it was only between 1903 and 1907 that the cathedral received much needed maintenance and rebuilding. It was the first time it had been cleaned since 1695 and many frescoes were discovered as a result. The devotion of the population to the cathedral is best summarised in the writings of the poet Agnes Miegel, born in Königsberg in 1879, who stayed until she was forced to flee in February 1945. 'You are always part of my life, like my father and my mother. Your bells wake me in the morning and send me to sleep in the evening.'

The RAF raids in August 1944 seriously damaged the cathedral but in no way destroyed it. The library, for instance, remained intact. There was no direct hit but fire spread from neighbouring buildings, which destroyed all the woodwork and led to the collapse of the roof. The site was abandoned after the war and some of the bricks were casually looted; others were specifically taken for use in various Soviet cities. The cobbles from the surrounding streets were relaid in Moscow's Red Square. The surrounding area was cleared in 1972, probably in preparation for the destruction of the site.

During the Soviet era, there was considerable dispute about the future of this ruin. Some felt it symbolised both the powerlessness and irrelevance of both Germany and religion. Others felt it was an inappropriate reminder of these former phenomena. In Kaliningrad *en route* to Britain in 1973, President Brezhnev certainly expressed his eagerness to destroy it, having just four years previously ordered the destruction of the castle ruins. Perhaps it was Kant's tomb that saved it, a complete and restored monument to the precursor to Marxist philosophy, beside a ruin of what he opposed. Local people reminded Brezhnev of the several references made by Lenin in his books to Kant.

Much of the vaulting collapsed in 1975 and some minimal restoration was done in 1976. Arguments went on as late as 1994, well after the demise of the Soviet Union, when views were still expressed that the whole area should become a sculpture park. However, that year saw the first service being held since the war and the burial of joint Russian and German capsules which included a memorial to the suffering of the German population. Four bells were restored during the following year and since then the roof has been completed and a museum has opened in the South Tower. An Orthodox chapel has been built in the North Tower, a compromise from the original Russian demands that the whole cathedral should be Orthodox. It has since been joined by a Lutheran one, and a Catholic one should follow in 2009. From 2002 to

2005, work concentrated on the interior windows and walls. The baptistery was completed early in 2000 with four stained-glass windows. The original designs were followed by local Russian glaziers and they depict John the Baptist, Konrad von Tierberg, the founder of Königsberg, and Martin Luther.

By 2006 reconstruction was basically complete, with two organs in place. These were built in Germany but were paid for by the Russian government; they are regarded as a gift from President Putin. The phoenix on top of the larger organ symbolises the revival of the city. Earlier restoration was largely paid for by the families of former inhabitants. Local writers are eager to point out that this organ has 112 stops, whereas the one in Riga Cathedral has only 90.

The cathedral museum already occupies several rooms in the South Tower and is regularly being extended. It shows the 1903–07 rebuilding plans, as well as others proposed earlier which were not in fact carried out. It also outlines plans for the next few years, including archaeological excavations under the former castle and university. One room is devoted to Königsberg city life around the cathedral and shows an extensive china and postcard collection. It has a model of the city as it looked in 1930. There are also some exhibits on the three Masonic lodges based in Königsberg until 1942. Several rooms are devoted to Kant. It is fortunate that much material on all these subjects survived during the Soviet period or was taken west by refugees in 1945. The whole collection is well lit and generously displayed. Labelling is, however, only in German and Russian.

The tapestry showing Kant's portrait was a gift from Belarus. The memorial to Kant on the north side of the cathedral has now been joined by others. One to **Duke Albrecht,** the founder of the university, was unveiled in August 2005 as part of the commemoration of the 750th anniversary of Königsberg. On the east side is one to the theologian Julius Rupp (1809–84). Others to famous Germans linked to the cathedral must soon follow.

German visitors always look east from Kneiphof Island to the former Lindenstrasse, now Oktyabraskaya. Until 2006, there was a view here across the road, but then the mock-German **Fishing Village** was built, a series of Gothic-style buildings which now include two hotels (Skipper and Kaiserkrug) and a tourist-information office. Although the name is new, it derives from the fact that fishing boats used to draw up here. The development is one of many signs that the German past of the city is at last being accepted by the local population and promoted, rather than hidden. The 'Lighthouse' Tower (⊕ *10.00–17.00 daily; longer in summer; admission R50*) next to the Skipper Hotel offers a good view of the cathedral.

There is one remaining brick building on the opposite side of Oktyabraskaya which dates from 1905 and was a Jewish orphanage for around 45 children. The synagogue, which had been built next door a decade earlier, was partially destroyed by the Nazis on Kristallnacht, 9 November 1938, and the site was then cleared in Soviet times. Unfortunately there is now a circus tent here and there are no immediate plans to develop the site in a more appropriate manner.

The street was also famous for the house of **Käthe Kollwitz**, an artist born there in 1867. Although she moved to Berlin in 1891, she kept close links with Königsberg until the rise of the Nazis. She never made a secret of her left-wing views, and her paintings – similar in many ways to those of the English artist L S Lowry – show the suffering of working-class people under various regimes. She was invited to Moscow in 1927 as part of a delegation to the celebrations of the tenth anniversary of the Russian Revolution. She courageously stayed in Germany during the Nazi era, feeling she would be more of an embarrassment by staying than by going into exile. Her work was banned from public exhibition during this time. Despite this political background, her house was not restored during the Soviet period and she was never mentioned in local publications of that era.

Looking south from the island, the former Stock Exchange, painted in a pastel blue, stands out on the riverbank. As a contrast to German Gothic and Soviet concrete, it is a welcome Florentine Renaissance façade and was built in the 1870s, when the town's prosperity was at its height. Like the cathedral, it is built on a foundation of deep piles; the exact number used was 2,202 and they are mostly 4.5m (15ft) deep. Statues were erected beside the four corners of the building, which depicted four continents, and hence the extent of Königsberg trade at the time, but these did not survive the war. The ground floor of the building is now a pretentious restaurant, Monetny Devor, one of the few places where the local rich like to flaunt themselves. Unlike their counterparts in other Russian cities, successful businesspeople in Kaliningrad tend to enjoy their wealth discreetly.

Walking north, back across the river, an incomplete Soviet-era office block, the 'Monster', as it is usually now called, dominates the skyline. It is built over the foundations of the famous **castle** (*Schloss* in German) that has haunted contemporary Kaliningrad. The castle dated from 1257 and dominated the German town throughout its history. All major ceremonies of state took place in its main reception room. Peter the Great stayed there and Frederick the Great accepted the surrender of the Russian army there at the end of the Seven Years War. In 1904 Russian and German Social Democrats were tried there, accused of smuggling Lenin's fledgling journal *Iskra* ('The Spark') into Tsarist Russia. The castle housed the Prussian Museum and then, during World War II, the Amber Chamber, which had been brought back from Tsarskoye Selo, outside Leningrad, by German troops. The museum curator, Dr Alfred Rohde, vowed he would not leave Königsberg in 1945 without his treasure and stayed behind when he might well have been able to flee. He died a few months later and the chamber was never seen again. One mosaic panel was finally rediscovered in Bremen in 1997 and was sent back to Russia in April 2000 in return for paintings taken by the former Soviet government which had belonged to the Bremen Art Gallery before the war. A small panel has been rebuilt for the Amber Museum in Königsberg but a full restoration was carried out for Tsarskoye Selo in 2003.

The former Amber Museum, which was also housed in the castle, boasted about 100,000 items, of which 11,000 were fortunately taken to Göttingen University in late 1944 for safe keeping and therefore survived. The rest of the collection was either destroyed or disappeared.

Much of the correspondence between Moscow and courageous local architects about the proposed destruction of the castle and a suitable replacement has recently come to light. To the politicians, the building represented 'centuries of German militarism and plunder' which should be replaced by a large modern civic building to display Soviet power in what had been the heart of the German city. The political activities of the exiled East Prussians in West Germany clearly influenced the final decision to remove all traces of the castle in 1969. They used the castle tower as the logo on all their campaign literature that lobbied vocally and frequently for the then West German government to continue its policy of regarding East Prussia as being 'temporarily under Soviet administration' rather than as being lost for good. It therefore made political if not aesthetic sense for this symbol of former German power to be eliminated. Architects pointed out the many historical links the building had with Russia, as outlined above, and how a Soviet war memorial could be incorporated into a restored building. Their pleas were ignored and a budget agreed for a new town hall.

The 25-year saga that followed showed Soviet planning and political bigotry at its very worst. An initial budget of 1.6 million roubles (about £500,000 or US$1 million at the official rate of exchange in 1969) was agreed for a 16-storey building. Over the first two years, around 1,100 concrete pillars, each 8m in length, were dug into the marshy ground beside the castle. Cynics were soon to point out that they did not have the firmness of those laid by the Germans 700 years before. Twenty workers were employed on the site between 1972 and 1976 and they completed six storeys. The next ten storeys took a further five years so the basic structure was finished in 1981. By then costs had increased to nine million roubles, a surprisingly capitalist problem in a country that had been cut off from a market economy for 30 years. There was no money for moving the local government and none for installing electricity and heating. In 1988 money was found to furnish half the building but this work was not completed by the time the Soviet Union collapsed in 1991. Nothing was done to the building until 2005 when minimal refurbishment was carried out so that it would not disgrace the 60th-anniversary celebrations of the liberation in 1945.

Excavation of the castle foundations started soon afterwards, financed by the German weekly *Der Spiegel*, and the site can now be visited (⊕ *midday–20.00 daily; morning visits for pre-booked groups by arrangements; admission R50*) The entrance is about 200m due south of the Kaliningrad Hotel, just before the bridge across to Cathedral Island. Some explanatory boards are in English. Fortunately, as with the House of Blackheads in Riga, the building was blown up from the ground floor so the foundations remain in relatively good condition. Pre-war residents remember a tunnel leading from here to the cathedral and the long-term aim must be to reopen this too.

Turning right along Moskovsky for about 100m, leaving behind the Monster and the Kaliningrad Hotel, the first major building on the right-hand side is the **Kaliningrad Regional Art Gallery** (*Moskovsky Prospekt 60–2; ⊕ 11.00–19.00 Tue–Sun; admission charges vary depending on the exhibition, from R50 to R250*). Soviet money fortunately did not run out here and the gallery opened in 1989, just in time to give a final overview of art throughout the USSR at that point.

That collection stayed for several years and it is in a way a pity that it is no longer on show. However, the temporary exhibitions that have replaced it are probably more appropriate. They usually have Königsberg-Kaliningrad as their theme, showing pictures by local artists from 1946 onwards, and nowadays photographs too. Much of what is shown now was banned in Soviet times as it was interpreted as showing excessive interest in a German past rather than in a Soviet future. Some galleries are usually open to contemporary artists wanting to sell their pictures. There is no café on the premises but the Pompeii (see page 267) is close by and can be recommended.

Cross Moskovsky and head towards the Lower Lake, called Schlossteich or 'Castle Lake' in German times. The surroundings of the lake had been made communal in 1900 and the path around it built in 1937. The **History and Art Museum**, on the eastern side of the lake, can easily be identified as a former German concert hall. In front of the museum, by the lake, is a monument to **Alexander Marinesko** unveiled in 2003. He was the submarine commander who sank the *Wilhelm Gutsloff* in the Baltic Sea on 30 January 1945, resulting in the worst maritime disaster ever, with about 9,500 passengers killed. The boat had been a cruise liner before the war, with a capacity of around 1,800 passengers, but on this occasion was a refugee ship heading towards Denmark which at the time was still under German occupation. Marinesko was a brilliant commander at sea but frequently took to drink on shore so instead of being received as a hero, he was sent to Siberia for three years. He was rehabilitated a few weeks before he died in 1963 but only became a Hero of the Soviet Union 27 years later in 1990. The sight of the statue horrifies many German visitors, who may have lost relatives in the disaster, and feel that Marinesko should not be honoured in this way.

The nondescript five-storey building on the western side used to be the town's most famous hotel, the Park, where on different occasions both Hitler and Molotov regularly stayed. Because of the notoriety of its former guests, this is now an office building.

The **History and Art Museum** (Историкоху дожественный музей) (*Klinicheskaya 21; ⊕ 10.00–18.00 Tue–Sun; admission R70*) has been totally transformed since the Soviet period. Most labels are in English and German. It originally consisted of the remains of the Prussian Museum collection, which had previously been housed in the castle. This was largely an archaeological collection, so did not cause political problems. It in fact enabled Soviet historians to claim a Slavic rather than a German origin for many of the artefacts. The museum has recently undergone considerable expansion, showing not only extensive material from pre-war Königsberg, but also from the early Soviet period in the 1950s. One can only hope that what is portrayed as a typical apartment from the 1950s is no longer typical of homes in the town outside. Fabrics, furniture, paintings and crockery from both eras have been salvaged. Some 'bourgeois' exhibits such as refined table linen and advertisements are displayed, as well as examples of the inflation banknotes from 1923 when they had to be constantly recycled and overprinted. Programmes and layouts are displayed for the major annual trade fair, the Ostmesse, which took place every autumn between 1920 and 1941.

The Königsberg room in other respects still shows considerable political bias. Far more is shown of the rise of the Communist Party than that of the Nazi Party, but no attempt is made to assess the Communists' failure to overcome the Nazis in the years prior to 1933. The banners, the photographs and the pamphlets all date from earlier. Some items would seem more appropriate for a car-boot sale than for a serious town museum. Beer mugs and ashtrays seem an odd choice of exhibit but anything gathered from former Königsberg has a magical significance for those who still remember it.

The Soviet room is now frank about issues that were formerly taboo. There are photographs of the destruction of the castle, and portraits of both Stalin and Khrushchev, leaders whose pictures were not shown elsewhere in the later Soviet times. Other exhibits have not been changed since the 1980s and are reminiscent of the Moscow 'Exhibition of Economic Achievements'. Several cosmonauts came from Kaliningrad so photographs of them with the Politburo abound and a display case is devoted to the presents given to them by visiting foreign statesmen, such as a cigar from Fidel Castro and a ring from Le Duan, the Vietnamese Prime Minister. The shop and stalls within the museum offer a variety and value impossible to find elsewhere in the town. They offer good selections of amber, lacquer, woodwork and paintings and some books likely to be of interest to foreigners.

Cross the lake on the footbridge and note the large memorial ahead which in 2007 replaced a more modest one than had stood previously to the left of the path. It commemorates Colonel Tulan and his French regiment that fought as part of the Soviet air force in 1942–44. In February 1944 the regiment was named Normandy Neman, the Neman (or Niemen) being the river that traditionally divided Russia from Germany (and which now divides Lithuania from Kaliningrad). The memorial notes that the regiment made 5,000 sorties, fought in 869 battles and destroyed 273 German aircraft. The back of the monument maps the routes taken by the pilots.

Next cross Proletarskaya which leads into the university. The buildings here date from the 19th century and were designed by August Stüler, one of the pupils of Karl Friedrich Schinkel, Germany's most famous architect of the early 19th century. They were all completed within a year between 1858 and 1859. Although seriously damaged at the end of the war, they could have been restored to show the original Italian façade but this was not done. It is necessary to wander inside for any memories of the 19th century. In the square which the university buildings surround, old sculptures are being restored and new ones being created. The original statue of Kant disappeared at the end of the war, but Marion Dönhoff paid for a replacement to be provided in 1992. Kant's name was given to the university in 2005. The statue replaced one of Ernst Thälmann which had been there for most of the Soviet era. He was the leader of the German Communist Party during the 1930s and he died in a concentration camp in 1944. He is still commemorated by a road with his name to the north of the Upper Lake.

In the centre of the square is the entrance to the **Bunker Museum** (Ълиндаж Ляша, ☉ *10.00–17.00 daily; admission R50*), sometimes called the Lasch Bunker after General Lasch, who had it built as his headquarters for the final defence of Königsberg in 1945. Several of the rooms are much as he would have left them on 10 April 1945 after signing the capitulation and surrendering himself to what would turn out to be ten years' imprisonment. The heating pipes, the telephone wires and the electric cables have all remained intact. When the museum opened in 1967, it provided the only picture of former Königsberg that local residents were allowed to have, with detailed models of the town layout and of the military formations. Even a German slogan (*Wir kapitulieren nie* – 'We will never surrender'), daubed on a wall, is included. The smallest exhibit is a ticket for the last train to Berlin that left on 22 January 1945. The leaflets dropped by the Russians stressed the futility of continued fighting and promised food supplies and family reunions to all who surrendered. Recently the museum has been extended to show the burial sites of troops from both sides.

Leave the museum in a westerly direction towards Lenin Prospekt. Turning left takes one back to the Hotel Kaliningrad after 100m. Readers of Russian will find the kiosks along here a good source of books, maps and magazines.

OCEANOGRAPHY MUSEUM AND KÖNIGSBERG MARITIME MUSEUM

Another sight within walking distance of the hotels is the **Oceanography Museum** (Музей истории мирового океана, *www.vitiaz.ru;* ☉ *11.00–17.00 Tue–Sun; admission R100, or R200 inc entrance to submarine & Königsberg Maritime Museum*) based in and around the ship *Vityaz*. This is now permanently moored on the Pregel about 700m from the hotel. During 2000 and 2001 the exhibitions were considerably extended and now include new buildings on the shore. *Vityaz* was built as a cargo boat in Bremerhaven in 1939 and launched with the name Mars, after a river in western Germany rather than the planet. It was never used as a cargo carrier, being taken over as a troop ship on the outbreak of war. In March and April 1945 it made several trips between Pillau, the port on the coast nearest to Königsberg, and Denmark, rescuing about 20,000 civilians from the oncoming Russians. When the British liberated Denmark from the Germans, they took over the boat and renamed it *Empire Forth* but it only stayed in British hands until February 1946 when it was 'returned' to the Russians, being seen as based in territory now belonging to them. This British name would have been most appropriate for the Russians in view of the territory they seized at the end of World War II, but they renamed it firstly *Equator* and then *Vityaz* ('Noble Warrior').

It was moved to Vladivostok and between 1949 and 1979 made constant oceanographic expeditions to the Pacific Ocean. It also made pioneering visits to Osaka and to San Francisco in 1958, the first in each case since the start of the Cold War. Jacques Cousteau was invited on board in Mombasa in 1967, again a symbol of an easier political climate. Its last expedition finished in Kaliningrad harbour where it would rot for ten years, becoming known as the 'rusty tin' until a restoration programme began in 1990. This was completed in 1994, partially with the help of surviving members of the Mars crew. (Meanwhile another *Vityaz* was built in 1981 and is now part of the Russian Black Sea fleet based at Novorossisk.)

The exhibitions are not limited to the life of the ship. One room covers the history of oceanography, the laboratories ships included, and two earlier boats that carried the name *Vityaz*. Pictures show the startled reaction of the inhabitants of New Guinea in 1870 to a white man when the captain of an earlier *Vityaz* landed. They assumed he had come from the moon, as his skin was a similar colour. The researches beneath the Pacific, including the measurement of the Marianas Trench, are covered extensively. The new political climate means that life on board in any era can be shown honestly, and where appropriate, ridiculed. The whims and needs of all former commanders,

Tsarist, Nazi or Soviet, are not hidden, be they for an absurdly large piano, a shredding machine or a portrait of Lenin. Mess rooms, too, with appropriate memorabilia, have been rebuilt. The museum authorities hope to set up a British room, if enough material from the 1945–46 period can be provided.

The 60th anniversary in 1999 of the building of the ship was a suitable pretext for further enlargement of the collections. One theme is 'Maritime Königsberg', showing the expansion of the harbour, firstly in 1901 when the canal to the sea at Pillau was widened, and secondly in the 1920s when Königsberg became eastern Germany's major port, following the loss of Danzig and Memel (now Gdansk in Poland and Klaipeda in Lithuania respectively) at the end of World War I. Many of the buildings dating from those times, such as the grain silos, can still be seen along the riverside. In 2000 a miniatures gallery was added with replicas of ships from Egypt, Greece, Japan and Fiji. More familiar to British visitors will be the models of the *Revenge* and of Elizabeth I knighting Francis Drake. Columbus and Queen Isabella have not been forgotten, nor has the *Santa Maria*. April 2000 also saw the conversion of several cabins into displays of coral reefs, sharks' jaws and underwater geological discoveries.

In July 2000 the opening to the public of a B-413 submarine (opening hours as above for *Vityaz*) greatly increased the scope of the museum. Originally built in 1969, it then travelled almost as much as *Vityaz*, being a frequent visitor to Cuba. The B-413 was the Soviet answer to the NATO Foxtrot submarines, being able to carry 22 torpedoes and to launch them from a depth of 100m. Only the small and the agile will be able to enjoy the displays on board as the interior has been maintained as closely as possible to the original. It is hard to believe that it housed 80 men for nine-month journeys; only the captain and the KGB agent had single rooms. An exhibition honestly portrays the history of the Russian/Soviet navy from 1834 until the present day. Tragedy and triumph are covered in equal measure.

The museum complex around *Vityaz* is probably the most dynamic institution in the whole Kaliningrad oblast. Each year there is expansion, the exhibits are regularly updated and the publications show a professionalism totally lacking elsewhere. In 2001 the Whale Pavilion was opened; it displays a whale 17m long which was captured in 1975 but which was then buried in the sand along the Baltic coast for the next 25 years in the hope that eventually a home would be found for it. The central museum building opened in 2003, covering in greater detail the whole field of oceanography and also introducing the theme of global warming.

In 2006 a further ship was added to the collection, the space-research vessel **Victor Patsayev**, named after a cosmonaut killed in space in 1971. It is gratifying how well this exhibition contributes to the Königsberg-Kaliningrad theme. Part of it tells the story of the early 19th-century astronomer Friedrich Wilhelm Bessell, and part the contribution made by Kaliningrad astronomers to the Soviet space programme. Visitors can enter the vessel only as part of an escorted group. Regular tours are held in Russian but tour operators can pre-book them in English for their groups.

The **Königsberg Maritime Museum** (Морской, ⊕ *11.00–18.00 Wed–Sun*) was opened in 2007 in one of the restored harbour buildings. Note that, unlike the rest of the complex, it is closed on Tuesday as well as on Monday. It is essentially a considerable extension of the exhibition on this theme on the *Vityaz*, but whereas the boat concentrates on the 19th century, the stress here is on the 20th, although a major exhibit is the shell of a wooden boat recently discovered in an amber mine on the coast. There are pictures from the winter of 1928–9, the last time the harbour froze. That the outlet to the sea is normally ice-free was a major reason for the USSR to demand it after World War II.

One of the other harbour buildings has been converted into a café and another to an aquarium so a whole day is recommended here. Many exhibits are outside on the harbourfront so can be enjoyed in good weather. A sculpture of Kant beside a bench reminds visitors of his frequent walks along the harbour front.

BEYOND THE CITY CENTRE

Many other sights within the city are too far to walk from the Kaliningrad Hotel but can be easily reached by bus or taxi. Tour operators abroad can pre-book English-speaking guides with their own cars and this is the most convenient way to visit other sites in the town and also for visits along the coast. The following itinerary can be done in a long day, or be divided into two days.

The first port of call must be at the **Amber Museum** (Музей янтарья, *Vasilevsky Sq; www.ambermuseum.ru;* ⊕ *10.00–17.30 Tue–Sun; admission R90*) housed in the Dohna Tower, one of six similar 19th-century fortifications that still dominate the city skyline. (General Dohna fought against Napoleon.) It replaced an earlier museum, which had been beside the mines at Yantarny on the coast. A few items come from the pre-war museum, which had been housed in the former castle. At the entrance, note the plaque that commemorates the capitulation of the German army on 10 April 1945.

Amber has formed the one thread that binds together the history of the region. Since 90% of the world's amber production comes from this area, its value was an incentive for many generations of conquerors and would-be conquerors. The Prussian tribes traded it with the Romans, who saw magical and practical value in it. Tacitus and Pliny the Elder both refer to it and gladiators wore it. Amber would become an important ingredient in medicine, in agricultural fertilisers and in varnish. It would strengthen fishing nets and be used in fumigation. The museum therefore presents a 2,000-year artistic and political history of the region through the 6,000 amber products displayed. The natural history goes back millions of years to the formation of fossilised resin, which is the basis of amber.

The most interesting exhibits are those from the Soviet period; models from Aesop's fables such as 'The Fox and the Grapes' are a surprising legacy but more obvious ones are the model Kremlins, dams, pylons, nuclear icebreakers and power stations with smoking chimneys. Examples of gifts to foreign dignitaries include jewellery boxes with the hammer and sickle emblem and statues of Soviet leaders. None have been deposed from the museum so Lenin, Stalin and Khrushchev sit peacefully side by side. There are some replicas of famous pieces in the Hermitage and Kremlin collections. The largest of these weigh over a kilo. Clearly the lost Amber Chamber (see page 272) cannot be forgotten in these surroundings, so some of the original panelling has been copied and paintings show how the complete original looked when it was displayed at Tsarskoye Selo, outside St Petersburg.

The prices in the museum shop are comparable to those charged elsewhere and quality is assured. Payment can be made in roubles or euros, or by credit card. The bookshop sells most of the small number of books and brochures available in English or German on Kaliningrad.

The museum is on **Vasilevsky Square**, named after the commander responsible for the final victory over the Germans. Marshall Vasilevsky was one of the very few Soviet military officials to start his career in World War I and to continue it throughout Stalin's rule, ending up as minister of defence after his successes in 1944 and 1945. The memorial at the centre of the square commemorates the fall of Königsberg, in particular 216 Heroes of the Soviet Union and 20 who received this award twice. On the opposite side of the road from the museum is a distillery; its shop sells vodka liqueurs at prices low even by Kaliningrad standards. Perhaps it is just as well nobody can really tell how dependent the local economy is on drink and cigarettes smuggled out to Poland and then on to the rest of Europe.

Proceeding west from the museum, along Chernyakhovskovo, the **Central Market** (Центральный рынок) is on the right-hand side of the road after about 800m. Between the first and second world wars, the halls housed the famous **Ostmesse**, an annual trade fair which brought together major traders from East Prussia with their opposite numbers in the Baltic countries and the Soviet Union. Being the largest building in Königsberg, it was also the centre for all political rallies during both the Weimar Republic (1920–33) and the subsequent Nazi era. President Ebert opened the building and the first fair in 1920 and Hitler, Himmler and Erich Koch, the Gauleiter of East Prussia during the Nazi era, all spoke here on several occasions.

Now it has a largely local function and for tourists gives a clear indication of what is available and what is fashionable. The 2,000 stands within the halls are clearly regulated with prices listed and satisfactory hygiene. A guide is useful since, when prompted, an otherwise banal stand can suddenly produce caviar or silk at prices much lower than elsewhere. Good picnic ingredients available here include German sausage, Polish ham, Lithuanian fruit, local cheeses and the famous Russian black bread. Few tourists can take advantage of all the fresh fish that arrives here at least once a day.

Chernyakhovskovo continues to **Ploshchad Pobedy** (Площадь Победы; 'Victory Square') the former Hansaplatz, which Gauleiter Erich Koch renamed after himself in 1933. It had by then become the business and administration centre of the town. In 2005 there were discussions about renaming the square so that the link with Soviet times could be broken. 'Redeemer' or 'Cathedral' Square seemed to be the most likely names, if there is to be a change. Another suggestion was 'Harmony' Square to mark the reconciliation between Germany and Russia, but by 2008 there had still been no change. On the north side of the square, a dominating statue of Lenin used to make clear who were now the masters here but it was removed in 2004 to allow a proper view of the Orthodox cathedral, due to be completed the following year. That Lenin had his back to the cathedral won the approval of some, but the fact that his base was made from gravestones taken from former German cemeteries was no longer acceptable.

Unlike in the Baltic countries, where the removal of Lenin statues was greeted with joy and television pictures to send around the world, it was only with subterfuge that it could be carried out in Kaliningrad. The mayor had to assure objectors that the statue was being 'removed for restoration', and not being dismantled for good. A few months later it was erected again, not here but at the southern end of Lenin Prospekt, and to add a cloak-and-dagger air to the operation, it was done in the middle of the night with no press coverage.

Lenin has been replaced by a victory column. It should be surmounted by an angel looking westwards, and one clearly visible from Lenin Prospekt, but in early 2008 lack of funds had still prevented it from being completed. Westwards was of course the direction the victorious troops took in 1945. The compass carved into the paving behind the column is regarded as the centre of Kaliningrad and distances are measured from here. At New Year a fir tree is erected for the annual celebrations. As in many other public areas of the town, the local authority has recently taken a great interest in landscaping the area properly. Cynics in 2005 said this was simply done to provide a suitable backcloth for a meeting between presidents Putin, Chirac and Schröder in July that year, but in fact this work has continued ever since.

Boris Yeltsin laid the foundation stone for the **cathedral** (⊕ *to the public 09.00–17.00 Sat, 15.00–21.00 Sun*) but lack of funds delayed progress on the building during the later 1990s. It was finally consecrated on 4 July 2006, Kaliningrad's City Day. This is the date in 1946 when the town name was changed from Königsberg to Kaliningrad. The interior remains incomplete, with bare walls and ceilings, but for the local community, the crucial factor is that it was built as an Orthodox church. For 38 years until 1988 they could not worship in public at all, and for the next 20 years they had to use converted Lutheran churches. There are no chairs, as believers stand through the service.

In the garden to the southeast of the square stands a statue of *Mother Russia*; she replaced Stalin on this plinth in 1974. The former North Station/Nordbahnhof, built in 1930, still functions as such but it now also includes offices of several government departments and private businesses. Foreign businesses such as the Hamburg Chamber of Commerce are in a new building behind the station on Sovietsky Prospekt (Советский проспект). The Town Hall building on the south side of the square dates from 1923 and is one of very few to have served the same function both in German and in Soviet/Russian times. Behind it a burial ground was discovered in 2006, which held 1,500 bodies of French soldiers retreating from Moscow in 1812. These were soldiers who died from earlier injuries, disease or starvation as there was no fighting then in this area. Of the 500,000 soldiers who invaded Russia, only 30,000 would be alive two years later.

Leaving Victory Square to the west, along Prospekt Mira (Проспект Мира, 'Peace Avenue'), note first the **bronze statue of the fighting bulls** on the right-hand side of the road. They are the work of sculptor August Gaul whose bronze animals became famous all over Germany before World War I. In early Soviet days the statue was moved to the zoo, but it was returned here to its original location in the late 1970s. Local people now read a contemporary theme into the statue, seeing it as a representation of Kaliningrad locked into battle with Moscow. Behind the statue note the Baroque entrance of the former courthouse, which dates from 1913. Beside the courthouse are the former postal headquarters constructed in 1924. This building now houses the senior staff of the Baltic Fleet so is one of the best maintained in the whole town centre. The statue of Peter the Great in front of this building was erected in 2006. He visited Königsberg four times to and from western Europe and took a great interest in the Russian navy.

The next major building on the right-hand side is the **Drama Theatre**, built in 1927 but given its current bolshoi façade by the Soviet regime. In the six years prior to the Nazi regime every German actor of note played here and the Soviets continued the high standards, once it was finally reopened in 1980. On the other side of the road is a statue of the German writer Friedrich Schiller (1759–1805) which was allowed to stay during the Soviet period, probably because his work was regarded as very 'progressive'. A rather implausible story is told to explain its survival at the end of the war: the words 'don't shoot' were allegedly daubed across it in both German and Russian.

Prospekt Mira now widens and soon the entrance to the **zoo** (Зоопарк) (⊕ *May–Sep 09.00–21.00 daily, Oct–Apr 09.00–17.00; admission R40*) comes up on the right-hand side. It was founded in 1896 and is the only institution in Königsberg/Kaliningrad to have had a continuous history through German, Soviet and now Russian times. It might well be the world's first theme park; its early posters were decades ahead of their time, the funfair was always as crucial as the collection of animals and no secret was ever made of its commercial intent. Slot machines competed with donkey rides, cycle races and tennis tournaments. There were free family days when cooking facilities would be provided, thereby encouraging long stays and extensive patronage of the fairground attractions. Within two years of its opening, it sold 25,000 annual season tickets, a present for which every young Königsberger yearned at Christmas. Its flamboyant first director Hermann Claass stayed in charge until his death in 1914, never letting his commercial flair interfere with the expansion and maintenance of the collection. Within a year of the opening there were 983 animals and by 1910 this number had increased to 2,126, including two Siberian tigers donated by Moscow Zoo.

The zoo closed on the outbreak of war in August 1914 but popular demand and the elimination of any threat from Russia enabled it to reopen in July 1918, before the end of the conflict. It was completely rebuilt during the 1930s and these buildings largely remain despite the zoo being a battleground in April 1945. The zoo stayed open throughout the war this time and the Soviet government even presented two elephants in 1940, while the cynical Nazi–Soviet pact was still in effect. Annual season tickets were printed for 1945 and were sold from Christmas 1944 until the following March. The director throughout the war was Dr Hans-Georg Thienemann whose father Johannes was founder of the bird sanctuary at Rossitten (see page 287).

Many stories circulate about the number of animals who survived through May 1945 – most of course were killed by the starving residents. Four is the most quoted figure, representing a hippopotamus, a deer, a fox and a badger. Several Russian soldiers tried to feed the hippopotamus, which had apparently lost its appetite. Conventional nourishment failed, but a fortnight of vodka, allegedly four litres a day, succeeded in reviving it. The hippopotamus is now therefore the zoo's logo. In the midst of the tragedy that engulfed Königsberg in the summer of 1945, it is good to find one amusing story.

The zoo reopened in 1947, it is claimed with a collection of 2,000 animals, though this figure is now doubted. For the local population, it is again a major attraction although they must feel frustrated at the rather rundown air it now presents. Around 300,000 come each year and a pet shop has been added to the traditional attractions. With a brochure printed in colloquial English, it is, however, well in advance of other Kaliningrad tourist sites in attracting foreign visitors. They are promised 'baboons with colourful bottoms' and 'apes who so closely resemble humans that they look like someone you have probably met before'. Hermann Claass would be proud of the marketing flair shown by his Russian successors. A winter garden is planned for 2009, so perhaps the opportunity will be taken then for modernisation throughout.

Almost opposite the zoo south of Prospekt Mira is the **Cosmonaut Memorial**, its circular format with the space in between portraying the journeys around the globe that Kaliningrad's most famous sons accomplished in the 1970s. One, Alexei Leonov, was the first to leave a spaceship while it was in orbit. Another, Victor Patsayev, was killed in a failed landing when his rocket returned to earth. (As noted above, the space-research vessel now part of the *Vityaz* collection was named after him.)

Leaving the zoo and continuing along Prospekt Mira out of town, Germany begins to take over the architecture from the Soviet Union. After 200m on the left, the **Luisenkirche** makes this point emphatically. It was built around 1900, paid for largely by one benefactor, Louis Grosskopf. He founded a cigar factory in 1857 but expanded the business so successfully that by 1900 he was employing 400 people there and had opened 18 shops around the town. The consecration of the church in 1901 commemorated the 200th anniversary of the crowning of King Frederick I in 1701. The German community worshipped here until 1948 when it was turned into a storeroom for gardening tools used in the surrounding park. Its conversion into a puppet theatre in 1976 possibly saved it from destruction as that was the last year in which German churches were still being pulled down.

A further kilometre along the same road brings up on the left the first new church to be built after the war. It uses the German name **Auferstehungskirche** ('Church of the Resurrection') and was completed in 1999 on land that had earlier been a German cemetery. The large Lutheran exile community in Germany had wanted to re-establish a church in Kaliningrad, theirs having been the predominant religion in the former East Prussia since the 16th century – both Martin Luther's son and daughter had been active in the area and were buried in Königsberg. Every former church considered for this gave rise to considerable difficulties. The current Russian organisation was in some cases not willing to move; in others the bureaucratic and financial hurdles in rebuilding turned out to be too great.

The church now serves a local Russian community, the Volga Germans, who have settled in Kaliningrad with the hope of eventually being resettled in Germany, and the increasingly large number of Germans who now work in Kaliningrad. Attending a service or a concert, or seeing all the voluntary activities that take place during the week, shows how strongly German/Russian reconciliation can work. The altar is of great significance, being assembled from bricks taken out of eight different ruined churches.

The oldest church in East Prussia, the **Juditterkirche**, is another kilometre or so along Prospekt Pobedya, but on the right-hand side. The Juditter suburb, (renamed Mendeleevo (**Менделеева**) was as sought after by successful Germans as it now is by successful Russians. The area offers space, greenery, cleanliness and above all privacy. The public parks near to the church rivalled the zoo as an attraction for children. Reminiscences from former East Prussians tell of collecting anemones in spring and acorns in autumn, of climbing trees, of open-air concerts, and the climax of the afternoon, buying peppermint drops and lemonade at the sweet shop. The church dates originally from the 13th century with the tower being added at the turn of the 15th century. It was extensively restored in 1906 and this revealed wall paintings which had been hidden for centuries. Although the church was totally untouched by the war and fighting, much of the intricate woodwork was plundered in the immediate aftermath and then 35 years of complete neglect left little of the former interior. Germans were allowed to continue worshipping here until their expulsion in 1948.

The ruins were given over to the Orthodox Church in 1984 and a basic restoration was completed in 1988. Services started in 1986, the first to be held in the Kaliningrad region since 1948. Official atheism had therefore lasted 38 years. It would take another two or three years before any other churches reopened. Given the vigorous support that the local Orthodox community gives to the church, the building is unlikely ever to return into Lutheran hands. However, the German cemetery beside the church is being slowly restored and a memorial plaque is planned to all Germans killed in Königsberg at the end of the war.

Another visit should be made within the town and that is to the **Brandenburg Gate**, Городские Ворота (it has kept the same name in Russian), situated south of the river on Ulitsa Bagrationa (**Улица Багратиона**) near to the main railway station. Architecturally, it has nothing in common with its Berlin namesake although being as large, trams and cars also go through it. Like six other similar gates that date from the early 19th century, it is a red-brick structure built so well that it survived both the RAF bombs and the subsequent Soviet onslaught. It even retains two statues, of General von Boyen and General von Aster, two prominent 19th-century commanders. The plaque with three figures who each played a prominent role at the Albertina (now Kant) University was unveiled in 2007. Ludwig Rhesa (1776–1840) was a theologian but more importantly a translator from Lithuanian into German and was responsible for introducing Lithuanian literature written in Prussia to the German-speaking population. Karl Burdach (1776–1847) was a physiologist, after whom a nerve was named. Christian Jacob Kraus (1753–1807) managed to be equally proficient in philosophy and economics (he introduced the ideas of Adam Smith to the German-speaking world) and also pioneered the serious study of Gypsy communities.

Some 2km east of the Brandenburg Gate is the **Friedländer Gate**, Городские Ворота Фридланские (*www.friedlander-tor.gazinter.net;* ⊕ *10.00–17.00 Tue–Sun; admission R50*). The exhibition here gives the history of the town's fortifications, including those that were removed in 1900 when the city was rapidly expanding, and also the damage suffered in World War II. Separately, there are some exhibits of day-to-day items from the early 20th century, similar to those in the Prussian Museum. One collection, ironically called 'Farewell to Arms', shows the weapons used by both sides in both world wars. Sadly, the detailed website is only in Russian.

Other gates from the fortifications set up in the mid 19th century were restored between 2004 and 2006. The quickest work was done on the King's Gate, **Königstor** (Королевские Ворота, ☉ *11.00–19.00, Wed–Sun; admission R50*), which had been a ruin since 1945, but which was suddenly transformed into a fully functional museum within four months between February and June 2005. The original architect was Friedrich August Stüler, who was active in this region but is best known for the Neues Museum and other large projects in Berlin. The gate is about a mile from the Prussian History and Art Museum, along ul Frunze, and three statues on the tower stand out immediately. They lost their heads during the 1945 fighting but now total recastings have been made of each one. On the left is the King of Bohemia Ottokar II (1230–1278), in the middle Duke Albrecht (1490–1568) who founded the Albertina University, and on the right Friedrich I of Prussia (1657–1713).

There are several exhibitions inside the building, but they are all subsumed under the title of 'The Grand Embassy' to show how international the city has always been except for the 45 years of total isolation between 1945 and 1990. One covers the twinning links the town now has, including those with Southampton in Britain and with Cork in Ireland. Another shows the links enjoyed in the early 20th century, when a large contingent of foreign consuls lived in Königsberg. A third is on the famous people who did not live there but who can be linked to the town, such as Copernicus, Peter the Great, Napoleon and Wagner.

Even though Lenin no longer dominates the square in front of the North Station, Kalinin still has to have his glory here in front of the **South Station** (Южный Вокзал). As most visitors, whether local or international, will arrive here or at the neighbouring bus station, he could always claim to be more prominent. The interior of the station was completely rebuilt in time for the 2005 celebrations, but surprisingly it has a very Soviet feel. Marble and chandeliers predominate. A small railway museum was opened in summer 2000 with two restored steam engines and the promise of more. Given the number of engines abandoned in marshalling yards around the country, it is a pity that this museum has not been enlarged. A large post office is at the western end of the station complex and beside it is an antique shop, full of Königsberg and Soviet memorabilia. There is another antique shop on the opposite side of the square, beside which is one of the larger bookshops in Kaliningrad.

The current home of the Kaliningrad Philharmonic Orchestra is in the former **Kirche zur Heiligen Familie** ('Church of the Holy Family'), known as Philharmonia in Russian. It is on the same road as the Brandenburg Gate, Ulitsa Bagrationa, and it is a walk of about 700m from there or from the station. Originally one of four Catholic churches in Königsberg built around 1900, it was saved from serious damage at the end of the war because it was surrounded by narrow streets. It therefore avoided the worst of the fighting and the bombardments. In the early 1970s, whilst other churches in Kaliningrad were still being pulled down, restoration started here and in 1980 it opened as a concert hall. An organ was added in 1982 and good standards of maintenance have been upheld ever since, together with equally good standards of catering in the crypt-café underneath.

EXCURSIONS FROM KALININGRAD

If time allows for only a one-day trip outside the town of Kaliningrad, this must be to the coast and along the **Curonian Spit** (Крушская коса) towards the Lithuanian border. It should be done by car and with a guide since it involves a number of stops and signing in many places is not good. Such a trip can start in **Yantarny** (Янтарный), which will very likely be the backbone of the Kaliningrad area's economy for the next 100 years, when the amber mine there is expected to run out, but well before then it may become a gambling centre with its dedicated hotels. Known as Palmnicken in

RETURN TO KÖNIGSBERG

Thomas Eichelbaum

My family left East Prussia in 1938 when I was aged 7: refugees from Hitler's Germany. We were to settle in New Zealand, on the opposite side of the world. My father had a globe of the world, and I was worried about where we were going, because looking at New Zealand on the globe, it seemed people had to walk upside down. My father said that wouldn't be a problem, and it wasn't; not being able to speak the same language was a greater worry, for a while. But New Zealand turned out to be a great choice for our new home.

Exactly 60 years later I returned to the place of my birth for the first time. My wife and I flew to Vilnius, then were driven to Kaliningrad, the city where I had been to kindergarten and (for two years) to school. As we crossed the border and moved deeper into the former East Prussia a number of memories came back. The light blue of the sky, the shape of the clouds, captured by pictures my grandfather used to paint, some of which we still have. Farmers haymaking, stacking the hay in round haystacks and transporting it by horse-drawn carts. Storks nesting on telegraph poles, some with large chicks. Swallows. Cobbled streets. As it grew dark, the road sweeping through avenues of trees in the countryside, the headlights catching reflector paint; vague childhood recollections of trips with my grandparents from Königsberg to Insterburg (Chernyakhovsk) to visit my grandparents there. We reach our hotel in Kaliningrad late at night and, despite the excitement, sleep well.

The next day, with our guide, we set out to look at Kaliningrad. The guide assures us that the trams have been replaced, but they seem to have been modelled on the ones I knew. I have a book with me, *Königsberg in 144 Pictures*, and recognise many of the buildings, although others have been destroyed. Some of the streets are familiar to me; Steindamm where my father had his office. Here the buildings have all gone, but the former shape of the streets is clear and unchanged. We come to the Hufenallee with its distinctive winding stretch and instantly I know where we are. I say to our guide, we are close to the zoo – around the next corner we come to the zoo entrance through which I was often taken as a child; it seems unchanged. A few minutes later, an unforgettable indescribable moment, we are outside the apartment building where my family was living in 1938.

German times, the village is on the coast about 35km kilometres from Kaliningrad. Its wealth is well disguised since the village houses have a forlorn look and its roads are poorly maintained. Bomb damage was minimal so older German tourists can recognise the layout and again enjoy Sunday afternoons along the beach.

There is now just one large open-cast mine in use, producing about 450 tonnes of amber a year, about 90% of world production. Water has now seeped into the others, although Russian children follow their German predecessors in collecting amber pieces from the beach when they have been washed up after storms.

There is a somewhat precarious viewing point from which the whole mine can be seen; strong footwear is necessary to reach it and an equally strong constitution to tolerate the dire environmental pollution that it causes. The site was privatised in 1990 and then renationalised three years later with the hope of returning most of the profits into government hands. The Baltic Germans in the 13th century had similarly tried to control this trade and although they publicly hanged private traders, they were as unsuccessful at controlling it as their 20th-century Russian successors. A small shop near the site is sometimes open for the purchase of amber; otherwise the Amber Museum in Kaliningrad is the best source.

By late 2008 there should be a proper memorial on the beach to the 6,000 Jews killed there and in the mine in January 1945. They had been taken to Königsberg from concentration camps about to be liberated by the Russians and were then force-marched to Yantarny. It is likely that about 8,000 started on the march but 2,000 died or were killed *en route*. Those who survived the march were then shot in the mine or on the beach. Only 13 survived. It was only in the late 1990s that the full story of what happened was properly recorded, given that all those responsible tried to keep the truth concealed and that – Kaliningrad being totally closed to foreigners – investigation on the spot was impossible. The memorial has been commissioned from Frank Meisler, best known in Britain for his sculpture at Liverpool Street railway station commemorating the arrival there of the Kindertransport, the trains that brought Jewish children to safety from Austria and Germany just before World War II.

RAUSCHEN/SVETLOGORSK If ever a reward could be made for the town in the Kaliningrad region least affected by the Soviet occupation it must go to Rauschen or, as it is still officially called, Svetlogorsk (**Светлогорск**). It is today developing as a health centre and as a summer holiday resort, largely for Russian tourists as the older generation of German tourists who returned in the early 1990s to relive their childhood memories has now largely died. The town is attractive in winter, too, particularly after a snowfall, as temperatures rarely drop much below freezing point, and day trippers from Kaliningrad keep it lively on a year-round basis at weekends.

The Russian name translates as 'bright city', the German one as 'to rustle'. Both are equally appropriate for a well-designed, spacious town full of trees and shrubs. The town's role as a seaside resort has remained constant, since with official Soviet status as a spa town, money could always be found for maintenance.

A good regular train service operates from Kaliningrad and the town is small enough to be explored in toto on foot. It was the introduction of this train service in 1900 that brought day trippers from Königsberg to Rauschen and so made it less exclusive than it had been in the 19th century. The Soviet Union, rather than Russia, intrudes with the street names. Marx, Lenin, Kalinin, Gagarin and the October Revolution are all remembered but, unlike in most other towns of the region, the statue of Lenin has been removed. Perhaps he may in due course be replaced by Prussia's King Friedrich Wilhelm I who first made the town famous in the early 18th century. Otherwise one could be in any small German town on the Baltic coast. At weekends, the town is as lively in the winter as it is in the summer. Its year-round population is some 4,000 compared with 2,500 before the war, but this trebles in the summer season when Russians come from all over the federation for their holidays and for medical treatment. Svetlogorsk likes to think of itself as the Sotchi of the north, rivalling this Black Sea resort in its facilities and in its prestige.

The red-brick Gothic church was designed by Friedrich August Stüler, famous for many grander buildings in Berlin, and architect of the King's Gate in Kaliningrad described above. It was consecrated in 1907, converted into a sports centre after the war but was then given to the Orthodox Church in 1990. Chamber music concerts are held there throughout the year. A second church was built in 1994 as a memorial chapel to 25 children killed when a military aircraft crashed into their kindergarten in May 1972. Following normal Soviet practice, no official mention of the crash was made at the time. The photographs inside are of the children and their teachers, but there are none of the air crew who also all died.

The promenade by the sea, with its funfair, sundial and stairway decorated with mosaics has survived largely intact. Some villas and sanatoria are newly built but most of the grand wooden villas with their intricate window designs and elaborate roofs date from around 1900. They are all at a discreet distance from each other, allowing for extensive shrubbery and flower gardens between them. Some are now in private hands, some still belong to state organisations, but all can be proud of their paintwork and varnish.

Sculpture from Rauschen's most famous artist, Hermann Brachert (1890–1972) has survived throughout the town. He fell out of favour with the Nazi regime on account of the pessimistic tone of many of his pieces. They did not allow him to teach or exhibit but fortunately they did not destroy his work and some of his most moving sculptures date from that era. He worked with equal effect in marble, limestone and bronze. His house in the neighbouring village of Otradnoye (Отрадное), formerly Georgenswalde, is now a museum.

Transport It is quite possible to visit Kaliningrad on a daily basis from Svetlogorsk by local train or vice versa. Trains go every hour in each direction to both Kaliningrad stations and the fare in early 2008 was R45 each way.

Telephone The dialling code for Svetlogorsk is 01153 and the '0' is still used when phoning from abroad.

Accommodation in Svetlogorsk/Rauschen

🏠 **Grand Palace** (32 rooms) Pereulok Beregocoy 2; ☏ 33232; e info@grandhotel.ru; www.grandhotel.ru. This hotel was assured of instant fame when it opened during the summer of 2005 & immediately greeted Vladimir Putin, Jacques Chirac & Gerhard Schröder for a brief summit meeting. This was the notorious occasion when Jacques Chirac criticised British food & perhaps lost the Paris bid for the 2012 Olympics in the process. In its restrained luxury, the Grand Palace is very un-Russian, but concentrates on what matters here: a private beach, a large terrace & 24hr room service. The best rooms of course look out over the sea; it would be a pity to come here just to have a hill view at the back instead. $$$$

🏠 **Falke** (58 rooms) Lenin 16; ☏ 32160; e info@ falke-hotel.ru; www.falke-hotel.ru. A lot of trouble has been taken with the décor here. Amber has been used to decorate the windows, & every room & corridor has original paintings. The sturdy red-brick façade certainly lends a tone of respectability to the hotel. There is an indoor swimming pool, AC in some rooms & more than usual have baths. It is a pity that the road outside, despite its name, is so ridden with pot-holes that arrival & departure are inevitably bumpy experiences. $$$

🏠 **Rus** (37 rooms) Verestschagin 10; ☏ 21445; e hotel_rusy@baltnet.ru; www.rus-hotel.narod.ru. Until the building of the Grand Palace, this was *the* hotel in Svetlogorsk. Everything is built on a lavish scale & its private grounds stretch to the sea. A winter garden is the most novel feature. It of course has a casino, tennis courts & a restaurant with probably the most extensive wine list in the region. The hotel achieved notoriety in February 2000 when Anatoly Sobchak, the former mayor of St Petersburg, died there from a heart attack after an evening of over-indulgence. He had been

helping with Vladimir Putin's presidential campaign. Although totally renovated in 2003, the hotel was closed in autumn 2007 for further renovation in time for summer 2008. $$$

🏠 **Azur Coast** (6 rooms) Dynamo 1a; ☏ 21523; f 21522. This large villa was opened as an exclusive hotel in 1999. Whilst only small, it offers the full range of hotel services. Its private grounds are sufficiently extensive to ensure privacy & tranquillity. With prices not being much higher than those in conventional hotels, the luxury is well worth the modest extra cost. $$

🏠 **Baltic Pearl** (20 rooms) Baltiskaya 15a; ☏ 21351. For many years, this was the most pleasant hotel in the whole Kaliningrad region, but by 2006 it had several other competitors. It is surrounded by woodland but is only 10mins' walk from the town centre. The family feel is unexpected & most welcome. The hotel offers ample grounds, a large indoor swimming pool, a sauna & a billiard room. Prices for meals & refreshments are very low, tea in spring 2008 costing R30 a cup & coffee R35. $$

🏠 **Universal** (34 rooms) Nekrasova 3; ☏ 74365; e unitour@inbox.ru; www.hotel-universal.ru. A major appeal of Svetlogorsk in recent years has been the careful restoration of the grand villas built in the early 20th century. This is one of several converted into a hotel. Accommodation is simple, but the addition of a large garden & a courtyard makes it a very congenial place to stay. Its pictures & maps on the wall are all of pre-war Rauschen & Königsberg. Presumably nobody has noticed that the maps are from the late 1930s when all the streets had been renamed after prominent Nazi leaders; it might have been tactful to choose some from a few years earlier. The hotel is about 200m from the railway station. $$

CURONIAN SPIT A 20km drive from Rauschen/Svetlogorsk is needed to reach the start of the Curonian Spit at Zelenogradsk (**Зеленоградск**), formerly Cranz. Not being granted any special status during the Soviet period and having been the scene of serious fighting in April 1945, what was once a glamorous, vibrant resort soon became a neglected village. It is changing much more slowly than other places in the region, but with the restoration of some large buildings in 2007–08, developments are clearly gambling on gentrification coming here in due course. The young people drifting around the streets clearly do not represent the success stories of the new regime. The Russian name translates as 'Green City', which perhaps aptly sums up the weeds growing in the streets and the moss that has gripped many former villas. A grotesque concrete walkway along the coast offers no consolation after seeing the main street through the town.

The Curonian Spit, however, will without doubt be worth the drive from Kaliningrad. Visitors with more time may well consider continuing their tour to Nida, just over the Lithuanian border. The spit is an 80km tongue of land which divides the Baltic Sea from the Curonian Lagoon. Half the territory belongs to Kaliningrad and half to Lithuania. The history of the spit shows nature at its most brutal. Humans fought the elements rather than each other in this area. Most visitors travelling on a calm summer's day will see an alternation of dunes and forests, interspersed with the occasional village. It is hard to believe that a graveyard of whole villages lies beneath the sea and sand just a few hundred metres away. In 2008, the website www.rybachy.com began to have some English-language material on all aspects of the spit, including information on the museums listed below.

That nature was finally controlled here is due to one man, Franz Epha (1828–1904), whose plans for forestation took 40 years to implement between 1860 and 1900, but which finally made the area secure. The Prussian regime encouraged the work initially to safeguard the road to the end of their empire and also to provide good communications with St Petersburg. If the rail network had developed sooner, this work might never have been carried out. Epha's work has been respected by all the governments that have ruled here since, by Nazis as much as by Communists, and now by the new independent regimes. A sand dune that was named after Epha shortly before he died has retained its name throughout the subsequent century, not being changed in the Soviet era. The isolation of the area at that time also spared it from development so animals roamed at will. Wild boar, beavers and elk now predominate in the pine forests, which take up 71% of the land on the Russian side. The spit is designated by both Russia and Lithuania as a national park and a small tax is charged for entry by car. Cars were banned from the spit between 1920 and 1940 so access was then by boat, bicycle or on horseback.

There are two main villages on the Russian side of the spit between Zelonogradsk and the Lithuanian border, Lesnoy (**Лесной**) and Rybachy (**Рыбачий**), Sarkau and Rossitten in German. In Lesnoy new money flaunts itself behind formidable metal grilles. One of the villas belongs to the Moscow Central Bank. It shows reasonable taste in architecture though one must regret the passing of many of the former more modest houses in the village.

Halfway between Lesnoy and Rybachy is the **Spit Museum** (⊕ *10.00–17.00 Tue–Sun; admission R30*), founded in 1987 in what had formerly been a Communist Party guesthouse. The first German guidebook to the area, produced in 1996, tells visitors not to be put off by the austere concrete exterior and that it really is worth entering. This is true. The year 1987 was sufficiently into the *glasnost* era for a detailed and honest history of the area to be given. An extensive collection of photographs, models and stuffed animals covers contemporary and past natural history.

More unexpected is the history of the gliding centre which was founded in Rossitten in 1920. This resulted from the ban on motorised aviation in Germany stipulated by the Versailles Treaty at the end of World War I. Although neither German nor Russian historians like to dwell on the matter, there was close co-operation between the USSR and Germany throughout the early inter-war period here. Soviet pilots came for training and Germans were in return invited to the Soviet gliding school in the Crimea. There had been similar co-operation between Imperial Germany and Tsarist Russia for a time after 1895 when gliding first began in this area. A recently erected plaque commemorates a world-record eight-hour flight undertaken in 1925 by a local pilot, Ferdinand Schulz. The inscription, carved in both German and Russian, proclaims that 'gliding should overcome frontiers and bring nations together'.

Seven kilometres further along the road towards **Rybachy**, or **Rossitten** in German (*www.zin.ru/rybachy*; ⊕ *Apr–Oct 09.00–18.00 daily; admission free*), the bird sanctuary founded by the German Ornithological Society in 1901 continues its work and welcomes visitors and helpers. It broke an earlier culture amongst the fishing community of killing local birds, mainly crows, for food. Now they are ringed and then released. The first and most famous director, Johannes Thienemann, ringed 103 himself in 1903. By 1936 this annual total had reached 140,000. The larger birds included seagulls, sparrowhawks, kestrels and buzzards. Regular smaller ones were robins, thrushes and wagtails. Thienemann was soon able to work out the migratory routes of the white stork through Hungary, Egypt and Kenya to South Africa. He remained as director until 1929. The German staff all fled in 1945 and it was not until 1956 that the sanctuary was reopened by the Russians. They gave it the name Fringilla, from the Latin for chaffinch which is one of the most common birds to be found there. In 1991 the very precise statistic was provided that 1,672,071 birds had been ringed since the reopening. Its traps are thought to be the largest in the world, one being 100m deep, 30m wide and 15m high. The birds fly in totally unaware that they are in a trap so around 60,000 can be ringed each year. The traps are relocated each season, facing north in the spring and south in the autumn to catch the birds on both their outward and return migrations. The large nets are renewed each year; songbirds in cages entice the migrants. By 2002, a lot of the exhibition material had been translated into English as well as into German. British and German researchers are now regularly at work there. Electronic chips are beginning to replace rings but the enormous cost of tracking them is limiting this research.

Just outside the sanctuary, the **Museum of Russian Superstition** (⊕ *Apr–Oct 10.00–17.00 daily; admission free*) opened in 2002 with a collection of 70 wooden carvings of spirits linked to water, forests and fields. It is planned to broaden the field of carving, so soon it should also have domestic utensils. The building is of course totally wooden.

In Rybachy/Rossitten itself, several wooden houses have preserved their original 19th-century carvings. The main building of interest is the red-brick village church, consecrated in 1873, and like the one in Svetlogorsk/Rauschen it was designed by August Stüler. The building was never damaged and the vicarage beside it is still intact. Even the bell and the windows remain. It was not used between 1945 and 1963 when it was taken over by the 'Dawn of Communism' fishing collective as a storage depot for their nets. In 1990 it was given to the Orthodox Church.

The Lithuanian border is a further 16km from Rybachy so this village is an appropriate point to finish the tour. By the summer of 2009 it may well be possible to return from Rybachy to Zelenogradsk by boat along the sea coast or along the lagoon. Another likely route is across the lagoon to Polessk. This second route would offer a semicircular journey starting to the west of Kaliningrad and then finishing in the east. In the summer of 2007 it was still necessary to retrace one's steps by road but the variety of tracks through the forest or along the dunes offer so many tempting stops that this is hardly an imposition.

Appendix I

LANGUAGE

Of necessity these are only basic words and phrases. Consult a dictionary if you would like to learn more.

USEFUL EXPRESSIONS

English	Estonian	Latvian	Lithuanian
hello	*tere*	*sveiki*	*laba diena*
goodbye	*nagemiseni*	*atā*	*viso gero*
good morning	*tere hommikust*	*labdien*	*labas rytas*
good evening	*head õhtust*	*labvakar*	*labas vakaras*
goodnight	*head ööd*	*ar labu nakti*	*labanakt*
yes	*jah*	*jā*	*taip*
no	*ei*	*nē*	*ne*
please	*palun*	*lūdzu*	*prašau*
thank you	*tänan*	*paldies*	*ačiu*
How much?	*Kui palju?*	*Cik?*	*Kiek tai kainuoja?*
When?	*Millal?*	*Kad?*	*Kada?*
Where?	*Kus?*	*Kur?*	*Kur?*
Excuse me please	*Vabandage palun*	*Atvainojiet, lūdzu*	*Atsiprasau*
I do not understand	*Ma ei saa aru*	*Nesaprotu*	*As nesuprantu*

USEFUL WORDS

English	Estonian	Latvian	Lithuanian
airport	*lennujaam*	*lidosta*	*aerouostas*
bus station	*bussijaam*	*autoosta*	*autobusu stotis*
railway station	*raudteejaam*	*dzelzceļa stacija*	*geležinkelio stotis*
toilet	*WC*	*tualete*	*tualet*
beer	*õlu*	*alus*	*alus*
coffee (with milk)	*kohv (piimaga)*	*kafija (ar pienu)*	*kava (su pienas)*
drinking water	*joogivesi*	*ūdens*	*vanduo*
juice	*mahl*	*sula*	*sultys*
mineral water	*mineraalvesi*	*minerālūdens*	*mineralinis vanduo*
wine (red, white)	*wein (pumane, valge)*	*vīns (sarkans, balts)*	*vynas*
sugar	*suhkur*	*cukurs*	*cukrus*

English	Russian
hello	здравствуйте [zdrahstvooytyeh]
goodbye	до свидания [dasvidanya]
good morning	доброе утро [dobriy dyen]
good evening	добрый вечер [dobriy vyechyer]
goodnight	спокойной ночи [spahkoynigh nochee]
yes	да [da]
no	нет [nyet]
please	пожалуйста [pazhalsta]
thank you	спасибо [spahseebah]
How much?	Сколько? [Skol ka?]
When?	яогда? [Kagda?]
Where?	υде? [Gdyeh?]
Excuse me, please	Извините, пожалуйста... [Izveeneetye, pazhalsta]
I do not understand	Я не понимаю [Ya nye panimayu]
airport	аэропорт [aeroport]
bus station	автовокзал [avtovokzal]
railway station	вокзал [vokzal]
toilet	туалет [tualyet]
beer	пиво [peeva]
coffee (with milk)	кофе (с молоком) [coffee (smolokom)]
drinking water	питьевая вода [peetyeva-ya vada]
juice	сок [sok]
mineral water	минеральная вода [meenyeralna-ya vada]
wine (red, white)	(красное, белое) вино [(krasna-yeh, byela-yeh) veeno]
sugar	сахар [sahar]

Appendix 2

FURTHER INFORMATION
GENERAL BOOKS

Baddiel, David *The Secret Purposes* Abacus 2005. The story begins in Königsberg shortly before the war.

Denny, Isabel *The Fall of Hitler's Fortress City: The Battle for Königsberg 1945* Greenhill Books, 2007. Despite the title, the book in fact covers the entire history of Königsberg, which has previously not been covered in any English-language book.

Dönhoff, Marion *Before The Storm: Memories of My Youth in Old Prussia* Knopf, 1990. Much of the literature on their former Heimat (homeland) produced by East Prussians is tendentious and superficial but voluminous. The Dönhoff is an exception, and fortunately one that has been translated into English. She has written many other books about both Königsberg and Kaliningrad but those are only in German.

Eksteins, Modris *Walking Since Daybreak* Macmillan, 2000. For the human dimension of the occupations during the 20th century, this is unlikely ever to be surpassed.

Fearley, Robert *The Latvian Issues* Silverwood Books, 2008. A history of 20th-century Latvia told through its stamps.

Königsberg Merian Live series. The best German guidebook. The many still in circulation that date from the early 1990s should be treated with great caution. The writers are still embittered about the loss of the area and the whole Soviet period is described in totally hostile terms.

Koster, Baldur *Königsberg: Architectur aus Deutscher Zeit* Husum, 2000. The definitive book on German architecture, it was the result of four years work there and shows how much has remained.

Landsbergis, Vytautas *Lithuania: Independent Again* 2000. Vytautas was the first Baltic independence leader to have written his memoirs. Walking the calm streets of Vilnius now, it is all too easy to forget the struggles needed to remove the Soviet occupiers. Music and politics have always been linked in his life so it is not surprising that two chapters in this book are called 'Debussy and Despair' and 'The Power of Music'. A third has the title 'Čiurlionis' in recognition of Lithuania's most famous composer.

Lane, Thomas; Pabriks, Artis; Purs, Aldis; and Smith, David J *The Baltic States: Estonia, Latvia, and Lithuania* Routledge, 2002. Three books brought together in one volume. Each provides short general histories on each country and then greater detail on the Soviet occupation and the transition to independence.

Manthey, Jürgen *Königsberg: Geschichte einer Weltbürgerrepublik* DTV, 2005. The year 2005, being the 750th anniversary of the founding of Königsberg, produced a number of commemorative books. Manthey's account is likely to be the definitive history of the German period for many years to come.

Mason, P M *Puppet Maker* 2005. A novel set in London and Latvia in the 1990s with flashbacks to pre-war Latvia.

Palmer, Alan *Northern Shores* John Murray, 2005. Effectively summarises a thousand years of very complicated history around the Baltic Sea.

Sumowski, Hans-Burkhard *Jetzt war ich ganz allein auf der Welt* DVA, 2007. Recollections of an eight-year-old orphan surviving in Königsberg after the death of his entire family.

Unwin, Peter *Baltic Approaches* Michael Russell, 1995. Unwin's many visits to the area and much research allows him to put the sudden transition of 1990–91 into a longer-term perspective; the book has in no way dated. His chapter on Kaliningrad is one of the very few sources in English on this area.

von Rauch, George *The Baltic States: Years of Independence* Hurst, 1995. Recommended for more detail on the 20 years of independence the Baltic countries enjoyed between 1920 and 1940.

Wieck, Michael *A Childhood under Hitler and Stalin* University of Wisconsin, 2003. The best account of life and death in Königsberg at the end of the war, written by a Jew who was under equal threat from both the Nazis and then from the Russians.

TRAVEL GUIDES Individual guides to Estonia, Latvia and Lithuania have been published by Bradt, offering in-depth coverage of each country. New editions of these books are published regularly.

Baister, Stephen and Patrick, Chris *Latvia: The Bradt Travel Guide* Bradt Travel Guides, 2007. All corners of Latvia, from the capital, Riga, to the 13th-century town of Cēsis, Sigulda National Park, the lakes of Latgāle and the coast at Jūrmala.

McLachlan, Gordon *Lithuania: The Bradt Travel Guide* Bradt Travel Guides, 2008. Highlights of this rapidly changing country include medieval cities, national parks, pristine beaches and colourful local festivals.

Taylor, Neil *Estonia: The Bradt Travel Guide* Bradt Travel Guides, 2007. A practical guide to Estonia's complex history and many attractions: Tallinn; the unspoilt countryside and islands; German manor houses and elegant resorts.

MAPS Jāṇa Sēta in Riga publish atlases of the Baltic countries and individual town plans for each capital and for many smaller towns as well. Their maps are available at Stanfords (*www.stanfords.co.uk*) in London, Bristol and Manchester and all over the Baltic countries. Their shop in Riga is at 83–85 Elizabetes. The Estonian map specialists are Regio, whose main outlet is the Apollo bookshop at Viru 23, close to the Viru Gate. They publish historical as well as contemporary maps of Tallinn. They also sell through Stanfords shops in the UK. There are no similar publishers to these two in Vilnius or in Kaliningrad, although a wide selection of locally produced maps is available. In Kaliningrad it is possible to buy bilingual maps produced in Germany giving both the former and the current names of all the streets in the town centre.

LOCAL PUBLICATIONS *Tallinn In Your Pocket* and the parallel publications for Riga and Vilnius are essential purchases on arrival. They cost only about £1.50/US$2.50 and this cover charge enables them to comment freely on local restaurants, museums and shops without being beholden to advertisers. They appear bi-monthly and are all on the website (*www.inyourpocket.com*) so this should be consulted for up-to-date information before departure. The *City Paper* covers all three Baltic capitals in one publication and, combined with practical information, has a wide range of articles on contemporary political topics. Its price is around £1.75/US$3.00 which again ensures editorial integrity. Its website (*www.citypaper.ee*) provides a far wider range of restaurant and hotel reviews than the written publication.

Kaliningrad has still to realise the potential of providing tourists with nice books as souvenirs of their visit. A locally produced guidebook in Russian has still to appear, let alone one in German or English. In Kaliningrad itself, visitors should look out for *Königsberg/Kaliningrad Now,* an excellent introduction to contemporary and former art and architecture produced by the local branch of the Centre for Contemporary Arts. This book was produced with a one-off subsidy for the 2005 celebrations but hopefully tourists in later years will still be able to obtain copies. Sets of postcards are easily available, both of pre-war Königsberg and of contemporary Kaliningrad. The cathedral has produced, in German only, a few booklets on its history.

From around 2000, the other three capitals began producing a plethora of large photographic albums and manageable booklets, a trend that showed no signs of abating in 2005. In Tallinn the little book *The Living Past of Tallinn* by Elena Rannu skilfully portrays the high life and the low life of the Upper Town throughout its history. Gustav German's *Estonia* published in 1996 in fact concentrates on photographs of Tallinn just before new building, rather than just restoration, took over in parts of the town. Sulev Maevali's *Architecture and Art Monuments in Tallinn* was first published in 1986 but it is regularly updated and has no equal in its detailed descriptions of church interiors. For exteriors turn to *History Reflected in Architecture*, which is in fact a catalogue of a photographic exhibition held in Tallinn in 2005. Tallinn deserves a lively book on its history but for the moment has to do with the rather ponderous *History of Old Tallinn* by Raimo Pullat published in 1998.

Most visitors to Riga return with the two books written by Andris Kolbergs together called *The Story of Riga*. One covers the history of the Old Town, the other Riga's expansion in the 19th century. Both are well illustrated with prints and contemporary photographs. A worthy extravagance for the coffee table is *Art Nouveau in Riga* by Janis Krastins which covers every building in this genre. *Riga: A City to Discover* by A Bruders manages to include 300 original photographs in a book almost pocket-size. *The Jews in Riga*, published by the Jewish Museum in 1991, covers all buildings linked with their history, both those still in use and those destroyed during the war. It also has a very useful history of their community.

It would be impossible to leave Vilnius without buying a Baroque book. The best is *Baroque in Lithuania*, which concentrates on architecture. *Baroque Art in Lithuania* covers porcelain, tapestry and painting. *Lithuania: Past, Culture, Present* does manage to do justice to all three ambitious themes within the space of 270 pages, both in the text and in the illustrations. The title *Lithuania: Facts and Figures* hardly sounds inviting but, although it is an official publication, it is written in a lively manner and has far more photographs than statistics. *Vilnius*, an annual publication in English of the Lithuanian Writers' Union, translates the best writing of the previous year and also has commentaries on art and film. *Vilnius 13.01.91* is a grim photographic reminder of the violence the capital had to endure in defending its independence from Soviet forces. (No individual authors are listed for these books as they all have several contributors.) The website www.booksfromlithuania.lt lists all Lithuanian fiction recently translated into foreign languages.

Many guidebooks produced in the Baltics suffer from the problem of being written for a local audience and then simply translated. Tomas Venclova's *Vilnius* is a clear exception to this pattern; having lived in exile in the USA from 1977 to 1990, he is able both to draw on his local knowledge and to present it warmly to an outside audience. He has a wide canvas, with an excellent historical introduction and a large number of drawings and photographs.

BOOKSHOPS Chapters earlier in this book include details of local bookshops with the best selection of recent English-language publications. The website www.amazon.com and www.amazon.co.uk websites are always up to date on material in English on each of the Baltic countries and the parallel www.amazon.de site similarly covers books published in German. The website www.amazon.fr covers the more limited, but now increasing number of books published in French on the Baltics.

WEBSITES

Baltic Times	www.baltictimes.com
City Paper	www.citypaper.ee
Estonian Tourist Board	www.visitestonia.com
Eurolines buses	www.online.ee/eurolines.com
In Your Pocket	www.inyourpocket.com
Latvian Tourist Board	www.latviatourism.lv
Liepaja	www.liepaja.lv
Lithuanian Tourist Board	www.tourism.lt
Tartu	www.tartu.ee

Index

Page numbers in **bold** indicate major entries; those in *italic* indicate maps

294

WIN £100 CASH!
READER QUESTIONNAIRE

Send in your completed questionnaire for the chance to win £100 cash in our regular draw

All respondents may order a Bradt guide at half the UK retail price – please complete the order form overleaf.

(Entries may be posted or faxed to us, or scanned and emailed.)

We are interested in getting feedback from our readers to help us plan future Bradt guides. Please answer ALL the questions below and return the form to us in order to qualify for an entry in our regular draw.

Have you used any other Bradt guides? If so, which titles? . . . .

. . . .

What other publishers' travel guides do you use regularly? . . . .

. . . .

Where did you buy this guidebook? . . . .

What was the main purpose of your trip to the Baltic cities (or for what other reason did you read our guide)? eg: holiday/business/charity etc. . . . .

. . . .

What other destinations would you like to see covered by a Bradt guide?

. . . .

Age (circle relevant category) 16–25   26–45   46–60   60+

Male/Female (delete as appropriate)

Home country . . . .

Please send us any comments about our guide to the Baltic cities or other Bradt Travel Guides. . . . .

. . . .

. . . .

. . . .

Bradt Travel Guides
23 High Street, Chalfont St Peter, Bucks SL9 9QE, UK
✆ +44 (0)1753 893444 f +44 (0)1753 892333
e info@bradtguides.com
www.bradtguides.com

CLAIM YOUR HALF-PRICE BRADT GUIDE!

Order Form

To order your half-price copy of a Bradt guide, and to enter our prize draw to win £100 (see overleaf), please fill in the order form below, complete the questionnaire overleaf, and send it to Bradt Travel Guides by post, fax or email.

Please send me one copy of the following guide at half the UK retail price

Title	Retail price	Half price
...	....	....	....

Please send the following additional guides at full UK retail price

No	Title	Retail price	Total
...	....	....	....
...	....	....	....
...	....	....	....

Sub total ....
Post & packing ....
(£2 per book UK; £4 per book Europe; £6 per book rest of world)
Total ....

Name . . . .

Address. . . . .

Tel . . . .   Email . . . .

☐ I enclose a cheque for £ . . . . made payable to Bradt Travel Guides Ltd

☐ I would like to pay by credit card. Number: . . . .

Expiry date: . . . / . . .   3-digit security code (on reverse of card) . . . . .

Issue no (debit cards only) . . . . .

☐ I would like to subscribe to Bradt's monthly enewsletter.

☐ I would be happy for you to use my name and comments in Bradt marketing material.

Send your order on this form, with the completed questionnaire, to:

Bradt Travel Guides BAL1
23 High Street, Chalfont St Peter, Bucks SL9 9QE
✆ +44 (0)1753 893444   **f** +44 (0)1753 892333
e info@bradtguides.com   www.bradtguides.com